D0881918

Heresy and the Politics of Community

A VOLUME IN THE SERIES
Conjunctions of Religion and Power in the Medieval Past
Edited by Barbara H. Rosenwein

A list of titles in the series is available at www.cornellpress.cornell.edu.

HERESY AND THE POLITICS OF COMMUNITY

THE JEWS OF THE FATIMID CALIPHATE

MARINA RUSTOW

Cornell University Press

Ithaca and London

Publication of this book was made possible, in part, by a generous grant from the Institute for Israel and Jewish Studies, Columbia University.

Copyright © 2008 by Cornell University

All rights reserved. Except for brief quotations in a review, this book, or parts thereof, must not be reproduced in any form without permission in writing from the publisher. For information, address Cornell University Press, Sage House, 512 East State Street, Ithaca, New York 14850.

First published 2008 by Cornell University Press
First printing, Cornell Paperbacks, 2014

Printed in the United States of America

Library of Congress Cataloging-in-Publication Data

Rustow, Marina.

Heresy and the politics of community: the Jews of the Fatimid caliphate / Marina Rustow.
p. cm. — (Conjunctions of religion and power in the medieval past)
Includes bibliographical references and index.
ISBN 978-0-8014-4582-8 (cloth : alk. paper)
ISBN 978-0-8014-5650-3 (pbk. : alk. paper)
1. Karaites—Egypt—History—To 1500. 2. Karaites—Syria—History—To 1500. 3. Jews—Egypt—History—To 1500. 4. Jews—Syria—History—To 1500. 5. Heresies, Jewish—History—To 1500. 6. Egypt—History—640–1250. 7. Syria—History—750–1260. I. Title. II. Series: Conjunctions of religion & power in the medieval past.

BM185.R86 2008

296.8'109620902 1—dc22 2008002314

Cornell University Press strives to use environmentally responsible suppliers and materials to the fullest extent possible in the publishing of its books. Such materials include vegetable-based, low-VOC inks and acid-free papers that are recycled, totally chlorine-free, or partly composed of nonwood fibers. For further information, visit our website at www.cornellpress.cornell.edu.

[Some of the disagreements between the Iraqi and Palestinian Rabbanites] make each group accuse the other of heresy. In fact, the religious divergence between the two groups is no smaller than that between both of them on the one hand and the Qaraites and the Ananites on the other.

—Abū Yaʿqūb Yūsuf al-Qirqisānī, *Kitāb al-anwār wa-l-marāqib* (937–38), Book I, 10:1

If in a study of human events we bracket the temporal dimension, we obtain a datum which is inevitably distorted because it has been cleaned of all power relationships. Human history does not unfold in the world of ideas, but in the sublunar world in which individuals are irreversibly born, inflict or endure suffering and die.

—Carlo Ginzburg, *Ecstasies: Deciphering the Witches' Sabbath* (1989), 16

CONTENTS

ILLUSTRATIONS

Illustrations

Maps

ACKNOWLEDGMENTS

Working with an epistolary corpus has entailed unexpected delights, among them the intimacy of reading words that were never intended for public consumption. It has also presented challenges, some of them insurmountable: letters that reached their destinations were folded in preparation for the journey, unfolded by readers, and refolded again before being unfolded by library conservators, sometimes too late; folds frequently ruined rows of writing or tore the paper, presenting the historian with the anguish of staring at holes where a crucial word or phrase once lay.

In facing the difficulties of decipherment and reconstruction, I have been aided considerably by the work of the scholars who preceded me. Where documents had been published more than once, I enjoyed the benefit of several opinions on how to read passages written in a difficult hand or whose ink has chipped or faded, or on how to fill lacunae left by holes, tears, and folds. I am truly grateful to the scholars who preceded me in studying this material. I have made every effort to compare their edited texts with the originals, digital photographs, or microfilms.

For allowing me access to Geniza material, I am grateful to a number of people and institutions. At the Taylor-Schechter Genizah Research Unit of the Cambridge University Library, my sincere thanks go to Stefan Reif, Ben Outhwaite, Rebecca Jefferson, Ellis Weinberger, and the Syndics of the Library for permission to publish reproductions of Geniza material. I am grateful to the Library of the Jewish Theological Seminary of America in New York for permission to publish one reproduction and to David Kraemer, Jerry Schwarzbard, Jay Rovner, David Wachtel, and Michelle Margolis for their help. I thank the Bodleian Library, University of Oxford, for permission to publish reproductions, and Lesley Forbes, Piet van Boxel, and Katie Guest. At the Jewish National and University Library, Jerusalem, my thanks go to Binyamin Richler, Ezra Chwat, and Avraham David. Thanks to the Center for Advanced Judaic Studies Library, University of Pennsylvania, for permission to reproduce two Halper images, and to Arthur Kiron, Seth Jerchower, and David McKnight of the Schoenberg Center for Electronic Text and Image. Thanks to Yaacov Choueka at the Friedberg Genizah Project, Jerusalem, and to Mark R. Cohen (whom I will thank in other guises) and Ben Johnston at the Princeton Geniza Project. At Emory University, I am grateful to Tarina Rosen,

Eric Nitschke, and Marie Hansen of the Woodruff Library, and to the Institute for Comparative and International Studies for research funds that enabled me to visit and cross-check the originals in 2005. Thanks also to Giuliano Tamani at Ca' Foscari University in Venice for allowing me access to the extraordinarily rich collection of works on medieval Hebrew manuscripts and on Jewish history and thought housed in his office.

I have also benefited from the help and expertise of many colleagues, teachers, students, and friends whose knowledge, ideas, criticisms, and advice improved this book and the process of writing it. I am particularly grateful to Barbara Rosenwein for insisting (but in a nice way) that I take my work a few steps further than I might have otherwise and inviting me to persevere in improving the book's execution, and to John Ackerman for his support for the project from inception to completion. I was fortunate to have Gavin Lewis as my copy-editor, and am grateful to Karen Laun for her unflappability, to Kate Mertes for the index, to the College and Graduate School of Emory University for defraying the costs of indexing, and to Michael Stanislawski and the Columbia University Institute for Israel and Jewish Studies for making the book's publication possible.

Stephen D. White was unstinting with good counsel, as were Patrick Allitt, Eric Goldstein, Jeffrey Lesser, Jonathan Prude, and Jerry Singerman. Fred Astren, Piero Capelli, Daniel Lasker, and an anonymous referee read the entire manuscript and shared with me their time, critical acumen, and knowledge. Sacha Stern generously helped me with calendar-related problems, and Ross Brann convinced me to revisit certain questions that I now see were central to the work. Mark Cohen read this book in past and subsequent incarnations and saved me from numerous errors; he was an exceptionally helpful and generous teacher and is now an ideal colleague. My other colleagues in Geniza studies, Elinoar Bareket, Arnold Franklin, Miriam Frenkel, Jessica Goldberg, Phillip Lieberman, and Roxani Margariti, will recognize here some shared questions and concerns; I have learned much from each of them and feel fortunate to have them as comrades. Thanks to Sinan Antoon for his poetic bilingualism and love of *sukhf*, to Alyssa Gray for help with questions related to the redaction of the Talmud, to Yaacov Lev for his encyclopedic knowledge of things Fatimid, and to Devin Stewart for paleographic and linguistic life-lines. For reading parts of the book, discussing particular problems, or generously answering my questions, I am grateful to Haggai Ben-Shammai, Elisheva Carlebach, Bruno Chiesa, Daniel Frank, Mordechai Friedman, Moshe Gil, Michael Glatzer, Jessica Goldberg, Benjamin Hary, Geoffrey Khan, Hayim Lapin, Phillip Lieberman, Judith Olszowy-Schlanger, Raymond Scheindlin, Gregor Schwarb, David Sklare, and Avrom Udovitch.

The graduate students in my seminar on heresy at Emory University in spring 2005 helped me deepen my thinking on many of the broad problems I raise in the book. Students at Emory and Ca' Foscari read with me some of the

Judeo-Arabic and Arabic documents in my corpus; their keen paleographic eye and iron grasp of Arabic grammar forced me to improve many of my translations. Nathan Hofer was a prompt and always entertaining research assistant; likewise, Kate McGrath, Daniel Domingues da Silva, Daniel Spillman, Uri Rosenheck, and Molly McCullers contributed to the project and the accuracy of its references.

Other debts are more difficult to define. The world of heresy would not have opened up so vastly without the many hours I shared writing (and not writing) with Tamer Elleithy, a certain complicity with Mark Pegg, and the comradeship of Federico Squarcini and Adrian Johnston; without Sam Haselby, the world of history would have remained a strange and lonely country. Without Yosef Hayim Yerushalmi I would never have discovered that world in the first place, and I could not have found my way around the Geniza or read its sources without Mark Cohen. Both of them have contributed to this book and to my formation as a historian in ways too pervasive to admit of further precision; so have Menaḥem Ben-Sasson, Richard Bulliet, and Michael Stanislawski. I hope that they will feel gratified to recognize their influence in these pages.

An Andrew W. Mellon Post-doctoral Rome Prize in Medieval Studies and time at the American Academy in Rome enabled me to complete the final revisions on the manuscript. For a particularly wonderful period there I am grateful to Adele Chatfield-Taylor, Carmela Vircillo Franklin, and Tom McGinn (who also read and commented on parts of the manuscript and offered much sage advice); to Deans Robert A. Paul and Cris Levenduski of Emory University for allowing me a year's respite from teaching; to my colleagues at Emory, especially Jeffrey Lesser and Clifton Crais, who encouraged me to seek time off; to Tom Burns, for helping it go smoothly; and to friends at the Academy: Arman Schwartz, for food, diversion, and one particularly memorable synopsis of a Herzog film; Jay Rubenstein, to whose dinner companionship I owe the *n*th and final version of the introduction; Dave King, for reassuring me that the heavens would yet open; Christopher MacEvitt, for opening trap-doors to a different book from the one I thought I was writing and for reading more than his fair share of chapters; Tom Bissell, for trying to convince me, sometimes successfully, that playing Guitar Hero was more urgent than work; Patricia Cronin, for insisting that work was, in fact, the most urgent thing of all; and Mona Talbott, Chris Boswell, and Mona Salinas, for sustaining me in myriad ways.

My siblings, siblings-in-law, and nieces have patiently observed the lengthy process of writing and revising this book and inquired about it in a manner that exceeded familial requirements; particularly memorable was a historiographic conversation with Ada Rustow, then eleven years old and curious about the differences between writing a history book and a historical novel. They have also tolerated my lapses in communication while I was writing or revising against deadlines, and despite those lapses, they know their love means more to me than books. Lulu, my accomplice, has contributed disappointingly little to my research but has made up for it by demonstrating the joys of short-term memory loss and forcing me out of the house with regularity. Piero Capelli has been a loving, entertaining, and quite distracting companion whose encouragement has sustained me and whose presence in my life has finally persuaded me that there is more to it than writing books. I dedicate this one to him with love.

NOTE ON TRANSLITERATION, TRANSCRIPTION, AND CITATIONS

Transcription of Arabic follows the conventions of the *International Journal of Middle Eastern Studies* except that elisions are not marked with apostrophes. Judeo-Arabic transcription follows the same rules. Hebrew transcription follows the conventions of the *Association for Jewish Studies Review* except that צ is transliterated as ṣ, ט is transliterated as ṭ, and final ה without a *mappiq* is not indicated.

English-language scholarship on the Qaraites has usually rendered them Karaites or Ḳaraites (or, in pre-nineteenth-century works, Caraites). Out of fidelity to the Hebrew *qara'im* and the Arabic *qarrā'iyyūn* (in their now standard transcriptions), I have spelled the name with a "q."

Similarly, the convention in Middle Eastern Studies is to transliterate Arabic proper names while in Jewish Studies it is to render familiar Hebrew names in their Anglicized forms, but this practice creates a confusing inconsistency for anyone working in both Arabic and Hebrew and writing about figures who rendered their names in both languages. Events of the late twentieth century have ensured the familiarity of at least some Hebrew names in their original forms to an English-speaking public. Except when speaking of characters from the Hebrew Bible, then, I have rendered both Hebrew and Arabic names following the rules above rather than using their English equivalents (thus I speak of Shelomo and Sulaymān, not Solomon and Sulaymān; and of the biblical Saul but of an eleventh-century Sha'ul). In the case of non-standard variants in Judeo-Arabic (e.g., Isḥaq for Isḥāq), I have retained the spelling of the name as it appears in the document I cite.

Patronymics are universally marked with b. whether they are masculine or feminine, Arabic or Judeo-Arabic (*ibn*, *ibnat*, *bint*), Hebrew (*ben*, *bat*), or Aramaic (*bar*, *berat*). But when a patronymic has become part of a family name used over several generations, I spell out *ibn* or *ben*.

When published works in Hebrew or Arabic include a title page in a European language, I have used it and indicated the original language. In other cases, and for all medieval works, I have given the original title in transliteration.

Finally, in quoting manuscript material, I use brackets to indicate additions to a text, including those made to facilitate comprehension and, occasionally, reconstructed lacunae. When the meaning of a text or my interpretation of it hinged on disagreements with previous editors over a reading or a reconstruction, I have noted this in footnotes. Double slashes surrounding a word indicate that the author or scribe added it above the line as an afterthought. I have used ellipses to signal both my omissions of text from a quoted work and lacunae in manuscripts, but I have usually also specified when I mean to indicate the latter. Those who would like further details as to the state of a manuscript can refer either to the originals or the published editions; to streamline the footnotes, I have cited manuscripts by shelfmark only and placed all references to published editions in the section on Manuscript Sources at the end of this work. In citing Geniza documents, I use a plus sign to refer to the shelfmarks of a severed document, or a "join" in genizologists' argot.

INTRODUCTION

This book is about the Jews of Egypt and Syria under the Fatimid caliphs (969–1171) and how they reorganized their community life in response to dramatic changes in the political geography of the Near East in the tenth and eleventh centuries. It is about two groups of Jews in particular: the followers of rabbinic Judaism, known as Rabbanites, who considered themselves bound by the accumulating corpus of postbiblical tradition contained in classical rabbinic literature and its commentaries; and Qaraites, who dispensed with that corpus, contested the rabbinic claim to exclusive authority in determining Jewish practice, and focused their exegetical and legal energies on the Bible instead.[1]

Most scholarship on Qaraism has styled it a "sect" of Judaism, a judgment that agrees with its condemnation as a heresy by medieval rabbinic religious authorities but does little to explain its role in the wider Jewish community. The term "sect" represents a commendable attempt to remove the stigma of judgment from groups whose coreligionists have deemed them heretics, but it still implies their marginalization. It also tends to reduce the complexity of the relationships between religious groups and make them appear static, substituting a sociological typology for a theological one and in so doing, bypassing the contingency and specificity of historical events.

I began writing this book to investigate whether the use of the term sect is justified in the case of Qaraism. Did the marginalization of Qaraite ideas and practices in the writings of certain rabbinic authorities entail their marginalization in politics, administration, economy, and physical space? Did Seʿadya b. Yūsuf al-Fayyūmī (882–942), the most prominent Jewish thinker of his generation and head of one of the central rabbinic academies in Baghdad, really neutralize the threat that Qaraism posed to Judaism through his tireless polemics in defense of rabbinic tradition? Leon Nemoy, editor of

[1] Syria translates the region known in Arabic as al-Shām. For definitions of regions and geographic terms, see the Guide to Places and People at p. 361. The term Rabbanite was a Judeo-Arabic coinage (*rabbānī*) distinguishing followers of the rabbis from the Qaraites. The Hebrew equivalent, *rabbanim*, designates the rabbis themselves, but under the influence of the Arabic term, also came to refer to their followers. On the vexed history of comparisons between Qaraite Judaism and Protestant Christianity, with reference to earlier studies, see Marina Rustow, "Karaites Real and Imagined: Three Cases of Jewish Heresy," *Past & Present* 197 (2007): 58–69.

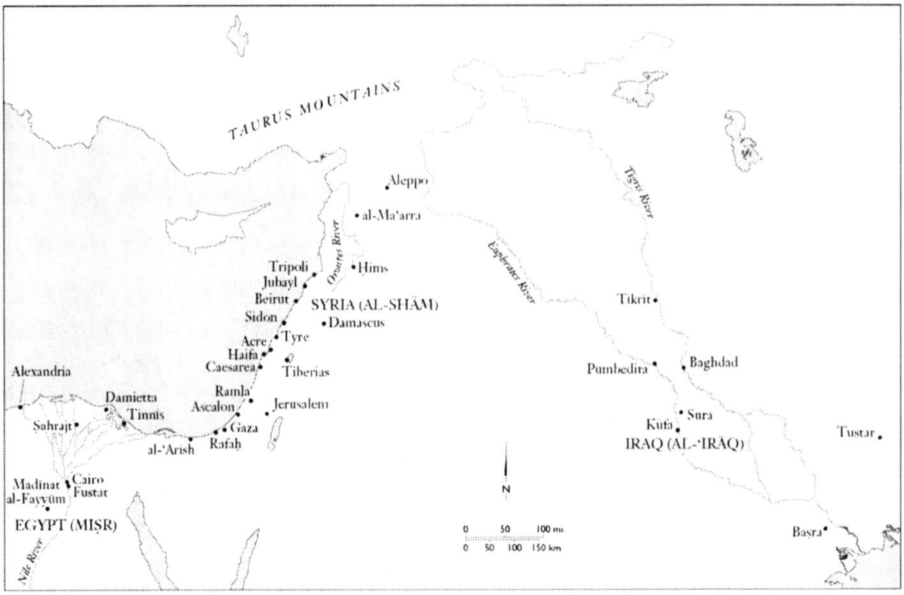

Map 1. The Medieval Near East

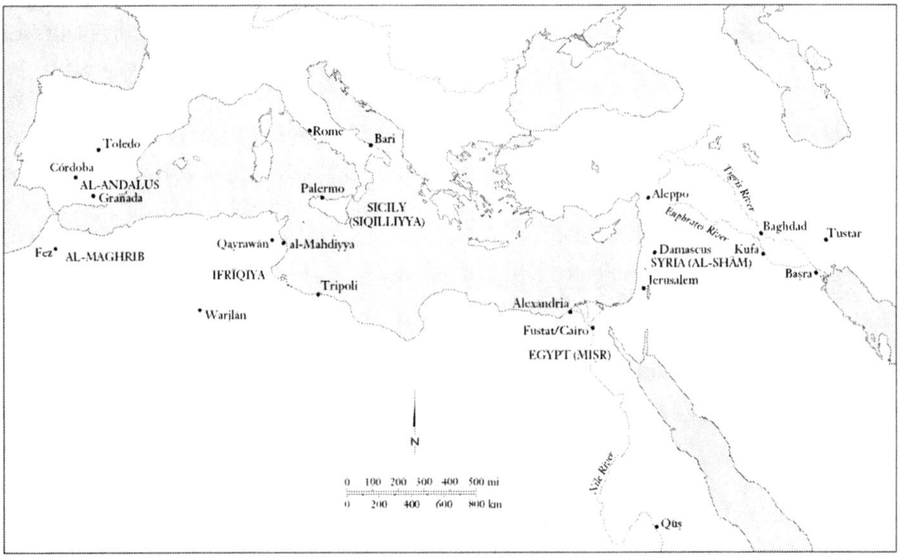

Map 2. The Medieval Mediterranean and Near East

the anthology of translated Qaraite texts that is still standard today, puts the matter as follows: "The suddenness of [Seʿadya's] attack and its effectiveness" brought about "a complete break" between Rabbanites and Qaraites and the Qaraites' "forced estrangement from the Rabbanite community." Nemoy extrapolated social history from polemical and prescriptive sources with little by way of other evidence, claiming that after Seʿadya, rabbinic Judaism and Qaraism parted company, and never did the twain again meet.[2]

The sources I have examined in writing this book suggest me that this "forced estrangement" never took place. Long after Seʿadya, Rabbanites and Qaraites remained in productive contact with one another in their writings and in daily life, marrying one another, cooperating in business ventures, and maintaining formal and informal alliances. Even more than that, together they reshaped the medieval Jewish community under Islamic rule to the extent that rabbinic authority now appears at best a partial explanation for why the Jewish community took the form it did. A long-standing scholarly consensus considers rabbinic power in communal administration to have been the great shaper of Jewish community life, dictating the norms according to which pre-modern Jews lived and the punishments they incurred for failing to adhere to them. The process of writing this book has convinced me that the shape of the Jewish community in medieval Egypt and Syria cannot be understood without accounting for the Qaraite role in it, a conclusion that may be suggestive for other historical periods and religious configurations as well. The question with which I began my research, then, whether the Qaraites were a sect, has led me to the wider problem on which this work focuses: What would the history of the Jewish community look like if viewed without the presumption that Qaraites were a sociologically separate group?

Until about 1200, the Jewish communities under Islamic rule constituted the vast majority of Jews worldwide, generally estimated at 90 percent. The political alliances and struggles between Rabbanite and Qaraite Jews over the course of the tenth and eleventh centuries were part cause and part symptom of a larger shift in the structure and governance of Jewish life in this vast area. Jews redrew their frameworks of religious authority and institutional power partly in response to changes in an empire that had reached its maximum expansion in the ninth century and, over the course of the tenth, fragmented into competing polities and dynasties. At the beginning of this period, Jewish religious consciousness was centered on the rabbinic academies of Palestine and Iraq; by its end, Jews had organized themselves into territorial administrations run by local leaders, and those administrations included Rabbanites and Qaraites alike. The disintegration of the old pattern of organization explains much about the subsequent history of medieval Jews and Judaism. But it is a change that thus far has been understood exclusively from the point of view of rabbinic Jews. In fact, the change itself was so intimately linked to the Qaraite

[2] Leon Nemoy, *Karaite Anthology: Excerpts from the Early Literature*, Yale Judaica Series 7 (New Haven, 1952), xx. See also idem, "Ḳaraites," in *EI*[2]; idem and J. E. Heller, s.v. "Karaites" in *Encyclopaedia Judaica* (Jerusalem, 1973), 10:761–81. An updated version of Nemoy's anthology culling literary texts from the Firkovich collections as well as documentary sources from the Geniza is a desideratum. For reference to a similar view on a parting of the ways, but revised by three centuries, see below, chap. 12 at n. 49.

members of the Jewish community as to be incomprehensible without taking them into account.

This book is an attempt, then, to bracket the pronouncements of medieval polemicists and heresiographers as to what the Rabbanites and Qaraites were and, instead, to filter the problem of Rabbanite-Qaraite relations through the finer analytical mesh of social and political history. I have approached my sources seeking answers to several questions: What was heresy to Jews of the tenth and eleventh centuries? Whom did they accuse of it, and how, when, and why did they lodge the accusation? Rather than asking only what those accused of heresy believed that made them vulnerable to the charge, I have asked here about the causes and consequences of the accusations—if there were any consequences at all.

The terms *min* (sectarian), *kofer be-ʿiqqar* (one who denies fundamental principles), and *apiqoros* (Epicurean)—all rabbinic epithets for heretics—are as old as rabbinic literature itself. At key points, rabbinic authorities attacked specific heresies and individual heretics in the frank admission that their actions were rendered more threatening by their beliefs.[3] Accusations of heresy in Judaism have included attempts to regulate belief and behavior through polemical discourse, excommunication, or other sorts of censure, not all of which were initiated by the same authorities. What makes the problem of heresy in Judaism a fascinating challenge for the historian is that the accusation's consequences varied enormously depending on who lodged it and in which circumstances. Only at very rare junctures was physical force mobilized against Jewish heretics. The consequences of an accusation of heresy usually ranged between excommunication and the progression of life in its normal course as though nothing had happened. This book aims to shed light on Jewish heresy by supplementing the accusations made in literary polemics with those in ritual, letters, and petitions, sources that allow one to judge the immediate context of the accusations and whether they were provoked by zeal in defense of the faith or by something else. It also aims to clarify the problem of Jewish orthodoxy and heresy by demonstrating that rabbinic Judaism could not enforce its authority without turning to power structures outside the Jewish community. What if those accused of heresy

[3] Judaism and Islam are usually taken to be religions of praxis in mistaken contradistinction to Christianity. But this is to compare unlike things—one religion's regulation of belief with the other's regulation of practice. Both Judaism and Islam have put forward notions of orthodoxy and heresy and Christianity has regulated behavior, even in the context of struggles over heresy. The important differences are the institutional structures through which religions prosecute heresy. See below, Epilogue; cf. Menachem Marc Kellner, *Dogma in Medieval Jewish Thought: From Maimonides to Abravanel*, The Littman Library of Jewish Civilization (Oxford, 1986); see Devin J. Stewart, *Islamic Legal Orthodoxy: Twelve Shiite Responses to the Sunni Legal System* (Salt Lake City, 1998), 45; Mark Gregory Pegg, *The Corruption of Angels: The Great Inquisition of* 1245–46 (Princeton, 2001), 45–46; Shannon McSheffrey, "Heresy, Orthodoxy and English Vernacular Religion," *Past & Present* 186 (2005): 47–80.

wielded enough power—either within the community or outside of it—to repel the accusation?

My argument, then, hinges on particulars—moments, individuals, incidents, and turns of phrase in letters. The texts, both their content and the very fact of their having been written and mailed, drive my larger arguments that the politics of community is an integral part of the history of religions and cannot be detached from it; and that histories of "mainstream" and "sectarian" groups, of the orthodox and the heretical, are inherently social and political histories, not merely histories of conflicting ideas.

SOURCES: THE CAIRO GENIZA

The narrative centers on the Fatimid territories of the southeastern Mediterranean—Egypt and Syria—in a period when Egypt was becoming the center of the Islamic world and its commercial hub, the hinge that joined the Mediterranean and Indian Ocean trades. It also glances westward at the Iberian peninsula and central North Africa, and eastward at Iraq and Iran. The period the book covers is in part a function of the availability of documentary sources, which become abundant toward the end of the tenth century, and in part a function of the First Crusade, which altered the landscape of Jewish politics by sending most Jews south from Syria to Egypt.

Most of my sources are letters. Letter-writing was a constitutive feature of Jewish social networks in the Mediterranean basin and the main medium in which Jews conducted politics from afar. Epistolary style had a hand in shaping the religious communities I investigate, communities that consisted of overlapping networks of individuals connected by bonds of loyalty that were frequently expressed in writing, sometimes elaborately so.

The sources all originated in Egypt or passed through there; most are documents preserved in the lumber-room of the Ben Ezra synagogue in Fustat, the old city of Cairo, known in the Middle Ages as *kanīsat al-shāmiyyīn*, the synagogue of the Syro-Palestinians, after the Rabbanite Jewish community that prayed there. Its lumber-room served as a kind of limbo for documents—a *geniza*—into which disused manuscripts were deposited in keeping with the custom not to discard pieces of writing casually if they contained the name of God but to store them until they could be given a proper burial. In practice, the custom of depositing worn books and disused documents in the Geniza came to include anything written in Hebrew script, whether or not it actually included God's name, as well as items in other alphabets (Arabic, Greek, and Latin). For reasons that are still not understood, the community of the Ben Ezra synagogue did not bury the contents of its *geniza* but stored them in perpetual limbo, while Cairo's temperate climate preserved them from paper and parchment's greatest enemy, mold.

This confluence of circumstances was enormously fortunate for future historians.[4]

Documents from the Cairo Geniza—as it is now called—form a staggeringly large corpus, estimated at more than a quarter of a million folio pages. Most of these date to the three centuries between 950 and 1250. The end-date marks a period when many of Fustat's Jews moved northward to Cairo proper, and probably began depositing their disused papers elsewhere. Of the total number of items preserved in the Geniza, roughly fifteen thousand are documentary texts such as letters, legal contracts, list, and accounts, the kind of material that comprises most of the corpus I studied in writing this book.

The existence of the Geniza was known outside Egypt as early as the eighteenth century, but it was not until the second half of the nineteenth that manuscript dealers, collectors, and library agents began removing its contents and selling, bequeathing, and acquiring them, thus creating an even greater dispersion of texts than the dispersion of Jews who produced them. Today whole quires, single folios, and crumbled *disjecta membra* alike are housed in libraries in Europe, the Near East, and North America. Torn halves or thirds of the same page have been identified in collections on different continents. The work of piecing together the Geniza's contents is still far from complete.[5]

Besides its intrinsic interest, the importance of the Cairo Geniza lies in the fact that hardly any archives have survived from the Near East before the advent of Ottoman rule in the fifteenth and sixteenth centuries. The Ottomans were great archivists whose collections outlasted their empire, but the previous Islamic dynasties that ruled Egypt—the Fatimids, Ayyubids (1171–1250), and Mamluks (1250–1517)—though they kept archives no less impressive, were the stepchildren of posterity compared with the Ottomans. That does not, however, mean there are no documents. Stephen Humphreys has justly described the history of the medieval Near East as "poor in archives but rich in documents," and documents that survive from the pre-Ottoman Near East did so in one of four ways: as copies or models in medieval works; in archives outside the Near East (Pisa and Venice, for instance, which preserved Egyptian documents related to trade and diplomacy); buried in the ground (such as the tens of thousands of Arabic papyri discovered in Egypt); or in the private keep of

[4] A small amount of the material cited in this work comes from the *geniza* of the Dār Simḥa synagogue of the Qaraites in Cairo, which, unlike the Ben Ezra Geniza, was probably a library. To distinguish the two *genizot*, I capitalize the word Geniza in the case of the Ben Ezra only. Much material from the Qaraite geniza is now housed in the Firkovich collections of the National Library of Russia, St. Petersburg (on which see further below). See further chap. 1, n. 54, and chap. 9, n. 22.

[5] A union catalogue and database of high-quality digital reproductions of all known Geniza documents is currently in preparation under the auspices of the Friedberg Genizah Project. The project currently estimates the total number of Geniza pages at 280,000, divided among thirty libraries, but final figures will be available only once the material is catalogued and photographed. Depending on the number of bifolios, the actual number may be higher; and documentary material often contains more than one text per page. For a preliminary report, see www.genizah.org.

religious institutions in the Near East itself. The Geniza falls into the last category, even if in other ways it resembles the third; but of all these kinds of collections it housed the largest amount of material by several orders of magnitude. Its contents are unrivalled not just in quantity but also in their scope, coherence, and the kinds of intimate details they provide the researcher, though one important distinction must be emphasized from the outset: the Geniza was not an archive. Archives are arranged for preservation, storage, and retrieval, whereas *genizot* are arranged for the opposite purpose: discarding refuse, albeit in a dignified manner.[6]

The Geniza's contents, then, offer historians the advantages of seeing items not meant for posterity, such as drafts of letters and official documents before they were finalized. They can also offer the concomitant disadvantage of uncertainty as to how the final version turned out. Drafts are easily distinguishable from final copies, since letters that were mailed bear addresses and evidence of having been folded; official copies of contracts bear witnesses' signatures and court validations. Sometimes, though, it is difficult to distinguish between a draft and a copy made later: letters, petitions, and contracts were used as writing samples and copied for practice by schoolchildren and more advanced scribes. Dating documents is also frequently difficult since documents tend to decay or tear at their extremities, where dates, signatures, and addresses usually lie; some of the material the Geniza preserved, such as accounts, lists, drafts of letters, and notes, is so singular that it cannot be dated in corroboration with other sources. Those difficulties increase the temptation to turn histories based on the Geniza corpus into synchronic, composite portraits that tell us generally about a span of three centuries while avoiding problems of relative chronology. I have attempted as much rigor as possible in constructing my argument on the basis of causality and chronological development, trying wherever possible to rely on material that is dated or whose date can be determined to within a decade or, in exceptional cases, to within a single caliph's reign.

The Geniza has changed and is still changing the way the history of the Near East is written—not just the history of its Jews but of its merchants, courtiers, craftsmen, city-dwellers and, occasionally, rural people, regardless of their religion. This book is a contribution to that history insofar as it attempts to recover the network of relationships between groups of Jews whose modes and means of politics tell us something about their time and place,

[6] R. Stephen Humphreys, *Islamic History: A Framework for Inquiry*, rev. ed. (Princeton, 1991), 40. I have also drawn here on his description of the Geniza as "a body of sources unequalled in medieval Islamic studies for its range, coherence, and intimacy" (ibid., 262). For overviews of the Geniza's contents and the history of its discovery, see S. D. Goitein, *A Mediterranean Society: The Jewish Communities of the Arab World as Portrayed in the Documents of the Cairo Geniza*, 6 vols. (Berkeley, 1967–93), 1:1–28, and the essays collected in S. C. Reif, ed., *The Cambridge Genizah Collections: Their Contents and Significance* (Cambridge, 2002).

about piety, politics, and power under the Fatimids and in the wider Islamic world. It is thus intended as a contribution to the history of the Near East, of its Jews, and of orthodoxy and heresy in religions more generally.

RABBANITES AND QARAITES BEFORE AND AFTER THE EUROPEAN DISCOVERY OF THE GENIZA

The first European scholars to visit the Geniza still imagined relations between Rabbanites and Qaraites to have consisted mainly in the composition of polemics refuting one another's beliefs. One of the first Hebrew manuscript collectors to penetrate the Geniza was the Russian Qaraite Abraham Firkovich (1786–1874). Firkovich was not a Qaraite of the sort I discuss in this book. He lived in a period of hostility between Rabbanite and Qaraite Jews in the Russian Empire; beginning in the late eighteenth century, Russian Qaraites had lobbied their government to exempt them from the crushing legal disabilities to which Jewish subjects of the czars were bound, including high tax burdens and extraordinarily long periods of military conscription. In 1837 the Qaraites of Russia were recognized as belonging to a religion separate from Judaism. Beginning in 1839, Firkovich began conducting archeological and manuscript research to prove that the Qaraites of the medieval Near East were the descendants of Khazars who had migrated southward from their kingdom between the Volga and the Dnieper Rivers to Jerusalem and Fustat. He was the first person in history to introduce a new, quintessentially modern question into the history of the Rabbanite-Qaraite division: ethnicity.[7]

Regardless of Firkovich's motives, scholarship owes a great debt to him. For a quarter-century, he traveled throughout the Near East with the avowed aim of acquiring manuscripts in Hebrew script (including Judeo-Arabic, or Arabic written in Hebrew characters), particularly manuscripts whose contents, colophons, or inscriptions linked them to medieval Qaraite communities. He reached Cairo in 1864, having already appeared at Rabbanite synagogues in the Crimea and Aleppo with edicts in hand entitling him to search their safes,

[7] On eighteenth- and nineteenth-century visitors to the Geniza, see Alexander Marx, "The Importance of the Geniza for Jewish History," *Proceedings of the American Academy for Jewish Research* 16 (1946–47): 183–85; Stefan C. Reif, *A Jewish Archive from Old Cairo: The History of Cambridge University's Genizah Collection* (Richmond, Surrey, 2000), 14–18; and Goitein, *Mediterranean Society*, 1:1–5. On Qaraite politics in the Russian empire and Firkovich's ethnic claims, see Philip E. Miller, *Karaite Separatism in Nineteenth-century Russia: Joseph Solomon Lutski's Epistle of Israel's Deliverance*, Monographs of the Hebrew Union College 16 (Cincinnati, 1993); Marina Rustow, Sharon Lieberman Mintz, and Elka Deitsch, *Scripture and Schism: Samaritan and Karaite Treasures from the Library of the Jewish Theological Seminary* (New York, 2000); Tapani Harviainen, "The Karaites in Eastern Europe and the Crimea: An Overview," in *Karaite Judaism: A Guide to Its History and Literary Sources*, ed. Meira Polliack, Handbuch der Orientalistik, pt. 1: Nahe und Mittlere Osten, 73 (Leiden, 2003), 636–39; Miller, "The Karaites of Czarist Russia, 1780–1918," ibid., 820–24.

archives, and *genizot* and enabling him to intimidate their custodians into letting him make off with large quantities of manuscripts. Sometimes, in exchange, he promised to help repair their crumbling buildings. Scholars are divided as to whether Firkovich left the Ben Ezra Synagogue with manuscripts from its Geniza; just as he began searching it, the letters that are the main source for his journey to Egypt break off, apparently because the family members to whom he had been writing now joined him in Cairo. But scholars do know why he went there: he was convinced that over the course of the Middle Ages, Rabbanite Jews had acquired manuscripts composed or copied by Qaraites.

Firkovich was correct in this conviction: synagogues in the Near East, including the Ben Ezra, possessed some of the oldest and most precious surviving manuscripts of the Hebrew Bible, dating to the late ninth, the tenth, and the early eleventh centuries, many commissioned and copied by Qaraites. As for the consequences that Firkovich drew from this conviction, even his admirers described him as a scholar "of the medieval type" who believed that Qaraite manuscripts belonged to the communities from whence they came and should be returned to them.[8]

Abraham Firkovich typified the enmity between Rabbanite and Qaraite Jews in the Russian Empire of the nineteenth century, an enmity he sustained and deepened and spread beyond the borders of Russia. Russian Qaraite leaders of his generation opted out of Judaism in part in order to exempt themselves from the anti-Semitic charge of having murdered the Christian savior—thereby implicitly accepting the legitimacy of this accusation in the case of their Rabbanite cousins. For these not very scholarly reasons, Firkovich felt himself justified in "ransoming" Qaraite codices from Rabbanite hands. The ruthless techniques he employed in acquiring them, manipulating his connections with local governors and intimidating synagogue custodians into offering him their treasures, make it easy to imagine the bitterness he must have left in his wake.[9]

Nonetheless, to accuse Firkovich of "medieval" tactics is unjust and inaccurate. This is not because his tactics merit defense, but because Rabbanites and Qaraites in the Middle Ages did not fight over manuscripts but presumed them

[8] Harviainen, "The Cairo Genizot and Other Sources of the Second Firkovich Collection in St. Petersburg," in *Proceedings of the Twelfth International Congress of the International Organization for Masoretic Studies* 1995, ed. E. J. Revell, Masoretic Studies 8 (Atlanta, 1996), 25–36 (see p. 35 for the question of his family members joining him in Cairo); idem, "Abraham Firkovich, the Aleppo Codex, and its Dedication," in *Jewish Studies at the Turn of the Twentieth Century: Proceedings of the 6th EAJS Congress, Toledo, July* 1998, ed. Judit Targarona Borrás and Angel Sáenz-Badillos (Leiden, 1999), 1: 131–36; idem, "Abraham Firkovich," in *Polliack, Karaite Judaism*, 875 (quoting Simon Szyszman); and on whether Firkovich removed items from the Ben Ezra Geniza, Haggai Ben-Shammai, "The Scholarly Study of Karaism in the Nineteenth and Twentieth Centuries," ibid., 10 n. 7, and below, chap. 9, n. 22.

[9] On Firkovich and the deicide charge, see Harviainen, "Abraham Firkovich," 882, and the references there in n. 32.

to be their joint heritage. The Geniza has proved Firkovich's suspicion right: precious codices composed or copied by Qaraites passed into Rabbanite hands over the course of the Middle Ages, many of them literally via ransom during the Frankish conquest of Palestine known as the First Crusade. But they did so not because Rabbanites usurped them from their Qaraite owners, but because the two groups were so closely allied that they pooled their funds and efforts to ransom them from the invaders and return them to what was, at the turn of the twelfth century, a united Jewish community under the aegis of a single chief administrative officer who served Rabbanites and Qaraites alike.[10]

Nor was this cooperation limited to times of war and crisis. Its history reaches back into the late tenth century, the first period for which we have documentation. Neither Firkovich nor any of his contemporaries knew this history, because it remained hidden in the Cairo Geniza. For them, as for most of nineteenth- and much of twentieth-century scholarship, Rabbanites and Qaraites were still normative and heretical, mainstream and sectarian.

The story of cooperation that the Geniza contained began to come to light at the beginning of the twentieth century through the work of two scholars: Solomon Schechter (1847–1915), who possessed a lifelong fascination with non-rabbinic forms of Judaism and brought the lion's share of the Geniza's contents to Cambridge, England, in 1897; and Jacob Mann (1888–1940), the first scholar to mine the Geniza collections for their documentary sources and piece together unknown chapters of Jewish history on their basis. Among the masses of Geniza papers—in Schechter's case, unsorted mountains; by Mann's day, rows and rows of boxes and binders—they found evidence that Rabbanites and Qaraites had married one another during the eleventh and twelfth centuries, contracting their marriages in deeds that safeguarded the religious practices of both bride and groom. Mann understood that these findings called for a total reevaluation of the historical relationship between the groups, their daily life as well as their administrative structures. He saw that Qaraites were an integral part of the Jewish communities of the eleventh and twelfth centuries, so much so as to cast doubt on the impact of the polemics of the tenth. He also saw that Qaraites were too numerous and influential for their Rabbanite contemporaries to ignore them or even to hate them very much: when one group of Rabbanites in the early 1030s importuned their leader "to be separated from the other party" (as Mann reported on the basis of a Geniza letter), he concluded (somewhat laconically) that "in those times the cleavage [between the two groups] was not so great." This recognition appears all the more remarkable for having come at a time when the history of Judaism, and even more so that of Qaraism, was studied principally as a literary-religious phenomenon.[11]

[10] On the ransom of codices, see below, chap. 12.

[11] Jacob Mann, *The Jews in Egypt and in Palestine under the Fāṭimid Caliphs: A Contribution to their Political and Communal History, Based Chiefly on Genizah Material Hitherto Unpublished*, 2 vols. (Lon-

But in his later work, Mann abandoned the social history he found in the Geniza and instead, turned toward Qaraite intellectual history and reconstructing the basic timeline and facts of Qaraite history. To that end, he set about publishing findings from manuscripts in the Firkovich collections, by then housed in the State Public Library in Leningrad and containing on the order of sixteen thousand manuscripts, most of them unknown elsewhere. His efforts brought great advances in the history of Qaraite literature and thought, and in retrospect this was an enormously fortunate shift in his scholarship, since most scholars would soon be denied access to large sections of the library during the decades of the Stalinist dictatorship. Mann died in 1940, at the peak of his career, and the social history project he had begun remained incomplete at the time of his death.[12]

A generation later, Zvi Ankori expounded magisterially upon the Geniza material Mann had discovered and argued for the profound interrelation between Rabbanites and Qaraites in the Middle Ages.[13] Though the focus of Ankori's book was the Qaraites of the Byzantine empire, he wrote with unusual nuance and breadth about Qaraites farther south and east under the Fatimids and Abbasids. Ankori took up Mann's task of narrating the social history of the groups, and his book argued for cooperation between them as strongly as Nemoy had argued for their permanent alienation just a few years earlier. But in light of subsequent Geniza finds, it has become clear that Ankori did not go far enough in his revisionism. In the fifty years since his book, Geniza studies have been utterly transformed by the multivolume works of S. D. Goitein and Moshe Gil, magna opera that include editions and interpretations of thousands of documents. Gil in particular has made it clear that the Geniza contained a greater quantity of material about Qaraites than Mann or Ankori realized, and even material composed by them—even though it was housed in the Rabbanite congregation of Old Cairo. This fact in itself invites a reexamination of the two groups' history of cooperation; and the story that Mann and Ankori told merits retelling solely on the basis of this wider corpus.

don, 1920–22), 1:138; and generally ibid., 1:88–93, 134, 138–39. Mann's picture of a Rabbanite camp forced to maintain peaceful relations with the Qaraites emerged most sharply in his discussion of Qaraite courtiers in Fatimid Cairo: Mann, *Texts and Studies in Jewish History and Literature* (New York, 1972 [1931–35]), 2:47. The most comprehensive evaluation of Mann's work is Gerson D. Cohen, "The Reconstruction of Gaonic History," originally published as the introduction to the 1973 reprint of *Texts and Studies* and reprinted in idem, *Studies in the Variety of Rabbinic Cultures* (Philadelphia, 1991), 99–155. Cohen notes that despite the abiding value of Mann's research, his works were marred by "forbidding expository techniques" (129).

[12] In Mann's preface, dated December 4, 1932, he refers to "a recent change in the policy of the authorities" of the State Public Library in Leningrad that had "made it impossible to obtain photostats of further material" and forced him, "with a keen feeling of regret," to conclude his research. Mann, *Texts and Studies*, x–xi.

[13] Zvi Ankori, *Karaites in Byzantium: The Formative Years*, 970–1100, Columbia Studies in the Social Sciences 597 (New York, 1959).

"MANY PEOPLE HAVE SWITCHED OVER TO THE OTHER SYNAGOGUE . . ."

One letter preserved in the Geniza, written probably around 1030, provides a striking introduction to the kinds of statements the Geniza has yielded that call for some rethinking of how Rabbanites and Qaraites related to each other in practice. The letter was written by a Rabbanite scribe, pharmacist, and perfumer in Ramla, Palestine, named Shelomo b. Ṣemaḥ; he wrote to a Rabbanite colleague in his network in Egypt, Efrayim b. Shemarya, from 1020 to 1047 head of the same Syro-Palestinian congregation in whose synagogue the Geniza was found.

The purpose of Shelomo b. Ṣemaḥ's letter was to warn his colleague against treating his congregants in an overbearing and high-handed fashion. "For haven't we in Palestine received numerous letters," he asked rhetorically, "the longest of which contains [the signatures of] thirty-odd witnesses, complaining that you are alienating the congregation with your haughtiness and domineering manner? Because of you and your son-in-law, many people have switched over to the other synagogue"—the Babylonian Rabbanite synagogue in Fustat, which paid fealty to Baghdad rather than Jerusalem—"and to the Qaraite congregations."[14]

That Efrayim b. Shemarya was accused of driving his congregants away was no small matter in a world pervaded by personal loyalties. Such obligations formed the architecture of professional and public life: horizontal ties with equals; hierarchical ties to patrons to whom one owed one's loyalty or clients to whom one promised protection and favor. This was as true of religious scholars of every persuasion as it was of caliphs, soldiers, courtiers, slaves, and long-distance traders. Efrayim b. Shemarya was told that he had failed to play his proper role in the patron-client nexus, arrogating its powers without offering any of its benefits. Without fanfare or commentary, Shelomo b. Ṣemaḥ warned him that his Rabbanite followers were as likely to join a Qaraite congregation as the rival Rabbanite one. This will seem extraordinary to anyone reared on intellectualist accounts of the Jewish Middle Ages, which claim that after the tenth century, Qaraism suffered a crushing defeat and was reduced to the status of a mere sect. In fact, for long after this supposed defeat, membership in either congregation was considered equally respectable. No one who "switched over . . . to the Qaraite congregations" risked self-marginalization. In a world of voluntary but binding alliances, each afforded its own particular

[14] T-S 10 J 29.13, in Judeo-Arabic (recto, lines 20–23). See Goitein, *Mediterranean Society*, 2:555 n. 44. For the view that Shelomo b. Ṣemaḥ served as scribe to the *yeshiva* (citing Bodl. MS Heb. b 13.54), see Moshe Gil, *Palestine during the First Muslim Period (634–1099)*, Hebrew, 3 vols. (Tel Aviv, 1983), secs. 804, 862. An updated version of volume 1 of this work was published in English as idem, *A History of Palestine*, 634–1099, trans. Ethel Broido (Cambridge and New York, 1992). In subsequent references to volume 1, I use the uniform title *History of Palestine* and section numbers to facilitate cross-referencing both versions. Volumes 2 and 3, which contain Gil's edition of Geniza documents, remain untranslated.

benefits. Some of Efrayim b. Shemarya's congregants were liable to join the Qaraite congregation because for them the politics of loyalty trumped religious ideology. Others reminded him via epistolary complaint to his ally in Palestine that his power depended upon his ability to cultivate their loyalty.

Statements like this one suggest the need to investigate more deeply the nature of Rabbanite and Qaraite religious commitments, and by extension, the contours of medieval Jewish political culture. While previous studies of Rabbanite-Qaraite relations have taken the nature of those religious commitments for granted, in the past fifteen years, the scholarly consensus has begun to change.

A generation of scholars in the post-Soviet era has now gained access to the Firkovich collections and turned to the task of identifying and understanding its vast contents and bringing to light the treasures of medieval Qaraite thought. The material itself has forced them to approach the task without the burden of preconceptions, since it reveals a more nuanced picture of Qaraism than any previously available. Those scholars have established the profound effect Qaraite thought had on rabbinic Judaism and the similarities and mutual influences of the two schools in a number of salient fields, among them biblical exegesis, linguistics, and philosophical theology. Their work is currently transforming our understanding not just of Qaraism and its relationship to rabbinic thought, which was more intimate than previously recognized, but our understanding of Islamic philosophical theology, of which Qaraites served as important transmitters.[15]

Several scholars in this field have thus objected to the term "sect" as a description of Qaraism and suggested instead the term "movement." They recognize that any application of the "sect" label carries a heavy theological and sociological freight. It implies dissent from the mainstream and stubborn separatism, and its use has produced an edifice of concomitant presumptions, in this case that medieval Qaraites remained palpably and insistently separate from the main body of the Jewish people. I agree entirely with the impulse behind this change, and without carping or caviling, wish only to point out that the term movement, too, has a history in both sociology and religious studies. For sociologists of religion, "sects" are separatist while "movements" are a fleeting stage on the path to either sectarianism or extinction. Movements are ephemeral; they either harden or die out once their mission has been accomplished. Both terms leave an unwanted residue on the phenomena they are used to describe.[16]

[15] Sabine Schmidtke, "The Karaites' Encounter with the Thought of Abū l-Ḥusayn al-Baṣrī (d. 436/1044): A Survey of the Relevant Materials in the Firkovitch Collection, St. Petersburg," *Arabica* 53 (2006): 108–42.

[16] Ben-Shammai, "The Karaite Controversy: Scripture and Tradition in Early Karaism," in *Religionsgespräche im Mittelalter*, ed. Bernard Lewis and Friedrich Niewöhner (Wiesbaden, 1992), 12 n. 4;

The best way around the problem of terminology, I think, is to listen to the sources and ask them what the Qaraites were. On this point, they speak clearly and volubly: in the medieval Islamicate world, Qaraism was a *madhhab* (pl. *madhāhib*), an Arabic term usually translated as "school of law" in the same sense in which both Sunnīs and Shīʿīs had schools of law that included both religious specialists and their loyalists.[17] The documents of the Cairo Geniza speak consistently of both Rabbanites and Qaraites as *madhāhib*, implying the combination of legal, theological, and institutional ideas and practices that also characterized the Islamic *madhāhib* beginning in the tenth century. The sources also use terms with more sociological heft—among them the Arabic *ṭāʾifa*, "party" or "group," or the Hebrew *kat*, meaning the same thing—but tellingly, they use them to describe both Rabbanites and the Qaraites, often in the dual form in Judeo-Arabic (*al-ṭāʾifatayn*, the two parties). Even the leaders of the rabbinic academies of Iraq and Palestine, the *geʾonim*, used the terms this way and without opprobrium. *Ṭāʾifa* and *kat* were political and social terms, usually used to distinguish a group from some other group, and entailed no ideological or religious program. Conversely, belonging to a *madhhab* entailed no particular set of political or sociological consequences.[18]

Judith Olszowy-Schlanger, *Karaite Marriage Documents from the Cairo Geniza: Legal Tradition and Community Life in Mediaeval Egypt and Palestine*, Etudes sur le judaïsme médiéval 20 (Leiden, 1998), 5–8; Polliack, *Karaite Judaism*, xvii; Ben-Shammai, "Scholarly Study of Karaism," 22. On the meanings of the term "movement" in classical sociology, see John C. Sommerville, "Interpreting Seventeenth-Century English Religion as Movements," *Church History* 69 (2000): 749–69.

17 Nimrod Hurvitz has argued that the translation "school of law" emphasizes the jurists and "ignores the huge following and social dynamics of the *madhhab*"; in his view, "religious community" "captures the social dimension of the *madhhab*." Hurvitz, "From Scholarly Circles to Mass Movements: The Formation of Legal Communities in Islamic Societies," *American Historical Review* 108, no. 4 (2003): 985 n. 4; see further idem, "Schools of Law and Historical Context: Re-examining the Formation of the Ḥanbalī *madhhab*," *Islamic Law and Society* 7 (2000):37–64, where he points to the dangers of projecting formalized *madhāhib* onto an early period characterized by informal disciple circles. For recent bibliography see *EI*², s.v. "madhhab." Cf. also Salo Wittmayer Baron, *A Social and Religious History of the Jews*, 2d ed., 17 vols., vol. 5 (New York, 1957), 211, and Ben-Shammai, "Karaite Controversy," 20. Both consider the term *madhhab* with regard to ʿAnan b. David, but the sources themselves support the designation for Qaraism throughout the Middle Ages.

18 Both *ṭāʾifa* and *kat* have been rendered in English as "sect," a modern translation that does not serve medieval contexts well. In postbiblical Hebrew, *kat* means group, occasionally with a semantic field of religious disagreements; see Palestinian Talmud, *Sanhedrin* 29:3, "twenty-four *kittot* of heretics [*minim*]"; but cf. ibid., *Pesaḥim*, 5:5–7, and *Bereshit rabba* 8, 84. In medieval letters Rabbanites are called *kat* more often than Qaraites; see Bodl. MS Heb. c 28.15r, lines 5–6, T-S 13 J 26.1, lines 10–11, ENA 2739.18, line 5, and T-S Misc. 28.231, line 10 for *kat ha-rabbanim* used in formal greetings. The Arabic *ṭāʾifa* also means group, party, or company of people and in the Qurʾān, its semantic field is usually religious belief, but not always with the connotation of difference (see, e.g., 24:2). In later medieval usage, it extends to social and political groupings of all kinds: Roy P. Mottahedeh, *Loyalty and Leadership in an Early Islamic Society* (Princeton, 1980), 158–59; Mark R. Cohen, *Under Crescent and Cross: The Jews in the Middle Ages* (Princeton, 1994), 114; *EI*², s.v. "ṭāʾifa" (Eric Geoffroy). The word has acquired connotations in modern Arabic that are misleading in the study of earlier periods: see Ussama Makdisi, *The Culture of Sectarianism: Community, History and Violence in Nineteenth-century Ottoman Lebanon* (Berkeley, 2000), and compare the use of the phrase "sectarian violence" (or "sec-

As *madhāhib*, Rabbanites and Qaraites established social and political networks with each other, competed for affiliates, acquired them, lost them, and allied themselves with other networks in religious pursuits, economic ventures, and high politics. Qaraites contributed funds to rabbinic institutions and maintained alliances with rabbinic scholars and communal leaders. Those leaders sought the protection and patronage of Qaraite notables, courtiers, and local governors. Scribes at rabbinical courts wrote legal documents for Qaraites, sometimes according to Qaraite specifications, and adapted parts of the Qaraite formulary for their own use. Rabbanites became Qaraites, Qaraites became Rabbanites, and those defections occurred frequently for reasons other than religious conviction. The sociological typology of sectarianism has tended to generate its own historical reality, one that does not accord with the preponderance of the evidence, which suggests that the Qaraites were not merely a part of the Jewish people but a central part of it, living among rabbinic Jews and forming alliances of all types with them. Their leaders shaped Jewish politics and community life. Their works changed medieval Jewish culture profoundly.

FROM ECUMENICAL TO TERRITORIAL COMMUNITIES

I have divided this work into four parts, and though the overall arrangement is chronological, each section bears a slightly different conceptual emphasis.

The chapters in Part 1 offer an anatomy of Jewish self governance under the caliphs. It presents the two main groups of Rabbanite Jews, the Iraqi and Palestinian congregations, and the Qaraites (chapter 1), and explains how those groups came to coexist in the towns and cities of the Near East in the late ninth and tenth centuries (chapter 2). It also presents the modes and methods of cultivating loyalty that bound the Jewish community together (chapter 3). The Jews of Egypt, Syria, northern Africa, Sicily, and the Iberian peninsula—all the regions under Islamic rule—claimed loyalty to one, and sometimes more than one, of these three groups and demonstrated their loyalty in various ways. The leaders of the central Jewish institutions in Baghdad and Jerusalem were acutely conscious of the necessity of securing their followers' loyalty and developed a complex system of titulature and ritual pageantry aimed at doing so. The idea that these leaders struggled to retain their centrality stands in some tension with the some of the master-narratives that have organized the study of medieval Jews in the twentieth century. The classical historiographic presumption of Jewish "communal autonomy"—the idea that Jews formed

---

tarianism" as code for it) in news reporting on Northern Ireland, Iraq, and Pakistan: the implication is that religious ideology is the chief motivation for such violence and one need not look for other causes.

something like a state within a state whose leaders ruled by sheer force of rabbinic law—has obscured some of the strong and durable ties that bound the rabbinic leadership to nonrabbinic Jews on the one hand and to sources of authority beyond the Jewish community, such as courtiers, government bureaucrats, and caliphs, on the other. Chapter 3 thus reframes the study of the Jewish community taking these sources of authority into account.

From the interplay of ecumenical, regional, and local authority in part 1, I turn in part 2 to changes in the politics of Jewish leadership in the fifty-year period after the Fatimid conquest of Syria, ca. 980 to 1030. Around 900, the Abbasid caliphate had stretched from the far Maghrib in the west to central Asia in the east, but in 945, the Abbasids endured the takeover of Baghdad and were reduced to puppet rulers, and by 1000, they had lost all of their territory west of Iraq. The drastic truncation of their territory by the Fatimid conquest and the loss of the wealthy provinces of Egypt (969) and Syria (970–95) exacerbated an economic crisis in their realm; that crisis, in turn, brought thousands of Iraqi and Iranian migrants westward in search of more favorable markets and turned the Fatimid capital at Cairo into the center of economic life in the Islamic orbit. The world was shifting westward. While the Jewish centers of leadership in Baghdad persisted for another century despite interregna and other crises, the centers in Jerusalem and Fustat gathered strength and organized their own sort of administrative authority over the Jewish communities of Syria and Egypt. The first century of Fatimid rule, then, brought repeated adjustments to the very nature of Jewish communal organization.

Because the Qaraite community also centered on Jerusalem and Fustat, they played a decisive role in the success of that reorganization—the subject of part 2. Qaraite literary works from Jerusalem at the dawn of Fatimid rule suggest a community of ascetics chafing under their domination by an oppressive rabbinic establishment. But Geniza sources suggest that those ascetics were only one part of a Qaraite system of leadership that also included more moderate Qaraite scholars as well as traders, financiers, and courtiers. Some of these Qaraites were appointed to political positions under the Fatimids that placed them at the center of the Jewish community (chapter 4); through their role in long-distance commerce, they served as links and nodes in the network of organization tying the rabbinic center in Baghdad to its loyalists in the Jewish communities of Egypt and Ifrīqiya (chapter 5). They served in roles so important to the Rabbanites and to the functioning of the wider Jewish community, in fact, that to ignore them would be to offer at best an incomplete account of that community's history, and at worst a misleading one.

Their centrality only increased in the 1010s and early 1020s, when a group of Egyptian Rabbanites in Fustat attempted to remove themselves from the jurisdiction of their leaders in Jerusalem and Baghdad. The rabbinic leadership of Jerusalem undertook an extraordinary campaign to bring the Egyptians to heel, and succeeded in doing so only by forging a countervailing alliance with the Qaraite notables of Fustat and Cairo (chapter 6). They recognized that these Qaraites were their surest and shortest route to the Fatimid chancery, which provided them with investitures for their own positions and therefore the possibility of political legitimacy. Once the leaders had begun petitioning the Qaraites for support, their followers joined them: over the course of the 1020s, Jewish communities all over the Fatimid realm began appealing to Qaraite courtiers for economic aid and intercession before the caliph (chapter 7). The Qaraites thus emerged as a third party in Jewish politics, the key to rabbinic leaders' attempts to connect themselves more securely with the Fatimid court.

In 1029, the course of these changes was interrupted by a crisis when a zealous faction of rabbinic Jews during a pilgrimage festival at Jerusalem attempted to excommunicate the Qaraites en masse and drive them out of the Jewish ecumene at the very least symbolically (chapter 8). This chapter is the fulcrum of the book's narrative because of what it says about the rabbinic leadership's political methods and their followers' initial resistance to them: for the leaders, pragmatic considerations trumped ideological ones, while the group who insisted on excommunicating the Qaraites repudiated their leaders' methods and the emerging possibility of a community with the Qaraites at its center. The excommunication attempt failed, in part because the Qaraites were already so central that no mass excommunication could have succeeded, and in part because the rabbinic leaders and the Qaraites themselves mobilized the intervention of the state against the ban's instigators. The crisis surrounding the ban revealed with even more clarity how power in the Jewish community depended on access to the Fatimid court, and thus in practice on the Qaraite courtiers.

But these events unfolded against the backdrop of alliances among the rank and file as well. Those alliances form the subject of the chapters in part 3, which are an interlude in the strictly chronological flow of chapters in parts 2 and 4. In Fustat, Tyre, and elsewhere, Rabbanites and Qaraites married one another and arranged for their children to do so (chapter 9). As Schechter and Mann knew, the couples formalized their marriages in contracts that stipulated respect for the religious customs of both bride and groom on pain of heavy fines. But as Schechter and Mann could not have suspected, the official representatives of the Rabbanite *madhhab*—the court clerks and judges who ran the rabbinical courts—not only approved of these marriages and wrote contracts for them, but also wrote legal documents for Qaraites according to Qaraite specifications even when no Rabbanite party was involved in the transaction (chapter 10).

Between ca. 1030 and 1100, the centrality of the Qaraites in rabbinic politics became an accepted fact of Jewish public life. Three successive contenders for the leadership of the Rabbanite community in Palestine and one in Fustat made no secret of their appeals for support not only among the Qaraite grandees but among ordinary Qaraites as well. Part 4 narrates how, over the 1030s,

Qaraite courtiers emerged as kingmakers in Jewish politics (chapter 11). Communities across the Levant in the 1020s had understood the uses of calling on Qaraite grandees in times of emergency; by the 1030s, the leaders began to understand the importance of Qaraite support in their campaigns for office and continued to seek it over the next fifty years.

In the latter part of the eleventh century, events beyond the ken of the Jews or even the Fatimid caliphs reshaped the political landscape of the Eastern Mediterranean. The Seljuks entered Jerusalem (1073), and no sooner had the Fatimids won it back (1098) when the Franks conquered it (1099) and massacred or exiled a good part of its population. The Jewish community—with a reconstituted administration in Tyre, Damascus, and finally Fustat—not only survived the chaos but, surprisingly, emerged even stronger than it had been before. A century of Rabbanite-Qaraite cooperation and experiments in high politics now enabled the Jews to respond to the exigencies of war and captivity. As the Latin kingdoms took over the eastern part of the Fatimid realm, the Jews concentrated their administration in Egypt—which now, after more than a century of Fatimid rule, became the undisputed center of Jewish life in the Eastern Mediterranean. It also became home to a new office of Jewish communal leadership, the *ra'īs al-yahūd* (head of the Jews) of the Fatimid empire (chapter 12). The old ecumenical structure of governance centered on the religious academies of Baghdad and Jerusalem had finally been broken apart and replaced by a local administration centered on Egypt, one that served a tripartite Jewish community of the former rabbinic loyalists to Baghdad and Jerusalem on the one hand and the Qaraites on the other.

The emergence of a territorial authority was a significant development in the history of the Jews because it signaled a new model of Jewish community: one in which leaders committed themselves to the administrative apparatus of the community—appointing judges and other officials, levying taxes, distributing charity—while transcending the local interests of the congregation.[19] It is here that one can begin to speak of a Jewish community in more formal administrative terms, and as an administrative structure the community owed everything to the long history of Rabbanite-Qaraite cooperation. The Qaraites were instrumental in remaking that structure, and their very presence as a third congregation—one that now shared a century of political collaboration with rabbinic institutions—hastened the transition from the ecumenical form

[19] I follow most historians of medieval Jewry in distinguishing between the congregation and the community since in larger towns or cities where there was more than one congregation, the community served joint functions. But the terms *qahal* and *jamāʿa* were used for both in Geniza sources and it is not always clear which is meant. The territorial office to which I refer here is yet a third configuration that subsumed some of the roles the congregations had hitherto retained even in the presence of a larger communal body. See Goitein, "The Local Jewish Community in the Light of the Cairo Geniza Records," *Journal of Jewish Studies* 12 (1961): 133–58; idem, *Mediterranean Society*, 2:51–55; and below, chapters 3 and 12.

of authority to the territorial one. The result was a Jewish diaspora that now broke apart into discrete units of governance centered on local leaders—much as the Islamic imperium itself had fragmented a century or two earlier.

The epilogue broadens the focus of the inquiry to consider the nature of heresy in religions without church hierarchies or councils to decide on orthodoxy. The triangular relationship between Rabbanites, Qaraites, and the Fatimid state rarely allowed for accusations of heresy against the Qaraites. But on the Iberian peninsula during the same period and slightly later, matters were different. Rabbinic Jews utilized the power of local governments to rout out the religious dissenters in their midst. In the atmosphere of high ideological tension occasioned by the wars of the Islamic south against the Christian north in Iberia, heresy took on a particular urgency among rabbinic Jews. In both contexts, access to power determined when, whether, and why dissenters were accused of heresy and how they were treated. The epilogue argues that the Iberian situation shaped later understandings of Rabbanite-Qaraite conflict in general, despite the specificity of the circumstances there. That fact, in turn, dictates caution in generalizing about heresy and religious schism while ignoring the specifics of context, time, and place.

ABBREVIATIONS

Add.	Additional
AH	anno Hegirae
AIU	Alliance Israélite Universelle (Paris)
Antonin	Antonin Collection (St. Petersburg)
Ar.	Arabic
AS	Additional Series
BL	British Library (London)
Bodl.	Bodleian Library (Oxford)
Cod.	Codex
CUL	Cambridge University Library (Cambridge)
DK	David Kaufmann Collection (Budapest)
EI[2]	*Encyclopaedia of Islam*, 2d ed., ed. P. Bearman, Th. Bianquis, C. E. Bosworth, E. van Donzel, and W. P. Heinrichs (Leiden, 2006)
EJ[2]	Encyclopaedia Judaica, 2d ed., ed. Michael Berenbaum and Fred Skolnik (Detroit, 2007)
ENA	Elkan Nathan Adler Collection (New York)
Firk.	Firkovich Collections (St. Petersburg)
Halper	Center for Advanced Judaic Studies (Philadelphia)
Heb.	Hebrew
P. Heid.	Papyrussammlung der Universität Heidelberg
JNUL	Jewish National and University Library (Jerusalem)
JTS	Jewish Theological Seminary of America (New York)
Leiden	Bibliotheek der Rijksuniversiteit (Leiden)
Misc.	Miscellaneous
Mosseri	Jacques Mosseri Collection (Cambridge)
NS	New Series
Or.	Oriental
PER	Papyrussammlung Erzherzog Rainer (Vienna)
RNL	Russian National Library (St. Petersburg)
Sel.	Seleucid (dating system)
T-S	Taylor-Schechter Collection (Cambridge)
West. Coll.	Westminster College (Cambridge)

PART I

THE SHAPE OF THE JEWISH COMMUNITY

CHAPTER ONE
THE TRIPARTITE COMMUNITY

From the tenth century onward, Mediterranean towns of any importance housed not two but three Jewish groups: Babylonian Rabbanites, Palestinian Rabbanites, and Qaraites. Each had its own houses of worship, and each its own scholastic academy: the Babylonians had two in Baghdad, called *yeshivot* (sing. *yeshiva*); the Palestinian Rabbanites had a *yeshiva* in Tiberias, which later moved to Jerusalem; and the Qaraites had an academy in Jerusalem, though they avoided calling it a *yeshiva*, a name with distinct Rabbanite overtones. Each group also ran its own judicial and administrative institutions. This arrangement meant that Jewish law was not territorial but personal: people living in the same town might claim loyalty to any one of these four academies and have their documents drawn up in the courts whose judges they ordained. Since congregational loyalties were removed from geographic origins, people whose families hailed from any region might join any one of the two Rabbanite congregations or opt for the Qaraite one.

Given the relative latitude Jews possessed to organize their loyalties, what were the principles according to which they chose one congregation over another? How did the three groups coexist, and how did they compete with one another for followers? In this chapter I will suggest some answers to these questions, taking each of the three scholastic centers in turn, Babylonian, Palestinian, and Qaraite. I will also examine the centers' histories and their relationships to their networks and to one another until the eleventh century. Many histories of the period have focused on one group to the exclusion of the other two. But their competition and jockeying for power defined Jewish life in the tenth and eleventh centuries. Without some sense of that jockeying, neither the medieval Jewish community nor medieval Judaism makes much sense in historical terms.

THE PROBLEM OF BABYLONIAN HEGEMONY

The period between the tenth century and the twelfth has been understood as one of a gradual but inevitable Babylonian Rabbanite triumph over the other varieties of Judaism. In fact it was a period of uncertainty and considerable complexity.

A Jewish historiographic tradition beginning in the Middle Ages has referred to the four centuries after the Islamic conquest of Iraq (ca. 640–1040) as the "gaonic period," after the *ge'onim* (sing. *ga'on*) who served as the academic principals, chief justices, and main administrators of the Babylonian *yeshivot.* (The Palestinian *yeshiva* had its own *ge'onim*, but they are not considered in the traditional periodization scheme.)

The importance of the Babylonian *ge'onim* lies in their having transformed the Babylonian Talmud, the great compendium of rabbinic teachings compiled over the course of the pre-Islamic centuries, into the principal legal text of rabbinic Judaism. The gaonic period is, then, understood as the era during which the Babylonian Talmud achieved its canonical and central status in Judaism, and Judaism, in turn, achieved the characteristic and recognizable form that it would hold until the dawn of the modern age.[1]

The *ge'onim* of Babylonia did indeed see their principal role as the transmission, interpretation, and promulgation of their Talmud and staked their authority on the claim that they received the rabbinic traditions it contained via an unbroken chain stretching back to God's revelation to Moses on Sinai. This was a claim on behalf of the superiority of their construction of Judaism over the others. The periodization of Jewish history in which the Babylonian *ge'onim* form the main link in the chain connecting talmudic antiquity with the Middle Ages therefore reflects a decidedly Babylonian rabbinic perspective. It has its origins in a number of post-gaonic works extolling the Babylonian *ge'onim*, the best known of which is a chronicle of Abraham ibn Dāwūd of Toledo (ca. 1160–61) arguing that Iberian Jews had inherited the mantle of the Babylonian gaonate.[2]

[1] This is the thesis of Robert Brody, *The Geonim of Babylonia and the Shaping of Medieval Jewish Culture* (New Haven, 1998); see especially 161. The date of the Babylonian Talmud's redaction is a notoriously thorny question whose answer depends on one's definition of redaction. Current estimates cluster around 600 or 650, with some opinions arguing for as late 700 or 750; the later date marks the first appearance of extratalmudic halakhic literature in Iraq and thus the first evidence that the Babylonian Talmud was regarded as a closed corpus (if not a rigidly fixed text), when rabbinic contributions to its interpretation took the form of independent works rather than interpolations. See David Weiss Halivni, *Midrash, Mishnah, and Gemara: The Jewish Predilection for Justified Law* (Cambridge, Mass., 1986); idem, *Sources and Traditions: Commentaries to the Babylonian Talmud, Tractate Bava Metsia* (Jerusalem, 2003), 12; Jeffrey L. Rubenstein, *The Culture of the Babylonian Talmud* (Baltimore, 2003), 3; Brody, *The Textual History of the She'iltot*, Hebrew (New York, 1991); Brody, *Geonim of Babylonia*, 3–11, 156–66, 210–13.

[2] On the problem of periodizing gaonic history, see Brody, *Geonim of Babylonia*, 3–18; on the self-conception of the Iraqi *ge'onim*, ibid., 35–53. The three important medieval chronicles disagree as to the exact chronological parameters of the gaonic period, but historical convention dates it to ca. 640–ca. 1040, even though the gaonate of Palestine is not considered in this periodization, the Iraqi gaonate was revived in the twelfth century and thus technically outlasted it, and the two tenth-century chronicles know nothing of its end. See the epistle of Natan ha-Bavli, written in the mid-tenth

The main difficulty in evaluating the historical accuracy of any claim to continuity is lack of evidence, and the Babylonian claim is no exception. Though the Babylonian *yeshivot* traced their origins to the period of Sasanid rule (224–651), the first concrete evidence of their institutional existence dates only to the Umayyad period (661–750). But even if we had evidence of the Babylonian *yeshivot* for every year of the first millennium of the Common Era, the importance of the gaonic claim would lie not in its veracity but in its status as ideology. The sense of continuity with the past was a central tenet of that ideology, and for Jews, that continuity was palpable.

Yet the *yeshivot* underwent major changes over the course of this period, even if many of them are still only hazily understood. As the Iraqi population urbanized massively and Baghdad grew into the largest and most important city in the Near East, the *yeshivot* moved there from Sura and Pumbedita, the tiny towns by the Euphrates where they had existed since pre-Islamic times. They are both attested in Baghdad by 900, and there they metamorphosed into cosmopolitan and outward-looking institutions, headed by *ge'onim* such as Seʿadya b. Yūsuf al-Fayyūmī (*ga'on* of Sura, 928–42), Shemu'el b. Ḥofni (*ga'on* of Sura, ca. 998–1013), and Hayya b. Sherira (*ga'on* of Pumbedita, ca. 1004–38), all of whom were educated outside the narrow confines of the *yeshivot* they came to serve.

Besides urbanization, the major demographic fact of the tenth century was westward migration, and it had a marked effect on the world of the *yeshivot*. As large numbers of Iraqis moved away from the immediate jurisdiction of the Babylonian *ge'onim*, the latter campaigned for the loyalty of Jews throughout the Mediterranean basin, in part through arguments for their unbroken custodianship of rabbinic tradition. This much is evident from the gaonic correspondence the Geniza has preserved, and in itself suggests that the uninterrupted tradition the *ge'onim* defended was perhaps more fragile than they would have liked. Indeed, the story of the Babylonian *yeshivot* is filled with significant

century, Hebrew text in A. Neubauer, ed., *Mediaeval Jewish Chronicles and Chronological Notes, Edited from Printed Books and Manuscripts*, 2 vols. (Oxford, 1887–95), 2:78–88; Judeo-Arabic fragments in Israel Friedlander, "The Arabic Original of the Report of R. Nathan Hababli," *Jewish Quarterly Review* o.s. 17 (1905): 747–61; and Menahem Ben-Sasson, "The Structure, Goals, and Content of the Story of Nathan Ha-Babli," Hebrew, in *Culture and Society in Medieval Jewry: Studies Dedicated to the Memory of Haim Hillel Ben-Sasson*, ed. M. Ben-Sasson, Roberto Bonfil, and Joseph Hacker (Jerusalem, 1989), 137–96; Sherira b. Ḥananya's epistle to the Jewish community of Qayrawān, written in 986–87, Aramaic text in B. M. Lewin, *The Epistle of Rav Sherira Ga'on* (Jerusalem, 1971 [1921]); and Margarethe Schlüter, *Auf welche Weise wurde die Mishna geschrieben? Das Antwortschreiben des Rav Sherira Gaon, mit einem Faksimile der Handschrift Berlin Qu. 685 (Or. 160) und des Erstdrucks Konstantinopel* 1566, Texts and Studies in Medieval and Early Modern Judaism, 9 (Tübingen, 1993); and Avraham ibn Dāwūd, *Sefer ha-qabbala*, written in 1160–61, Hebrew text with English translation in Gerson D. Cohen, *A Critical Edition with a Translation and Notes of the Book of Tradition (Sefer ha-qabbalah)* (Philadelphia, 1967). For an overview of scholarship on the gaonic period, see idem, "Reconstruction of Gaonic History."

ruptures. Sura closed its doors for four decades (943–87), and around 1040, both Babylonian *yeshivot* closed down and would not reopen until the twelfth century, by which point they were a mere shadow of their former selves.[3]

The closure of the *yeshivot* in the mid-eleventh century is usually explained as a side-effect of their success. The Babylonian rabbinic construction of Judaism, this argument runs, had won the loyalties of Jews from Iran to the Atlantic coast; the independent centers of the Mediterranean inherited the gaonic teachings and now took the mantle of leadership from the *ge'onim* themselves. The story of the reorganization of Jewish communities into territorial units thus follows an arc of triumph and fragmentation, one parallel to a prevalent version of the political history of the Islamic empire, which had been centered on the ecumenical caliphates of the Umayyad and Abbasid dynasties and then shattered into rule by local territorial dynasties that either swore fealty to the center or claimed to have superseded it.

But in this narrative, the ultimate triumph of the peripheries is never held to have challenged the importance of the center. The Babylonian Rabbanite construction of Judaism is understood to have emerged victorious, and even to have vanquished the Palestinian one on its own turf. The Qaraites, for their part, are seen as having been reduced to an insignificant sect permanently separated from the main body of the Jewish people by the mid-tenth century at the latest.

In fact, it is unclear just how much loyalty the Babylonian *yeshivot* commanded outside Iraq before 900 because the sources are too thin to permit anything but speculation. The Palestinian *yeshiva* (a near complete mystery before the discovery of the Geniza) offered it vigorous competition, while the local communities of the Mediterranean ran their own daily affairs rather than requiring continual directives from the center. The Qaraites, for their part, played so central a role in the reorganization of the local Jewish communities that one should not imagine them watching all these developments from the sectarian sidelines.

The Conundrum of Gaonic Power

Though tenth-century sources report that the gaonate arose around the time of the Arab conquest of Iraq (ca. 640), in fact, evidence of what the *ge'onim* were and did in the seventh and eighth centuries is sparse, and there is a persis-

[3] On the academies' claims to antiquity, see Brody, *Geonim of Babylonia*, 4–35; on legal enactments dating to 650–51 and 786–87, ibid., 9 and 62–63; on the few extant responsa dating earlier than 760, ibid., 185–86 n. 2, where Brody notes that many of those attributions have been questioned. For the thesis that until the Islamic conquests the academies were no more than informal disciple circles without institutional continuity, see David M. Goodblatt, *Rabbinic Instruction in Sasanian Babylonia*, Studies in Judaism in Late Antiquity 9 (Leiden, 1975), and for a discussion, Rubenstein, *Culture of the Babylonian Talmud*, 16–21.

tent temptation to project the structure and function of the *yeshivot* in the better-known period after 900 back onto the earlier and more murky one. Regardless of the situation before 900, Geniza evidence confirms that by the tenth century, the Babylonian *ge'onim* had disseminated their Talmud beyond the closed circle of the *yeshivot*, and by the eleventh, it played a central role in Jewish scholarship not only in the Arabic-speaking Jewish world but as far away as Christian Europe, where the great scholar Shelomo b. Yiṣḥaq of Troyes in Champagne (known as Rashi, 1040–1105) composed a running commentary on most of it. But what role the Babylonian Talmud played in the lives of masses of Jews in an age when male literacy scarcely ever exceeded single-digit percentages is a separate and still unanswered question.[4]

The accomplishments of the Babylonian *ge'onim* would still be impressive even if we restricted them to having amassed loyalists as far away as Iberia and disseminating the Talmud as far away as the Rhineland. There are two standard explanations for the Babylonian achievement.

One is that there was a causal connection between the political events of the first four hundred years of Islamic empire and the spread of Babylonian rabbinic Judaism. The Islamic conquests, surely one of the most momentous events in world history, were no less momentous for the world's Jews, the vast majority of whom they brought under a single political aegis for the first time since Alexander of Macedon a millennium earlier. But while the Macedonian territories fragmented after only a decade, the Islamic empire held together—more or less—for three hundred years. That must have meant something for the unity of the Jews, and for the power the *ge'onim* held over them.

This explanation first appeared at the dawn of modern Jewish history-writing. "The further the rule of Umayyad caliphs extended," wrote Heinrich Graetz in the 1850s, "the more followers the Babylonian Jewish leaders gained. Every conquest of the Mohammedan generals extended the borders of exilarchal and gaonic rule."[5] In this account, political unity enabled the spread of rabbinic Judaism; in others, the fact that the Abbasids founded their capital in 762 at Baghdad on the Tigris, about two days' journey from the academies of Sura and Pumbedita, meant that the Babylonian *yeshivot* suddenly found themselves at the center of the civilized world, and this confluence of events contributed to their dominance over world Jewry.[6]

[4] For this estimate, see Rustow, "Literacy, Orality, and Book Culture among Medieval Jews," *Jewish Quarterly Review* (forthcoming).

[5] Heinrich Graetz, *Geschichte der Juden von den ältesten Zeiten bis auf die Gegenwart*, 4th ed., 11 vols. (Leipzig, 1906–9), 5:141 (rev. Hebrew trans. [Warsaw, 1890], 3:141–42).

[6] For a summary of the scholarly consensus, see Mark R. Cohen, "Administrative Relations between Palestinian and Egyptian Jewry during the Fatimid Period," in *Egypt and Palestine: A Millennium of Association (868–1948)*, ed. Amnon Cohen and Gabriel Baer (Jerusalem, 1984): 134. On the locations of Pumbedita and Sura, see Aharon Oppenheimer in collaboration with Benjamin Isaac and Michael Lecker, *Babylonia Judaica in the Talmudic Period*, Beihefte zum Tübinger Atlas des

The other explanation focuses on the principal written works of the *ge'onim*: commentaries on the Talmud; discussions and monographic treatments of problems in Jewish law; and responsa (Heb. *she'elot u-teshuvot*, literally, "questions and answers"), rulings on legal questions that sometimes consisted principally of talmudic exegesis. Though the first gaonic responsum is estimated to date to some time before 689, this is only an estimate. Gaonic responsa are not well attested until the ninth and tenth centuries, and by that point they were mailed to parts of the Jewish world from Iran to Iberia over distances previously unthinkable.[7] A functioning system of letters as tools of religious instruction and regulation required a reliable and efficient system of mails, and indeed, although the Umayyads had established one along with the system of roads on which it depended, its use was restricted principally to government intelligence and administration. In the late ninth century, the Abbasids centralized the system, founded a *dīwān* to administer it, and transformed the flow of written information in the empire, with a host of private carriers following suit.[8] Many of the responsa preserved in the Geniza survived because they were sent to faraway places in Egypt, Ifrīqiya, al-Andalus, and Sicily. Responsa, then, are thought to have constituted the principal mechanism by which the *ge'onim* established their legal authority. This second explanation is congruent

Vorderen Orients, Reihe B (Geisteswissenschaften) Nr. 47 (Wiesbaden, 1983), 362–64 (citing Natan ha-Bavli at n. 69) and 417–18. Pumbedita (in Sasanid usage, Anbār) was about five kilometers upstream from al-Fallūja on the Euphrates near the Nahr ʿĪsā; Sura was midway between the east branch of the Euphrates and the ruins of Babylon, on the Nahr Sūrā (now Shaṭṭ al-Ḥilla), a main subsidiary of the Euphrates, about fifteen kilometers north of the later town of al-Ḥilla (founded in 1102; see *EI*[2] s.v. "al-Ḥilla" [Jacob Lassner]). On the distances and travel times, see Jacob Obermeyer, *Die Landschaft Babylonien im Zeitalter des Talmud und des Gaonats* (Frankfurt am Main, 1929), 251; Babylonian Talmud, *Makkot* 5a and *Yevamot* 116a (on a fast service called the Flying Camel, *gamla pirḥa*, which reduced the distance between Nehardea and Sura from two days to one). In the Middle Ages, there was still a mail route between al-Anbār (Pumbedita) and Baghdad that the Arab geographers measured as twelve *farsakhs*, about 62 km. See *EI*[2], s.v. "al-Anbār" (M. Streck [A. A. Duri]) and the sources cited there.

[7] Simḥa Assaf, *Tequfat ha-ge'onim ve-sifrutah* (The gaonic period and its literature), ed. Mordecai Margaliot (Jerusalem, 1976), 133; see also Brody, *Geonim of Babylonia*, 185–201. The rabbinic *teshuva* is the equivalent of the Islamic *fatwā*, but there is no evidence that the former was developed in imitation of the latter. Both may have continued an earlier Roman and Byzantine pattern of ecclesiastical leadership via epistles, or perhaps the earlier Jewish one of disseminating halakhic letters, but as Brody writes, "it was only in the Geonic period" that writing and sending responsa "became a central facet of rabbinic activity" (*Geonim of Babylonia*, 185). Cf. Menachem Elon, *Jewish Law: History, Sources, Principles*, ed. A. Philip and Muriel Berman, 4 vols. (Philadelphia, 1994), 3:1454–56; Rina Drory, *The Emergence of Jewish-Arabic Literary Contacts at the Beginning of the Tenth Century*, Hebrew (Tel Aviv, 1988), 61–64, and eadem, *Models and Contacts: Arabic Literature and Its Impact on Medieval Jewish Culture* (Leiden, 2000), 131–34.

[8] See *EI*[2], s.v. "Barīd" (Dominique Sourdel); Adam Silverstein, *Postal Systems in the Pre-Modern Islamic World* (Cambridge, 2007), chaps. 2 and 3; Goitein, "Commercial Mail Service in Medieval Islam," *Journal of the American Oriental Society* 84 (1964): 118–23, with references to earlier studies; idem, *Mediterranean Society*, 1:281–95; and Abraham L. Udovitch, "Time, the Sea, and Society: Duration of Commercial Voyages on the Southern Shores of the Mediterranean during the High Middle Ages," *Settimane di studio del Centro Italiano di Studi sull'Alto Medioevo* 25 (1978): 503–46.

with the first in focusing on political unity as the cause of gaonic hegemony, but it emphasizes communication rather than proximity to governmental power as the means of its spread. And while the first set of answers leans on state power for their explanatory force, the second set focuses on the authority of the *ge'onim* themselves.

Both answers to the conundrum of gaonic power—the Islamic state and the force of rabbinic law—seem plausible on their face, but appear wanting when one examines the period's sources more closely. Linking Babylonian rabbinic power to the Abbasid dynasty reflects an understandable and even commendable desire to search for explanations beyond inner-Jewish developments. But it also reflects a bias toward identifiable institutions such as states over more complex and informal networks, and a focus on the power of coercion over that of persuasion.

In fact, there is not a word in the sources attesting to a direct relationship between the *ge'onim* and the Abbasid caliphs before the thirteenth century. Political unity does not necessarily entail religious homogenization. Two centuries after they came under caliphal rule, subjects of the Islamic empire still spoke a wide variety of languages and represented a congeries of religious traditions. If linguistic Arabization and religious Islamization were slow (and separate) processes that did not gain momentum until the ninth and tenth centuries, depending on the region, so, too, the degree and rate of Jewish religious homogenization should be neither assumed nor overstated. The outlying communities were willing to cede authority to a far-off spiritual center in Baghdad where textual or other abstract questions were concerned, but they hardly waited for the next ship or caravan to supply them with gaonic dictates in quotidian matters. The *ge'onim*, for their part, waited less than patiently for revenues from their followers abroad, as their letters suggest. It may be that the gaonic centers needed the peripheries more than the peripheries needed the centers.[9]

Partly because of its focus on law, then, older scholarship on the gaonic period tended to depict Babylonian hegemony as an orchestrated battle that succeeded simply by being waged, or the *ge'onim* as having become powerful merely by writing works and having them copied, disseminated, and preserved.[10] In fact, Jews in the Islamic Mediterranean paid symbolic and intellectual fealty

[9] On the relationship between the Abbasid caliphs and the Iraqi *ge'onim*, see chap. 3, 67–68. For a discussion and definition of the term "state" in this context, see chap. 3, n. 5. On rates of conversion to Islam, see Richard W. Bulliet, *Conversion to Islam in the Medieval Period: An Essay in Quantitative History* (Cambridge, Mass.,1979). Bulliet focuses on Iran and extrapolates to various other regions based on varying historical conditions. His methods and conclusions have been debated but the questions he asks about the correlation between conversion and innovation diffusion remain salient.

[10] See especially Louis Ginzberg, *Geonica*, 2 vols. (New York, 1909); Assaf, *Tequfat ha-ge'onim ve-sifrutah*; Sheraga Abramson, *In the Centers and the Peripheries during the Geonic Period: The History of the Geonim and Exilarchs in Palestine and Babylonia and the Sages of Egypt and North Africa, based on Geniza Documents*, Hebrew (Jerusalem, 1965).

to the *ge'onim* while retaining their independence in the day-to-day practice of Jewish law.[11] From an administrative point of view, moreover, Babylonian gaonic hegemony was never fully achieved. At no point during the existence of the Babylonian *yeshivot* did they command the unquestioned loyalties of a majority of world Jewry. Up until their closure, they engaged in bitter and continuing struggles over the fealty—and financial contributions—of the Jews outside Iraq.

Westward Migration

It is nonetheless possible to establish a relationship between Islamic empire and rabbinic Judaism if one seeks it not in the ascendancy of the Abbasids but in their decline and the concomitant migration of Jews from the Iraqi and Persian provinces under Babylonian jurisdiction westward in the late ninth and tenth centuries. Those migrations facilitated the growth of durable links between the center and the peripheries.

The decline of the Abbasid center began in lower Iraq and Khuzistān with the Zanj slave revolt of 869–83, which sapped the caliphate's energies and weakened the already precarious hold it exerted on the central Islamic lands. It accelerated during the utterly disastrous reign of al-Muqtadir (908–32), who was installed as a child by a powerful group of courtiers, was deposed the minute he ascended the throne (908), lost Ifrīqiya to the Fatimids (909), endured the pillaging of Mecca, Baṣra, and Kufa (923–30), exhausted the treasury with profligate spending that provoked a military rebellion in Baghdad during which he was deposed again (929), and was finally killed.

During these decades, the Iraqi economy declined precipitously along with Iraq's institutional structures. Then, in 945, condottieri from Daylam south of the Caspian Sea entered Baghdad and reduced the caliphate to a pale shadow of its former self. As the Buwayhid dynasty they ruled the Abbasid realm for the next century, but the caliph would remain a puppet for the next five centuries. The last blow came in 969, when the caliphate lost the wealthy province of Egypt to the Fatimids, who over the next two decades conquered Syria, thus extending their rule right up to the border of Iraq itself. It was then that Cairo emerged as the undisputed center of the Near Eastern world. Vast numbers of people left the collapsing Abbasid heartland and entered the Mediterranean and Indian Ocean trade routes, a tide of migrants that did not taper off until the Seljuk invasions of the eastern Mediterranean in the third quarter of the eleventh century.

Contemporary commentators were not unaware of the momentous shift westward. The geographer al-Maqdisī (d. ca. 990) proclaimed that Fustat had

[11] See particularly the works of Ben-Sasson, chap. 3, n. 14.

now abrogated Baghdad, which "has been superseded until the day of Judgment; [Egypt's] metropole has now become the greatest glory of the Muslims." (Al-Maqdisī himself was a product of these migrations: his maternal grandfather had left Qūmis in Iran for Palestine.) Members of the literate classes featured prominently among these migrants, including merchants and high government functionaries who possessed skills in writing and administration and now filled the ranks of local government bureaucracies in Syria, Egypt, and Ifrīqiya. There were numerous Jews among these literate migrants, too, and they were a potent force in the transplantation of Iraqi loyalties to the west—and in the political struggles that form the subject of this book.[12]

During the tenth and eleventh centuries, the Jewish communities of the Islamic Mediterranean were teeming with Iraqis. Their arrival in Fustat, Qayrawān, Palermo, and numerous cities and towns in Syria–Palestine facilitated the spread of Babylonian traditions and expedited the efforts of the Babylonian *ge'onim* to win loyalists in the Mediterranean communities. Though it was not a given that people of Iraqi origin would offer fealty to the *yeshivot* in Baghdad, their migration meant that in a palpable and, ultimately, historically important way, the center now inhabited the periphery. Logistically as well, the presence in the Mediterranean of long-distance traders with ties to Iraq made it easier for the *ge'onim* of Baghdad to send responsa to the Mediterranean centers and demand donations in return.

Even so, more than uncontested hegemony, the result of this migration was protracted conflict. In the mid-tenth century, while Iraq was collapsing and the academy of Sura was closed, Iraqi immigrants managed to establish their own congregations in parts of Palestine where Jews had always followed the Palestinian rite. These included Banyas and possibly even Tiberias, the very seat of the Palestinian *yeshiva*. There were further stirrings of an autonomous Iraqi administrative body in Ramla ca. 1030, but the Palestinian *ga'on* crushed it by appealing to the Fatimid caliph.[13] (Though there is no evidence of Abbasid support for the Babylonian *ge'onim*, there is ample evidence of Fatimid support for the Palestinian *ge'onim*, a subject I will take up in chapter 3.)

It is important to try to reimagine how the drama of westward migration unfolded from a ground-level perspective because its outcome—the Babylonian

[12] Muḥammad b. Aḥmad al-Muqaddasī (al-Maqdisī), *Aḥsan al-taqāsīm fī maʿrifat al-aqālīm* (The best divisions for knowledge of the regions), ed. M. J. de Goeje, Bibliotheca geographorum Arabicorum 3 (Leiden, 1906), 193; on his forebears, 357 (cf. 188). On the migration, see Goitein, *Mediterranean Society*, 1:30–33; Eliyahu Ashtor, "Un movement migratoire au haut moyen âge: Migrations de l'Irak vers les pays méditerranéens," *Annales: Economies, sociétés, civilizations* 27 (1972): 185–214. Few scholars have noted the impact of Iraqi migration on the spread of Babylonian rabbinic tradition. The exception is Cohen, "Administrative Relations," 119–20. Cf. Goitein, *Mediterranean Society* 1:30–31, 2:5–14, and Cohen, "The Reconstruction of Gaonic History," 137–38.

[13] S. D. Goitein, "Congregation versus Community: An Unknown Chapter in the Communal History of Jewish Palestine," *Jewish Quarterly Review* 44 (1954): 294, and below, chaps. 2 and 4.

challenge to the Palestinians on their own soil—was so full of paradoxes: the Iraqi descendants of the Judean exiles who had remained in Persia under Cyrus the Great now claimed ascendancy over the followers of the Jerusalem *yeshiva* itself; the apotheosis of the Babylonian construction of rabbinic Judaism became possible not because the followers of the *ge'onim* had triumphed through their religious ideology but because economic duress had forced them to move west.

Babylonian gaonic hegemony is, then, best understood as an ongoing struggle whose successes depended on far-flung networks of followers—followers who might shift their loyalties at any moment to one of the other two congregations. While the medieval Jewish chronicles paint Babylonian hegemony as a series of campaigns from a strongly organized center that imposed its will on the peripheries through law, Geniza evidence attests to the continuing efforts of the Babylonian *ge'onim* to cultivate and hold adherents.

RABBINIC ACTIVITY IN PALESTINE

The Rabbanite *yeshiva* of Palestine led an even more disjointed existence than the Babylonian *yeshivot*. Any account of it is hampered by a paucity of sources before the period of Fatimid rule from Cairo (969–1171), but it is clear that during the ninth and early tenth centuries, it was based in Tiberias in Galilee. When it first assumed some semblance of institutional form is, however, unclear and badly attested. In the tenth century, the *yeshiva* moved from Tiberias to Jerusalem, where it remained until the Seljuk and Frankish conquests forced it northward to Tyre and Damascus, and finally southward to Fustat.

Despite all this disruption, the Palestinian *yeshiva* outlasted the Babylonian *yeshivot*. In the early eleventh century it repelled several attempts by local Iraqis to form their own independent jurisdiction. After the fall of the *yeshivot* in Baghdad, it absorbed many Iraqi loyalists, and by the time it moved to Fustat in 1127, it had inherited the entire administrative infrastructure of the Babylonian community. When a latter-day Babylonian *yeshiva* opened in Baghdad in the twelfth century, the great sage of Fustat, Moses Maimonides (1138–1204), a leader of the Palestinian-rite synagogue in which the Geniza was kept, ridiculed its *ga'on*, Shemu'el b. ʿAlī (r. 1164–94), as "an ignoramus in every respect," while corresponding with what he deemed more serious scholarly centers elsewhere. All this already suggests that there is more to the putative Babylonian triumph than meets the eye.[14]

[14] On the dates of the *yeshiva*'s arrival in Jerusalem, see Gil, *History of Palestine*, sec. 738. On its arrival in Tyre, its move to Fustat and its merger with the office of head of the Jews (*ra'īs al-yahūd*), see chap. 12. For Maimonides' opinions of Shemu'el b. ʿAlī, see below, chap. 3, 84–85.

Yet while the Babylonian *ge'onim*—especially those of the tenth and eleventh centuries—left a record of responsa, commentaries, and monographic studies of Jewish law and liturgy that their followers copied and preserved, next to nothing has survived attesting to the scholarly and spiritual activities that must have lain at the heart of the Jerusalem *yeshiva*'s activities during the same period. But this dearth of literary works is offset by thousands of letters and legal documents preserved in the Geniza that bear the signatures of the Palestinian *ge'onim*, as against a tiny number of such documents for the Babylonian *ge'onim*. The result is that we know much more about how the Jerusalem *yeshiva* ran its quotidian affairs during a period when it functioned as a high court, a legislative body, and the principal administrator of the Rabbanite communities under Fatimid rule than we do about its function as a scholastic center.

Prior to the eleventh century, by contrast, the situation is almost precisely the reverse. Little survives by way of administrative or personal correspondence from the *yeshiva* of Palestine, but there is an enormous corpus of exegetical and other scholastic materials of Palestinian provenance, much of it of anonymous authorship. These include not only the Palestinian Talmud (a finished product by the fifth century) but numerous collections of *midrash* (biblical exegesis and homilies) and *piyyuṭ* (liturgical poetry), two areas in which the Palestinians seem to have excelled. These collections came into being between the fifth century and the tenth, with the preponderant majority dating to the first three centuries of the Islamic era. But despite the abundance of Palestinian literature, to what degree the Palestinian *ge'onim* conceived of themselves as the authoritative interpreters and transmitters of these works is entirely unknown, as is the degree to which they attempted to promulgate their own Talmud. The first evidence of the transmission of the Palestinian Talmud comes from Qayrawān in North Africa, which suggests that the Palestinian Talmud was indeed transmitted beyond Palestine's borders, but the role of the Palestinian *ge'onim* in doing so remains obscure.[15]

Any question of continuity between the Palestinian Jewish communities in late antiquity and the early Islamic period is, then, a matter of conjecture. The circumstantial evidence is suggestive: Tiberias became an important Jewish center after the emperor Hadrian exiled the Jews from Jerusalem in 135 CE (they were readmitted to Jerusalem only after the Arab conquest in 638) and the center of Jewish life shifted north to Galilee. Between the second and fourth centuries, Tiberias changed from a pagan city to a recognizably Jewish one whose Jewish inhabitants observed more and more distinctively Jewish

[15] See Shmuel Safrai, ed., *The Literature of the Sages*, Compendia rerum Iudaicarum ad Novum Testamentum, 2:3:1 (Assen, Netherlands, 1987): 312–14, and Grossman, "The *Yeshiva* of Eretz Israel, Its Literary Output and Relationship with the Diaspora," in *The History of Jerusalem: The Early Muslim period, 638–1099*, ed. Joshua Prawer and Haggai Ben-Shammai (Jerusalem, 1996), 225–69.

practices, though not necessarily rabbinic ones. Most of the Palestinian Talmud was redacted at Tiberias in the mid- to late-fourth century. Tiberias was also the administrative center of the Jewish population and the seat of the Jewish *nasi*—the patriarch invested by Rome with authority over the Jews. All these facts hint at the possibility that the Jewish institutions of late antique and early medieval Tiberias may have existed in continuity, even if they still offer no firm evidence to that effect. Though the patriarchate itself was abolished by the emperor Theodosius II (408–50) some time between 415 and 429, the Theodosian code of 438 nonetheless persisted in portraying the Jews as a religious community with a clergy under the jurisdiction of an episcopal office. The elimination of the patriarchate apparently altered but did not abolish this basic administrative structure, which is in keeping with evidence for the existence of a Jewish *ga'on* in ninth-century Tiberias heading some administrative institution.[16]

But that does not amount to an argument for continuity, and the institutional setting of Palestinian rabbinic activity from the fifth century to the ninth remains a vast blank, with one exception: a ninth-century chronicle claiming that in 520, the Babylonian exilarch (*resh galuta*), Mar Zuṭra, became "head of the Sanhedrin" in Palestine, the ancient high court of seventy judges—an institution otherwise utterly unattested during this period. That information is too late and too little to warrant the conclusion that either the Sanhedrin or the Palestinian *yeshiva* that claimed to have inherited its function existed in the early sixth century, let alone continuously throughout this period. The first firm evidence of a *yeshiva* in Tiberias appears only in the ninth century.[17]

Nor does it bring us any closer to understanding the *yeshiva* as a scholastic center, even though numerous learned works emanated from Jewish Palestine during these centuries. The difficulty of integrating Palestinian rabbinic literary output with later information about the administrative structure of the Jewish community is exacerbated by a division of scholarly labor according to

[16] *Codex Theodosianus*, 16.8.22, 16.8.29. See Günter Stemberger, *Jews and Christians in the Holy Land: Palestine in the Fourth Century*, trans. Ruth Tuschling (Edinburgh, 2000 [1987]), 262–66. On this basic administrative structure, which stood in tension with the Roman and Byzantine one of citizens organized into municipalities under provincial governors, see Seth Schwartz, "Rabbinization in the Sixth Century," in *The Talmud Yerushalmi and Graeco-Roman Culture*, ed. Peter Schäfer (Tübingen, 2002), 59; idem, *Imperialism and Jewish Society, 200 BCE to 640 CE*, Jews, Christians, and Muslims from the Ancient to the Modern World (Princeton, 2001), 192–206. See further ibid., introduction; 145–53 and 205; chap. 9; idem, "Historiography on the Jews in the 'Talmudic period' (70–630 CE)," in *The Oxford Handbook of Jewish Studies*, ed. Martin Goodman (Oxford, 2003): 79–114; and Catherine Hezser, *The Social Structure of the Rabbinic Movement in Roman Palestine*, Texte und Studien zum antiken Judentum 66 (Tübingen, 1997). On the date of the redaction of the Palestinian Talmud see Stemberger, *Jews and Christians in the Holy Land*, 289–94; and most recently Elizabeth Shanks Alexander, *Transmitting Mishnah: The Shaping Influence of Oral Tradition* (Cambridge, 2006), 81–82 n. 9.

[17] Cf. Gil, *History of Palestine*, secs. 729–32, and see further ibid., secs. 732–35.

which the Palestinian literary corpus—even works whose redaction postdates the Islamic conquest—has tended to remain the preserve of scholars of rabbinic literature whose chronological center of gravity lies in late antiquity. That division of labor is justifiable on the grounds that the later rabbinic corpus is modeled on the earlier one, and in literary terms, must be understood in light of it. But those who study the institutional workings of the later Palestinian *yeshiva*—myself included—leave the study of its scholarly corpus to specialists in rabbinic literature, with the result that the relationship between the scholastic and administrative functions of the *yeshiva* before the eleventh century still remains elusive.

In some ways, the entire problem has been upstaged by a single event of the early tenth century that, according to common consensus, marked the final and decisive Palestinian submission to Babylonia and the point after which the Palestinian *yeshiva* putatively stopped mattering because it became intellectually dependent on Baghdad: the calendar controversy of 921–22.

The Calendar Controversy

This celebrated dispute pitted the leaders of the Palestinian *yeshiva*—the *ga'on* Me'ir and his son Aharon b. Me'ir—against the Egyptian Se'adya b. Yosef al-Fayyūmī. Se'adya was not yet *ga'on* of Sura (he would be appointed in 928), but he was about to prove himself a zealous champion of the Babylonian cause. There is general scholarly agreement that victory in the calendar controversy earned the Babylonian camp the loyalty of Jews and acknowledgement as superior to the Palestinians. After the calendar controversy, it is said, Palestinian Judaism could no longer compete with the strengths of Baghdad in Jewish law and administration. As the rest of this book will make clear, matters were not so simple: the Palestinian *ge'onim* continued to engage in vigorous and successful efforts to block Iraqi incursions into their jurisdiction.[18]

The Jewish Calendar

To understand the dispute—as well as some things I am going to say about the Qaraites in chapter 2—it will help to know how the Jewish calendar works, and when it does not work, why not.[19]

The basic problem facing the ancient Israelite calendar—and the later Jewish one based on it—was how to reconcile the lunar months the Torah presumes with the agricultural or solar cycle it commands. Twelve lunar months

[18] See, for example, Henry Malter, *Saadia Gaon, His Life and Works* (Philadelphia, 1921): 69–88, and cf. Brody, *Geonim of Babylonia*, 120.

[19] Most of the explication of calendars in this section is based on Sacha Stern, *Calendar and Community: A History of the Jewish Calendar, Second Century BCE–Tenth Century CE* (Oxford, 2001), and on personal communication with George Saliba (May 2003) and Stern (February–May 2005).

add up to a span roughly eleven days shorter than the solar year. Keeping the calendar running therefore required making two decisions: how often to reconcile the lunar year with the solar one by inserting an intercalary thirteenth month; and how to determine when the months began.

I will start with the problem of months first. Most Jewish calendars of antique vintage opted to declare months at the new moon. But there was still some disagreement over whether the crucial event was the conjunction—when the moon is poised between the sun and the earth and one can not see it in the sky—or the appearance of the crescent moon a day or two after the conjunction. The second method possessed the advantage of empirical verifiability, and so months were declared when someone actually saw the crescent moon.

But this method had drawbacks, too: cloudy skies could make it impossible to see the crescent moon for months on end. The crescent moon also appears at different times in different places. To avoid the latter problem, by ca. 200 CE the rabbis decided that the crescent moon sighting that mattered was the one reported to the rabbinic court in Palestine, a decision attested in the Mishnah in a passage that demonstrates that calendars are principally social conventions whose regulation is a function of institutional power.[20] The rabbis also developed a system of beacons for announcing the new moon to the communities of the diaspora. As for cloudy skies, there needed to be a backup method to determine whether and when the new moon had appeared. Though astronomers in late antiquity possessed the knowledge necessary to predict the new moon mathematically, Jewish authorities still relied in the main upon empirical methods, and continued to determine the new moon empirically as late as the tenth century.[21]

Intercalating the year presented a different set of problems. The Torah commands proclaiming a new year in the month of Nisan, in the spring (even though the holiday celebrating the New Year, Rosh ha-Shana, occurs in the fall, at the beginning of the seventh month). But because twelve lunar months are shorter than a solar year, within a matter of years the discrepancy would put Nisan too early for Passover to remain a spring holiday. The intercalary month was devised to correct the discrepancy.

But the problem still remained of when to insert the intercalary month. Should there be a milestone the passing of which would trip an intercalation, such as the vernal equinox or the maturing of specific crops, or a fixed rhythm of intercalations? Exodus 34:18 and Deuteronomy 16:1 command the Israelites to observe Passover "in the month of *aviv*," a word variously interpreted to

[20] Mishnah, *Rosh ha-Shana* 2:2–5.

[21] Stern, *Calendar and Community*, 227–28. This last point is generally overlooked in scholarship on Qaraites, which presumes lunar observation to have been a strictly Qaraite method; see below, chap. 2.

mean "spring" (some time after the vernal equinox) or "the ripening barley crop" (an interpretation that necessitated following the progress of the barley crop in Palestine in order to determine whether Nisan should be declared or held off by an intercalary month). The latter interpretation is attested both among Qaraites (with whom it eventually became associated) and in classical rabbinic literature.[22]

Eventually, Rabbanite Jews decided to follow a fixed cycle of intercalations. For this purpose, they adopted the Metonic system, an ancient nineteen-year cycle containing seven intercalated years, since it most closely brought the lunar year into line with the solar one.[23] It also allowed the Babylonians to keep up in case of attenuated communication with Palestine. In determining the months, the Babylonians probably used lunar tables, but they would defer to the Palestinians' empirical observations if these reached them in time. The Palestinians, too, had recourse to a calendar of conjunctions in case of cloudy skies. When Babylonia and Palestine came up with different dates, there was a protocol for which one to follow: Palestine always took precedence.[24]

There the technical details end and questions of institutional power begin.

The Babylonian Bid for Precedence

Both prerogatives—intercalating the year and declaring the new months—belonged to the Jewish communal leadership of Palestine: the *nesi'im* and, after them, the *ge'onim* of Tiberias, who declared annually whether there would be an intercalary thirteenth month and announced the start of each new month according to lunar observation. But next to nothing is known about the operation of this system in the period between the abolition of the *nesi'im* in the early fifth century and the first evidence of the gaonate in Palestine in the early ninth. In the early ninth century, the traditional Babylonian dependence on Palestine in calendation loosened. Why is a matter of conjecture. One convincing answer is that Abbasid advances in astronomy enabled the Jews to develop a fixed calendar that did not need to be verified through empirical observation.

22 A rabbinic interpretation of *aviv* as the barley crop is attested in the Tosefta, *Sanhedrin* 2:2–3 (Stern, *Calendar and Community*, 161 n. 22), and among eleventh-century rabbinic commentators for whom it probably had no practical ramifications. A third interpretation—the ripening of tree-fruits—is also attested in rabbinic literature (ibid., 161). Eleventh-century Qaraite letters bearing witness to the state of the barley crop in Palestine survived in the Geniza. Bodl. MS Heb. b 11.10, in Judeo-Arabic: letter of the Qaraite Moshe b. Yiṣḥaq in Jerusalem to a Qaraite leader in Fustat, 1044. T-S 12.147, in Judeo-Arabic: copy of a Qaraite testimony on the state of the barley crop near Gaza, March 1052.

23 For a mathematical explanation of the intercalary cycles, see Abu l-Rayḥān Muḥammad b. Aḥ-mad al-Bīrūnī, *al-Āthār al-bāqiya ʿan al-qurūn al-khāliya* (The remaining traces of past ages, composed ca. 1000) in C. Edward Sachau, *Chronologie orientalischer Völker von alBīrūnī* (Leipzig, 1923), 52–55; idem, *The Chronology of Ancient Nations: An English Version of the Arabic Text of the Āthārul-bākiya of alBīrūnī* (Frankfurt, 1984 [1879]), 62–64.

24 Stern, *Calendar and Community*, 263 et passim.

The first evidence that Babylonian Jews possessed a fixed calendar is found in a work of 823–24 by Abū ʿAbd Allāh Muḥammad b. Aḥmad al-Khwārazmī, an astronomer and mathematician at the Abbasid court in Baghdad.[25] If the passage is not a later interpolation into al-Khwārazmī's work, then as early as the first quarter of the ninth century, Babylonian Jewish authorities were capable of anticipating all the Palestinian calendar proclamations. That meant that in theory, they were also capable of declaring total independence from Palestine in calendrical reckoning. But they did not. Rather, they continued to defer to the Palestinians—calendars being, in practice, bound to human hierarchies.

There is further evidence of Babylonian submission to the Palestinians about a decade later. In 835–36, an Iraqi exilarch announced that according to his calculation, Passover 836 should fall on a different date from the one decreed by the Palestinian *gaʾon*, but that he would defer to the Palestinian decree "lest Israel be split into factions."[26] That the exilarch offered such a justification confirms that the Iraqis' new scientific means of calculating the conjunction had made it possible for them to supplant the Palestinian courts in calendrical matters, but they had chosen not to do so for the sake of unanimity. Until the Iraqi advance in calendar calculation in the ninth century, writes Sacha Stern, "the survival of this Palestinian rabbinic monopoly" from late antiquity had been "not a mere archaism but an inherent necessity," the only way to safeguard the unity of the Jewish calendar, since a single method of calendation had not yet been established.[27] Despite the Babylonians' technological advance, they deferred to Palestine and the matter did not erupt into open strife—until the tinder was lit by the irascible personality of Seʿadya b. Yosef.

In the summer of 921, the Palestinian *gaʾon* Meʾir, or possibly his son Aharon b. Meʾir, announced the calendar for the following three years from Tiberias.[28] His dates did not agree with the Babylonian reckoning. Rather than deferring, as was the custom, the *geʾonim* of Sura and Pumbedita opposed the Palestinian proclamation. Seʿadya recognized clearly that this was an opportunity to proclaim Babylonian precedence and turned the disagreement into an international power-struggle by addressing letters to the Palestinian *gaʾon* and the

[25] Ibid., 185.

[26] T-S 8 G 7.1, in Aramaic, verso, line 15.

[27] Stern, *Calendar and Community*, 189.

[28] Gil argues that Aharon b. Meʾir made the calendar announcement on his father's behalf, probably on analogy with the *gaʾon* Shelomo b. Yehuda's son having declared excommunications a century later in 1029 and 1038 (see below, chap. 8, 213–14 and chap. 11, 306). Gil, *History of Palestine*, sec. 785; and see idem, *In the Kingdom of Ishmael*, Hebrew, 4 vols. (Tel-Aviv, 1997), vol. 1, secs. 142–43, 162. An English translation of vol. 1 of this work has now been published as Gil, *Jews in Islamic Countries in the Middle Ages*, trans. David Strassler, Etudes sur le judaïsme médiéval 28 (Leiden, 2004), but it cannot always be trusted and should be cross-checked against the Hebrew original. I use the first title and cite by section number to facilitate cross-referencing.

Jewish communities of Egypt attempting to convince them of the correctness of the Babylonian method. The key issue dividing the two centers was a difference of less than an hour that dictated the beginning of the month of Tishri in 924, but had a ripple effect beginning with Passover in 922.

For one year, from the fall of 921 until the New Year in 922, the Jewish world was riven in twain as some followed the Babylonian calculation and others followed the Palestinian. In one particularly memorable episode from the conflict, the Jews of Fustat waited for the appearance of the new moon, which obliged the Palestinians by appearing on the day on which they had predicted it, one day earlier than it should have by the Babylonian reckoning. Some Jewish communities celebrated the New Year in the fall of 922 according to the Palestinian system. But after that point, the controversy seems to have been resolved in favor of the Babylonian method—or so most scholars have presumed, since no more is heard of the Palestinian side in the debate.[29]

Beside absence of evidence, the reason that modern scholars have understood this event as the final battle in the Babylonian struggle for authority over Palestine is, briefly, presentism: since the algorithm that Seʿadya employed to determine the calendar is the same one in use today, most accept that the controversy of 921–22 was the last time Jews ever disagreed over how to mark the calendar. But even after 922, some rabbinic Jews ignored that algorithm and still preferred empirical methods of calendation instead.

We have this on the authority of two medieval witnesses, Sahl b. Maṣliaḥ in the tenth century and Levi b. Yefet in the early eleventh. Granted, both are Qaraites and may show a bias toward empirical methods of calendation, which many Qaraites advocated and practiced (see further below). But since Levi b. Yefet's code of law (composed ca. 1006–7) also admits that there were Qaraites who observed the Rabbanite calendar, he can be presumed an honest observer. If these accounts are correct, then there continued to be some measure of diversity in matters of calendation as late as the early eleventh century, a possibility that suggests that the calendar controversy of 921–22 represented a climax of jurisdictional conflict between the Babylonians and the Palestinians but not yet its denouement. Indeed, the conflict smoldered on over the first half of the eleventh century, and after the fall of the *yeshivot* of Baghdad ca. 1040,

[29] The letters preserved from the controversy are collected in Ḥayim Yeḥiel Bornstein, *Maḥloqet Rav Seʿadya gaʾon u-Ven Meʾir* (Warsaw, 1904); see Gil's new editions of copies of Seʿadya's letters to Egypt and Palestine: Halper 332; Bodl. MS Heb. f 56.82–83; T-S 6 Ja 1; and MS Levi+West. Coll. Bib. 6.52+Bodl. MS Heb. c 13.22. For summaries of the controversy see Brody, *Geonim of Babylonia*, 118–20, and the earlier literature cited there; Jacob Katz, "Rabbinic Authority and Authorization in the Middle Ages," in *Studies in Medieval Jewish History and Literature*, ed. I. Twersky (Cambridge, Mass., 1979), 128–45; Gil, *History of Palestine*, secs. 784–89, 926 (where he notes evidence of some Qaraite involvement, oddly enough on the side of Seʿadya); and idem, *In the Kingdom of Ishmael*, secs. 142, 143, 162. On the technical aspects of the controversy, see Arnold A. Lasker and Daniel J. Lasker, "642 Parts—More Concerning the Saadya-Ben Meir Controversy," Hebrew, *Tarbiẓ* 61 (1991): 119–28.

at least one Palestinian *ga'on*, Evyatar ha-Kohen b. Eliyyahu (1083–93, 1094–ca. 1112), reasserted the traditional prerogative of proclaiming the calendar—with the claim that the *ge'onim* of Palestine had received the esoteric secrets of the proper method of calendation in an unbroken chain of transmission stretching back to the third day of creation.[30]

The scholarly consensus that Seʿadya effected a final Babylonian Rabbanite triumph over Palestine parallels the consensus about his anti-Qaraite polemics, which led most scholars to believe that he defused the threat of Qaraism once and for all. But on both questions, Seʿadya's "triumph" has been projected forward as permanent in spite of later evidence that his victories did not settle matters once and for all.

A Babylonian "Triumph"?

It has recently been suggested on other grounds that by the eleventh century, the Palestinian *yeshiva* had submitted to the authority of Baghdad. The evidence is a letter written by Shelomo b. Yehuda, who would eventually accede to the gaonate of the Jerusalem *yeshiva* (1025–51), in which he mentions that one of his three sons, Yaḥyā, was studying with Hayya Ga'on (1004–38) at Pumbedita.

"A letter from Yaḥyā arrived at the end of [the month of] Ḥeshvan from Baghdad," Shelomo b. Yehuda writes to an unknown recipient, "together with a letter from our lord the *ga'on* Hayya, may his Rock preserve him. He said that he is sitting and repeating *Halakhot gedolot* before [the *ga'on*]."[31] The work his son was learning, *Halakhot gedolot* (The Great [Book of] Laws), was a (probably) mid-ninth century compendium by a certain Shimʿon Qayyara of Baṣra about whom nothing is known. It was one of the most continuously studied rabbinic works of the medieval period, and contained both Babylonian and Palestinian talmudic traditions, the former in greater abundance.[32]

[30] Sahl b. Maṣliaḥ in Simḥa Pinsker, *Lickute Kadmoniot: Zur Geschichte des Karaismus und der karäischen Literatur* (Vienna, 1860), 33; Levi b. Yefet, *Sefer ha-miṣvot*, quoted in Ankori, *Karaites in Byzantium*, 303–4 (Hebrew text in n. 31), on the basis of a late-sixteenth- or early-seventeenth-century copy of a Hebrew translation of the Arabic original (Leiden, Or. 4760, MS Warner 22, 19r–19v). For the Arabic original, see Ben-Shammai, "Qeṭaʿ ḥadash me-ha-maqor ha-ʿaravi shel Sefer ha-miṣvot le-Levi ben Yefet ha-qara'i," *Shenaton ha-mishpaṭ ha-ʿIvri* 11–12 (1985): 99–133 (BL Or. 2577, possibly an autograph, copied 1024; see fol. 89b; BL Or. 2564, copied in 1045 from an autograph; fols. 11–18 only; and BL Or. 2563, copied after the author's death; fols. 90–100); and Yosef Algamil, *Sefer ha-miṣvot le-rav Levi b. Yefet ha-Levi ha-mekhune Abu Saʿid*, 5 vols. (Ashdod, 2004), 1:26–27, esp. n. 24. According to the plain meaning of the passage, Qaraites still used mathematical methods in the early eleventh century, when Levi was writing. Cf. Gil, *History of Palestine*, sec. 928; and Ankori, *Karaites in Byzantium*, 305–8.

[31] T-S 13 J 13.14, in Hebrew, recto, margin, lines 13–21. The addressee is [?] b. Avraham, whom Gil assumes is Yiṣḥaq ha-Kohen b. Avraham ibn Furāt.

[32] Ezriel Hildesheimer, ed., *Sefer Halakhot Gedolot*, 3 vols. (Jerusalem, 1971–87); on the work's authorship, see Neil Danzig, *Introduction to Halakhot Pesuqot with a Supplement to Halakhot Pesuqot*,

It appears striking indeed that Shelomo b. Yehuda, later the *ga'on* of Palestine, should send his son to study in Baghdad with Hayya rather than educating him at home. But it would be overly hasty to see this as an admission of Babylonian triumph on the part of the future Palestinian *ga'on*—particularly this Palestinian *ga'on*. After Shelomo b. Yehuda acceded to the gaonate of Jerusalem in 1025, he fought the Babylonians tooth and nail, doing everything in his power to break their dominance over the Jewish communities of Egypt and Syria. He waxed extraordinarily irate when Hayya attempted to encroach on his jurisdiction in Egypt, and even traveled to Fustat to excommunicate the Iraqi congregation on a flimsy pretext in a special graveside ceremony the purpose of which was to intimidate the Iraqis into obeying his authority.[33] Shelomo b. Yehuda is the last *ga'on* one should imagine admitting Iraqi supremacy.

There were other reasons why Shelomo b. Yehuda might have sent his son to Baghdad. Baghdad was thought superior to Jerusalem in Jewish law, an impression borne out by the number of preserved legal works of Iraqi provenance. But an admission of Babylonian superiority in law does not amount to a Palestinian admission of defeat in administration. Besides, Hayya was already a nearly legendary figure, as attested by the number of stories that circulated about him even during his lifetime.[34] Finally, by the eleventh century, the gaonate of any *yeshiva* was more easily attained with some claim to far-flung contacts.[35] Shelomo b. Yehuda himself was a Maghribī, one of the many immigrants from the western part of the Islamic world who came east in the eleventh century; a rival of his was from Gaza, but had studied in Qayrawān and would use his contacts in Ifrīqiya and Fustat to his advantage in attempting to usurp Shelomo b. Yehuda's position. By sending his son to Baghdad, Shelomo b. Yehuda may have been ensuring that he would be better poised to make inroads into the Babylonian communities of Syria and Egypt on his return.[36]

Hebrew, 2d ed. (New York, 1993), 175–80; and Brody, *Geonim of Babylonia*, 217, 223, 228–29. It is striking that Yaḥyā b. Shelomo was said to be studying *Halakhot gedolot* rather than the Babylonian Talmud. This confirms the evidence of other sources that compendia, codes, and digests were in wider circulation than the Talmud itself among advanced students.

[33] T-S 20.102.

[34] See, for instance, Bodl. MS Neubauer 356, fol. 127r, Ibn ʿAqnīn, *Inkishāf al-asrār wa-ẓuhūr al-anwār*, in A. S. Halkin, ed., *Divulgatio mysteriorum luminumque apparentia, commentarius in Canticum Canticorum* (Hitgallut ha-sodot ve-hofaʿat ha-me'orot: Perush Shir ha-shirim) (Jerusalem, 1964), 493–94; and the additional citations in Gil, "The Jews in Sicily under Muslim Rule in the Light of the Geniza Documents," in *Italia Judaica: Atti del convegno internazionale, Bari 18–22 maggio 1981*, Pubblicazioni degli Archivi di Stato, Saggi 2 (Rome 1983), 95 n. 30; and Goitein, *Mediterranean Society*, 1:52, at n. 62.

[35] Brody himself suggests that "the Palestinian Jews of this period (like their Muslim contemporaries) considered it desirable for developing scholars to travel widely to amass a wide range of 'traditions'" (*Geonim of Babylonia*, 120 n. 70), but dismisses this as a "seemingly less plausible explanation"; it may simply have been the claim of a Babylonian scholarly pedigree that motivated the *ga'on*'s son to study in Baghdad.

[36] My thanks to Nathan Hofer for this excellent suggestion.

Similar caution is in order when considering the putative triumph of the Babylonian Talmud over the Palestinian. It is true that Shelomo b. Yiṣḥaq (Rashi) of Champagne knew the Palestinian Talmud only at second hand; but his successors, the Tosafist commentators of the thirteenth century, knew it profoundly. It is also true that the great talmudic commentator Yiṣḥaq b. Yaʿaqov al-Fāsī (1013–1103) of Qayrawān and Fez ruled that when the two Talmuds disagreed with one another, the Babylonian one took precedence, on the (historically flawed) reasoning that because it had been redacted later, its authors knew the other's decisions and disagreed with them for good reason.[37] His teachings became the basis of all subsequent rulings, particularly in the Iberian peninsula. But though al-Fāsī established the Babylonian Talmud's legal authority over the Palestinian, he also incorporated the Palestinian Talmud into his own legal works. Maimonides, who was born in Córdoba but spent most of his life in Egypt, also made ample use of the Palestinian Talmud, composed a digest of it, and occasionally rendered decisions that agreed with it in contradiction of the Babylonian.[38] The Palestinian Talmud continued to be known in Provence, as evidenced by the now lost commentary of a certain Yiṣḥaq ha-Kohen, a younger contemporary of Maimonides.[39] The Babylonian Talmud did not suppress the Palestinian Talmud, even if it was considered the principal basis of Jewish law.

There was, then, no final Babylonian triumph during the gaonic period. To look for one is to write history backwards—to use present monopolies to limit our interpretation of a past full of contingencies. It may be more fruitful to see the question of when the Babylonian construction of Judaism triumphed throughout the Jewish world as having either many answers or none. It triumphed in the twelfth century, when the rabbinic authorities of Christian Europe memorialized the Iraqi *geʾonim* as the authentic links in a chain connecting them with the rabbis of late antiquity.[40] It triumphed again in the thirteenth century when the Tosafist commentators of northern France and Germany wrote a vast set of commentaries in which, among other things, they attempted to reconcile local Jewish customs with the text of the Babylonian Talmud and thus bring Jewish practice closer to the talmudic text. One cannot really say that it triumphed at the first public Talmud disputation in Paris in 1240—it lost, and cartloads of manuscripts were publicly burned as a result—but it is no accident that church and state authorities began to put the Talmud on trial only then, as it became central to the practice of Judaism. It triumphed again in 1523 when the Christian printer Daniel Bomberg of Venice published the

[37] Alfasi ad Babylonian Talmud, *Eruvin* 104b.

[38] Safrai, *Literature of the Sages*, 314–15.

[39] The first extant commentary was written by a Spaniard, Shelomo Sirillo, who migrated to Palestine after the expulsion of 1492; ibid., 315 (where the name is transliterated as Syrileio).

[40] See further chaps. 6, 7, Epilogue.

editio princeps, which allowed the Babylonian Talmud to circulate among an exponentially greater number of readers, accompanied by the commentaries of both Rashi and the Tosafists; but in the same year, the Bomberg atelier also produced the *editio princeps* of the Palestinian Talmud. And it triumphed again in the twentieth century, when greater literacy and increased access to traditional Jewish texts entered the educational lives of observant Jews on an unprecedented scale, particularly, in the last third of the twentieth century, the lives of a large segment of Jews who had hitherto almost never studied the Talmud: women. And so the question of the triumph of the Babylonian Talmud and of rabbinic authority in general continues to hold a kind of exaggerated fascination for the modern age, in which printing and mass literacy have made the Babylonian Talmud even more widely known among observant Jews than it was in the Middle Ages.[41]

The gaonic period has been viewed principally in terms of a struggle between Babylonia and Palestine over whose corpus of rabbinic texts would remain central to Judaism. In fact the major Jewish centers included not two options but three.

THE QARAITES

Among those who left Iran and Iraq and migrated westward in the tenth and eleventh centuries, Qaraites featured prominently. Those migrations thus precipitated the spread not only of Babylonian rabbinic loyalties, but of the scholarly methods and techniques that lay at the heart of Qaraism, including linguistics and a commitment to reason as an interpretive tool and as a check against the received knowledge embedded in tradition. Those who made a name for themselves in the intellectual life of the west brought with them their expertise in the Islamic philosophical traditions and Arabic linguistic studies prevalent in Iraq, and those fields now grew rapidly in the west.

Palestine and Egypt are the most frequently attested destinations of Qaraite migration. In Palestine, a "golden age" of Qaraite scholarship began around 950 and continued until the Crusader conquests of ca. 1100 exiled many to

41 On the twentieth century, see Haim Soloveitchik, "Rupture and Reconstruction: The Transformation of Contemporary Orthodoxy," *Tradition* 28 (1994): 64–130. See also Schwartz, "Rabbinization in the Sixth Century," 55, who observes that rather than supposing that rabbinic Judaism emerged victorious at some definite point and then attempting to determine when, one should concentrate instead on the tension created "by the introduction of rabbinic Judaism into the larger social system of Judaism" over the course of many centuries. Talmud study has been utterly transformed in the age of mass literacy, globalization, and the internet: see the large number of websites devoted to the study of a page per day (*daf yomi*) of the Babylonian Talmud in a seven-and-a-half-year cycle coordinated worldwide. In 2005, the event marking the completion of the eleventh cycle attracted some fifty thousand Talmud enthusiasts in the New York area alone.

Egypt and elsewhere. Its legacy includes several refutations of Seʿadya's polemics against Qaraism, and perhaps most importantly, a new kind of biblical commentary characterized by attention to lexical, grammatical, and other linguistic details of the Hebrew text. This kind of biblical exegesis set the standard for most medieval commentaries on the Hebrew Bible. In Egypt, migrants made equally important contributions to scholarship, though scholars are just beginning to pry those contributions from the manuscripts of the Firkovich collections. It now appears that Qaraites were instrumental in transplanting philosophical rationalism, and the *muʿtazilī* traditions of Baṣra in particular, onto Egyptian soil. This was a development as central to Islamic philosophy as to Jewish history.[42]

By the tenth century, Qaraites were spread all over Syria, Egypt, and Ifrīqiya. The major Qaraite centers were in Jerusalem, Ramla, Tyre, Fustat, and the new city of Cairo. A host of smaller towns also contained Qaraite populations, including—moving more or less clockwise around the Mediterranean—in Syria: Aleppo, Damascus, Tiberias, and Acre; in the coastal region north of Sinai: Gaza and al-ʿArīsh; in Egypt: Damietta, Tinnīs, Ṣahrajt, and Alexandria; in northern Africa: Tripoli, Qayrawān, and Warjlān. There were also Qaraites in various towns in al-Andalus and Byzantine Asia Minor.[43]

Early Qaraism in the Context of Its Times

The difficulties of offering a meaningful general description of Qaraite history in this period are both substantive and historiographic. Works in manuscript still far outnumber what scholars have studied and published, and the risk is thus greater than normal that any generalizations I make will soon be rendered obsolete. But perhaps the greatest challenge to rendering medieval Qaraism in synthetic or synchronic form is that a central part of the Qaraite program was to avoid having too coherent a program. Major Qaraite figures disagreed radically on the fundamentals of law and theology, a fact considered healthy and desirable even by those who thought their opinion the only correct one. The Iraqi Qaraite Abū Yūsuf Yaʿqūb al-Qirqisānī wrote in 937–38 that "hardly two [Qaraites] are to be found who agree on everything."[44] A century

[42] See above, Introduction, n. 15, and below, chap. 2, n. 8.

[43] Olszowy-Schlanger, *Karaite Marriage Documents*, 46–47, derives this list from direct evidence and toponymic *nisba*s. Many of these communities are abundantly represented below; on Tinnīs, see chap. 7, n. 24, chap. 9, nn. 11, 36, 39.

[44] Abū Yūsuf Yaʿqūb al-Qirqisānī, *Kitāb al-anwār wa-l-marāqib [Book of lights and watchtowers]: Code of Karaite Law*, ed. Leon Nemoy (New York, 1939–43), Book I, 2:21 (14); Bruno Chiesa and Wilfrid Lockwood, *Yaqub al-Qirqisani on Jewish Sects and Christianity: A Translation of "Kitab al-anwar," Book 1, with Two Introductory Essays*, Judentum und Umwelt 10 (Frankfurt, 1984), 104; Nemoy, "al-Qirqisānī's Account of the Jewish Sects and Christianity," *Hebrew Union College Annual* 7 (1930), 330.

later, Shelomo b. Yehuda, *ga'on* of Jerusalem, complained—not without humor—that the Qaraites differ from one another so much that "each person forms his own *madhhab*."[45] Nonetheless, a few things must be said by way of introduction. Given the preponderance of literary studies over historical ones, I shall try to emphasize the context in which so much intellectual development was taking place.

Major programmatic statements by ninth- and tenth-century Jews—Rabbanites and Qaraites alike—reflect a shared concern with the transmission of religious knowledge and the possibility of knowing right and wrong actions independently from the authority of transmitted tradition. This was in keeping with the great religious and philosophical debate of the age, among Muslims and Jews alike: the struggle between reason (*ʿaql*) and tradition (*naql*). Qaraites beginning in the ninth century accused Rabbanism of accepting laws and interpretations unthinkingly and following them blindly. The Qaraites, for their part, did not reject all of rabbinic law wholesale, but they rejected the rabbinic claim to exclusive authority in deciding Jewish law. The Persian Qaraite Dani'el al-Qūmisī (active ca. 870–910) first expressed that critique by calling rabbinic law "an ordinance of men, learned by rote" (Isaiah 29:13), that is, human laws (rather than divine ones) transmitted uncritically.[46] A Judeo-Arabic gloss on this statement in the sole surviving manuscript of al-Qūmisī's sermon—preserved in the Geniza—points in a single word to the parallel Islamic theological debate: *al-taqlīd*, imitation or blind obedience, a term used in Islamic law and theology to describe a range of positions from mere adherence to a particular school of thought or *madhhab* to slavish compliance with previous authorities.[47] One of the unintended consequences of the Qaraite challenge to tradition was that it drove Rabbanites such as Seʿadya to articulate ever more extreme arguments on behalf of the unbrokenness of rabbinic

45 *Kull wāḥid minhum ʿalā madhhab.* T-S 13 J 19.16 and T-S 13 J 16.15 (see chap. 8, 219–20, where the passage is translated in full and discussed).

46 Bodl. MS Heb. d 36.13–18, here fols. 15r, line 1, and 17r, line 22. See Daniel Frank, "Karaite Exegesis," in *Hebrew Bible, Old Testament: The History of its Interpretation, vol. 1: From the Beginnings to the Middle Ages (Until 1300), pt 2: The Middle Ages*, ed. Magne Sæbø (Göttingen, 2000), 112; and idem, *Search Scripture Well: Karaite Exegetes and the Origins of the Jewish Bible Commentary in the Islamic East* (Leiden, 2004), 5 n. 18. Less than a century after al-Qūmisī, Sahl b. Maṣliaḥ similarly warned his coreligionists against "relying upon the ordinance of men, learned by rote": see his polemical treatise against Yaʿaqov b. Shemu'el, in Pinsker, *Lickute kadmoniot*, app. 2, 31; English translation in Nemoy, "The Epistle of Sahl ben Maṣlīaḥ," *Proceedings of the American Academy for Jewish Research* 38–39 (1970–71): 145–77. So did Ibn Nūḥ: idem, "Nissi ben Noah's Quasi-Commentary on the Decalogue," *Jewish Quarterly Review* 73 (1983): 328.

47 See *EI*[2], s.v. "Taḳlīd" (Norman Calder); Wael B. Hallaq, *Authority, Continuity, and Change in Islamic Law* (Cambridge, 2001), chap. 4; Naphtali Wieder, *The Judean Scrolls and Karaism* (London, 1962), 71–72, 259–63; Frank, *Search Scripture Well*, chap. 1 (esp. 28–31); the Judeo-Arabic glosses on al-Qūmisī, Bodl. MS Heb. d 36.17r, line 22 and 17v, line 11; and the remarks in Mann, "A Tract by an Early Ḳaraite Settler in Jerusalem," *Jewish Quarterly Review* 12 (1921–22), 265.

transmission and its centrality to any understanding of God's commandments.[48]

The legal consequences of these theological disagreements centered on the interpretation of biblical commandments: while the Rabbanites considered themselves bound to the accumulating corpus of legal precedent contained in the Mishnah and Talmud, the Qaraites cast these off as layers of interpretation. They did not, however, profess a *sola scriptura* principle, and by the tenth century were developing principles of jurisprudence according to which the Bible was only one source of law among several.[49]

As for what this meant in practice, I will begin with the best-known example. In Exodus 35:3, Moses tells the Israelites that God has commanded them not to "burn fire in any of your dwellings on the Sabbath." Does the verb to "burn" mean to light a new flame or allow a fire to burn? For Qaraites the verse was an injunction against using fire on Friday evenings, while for Rabbanites, it simply meant not starting one, while sitting by a lamp lit before sundown on Friday was permitted. In a similar vein, for Qaraites sexual intercourse was prohibited on the Sabbath since it entailed performing labor and could lead to ritual impurity, while Rabbanites not only permitted but encouraged it as Sabbath enjoyment. But Qaraite law did not always choose the more restrictive path: it forbade the mixing of meat and dairy only under certain circumstances, while the Rabbanites forbade it altogether based on a series of hermeneutical justifications. The Qaraites did, however, prohibit eating certain parts of animals that were permitted to Rabbanites, such as the tail of fat-tail sheep (*ḥelev*, Leviticus 3:9), and each group developed rules for butchering animals that were so complex as to exclude not only members of the other group from doing so but anyone not versed in law and theology. Finally, differences in methods of calendation meant that Qaraites and Rabbanites often observed the same festivals and fasts on different days (see below). Most of these legal differences will reappear over the course of this book, but one thing must be

[48] Seʿadya extended and bolstered the concept of a divinely revealed Oral Law, as against discretionary scriptural exegesis. For some examples, see Brody, *Geonim of Babylonia*, 96–99; for an excellent analysis of this shift in rabbinic thinking and Seʿadya's role in it, see Jay Harris, *How Do We Know This? Midrash and the Fragmentation of Modern Judaism* (Albany, 1995), 76–81. See also Alexander Guttman, "Tractate Abot: Its Place in Rabbinic Literature," *Jewish Quarterly Review* 41 (1950): 190–93, who argues that the rabbinic chain of tradition in *Avot* was a late stratum added under the influence of *ḥadīth* scholarship. The *ge'onim* ʿAmram b. Sheshna and Seʿadya included it in their liturgies as a traditionist polemic, and by the eleventh century it was an established practice to read Avot aloud on the Sabbath.

[49] Tenth- and eleventh-century works suggest a direct relationship between Qaraite and Islamic hermeneutics in both jurisprudence and exegesis (*uṣūl al-fiqh* and *uṣūl al-tafsīr*). See Gregor Schwarb, "Capturing the Meanings of God's Speech: The Relevance of Uṣūl al-fiqh to an Understanding of Uṣūl al-tafsīr in Jewish and Muslim Kalām," in *A Word Fitly Spoken: Studies in Mediaeval Exegesis of the Hebrew Bible and the Qur'ān Presented to Haggai Ben-Shammai*, ed. Meir M. Bar-Asher, Simon Hopkins, Sarah Stroumsa, and Bruno Chiesa (Jerusalem, 2007), 111–56.

emphasized from the outset: their importance in the lives of the two groups varied depending on context. Some of the most reliable evidence of how the differences played themselves out in practice are clauses in eleventh- and twelfth-century marriage contracts that safeguard the rights of Rabbanite and Qaraite spouses in mixed couples to their own form of observance. In other words, religious differences could be lived with when necessary. I will say more about this in Part Three.[50]

Moreover, even as Rabbanites and Qaraites maintained divergent theories of religious tradition, some key issues united them. One was a renewed focus on Jerusalem and an attempt to integrate it into the religious geography of Judaism on a practical rather than merely literary level. Al-Qūmisī is again the earliest known Qaraite to have articulated this commitment. Some time after 874, he left Dāmghān (southeast of the Caspian Sea) and traveled westward, settling in Jerusalem, where he either found or founded a community of "mourners of Zion" (*aveley ṣiyyon*) who engaged in ascetic practices, including abstaining from meat and wine and reciting prayers in mourning for the destroyed Jerusalem Temple. But the movement of which he is known as the earliest and most vociferous champion was not an exclusive Qaraite preserve; the mourners of Zion left their stamp on the rabbinic liturgy for the fast of the Ninth of Av (which commemorates the destruction of the First and Second Temples).[51]

Nor were Jews the only ascetics to set the sanctity of Jerusalem above other ideals. Al-Qūmisī himself even complains that Christians and Muslims came to Jerusalem on pilgrimage, but where were the Jews? "Do not the nations other than Israel come from the four corners of the earth to Jerusalem every month and every year in the awe of God?" he protested. "What, then, is the matter with you, our brethren in Israel, that you are not doing even as much as is the custom of the Gentiles in coming to Jerusalem and praying there?"[52] Pilgrimage was partly a testimony to new horizons of geographic mobility, and

[50] Ankori, *Karaites in Byzantium*, passim; Goitein, *Mediterranean Society*, 5:312–13; Olszowy-Schlanger, *Karaite Marriage Documents*, 120–26; Frank, "Karaite Ritual," in *Judaism in Practice from the Middle Ages through the Early Modern Period*, ed. Lawrence Fine (Princeton, 2001), 248–64.

[51] On al-Qūmisī's emigration, see Ben-Shammai, "Fragments of Daniel al-Qūmisī's Commentary on the Book of Daniel as a Historical Source," *Henoch* 13 (1991): 259–82. On the Qaraite mourners (and Rabbanites among them), see Ankori, *Karaites in Byzantium*, 256–57; Haim Hillel Ben-Sasson, "The Karaite Community of Jerusalem in the Tenth–Eleventh Centuries," *Shalem* 2 (1976): 1–18; the literature cited in Gil, *History of Palestine*, sec. 827 n. 100; Frank, "The *Shoshanim* of Tenth-century Jerusalem: Karaite Exegesis, Prayer, and Communal Identity," in *The Jews of Medieval Islam: Community, Society, and Identity*, ed. idem (Leiden and New York, 1995): 199–245; idem, *Search Scripture Well*, 165–203; and Yoram Erder, "The Mourners of Zion: The Karaites in Jerusalem of the Tenth and Eleventh Centuries," in Polliack, *Karaite Judaism*, 213–35.

[52] Bodl. MS Heb. d 36.13–18, in Mann, "Tract by an Early Ḳaraite," 285 (lines 15–17); Nemoy, "The Pseudo-Qumisian Sermon to the Karaites," *Proceedings of the American Academy of Jewish Research* 43 (1976): 77 (Eng.), 100 (Heb.).

al-Qūmisī's invidious comparison of the Jews with their more devoted Christian and Muslim counterparts suggests that he was in part motivated by cultural competition.

Al-Qūmisī's rejection of worldly pursuits even took on a certain shrill character against the background of the rise of long distance trade in the late ninth century. "Now you, our brethren in Israel, do not act this way," he thundered with contempt for the economic pursuits of his coreligionists. "Hearken to the Lord, arise and come to Jerusalem, so that we may return to the Lord. Or if you will not come because you are running about in tumult and haste after your merchandise, then send at least five men from each city in the diaspora, together with their sustenance, so that we may form one sizable community to supplicate our God at all times upon the hills of Jerusalem."[53] Remarkable here is not only al-Qūmisī's dogged idealism in attempting to persuade some Jews to abandon material pursuits in favor of pilgrimage and asceticism, but also his frank admission that others would better serve the movement by staying home and sending contributions. In that sense, his asceticism was a product of its time, and not merely a reaction against it: it depended vitally upon the possibility of establishing a diocesan infrastructure, something imaginable only in a geographically mobile world and something eminently comparable to the system the *ge'onim* of Iraq had established, in which the sacred centers depended precisely upon the diaspora's "running about in tumult and haste after merchandise."

Qaraite Communal Organization

Although Qaraites in the tenth and eleventh centuries were responsible for one of the most extraordinary outpourings of literary creativity in all of Jewish history, the social and institutional contexts within which they worked are still poorly understood. In part this is because scholarship on Qaraism has concentrated on intellectual production rather than social and institutional history, an understandable choice given the disproportion of surviving literary to documentary materials. Still, much documentary material relating to Qaraites was preserved in the Cairo Geniza (one of the purposes of this book is to understand why). The literary materials also frequently contain vital clues as to the historical contexts in which they were written and read, including colophons, dedications, and readers' inscriptions.[54]

[53] Bodl. MS Heb. d 36.13–18, in Mann, "Tract by an Early Ḳaraite," 285 (lines 23–26); Nemoy, "Pseudo-Qumisian Sermon," 78 (Eng.), 100 (Heb.).

[54] For the historiography and the current state of Qaraite studies, see Frank, "The Study of Medieval Karaism, 1959–1989: A Bibliographical Essay," *Bulletin of Judaeo-Greek Studies* 6 (1990): 15–23; idem, "The Study of Medieval Karaism, 1989–1999," in *Hebrew Scholarship and the Medieval World*, ed. Nicholas De Lange (Cambridge, 2001): 3–22; Polliack, "Medieval Karaism," in Martin Goodman, ed., *The Oxford Handbook of Jewish Studies* (Oxford, 2002), 295–326; and the essays in Polliack, *Karaite*

Those sources suggest that unlike the Iraqi and Palestinian *ge'onim*, the Qaraites of Jerusalem did not combine their academic, administrative, and legal bodies into one institution. The Qaraites ran an academy in Jerusalem in the late tenth and eleventh centuries, called a *majlis*, which doubled as a center of learning and a house of worship. It is unknown when it was founded.

Meanwhile, the community's judicial and administrative functions were served elsewhere in Jerusalem, by leaders called *nesi'im*. (Though the Qaraite *nesi'im* held the same title as the *nesi'im* of Roman Palestine, the former claimed descent from the Babylonian Davidic line that had produced both the exilarchs and 'Anan b. David in the mid-eight century; 'Anan was regarded as having founded Qaraism, though matters were more complex, as I will explain below.) During the tenth and eleventh centuries, there were two separate dynasties of Qaraite *nesi'im*, one in Fustat and the other in Jerusalem. When the Fustat line died out in the 1050s, the Jerusalem line moved there and replaced it.[55]

The Qaraite *nesi'im* were parallel to the *ge'onim* in the sense that they adjudicated court cases, but unlike the *ge'onim*, they were not attached to the central academy and did not run it. There was a whiff of royalty attached to the symbolism surrounding the Qaraite *nesi'im*. Qaraite marriage contracts listed their names in a manner comparable to the ways in which Rabbanites mentioned their *ge'onim* and exilarchs in prayers and followers of a particular *ga'on* marked their official correspondence with his signature-cipher *('alāma)*. References to leaders carried semiotic weight. If they were not consciously modeled after the insertion of the caliph's name into the sermon in congregational mosques, they would have conjured up a comparable set of associations.

The existence of a Qaraite version of the Davidic dynast must have echoed in three related realms of meaning. First, the *nasi* offered Qaraites a tangible claim to continuity with the biblical past through descent from the ancient Israelite kings, and the symbolic importance of this concrete connection to the biblical text must have been all the greater given the Qaraite project of living in dialogue with it. Second, the *nasi* offered the Qaraites a claim to legitimacy, sanctity, and royalty among Muslims, for whom David was a prophet; Davidic ancestry placed these Jewish leaders in a special category.[56] Last, the *nasi*

Judaism. The Qaraites did have their own geniza in Cairo, but what survives from it are books and parts of books, and only an exiguous number of documents such as contracts and letters. This may be because the Qaraites interpreted the practice of *geniza* more narrowly than the Rabbanites of the Ben Ezra and deposited only books there; or because the Qaraite *geniza* was a library rather than a holding tank for discarded books; or else because the two collectors known or presumed to have taken material from it, Abraham Firkovich and Solomon Schechter, concentrated on the larger prizes. See also below, chap. 9, n. 22.

[55] On the Qaraite *nesi'im*, see Gil, *History of Palestine*, secs. 926–27 (with a genealogical tree); and Olszowy-Schlanger, *Karaite Marriage Documents*, 143–55 (with genealogical tree on 155).

[56] Here I have adapted the arguments about Rabbanite *nesi'im* made by Arnold E. Franklin, "Shoots of David: Members of the Exilarchal Dynasty in the Middle Ages" (Ph.D. diss., Princeton University,

offered the Qaraites another weapon in their arsenal of counterclaims against the Rabbanites, whose *nesi'im* commanded increasing attention and inspired popular fervor over the course of the eleventh and twelfth centuries.[57] It was the genealogical theater of the Qaraite attack on Rabbanism, as distinct from the scholarly one, in which the Qaraites contested in a tangible way the rabbis' claims to be the sole continuation of the ancient biblical line. That the Qaraite *nasi* was a distant cousin of the Rabbanite one must also have figured somewhere in the consciousness of the two groups: in claims to kinship, as in scholarly polemics, the two groups claimed distinctiveness from one another while admitting that they were, ultimately, connected.

In any event, the Qaraite *majlis* seems to have enjoyed some independence from the functions and prerogatives of the *nesi'im*, and this separation of the scholarly and administrative branches reflects two central characteristics of Qaraism: openness and diffuseness. Having abandoned the rabbinic idea of a singular tradition (even a heterophonic one), Qaraites perhaps found it unnecessary to consolidate their scholarly and leadership functions under a single administrative aegis.

This diffuseness is evident in the letter I cited in the Introduction by Shelomo b. Ṣemaḥ of Ramla: he tells Efrayim b. Shemarya that his congregants are switching to the Babylonian Rabbanite synagogue in Fustat and the Qaraite congregations, in the plural.[58] The word I translated there as congregations is *majālis* (sing. *majlis*) in Arabic, semantically equivalent to the Hebrew *yeshiva* (both are places of sitting in council), but with a broader range of uses. A *majlis* was the office or chamber in which caliphs, courtiers, and other high government functionaries held public audiences. By extension it was also a learned salon, and in this sense teachers held their own *majālis*. Among the Qaraites, *majālis* were places of both study and prayer, and the sources describe them as multiple.[59] Similarly, Sahl b. Maṣliaḥ, a Qaraite of late tenth-century Palestine, expresses his belated thanks toward the Arab conquerors for having allowed the Qaraites to establish "places in [Jerusalem] for reading and expounding and praying at any time and setting up night watches," a statement that suggests that the Qaraites combined places of study and worship and had many of them. "Setting up night watches," by contrast, refers to circumambulating the walls of Jerusalem, and should not be taken as a reference to some administrative function being served in the same institution. Apparently the *nesi'im* and their administration were sepa-

---

2001); and idem, "Cultivating Roots: The Promotion of Exilarchal Ties to David in the Middle Ages," *Association for Jewish Studies Review* 29 (2005): 91–110.

[57] On connections (including marriages) between the Qaraite *nesi'im* and the Tustarīs (see next chapter), see Moshe Gil, *The Tustaris, Family and Sect*, Hebrew (Tel Aviv, 1981), 59–60.

[58] Introduction at n. 14.

[59] Cf. Gil, *History of Palestine*, sec. 936; and Goitein, *Mediterranean Society*, 2:166.

rate from the *majlis*, and the main *majlis* in Jerusalem was exalted above the other *majālis* there.[60]

This separation of scholarly and administrative functions is reflected in a scholarly chronicle of the fifteenth century by the Iraqi Qaraite David b. Seʿadel ibn al-Hītī, who informs us that Abū Yaʿqūb ibn Nūḥ, an Iraqi who migrated to Jerusalem and wrote numerous biblical commentaries, "had an academy in Jerusalem."[61] Ibn al-Hītī uses the phrase "dār . . . li-l-ʿilm" (house . . . for study) a frustratingly vague expression that sounds highly informal but may reflect later Iraqi usage rather than eleventh-century Palestinian terminology. It is possible that this academy was a continuation of the one to which Sahl b. Maṣliaḥ refers, but the fact that Ibn al-Nūḥ's name is so closely associated with it raises the question of whether he ran a disciple circle rather than a full-fledged institution. Questions of this type—formal institution versus informal network—recur in material from this period. It may simply be that these questions reflect the biases of modern historians, who are accustomed to looking for institutions, and that the reality was somewhere between the two: a disciple circle dependent on one main teacher or several, but one expected to continue on over the course of generations.

The colophon of a Qaraite biblical codex dated 1016 confirms that the academy—however formal or informal it was—served scholastic but not administrative or legal functions. The colophon announces that the Qaraites of Jerusalem had received the codex as a donation from a certain Ḥasūn b. Yaʿqūb b. Yūsuf b. Kushnām (the first three names are Arabic and the fourth is Persian: another descendant of westward migrants). He, in turn, entrusted it to the Qaraite *nasi* Shelomo b. David b. Boʿaz, and the *nasi* ordered it to remain in the *ḥaṣer* ("court" or "compound") of Ibn Nūḥ (here, called Yūsuf b. Bakhtawayh).[62] This suggests some kind of a library. It also suggests that the Qaraite *nesiʾim* attended to the community's legal and administrative functions somewhere outside the academy.

[60] Sahl b. Maṣliaḥ's epistle: Avraham Eliyyahu Harkavy, *Meʾassef niddaḥim: meqorot be-toldot Yisraʾel u-ve-sifruto* (Jerusalem, 1970 [1879]), 197–212 (here, 199); Wieder, *Judean Scrolls and Karaism*, 103 n. 2; and cf. Gil, *History of Palestine*, sec. 936 n. 20.

[61] BL MS Or. 2402, 188 verso, in G. Margoliouth, "Ibn al-Hiti's Chronicle of the Karaite Doctors," *Jewish Quarterly Review* 9 (1897): 433; see also Ankori, "Ibn al-Hītī and the Chronology of Joseph al-Baṣīr the Karaite," *Journal of Jewish Studies* 8 (1957): 71–81; Geoffrey Khan, María Ángeles Gallego, and Judith Olszowy-Schlanger, *The Karaite Tradition of Hebrew Grammatical Thought in Its Classical Form: A Critical Edition and English Translation of* al-Kitāb al-kāfī fī al-luġa al-ʿIbrāniyya by *ʾAbū al-Faraj Hārūn ibn al-Faraj*, Studies in Semitic Languages and Linguistics 37 (Leiden, 2003), 1–25; Khan "Editor's Introduction" in idem, ed., *Exegesis and Grammar in Medieval Karaite Texts*, Journal of Semitic Studies Supplement 13 (Oxford, 2001), 7; and ibid., 5, where he suggests that Ibn Nūḥ must have directed the academy by 1002–3 at the latest.

[62] 2 Firk. Cod. 223; see Gil, *History of Palestine*, sec. 936 n. 20. T-S 16.171r (dated 1003) connects Ḥasūn with Ibn Nūḥ via a certain Abū Bishr Nisi b. Aharon ibn Bakhtawayh, probably Ibn Nūḥ's nephew. See Olszowy-Schlanger, *Karaite Marriage Documents*, 49.

As for how the educational and judicial branches of the Qaraite administrative apparatus functioned, the Geniza sheds some light on the matter in the form of a moving letter written by an otherwise unknown Jerusalem Qaraite named Natan b. Yiṣḥaq. who writes to his "noble teacher" (*al-muʿallim al-jalīl*) Shelomo b. David b. al-ʿArīshī in Fustat, some time in the mid-eleventh century. Only the top half of the letter has been preserved, but it furnishes information not easily gathered from literary evidence.[63]

> To my lord the teacher Shelomo b. David ibn al-Arīshī, may God preserve him, from his disciple Natan b. Yiṣḥaq. My letter to you, my lord, may God lengthen your existence and make your glory eternal and strengthen your benefactions, from Jerusalem, there having elapsed four days of the month of Shevaṭ; God makes his blessings known to us and to you.
>
> I inform you that I have longed for you very much, with the strongest possible longing, and that every time I pass by the *majlis* and I do not see you in it, the world oppresses me. I ask God that He not withdraw himself from you and that He hasten [my] meeting with you in a good state and in good health, amen. And I inform you further that I always inquire about you, in every moment, and always ask everyone about you.
>
> I attended the lesson of the Shaykh Abu l-Faraj ibn Asad, may God strengthen him, at the time of the two-dinar payment to him, and I attended it, and also at the time of the half-dirham payment to him . . . attended it.[64]
>
> And when we heard your news, I was very happy. And your sons . . . the girl . . . healthy . . .

Before it breaks off, the letter refers to the same academy that Ibn al-Hītī describes, calling it a *majlis*. The teacher holding lessons there is Abu l-Faraj Furqān ibn Asad, known in Hebrew as Yeshuʿa b. Yehuda, a jurist and exegete who had also studied at Ibn Nūḥ's academy under two great Qaraite scholars of the second quarter of the eleventh century, Abū Yaʿqūb Yūsuf b. Ibrāhīm al-Baṣīr ("the blind," d. ca. 1047, author of many volumes of responsa and commentaries on biblical books), and Abu l-Faraj Hārūn b. al-Faraj (a linguist to whom I shall return). As far as one can tell from the letter, the fund collection for the Qaraite academy occurred on a regular but still ad hoc basis in conjunction with lessons. Perhaps students who came from abroad were responsible for

63 T-S 8 J 20.12.

64 "Lesson": *nawba*. See also Mosseri VII 200 (L 268) and Halper 354, verso, where *nawba* is also used in the sense of "repeated lecture" or "repeated performance," a meaning that Goitein notes is missing from Arabic dictionaries, *Mediterranean Society* 2:561 n. 7. See also Gil, *History of Palestine*, 2:531, note to line 8, and Frenkel, *"The Compassionate and Benevolent": The Leading Elite in the Jewish Community of Alexandria in the Middle Ages*, Hebrew (Jerusalem, 2006), doc. 20, note to line 6. In Arabic music (especially the Andalusī tradition of the Maghrib), a *nawba* is a suite or exposition of a particular *maqām* or mode, a meaning related to the one here; for medieval and modern references see *EI*² s.v. *nawba* (Owen Wright).

making collections in their communities and giving them to the academy when they came for lessons—a speculative interpretation developed on loose analogy with the Rabbanite *yeshivot*. In any case the letter suggests that the *majlis* was the beneficiary of income from its students and followers.

The Qaraite *nesiʾim*, meanwhile, probably received revenues through taxes or donations, and served in turn as benefactors of the Jewish community, Rabbanite and Qaraite alike.[65] In any event, the medieval Qaraite *nesiʾim* were closer to their rabbinic predecessors in the Roman and Byzantine periods than were the medieval Rabbanite bearers of the same title: while all medieval *nesiʾim*, Rabbanite and Qaraite alike, traced themselves back to the Israelite monarchy via the Davidic line of Babylonian exilarchs, the Rabbanite *nesiʾim* held no institutional power but considerable sentimental appeal, serving as a kind of honorary royalty, a mere residue of kingship in the absence of sovereign territory.[66] Qaraite *nesiʾim*, by contrast, carried institutional prerogatives and sovereign leadership over the Qaraite community, and like the patriarch in Tiberias under Roman rule, held the office hereditarily. The Qaraites had begun to claim their own line of *nesiʾim* by the ninth century. Like the Rabbanite line, the Qaraite one traced itself back to the Israelite monarchy via the Babylonian exilarchal family, but through ʿAnan b. David, the putative founder of Qaraism, who never served as exilarch.

The Qaraite *nesiʾim* were, then, parallel to the *geʾonim* in the sense that they adjudicated court cases and gave their imprimatur to legal responsa, but different in that they did not claim to be the chief promoters of scholastic education.

Nesiʾim Who Were *Geʾonim*

There is one early and important exception to this division of scholastic and judicial functions: between ca. 860 and 893, two *nesiʾim* in the line of ʿAnan b. David assumed the gaonate of the *yeshiva* at Tiberias. It is extremely surprising to see non-Rabbanite Jews as *geʾonim*. But the evidence is clear, despite the otherwise impenetrable obscurity of the *yeshiva*'s history in the ninth century: a Qaraite memorial genealogy lists a pair of brothers, Yehoshafaṭ and Ṣemaḥ b.

[65] See T-S Misc. 35.43 (chap. 7, 195–96); T-S 13 J 17.17 (Shelomo b. Yehuda showers the *nasi* Ḥizqiyahu with praise for helping him obtain help from the Tustarīs in Fustat, see chap. 6, 172); and T-S 13 J 15.11 (the Qaraite *nasi* guarantees some large amount of money, possibly to help debt prisoners; chap. 11, n. 58). See Gil, *History of Palestine*, sec. 927; and Olszowy-Schlanger, *Karaite Marriage Documents*, 151 n. 34.

[66] Rabbanite claimants to the title *nasi* proliferated over the course of the Middle Ages in Iraq, Syria, Egypt, and ultimately the rest of the Mediterranean and western Europe. For a comprehensive and nuanced interpretation of the phenomenon among medieval Rabbanites, see Franklin, "Shoots of David." On the Roman office of the patriarchate and its eventual abolition, including a summary of sources and scholarship, see Stemberger, *Jews and Christians in the Holy Land*, 230–68, esp. 261–66.

Yoshiyyahu, as great-grandsons of ʿAnan b. David, and gives Yehoshafaṭ's title as "rosh yeshivat geʾon Yaʿaqov," a title used exclusively by *geʾonim.* Meanwhile, a Rabbanite list of heads of the *yeshiva* in Tiberias contains the name of the other brother, Ṣemaḥ, son of Yoshiyyahu b. Shaʾul b. ʿAnan (b. David), who is titled *nasi* and *rosh yeshiva.* After Ṣemaḥ's death, the gaonic succession returned to the previous family of Rabbanites and remained permanently in Rabbanite hands. The period of Ananite control over the *yeshiva* left smoldering resentments: the *gaʾon* Meʾir or his son Aharon b. Meʾir, Seʿadya's adversary in the calendar controversy of 921–22, would later claim that "one of the descendants of ʿAnan" killed an ancestor of his.[67]

This interlude suggests that—at least in the late ninth century—the *yeshiva* was not an exclusively Rabbanite institution. It also casts light on rabbinic Judaism in Palestine, which had a more inclusive character than the rigidly zealous Babylonian variety, and in turn on Seʿadya's eagerness to put an end to the Palestinian *gaʾon* Meʾir's independent exercise of calendrical prerogatives in 921–22: for Seʿadya, the Rabbanites of Babylonia and Palestine had to close ranks against nonrabbinic Jews. Otherwise, they would have had to face a united front comprising Palestinian Rabbanites, Qaraites, and Ananites (I will have more to say about this, and about the differences between Qaraites and Ananites, in chapter 2).

THE TRIPARTITE JEWISH COMMUNITY IN THE TENTH CENTURY

Iraqi *geʾonim* after Seʿadya never attempted to close ranks the way he had. On the contrary: they accepted Palestinian Rabbanites and Qaraites as equal competitors for Jewish loyalties (see chapter 5). The Palestinian *geʾonim*, for their part, were so closely allied with the Qaraites over the course of the eleventh century as to suggest that Seʿadya's efforts never permanently altered the politics of the tripartite Jewish community. The periods both before and after Seʿadya, then, attest to a considerable degree of cooperation between Rabbanites and Qaraites, a fact that dictates caution in reading his polemics (and the Qaraite counterpolemics they inspired) as representing a generalizable or eternal state of alienation.

This was the structure of the tripartite Jewish community after Seʿadya. There was vigorous competition among the three groups. Each one made different kinds of claims on behalf of its own supremacy. The Palestinians mobilized their claim to custodianship of the ancient sacred center. The Babylonians

[67] The list of *geʾonim*: T-S NS 312.82, a fragment Gil identifies as written by Sahlān b. Avraham, lines 1–4. The Qaraite memorial list: T-S 12.138. See Gil, *History of Palestine*, sec. 852, and Olszowy-Schlanger, *Karaite Marriage Documents*, 144–46. Murder by a descendant of ʿAnan: Gil, *History of Palestine*, sec. 849.

responded with progressively more sweeping claims to seamless continuity with the biblical past via an unbroken chain of rabbinic tradition. The Qaraites called the validity of that tradition into question and made their own claims on behalf of a connection with Palestine. All these ideologies emerged in response to two broad sets of developments over the course of the tenth century: the fragmentation of Islamic empire and a rapid and marked increase in the production of literary texts in Arabic. In the next chapter I will trace those developments and the transformations they occasioned in Jewish thought, literature, and institutional life. New types of scholarship and new techniques for transmitting it came to play a central role in the identity and administrative organization of all three groups of Jews.

CHAPTER TWO
JEWISH BOOK CULTURE IN THE TENTH CENTURY

Hardly any documentary sources have survived that attest in detail to the workings of the Jewish community during the ninth and tenth centuries. But for Babylonian Rabbanites, Palestinian Rabbanites, and Qaraites, this was an important period during which the groups worked out their ideological programs in response to one another. It was a period of both polarization and significant mutual influence: each group adopted some of the other's intellectual tools, literary genres, and fields of interest; but the nature of the sources from this period—most of them literary, some datable only within the range of a decade or two—permits only glimpses of these transformations. Nonetheless, when viewed together, the changes from the beginning of the ninth century to the end of the tenth explain why scholastic loyalties took the form they did in the eleventh, and why the rabbinic academies in Baghdad and Jerusalem struggled so bitterly over the loyalties of Fatimid Jews.

The major developments fall under four main rubrics. First, broad changes in modes of literary transmission distinguished this period from the ones that preceded it. As the volume of textual production in the Arabic-speaking world increased exponentially, Jews responded to the erosion of oral transmission as a method of scholarship. For Babylonian Rabbanites, who were committed at least in theory to oral transmission of the Babylonian Talmud, that erosion presented a particularly difficult dilemma; they partially resolved it by making increasingly vehement claims on behalf of oral transmission as the best way to ensure the continuity of rabbinic tradition. Those claims were pitched against the Qaraites; they were also at odds with the reality of textual transmission among Jews, which was, by and large, not oral but written.

Second, the late ninth and tenth centuries marked the appearance of the first individual, named Jewish authors since the Hellenistic age. This development was intimately linked to the history of the Rabbanite-Qaraite debate. As Qaraites experimented with new genres and a new literary system, Rabbanites could not help but respond to the challenge in some way. The result was the production of new kinds of literature by Jews from both groups.

Third, Jews began to accord a new centrality to the Bible within the wider Jewish literary canon and to biblical studies as a scholarly pursuit. This change began among the Qaraites (who in turn were responding to the wider Arabophone literary culture), but it came to affect the Rabbanites profoundly. One of the most important innovations was the masoretic text of the Bible. Its creation and diffusion were intimately bound up with the history of Rabbanite-Qaraite relations.

Finally, both Rabbanites and Qaraites began to make new kinds of historical claims in the service of communal identity and religious legitimacy. Both sides embraced history as a mode of self-legitimation, and the result was that both groups exaggerated their differences by making them seem older and more primordial than they actually were. The Qaraite embrace of historical claims is particularly paradoxical, but it, too, holds numerous clues to the otherwise mysterious history of Rabbanite-Qaraite relations in the ninth and tenth centuries.

In what follows, I will take each of these developments in turn, paying special attention to their social and institutional context.

ORALITY, LITERACY, AND BOOK PRODUCTION

The fourth Islamic century witnessed an explosion of literary production among Muslims in various fields, including history, philosophy, the sciences, belles-lettres, poetry, ethics, administration, and epistolography.[1] In part this had to do with the exponential rate of growth of speakers of Arabic; and in part it had to do with the introduction of paper manufacture to the Near East. Papermaking techniques spread from China to Iraq in the eighth century and then rapidly westward; paper presented authors and copyists with a writing surface less expensive than parchment and more convenient than papyrus, and it took hold so firmly that over the course of the tenth century, papyrus became outmoded even in Egypt, its center of manufacture. Though Judeo-Arabic literature had its beginnings in the late ninth century, it witnessed a veritable explosion in the tenth, a proliferation facilitated by paper, the adoption of the codex, and the near universal acceptance of written transmission as a mode of passing on knowledge.[2]

[1] On tenth-century literary innovation in Arabic, see M. J. L. Young, J. D. Latham, and R. B. Serjeant, eds., *Religion, Learning, and Science in the ʿAbbasid period*, Cambridge History of Arabic Literature (Cambridge, 1990); Julia Ashtiany, *ʿAbbasid Belles-Lettres*, Cambridge History of Arabic Literature (Cambridge, 1990).

[2] This section is based on Rustow, "Literacy, Orality, and Book Culture," and indebted particularly to Shawkat Toorawa, *Ibn Abī Ṭāhir Ṭayfūr and Arabic Writerly Culture: A Ninth-century Bookman in Baghdad* (Richmond, Surrey, 2005).

The codex format had long been in use among Christians. It began in the first century and was widespread by the fifth, but the Jews had avoided it scrupulously in favor of the scroll, probably due to its association with Christian books. But since codices offered greater convenience than the scroll for the purposes of cross-referencing, it is not surprising that the Jews would eventually adopt it too, particularly in an age when textual memory may have been eroding. The turning point for Jews was Muslim adoption of the codex. Once Muslims adopted it, it seems it no longer bore a Christian stigma in Jewish eyes. Indeed the earliest reference to a Jewish codex dates from ca. 800–850, and the word used to describe it in an Aramaic text is borrowed from Arabic (*muṣḥaf*).[3] It is probably not entirely accidental that so few Jewish works survive in copies that date to before 900: the number of books produced after that point was probably simply much greater.

Rabbinic conceptions of writing and orality, too, changed drastically. Jewish religious scholars adopted written transmission with enormous rapidity compared with contemporaneous Muslim religious scholars. Muslim scholars so profoundly mistrusted written transmission that, in principle, they required books to be copied not from other manuscripts but by having their contents read aloud by an authorized transmitter. These scholars considered the oral intermediary to be necessary to the work's proper transmission, at least in theory: authors were expected to declaim the written texts of their works before audiences who transcribed them and then became licensed to transmit them orally themselves. The Islamic system of granting licenses (*ijāzāt*) to transmitters to copy and recite works constituted a mechanism for maintaining a scholarly monopoly on the transmission of knowledge, especially given the exponentially greater population of Muslims and the broad area over which they were now dispersed. But strangely, the Jews never developed a system of licensing.

This is strange because the necessity of the oral intermediary probably had its origin in Hellenistic models of education, and it is attested among late antique Jews. But the Jews abandoned it and instead copied books from other books. It is even stranger when one considers that rabbinic teachers stood at the end of a long history of using the very same methods of oral recitation that their Muslim contemporaries now did.[4]

By the tenth century, the oral monopoly on textual transmission applied only to one Jewish text: the Babylonian Talmud, which the Iraqi *ge'onim* con-

[3] Malachi Beit-Arié, *Hebrew Manuscripts of East and West: Towards a Comparative Codicology*, The Panizzi Lectures 1992 (London, 1993), 10–11; *EJ*, s.v. "Masorah" (A. Dotan), citing *Halakhot gedolot*.

[4] Martin S. Jaffee, *Torah in the Mouth: Writing and Oral Tradition in Palestinian Judaism, 200 BCE–400 CE (New York*, 2001), 126–56; idem, "The Oral-Cultural Context of the Talmud Yerushalmi: Greco-Roman Rhetorical Paideia, Discipleship, and the Concept of Oral Torah," in *Transmitting Jewish Traditions: Orality, Textuality, and Cultural Diffusion*, ed. Yaakov Elman and Israel Gershoni (New Haven, 2000): 27–73.

tinued to insist had to be learned orally. But, as with Islamic book transmission, that insistence was in some cases only theoretical, since the exigencies of geographic dispersion had already seen to it that the Babylonian Talmud was disseminated in writing. Indeed, some of the oldest surviving texts of the Babylonian Talmud are copies of sections that the *ge'onim* wrote and mailed to their followers in Egypt, Ifrīqiya, and elsewhere. But by the eleventh century, we learn from the Babylonian *ga'on* Hayya b. Sherira (1004–38), there were written copies of the Babylonian Talmud circulating within the *yeshiva* of Pumbedita itself. Not only that: in one instance, Hayya admitted that the version of the text they contained was more authoritative than the oral one. Queried from abroad on the correct reading of a passage of the Mishnah, Hayya had this to say: "They taught us [the passage] this way originally . . . and we have heard that in Palestine they recite [it nearly the same way], and here too there are copies that are written so. And this made sense to us, and we said in the academy . . . that this version is more accurate, but the elders . . . protested against us vehemently over this."[5]

Hayya, then, emended the oral version of the text current at Pumbedita on the basis of two variants: the oral version from Palestine and written copies of the text that circulated in his *yeshiva*. He admits frankly that written versions in this case contained better readings, even though the older members of the *yeshiva* protested. Even so, the Talmud was the only text that Jews continued to insist be transmitted orally, even if that insistence went increasingly unheeded.

The difference between Muslim suspicion of writing and the Jewish embrace of it has to be explained somehow. In part, it owes to the fact that there were fewer Jews than Muslims, and their paucity helped scholars and religious experts to preserve institutional monopolies over texts like the Talmud—but only in part. One still has to explain why rabbinic scholars, who had used oral transmission for centuries, allowed this system to lapse.

Rina Drory has argued that the shift to written transmission came as a result of Qaraite innovations in the transmission of sacred and other literature. By the tenth century, Qaraites had already so thoroughly broken the traditional Jewish patterns of oral transmission, she argues, that the Rabbanites, too, now had to embrace writing.[6] I have independently reached the same conclusion: As Rabbanites and Qaraites competed with one another for followers and responded to the same broader cultural developments, and Qaraites adopted the most important intellectual and technological developments of their age, the Rabbanites could not watch and do nothing.

[5] Cited in Brody, *Geonim of Babylonia*, 158; cf. his interpretation ibid., 157–58.

[6] See especially Rina Drory, "Le rôle de la littérature karaïte dans l'histoire de la littérature juive au Xe siècle," *Revue des études juives* 159 (2000): 107–8.

Already in the late ninth century, the Qaraites became the first Jews to adopt what Drory has called "the basic Arabic principle of organizing the literary repertoire around one sacred text," something Arabic literature had accomplished two centuries earlier.[7] That sacred text was the Hebrew Bible. That is not to say that Rabbanites had neglected the study of the Bible. But the Qaraites began to study it scientifically; they developed Hebrew linguistics and lexicography and reinvented the running commentary to explicate the Bible verse by verse.[8]

Traditional rabbinic-style midrashic exegesis, of the type produced over the period from the dawn of the Common Era until the close of the first millennium, was loosely and tangentially organized. Among the earliest surviving Jewish scriptural commentaries that departed from this traditional method of explication were those of the Qaraite Dani'el al-Qūmisī, active in Palestine ca. 870–910. His commentaries hewed more closely to the plain sense of the text, a signal change that eventually transformed the genre for both Qaraites and Rabbanites. Al-Qūmisī also wrote his commentaries in Hebrew rather than the Aramaic that had dominated the genre: like commentaries on the Qur'ān, biblical commentaries could now be written in the language of scripture itself. Al-Qūmisī also worked with another innovative technique: his own name and an authorial voice, in contradistinction to the collectively and anonymously authored and edited rabbinic compendia of classical rabbinic midrash.[9]

Over the course of the ninth and tenth centuries, Jewish literature in Hebrew, Judeo-Arabic, and Arabic was utterly transformed by these and other innovations. According to Drory, the Qaraites, unfettered by rabbinic tradition, were at their forefront. She also argues that they removed the discomfort and embarrassment when rabbinic circles considered adopting three elements of the contemporaneous Arabic literary system: written works designed for a public readership (as distinct from private notes to facilitate oral transmission); texts written in the name of an individual author using an authorial first person; and attention to literary form and structure, rather than thematic, mnemonic and/or associative schemes of organization.[10] Before the tenth century, in Drory's view, new works of rabbinic literature strove to fit themselves into the old canonical genres and conceal their novelty—hence the anonymously authored

[7] Drory, *Models and Contacts*, 135; eadem, *Emergence of Jewish-Arabic Literary Contacts*, 81–94; and above, n. 1.

[8] Meira Polliack, *The Karaite Tradition of Arabic Bible Translation: A Linguistic and Exegetical Study of Karaite Translations of the Pentateuch from the Tenth and Eleventh Centuries C.E.* (Leiden, 1997).

[9] Frank, *Search Scripture Well*, esp. 4 (and n. 12); Drory, "Rôle de la littérature karaïte," 99–111; Polliack, *Karaite Tradition of Arabic Bible Translation*, 26–36.

[10] Drory, *Emergence of Jewish-Arabic Literary Contacts*; eadem, "Rôle de la littérature karaïte"; eadem, *Models and Contacts*, 134–38.

midrash collections compiled in Palestine during first four centuries of Islamic rule. After that point, rabbinic literature assimilated these innovations and used them in a remarkable outpouring of scholarly works.

The figure who did the most to import the new models into the rabbinic canon was Seʿadya b. Yūsuf al-Fayyūmī (882–942). On its face, this is paradoxical: these innovations had been the preserve of Qaraites, and Seʿadya was a vicious polemicist against Qaraism. Both in spite of his zealous anti-Qaraism and precisely because of it, Seʿadya adopted all these innovations. He wrote in disciplines and genres that had previously been the preserve of Muslims, Qaraites, or Palestinian Rabbanites, but largely untouched by the Babylonian Rabbanites: systematic theology, linguistics, liturgical poetry, polemic, biblical exegesis, and translation. Testimony to his drive to best his opponents at their own game, he also became the first Babylonian *gaʾon* to make use of the Palestinian Talmud itself. All of these innovations worked in the service of his campaign on behalf of Babylonian supremacy. Robert Brody has aptly called Seʿadya a "revolutionary champion of tradition." Most would concede him that label merely in light of inner-rabbinic developments, but Drory's argument about the elements of the Qaraite and Muslim literary systems that he adopted makes it evident just how revolutionary he was.[11]

THE BIBLICAL TEXT

Concurrently with all this, there occurred one of the most important literary developments of this relatively murky period, one in which Rabbanites and Qaraites alike had a hand: the invention of a new written system of transmission for the text of the Hebrew Bible. The history of Rabbanite-Qaraite cooperation in the project sheds light on some important institutional changes that, in turn, bore an impact on the events I narrate in the rest of this book.

The textual transmission of the Hebrew Bible occurred in three major stages over the course of fifteen centuries.[12] During the first stage, the number of biblical books were stabilized, as was the consonantal text. This process concluded in late antiquity. During the second stage—on which my discussion will focus—vowels and a system of symbols or numes to guide the chanting of the text were added to the consonantal text. Textual variants were adjusted or reconciled with one another, at least to some extent. The result was the

[11] Brody, *Geonim of Babylonia*, 239–48. Drory readily acknowledges that most extant Qaraite literature dates from Seʿadya's lifetime or after. But al-Qūmisī is a weighty exception, and Seʿadya's polemics demonstrate that a significant Qaraite literature preceded him.

[12] See Ernst Würthwein, *The Text of the Old Testament: An Introduction to the Biblia Hebraica*, trans. Erroll F. Rhodes, 4th ed. (London, 1979 [1973]); and Angel Sáenz-Badillos, *A History of the Hebrew Language*, trans. John Elwolde (Cambridge, 1993 [1988]), 70–111.

so-called masoretic text of the Bible, from the Hebrew word *masora*, transmitted tradition; the generations of scholars who created it are called Masoretes.

The work of the Masoretes extended over the eighth and ninth centuries, but the earliest concrete evidence of the existence of masoretic manuscripts dates to the late ninth century and so to the end of masoretic activity.[13] Those manuscripts also date to precisely the era in which Jews were adopting the codex format, and the important surviving masoretic manuscripts are codices rather than the older form the text of the Hebrew Bible took, the scroll. There were two masoretic traditions in circulation, a Babylonian and a Tiberian. There had also been a Palestinian tradition, but since there is a near total lack of evidence about it as distinct from the Tiberian tradition after the tenth century, it is safe to assume that at some point, the two traditions merged.[14]

The third stage of biblical transmission finally produced a *textus receptus* in the form of the second edition of the Hebrew Bible, printed at the Bomberg atelier in Venice in 1524–25. For the sake of this edition, a certain Yaʿaqov ben Ḥayyim studied myriad contradictory medieval manuscripts and lists of variant readings, and to judge by his comments, it was a Sisyphean labor.[15]

Despite the variants of which Yaʿaqov ben Ḥayyim complained, by the twelfth century, some version of the masoretic text had been accepted so broadly as the canonical one that Rabbanites and Qaraites alike expressed the view that the Torah had been revealed to Moses on Sinai with its masoretic marks already in place. This is somewhat surprising in light of the fact that the *ge'onim* themselves held and stated plainly that the original scroll given to Moses on Sinai contained consonants only. The wildly anachronistic opinion that the *masora* was revealed on Sinai went unchallenged until 1538, when the Italian humanist Elia Levita (1469–1549) published his book *Masoret ha-masoret*

[13] Chiesa determines the *terminus post quem* of masoretic activity on the basis of the silence of either Talmud on the existence of vowel points or dots; *The Emergence of Hebrew Biblical Pointing*, Judentum und Umwelt (Frankfurt, 1979), 36–37 (as to cantillation marks, see his comments there). That terminus has to suffice for the Babylonian system given the lack of positive testimony as to its inception. For the Tiberian, see the masoretic list Chiesa quotes on 38–40 (also discussed below). Though the Cairo Codex of the Prophets contains a colophon stating that it was written by Moshe Ben Asher in 894–95, apparently it was copied in the late tenth or early eleventh century together with the colophon (it nonetheless offers evidence for a ninth-century Qaraite commission of a masoretic codex). Mordechai Glatzer, "The Aleppo Codex: Codicological and Paleographical Aspects," Hebrew, *Sefunot* 19 (1989): 250–59; for the colophon, see Paul Kahle, *The Cairo Geniza*, 2d ed. (Oxford, 1959 [1947]), 110–14.

[14] On what the "Palestinian" *masora* may have been before it merged with the Tiberian, see Chiesa, *L'Antico Testamento ebraico secondo la tradizione palestinese* (Turin, 1978); idem, *Emergence of Hebrew Biblical Pointing*, 11 at n. 37; 16 (citing the *Maḥzor* of Simḥa b. Shemu'el of Vitry, d. 1105 CE, the only source that claims the Palestinian tradition was different from the Tiberian); 35–36; 56–57, n. 37; and cf. Sáenz-Badillos, *History of the Hebrew Language*, 91–92.

[15] Moshe Greenberg, "The Stabilization of the Text of the Hebrew Bible, Reviewed in the Light of the Biblical Materials from the Judean Desert," *Journal of the American Oriental Society* 76 (1956): 158, and more generally, Würthwein, *Text of the Old Testament*, 12–41.

(The tradition of the *masora*), arguing that vowel points had been added to the consonantal text only late in its diffusion. Levita's view still met with resistance, most notably from the illustrious Jewish humanist Azarya de' Rossi (ca. 1511–77) and the Christian Hebraist Johannes Buxtorf (1564–1629). The shared Jewish and Christian interest in the history of the Bible's transmission is a fascinating chapter in the history of the Renaissance and the contest between humanist values and religious ones.[16] But the belief in the sanctity and antiquity of the masoretic text also covered the tracks of its reception and transmission and made them somewhat impervious to analysis.

Partly as a result, the masoretic text has been seen as a "tradition" in the weak sense, a snapshot of how people had already come to learn and recite the Bible. In fact, masoretic texts were something new. The Masoretes invented new signs and symbols—vowel points and cantillation marks—to convey the sound of the text in writing; the shift toward writing was a symptom of the broader move from oral to written transmission in general. The masoretic project also involved collating texts, researching biblical grammar, and making decisions about how Hebrew should be pronounced, all activities that presume a conscious scholarly intent, not the mere preservation of a tradition. The *masora* can also be understood as a response to the project to fix the text of the Qur'ān and give it vowels, numes, and diacritical points.

But understanding the *masora*'s history is further complicated by a lack of evidence. There are no complete masoretic manuscripts datable to earlier than the tenth century—not to speak of the near total lack of Hebrew manuscripts dating between the first the late ninth centuries. This makes it almost impossible to know anything about the masoretic schools other than what one can glean from the painstakingly technical work of comparing the surviving masoretic manuscripts and fragments or from vague or indirect statements about masoretic activity in medieval works. This kind of painstaking labor, particularly that of Bruno Chiesa, has demonstrated that by the tenth century, the Tiberian *masora* had already been adopted as canonical. This is a salient fact not just because of what it says about the history of the biblical text. It also offers us precious information about the politics, scholarly traditions, and scholastic loyalties of the Jewish communities under Islamic rule and how they shifted during this period.

Two points should suffice to make this clear. First, the Tiberian *masora* held such decisive sway that the Babylonian *masora* adopted elements of it and Babylonians themselves came to participate in its production and dissemination.[17] This means that for all the Babylonians' aspiration to superiority in Talmud

[16] Chiesa, *Emergence of Hebrew Biblical Pointing*, 5–8, who also cites a lone twelfth-century statement that the original Torah scroll was not pointed, cited in the Maḥzor Vitry; but both this and the gaonic statements should be understood not as historical evidence that the *masora* was late but as justifications of the practice of using unpointed texts for liturgical purposes.

[17] Chiesa, "La tradizione babilonese dell'Antico Testamento ebraico," *Henoch* 6 (1984): 181–204.

and the calendar, they acknowledged that the Palestinians dominated matters related to the Bible.

Second, the Tiberian tradition was the accepted among Rabbanites and Qaraites alike. That is a seemingly simple statement on its face—after all, both held the Bible to be a sacred and canonical text. But in fact it contains a welter of historical implications that I shall now try to map out via the story of one biblical codex.

The Tāj

The oldest complete text of the Hebrew Bible that survived the Middle Ages was a manuscript known as the Aleppo Codex, in the Middle Ages called simply the Crown (Tāj in Arabic, Keter in Hebrew). I say "was" rather than "is" because a third of it disappeared in 1947, but not before scholars had had a chance to copy some of the inscriptions it contained attesting to its own history.

The Tāj was the work of the Tiberian Masorete Aharon ben Asher, and it was completed ca. 900. During its early years, until the end of the eleventh century, it had been a prized possession of the Qaraite community in Jerusalem, as one inscription attests. By the twelfth century, it had moved to the Jewish community of Fustat, where the greatest Rabbanite legal authority of the Middle Ages, Maimonides (1138–1204), codified the rules for writing certain sections of Torah scrolls on its basis. "Since I have seen great confusion in these matters in all the scrolls that I have seen," he wrote,

> and the Masoretes who write and compose [treatises] . . . contradict each other in such matters in keeping with the scrolls on which they base themselves, I decided to write down here all the sections [in question] of the Torah. . . . The copy on which I base myself in these matters is the one known in Fustat, which contains the twenty-four books, which was formerly in Jerusalem serving as a model by which copies were corrected. Everyone used to rely on it, for Ben Asher corrected it, scrutinized it for years and corrected it many times."[18]

[18] Maimonides, *Mishne Torah*, Hilkhot Sefer Torah 8:4, quoted in Chiesa, *Emergence of Hebrew Biblical Pointing*, 13 (see also his comments on 14). As to which codex is meant, see Rudolf Kittel, Karl Elliger, Wilhelm Rudolph, Hans Peter Ruger, and G. E. Weil, *[Torah, Neviim u-Khetuvim]=Biblia Hebraica Stuttgartensia*, ed. A. Schenker, 5th ed. (Stuttgart, 1997), xii; Paul Kahle, "The Hebrew ben Asher Bible Manuscripts," *Vetus Testamentum* 1 (1951): 161–67; I. Ben-Zvi, "The Codex of Ben-Asher," *Textus* 1, no. 7–9 (1960): 7–9; M. H. Goshen-Gottstein, "The Authenticity of the Aleppo Codex," ibid. (1960): 17–19, 24; idem, "A Recovered Part of the Aleppo Codex," ibid. 5 (1966): 53–59; idem, "The Aleppo Codex and the Rise of the Massoretic Bible Text," *Biblical Archeologist* 42:3 (1979): 145–63; Jordan S. Penkower, "Maimonides and the Aleppo Codex," *Textus* 9 (1981): 40–43; and cf. Goitein, "New Documents from the Cairo Geniza," *Homenaje a Millás-Vallicrosa* (Barcelona, 1954), 1:713–16 (on Bodl. MS Heb. c 28.23, a twelfth-century document describing negotiations toward the restoration of a precious Torah scroll called "the brother of the Tāj").

The fact that both Qaraites and Rabbanites regarded the Tāj as the most accurate and important witness to the biblical text has led to a clamorous scholarly disagreement as to whether the Ben Asher family, who produced it, was Rabbanite or Qaraite. The votes tally about equally on either side of the debate, but the arguments for the Ben Ashers' Qaraism, which had more champions early on, have now gained ground again. A piece of evidence usually mustered in the debate is the fact that Aharon ben Asher's father, Moshe ben Asher, copied a codex of the Prophets in 894–95 in response to a Qaraite commission. On the other side, Maimonides' admiration for the Tāj has prompted some scholars to insist that the Ben Ashers were Rabbanites, for how could the great rabbinic sage lend his imprimatur to a product of Qaraite scholarship? In fact Maimonides did not canonize the text of the Tāj; he only confirmed the importance it had already achieved, since in Jerusalem in the eleventh century it had already come to serve "as a model by which copies were corrected." Others have noted that all the major masoretic codices, including the originals produced by the Ben Ashers, were either commissioned by Qaraites or preserved in Qaraite libraries: the Tāj; the original from which the Cairo Codex was copied; and the Leningrad Codex, a complete Hebrew Bible of 1008–9 that (like the Cairo Codex) seems to have been copied from a Ben Asher codex now lost.[19]

One problem with the Ben Asher debate is that both sides of it claim to know what it meant to be a Rabbanite or a Qaraite at the turn of the tenth century. This certainty is achieved by projecting the conclusions culled from later evidence of Qaraism backward in time. But evidence of Palestinian Qaraism ca. 900 is restricted to al-Qūmisī and some anonymous authors ascribed to his circle. They offer us, at most, evidence of a circle—one whose surviving sermons probably exhibited extreme doctrinal fervor even for their day. But if we turn the question around and ask what masoretic history can teach us about Rabbanites and Qaraites at the turn of the tenth century, the results are more promising. As Geoffrey Khan and Meira Polliack have noted, medieval sources call the Masoretes of the eighth and ninth centuries *baʿaley miqraʾ* ("experts in scripture"), the same name by which the Qaraites would come to be known in the ninth and tenth. The name designated an intellectual trend and a scholarly project first, and only later, as the debate between the "party of scripture" and the "party of tradition" polarized, its use became reserved exclusively for

[19] The Leningrad Codex was preserved by Egyptian Qaraites until the nineteenth century, when Firkovich brought it to Russia (at the Russian National Library it bears the shelfmark 1 Firk. Heb. B 19a). Firkovich attempted to acquire the Tāj as well, but did not succeed. See Harviainen, "Abraham Firkovich, the Aleppo Codex, and Its Dedication." For an exhaustive bibliography on the question of whether Ben Asher was Qaraite, see Chiesa, *Emergence of Hebrew Biblical Pointing*, 77–79 n. 106, and now Rafael Zer, "Was the Masorete of the Aleppo Codex of Rabbanite or Karaite Origin?" Hebrew, *Sefunot* 23 (2003): 573–87, who argues on the basis of a scholion in the manuscript that its scribe was a Qaraite, but remains agnostic on the question of whether Ben Asher was really the scribe.

Qaraites. In the eighth and ninth centuries, meanwhile, a group of Jewish scholars held as a matter of common concern the task of producing an authoritative text of the Hebrew Bible. There is no evidence that they also endeavored to produce sharp scholastic distinctions or declarations of a scholastic monopoly on biblical study.[20]

This hypothesis finds partial confirmation in a list of Tiberian Masoretes ordered by generation found in a tenth-century grammatical treatise. Assuming twenty-five-year generations, the first Masoretes on the list date to ca. 775–800, before Qaraism existed at all. The masoretic project, then, was older than the first evidence of Qaraites. Further on in the list, in the second generation, ca. 800–825, there appears a certain Pinḥas "head of the academy" (*rosh ha-yeshiva*)—that is, *ga'on* of the *yeshiva* at Tiberias—an indication that Rabbanites were involved in the project. That generation also produced the eponymous Asher the elder, father of the Ben Asher dynasty, and his progeny are listed as the main representatives of the Tiberian masoretic school for another four generations, until Aharon ben Asher, the last representative, in ca. 900–925.[21]

The identical name designating first these *baʿaley miqra'* and later the Qaraites suggests that the Qaraite movement grew out of the masoretic focus on scripture—not the other way around. The presence of one of the Palestinian *ge'onim* on the list further suggests a working group distinctly uninterested in creating distinct institutional or scholastic identities.[22]

As for what created Rabbanism as a self-consciously anti-Qaraite movement, previous scholars correctly point to Seʿadya b. Yūsuf al-Fayyūmī in the 920s and 930s. But it must be remembered that Seʿadya did not merely polemicize against the Qaraites; he also learned from them. One of Seʿadya's teachers is said to have been a certain Abū Kathīr Yaḥyā b. Zakariyyā the Rabbanite (d. ca. 932–33), a *kātib* (government appointee) in Tiberias, a contemporary of Aharon ben Asher, and among the important Masoretes of his

[20] Al-Qūmisī's "circle": e.g., the anonymous author of JTS Schechter Geniza, 17r–18v. See also Frank's comments in *Search Scripture Well*, 28–29 n. 108. *Baʿaley miqra'*: Khan, *The Early Karaite Tradition of Hebrew Grammatical Thought: Including a Critical Edition, Translation and Analysis of the* Diqduq *of Abū Yaʿqūb Yūsuf ibn Nūḥ on the Hagiographa* (Leiden, 2000), 20, and in general, 12–25; see also Polliack, "Medieval Karaism," 312. The term *baʿaley miqra'* is reflected in the Qaraite *ketubba* formulary, which enjoins observance of commandments and customs "according to the way of the Qaraites [*ke-derekh baʿaley miqra'*]"; see, e.g., ENA 4020.38, line 3. Binyamin al-Nahāwandī uses the term; Baron noted it to be the first designation of the Qaraites as such, but it may have represented something between scriptural experts in general and a defined movement. Cf. Baron, *Social and Religious History*², 5:225. See also M. A. Friedman, "Qara'(im) = ben(ey) miqra'; baʿal(ey) miqra'," *Lĕšonénu* 39 (1976–77): 296–97, and Goitein, *Mediterranean Society*, 5:372.

[21] Chiesa, *Emergence of Hebrew Biblical Pointing*, 84 n. 133.

[22] Khan, *Early Karaite Tradition*, 25, who also notes that the other Hebrew term by which the Qaraites came to be identified, *qara* (pl. *qara'im*), is attested several times in the Babylonian Talmud referring to those who occupied themselves with the biblical text and its linguistic details.

day.[23] From the former, Seʿadya gleaned the fruits of two and a half centuries of Tiberian masoretic tradition; against the latter, he seems to have written an anti-Qaraite polemical poem.[24] That Ben Asher was a Qaraite is a fact known only on the basis of this poem (if the Ben Asher in the dedication really is the Masorete in question)—that is, known only from the fact that Seʿadya saw fit to call him a heretic; but we know nothing of what it may have meant that he was a Qaraite. We do know, however, that Seʿadya then went on to become the first Rabbanite to claim the field of biblical studies as a rabbinic preserve, insisting in his philosophical and polemical statements against the Qaraites that scripture was incomprehensible without the aid of rabbinic exegesis and tradition.

Meanwhile, both sides of the Ben Asher debate have mustered evidence that, though it has little to do with the Ben Ashers themselves, touches instead on the question of the transmission and reception of their work. Maimonides' approbation of the Tāj is actually a very weak argument for the Ben Ashers having been Rabbanites, but a sound one for widespread acceptance of Ben Asher's work regardless of his scholastic affiliation. Similarly, the Qaraite custodianship of the major masoretic codices tells us nothing about the Ben Ashers, but suggests that there is something to be learned about the early Qaraites from the diffusion of the Ben Ashers' work. In short, reframing the history of the Tiberian *masora* in terms of its reception and transmission opens a wide vista onto the history of tenth-century Palestine and its changing Jewish community.

The Reception of the Tiberian *Masora*

What caused the Tiberian tradition to become the dominant one in the first place?

[23] Al-Masʿūdī, *Kitāb al-tanbīh wa-l-ishrāf*, quoted in Mann, *Jews in Egypt and in Palestine*, 2:375, and in Chiesa, *Emergence of Hebrew Biblical Pointing*, 11–12, 60 n. 41. Al-Masʿūdī calls him "min al-ashmaʿat," "a traditionalist" (an Arabic neologism from Aramaic); but al-Bīrūnī, *al-Āthār al-bāqiya ʿan al-qurūn al-khāliya*, uses the same term to describe the Qaraites: Sachau, *Chronologie orientalischer Völker*, 58 (Arabic), and idem, *Chronology of Ancient Nations*, 68. This seems to be simply an error on al-Bīrūnī's part, unless Seʿadya really studied with a Qaraite. On *kātib* here as government bureaucrat rather than scribe, see Chiesa, *Emergence of Hebrew Biblical Pointing*, 59 n. 40. Abū Kathīr Yaḥyā b. Zakariyyā has been identified unconvincingly with the Hebrew grammarian ʿEli ben Yehuda ha-Nazīr: Nehemya Allony, "ʿElī ben Yehuda Hannazīr and His Treatise '*Kitāb uṣūl al-lugha al-ʿibrāniyya*,'" Hebrew, *Lĕšonénu* 34 (1969–70): 80–81.

[24] "Essa meshali" ("I shall take up my parable"), preserved in the Geniza; it contains a superscription dedicating it to a certain Ben Asher, possibly a member of the masoretic family, but the identification is not certain. B. M. Lewin, "Essa meshali le-RaSaG" (Seʿadya's 'I shall take up my parable'), in *Rav Seʿadya Gaʾon: qoveṣ torani–maddaʿi*, ed. J. L. Fishman (Jerusalem, 1943), 481–532; Baron, *Social and Religious History*², 6:246; Benjamin Klar, *Meḥqarim ve-ʿiyyunim: ba-lashon, ba-shira u-va-sifrut*, ed. A. M. Habermann (Tel-Aviv, 1954), 276–319; Gil, *History of Palestine*, sec. 294; Brody, *Geonim of Babylonia*, 97 n. 58; Ezra Fleischer, "Saadya Gaon's Place in the History of Hebrew Poetry," Hebrew, *Peʿamim* 54 (1993): 11 n. 28.

Here again, westward migration played a role. Chiesa points out that the Ben Asher family's rise to prominence coincided with the first migrations of Iraqi Qaraites to Palestine in the mid- to late ninth century. Iraqi Qaraites participated in the masoretic school in Tiberias, he argues, and this gave the Tiberian *masora* its edge over the Babylonian version: If even the Babylonians themselves accepted the Tiberian reading, how could anyone argue with them? Their migration also offered the Tiberian Masoretes a new infusion of linguistic knowledge and talent from the east, which in the ninth century was known for its experts in linguistics.[25] The infusion of Iraqis to Tiberias, Chiesa suggests, propelled the acceptance of the Tiberian *masora* in the east and precipitated the decline of the Babylonian one everywhere.[26]

To that argument, Drory adds some consideration of the material history of the text's reception. Moshe ben Asher wrote his codex of the prophets in the late ninth century in response to a Qaraite commission; from that point forward, Qaraites continued to commission copies of Tiberian masoretic codices for both personal study and liturgical use. Qaraite sponsorship, she argues, promoted the wide dissemination of the Tiberian tradition. Once the Qaraites had diffused it, the Rabbanites accepted it as well.[27]

Both reasons are plausible, principally because they attend to questions of demographics, power, and material history, rather than taking for granted some putative superiority of the Tiberian text over the other ones. But that was not how medieval Jews saw the matter. Just at the point when all Jews who cared about the Bible had come to accept the dominance of the Tiberian tradition, they began to express their belief in its superiority and purity—and they did so just as vociferously as the Babylonian *ge'onim* promoted their belief in the unbroken transmission of rabbinic tradition.

Thus the Iraqi Qaraite Abū Yūsuf Yaʿqūb al-Qirqisānī, in his history of Jewish schisms (937–38), recounts a debate he conducted with a student of Seʿadya's named Yaʿqūb b. Efrayim al-Shāmī. Al-Shāmī set out to convince al-Qirqisānī of the Babylonian *masora's* superiority, but he made the mistake of doing so precisely at a point when the Tiberian one had begun to replace it even in Iraq. As zealous a champion of Iraqi supremacy as his teacher, al-Shāmī claimed

[25] Chiesa, *Emergence of Hebrew Biblical Pointing*, 84 n. 133. The al-Qūmisī sermon (datable to the last third of the ninth century) seems to presume the existence of a community in Jerusalem (Mann, *Texts and Studies*, 2:3–8); Salmon b. Yeruḥim claims that Qaraites began to settle there after Binyamin al-Nahāwandī, i.e., in the second half of the ninth century (Pinsker, *Lickute Kadmoniot*, 22, quoted in Mann, *Jews in Egypt and in Palestine*, 1:60 n. 3); and see the discussion in André Paul, *Ecrits de Qumran et sectes juives aux premiers siècles de l'Islam: Recherches sur l'origine du Qaraïsme* (Paris, 1969), 100–102, which requires rethinking in light of the distinction between Ananism and Qaraism; see Ben-Shammai, "Between Ananites and Karaites: Observations on Early Medieval Jewish Sectarianism," in *Studies in Muslim-Jewish Relations*, ed. Ronald L. Nettler (Chur, 1993), 25 n. 1, and also idem, "Fragments of Daniel al-Qūmisī's Commentary."

[26] Chiesa, *Emergence of Hebrew Biblical Pointing*, 41–42, esp. 41.

[27] Drory, *Models and Contacts*, 142.

tendentiously that that the Palestinians "are many fewer than those who have adopted the Babylonian reading," while the Babylonian tradition was both more correct and more widespread. "The Babylonian reading has filled the world," al-Shāmī hyperbolizes, "for it extends from Raqqa to China, throughout those countries and among most of the inhabitants of the [Iraqī] Jazīra, Khurāsān, Fārs, Kirmān, Iṣfahān, Yamāma, Baḥrayn, and the Yemen, and so on."[28]

Al-Qirqisānī counters al-Shāmī by pointing out that actually, the Tiberian reading is not only prevalent among Byzantine and Maghribī Jews; in the east it is already considered superior to the Babylonian reading, even among those who have not yet had much exposure to it. Who could possibly doubt, he asks al-Shāmī,

> that the Palestinian reading is the authentic one, and that it is the one in which God addressed His prophets? Besides, in our days there is no one among those who study philology and grammar in Iṣfahān, Baṣra, Tustar, and other places [in the east known for their linguistic scholarship] who does not prefer the Palestinian reading, who does not judge it to be the correct one, and who does not hold that grammar can be expounded only by means of it. In addition, some of their elders who do not use the Palestinian reading and are acquainted only with the Babylonian one, having only heard of the Palestinian reading by hearsay, when they want to speak about language and grammar speak only of the Palestinian language, to the exclusion of any other.[29]

Al-Qirqisānī, then, testifies that in his day, the Tiberian tradition had already begun to dominate the Babylonian one even in Iraq itself, where only the older generation remained unversed in it. Both systems were known, but the Babylonian had started to be edged out, "or, rather," Chiesa notes, "banished to remote areas" east and south of Iraq that had once been centrally located in the Abbasid heartland but were now depleted by migration westward and marginalized in the study of the Bible.[30]

But that is not the only argument al-Qirqisānī musters. When al-Shāmī attempts to defend the validity of the Babylonian tradition, al-Qirqisānī counters that the Babylonian tradition has been corrupted by exposure to the

[28] Al-Qirqisānī, *Kitāb al-anwār wa-l-marāqib*, Book II, 16:2; quoted in Chiesa, *Emergence of Hebrew Biblical Pointing*, 19 and 24 (I have slightly altered his translation).

[29] Al-Qirqisānī, *Kitāb al-anwār wa-l-marāqib*, Book II, 17:5–6; quoted in Chiesa, *Emergence of Hebrew Biblical Pointing*, 21, 23, 25, and 26 (I have slightly altered his translation). Al-Qirqisānī goes on to hint ("darkly," as Chiesa notes) that "if Palestinians and Babylonians together changed and transformed what was imposed on them [by God] on account of the supremacy [*ghalba*] of the rabbis, of their dominion [*istilā'*], and their authority [*tamakkun bi-ri'āsa*], it would still not be denied that it was the Babylonians who changed and modified the reading" rather than the Palestinians (Book II, 17:5; Chiesa's commentary, ibid., 29).

[30] Ibid., 17; see also 27.

Aramaic speech of its environment and rabbinic distortions in transmission, while the Palestinian one remains free of taint.[31] Al-Qirqisānī the Qaraite, in short, makes use of a technique worthy of Seʿadya: the argument for the validity of a tradition by virtue of its unbroken transmission. But while Seʿadya used the unbroken transmission of rabbinic interpretation against the Qaraites, al-Qirqisānī used the unbroken transmission of the biblical text against the Rabbanites. Both arguments attest to anxieties about the rupture of scholarly traditions in an age of written transmission: each claims for his side the distinction of continuity.

Al-Qirqisānī demonstrates the Qaraite promotion of the Tiberian masora and the Qaraites' role in spreading it and its good repute. But he was not the only one to defend the purity and authenticity of the Tiberian *masora*. A wealth of evidence first mustered by Chiesa testifies to a widespread belief that the Jews of Tiberias possessed a superior understanding of the pronunciation and grammar of Hebrew. This belief was so widely held that Rabbanite and Qaraite scholars alike repeated it over the course of the three centuries beginning with the generation before al-Qirqisānī. Though they all believed that the superiority of the Tiberian tradition of Hebrew had led the Tiberians to produce a superior *masora*, in fact their statements should be read as evidence that once it was considered superior, an ideology developed as to the superiority of the native traditions of the Tiberians. Not only that, they all expressed this ideology without regard for whether these Tiberians were Rabbanite or Qaraite.

"The Excellence Which Originated from the City of Tiberias"

The earliest proponent of the view is ʿEli b. Yehuda ha-Nazir, a native of Tiberias, who recounted in a linguistic treatise of ca. 915 (preserved in fragments in the Geniza) the time and trouble he had devoted to studying the language of the Bible. When he had doubts about the accuracy of his work, he added, he would go outside to test his results.

> I used to spend much time sitting in the squares and streets of Tiberias, listening to the speech of the marketplace and the simple people. I would observe their language and its grammar in order to see whether something in my grammar was lacking or there was something incorrect in my understanding and in the pronunciation of Hebrew and the various dialects of Aramaic [Siryānī], by which I mean the language of the *targum* [the Aramaic Bible translation] and so on, which is very close to Hebrew, as I have said above. . . . My findings turned out to be true and correct, with God's help, strength, and power, not because of

[31] Al-Qirqisānī, *Kitāb al-anwār wa-l-marāqib*, Book II, 16:1–2 and 17:3–7 (135–36, 138–41); quoted in Chiesa, *Emergence of Hebrew Biblical Pointing*, 18–27.

something that I have merited but with His support, may He be exalted and glorified.[32]

The suggestion that Hebrew was spoken in Tiberias in the tenth century seems far-fetched, especially given ha-Nazir's contention that it was "simple people" who spoke it (this detail disqualifies analogies with Latin as a spoken language among the students of premodern Oxford or Cambridge). Aramaic is more plausible. But the truth of ha-Nazir's statement is not the point. Rather, it is his belief that Tiberian Hebrew was superior to all the others and the terms in which he casts that belief: terms borrowed directly from the literary ideology surrounding the Qur'ān. Just as Muslims had developed ideals about the purity of Bedouin Arabic and mustered them in debates about the inimitability (*iʿjāz*) of the Qur'ān and its language, Jews now reclaimed the language of their sacred text and claimed for it a locus of production in its purest state.[33]

Thus a tenth-century Rabbanite scholar at the Fatimid court in al-Mahdiyya, Abū Sahl Dunash b. Tamim (ca. 890–960), held that "the natives of Palestine and Tiberias are perfect in Hebrew, inasmuch as they hold that language by inheritance . . . while others know it by means of literary tradition." Here again, we see anxieties about the reliability of written transmission. Similarly, in the second half of the tenth century, the Qaraite David b. Avraham al-Fāsī spoke of the Tiberians as possessing "purity of language and pronunciation." Another Qaraite scholar concurred that "the correct reading [of the Bible] is the excellence which originated from . . . the city of Tiberias."[34] In the *Kitāb hidāyat al-qārī* (Guide for the reader), the eleventh-century Qaraite linguist Abu l-Faraj Hārūn b. al-Faraj commented on the phonetics of the Tiberian system and the correct pronunciation of Hebrew, about which he had this to say:

> It is a commonplace that the way of the land of Israel is the original, and this is what is called the Tiberian reading [*al-qur'ān al-ṭabarānī*]. What we have said is confirmed by the fact that any scholar who travels to distant lands is eagerly begged by the exiles there to teach their children the reading of the land of Israel: they absorb it from him and make him sit [among them] in order to learn it from him rigorously. Anyone who has come from the diaspora to the land of Israel behaves like a foreigner in his anxiety to learn the reading of the land of Israel and in his abandonment of his own.[35]

[32] T-S Ar. 32.17, verso, lines 9–17.

[33] Chiesa, *Emergence of Hebrew Biblical Pointing*, 35; Drory, *Emergence of Jewish-Arabic Literary Contacts*, 138–49.

[34] All these sources cited in Chiesa, *Emergence of Hebrew Biblical Pointing*, 9–13; see also Drory, *Emergence of Jewish-Arabic Literary Contacts*, 135–55.

[35] Quoted in Chiesa, *Emergence of Hebrew Biblical Pointing*, 31 and 33 from 2 Firk. 2390, 5b (I have slightly modified his translation). The author of the treatise is identified and the text published in Ilan Eldar, *The Art of Correct Reading of the Bible*, Hebrew (Jerusalem, 1994).

As far away as al-Andalus, the Rabbanite grammarian Abu l-Walīd Yona ibn Janāḥ (ca. 990–1050) called the Tiberians "the purists among the Jews with regard to language," who "outdo all of them in speech." As late as the twelfth century, Avraham ibn ʿEzra of Tudela (1089–ca. 1164) admired the scholarship of the Tiberians, even though by his time the Jewish scholarly center there had long ceased to exist, saying, "I saw some books scrutinized by the Tiberian sages and fifteen among their elders swore that they had considered every single word and point three times."[36]

All these testimonies attest to a belief in the superiority of the Tiberian tradition of reading the biblical text. But we should not let these paeans to Tiberian Hebrew mislead us into imagining that the belief in its superiority led to its being canonized among the Jews. The belief in the purity of Tiberian Hebrew was an *effect* of the Tiberian tradition's dominance, not its cause. The earliest instance of the ideology dates to ca. 915, while the Tiberian tradition had already come to be diffused, accepted, and canonized in the late ninth or early tenth century.

Over the course of the next three hundred years, that ideology would be repeated by Qaraites and Rabbanites alike, even Rabbanites who in other contexts made much of their anti-Qaraism. All regarded Tiberian Hebrew and the Tiberian *masora* as their common patrimony. Jews in the Middle Ages may have regarded Babylonia as the most important center of talmudic studies, but they acknowledged Palestine's dominance in matters related to the Bible.

HISTORICAL CLAIMS

That even Qaraites like al-Qirqisānī cast their claims on behalf of Tiberias in terms of its textual transmission is somewhat paradoxical. What need would a Qaraite have for arguments from transmission? The basis of the Qaraite claim to expertise was a scientific one, founded on the study of linguistics in the service of exegesis. In casting off rabbinic tradition, the Qaraites declared that they had no use for continuity in transmission. Yet the Qaraites mustered arguments from history increasingly over the course of the tenth century.

Classical rabbinic literature contains implicit claims about the continuity of rabbinic discipleship. Chains of transmission detail the masters and disciples in whose names particular dicta were transmitted, though the chains are never as long or detailed as they became in the transmission of *ḥadīth* among Muslims. But the rabbinic literature of late antiquity had not yet developed a thoroughgoing theory of transmission.

[36] Chiesa, *Emergence of Hebrew Biblical Pointing*, 9–13; see Drory, *Emergence of Jewish-Arabic Literary Contacts*, 135–55.

By the tenth century, all this changed. Gaonic literature of Iraqi provenance now elevated claims of transmission from local statements of discipleship to general guarantees of the authenticity of the entire body of rabbinic tradition. The Babylonian *ge'onim* did so partly under the influence of Islamic religious epistemology and its emphasis on the transmission of knowledge; and partly in response to the challenge of the Qaraites, who rejected the authority of rabbinic tradition.

The most extreme version of the rabbinic argument came, once again, from Seʿadya, who claimed with characteristic hyperbole that without transmitted tradition, it would be impossible to know anything with certainty—even whether one is "the son of his mother, let alone the son of his father." In Seʿadya's hands, scholarly continuity (within legitimate chains of rabbinic discipleship) became not just an incidental fact of rabbinic transmission but an epistemological necessity, the sole means of legitimating religious knowledge.[37] Likewise, several decades later, in 986–87, Sherira b. Ḥananya, *ga'on* of Pumbedita (968–1004), sent a responsum to the Jews of Qayrawān in Ifrīqiya in which he explained how the Mishnah and the Talmud were composed and detailed the entire chain of transmitters from biblical times to the *ge'onim* of Babylonia.[38]

The Qaraites might have responded by rejecting claims to religious authority via arguments from history. But they did not. Instead, they returned fire in kind, using historical arguments particularly in the context of anti-Rabbanite polemics. The paradox this represents is worthy of some consideration. It shows the influence of rabbinic thinking on Qaraism. It also shows the extent to which both schools of Judaism were responding to the modes and methodologies of *isnād*, the listing of authorities that Muslims considered an essential guarantor of the authenticity of tradition, particularly from the ninth century onward.[39]

The Qaraite adoption of historical claims in the service of self-legitimation is reflected most abundantly in the story of Qaraism's origins and how it changed during this period. Qaraism proper originated in the ninth century with the Persians Binyamin al-Nahāwandī (ca. 850) and Dani'el al-Qūmisī (ca. 870–910). But in the tenth century, Qaraites began to trace their origins further back, to ʿAnan b. David, the scion of the Babylonian exilarchal house during the reign the Abbasid caliph al-Manṣūr (754–75).[40]

[37] Quoted in Brody, *Geonim of Babylonia*, 244–45; see further 245–48.

[38] For editions see chap. 1, n. 2.

[39] On historical claims in the service of Qaraite identity, see Fred Astren, *Karaite Judaism and Historical Understanding*, Studies in Comparative Religion (Columbia, 2004). On rabbinic arguments from history in the service of tradition, see Gershom Scholem, "Revelation and Tradition as Religious Categories in Judaism," in *The Messianic Idea in Judaism and Other Essays on Jewish Spirituality* (New York, 1971): 282–303; Cohen, *Sefer ha-qabbalah*; Yosef Hayim Yerushalmi, *Zakhor: Jewish History and Jewish Memory*, The Samuel and Althea Stroum Lectures in Jewish Studies (Seattle, 1996 [1982]), chapters 1 and 2.

[40] Al-Qirqisānī, *Kitāb al-anwār wa-l-marāqib*, Book I, 2:14; Chiesa and Lockwood, *Yaqub al-Qirqisani on Jewish Sects and Christianity*, 103; Nemoy, "al-Qirqisānī's Account," 328.

At first blush, this, too, is paradoxical. ʿAnan b. David composed a code of law (which has survived only in fragments) in Aramaic, a language inextricably associated with classical rabbinic literature and eschewed by the Qaraites. Indeed, ʿAnan's code retained some elements of rabbinic legal methodology, though he discarded others. Though he cast off the binding obligation of rabbinic precedent, his rejection of the traditions and methods of the Rabbanite milieu in which he had been trained was only partial.[41]

After the tenth century, however, all histories of Qaraism attributed its origins to ʿAnan b. David. Ḥaggai Ben-Shammai has offered a convincing reconstruction of how this change came about.[42] Until the tenth century, Ananism had been a separate movement. Indeed, sources mention a group called the ʿAnāniyya (Ananites) as distinct from the Qaraites. An echo of this can be heard in Daniʾel al-Qūmisī, who (according to al-Qirqisānī) initially extolled ʿAnan, but by ca. 900 had come to regard him as "the greatest of fools." Al-Qūmisī was not alone in his violent rejection of ʿAnan: during the same period, a large part of the Ananite movement in Jerusalem became Qaraite, in the sense that they adopted the Qaraite commitment to scripture and moved further away from the rabbinic exegetical techniques and legal methods associated with ʿAnan. They may have done so under al-Qūmisī's influence. Even ʿAnan's descendants in the exilarchal line, the *nesiʾim*, adopted Qaraism, a move that had lasting influence on the story of Qaraite origins.[43]

According to Ben-Shammai's reconstruction, the Ananite *nesiʾim* quickly rose to leadership in the Qaraite community of Jerusalem. They may have done so partly on the strength of their Davidic genealogy (one should perhaps also see this in light of proliferating claims among Muslims of descent from the line of ʿAlī).[44] In the course of the merger, the *nesiʾim* grafted ʿAnan as totem and founding ancestor onto Qaraism. Qaraites, for their part, did not deny the claim to Ananite lineage because they stood to benefit from the prestige of a more ancient and illustrious pedigree than they in fact possessed. Claims to scholarly superiority may have attracted a small following of intel-

[41] Harkavy, *Studien und Mittheilungen aus der Kaiserlichen Öffentlichen Bibliothek zu St. Petersburg*, vol. 8 (St. Petersburg, 1903) and the additional published fragments mentioned in Ben-Shammai, "Between Ananites and Karaites," 26 nn. 4–5 (and note his distinction between Geniza fragments of Anan's book and sections quoted in later works, 19).

[42] Ben-Shammai, "Between Ananites and Karaites," 19–29. See also Gil, *In the Kingdom of Ishmael*, secs. 160–63.

[43] Ben-Shammai, "Between Ananites and Karaites," 24. Al-Qūmisī quoted in al-Qirqisānī, *Kitāb al-anwār wa-l-marāqib*, Book I, 1:3; Chiesa and Lockwood, *Yaqub al-Qirqisani on Jewish Sects and Christianity*, 95; Nemoy, "al-Qirqisānī's Account," 321. For al-Qūmisī's later opinion of Anan, see also his commentary on the book of Daniel, T-S 10 C 2.2, fol. 2a, lines 1–4. For the hypothesis that al-Qūmisī convinced Ananites to become Qaraites, see Ben-Shammai, "Between Ananites and Karaites," 24.

[44] See Teresa Bernheimer, "A Social History of the ʿAlid Family from the Eighth to the Eleventh Century" (Ph.D. diss., Oxford University, 2006).

lectuals, but standing among the masses probably required some version of an appeal to history.

A hint of the Ananite-Qaraite merger is revealed in the work of the Qaraite biblical commentator Yefet b. ʿEli (last third of the tenth century). Yefet was the first to attribute to ʿAnan b. David an Aramaic dictum enjoining his followers to "search scripture well" (*ḥappisu be-orayta shappir*), that is, to study the biblical text rather than relying on received opinion. That means that by the late tenth century, the quintessentially Qaraite ideal of scripturalism had been retrojected onto ʿAnan, whose methods were not scripturalist at all.[45]

That ʿAnanism was grafted onto Qaraism in the tenth century shows that historical claims served as buttresses for religious authority even among the Qaraites. The separation of powers between the administrative-judicial and scholarly wings of the Qaraite community in eleventh-century Jerusalem, which I discussed in the last chapter, may have been a residue of the merger: the administrative leadership of the *nesiʾim* descended from the Ananites while the scholarly activities of the academy continued the Qaraite tradition of textual study.

It also casts light on a mysterious period between ca. 860 and 893, when the Ananite *nesiʾim* Yehoshafaṭ and Ṣemaḥ b. Yoshiyyahu rose to the gaonate of the *yeshiva* in Tiberias. It would be a mistake to see them as Qaraite *geʾonim*, since the Qaraite movement had not yet merged with the exilarchs in the line of ʿAnan, and this lessens the paradox of an avowedly antirabbinic group such as the Qaraites leading the *yeshiva*. But once the Qaraites claimed the Ananite exilarchs as their own, they avidly preserved the memory of two of their leaders having held the highest post of the *yeshiva*. That is why a Qaraite memorial list proudly appends the title *rosh yeshivat geʾon Yaʿaqov* to Yehoshafaṭ's name. I will have more to say about these Ananite *geʾonim* further on.[46]

The merger between ʿAnanism and Qaraism is also a prime example of how histories of religious movements tidy up messy and gradual processes of evolution and replace them with linear narratives featuring a founder with a clear agenda and followers. By the twelfth century, the notion that ʿAnan was the first Qaraite had metamorphosed into a full-fledged foundation myth, according to which he broke from the rabbinic establishment when he was passed over for the exilarchate in favor of his younger brother Ḥananya. In a fit of pique, the legend claims, ʿAnan "set up a dissident sect in secret," for which he was condemned to death and thrown into an Abbasid prison. There, it is said,

[45] Ben-Shammai, "Between Ananites and Karaites," 22, 27 n. 34. On the problem of the dictum's historicity, see Frank, *Search Scripture Well*, 22–32, who convincingly interprets its historical development and transmission in manuscripts of Yefet's work as a mirror of the origins and early history of Qaraism.

[46] See also above, chap. 1, 33–34.

he shared a cell with one of the founders of the four Sunnī Islamic *madhāhib*, who instructed him in the art of religious schism.

The myth was first reported by a twelfth-century Byzantine Qaraite, Eliyyahu b. Avraham, who claimed to relate it from an unnamed Rabbanite source.[47] The account succeeds as anti-Qaraite propaganda, discrediting the movement as the product of wounded pride; it also suspiciously parallels twelfth-century Christian slanders of Muḥammad as a Christian cleric who out of ambition, or having been passed over for election as patriarch, turned heresiarch and founded Islam.[48] It shows the medieval propensity to compress historical processes into single, mythologized events. More importantly for our immediate purposes, the myth was accepted by Qaraites as well—a hint that historical claims, even false ones, were gladly accepted if they worked for the purposes of building communal cohesion and claims to legitimacy.

The fullest embrace of historical claims in any Qaraite work of the tenth century is surely to be found in al-Qirqisānī's heresiography of Judaism. Among other things, al-Qirqisānī dates the origins of religious dissension to the split between the kingdoms of Israel and Judah in the tenth century BCE. For al-Qirqisānī, the next important milestone in the history of dissent comes after the restoration of the Temple cult in Jerusalem in the late sixth century BCE, when the Rabbanites strayed from the true path.[49] Of course "Rabbanites" cannot be said to have existed at such an early date. By admitting this anachronism, al-Qirqisānī tacitly accepts the rabbinic claim to continuity with the biblical past (a claim the Qaraites could perhaps have made as convincingly for themselves). His history instead paints the Qaraites as the renewers of a true faith that had been eclipsed at some even earlier date. Thus he stops

[47] Eliyyahu b. Avraham, *Ḥilluq ha-qara'im ve-ha-rabbanim*, in Pinsker, *Lickute kadmoniot*, 2:103. Pinsker identified the earlier Rabbanite polemicist with Seʿadya; see also Samuel Poznanski, *The Karaite Literary Opponents of Saadiah Gaon* (London, 1908), 72–74, and for a skeptical view, Nemoy, "Anan ben David: A Reappraisal of the Historical Data," in *Semitic Studies in Memory of Immanuel Löw*, ed. Alexander Scheiber (Budapest, 1947), reprinted in *Karaite Studies*, ed. Philip Birnbaum (New York, 1971), 313–14. Another Qaraite work claims that Anan's cellmate was Abū Ḥanīfa; see Poznanski, "Anan et ses écrits," *Revue des études juives* 44 (1902), 167 n. 2 and the reference to Harkavy in Baron, *Social and Religious History*², 5:388–89 n. 1.

[48] On the image of Muḥammad in the medieval West with extensive references to Latin sources see *EI*², s.v. "Muḥammad" (Albrecht Noth and Trude Ehlert); and Guibert of Nogent (1052–1124), according to whom Muḥammad was the student of an Egyptian hermit who had been passed over for the patriarchate of Alexandria due to his heterodox beliefs: R. B. C. Huygens, ed., *Guibert de Nogent: Dei gesta per Francos et cinq autres textes*, Corpus Christianorum, Continuatio Mediaevalis 127a (Turnhout, 1996), 94–100 (thanks to Jay Rubenstein for kindly sharing this reference with me). Petrus Alfonsi (1062–after 1121) relates a variant on this theme according to which Muḥammad's teachers, a heretical Jacobite archdeacon and two heterodox Jews, encouraged him to spread his faith through political means: Reginald Hyatte, *The Prophet of Islam in Old French: The Romance of Muhammad (1258) and The Book of Muhammad's Ladder (1264)* (Leiden, 1997), 11–12. On other possible precedents, see Cohen, *Sefer ha-qabbalah*, xxxviii.

[49] Al-Qirqisānī, *Kitāb al-anwār wa-l-marāqib*, Book I, 2:1–4; Chiesa and Lockwood, *Yaqub al-Qirqisani on Jewish Sects and Christianity*, 95–100; Nemoy, "al-Qirqisānī's Account," 322–25.

short of claiming greater antiquity for the Qaraites, but by retrojecting the schism he reveals the assumptions he shared with his exact contemporary, Seʿadya, the arch-retrojector.

One of the effects of all this retrojection was to map a simple, linear history of schism onto a more fluid and complex process. Such histories of origin are always implicitly essentialist: the notion that Qaraism branched off from Rabbanism in the ninth century (or the eighth) implies that both began fully formed and remained unchanged in the process.[50] In fact their histories were so closely intertwined that they shared more than divided them, and defined themselves in contradistinction to one another progressively over the course of several centuries.

The history of calendar differences between Qaraites and Rabbanites is a prime example of this sort of progressive contradistinction. In chapter 1, I discussed the importance of the calendar as a locus of institutional power. The history of the calendar in the Rabbanite-Qaraite debate still remains to be written, in part because most scholarship has accepted the later medieval notion that calendar differences were the main issue driving the Qaraites (and Ananites) apart from the Rabbanites. Here, too, the process of contradistinction was more gradual and more complex, and therefore has much to teach us—about the history of the groups, about how they represented that history, and about the purposes for which they deployed those representations.

The Calendar

The story of calendar differences—first briefly, then in more detail—is as follows.[51] By the end of the tenth century, Qaraites had become champions of a rigorous calendrical empiricism, requiring observation of the new moon to determine the months and monitoring of the barley crop in Palestine to determine whether the year should be intercalated. Rabbanites, meanwhile, insisted on the use of astronomical calculation or mathematical prediction in both areas.

Also beginning in the tenth century, those differences in method were said to date to Qaraism's origins—which, in turn, were retrojected onto ʿAnan b. David. But they turn out to have come into being only gradually over the course of the ninth and tenth centuries. It was only in the ninth century that the calendar became a point of ideological distinction between the two groups.

[50] See the still excellent arguments of Marshall Hodgson, "How Did the Early Shiʿa Become Sectarian?" *Journal of the American Oriental Society* 75 (1955):1–13; and more recently and with much more detail, Hossein Modarressi, *Crisis and Consolidation in the Formative Period of Shiʿite Islam: Abu Jaʿfar ibn Qiba al-Razi and his Contribution to Imamite Shiʿite Thought* (Princeton, 1993).

[51] For an explanation of the problem of determining months and years in the Jewish calendar, see chap. 1, 15–17.

The lived distinction would take even longer to establish: as late as the tenth century, each group used elements of both methods. Medieval writers confirm that calendation was not divided along party lines.

To untangle the skein of events it helps once again to distinguish between the two basic problems inherent in the Jewish calendar: intercalating the year and determining new months. Each of those elements of the calendar followed a slightly different trajectory over the course of the period in question.

Intercalating the Year

The earliest reference to Qaraites intercalating the year is in al-Qirqisānī's heresiography of 937–38. This is quite late, given that there, he attributes the requirement to intercalate the year via observation of the barley crop to ʿAnan b. David in the eighth century.[52] But ʿAnan mentions nothing about the calendar in extant fragments of his code of law, and al-Qirqisānī knew even less of ʿAnan's code than we do, since he lacked access to the original text. Rather, he made this claim on the basis of epitomes or perhaps even of conjecture.[53] While the veracity of his claim cannot be trusted, it shows that by his day, Qaraism had been so thoroughly associated with empiricism in intercalating the year that he found it plausible to attribute it to the very origins of the religious restoration that he attributed to ʿAnan.

In fact the first Qaraites to call for empirical intercalation were al-Nahāwandī and al-Qūmisī, who postdated ʿAnan by a century. But even during al-Qūmisī's day, empirical calendation was still only an ideology and practiced only by some adherents.[54] We have this on the testimony of al-Qūmisī himself, who notes ca. 900 that some Qaraites (*baʿaley miqraʾ*) do not intercalate the year according to the barley crop.[55] We have it even later, ca. 1006–7, from Levi b. Yefet, who informs us that Iraqi Qaraites used a mathematical cycle of intercalations, just as their Rabbanite counterparts did.[56] Methods of intercalation, then, had not yet become thoroughly polarized along scholastic lines, even in al-Qirqisānī's day. They had, however, emerged as an important point of ideological distinction.

The reason why is not difficult to discern: the calendar controversy of 921–22 had made the calendar an issue of ideological and institutional contention across the entire Jewish world. Around 900, al-Qūmisī had called for in-

[52] Al-Qirqisānī, *Kitāb al-anwār wa-l-marāqib*, Book I, 13:2; Chiesa and Lockwood, *Yaqub al-Qirqisani on Jewish Sects and Christianity*, 146; Nemoy, "al-Qirqisānī's Account," 384.

[53] Ben-Shammai, "Between Ananites and Karaites," who demonstrates convincingly that ʿAnan's code of law circulated in the tenth century in the west (on the Iberian peninsula) but not the east.

[54] Al-Nahāwandī: in Harkavy, *Studien und Mittheilungen*, 8:176; English translation in Gil, *History of Palestine*, sec. 928. Al-Qūmisī: Mann, "Tract by an Early Ḳaraite," 285; Nemoy, "Pseudo-Qumisian Sermon," 76 (". . . to observe the month of the *aviv* in its proper time and to observe His precepts").

[55] See the text cited by Ankori, *Karaites in Byzantium*, 220 n. 29; cf. the text on 311–12.

[56] See chap. 1, n. 30.

tercalating the year via observation of the barley crop as a point of Qaraite ideology; in the 920s, intercalation became a polemically charged issue at the center of a Babylonian-Palestinian Rabbanite struggle for control over Jewish religious practice; and in the 930s, al-Qirqisānī (or his informants) attributed Qaraite empirical calendation to a much earlier period—one that even preceded the existence of Qaraism.

As for calendation among Rabbanites, the calendar controversy of 921–22 itself confirms that by al-Qirqisānī's own time, let alone in al-Qūmisī's several decades earlier, Rabbanites had not yet established uniform methods of calendation either.

Determining the Months

Though determining the months empirically—that is, witnessing the crescent moon—is usually identified with the Qaraites, the practice was not associated with them until even later, in part because Rabbanites still engaged in it until at least the tenth century.

In fact, al-Qirqisānī noticeably refrains from associating ʿAnan and witnessing the crescent moon. He does, however, attribute it to al-Nahāwandī, but in modified form: al-Nahāwandī, he tells us, enjoined witnessing the crescent moon for two months of the year (Nisan and Tishri), while for the rest, he allowed calculation. This was not, however, a sweeping injunction that Qaraites witness the crescent moon every month. That would appear only a generation later, with al-Qūmisī.[57]

Al-Qūmisī famously ordered his followers in Palestine to practice lunar observation, telling them, "Now you are amidst the kingdom of Ishmael, who favor those who observe the month via the moon; why, then, do you fear the rabbis?"[58] This injunction is usually read as a claim that since the Muslims rulers, unlike the Rabbanites, determine the months empirically, Qaraites should cast off their fear of the Rabbanites. But that is not what the passage says. All al-Qūmisī claims is that the Muslims favor those who fix the new months by lunar observation. He does not claim that the Qaraites were the only Jews who did so.

A few decades later, Al-Qirqisānī confirms this: he tells us that the Rabbanites, too, fixed the new months by lunar observation, and even complains about their inconsistency in using empirical methods in fixing the months but mathematical ones in fixing the year. The Rabbanites "admit that the beginnings of months should be fixed by the appearance of the new moon," he writes, "but they

[57] Al-Qirqisānī, *Kitāb al-anwār wa-l-marāqib*, Book I, 14:2; Chiesa and Lockwood, *Yaqub al-Qirqisani on Jewish Sects and Christianity*, 148; Nemoy, "al-Qirqisānī's Account," 387.

[58] For the full passage, see chap. 4, 117. cf. Nemoy's translation, "Pseudo-Qumisian Sermon," 78.

contradict themselves by adopting intercalation."[59] Further confirmation comes in the Seʿadya–Ben-Meʾir controversy of 921–22. At the peak of the controversy, we read in a letter preserved in the Geniza, the Jews of Fustat stood waiting for the new moon, which appeared when the Palestinian Rabbanite camp predicted it would, a day earlier than it should have according to the Babylonian calculation. For the Rabbanites, it should not have mattered when the crescent moon deigned to show itself in the sky: a rabbinic pronouncement was a rabbinic pronouncement. The fact that the Jews of Fustat waited to see the new moon demonstrates that the Qaraites had no monopoly on empirical calendation. Al-Qirqisānī tells us, then, that two decades *after* Seʿadya's "victory" in the calendar controversy of 921–22, Rabbanites continued to determine the months via what would later become the "Qaraite" method, empirical observation. The Qaraite method of empirical calendation was not a deviation from some hoary and uniform Rabbanite practice: rabbinic methods remained in flux, too.

That, in turn, means that al-Qūmisī's own insistence on lunar observation for Qaraites must be interpreted differently. In his day, Rabbanites still used this method. He cannot therefore have been telling his followers that doing so would distinguish them from the Rabbanites, because it would have done no such thing. He must have been advocating something more than just lunar observation. The most plausible answer is that he was advocating lunar observation free from the authority of the Palestinian *yeshiva* and its pronouncements about the calendar. "Why, then, do you fear the rabbis?" means, in effect, "Why do you fear the *yeshiva*?" The battle al-Qūmisī was fighting was not against mathematical methods of calendation, but against the *yeshiva*'s monopoly on empirical ones.

This interpretation finds support in the institutional context in Palestine during al-Qūmisī's time, the close of the ninth century. Until 893 the *geʾonim* of the *yeshiva* in Tiberias were Ananites, Yehoshafaṭ and Ṣemaḥ b. Yoshiyyahu. After them, the succession of the gaonate returned to the old Rabbanite clans. One can understand why al-Qūmisī might have wanted to declare his secession from the authority of the *yeshiva*—both from the old Ananite leadership, since by now he considered ʿAnan "the greatest of fools," and from the new Rabbanite leadership as well. Fixing the months visually without the *yeshiva*'s pronouncements helped him to do so.

This, in turn, may shed some light on al-Qūmisī's urgent call to Jews to settle in Jerusalem. He is usually understood to have been addressing himself

[59] Several paragraphs later he goes on to say, "They make compulsory the practice of searching for the *aviv* and fixing the date of Passover according to it, but contradict this with their doctrine of intercalation," a statement that suggests (as Levi b. Yefet would seventy years later) that some Rabbanites still used empirical methods only. Al-Qirqisānī, *Kitāb al-anwār wa-l-marāqib*, Book I, 3:27, 31; Chiesa and Lockwood, *Yaqub al-Qirqisani on Jewish Sects and Christianity*, 114, 116; Nemoy, "al-Qirqisānī's Account," 342, 344.

to Qaraites outside Palestine. But perhaps he was addressing himself to Qaraites in Tiberias as well. Moving to Jerusalem, he told them, would free them from the Rabbanites and their dominance over the *yeshiva*. It would also permit them to determine the months with their own lunar observations.

A century later, writing ca. 1000, the Muslim astronomer and polymath al-Bīrūnī (973–1048) noted that the Qaraites are those who watch the barley crop and the crescent moon. By his time, those practices were considered Qaraite ones. But then he reveals something important: the originator of the system, he tells us, was not ʿAnan b. David in the eighth century, nor al-Nahāwandī nor al-Qūmisī in the ninth, but ʿAnan's great-grandson, ʿAnan b. Daniʾel (b. Shaʿul b. ʿAnan b. David) at the end of the ninth century. It is impossible to evaluate the truth or precision of this claim. But it is significant that al-Bīrūnī does not attribute Qaraite empiricism to the much better-known ʿAnan b. David, in spite of the fact that Qaraism was already thought to have originated with him. Even al-Bīrūnī preserves the memory that Qaraite calendrical empiricism was a relatively late adoption. Nor does he ascribe Qaraite practices to Ananites before the late ninth century, the period of the merger. This merely confirms what the silences and omissions in the other sources suggest: that the dispute over methods of calendation deepened only gradually, taking hold over the second half of the tenth century.[60]

The Changing History of the Jewish Calendar

What, then, were the origins of the claim that empirical calendation had always been a Qaraite practice and calculation a Rabbanite one?

The earliest and most vocal source on the matter is the twelfth-century Byzantine Qaraite Eliyyahu b. Avraham, the same author who recounted the legend about ʿAnan b. David founding Qaraism. Here, too, Eliyyahu b. Avraham quotes an unnamed Rabbanite polemicist's claim that Jews had "always" "maintained that rule [of calculated calendation]"—that they had never done things any other way. The source was probably Seʿadya. Eliyyahu attempts to refute the statement, which he finds a patent exaggeration, by arguing that calculated calendation "was the situation [among the Jews] until the rise of the kingdom of the Ishmaelites, who innovated the principle of seeking the new moon. Then ʿAnan the Exilarch stood up and strove for power, and he followed them [the Muslims] so that they might help him." Eliyyahu makes two claims: that the Jewish calendar had been determined by calculation since time immemorial, and that ʿAnan changed all this in the eighth century. In the first claim, he concedes the point he should have attempted to refute, namely, that Jews had

[60] Al-Bīrūnī, *al-Āthār al-bāqiya ʿan al-qurūn al-khāliya*, in Sachau, *Chronologie orientalischer Völker*, 58–59 (Arabic); Sachau, *Chronology of Ancient Nations*, 68–69 (English); cited in Ben-Shammai, "Between Ananites and Karaites," 28 n. 48, with reference to previous discussions.

"always" calculated calendation. In the second, he is hopelessly vague. How did ʿAnan "strive for power," and in what way did he follow the Muslims—by determining the months through observation of the crescent moon? He goes on to specify that after ʿAnan "came Benjamin al-Nahāwandī, who modified some of ʿAnan's pronouncements. Finally, people who claimed to be wise stood up and abolished calendar computation altogether."[61] Though here, too, he declines to offer any specificity, he is clearly saying that the Qaraite empirical methods were worked out gradually, over the course of several centuries.

Eliyyahu's testimony is usually taken to indicate that the Qaraites introduced empirical calendation from the very beginning and that ʿAnan used it as a way of winning Muslim favor and distinguishing his "sect" from that of the Rabbanites. But this is not what he says. He says that it was not until *after* al-Nahāwandī that computation was totally abolished among the Qaraites—a point that confirms what we know from al-Qirqisānī, that both ʿAnan and al-Nahāwandī had permitted computation or elements of it.

A fully mature disagreement over the calendar from the beginnings of the Rabbanite-Qaraite schism is a point of nearly universal consensus among scholars of Jewish studies. Even scholars who reject the historicity of the legend of ʿAnan founding his "sect" in an Abbasid prison take it as axiomatic that disagreement over the calendar was a reason for the Qaraite schism.[62] But matters were more complex. In the ninth century, empirical calendation began in some quarters to be considered a distinctively Qaraite practice. Over the course of the tenth century—the same period during which ʿAnan came to be seen as the founder of Qaraism—the Qaraites were progressively associated with a thoroughgoing calendrical empiricism.

Similarly, most scholars have assumed that the Rabbanite calendar originated in late antiquity. The event usually cited is an edict by the Jewish patriarch Hillel b. Yehuda, who purportedly decreed in 359–60 the use of a fixed cycle of

[61] Eliyyahu b. Avraham, *Ḥilluq ha-qara'im ve-ha-rabbanim*, in Pinsker, *Lickute kadmoniot*, 2, appendix 12, 99–106 (this passage on 95). Cf. Ankori, *Karaites in Byzantium*, 294.

[62] Thus Gil, *In the Kingdom of Ishmael*, secs. 160–62. Ankori is chiefly responsible for the notion that the calendar was a Qaraite "rallying cry of anti-Rabbanite dissent" and the main barrier to social cooperation (*Karaites in Byzantium*, 305), an argument that contradicts his own evidence, such as the statement of Levi b. Yefet cited above (chap. 1, n. 30) and the clauses in marriage contracts safeguarding each spouse's calendar observances (see chap. 9). Ankori was heavily influenced by Shemaryahu Talmon's work on the Dead Sea Scrolls, which argued that calendar differences had caused the Qumran sect to withdraw from Jerusalem, and both formulated overly general sociological laws about calendars as the main motor behind religious schisms "whatever their time and place." Ibid., 293–99; Talmon, "Yom Hakkippurim in the Habakkuk scroll," *Biblica* 32 (1951): 563; idem, "The Calendar Reckoning of the Sect from the Judaean Desert," in Chaim Rabin and Yigael Yadin, eds., *Aspects of the Dead Sea Scrolls*, Scripta Hierosolymitana 4 (Jerusalem, 1958), 163–64. But calendars do not create schisms; people do. See Albert I. Baumgarten, *The Flourishing of Jewish Sects in the Maccabean Era: An Interpretation*, Supplements to the Journal for the Study of Judaism 55 (Leiden, 1997), introduction and 36 n. 116, and Schwartz's comments in his review of that work, *Association for Jewish Studies Review* 24 (1999): 377.

intercalations of a thirteenth month. But as Günter Stemberger and Sacha Stern have each noted, the first mention of this decree appears in a late source, a work on the calendar composed in 1123 by a rabbinical authority and astronomer of Barcelona, Avraham b. Ḥiyya (d. 1136), who quotes it from a responsum of a certain unidentified Hayya *ga'on*—at the earliest, a ninth-century source. Moreover, Avraham b. Ḥiyya's was hardly the only medieval tradition to attribute a fixed calendar to an early rabbinic authority. Other medieval authors supply different testimonies, few of which agree with one another. Among them are al-Qirqisānī and, in the late tenth century, the Qaraite Yefet b. ʿEli; and the Rabbanites Evyatar *ga'on* in the late eleventh century, Maimonides in the late twelfth, and Yiṣḥaq Yisra'eli in the early fourteenth. All retroject a later medieval situation onto late antiquity, but they each identify a different moment and figure as the originator of the fixed, calculated calendars. For unclear reasons, it is Avraham b. Ḥiyya's Hillel tradition that later Jewish tradition and most modern scholarship adopted as authoritative.[63]

As Stern has shown, the first evidence of the existence of the current rabbinic calendar dates to Seʿadya and can only have predated him by two or three generations. Even then, it was not uniformly observed among Rabbanites, as the calendar controversy of 921–22 shows. Even later, ca. 1006–7, Levi b. Yefet, the son of Yefet b. ʿEli, argued that the Rabbanites of Palestine used empirical methods and the Qaraites of Babylonia used mathematical ones—even though he must have known his father's claim on behalf of the antiquity of the Rabbanite calendar. Only if the rabbinic calendar is presumed to have existed before it really did can the Qaraites be said to have deviated from it. In fact, both the Rabbanite and Qaraite methods of calendation were worked out gradually, and each in contradistinction to the other.

"A Festival of Their Own Invention"

One other text, familiar to all students of Qaraism, has been read nearly universally through the lens of the idea that the calendar was the main motor of the Rabbanite-Qaraite schism.

Once again, the source is al-Qirqisānī's work of 937–38. Al-Qirqisānī writes that he once asked a student of Seʿadya named Yaʿqūb b. Efrayim al-Shāmī why

[63] Stemberger, *Jews and Christians in the Holy Land*, 249–58; Stern, *Calendar and Community*, 175–81, 233. It is unclear whether Avraham b. Ḥiyya intends Hayya b. Naḥshon, *ga'on* of Sura (889–96); Hayya b. David, *ga'on* of Pumbedita (890–97); or Hayya b. Sherira, *ga'on* of Pumbedita (1004–38). Al-Qirqisānī also cites the invention of the intercalary cycle (though by Yiṣḥaq Nappaḥa, not Hillel b. Yehuda) in the name of a certain Hayya, *ra's al-mathība*, and if he is citing the same authority that Avraham b. Ḥiyya cites, this would rule out Hayya b. Sherira. Al-Qirqisānī also reports that a certain Hayya *ga'on* and his father translated a work of ʿAnan b. David (probably his *Sefer ha-miṣvot*) from Aramaic to Hebrew; see Assaf, *Tequfat ha-ge'onim ve-sifrutah*, 120–21, Gil, *In the Kingdom of Ishmael*, secs.161 and 203, and Nemoy, "al-Qirqisānī's Account," 328 n. 37; and the references in Ben-Shammai, "Between Ananites and Karaites," 26 n. 13.

the Rabbanites refused to marry Qaraites but permitted themselves to marry the ʿIsawīyya, followers of the seventh-century messianic leader Abū ʿĪsā al-Isfahānī. Yaʿqūb al-Shāmī replied, "Because they [the ʿIsawīyya] do not disagree with us over the festivals."[64]

Virtually all scholars have read Yaʿqūb al-Shāmī's statement as referring to methods of calendation: Rabbanites do not marry Qaraites because they do not agree over how to determine when the holidays fall. After all, if husband and wife fast or refrain from labor or observe other commandments on different days, how could they possibly live under the same roof?

Stern has noted that al-Qirqisānī himself does not interpret al-Shāmī's answer this way. Rather, al-Qirqisānī says that al-Shāmī's answer shows that Rabbanites "regard open apostasy more favorably than disagreement over a festival of their own invention."[65] A "festival of their own invention," Stern notes, is not the same as the entire calendar. Instead it refers to the rabbinic requirement for diaspora Jews to observe a second festival day, a measure instituted to ensure that all Jews would observe the festivals at the same time, even when the calendar pronouncements from Palestine failed to reach them in a timely manner.[66] That issue was one on which Rabbanites themselves were so divided that Seʿadya claimed the second festival day to have been revealed on Sinai—a retrojection that the later *gaʾon* Hayya b. Sherira (d. 1004) dismissed as a patent exaggeration for polemical purposes, a slight and slender "reed to ward off the heretic."[67]

Al-Shāmī was not, then, criticizing the Qaraites for their methods of calendation in general, but only for refusing to observe the second festival day. Al-Qirqisānī retorted by pointing out that the Rabbanites had raised their second festival day to the absurd level of a commandment whose importance eclipsed even the fundamentals of Jewish belief. Seʿadya's defense of its antiquity shows precisely that the matter was hotly contested—so hotly that his student al-Shāmī reported *it*, and not methods of calendation in general, as the principal marker distinguishing Rabbanites from Qaraites. (As for Rabbanites and Qaraites marrying one another, the documentary evidence of the eleventh

64 Al-Qirqisānī, *Kitāb al-anwār wa-l-marāqib*, Book I, 11:2; Chiesa and Lockwood, *Yaqub al-Qirqisani on Jewish Sects and Christianity*, 144; Nemoy, "al-Qirqisānī's Account," 382.

65 Al-Qirqisānī, *Kitāb al-anwār wa-l-marāqib*, Book I, 11:2; Chiesa and Lockwood, *Yaqub al-Qirqisani on Jewish Sects and Christianity*, 145; Nemoy, "al-Qirqisānī's Account," 382.

66 Stern further notes than there is a paradox embedded in the very institution of two-day festivals in the diaspora: it began as a way of ensuring that Jews in the land of Israel and in the diaspora celebrated their festivals at the same time, but "meant that the Diaspora would observe a *different* calendar—with two-day rather than one-day festivals—in order to observe the *same* calendar, i.e. celebrate the festivals on the same day. This paradox was perhaps the clearest expression of the impossibility, at least in the context of the ancient world, of implementing worldwide calendrical unity with an empirical calendar. Calendrical unanimity was bound to remain, in this sense, an unfulfilled ideal." Stern, *Calendar and Community*, 243; 19–20.

67 Brody, *Geonim of Babylonia*, 98.

and twelfth centuries shows that so long as the couple's various observances were negotiated in advance as part of the terms of the marriage, living under the same roof posed no great difficulty.)[68]

The development of the calendar controversy suggests something of the hesitations and uncertainties that polemical and prescriptive sources erased in favor of clean schisms and essential polarities. It also shows that by the tenth century, Qaraites had joined the Rabbanites in making historical claims in the service of self-legitimation.

FROM DIOCESAN CENTERS TO TERRITORIAL COMMUNITIES

Three generations after al-Qūmisī's move to Jerusalem, by the third quarter of the tenth century, the city had already turned into a remarkably productive center of Qaraite scholarship. Some time after the calendar controversy of 921–22 but before ca. 960, the Rabbanite *yeshiva* quit Tiberias for Jerusalem as well, under circumstances still hardly understood.[69] Why did the *yeshiva* not move there earlier? Jews had been permitted back to Jerusalem by its Muslim conquerors as early as 638.[70] One can only imagine that attachment to the masoretic project was one reason it had stayed in Tiberias. When it did move to Jerusalem, it may have been to challenge the Qaraite center there. The *yeshiva* may have sought to be closer to the old priestly center of Judaism, or the move may have been pitched against the Babylonian claim to authority in the wake of the calendar controversy, an effort to reassert some of the traditional prerogatives of the land of Israel, including proclaiming the calendar. Or perhaps the impetus was simply the sack of Tiberias by the Qarmaṭīs in 964 or the Fatimid conquest five years later.[71]

Unfortunately, these matters remain obscure. But in the late tenth century when documentary sources from the Geniza bring them into sharper focus, the Palestinian Rabbanites, emboldened by the Fatimid conquest of Palestine, began to assert their hold over the Jewish communities of Egypt. Meanwhile, the Babylonian *ge'onim*, having absorbed new types of learning from both Qaraite and Palestinian Rabbanite sources, worked hard to cultivate the loyalties of Jews in Egypt, Ifrīqiya, Sicily, and al-Andalus. And there were Qaraites to be found not just in Jerusalem but all over Syria, the eastern Mediterranean

[68] See below, chap. 9.

[69] Gil, *History of Palestine*, sec. 738.

[70] On the readmission of the Jews to Jerusalem—and the still murky possibility that they were invited to clean the site of the Temple in what they imagined to be preparation for its reconstruction—see ibid., secs. 82–87.

[71] On the Qarmaṭīs and the sack of Tiberias, see *EI*[2], s.v. "Ḳarmaṭī" (Wilferd Madelung). On the Fatimid conquest, see Thierry Bianquis, *Damas et la Syrie sous la domination fatimide 359–468/969–1076: essai d'interprétation de chroniques arabes médiévales*, 2 vols. (Damascus, 1986), 41–42.

littoral, Egypt, and northern Africa. That is why the rabbinic academies in Baghdad and Jerusalem, over the course of the late tenth and early eleventh centuries, extended their battle for Jewish loyalties from the academic centers to the communal peripheries, even as the Jews turned away from the ancient spiritual centers and reorganized into smaller geographic units. The Qaraites played key roles in the service of both Rabbanite camps. So did the Fatimid state. The form and content of Jewish politics during this period—and the triangular alliances between Rabbanites, Qaraites, and the Fatimids—are the subject of chapter 3.

CHAPTER THREE
THE LIMITS OF COMMUNAL AUTONOMY

Historians of Jewish civilization have long agreed that Jews under Islamic rule in the Middle Ages enjoyed "communal autonomy," a degree of self-government that enabled them to practice their religion freely, to appoint judges and establish their own courts of law, to establish systems of social welfare and institutions of learning, and to run their collective affairs generally free from the intrusions and interference of the ruling powers under whom they lived.

For the caliphs who devised this system—so the theory runs—delegating self-government to protected non-Muslim communities (*dhimmīs*) was an efficient way to rule a large empire. For Jews, self-government allowed a measure of internal coherence that offset the growth of a diaspora of unprecedented proportions. The basic structure of the system is said to have been pyramidal: *dhimmīs* recognized a single communal leader, whom the caliphs in turn recognized as the point of contact between themselves and the community.[1]

How this process of caliphal recognition worked remains, in practice, elusive. In Iraq, the only surviving records attesting that the *ge'onim* enjoyed direct caliphal recognition are too late to be helpful: three thirteenth-century records of investiture by the Abbasid caliphs. But these tell us nothing about the "classical gaonic period" (ca. 640–1040).[2] Before then, the Babylonian

[1] For some useful and appropriately cautious generalizations about Jewish communal autonomy, see Baron, *The Jewish Community: Its History and Structure to the American Revolution*, 3 vols. (Philadelphia, 1942): 1:21–25; and on how it played out in the medieval Islamic world, idem, *Social and Religious History*[2] 5:5–81. See also below, n. 13.

[2] Brody, *Geonim of Babylonia*, 337–40. The three investitures: copy of a rescript granted to Dani'el b. El'azar b. Hibat Allāh in 1209, in Abū Ṭālib Tāj al-dīn 'Alī b. Anjab Ibn al-Sā'ī, *al-Jāmi' al-mukhtaṣar* (The comprehensive abridgement), ed. Muṣṭafā Jawād (Baghdad, 1934), 9:266–69, translated in Norman A. Stillman, *The Jews of Arab Lands: A History and Source Book* (Philadelphia, 1979): 178–79; and identical transcripts of ceremony appointing the *ge'onim* Dani'el b. Shemu'el b. Abi l-Rabī' and Eli b. Zekharya al-Arbilī as heads of the Rabbanite Jews in 1247–48 and 1250, in a thirteenth-century historical work of uncertain authorship, Ibn al-Fuwaṭī, Kamāl al-dīn 'Abd al-Razzāq b. Aḥmad (attributed to), *al-Ḥawādith al-jāmi'a wa-l-tajārib al-nāfi'a fi l-mi'a al-sābi'a* (The comprehensive events and useful experiences of the seventh century), ed. Muṣṭafā Jawād

ge'onim seem to have negotiated with the Abbasid caliphs via the mediation of Jewish courtiers; whether they received official investiture remains a matter of speculation.[3]

We are only slightly better off when it comes to the Iraqi exilarch (*resh galuta*). Medieval Jewish sources say that he ran his own academy in the shadow of Sura, while modern historians have credited him with even more than this, styling him the caliph's designated official in representing the Jewish minority. That theory stems in part from an analogy with the role of the *katholikos*, the head of the Nestorian Christian community in Iraq, for whom a written record of caliphal appointment has been preserved from 1138. But it is unknown whether the Jewish exilarch also received such a caliphal appointment. Only two accounts of exilarchal accessions to office have survived, both in Jewish accounts. The first, from the tenth century, describes how the Jews installed the exilarch with great pomp and ceremony, but says nothing about the caliphs; that account is the profoundly tendentious composition of a certain Iraqi named Natan ha-Bavli, who arrived in Ifrīqiya in the mid-tenth century and set about telling tales of the Jewish community in Baghdad that he filled with an aura of courtly ritual. He emphasized that the caliph used to receive the exilarch in his *majlis* when the latter wished to present petitions on behalf of the Jewish community, and he described the ritual surrounding the installation of the exilarch in terms evoking the ceremonial of the Abbasid court—then in the process of collapse. Thus did Natan ha-Bavli try to convince the Jews of Ifrīqiya to offer the Iraqi *yeshivot* their allegiance, though at the time of his writing, Sura had probably already been closed and would remain so for four decades (943–87). It is the quintessential account of a tradition recorded for outsiders with embellishments just at the moment when both the tradition and the worldly power on which it rested were in steep decline. In fact Natan ha-Bavli's account is so full of partial truths and exaggerations that it is difficult to know whether it represents anything beyond what he imagined might impress the Jews of Ifrīqiya. Yet even Natan, who would have been most likely to emphasize a direct relationship between the caliph and the exilarch, says nothing of a caliphal investiture. The second account is by the Iberian traveler

(Baghdad, 1932), 218 (Jawād later showed the work's title and ascription to Ibn al-Fuwaṭī, 1244–1323, to be doubtful; see *EI*[2], s.v. "Ibn al-Fuwaṭī," Franz Rosenthal), both passages translated in Stillman, *Jews of Arab Lands*, 181 and 182.

[3] Natan ha-Bavli speaks of a certain Naṭīra, a *jahbadh* or financier at the Abbasid court under al-Muʿtaḍid (892–902), and reports that Seʿadya's rival Khalaf ibn Sarjado "paid sixty thousand dirhams of his own to remove Seʿadya from his position," which Cohen reads as a bribe to the caliph. But Cohen adds that caliphal investitures of *ge'onim* may have ceased between the tenth and the thirteenth centuries; Cohen, "Administrative Relations," 117–18 n. 13. Seʿadya mentions a second *jahbadh*, Aharon b. ʿAmram, "the diadem of Israel, our precious and pleasant jewel . . . savior of the generation, who has not inclined his ear away from God's laws"; Bodl. MS Heb. d 74.31 verso, lines 4–5. See Gil, *In the Kingdom of Ishmael*, sec. 363, and in general, ibid., secs. 355–67; and Walter J. Fischel, *Jews in the Economic and Political Life of Medieval Islam* (New York, 1969 [1937]).

Binyamin of Tudela, who visited Baghdad ca. 1170 and describes the exilarch as "possessing great authority [*serara*] over all the communities [*qehillot*] of Israel at the hands of the Commander of the Faithful, the lord of the Ishmaelites," which suggests that Binyamin believed that the exilarch's power stemmed from a caliphal investiture, but does not say it outright.[4]

We are much better served by sources for the workings of the Palestinian gaonate under the Fatimid caliphs (969–1171). These sources, all of them preserved in the Geniza, contain a richer yield than their counterparts in Iraq: extending over the course of the eleventh century and reaching back into the tenth, they offer us precious details about the process of negotiation between the *ge'onim* and the caliphs. Those sources make it clear that the relationship between the *ge'onim* and the caliphs was (as I suspect was the case in Iraq) indirect, mediated by Jewish courtiers and other notables in Fustat. (They are, unfortunately, unyielding on gaonic politics during the preceding period of Abbasid rule over Palestine, 750–970s.)

There is much to be learned from those sources about the internal politics of the medieval Jewish communities under Muslim rule, about their external politics toward the state, and about the notion of Jewish communal autonomy in general. In the first years of the eleventh century, for instance, the Jews negotiated with the Fatimid court via members of the Iraqi congregation in Fustat; by the 1020s, the main intercessors were Qaraites. The shift bore a number of consequences in Jewish communal politics, including the kinds of close alliances between Rabbanites and Qaraites that it would have been impossible to imagine on the basis of literary sources (those alliances are the subject of Parts Two and Four, but I will also touch on them further on in this chapter). The Geniza sources thus shed light on the structure of the Jewish community during the Middle Ages, and challenge the pyramidal paradigm.

This chapter offers an introduction to that structure, especially the relationship between the Jewish leadership and the state.[5] Contrary to the usual

[4] Ben-Sasson, "Natan ha-Bavli"; for editions of the text, see chap. 1, n. 2; Binyamin of Tudela in Marcus Nathan Adler, *The Itinerary of Benjamin of Tudela: Critical Text, Translation and Commentary* (London, 1907), 61; for the *termini post* and *ante quem* of his visit (1166–71) see ibid., n. 2 of the translation; Brody, *Geonim of Babylonia*, 26–30; Gil, *History of Palestine*, sec. 746. For the Nestorian *katholikos*'s edict of appointment, see Lawrence I. Conrad, "A Nestorian Diploma of Investiture from the Tadhkira of Ibn Ḥamdūn: The Text and its Significance," in *Studia Arabica et Islamica: Festschrift for Iḥsān ʿAbbās on his Sixtieth Birthday*, ed. Wadād al-Qāḍī (Beirut, 1981): 83–104.

[5] The use of the term "state" in medieval contexts has occasioned debate among historians of Europe; for a summary see Rees Davies, "The Medieval State: The Tyranny of a Concept?" *Journal of Historical Sociology* 16 (2003): 280–300. Its use is justified in the context of the Fatimid empire, which had all the qualities of states as defined in Max Weber, "Politik als Beruf," in *Gesammelte Politische Schriften* (Munich, 1921), 396–450: a monopoly on legitimate violence, extraction of wealth through taxation, a developed administrative apparatus, and so forth. These qualities were, moreover, palpable to those who lived under its dominion: the letters I cite throughout this book use the terms *dawla* (dynasty) and *sulṭān* (dominion) in Arabic and *malkhut* (dominion, kingdom) in Hebrew. The abstractions of government, authority, and administration were also thinkable, even if they were understood

theories about the structure of the Jewish community, the Fatimid example suggests that the relationship between the caliph and the Jewish community was not compressed into a single point of contact. Rather, there was a much wider network of Jewish leaders who offered access to government support and protection. One of the implications of this was that the *ga'on* of Jerusalem, and after 1065, the new Jewish office of the *ra'īs al-yahūd* (head of the Jews), had to work hard to cultivate alliances with the entire network of leaders, because their own authority depended on how well they could mobilize state support for their positions, and how well they could do that, in turn, depended on their allies outside the immediate circle of the rabbinic elite. The classical theory of pyramidal rule and communal autonomy in fact conceals more than it reveals about the inner workings of the Jewish community. The evidence at our disposal suggests the weakness of that model. A better model for the Fatimid period looks like a loose network rather than a tight pyramid.

THE LIMITS OF AUTONOMY

"Communal autonomy" and its effects have been overstated in studies of medieval Jewish history since the inception of the field in the nineteenth century. To some extent, this was a product of the historical discipline's habitual focus on nations and institutions. It also emerged from misplaced confidence in statements about Jewish autonomy in rabbinic and royal edicts alike.[6]

The earliest studies of the gaonic period emphasized the power that the Iraqi rabbinic leadership supposedly exercised over Jews in the entire Islamic empire, from Iran to al-Andalus. Only in this way, it seemed, could one explain how the authority of the *yeshivot* managed to spread westward after the Islamic conquests. Heinrich Graetz wrote of the dominance that the Iraqi exilarchs and *ge'onim* extended over medieval Jews across the Islamic world. Louis Ginzberg held that the Islamic conquests vested the *ge'onim* "with great power and unquestioned authority" and posited a direct connection between the caliphs and gaonic authority: "what the spiritual leaders of the people secured from the new rulers was the permission to call into being, by the side of the Exilarchate, a religious authority with definite power and competence." Ginzberg thus attempted to link the history of the Jews, as he put it, to "more than the

---

as comprised of personal bonds; similarly, as Goitein argued, the use of Islamic law and institutions by non-Muslims constituted a certain approximation of public law.

[6] On this problem, see most recently the excellent analyses in Elka Klein, *Jews, Christian Society, and Royal Power in Medieval Barcelona* (Ann Arbor, 2006), especially 26–51, and Jonathan Ray, *The Sephardic Frontier: The Reconquista and the Jewish Community in Medieval Iberia* (Ithaca, 2006), 104–11.

merely Jewish conditions prevailing in Babylonia"; there seemed no other way to explain the success of the gaonate. Yet there was still no evidence of a link between the caliphs and Jewish self-government beyond the exilarch's power to collect the *dhimmī* head-tax (*jizya*) from the Jews.[7]

Over the course of the twentieth century, the notion of Jewish autonomy took on a life of its own, mainly by becoming detached from any theory of a relationship to the state. What replaced the state as the main motor of communal autonomy was rabbinic power itself.[8] Emblematic was the article "Gaon" in the *Encyclopaedia Judaica* (1973), which held that "The *ge'onim* were considered the intellectual leaders of the entire Diaspora" and that "their decisions and responsa had absolute legal validity in most Jewish communities," an exaggerated claim unless one understands the phrase "absolute legal validity" to entail nothing whatsoever of actual observance and enforcement.[9] Goitein, too, introduced his volume on the Jewish community by presenting "juridical autonomy" as "one of the most essential aspects of Christian and Jewish life in the countries of Islam during the High Middle Ages," though he arrived at a more nuanced picture of the complex interrelationship between Jewish communal heads and the state.[10] All these authors suggested that the absolute sway of rabbinic authority owed to the unfailing piety of medieval Jews, but perhaps what really swayed them was the search for self-sufficient and even state-like Jewish institutions in the premodern diaspora. The theory of autonomy assumed a nationalist cast. Goitein called the Jewish community of the medieval Near East a "state within a state," and Gil, too, has argued that

[7] Graetz: see chap. 1, n. 5; Ginzberg, *Geonica*, 2 vols. (New York, 1909), 1:53, and in general, 1:1–71. Graetz set the agenda for an overemphasis on rabbinic law (and adherence to it) as the central facet of Jewish civilization, but it was Yitzhak Baer who reinterpreted Jewish history through the lens of the continuity of institutions (in keeping with his romantic nationalist bent), reading the Jewish "community" as a substitute for political sovereignty: Baer, *A History of the Jews in Christian Spain*, trans. Louis Schoffman, 2 vols. (Philadelphia, 1961 [1945, 1959]), 1:87 (on the Jewish community as a separate political body) and index, s.vv. "Autonomy of Jewish community," "Criminal jurisdiction of Jewish community," and "Jewish community, structure and jurisdiction"; idem, "Ha-yesodot ve-ha-hatḥalot shel irgun ha-qehillot bimey ha-benayim," *Zion* 15 (1950): 1–41. This centralistic approach has also characterized historiography on Jews in the pre-Islamic periods in Byzantine Palestine and Sasanian Iran; for historiography and critique, see Schwartz, "Big Men or Chiefs: Against an Institutional History of the Palestinian Patriarchate," in *Jewish Religious Leadership: Image and Reality*, ed. Jack Wertheimer (New York, 2004), 1:155–73; idem, "Historiography on the Jews in the 'Talmudic Period,'" 79–114; and Goodblatt, *Rabbinic Instruction in Sasanian Babylonia*, 1–59.

[8] This approach was indirectly created by Baer; see above, n. 7, and Mark R. Cohen, "Jewish Communal Organization in Medieval Egypt: Research, Results and Prospects," *Judaeo-Arabic Studies* (1997): 73–86.

[9] Now updated in *EJ*², s.v. "Gaon," 7:380–86 (quotations on 382); authors are listed as Simḥa Assaf and Jehoshua Brand, presumably the latter on the basis of notes from the former's Hebrew University lectures (Assaf died in 1953). For similar approaches, see also Baron, *Social and Religious History*², 5: 3–4, 13, 16, 47–49; Günter Stemberger, *Il Giudaismo classico: Cultura e storia del tempo rabbinico (dal 70 al 1040)*, trans. Daniela Leoni and Luigi Cattani (Rome, 1991 [1979]): 302–6; Brody, *Geonim of Babylonia*, xx.

[10] Goitein, *Mediterranean Society*, 2:3; cf. ibid., 2:404–5.

medieval Jews were a "nation"—"always more of a nation than all those nations settled on their own land," he adds—though one held together not by territory but by "strong communal organization and central institutions of leadership."[11]

Presumptions about the strength of Jewish institutions have tended to produce in their wake concomitant presumptions of a coherent and clearly bounded Jewish community. Even claims about the more limited privilege of Jewish judicial autonomy have been elevated to an overarching principle that supposedly shaped and governed Jews' daily lives and consciousness, as though the Jews' right to seek justice in their own courts—and their leaders' understandable determination to prevent them from going to other courts—meant that Jewish communities were legally, administratively, and logistically independent from non-Jews in practice. The danger here is mistaking prescription for reality, to the point where historians have refused to believe that medieval Jews might seek justice in Islamic courts, or have depicted those Jews who called the authority of the state down upon fellow Jews as treasonous.[12]

Like all models, then, "communal autonomy" is useful to the extent that it facilitates comparison across Jewish societies and contexts, but misleading when mistaken for an empirical fact. The official leadership of the Jewish community was one of a number of competing systems of power. Jewish grandees of various kinds exercised power in the community by virtue of their positions in government or else by virtue of their wealth, and bypassed the system of rabbinic authority. Not only did the rank and file resort to Islamic courts when doing so brought them some advantage; their leaders made sure that their contracts were enforceable there. Leaders of both the middle and high ranks turned the state against their enemies when it served them to do so, as a normal part of Jewish politics. They were able do this

[11] Ibid., 2:1; Gil, *History of Palestine*, sec. 728. The Hebrew word he uses is *umma*, not to be confused with its Arabic and Judeo-Arabic homonym (below, chaps. 5 and 6).

[12] See, e.g., Hartwig Hirschfeld, "A Karaite Conversion Story," in *Jews" College Jubilee Volume* (London, 1906): 83–84; William M. Brinner, "A Fifteenth-Century Karaite-Rabbanite Dispute in Cairo," in *The Majlis: Interreligious Encounters in Medieval Islam*, ed. Mark R. Cohen, Hava Lazarus-Yafeh, Sasson Somekh, and Sidney H. Griffith (Wiesbaden, 1999), 185; and cf. Tamer el-Leithy, "Coptic Culture and Conversion in Medieval Cairo, 1293–1524 A.D." (Ph.D. diss., Princeton University, 2005); and Mark R. Cohen, "Jews in the Mamluk Environment: The Crisis of 1442 (a Geniza Study)," *Bulletin of the School of Oriental and African Studies* 47 (1984): 425–48. On Jews in Islamic courts under the Fatimids, see Goitein, *Mediterranean Society*, 2:395–407, 3:280–84, 331 and 599 n. 19; T-S 13 J 33.12 (analyzed below, chap. 8, 230–31); T-S 13 J 30.3 (below, chap. 6, 169–71); and Bodl. MS Heb. b 11.12 (chap. 6, n. 33). See also the important contributions to the question in Joseph Hacker, "Jewish Autonomy in the Ottoman Empire: Its Scope and Limits: Jewish Courts from the Sixteenth to the Eighteenth Centuries," in *The Jews of the Ottoman Empire*, ed. Avigdor Levy (Princeton, 1994): 153–202; Najwa al-Qattan, "Dhimmis in the Muslim Court: Legal Autonomy and Religious Discrimination," *International Journal of Middle East Studies* 31 (1999): 429–44; and Uriel Simonsohn, "Communal Boundaries Reconsidered: Jews and Christians appealing to Muslim Authorities in the Medieval Near East," *Jewish Studies Quarterly* 14 (2007), 328–63.

because the limited autonomy of the Jewish community rested on a basic paradox: the harshest punishment at the Jews' disposal was excommunication, while Jewish leaders depended on the state to administer sanctions such as imprisonment and other corporal punishment. Excommunication was frequently insufficient to convince wrongdoers to change their ways. The only exercise of full communal autonomy came when bans of excommunication functioned perfectly, the entire community stopped speaking or doing business with the offender, and he or she repented. But offenders could always flee to another town or straight into the bosom of Islam, and rabbinic authorities were well aware of those risks. When they condemned their followers for going outside the Jewish juridical system or "informing on" fellow Jews, what they were really condemning was not the practice itself, in which they themselves engaged when it served them, but the challenge it posed to their own authority.[13]

In a sense, then, though *dhimmī* autonomy is held to have been a function of caliphal protection, in practice they were related not directly but inversely: the more Jewish leaders tried to force their followers to observe rabbinic law by having state authorities flog or imprison offenders, the more they compromised their autonomy. Efforts to create a tighter system only created a more porous one. Jewish autonomy was perhaps an ideal to which leaders aspired or an ideology they promoted among their followers, but it was not a concrete fact. Bracketing the questions of the intent with which they propagated the ideology—and the reasons people accepted it—one of its effects was to prevent some Jews, some of the time, from rebelling against their leaders.

GE'ONIM, MERCHANTS, AND COURTIERS

Describing the structure of Jewish communal authority in the medieval Near East is not made easier by the lopsided state of the evidence. Before the tenth century, the sources consist mainly of the responsa and other works written by the Babylonian *ge'onim*; after, they include administrative and mercantile correspondence from Palestine, Egypt, Ifrīqiya, and Sicily. Menaḥem

[13] The question of whether medieval Jews enjoyed the right of corporal punishment requires a thorough comparative investigation that goes beyond prescriptive and scholastic sources. Meanwhile see Simḥa Assaf, *ha-ʿOnashin aḥarey ḥatimat ha-talmud: ḥomer le-toldot ha-mishpaṭ ha-ʿivri* (Punishments after the close of the Talmud: Material toward the history of Jewish law) (Jerusalem, 1922); Baron, *Social and Religious History*², 5:45–46, 56–58, 312 n. 55, 316 n. 69; idem, *Jewish Community*, 2:220–28; Goitein, *Mediterranean Society*, 2:330–34; and below, chap. 4, n. 8. In every instance I have found of Fatimid Jews administering corporal punishment, they do so through the state (T-S 18 J 1.6, quoted in Goitein, *Mediterranean Society*, 2:330, is unlikely to be an exception). See also T-S Misc. 35.11, T-S 13 J 19.16, and T-S 13 J 16.15, discussed below, chap. 8.

Ben-Sasson has noted this imbalance and the imprint it has left in the scholarship on medieval Near Eastern Jews, which describes their communal organization "in either a gaonic or a Mediterranean framework," that is, as a function of the power of the *yeshivot* or else of the social and mercantile networks that operated independently from the rabbinic centers. Gil and Ben-Sasson have both done much to advance the cause of integrating these two frameworks. They have done so principally by arguing that the local Mediterranean Jewish communities founded on mercantile wealth became independent from the *ge'onim* before the tenth century, the point previously considered to mark the rise of Jewish communities independent of Iraqi control. In fact, the two frameworks overlapped, in ways that have yet to be fully understood. As Ben-Sasson has argued, replacing the "gaonic" and "Mediterranean" frameworks with more precise categories—filtering the evidence through a finer mesh—better serves the cause of constructing a more integrated picture.[14]

In order to comprehend Jewish communal authority in its full complexity, it helps to distinguish not two but five overlapping strata of religious and communal organization. (1) Religious and scholarly loyalties: What led rabbinic Jews to express fealty to one or more of the *ge'onim* and to seek titles from them? (2) Synagogue attendance: How did Jews choose where to pray and thus which rite to follow (Babylonian, Palestinian, or Qaraite)? (3) Educational decisions: What drew the many young scholars who traveled in pursuit of knowledge to attend institutions of learning in Córdoba, Qayrawān, Fustat, Jerusalem, or Baghdad? (4) Administrative structure: Why did Jews donate money to particular religious and educational institutions? (5) Legal services: In which kind of court did one have contracts drawn up and cases adjudicated? Once these finer categories are in place, the various forms of loyalty they describe combine in ways that flout one's expectations. Loyalties hardly ever divided neatly along party lines. Qaraites attended their own synagogues and felt no obligation to the major products the *yeshivot* had to offer—the Talmud and the legal responsa of the *ge'onim*—but donated money to the *yeshivot* nonetheless, assisted them with administrative functions, and utilized the court sys-

[14] Ben-Sasson, "Varieties of Inter-Communal Relations in the Geonic Period," in Frank, *Jews of Medieval Islam*, 17–31. See also Ben-Sasson, *The Emergence of the Local Jewish Community in the Muslim World: Qayrawan*, 800–1057, Hebrew, 2d rev. ed. (Jerusalem, 1997); idem, "Fragmentary Letters from the Geniza: Concerning the Ties of the Babylonian Academies with the West," Hebrew, *Tarbiz* 56 (1987): 171–209; idem, "Religious Leadership in Islamic Lands: Forms of Leadership and Sources of Authority," in Wertheimer, *Jewish Religious Leadership: Image and Reality*, 1:177–210; and idem, "Maghrib-Mashriq Ties from the Ninth to the Eleventh Centuries," Hebrew, *Pe'amim* 38 (1989): 35–48. See also Gil, *In the Kingdom of Ishmael*. The gaonic model to which Ben-Sasson refers can be found especially in Assaf, *Tequfat ha-ge'onim ve-sifrutah*, and Abramson, *In the Centers and the Peripheries*; for a masterful summary of this scholarship updated to reflect recent research, see Brody, *Geonim of Babylonia*. The Mediterranean model can be found in the work of Goitein and his students (especially Gil and Cohen), cited extensively below.

tems they ran and sanctioned.[15] Such multiple allegiances are nearly impossible to explain using monolithic models of religious loyalty or a centralistic model of rule by the Babylonian *ge'onim*. Similarly, Rabbanite Jews in Qayrawān, Palermo, and Fustat sought ordination from the Palestinian and Babylonian *yeshivot* simultaneously, while soliciting responsa from the latter and sending money to all three.[16] To earlier historians, this represented nothing but the struggle between Palestinian and Babylonian rabbinic authorities for the loyalties of the outlying communities, a struggle supposed to have originated long before the Islamic conquests. In fact such explanations presume rather than demonstrate that loyalties must be exclusive. In practice, Jews seemed to have sensed no contradiction in offering fealty to more than one institution.

All of this fits with the tenor of social and political relations in the tenth, eleventh, and twelfth century Near East. Systems of leadership relied primarily upon patronage relationships, in which protection from above was exchanged for loyalty from below. Those relationships were individual rather than collective ones and changed according to mutual political advantage, economic opportunity, rising and falling social capital, and other contingencies. But they were also considered binding, entailing obligations for both sides. Such patterns have also been noted by social historians investigating leadership hierarchies and social networks among Muslim state officials and the *'ulamā'*. Abraham L. Udovitch has described the medieval Near East as a system in which "political power was not clearly defined and political roles, consequently, tended to be ambiguous. In Fāṭimid Egypt (and certainly elsewhere in the medieval Islamic world), this ambiguity was not restricted to politics. It represented a style of interaction. A flexible definition of roles extended beyond the political sphere and penetrated into the economic, social and even religious domains." This flexibility was a central feature of the Jewish communities under Islamic rule as well. Knowing this helps make sense of evidence that has hitherto seemed difficult to explain; it also sheds light on the Iraqi *yeshivot* themselves, the very epicenters of supposedly monolithic rabbinic power, by pointing out that they did not exert raw power (after all, they lacked access to the means of physical force) but hegemony, a system that encouraged voluntary loyalty through various types of reward.[17]

[15] On Qaraite donations to the Jerusalem *yeshiva*, see below, chap. 7. On other forms of Qaraite aid to the Baghdad *yeshivot*, see chaps. 4 and 10. On Qaraites making use of rabbinical courts, see chaps. 9 and 10.

[16] Ben-Sasson, *Emergence of the Local Jewish Community*; idem, "The Emergence of the Qayrawan Jewish Community and Its Importance as a Maghrebi Community," *Judeo-Arabic Studies* (1997): 1–14; idem, "Jewish Leadership in Islamic Lands."

[17] Udovitch, "Merchants and *Amirs*: Government and Trade in Eleventh-century Egypt," *Asian and African Studies* 22 (1988): 54. See also Goitein, discussed extensively below; Bulliet, *The Patricians of Nishapur: A Study in Medieval Islamic Social History* (Cambridge, Mass., 1972); Udovitch, "Formalism and Informalism in the Social and Economic Institutions of the Medieval Islamic World," in *Individualism and Conformity in Classical Islam*, ed. Amin Banani and Spiros Vryonis (Wiesbaden, 1977),

This new model bears important consequences for the idea of Jewish communal autonomy. It forces one to admit that there were a great many points of contact between Jewish leaders and the Muslim dynasts and bureaucrats who granted them the latitude to govern themselves. Jewish leadership operated both outside and inside the channels recognized by rabbinic power and even by the state. Even the official Jewish leadership drew on sources of authority outside the rabbinic system: Jewish merchants and courtiers in the entourages of amirs, caliphs, and sultans received honorific titles from the rabbinic academies *after* they had made a name for themselves in trade or politics. The *yeshivot* were political institutions, even if the type and extent of the sovereignty they enjoyed is still poorly understood.

Jewish leadership, then, cannot be fully understood when it is stripped of its ties to the world outside the Jewish community. Not only that: the relationships reflected in both the form and content of the period's documentary sources demonstrate that the links between Jews and the state brought mutual advantage.

COURTLY POLITICS AND JEWISH POLITICAL CULTURE

The thesis that political roles were characterized by flexibility while ties between individuals were iterated and reiterated in formal and binding terms emerges especially clearly in the form, functions, and contents of letters and petitions from the period. One of the clearest expressions of that mixture of formalism and informalism is the use of titulature in political contexts. The state and the *yeshivot* maintained separate systems of titulature that overlapped at various points, but they also exhibited subtle differences that speak to the tenor and tenure of power in each system.

Titles in Courtly Contexts

This system was in keeping with court culture of the tenth and eleventh centuries. In Abbasid Baghdad and Fatimid Cairo alike, titles (*alqāb*, sing. *laqab*) functioned first and foremost as forms of investiture (though not the only ones). They served tangible political functions.

61–81; Mottahedeh, *Loyalty and Leadership*; idem, "Bureaucracy and the Patrimonial State in Early Islamic Iran and Iraq," *al-Abhath* 29 (1981): 25–36; Jonathan P. Berkey, *The Transmission of Knowledge in Medieval Cairo: A Social History of Islamic Education* (Princeton, 1992); and the response of Carl F. Petry, "Educational Institutions as Depicted in the Biographical Literature of Mamluk Cairo: The Debate over Prestige and Venue," *Medieval Prosopography* 23 (2002): 101–23; Daphna Ephrat, *A Learned Society in a Period of Transition: The Sunnī 'Ulamā' of Eleventh-Century Baghdad* (Albany, 2000); and Michael Chamberlain, *Knowledge and Social Practice in Medieval Damascus, 1190–1350* (Cambridge, 2002).

Alqāb took on particular forms depending on the dynastic context, and regnal titles of caliphs were part of this phenomenon. Fatimid regnal titles were all compounds on God's name indicating the theocratic claims of the caliphate. The Abbasids also initiated the phenomenon of granting governmental officials *alqāb* in recognition of services they had performed, and officials wore them like badges of honor. Titles were, then, one of the chief methods caliphs used to bestow benefactions (*niʿam*, sing. *niʿma*) upon those who served them, especially court appointees, but also those without formal functions at court.[18]

This idea finds expression, for example, in the work of a Fatimid chancery official, Abu l-Ḥasan ʿAlī b. Khalaf al-Kātib, who writes in 1045–46 that *alqāb* "are among [the caliph's] benefactions [*niʿam*] that he bestows upon his slaves." *Niʿma* is a term of art in medieval Islamic politics: it indicates a type of favor or benefit that required its recipient to render loyalty and service in exchange; those in turn obligated his patron to bestow further *niʿma*. In the Qur'ān, the term describes God's munificence toward humans, whose ingratitude was synonymous with apostasy; but it quickly came to have a central meaning in human-human relationships, especially political ones, where the exchanges were equally binding.[19]

The type of relationship resulting from such an exchange might appear surprisingly formal to modern readers. Its formality lay partly in the fact that it was so widespread in medieval Near Eastern contexts as to suggest a universally agreed-upon code of conduct. That explains, for instance, Abu l-Ḥasan ʿAlī b. Khalaf al-Kātib's description of the caliph's "slaves" where we might say "subjects." The higher the patron—or the higher he or she was imputed to

[18] On *alqāb*, see Leone Caetani and Giuseppe Gabrieli, *Onomasticon Arabicum, ossia repertorio alfabetico dei nomi di persona e di luogo contenuti nelle principali opere storiche, biografiche e geografiche, stampate e manoscritte, relative all'Islām: Fonti–introduzione*, 2 vols., vol. 1 (Rome, 1915), 144–73 (on sobriquets); 173–222 (on honorifics and titles); Goitein, *Mediterranean Society*, 2:355–57; *EI*², s.vv. "Ism" (H. Fleisch), "Laḳab" (Clifford Edmund Bosworth); and Bosworth, "The Titulature of the Early Ghaznavids," *Oriens* 15 (1962): 210–33. Sobriquets—both the *laqab* and the *kunya* (pl. *kunā*, generally bestowed at birth, or at manumission if one had been a slave)—were donned like vestments, and appearing without one was believed to compromise one's dignity. Jews generally refer to government officials by their titles, and Geniza documents are a great untapped source of Fatimid titulature, particularly for courtiers and provincial officials (both Muslim and non-Muslim) who do not appear in the medieval narrative sources.

[19] Ibn Khalaf, *Mawādd al-bayān*, quoted in Abu l-ʿAbbās Aḥmad b. ʿAlī al-Qalqashandī, *Ṣubḥ al-aʿshā fī ṣināʿat al-inshā* (Daybreak for the dim-sighted in the art of diplomatic), 15 vols. (Cairo, 1964), 8:341–47 (here, 341). Ibn Khalaf's chancery manual was for a long time believed to be lost, but in the early 1970s an incomplete copy was located in the Süleymaniye Library in Istanbul (Fatih MS 4128, a twelfth-century copy); it has now been published in facsimile: Abu l-Ḥasan ʿAlī al-Kātib ibn Khalaf, *Mawādd al-bayān* (The substance of eloquence), ed. Fuat Sezgin (Frankfurt, 1986). A critical edition of the work on the basis of this manuscript and the quotations in al-Qalqashandī is a desideratum. On the author and his work, and for the identification of the manuscript, see Abdel Hamid Saleh, "Une source de Qalqašandī, Mawādd al-Bayān, et son auteur, ʿAlī b. Ḫalaf," *Arabica* 20 (1973): 192–200. On *niʿma*, see Mottahedeh, *Loyalty and Leadership*, below, n. 29.

be—the more likely the client was to call him- or herself a slave. The term recurs not just with reference to caliphs but in petitions to private individuals and even in particularly ornate personal letters.

Both extremes of the hierarchy were, then, somewhat predictable, with rulers at the top and "slaves," both literal and metaphorical, at the bottom. But everything in between was subject to negotiation. Precisely because titles served relative, semiotic functions, they were susceptible to a particular weakness: inflation. Tenth- and eleventh-century accounts even complain of this. The Persian polymath al-Bīrūnī (ca. 973–1048) expressed his irritation with title inflation this way: "When the Abbasids had decorated their assistants, friends and enemies indiscriminately with vain titles compounded with the word *dawla*"—the word for dynasty or realm, as in *amīn al-dawla*, faithful one of the realm—"their empire perished, for in this they went beyond all reasonable limits," he complains. "This went on so long that those who were especially connected to their court claimed something new [even more exalted titles] in order to distinguish themselves from the others. Thereupon the caliphs bestowed double titles. But then the others, too, wanted the same titles, and knew how to make their point through bribery, so it became necessary again to create a distinction between this class and those who were directly connected to their court. So the caliphs bestowed triple titles, adding as well the title of Shāhanshāh [king of kings]. In this way the matter became utterly opposed to common sense and clumsy in the highest degree, so that he who mentions them becomes tired before he has even begun, he who writes them wastes his time and writing, and he who uses them in address runs the risk of missing the time for prayer."[20]

So, too, the poet and prose stylist Abū Bakr Muḥammad b. al-ʿAbbās al-Khwārazmī (934–93) complained in verse that title inflation had flattened social distinctions:

What do I care that the Abbasids have thrown open
  The gates of *kunā* and *alqāb*?
They have conferred titles on a man whom their ancestors would not have
  Been satisfied to make a doorkeeper of their outhouse.
The dirhams in the hands of our caliph are few,
  Thus he lavishes people with *alqāb*.[21]

[20] al-Bīrūnī, *al-Āthār al-bāqiya ʿan al-qurūn al-khāliya*, Sachau, *Chronologie orientalischer Völker*, 132; Sachau, *Chronology of Ancient Nations*, 129 (I have slightly altered his translation).

[21] "Mā lī raʾaytu bani l-ʿAbbāsi qad fataḥū / mina l-kunā wa-mina l-alqābi abwāban // wa-laqqabū rajulan law ʿāsha awwaluhum / mā kāna yarḍā bihi li-l-ḥushshi bawwāban // qalla l-darāhimu fī kaffay khalīfatinā / hādhā fa-ʾanfaqa fi l-aqwāmi alqāban." Quoted in the anthology (ca. 1000) of Abū Manṣūr ʿAbd al-Malik b. Muḥammad b. Ismāʿīl al-Thaʿālibī, *Yatīmat al-dahr fī maḥāsin ahl al-ʿaṣr* (The incomparable of the age in the merits of its people), ed. Muḥammad Muḥyi l-Dīn ʿAbd al-Ḥamīd, 4 vols. in 2 (Cairo, 1956–58), 4:230, ed. Ibrāhīm Shams al-Dīn, 6 vols. (Beirut, 2000), 4:264; see Adam

The last line refers to the Abbasid practice of allowing provincial rulers to buy titles in exchange for cash payments or luxury goods.

The fact that titles were subject to inflation confirms that they bore meaning only in relationship to other titles. But since they could only be granted from above, they continued to bear meaning. Likewise, the power to confer titles distinguished superiors in the hierarchy from their inferiors.

Honorifics

Different from formal *alqāb* were honorific terms of address. While *alqāb* were conferred by superiors and served as markers of status, honorifics were offered up from below by petitioners, correspondents, panegyrists, and sycophants of all kinds—inferiors who did not exert the power to confer formal titles. True, inferiors were expected to use the titles that had been granted to their superiors from above. But inferiors could not bestow formal *alqāb*. They could only lavish their superiors with honorifics, which were softer and less stable than titles and occupied a place outside the tightly relational system of formal titulature.

Honorifics, then, admitted of greater latitude in their usage. In submitting petitions to the Fatimid chancery, for instance, etiquette required naming an official by his *laqab* (and perhaps also his *kunya*), but supplication and flattery required adding honorifics in the form of additional blessings and terms of praise. Some of those honorifics eventually attached to a certain ruler in perpetuity; the petition form in Egypt went so far as to develop an entire code of formal terms of address. But it was never a fixed template and admitted of significant variation even in a given time and place.[22]

This is one effect of the mixture of formalism and informalism that characterizes the period's political relationships and its textual remains alike. The informal side lay in the fact that the Fatimids heard petitions in open court (*al-tawqīʿ ʿala l-qiṣaṣ*); they made particularly wide use of the petition format as a means of administration. Anyone could petition the Fatimid chancery to request redress in matters great or small. Though there was no guarantee of

---

Mez, *The Renaissance of Islam*, trans. Salahuddin Khuda Bukhsh and D. S. Margoliouth (New York, 1975 [1937]), 87; Bosworth, "Titulature of the Early Ghaznavids," 213 (whose page reference in ʿAbd al-Ḥamīd's edition of al-Thaʿalibī should be corrected).

22 Paul Balog, "Pious Invocations Probably Used as Titles of Office or as Honorific Titles in Umayyad and Abbasid Times," in *Studies in Memory of Gaston Wiet*, ed. M. Rosen-Ayalon (Jerusalem, 1977), 61–68. Balog notes that certain rulers' names carried a specific set of blessings for their entire lives which then hardened into titles, a continuum I have also found, though the differences deserve emphasis as well.

receiving an answer, numerous petitions were either answered directly and ratified or redrafted as edicts.[23]

The formal side lay in the fact that petitions had to adhere to a certain structure in order to be effective, and that structure hardened over time and grew more formalized.[24] Petitions of the twelfth century include a greater proportion of formulaic language than those from the eleventh. A petition from the early years of al-Mustanṣir's caliphate (1036–94) opens, as usual, with the *tarjama* (the name of the petitioner, styled the "slave of" the ruler with all his titles) and *basmala* (the invocation of God); it then introduces the request simply as follows: "The slave of our lord [the caliph], God's blessings be upon him, seeks refuge with God, may His name be blessed, and with the justice of the prophetic dynasty," before specifying the details of the case.[25] "Seeking refuge" (*istijār*) is another a term of art: it serves as a way of invoking the patron-client relationship and asking for protection, and thus as a code for requesting some special favor. But why would one "seek refuge with God" rather than one's patron? One acknowledged that at the apex of the clientage pyramid stood God, not the caliph, and so one mentioned the former first.[26] The *niʿma* that God bestowed on humans was the model for all the benefactions that humans bestowed on one another; it was the stable term that held the system in place.

Yet even the formula in this petition seems rather curt compared to one submitted to a vizier of the last Fatimid caliph, al-ʿĀḍid (1160–71), in which the comparable section reads: "The slave kisses the earth and reports to the exalted council of the just ruler, the most excellent lord, commander of the armies, sword of religion, the protector, the defender, may God guard him and support religion through him and comfort the commander of the faithful by his long life, may he give him lasting power, exalt his word, and firmly establish his orders and might upon the face of the earth; and reports . . ." (the *narratio* of the petition follows).[27] All of the epithets applied here to the vizier, from "the just ruler" until "the defender," are in fact adjectives modifying the

[23] S. M. Stern, "Three Petitions of the Fāṭimid Period," *Oriens* 15 (1962): 187–88; idem, *Fāṭimid Decrees: Original Documents from the Fatimid Chancery* (London, 1964); idem, "A Petition to the Fāṭimid Caliph al-Mustanṣir Concerning a Conflict within the Jewish Community," *Revue des études juives* 128 (1969): 203–33; D. S. Richards, "A Fāṭimid Petition and 'Small Decree' from Sinai," *Israel Oriental Studies* 3 (1973): 140–58; Khan, *Arabic Legal and Administrative Documents in the Cambridge Genizah Collections* (Cambridge, 1993), 303–5; *EI*[2], s.v. "Diplomatic" (W. Björkman); and further references in Mark R. Cohen, *Poverty and Charity in the Jewish Community of Medieval Egypt* (Princeton, 2005), 175 nn. 6–7.

[24] Khan, "The Historical Development of the Structure of Medieval Arabic Petitions," *Bulletin of the School of Oriental and African Studies* 53 (1990): 8–30.

[25] T-S Ar. 42.158.

[26] Cf. Cohen, *Poverty and Charity*, 182. Jewish petitions for alms use a range of structures and rhetorical devices also found in Arabic petitions to rulers.

[27] T-S Ar. 51.107. On the standardization of the phrase "the slave kisses the ground" in petitions starting with the reign of al-ʿĀmir (1101–30), see Khan, *Arabic Legal and Administrative Documents*, 310–12.

word "council" (*majlis*); they do not function as titles or honorifics of the vizier himself. Justice, excellency, protection, and so forth are his attributes, but grammatically they do not modify him. They thus cannot be considered to operate within the universe of formal *alqāb*. At the same time, the use of honorifics like these was not a matter of mere politeness but a fundamental element of diplomatic protocol whose neglect could cost the petitioner his or her success.[28]

Keeping in mind the difference between formal *alqāb* and informal honorifics helps explain how courtly actors created and re-created the social hierarchies into which they fit themselves. *Alqāb* were formal, honorifics informal; at the same time, both served important semiotic and communicative functions. Formulaic language was, then, neither merely decorative nor rote and meaningless. It partook of social meaning and created it.

Roy Mottahedeh has offered the most evocative and complete description to date of patronage in his study of the political culture of tenth- and eleventh-century Iraq and Iran. Fundamental to his study is the insight that many of the texts of this period are characterized by a kind of linguistic formalism that makes them replete with technical terms whose importance can be easily overlooked. He explains this formalism as an effect of "a scripturalist tradition in which an immutable text lies at the heart of religious study": because scripture is revealed, it is fixed, stable, and enduring; its words continue to convey certain meanings and reverberations even when they are used in other contexts.[29] *Niʿma* is one of these terms. *Niʿma* begins its career as a description of what God bestows on humans, but comes to pervade political relationships while never quite losing the implication that to bestow *niʿma* is to imitate God. In politics a common way of describing ingratitude was *kufr al-niʿma*, literally denial of benefaction, but the verb is the same one used for apostasy, as though failing to repay *niʿma* to a human benefactor is tantamount to breaking one's pact with God.

In practice, this kind of linguistic formalism was a habit of mind that extended beyond the language of scripture and affected social relationships of all kinds. The key to grasping the tenor of communication in many Arabic and Judeo-Arabic sources of the tenth and eleventh centuries, then, lies in recognizing when words are laden with meaning, in distinguishing between technical terms and everyday language.

[28] On *nisba* adjectives modifying the noun *dīwān*, see Khan, *Arabic Legal and Administrative Documents*, 107. In the context of international negotiations, improper use of titulature could actually lead to war. See Bosworth's argument that the Mamluks' broad sphere of international negotiations fostered their unusually intense concentration on matters of chancery practice: "Christian and Jewish Religious Dignitaries in Mamluk Egypt and Syria: Qalqashandi's Information on Their Hierarchy, Titulature, and Appointment," *International Journal of Middle East Studies* 3 (1972), 59–60.

[29] Mottahedeh, *Loyalty and Leadership*, 9; see also ibid., 5–6, 41, 72–84.

Titles among the Jews

Jewish sources exhibit the courtly distinction between formal titles conferred from above and informal honorifics or terms of address conferred from below.

All three *yeshivot* used titles in a formal way, which is to say that through titles they recognized a strict hierarchy among the *yeshiva*'s supporters. One could not simply assume a *yeshiva* title: it had to be bestowed by one of the *ge'onim*. Bestowing titles was also one of the main means by which the hierarchy of the rabbinic *yeshivot* cultivated loyalty.

At the lower ranks, the *yeshivot* distributed the title of ordinary member or associate (*alluf* in the Iraqi *yeshivot*; *ḥaver* in the Palestinian), which authorized their bearers to serve as judges in local communities. Most community officials in the Palestinian congregations also received salaries or payments in kind (loaves of bread, for instance), together with the promise that the *jizya* would be paid for them annually (we are woefully ignorant of how this worked in the Babylonian community). The community funded these expenditures through taxes, fines, and special collections on behalf of the scholars and the community chest. But not all *ḥaverim* took up positions or received salaries.[30] Regardless of emolument, and even when a *ḥaver* was granted a title from above, in practice his authority depended upon the willingness of his local followers to comply with his rulings.

Further up the ranks, members of the Palestinian *yeshiva* held titles in the form of Hebrew ordinals from seventh through third (*shevi'i*, *shishi*, *ḥamishi*, *revi'i*, and *shelishi*), and above that, *av bet din* (president of the court) and *ga'on*, a shortened version of *rosh yeshivat ge'on Ya'aqov*, "the head of the *yeshiva* of splendor of Jacob" (in various biblical passages, the last two words refer to the people Israel).[31] The ordinal titles of members of rank exemplify in its purest form the tendency of titles to convey relative rather than absolute meaning.[32]

That is an important point, because titles frequently offer the historian of the Jewish community only an illusory precision. They appear to specify something quite precise—rank in a hierarchy—but they almost never indicate the actual prerogatives associated with their bearers' official functions. Titles

30 Goitein, *Mediterranean Society*, 2:121–26. On titles as an incentive for the establishment of pious foundations (*awqāf*) and contributions to them, see Gil, *Documents of the Jewish Pious Foundations from the Cairo Geniza* (Leiden, 1976), 11.

31 Nahum 2:3; Amos 8:7; Psalms 47:5. It has also been suggested that *yeshiva* (in the construct state) functions in apposition to *ge'on Ya'aqov*, thus "head of the *yeshiva* that is the splendor of Jacob" (i.e., the splendor of the people Israel). For references, see Brody, *Geonim of Babylonia*, 49 n. 61.

32 See Elinoar Bareket, *Fustat on the Nile: The Jewish Elite in Medieval Egypt* (Leiden, 1999), 31–43 with reference to previous studies.

were conferred by superiors, and thus functioned as markers in a system whose value was relative and therefore primarily semiotic; they indicated rank but not role. The precise prerogatives exercised by the *ga'on* of the Jerusalem *yeshiva* in the eleventh century, for instance, are still a matter of debate (to which I shall return). But this fact should not be taken to mean that titles were merely empty markers. On the contrary: the system was based on exchanges of patronage for loyalty according to well-defined gestures.

As at court, in the *yeshivot* titles were granted in official ceremonies, with maximum publicity. The Jerusalem *yeshiva* conferred its titles at the convocation on Hoshaʿna Rabba on the Mount of Olives (see chapter 8), the largest pilgrimage festival of the year. (The Fatimids, too, bestowed titles publicly, accompanying them with gifts of vestments, sabers, and mounts.)[33] The public conferral of titles contributed to their potential to translate into real status: it publicized the investiture of power. Titles both served as markers of status and created links in the network binding the outlying centers to the central *yeshivot*; in practice, this meant that titles manufactured loyalty. The *ge'onim* knew this, and bestowed titles as a way of persuading scholars from Mediterranean communities such as Fustat and Qayrawān to secure their loyalties to one *yeshiva* over another. Rather than simply conferring authority on their bearer, in some contexts titles became a means of conferring power on those who bestowed them.[34]

That meant that *yeshiva* titles were simultaneously stable and unstable. They were stable in the sense that one could not simply arrogate membership or one of the ordinal titles; they had to be granted by a *ga'on*. But nor did they indicate the bearer's scholarly achievement. Titles were granted to those who had made significant donations to the *yeshiva* or raised funds on its behalf, and the latter were sometimes but certainly not always its most learned members. Titles were also granted to people who had never set foot in one of the *yeshivot*. Their primary function was to encourage fealty, and that lent them a certain lack of stability. In certain courtly contexts, of course, titles also served the purpose of promoting loyalty; the difference is one of emphasis. In the Jewish context, all three *yeshivot* resorted to cultivating networks of loyalty through titulature precisely because institutional affiliations were fluid. Because the *yeshiva* system functioned not on the basis of clear territorial jurisdictions but of loyalty regardless of geographic origin, the granting of titles turned into bids for loyalty. Caliphs, by contrast, had courts, territories, and armies. Precisely because the Jewish community

[33] al-Qalqashandī, *Ṣubḥ al-aʿshā*, 8:341–42, who quotes from Ibn Khalaf, *Mawādd al-bayān*. The last Abbasid viziers evidently also granted vestments to their gaonic appointees; see above, n. 2. On the ceremonies accompanying the conferment of titles, see further Caetani and Gabrieli, *Onomasticon Arabicum*, 209–212.

[34] On granting of titles by the *yeshiva*, see Goitein, *Mediterranean Society*, 5:261–72.

was not a state, titles among Jews performed a particularly heavy kind of labor.[35]

The very titles *ga'on* and *khalīfa* (caliph) further illustrate this distinction. Both contained absolute claims to authority, including powers and prerogatives that were the bearer's exclusive preserve. In the *ga'on*'s case, those powers included dispensing titles, stipends, and shares of tax revenue. The titles *ga'on* and caliph were also similar in that both theoretically lay claims to exclusive authority while, in practice, both could be held by two or three incumbents at a time. After the Abbasids had held the title *khalīfa* for a century and a half in exclusivity, the Fatimids claimed it (909) followed closely by the Umayyad *amīr* of Córdoba (929); all bore it simultaneously over the course of the tenth and early eleventh centuries while claiming different territories (or going to war). The three Jewish *ge'onim* (two in Baghdad and one in Jerusalem) also bore the same title with respect to different jurisdictions, but those jurisdictions were not delimited territorially. That also meant that the titles they dispensed functioned principally, not incidentally, as bids for loyalty and, thus, for power.[36]

Titles in the Jewish community may have been as susceptible to inflation as titles at court. But significantly, I have found no evidence of title inflation among Jews during the Fatimid period. Late in the twelfth century, Maimonides complained, "In Palestine I have seen men called *ḥaverim*, and in other places men may be styled heads of academies, when they are not even freshmen students." He directed this comment at the latter-day Babylonian *ga'on* Shemu'el b. ʿAlī (d. 1194), whom he famously considered a beggar and "a poor old man, truthfully an ignoramus in every respect," whose authority lay solely in the titles he dispensed: "each and every individual hangs expectantly on each word pronounced from the [Babylonian] academy in anticipation of being

[35] The question of Qaraite titles requires a thorough investigation. See meanwhile Wieder, *Judean Scrolls and Karaism*, 90–91, and cf. Gottheil-Worrell 35; Gil, *History of Palestine*, sec. 936 n. 20; Goitein, *Mediterranean Society*, 1:169 and n. 21; Gil, *In the Kingdom of Ishmael*, secs. 163, 220; Pinsker, *Lickute kadmoniot*, 2: 174–75.

[36] This partly contradicts the current scholarly consensus that the *ge'onim* of Sura and Pumbedita and the exilarch in Baghdad held *reshuyot* or territorial jurisdiction over separate parts of Iraq, Iran, and Yemen. In fact the descriptions of the gaonic *reshuyot*, most notably the account of Natan ha-Bavli, do not pretend to completeness, and the ongoing battles over the loyalties of Jews in Egypt, Ifrīqiya, and Sicily suggest that the situation was far from clear even to the *ge'onim* themselves. See Goitein, *Mediterranean Society*, 2:106–7; Gil, *History of Palestine*, sec. 728; and Ben-Sasson, "Varieties of Inter-Communal Relations in the Geonic Period," 20 (the latter two offer a picture more clear-cut than the evidence allows); cf. Brody, *Babylonian Geonim*, 123–32. The entire question deserves further investigation. On the caliphal title, its claims, and its early development, see Patricia Crone and Martin Hinds, *God's Caliph: Religious Authority in the First Centuries of Islam* (Cambridge, 1986). The title *khalīfa* was also used in a Jewish context to designate the representative of the Jerusalem *ga'on*, as when it was applied to the head of the Rabbanite Jews in Fustat during the first half of the eleventh century; it was also applied to the bishop of Ifrīqiya. Goitein, *Mediterranean Society*, 2:8.

honored by an epithet."[37] Maimonides' complaints differ from al-Bīrūnī's and al-Khwārazmī's: the former complained not of a caliph or a dynasty but of a single leader whose authority depended vitally on the respect he commanded among rabbinic leaders. By accusing the *ga'on*'s followers of seeking only the benefits derived from titles, he was, in effect, unmasking the gaonic system as interested only in self-perpetuation and otherwise devoid of content. Feeling his father's irritation, Avraham Maimonides (d. 1237) dismissed all titulature as nothing but empty ceremony: "It is known among all men of reason and understanding that most of these titles that people use for one or another purpose are vain and senseless words applied by wise persons sparingly and with discomfort. Only pretenders in quest of power indulge them to excess, because with them rests all their greatness and dignity."[38] But these Maimonidean objections are nowhere in evidence in the tenth and eleventh centuries, when institutional structures in the Jewish community were softer and titles served to delineate meanings that, in part, compensated for the lack of clear and continuous institutional power.

Honorifics

Honorifics also appear in Jewish letters, official documents, petitions, and other contexts in which they serve to distinguish their bearers from others, to flatter them, or to indicate loyalty towards them; but they were basically the preserve of inferiors.

Thus a Qaraite courtier to whom the Fatimid caliph had granted the title *sanī al-dawla* (exalted one of the realm) was addressed by Jews with the Hebrew honorific *ha-sar ha-addir* (the mighty prince)—not a gaonic title but a mere honorific commonly bestowed by Jews on Jewish courtiers. A second Qaraite courtier, David b. Yiṣḥaq, who served in the *dīwān al-kharāj* (bureau of taxation), was also called *ha-sar ha-addir*, as well as *rozen ha-zeman* (the ruler of the age), an honorific that Jews frequently accorded to courtiers from among their own ranks. A Rabbanite panegyrist of the same period, Yiṣḥaq ibn Khalfūn, calls the Qaraite notable David b. Bapshād *sar ha-adama* (the prince of the land) and *sar bet yisra'el* (prince of the Jews); the latter honorific was also granted to the Qaraite noble Abu l-Faḍl ibn Shaʿyā at the turn of the twelfth century. These honorifics indicated simply that their bearers held some government appointment. (The disproportion of Qaraites in these examples

[37] Moses Maimonides, commentary on Mishnah *Bekhorot* 4:4, cited in Baron, *Social and Religious History*^{2} 5:313 n. 58; Maimonides, letter to his disciple Yosef b. Yehuda, in D. Z. Baneth, ed., *Mose ben Maimon: Epistulae* (Jerusalem, 1985 [1946]), 56, lines 6–7 ("fa-kayfa iltafa'tu li-shaykhin maskīnin ḥaqīqatan jāhilin bi-kulli shay'"); 54, line 14, to 55, line 1 ("anna l-nāsa kullahum mustaṭliʿūna li-kulli amrin masmūʿin min al-yeshiva aw tashrīf bi-sm"—without the word *laqab*).

[38] Avraham Maimonides, *Responsa*, quoted in Baron, *Social and Religious History*^{2}, 5:48.

represents not a general disproportion of Qaraites at court, but a specific one of Qaraites in the correspondence of the Palestinian rabbinic elite from the Geniza, more on which in Part Two.)[39]

A famously misunderstood piece of Hebrew titulature is the word *nagid*, meaning chief or prince. The term was used equally by superiors and inferiors, a fact that underlines the importance of distinguishing rigorously between the use of titles and honorifics in the sources. As a title, *nagid* appeared for the first time in 1015, when the *ga'on* of Pumbedita, Hayya b. Sherira (1004–38), bestowed it on Abū Isḥāq Avraham b. ʿAṭā of Qayrawān, a physician in attendance at the court of the Zirid governors of Ifrīqiya. Here, power vested by the state attracted gaonic recognition through titulature. As Mark Cohen notes, the title *nagid* "did not *establish* Ibn ʿAṭā's power" in Ifrīqiya; "it acknowledged and reinforced the status and authority that he already possessed by virtue of his connections with the Tunisian rulers [the Zīrids] and his prominent role in Jewish communal affairs."[40] In 1027, the same title was granted to the poet, talmudist, and philosopher Shemu'el ibn Naghrilla (993–1056), though here, before the *amīr* of Granada appointed him vizier.[41] What did the title mean? That a *ga'on* had seen fit to bestow it on someone. It may have inspired the awe of those lower in the hierarchy, but it carried no special privileges. For this reason, Goitein dismissed as a moot question whether Maimonides bore the title *nagid*: an answer would tell us only whether someone was willing to confer it on him.[42]

The title *nagid* could also function as an informal honorific, as when an anonymous panegyrist of the early 1020s bestowed it on mere children, the sons of the Qaraite military governor of Palestine ʿAdaya b. Menashshe ibn al-Qazzāz.[43] This illustrates the distinction I am emphasizing here: when Hayya Ga'on conferred the title from above, it functioned as a *laqab*; when the anonymous poet conferred it from below, it remained an informal honorific. The same word could function as either depending on who was bestowing it and in what context.

[39] Goitein: to the ranks of the *sarim* "belonged high government officials and agents, great doctors (often acting as parttime or fulltime court physicians), chief judges, and leading businessmen, especially if they were learned enough to act also as community leaders. These were 'the notables connected with the government and well known to it'" ("sarim qerovim la-malkhut ve-nodʿim bah"). *Mediterranean Society* 1:76, citing T-S 16.171, line 21. On the number of Rabbanites and Qaraites at court, see below, chap. 4.

[40] The full title he used was *negid ha-gola*, prince of the diaspora. Mark R. Cohen, *Jewish Self-Government in Medieval Egypt: The Origins of the Office of Head of the Jews, ca. 1065–1126* (Princeton, 1980), 30–31 (emphasis in original). For a discussion of the history of the debate on the title *nagid*, see ibid., 3–49. The letters from which Goitein deduced Ibn ʿAṭā's appointment as *negid ha-gola* are ENA 2 B and Bodl. MS Heb. d 65.9; for references see ibid., 30 n. 86, and for other instances of *nagid* as a generic term of praise, ibid., 39–40 n. 114.

[41] For speculation on who granted the title to him, see Baron, *Social and Religious History*[2], 5:311–12, n. 54.

[42] Goitein, *Mediterranean Society*, 2:26.

[43] T-S 32.4, line 41.

Titles vs. Prerogatives

Medieval leaders and commentators themselves were painfully aware of the weaknesses of titles and limits of the power they conferred. In fact, the tendency of titles to come uncoupled from prerogatives was a particular characteristic of Jewish offices and the limits of force and sovereignty in Jewish leadership institutions. Al-Bīrūnī says as much ca. 1000. First, he remarks that after the Buwayhids took over Baghdad in 945, "the authority that remained with the Abbasid [caliph]s was only a matter of religion and theology, not a political or secular one [*amr dīnī iʿtiqādī lā mulkī dunyāwī*]." The Abbasid dynasts still bore the title caliph, he notes, but they exercised a greatly reduced number of its prerogatives. He then exemplifies this by comparing the post-Buwayhid caliphate to "the dignity of the exilarch [*ra's al-jālūt* or *resh galuta*] among the Jews, who exercises a sort of religious authority without any actual dominion or realm [*min ghayr mulk wa-lā dawla*]." The comparison may have stemmed only from his presumption that real power depends on dominion and realm; in any case, the link between titles and prerogatives was seen as a particularly weak one among the Jews. (This is our best answer to Natan ha-Bavli and the tales he told in Ifrīqiya. For Natan, the exilarch was like the caliph since the investiture of both entailed great pomp and ceremony. For al-Bīrūnī, they were alike in that both wielded only a nominal dominion.)[44]

Jewish leaders, too, were acutely aware of the danger that their prerogatives might come unlinked from their titles. After the Palestinian *ga'on* Shelomo b. Yehuda (1025–51) had successfully defended his position from the usurper Natan b. Avraham of Gaza (1038–42), a board of overseers took charge of the *yeshiva*. The *ga'on* complained bitterly of the reform, saying, "I have the title but not the power of my office."[45] The gaonate of Iraq suffered a similar blow in the ninth century, when ʿAmram bar Sheshna had expected to become *ga'on* of Sura but, instead, had to endure the appointment of Naṭronay b. Hilay (857–65). Without the title of *ga'on*, ʿAmram nonetheless assumed some of the prerogatives by founding an academy of his own (857–75) and issuing responsa to followers in Iraq and abroad (including, famously, a prayerbook he wrote at the request of a certain Yiṣḥaq b. Shimʿon of Iberia).[46]

Embedded in the title *ga'on*, then, was a claim to jurisdiction over all the Jews. But the office was subject to weaknesses, including interregna and rival

[44] al-Bīrūnī, *al-Āthār al-bāqiya ʿan al-qurūn al-khāliya*, in Sachau, *Chronologie orientalischer Völker* 132; Sachau, *Chronology of Ancient Nations* 129 (I have altered his translation).

[45] T-S 12.217, line 21.

[46] Brody, "Rav ʿAmram bar Sheshna—Ga'on of Sura?" Hebrew, *Tarbiẓ* 56 (1987): 327–45; idem, *Geonim of Babylonia*, 191–93; on the whereabouts of Yiṣḥaq b. Shimʿon, see Cohen, *Sefer ha-qabbalah*, 53, notes to lines 114–15.

gaonates—effects (and further causes) of the semiformal nature of gaonic authority.

GAONIC INVESTITURE

One way to stabilize the gaonic office was to have it conferred from above. That leads us back to the connection between the *ge'onim* and the state.

The earliest surviving evidence of gaonic investiture by caliphs are petitions from the Fatimid period. They reveal much about how the Jewish communal leadership negotiated with the chancery. They also fully reveal the paradoxes of Jewish communal autonomy at work.

In theory, the political authority of the gaonate was rooted in arguments from scripture, tradition, and continuity with the rabbis of classical antiquity, who themselves claimed continuity with the biblical past. But in practice, the *ge'onim* recognized their need for investiture by some worldly authority.

A statement in a responsum of Shemu'el b. Ḥofni, *ga'on* of Sura (998–1013), bears on the subject. The responsum is of a type common during the gaonic period: it answers a question having no practical consequences in the lives of Jews; those who submitted the query seemed to have done so solely to have the *ga'on* teach them something and thus express their fealty to him. "It has been asked," Shemu'el b. Ḥofni writes, "why it is written, 'Thou shalt establish judges and officers in all thy gates' [Deuteronomy 1:18], in the [second person] singular and not in the plural." The *ga'on* then expounds upon this verse as the basis for the gaonic prerogative to appoint judges, but in so doing, admits that scriptural justification is not always enough. "The answer," he writes, "is this."

> The verse is addressed to the spiritual leader on whom it is incumbent to appoint judges in Israel, just as Moses said, "Get you wise and capable men, who are well known among your tribes, and I will make them heads over you" (Deut. 1:13). Without the appointment by Moses, the election by the people was not valid. Even Joshua's office, although he was chosen by God, was complete only after his investiture by Moses. The same is true of Saul and Samuel [Samuel anointed Saul as king, 1 Samuel 10]. All this proves that installation in an office is incomplete unless it is done by the spiritual leader of any given period. In the absence of such leadership, however, each community is at liberty to make its own choice.[47]

[47] Quoted in Goitein, *Mediterranean Society*, 2:4; original text in Harkavy, *Me'assef Niddaḥim*, 14:222, n. 123. I have altered Goitein's translation slightly.

This responsum addresses the problem of how the Jewish judiciary gains its authority. It does not, however, directly address the question of what the relationship is between Jewish judges and the non-Jewish government. Judges should be confirmed in office from above, writes the *ga'on*, but "in the absence of such leadership," the appointment may be made by the community, from below. The passage nonetheless suggests that installation in any office should ideally be performed by "the spiritual leader of any given period" should one be available. Shemu'el b. Ḥofni is vague as to who this "spiritual leader" might be. Was he referring to a Jewish prophet like Samuel (but the rabbis held prophecy to have ended long ago in antiquity)? A king like Saul (but Jewish kingship, too, was a thing of the past)? The exilarch, who claimed descent from the kings of Israel and Judah? Or some other "spiritual leader"? Responsa are usually sparing in their inclusion of verifiable historical information, and this one may not have been meant to provide pragmatic instruction. Since the *ge'onim* of Sura and Pumbedita in Shemu'el b. Ḥofni's day did not receive appointments from the Abbasid caliphs or the Buwayhid *amīr*s of Iraq, one is left in the dark as to whether he may have entertained the possibility of a non-Jewish leader granting the *ge'onim* legitimacy, even through the mediation of the exilarch, or whether he considered himself to have been appointed by the community.

Further west, however, the *ge'onim* of Jerusalem tacitly recognized the Fatimids as the leaders of their age—political if not spiritual. When exigencies made them conscious of the need to link their authority to the state, they applied to them for documents of investiture.

The petitions of investiture that have left their traces in the Geniza—all of them discovered and first published by Goitein—fall into three categories. The first type includes petitions that *ge'onim* submitted when they first rose from *av bet din* to assume the chair of *ga'on*. The procedure suggests some agreement with Shemu'el b. Ḥofni's statement that "installation in an office is incomplete" unless it is confirmed from above.

The second type is the petition that a *ga'on* submitted when the caliph died and a new caliph replaced him. This suggests that the Jerusalem *ge'onim* petitioned the chancery for rescripts of appointment at every important political juncture: when a new *ga'on* acceded to office, or when a new caliph ascended the throne.[48] The *ga'on*'s power was tied not to the caliphate in any abstract sense, but to the particular caliph in question. The relationship was essentially

[48] I follow scholars of Fatimid chancery practice in using the word rescript to indicate an edict issued by the Fatimid caliph in response to a petition. Often rescripts would consist merely of the original petition itself plus the ratifying signature of the caliph or one of his ministers. The terms these documents use for themselves are "report" (*qiṣṣa*), "petition" (*ruqʿa*), "rescript" (*tawqīʿ*), and "decree" (*sijill*) with the understanding that the first two represented initial steps on the way to the third or fourth. In practice, the first two and last two terms were used interchangeably: see, e.g., Khan, *Arabic Legal and Administrative Documents*, 458.

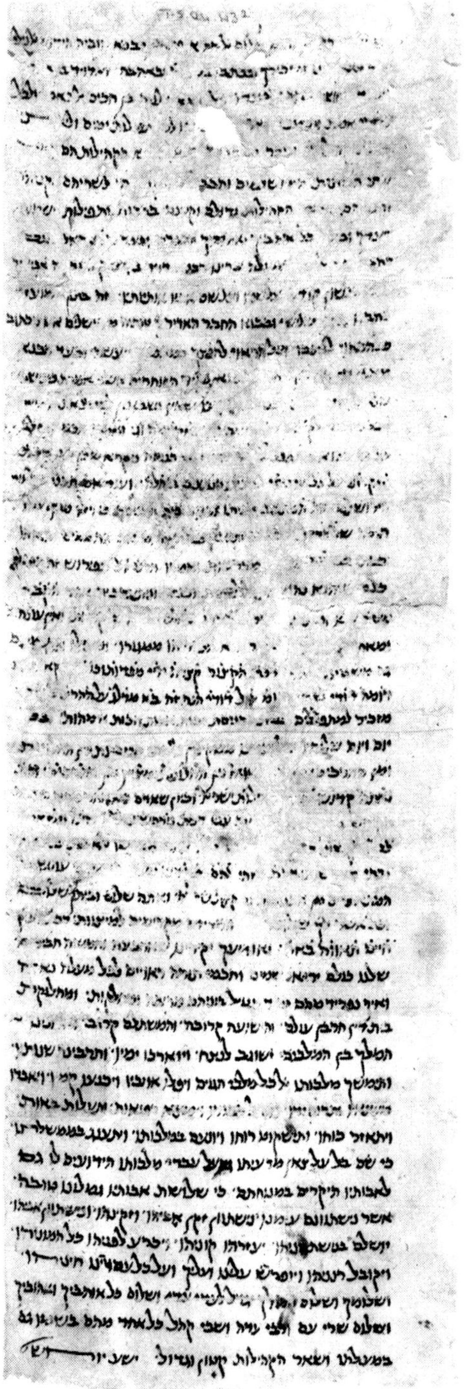

Fig 1. A *ga'on* seeks confirmation in office from the caliph: letter of Shelomo ha-Kohen b. Yehosef, *ga'on* of the Jerusalem *yeshiva*, asking his Rabbanite and Qaraite supporters in Fustat-Cairo to procure a rescript of investiture for him from the Fatimid caliph al-Ẓāhir. In Hebrew, probably spring 1025. Cambridge University Library, T-S 24.43r.

a tie of personal patronage, and had to be reaffirmed when one party to the relationship changed. That is in keeping with the nature of authority in the medieval Near East. Even when a caliph, governor, or any other high-ranking state officer "distributed alms," writes Goitein, "or opened his granaries in a time of famine, or founded a hospital or a caravanserai, or even built an aqueduct, he did so not as the representative of the government, but as a pious, powerful, and munificent Muslim."[49] Mottahedeh, too, has noted that even the strictly political kind of *niʿma* "remained largely concerned with ties between individuals. . . . No abstract gratitude to the state is imaginable. Some forms of *niʿmah*, like public works, . . . were transactions between a single man and an abstractly defined category of men; but those men were presumed to be grateful individually, and 'to invoke God's blessing' on the donor rather than to be grateful in any corporate fashion."[50]

The third type of petition was one the *gaʾon* submitted to the caliph to shore up his own authority when his power was threatened by a rival.

All the surviving petitions, then, derive from moments of succession or rivalry. But the *gaʾon* was not the only one who gained by the process. By petitioning the caliph and the chancery for recognition, the *gaʾon* confirmed his own power and implicitly and reciprocally affirmed that the caliph was his highest protector. A rescript, then, had the potential to confirm not just one but both parties in the patron-client relationship.[51]

The Rescripts

The earliest surviving evidence of the process dates from 1025, when Shelomo ha-Kohen b. Yehosef, having been appointed *gaʾon* by the curia of the Jerusalem *yeshiva*, solicited a rescript from the chancery of the Fatimid caliph al-Ẓāhir (1021–36) confirming him in office (see fig. 1).

The evidence comes in the form not of the petition itself, but of the letter that the new *gaʾon* sent to a group of Jewish notables in Cairo asking them to write the petition on his behalf. All of these men derived their power from their mercantile and political activities. Among them were Qaraites then serving the Fatimid court. The *gaʾon*'s letter offers us even more information than the petition alone might have, since it contains the names of his allies in Cairo and traces of the route he used to reach the chancery.[52]

[49] Goitein, "Minority Selfrule and Government Control in Islam," *Studia Islamica* 31 (1970): 102.

[50] Mottahedeh, *Loyalty and Leadership*, 77–78.

[51] Cohen, "Administrative Relations," 117.

[52] T-S 24.43, in Hebrew. Goitein dated this letter to 1022–24, but Gil has shown that Shelomo ha-Kohen b. Yehosef served as *gaʾon* for less than half a year, from spring to August 1025. See Goitein, "New Sources on the Palestinian Gaonate," in *Salo Wittmayer Baron Jubilee Volume on the Occasion of His Eightieth Birthday*, ed. Saul Lieberman and Arthur Hyman (Jerusalem, 1974): 503–37; idem, *Mediterranean Society*, 2:16–17; Gil, *History of Palestine*, chronology (appendix).

Goitein found it perplexing that a high-ranking leader such as the *ga'on* would resort to mediation, asking a coterie of grandees to approach the chancery instead of doing it himself. (He did not realize that the courtiers were Qaraites; I will return to that piece of the story in chapter 5.) He offered that "the *Ga'on* himself could not apply. This would have been bad form; the old principle 'do not seek honor (i.e., office)' was as valid in Islam as in Judaism."[53] But humility is surely not the only motive that required the *ga'on* to seek mediation.

To explain this, it helps to look at the *ga'on*'s petition from the caliph's point of view. To the *ga'on*, the caliph was the only authority high enough to confer and thus stabilize his power. But from the caliph's perspective, the Jewish courtiers were more powerful than the *ga'on*. Between the caliph and the *yeshiva* stood the Egyptian Jewish notables, including the *ga'on*'s followers and supporters, who could serve as witnesses to his worthiness of appointment and to the degree of support he enjoyed among the Jews—a key consideration for the caliph. The conflict between the relative values accorded the *ga'on* in these two separate political systems could be resolved only by attaching the two networks via the courtly intermediaries. From the perspective of the chancery itself, this stands to reason. But in light of the theory of Jewish communal autonomy, it was difficult to admit that Jewish courtiers held more power than the *ga'on*. The only way to resolve the paradox is to admit that in certain circumstances, the *ga'on* was not, in fact, the highest-ranking leader in the Jewish community.

Another aspect of the petition seems puzzling. The draft of the petition that the *ga'on* sent to his allies in Egypt is in a florid Hebrew, much of it rhymed prose. Why did the *ga'on* not write it in Arabic, or at least in Judeo-Arabic, the more common (though not exclusive) language of political correspondence? That way, his intermediaries would have had merely to render the document into Arabic script. Writing in florid Hebrew probably represented his efforts to act the role of *ga'on*. Since Arabic rhymed prose (*saj'*) was an important feature of chancery protocol, his Hebrew letter served the purpose of rendering the lofty tone of the petition without its literal wording. It also suggests that the *ga'on* knew that the petition would have to be redrafted anyway by those more familiar than he with the conventions of the chancery. It highlights his dependence on intermediaries, courtiers trained in *inshā'*, the styles and methods of government document-production, who could be relied upon to draw up an appropriately worded petition and therefore an effective one. Their connections at court also offered the petition a better chance of being ferried through the chancery. The *ga'on* was, it seems, well aware of his dependence on the Jewish courtiers and the fact that, in practice, his authority over the community depended on them.

[53] Goitein, "New Sources on the Palestinian Gaonate," 523.

The petition reads as a faithful rendering of Arabic diplomatic into Hebrew: "May our lord his honor the caliph, son of caliphs, be exalted forever; may his days be prolonged and his years multiplied and his reign endure longer than that of all the kings of other nations. . . . For he looks after his flock and the slaves of his dominion, who have been known to him and also to his esteemed fathers in their [eternal] rest. For three of his ancestors have shown their kindness to us, and we possess their rescripts, the rescript of his grandfather, his great-grandfather and his father. Let him complement those by his own rescript."[54]

The penultimate sentence demonstrates that the previous *ge'onim* of Jerusalem had procured writs of appointment from the first three Fatimid caliphs in Cairo: al-Muʿizz (969–75), al-ʿAzīz (975–96), and al-Ḥākim (996–1021).[55] None of those petitions has surfaced, an unfortunate fact since they might reveal something about the development of the gaonic office in the transition to Fatimid rule over Jerusalem. It is even possible that the Jerusalem *ga'on* began petitioning the government for ratification only when the Fatimids conquered Jerusalem ca. 970: since there is no evidence that the Babylonian *ge'onim* maintained direct contact with the Abbasids in the tenth century, then it is hard to believe that the Palestinian *ge'onim* would have sought ratification from them either. From the very beginning of Fatimid rule, however, and soon after the Palestinian *yeshiva* moved from Tiberias to Jerusalem, the Jerusalem *ga'on* sought the caliph's ratification; he must therefore also have developed a network of supporters close to the court.[56]

Shelomo ha-Kohen b. Yehosef died just half a year later. Scanty evidence has survived of the procedure by which his successor, Shelomo b. Yehuda (1025–51), petitioned the chancery on his appointment (there is indirect evidence, to which I will return in chapter 7). The Geniza has, however, yielded the petition he submitted (again via supporters) when the caliph al-Ẓāhir died in 1036 and al-Mustanṣir (1036–94) succeeded him. This, then, is a petition of the second type, submitted by a reigning *ga'on* at the accession of a new caliph.[57]

This petition, too, was written not by the *ga'on* himself, but by his Egyptian supporters. It thus represents the second phase in the process by which *ge'onim* requested investitures: after he wrote to his supporters in Cairo, they drafted

[54] T-S 24.43, lines 38–47. I have altered Goitein's translation (ibid., 520–21). The word the *ga'on* uses for rescript is *nishtevan*; see chap. 7, n. 19.

[55] This is a claim from which Goitein recoils for reasons I cannot discern ("New Sources on the Palestinian Gaonate," 521 n. 33).

[56] On the question of when the *yeshiva* moved from Tiberias to Jerusalem, see Gil, *History of Palestine*, sec. 738.

[57] Halper 354, verso, in Arabic. For a discussion of the document's dating, see chap. 11, 294–96.

the petition and had it submitted to the chancery on his behalf. It also offers us a piece of evidence missing from the first document: a list of the prerogatives the *ga'on* had exercised in his eleven years in office and hoped to exercise in the future. Those included supreme authority to arbitrate questions in Jewish religion and law; the sole right to impose coercive sanctions, especially the ban of excommunication; and the exclusive power to appoint judges, cantors, butchers, and associates of the *yeshiva* (*ḥaverim*). The petition further confirms that his title was *ra's al-mathība*, head of the *yeshiva*, and adds, just to be clear, that "the Jews are not permitted to disapprove of or to object to his decisions or actions." The document also stipulates that the *ga'on*'s jurisdiction is over "the party known as the Rabbanite Jews" (*al-ṭā'ifa al-maʿrūfa bi-l-yahūd al-rabbānīn*)—to the exclusion of the Qaraites and the Samaritans (whom the Fatimids considered a Jewish group)—a point to which I shall return.[58]

Goitein notes that this second petition finds its parallel in an edict that al-Ẓāhir had issued to a Coptic monastery on his accession in 1021 ensuring that its *dhimmī* privileges would remain in effect during his reign.[59] Considered as a group, all three attest that the legal and administrative position of minority communities—and their leaders—needed to be confirmed and ratified despite the supposedly universal validity of *dhimmī* judicial autonomy. That autonomy was tied to individual office-holders—a point that should caution us against generalizing too confidently about the legal and administrative status of the Jewish community under Islamic rule.

The final type of petition—submitted for defense against rivals—is best illustrated by a document that Shelomo b. Yehuda submitted to al-Ẓāhir some time during his reign, perhaps ca. 1030, preserved in the Geniza in a Judeo-Arabic copy (see fig. 2). The threat to Shelomo b. Yehuda's jurisdiction came, as one might expect, from the Babylonians, who had already established

[58] Ibid., verso, line 4. Judeo-Arabic and Arabic documents are inconsistent in their spelling of the Arabic terms for Rabbanites and Qaraites: this one has *rabbānīn* while others have *rabbāniyyīn*, and similarly the Qaraites appear as either *qarrā'īn* or *qarrā'iyyīn*. Goitein called this document the draft of a letter requesting the *ga'on*'s confirmation in office (Goitein, "New Sources on the Palestinian Gaonate"); Cohen specifies that it is the draft of "a petition to the Fatimid government" (*Jewish Self-Government*, 28 n. 81), a designation now justified in light of Khan's research on Fatimid petitions in *Arabic Legal and Administrative Documents*. See also the Arabic petition T-S NS 320.45, which the Jews submitted on al-Mustanṣir's accession in 1036 requesting that he confirm an Alexandrian judge in office; it is not immediately evident how that petition fits with this one, which states that the *ga'on* has the exclusive power to appoint judges to rabbinical courts in the Fatimid realm. Evidently Shelomo b. Yehuda had appointed the judge himself and now asked the caliph to recognize his jurisdiction over Alexandrian Jews—a fact that suggests that the Jewish administrative structure was even more dependent on the chancery than the system of gaonic investiture let on. See also below, chap. 6, p. 161: Elḥanan b. Shemarya also solicited (and received) caliphal recognition as chief judge in Fustat, but in a period when the *ga'on* of Jerusalem was particularly weak. This, in turn, sheds light on the politics of Shelomo b. Yehuda, who was attempting to invest the gaonate with new strength.

[59] Goitein, "New Sources on the Palestinian Gaonate," 523. The monastery's decree was edited by Stern, *Fāṭimid Decrees*, 15–22.

Fig. 2. A *ga'on* defends his position: copy of a petition from Shelomo b. Yehuda, *ga'on* of the Jerusalem *yeshiva* (1025–51), to the Fatimid caliph al-Ẓāhir attempting to prevent the Babylonian-Iraqi community of Palestine from seceding from his jurisdiction. In Judeo-Arabic, ca. 1030. This copy was probably a writing exercise. Jewish Theological Seminary of America, ENA 4020.65r.

their own community in Palestine and were now attempting to install their own *ra'īs* (chief), in the form of one Yūsuf al-Sijilmāsī, head of the Iraqi synagogue in Ramla.[60]

[60] ENA 4020.65, in Judeo-Arabic. Goitein initially dated this acephalous fragment to the tenth century because of the acute tension it reflects between the Palestinian and Babylonian *yeshivot* ("Congregation versus Community," 295), but he later revised his opinion to the reign of al-Ḥākim (996–1021). Goitein, "Petitions to the Fatimid Caliphs from the Cairo Geniza," *Jewish Quarterly Review* 45 (1954): 31; see also Khan, "Historical Development," 19. Gil, however, dates it to ca. 1030 since he identifies the Iraqi in question as Yūsuf al-Sijilmāsī (here also called Ibn al-Sijilmāsī), head of the Iraqi congregation of Ramla, who was active in the early 1030s. I follow his dating: if al-Sijilmāsī was attempting to launch an independent Iraqi community in Palestine, this might explain his bid for peace with the Qaraites (see chap. 11); and Khan's research on Arabic petitions has made it possible to judge the formulaic language in line 24 as dating comfortably to the reign of al-Ẓāhir (1021–36) or early in the reign of al-Mustanṣir (1036–94); Khan, *Arabic Legal and Administrative Documents*, docs. 70, 73, 75, 77 (in the twelfth-century petitions, the corresponding language has changed). Gil further identifies the handwriting as that of Avraham ha-Kohen b. Yiṣḥaq ibn Furāt, but this identification should be taken as conjectural. See further Gil's comments, *History of Palestine*, sec. 771.

It was not the first time the Iraqis had attempted to secede. The Babylonian community of Fustat had tried to break away from the authority of the Jerusalem *ga'on* during the early 1020s as well. But while Shelomo b. Yehuda's predecessor had quenched the fires of Babylonian rebellion by forging alliances with Qaraites in the capital, he took the extra precaution of appealing directly to the caliph to bolster his authority—an effort in which his Qaraite connections may have helped him. The document suggests that Ibn al-Sijilmāsī's party, too, had petitioned the caliph for recognition of their candidate as leader of the Babylonians; the *ga'on* now tried to block it by submitting a petition of his own.[61]

His petition allows us a precious glimpse of jurisdictional squabbles between the Babylonian and Palestinian communities. It also sheds light on how the *ga'on* conceived of his authority, how he hoped to exercise it, and most importantly, how he linked it to the political legitimacy of the state. Petitions are not always interpreted as bearing any discernable relationship to the political life of the Jewish community as it was defined by its members, but are rather presumed to translate a complex internal Jewish situation into formulae designed for the benefit of bureaucrats unversed in the fine points of Jewish communal administration. Such presumptions rest on the notion that Jews of the political classes lived in a world hermetically sealed—or at least formally autonomous—from Muslim officialdom. In fact, Jews spoke a shared language of political legitimacy and used it not merely when communicating with the chancery but among themselves as well. This petition, then, tells us something about how the *ga'on* construed his relationship to the caliph. The seemingly standard or formulaic form of the petition also carries a more muscular set of meanings. It presents in compact form a range of justifications for gaonic authority, in the form of two distinct arguments on behalf of the *ga'on*'s right to supreme leadership of the entire Rabbanite community in Palestine. The first links his authority to the caliph's; the second justifies his authority through Jewish law.

The *ga'on* first argues that his authority is both a reflection of the caliph's and reflects back on him. Maintaining order in the Jewish community, he states, depends upon the *ga'on*'s unquestioned authority, for "when it is permitted for there to be two chiefs, it is permitted for there to be three and even more. This would lead to denunciations [*al-fitan*] without end, to the robbing of goods and land, to the rape of women and the abrogation of rights [*hatak al-ḥarīm wa-baṭalat al-ḥuqūq*]."[62] Weakening his authority, he suggests, will undermine the very basis of Authority itself. He may also be referring directly to rabbinic arguments for Jewish communal autonomy: the word *fitan* invokes

[61] On the Iraqi secession of the early 1020s, see chap. 6.

[62] ENA 4020.65; cf. Goitein, "Congregation versus Community," 302, and Gil, *History of Palestine*, 2:570.

the long history of rabbinic screeds against Jews who denounce other Jews, *malshinim* (Heb., literally, slanderers), who by inviting non-Jewish authorities into the community's affairs threaten its autonomy. Here, however, the *ga'on* invites the government to resolve the jurisdictional dispute between him and his rival. He states plainly that he is to be the designated link between the community and the caliph.

For if the caliph grants the Iraqi leader the same benefaction (*niʿma*) he has granted the *ga'on*, the *ga'on* continues, "the *niʿma* bestowed [upon me] would then be no *niʿma* at all, and it would be impossible to obtain even what the simplest man owes." It is worth saying a bit more about *niʿma* here, because the *ga'on* invokes it repeatedly. Mottahedeh, the modern expositor of the ethics of medieval *niʿma*, points out that its importance lay not only in its power to create binding relationships of patronage, but conversely, in its power to unbind them: "since one acknowledged ties by accepting *niʿmah*, a man could cast off ties, and in particular could cast off his allegiance, by claiming that no *niʿmah* had been given by the other party."[63] By petitioning the caliph not to grant Ibn al-Sijilmāsī the same authority he had been granted, for then "the *niʿma* bestowed [upon me] would then be no *niʿma* at all," he is, in effect, warning the caliph that he would be acting within the bounds of propriety to withdraw his loyalty. If this seems bold for a *dhimmī* dependent, one should bear in mind that he did so to stress that his relationship with the caliph was binding on both sides. The bestowal of *niʿma* had required the *ga'on*'s gratitude and created a bond between the two men; withdrawing that *niʿma* ruptured the bond. Later he rephrases this, asking the caliph not to allow the Iraqi leader "to split apart [*tashaʿʿuth*] what has been bestowed upon the slave [the *ga'on*], for when someone shares this *niʿma* with him, it turns into vengeance [*niqma*]." (The pun in the last line is probably deliberate.)

Further on in the petition, the *ga'on* invokes caliphal precedent, linking his authority to that of the state in precisely the same way he would do before al-Mustanṣir in 1036. "The pure presence [the caliph] has made grants in numerous writs [*sijillāt*] to many leaders over time," he writes, "a fact of which the archives [*al-dawāwīn*] offer proof, but they have not made for any one of them a partner in what they have bestowed upon them. For the *sijill* of the government, may God bestow glory upon its victories, is laid down." The Fatimids kept archives; its written documents served as proof of the *ga'on*'s own privileges; the benefactions his predecessors had received from previous caliphs served as precedent and justification for his own.[64]

[63] Mottahedeh, *Loyalty and Leadership*, 77.

[64] This document should thus be understood in light of the section on the Fatimid archive (*khizāna*, the exact equivalent of the Hebrew *geniza* [Ezra 6:1], though *genizot* were not archives) in the chancery code of the Fatimid *kātib* Ibn al-Ṣayrafī (d. 1147): Tāj al-Ri'āsa Amīn al-Dīn Abu l-Qāsim ʿAlī b. Munjib ibn al-Ṣayrafī, *Qānūn dīwān al-rasā'il*, ed. ʿAlī Bahjat (Cairo, 1905), 142; French translation in

Conversely, if the caliph allowed Ibn al-Sijilmāsī to get away with his designs, he would be breaking with the precedent set by his illustrious ancestors, who justified the caliph's own rule. Gaonic authority and caliphal authority are, the *ga'on* implies, bound up with each other: weaken one and you weaken the other.

Then Shelomo b. Yehuda enlists arguments from Jewish tradition, resorting to the preposterous claim that the Bible itself prohibits challenging the sovereignty of the Jewish leader of Jerusalem. (Perhaps he allowed himself to say this since he knew that neither the caliph nor the Jewish courtiers would contradict him.) "It is the law of our *madhhab*," he wrote, "that there should be no chiefdom above the chiefdom of Jerusalem, for the Holy City is the place towards which [Jews] turn in prayer, and God, may He be exalted, has ordered them to obey the command of the leader in Jerusalem and to follow his command, and he who disobeys him disobeys God. This is witnessed in their [i.e., our] Torah."[65] Although the Iraqis are allowed to maintain their own synagogues in Palestine, he argues, they are to be allowed nothing else: no judges, no officials, no separate communal organizations. They enjoy the permission to worship in synagogues separate from those of the Palestinians, but not to organize public offices or develop an independent communal structure. That they enjoy freedom of worship at all owes only to the fact that "they have the custom of observing a second day [of holiday] after they have observed [the first day] with us. The chiefs of Jerusalem [the *ge'onim*] permitted them this as a special favor so that they could pray there on the day of their holiday which is on the morrow of our holiday, which they keep together with us, but [they permitted them] nothing else. The proof of the truth of what the slaves have said is that in al-Shām there are various towns in which the Iraqi synagogues are solely for prayer, and they have neither a judge [*ḥākim*] nor any other official [but rely on the officials of the Palestinian congregation instead]. Everything they are allowed to do is granted to them as a favor by the chief [the *ga'on*] who is in Jerusalem at any given time."

Thus did the *ga'on* articulate the precise contours of his authority over Fatimid Jews—as usual, only when it was threatened: the Iraqis are entirely under the jurisdiction of the Jerusalem *ga'on*, since he has granted them the right to worship in their own synagogues according to their diasporic customs; he grants them nothing more.

Henri Massé, "Ibn el-Çaïrafi: Code de la Chancellerie d'Etat (période fâtimide)," *Bulletin de l'Institut français d'archéologie orientale* 11 (1914), 108–109; Ibn al-Ṣayrafī, *al-Qānūn fī dīwān al-rasā'il wa-l-ishāra ilā man nāla al-wizāra*, ed. Ayman Fu'ād Sayyid (Cairo, 1990), 34–38.

[65] It is common for letters of this period to alternate between first and third person. In this case, the third person possessive can be understood as referring to *al-'abīd*, "the slaves." Similarly, the caliph is usually referred to as *al-ḥaḍra*, "the Presence," and thus in the third-person feminine singular.

These three petitions represent traces of the attempt to fix and define for the gaonic office a set of prerogatives that, by everyone's admission, fluctuated from incumbent to incumbent. The prerogatives the petitions outlined cannot be projected backwards and forwards in time, no matter how much we would like to form some composite or continuous portrait of gaonic power. The petitions cannot be read as the records of an institution that transcended the lives and personalities of the people who created it. They are less than that, but also more: they demonstrate that the political theology of the Jews partook of the means and methods at its disposal. Saying that the gaonic office had a semi-institutionalized character is not to say that it was weak, illegitimate, or irrelevant. On the contrary: it is only to point out that it spoke in the language of its time and place, that of leadership offices in the medieval Near East. As well, saying that Jewish leaders drew their authority from the state is not to say that they exerted power over their followers by force rather than persuasion. It is only to say that Jewish elites governed their communities not only by means of religion but also by means of politics.

THE JURISDICTION OF THE JERUSALEM *GAʾON*

Despite a relatively healthy quantity of evidence attesting to the *gaʾon*'s power, its extent, and its limits during the first half of the eleventh century, the question of whether his jurisdiction included the Qaraites has remained subject to debate—even though the investiture petition of 1036 explicitly limits his authority to "the party known as the Rabbanite Jews."

Part of the difficulty stems from the fact that Goitein, the first to grapple with the problem, phrased matters ambiguously, describing the Jerusalem *yeshiva* as "the highest authority of the Jews in the Fatimid Empire"—implying (but not meaning) all the Jews.[66] By "Jews," Goitein meant only "Rabbanite Jews"; he never discussed what place the Qaraites held in the hierarchy of Jewish communal leadership. This fact is in itself telling; it reveals the extent to which the second set of theories about Jewish communal autonomy that I discussed above—those that presume rabbinic authority as its main

[66] Goitein, *Palestinian Jewry in Early Islamic and Crusader Times in Light of the Geniza Documents*, Hebrew, ed. Joseph Hacker (Jerusalem, 1980), 52; Goitein, "New Sources on the Palestinian Gaonate," 529–30. Contrary to what Goitein's language implied, he believed that the *gaʾon* headed the Rabbanites alone, a point I emphasize because Shulamit Sela later claimed that Goitein "projected backwards, from the inclusive authority of the head of the Jews who was responsible for the three sects on to the *gaʾon*, head of the *yeshiva*. This idea was spelled out in the title he chose for his article: 'The head of the Palestinian Academy as head of the Jews in the Fāṭimid Empire'" (Sela, "The Head of the Rabbanite, Karaite and Samaritan Jews: On the History of a Title," *Bulletin of the School of Oriental and African Studies* 57 [1994]: 266). In fact Goitein makes no such claim in that article, and gave it that title because for him Jews meant Rabbanites. Gil makes the claim that Sela attributes to Goitein; see below.

motor—had come to shape even the most inductive and document-based research.

Gil, too, has devoted considerable attention to the place of the Qaraites within the Jewish community and has espoused the position that Goitein mistakenly implied: that the *ga'on* served as the de facto head of all the Jews, Qaraites included, until the 1060s, when the office of *ra'īs al-yahūd* in Fustat came to unite all of Fatimid Jewry, Babylonians, Palestinians, and Qaraites, under the same administrative aegis. "From a document first identified and edited by Goitein," Gil writes, "it emerges, without any doubt, that the *Gaon* who headed the Palestinian *yeshiva* was the recognized leader of the Jewish communities within the framework of Fatimid rule and was accepted as such by the authorities."[67] Unlike Goitein, Gil was not unintentionally overstating matters: he held that "the *yeshiva* was the recognized representative of all the Jews, including the Qaraites; this despite the fact that there is no explicit evidence to that effect in the sources, and that sometimes one might even understand the opposite"—that is, that the Qaraites represented the *ga'on*.[68] While officially, the Qaraite courtiers and other communal leaders were informal intermediaries between the *yeshiva* and the Fatimid court and formal power was in the *ga'on*'s hands, including, according to Gil, power over the Qaraites, sometimes, Gil writes, it seemed that the Qaraite courtiers held all the formal power, while the *ga'on*'s power was informal. This is not far from what I believe to be the correct interpretation, but the situation is less than explicit in his statement on the matter, and one need not go so far as to dismiss the evidence in order to resolve the contradictions it presents. Below, I will attempt to resolve those considerations by considering the titles, offices, prerogatives, and modes of formal and informal leadership in the Jewish community. But before I do, I owe it to two students of Gil's, Shulamit Sela and Elinoar Bareket, to discuss their arguments on the subject, since they, too, remained unsatisfied with the contradictions in the evidence and tried to resolve them.

The Qaraites and the Office of *Ra'īs al-Yahūd*

Sela ventured the hypothesis that in the second quarter of the eleventh century, the Qaraites held a formal role within the structure of Jewish administration: the office of *ra'īs al-yahūd*.[69]

[67] Gil, *History of Palestine*, sec. 746.

[68] Gil, *Tustaris*, 45. Quoted also in Sela, "The Headship of the Jews in the Fāṭimid Empire in Karaite Hands," Hebrew, in *Mas'at Moshe: Studies in Jewish and Islamic Culture Presented to Moshe Gil* ed. Ezra Fleischer, Mordechai A. Friedman, and Joel L. Kraemer (Jerusalem, 1998), 257, where she turns that theory on its head; and in Bareket, "Rais al-Yahud in Egypt under the Fatimids: A Reconsideration," Hebrew, *Zemanim* 64 (1998): 40. See also Gil, *Tustaris*, 25.

[69] Sela, "Head of the Rabbanite, Karaite and Samaritan Jews"; eadem, "Headship of the Jews in the Fāṭimid Empire in Karaite Hands."

In claiming that the office existed before the 1060s, Sela was arguing against the reigning scholarly consensus but returning to an earlier one according to which the Fatimids had established the office on their conquest of Egypt in 969. Sela then began to fill in the chain of putative incumbents of the office from 969 until the 1060s, a task that Bareket completed.[70] The Qaraite candidates Sela put forward—David ha-Levi b. Yiṣḥaq and Ḥesed al-Tustarī—appeared in dozens of documents called by titles such as *rayyis* in Judeo-Arabic or *rosh* in Hebrew; both read these to mean *ra'īs al-yahūd*.[71] This part of their thesis had, however, already been refuted by Cohen, who pointed out desultory uses of the term *ra'īs* as an honorific before the position of *ra'īs al-yahūd* was established in 1065.[72]

And indeed, many individuals are called *ra'īs* in the Geniza corpus and in medieval Arabic literature: *ge'onim*, judges, court physicians, heads of merchant partnerships, tribal chieftains, Coptic bishops, and Muslim *'ulamā'*. As early as the 990s, Ṣemaḥ b. Yiṣḥaq, *ga'on* of Sura (ca. 987–99), called Shemarya b. Elḥ anan by the full title *ra'īs al-yahūd* in recognition of the Babylonian congregation he led in Fustat.[73] But the *ga'on* did not use this phrase as a formal title; he merely meant to indicate that Shemarya was the head of the Iraqi Jewish congregation in Fustat. Had Ṣemaḥ wished to grant Shemarya a formal title, he would have

[70] Bareket, "Rais al-Yahud in Egypt under the Fatimids," 40–42. Bareket's chain of incumbents includes the mysterious Palṭiel (see below, n. 84), Shemarya b. Elḥanan, and Elḥanan b. Shemarya (see chap. 6); the Qaraite governors Menashshe ibn al-Qazzāz and his son 'Adaya (chaps. 4, 5 and 8); Ḥ esed al-Tustarī (whose dates she offers as 1026–49; see below, chaps. 5, 6, 7, 9, 11); David b. Yiṣḥaq (esp. chaps. 7, 10, 11; in claiming his headship as 1049–55, she contradicts Sela); and Avraham ibn Furāt (1055–62). Many of these men are called by lofty titles such as *rosh* or *ra'īs*, but nothing suggests that they occupied an office resembling the headship of the Jews in its later incarnation. The effectiveness of the Fatimid military and political appointees in Jewish communal affairs derived precisely from their appointment from *outside* the Jewish community. See also idem, "Abraham ha-kohen b. Isaac ibn Furat," Hebrew, *Hebrew Union College Annual* 70–71 (1999–2000): 1–19.

[71] The former is an alternate form of *ra'īs*, as al-Qalqashandī affirms. Sela, "Headship of the Jews in Karaite Hands."

[72] Cohen, *Jewish Self-Government*, 166–68; see also Mottahedeh, "Administration in Buyid Qazwin," in *Islamic Civilisation 950–1150*, ed. D. S. Richards (Oxford, 1973): 35; idem, *Loyalty and Leadership*, 129–36. In a letter of 1057, a Jerusalem Rabbanite calls 'Anan b. David "the head of the Qaraites and their ancestor" (*rayyisuhum wa-qadmon al-qarrā'īn*); T-S 13 J 9.4, verso, lines 11–12.

[73] Mosseri Ia 10.2 (L 279), cited in Cohen, "Administrative Relations," 126–27 n. 47. See also the testimony (*ḥujja*) published in Richard J. H. Gottheil, "An Eleventh-Century Document Concerning a Cairo Synagogue," *Jewish Quarterly Review*, o.s. 19 (1907): 467–539. The document purports to date from 1037–38 and gives the title of a certain Abu l-'Imrān Mūsā b. Ya'qūb b. Isḥāq as "head of the party of the Jews, the Rabbanites, Qaraites, and Samaritans" (*ra'īs 'alā ṭā'ifat al-yahūd al-rabbāniyyīn wa-l-qarrā'īn wa-l-sāmira*), but it is almost certainly a later copy whose scribe altered the original wording, "head over the party of the Rabbanite Jews" (*ra'īs 'alā ṭā'ifat al-yahūd al-rabbāniyyīn*), adding the Qaraites and Samaritans in order to bring the title into line with contemporary usage (and also perhaps to include the wider Jewish community among the original beneficiaries of the *waqf* in question). It cannot be taken as evidence that the office of *ra'īs al-yahūd* existed in 1037–38. See Goitein's comments, *Mediterranean Society*, 2:243; Cohen, *Jewish Self-Government*, 35 n. 99; Rustow, "Rabbanite-Karaite Relations in Fatimid Egypt and Syria: A Study Based on Documents from the Cairo Geniza" (Ph.D. diss., Columbia University, 2004), 207–16; and cf. Sela, "Head of the Rabbanite, Karaite and Samaritan Jews," 262–63.

granted him one of those in use in the *yeshiva*. David b. Yiṣḥaq, too, was called by legions of fancy-sounding Hebrew titles over the course of the 1020s, including *ha-sar ha-addir* (the mighty lord), *ha-sar ha-kabir ve-ha-rosh ha-addir* (the great lord and the mighty chief), *zeqan ha-dor* (elder of the generation), and *pe'er shetey ha-pe'ot* (glory of the two parties)—three of those titles in one document alone.[74] Sela read them as proof that David b. Yiṣḥaq was not merely *a* leader, but *the* leader of the Jewish community. But what of questions of form and context: who offered him these titles and to what ends? In fact, he was granted all of them from below in solicitations for money and intercession of various sorts, as honorifics to inspire his generosity. None of the documents in which he appears mentions specific prerogatives he held as an officer in the Jewish community.

The same is true of the other Qaraite candidate whom Sela proposed for the office, Abū Naṣr Ḥesed (al-Faḍl) al-Tustarī. And the same is true of one of Bareket's candidates, the Qaraite military governor of Palestine, ʿAdaya b. Menashshe ibn al-Qazzāz, dubbed *rosh ha-rashim* (highest chief) by an anonymous panegyrist of the early 1020s, a Hebrew rendering of the Arabic title *ra'īs al-ru'asā'*. This was a phrase of high respect or of rank flattery, but it was not an indication of communal office. Similarly when the poet bestowed the title *nagid* on ʿAdaya's sons: though that title was later associated with heads of the Jews in the Fatimid empire, in this case it served as an honorific bestowed on mere children. (In fact, even the title *nagid* was not attached permanently to the office of *ra'īs al-yahūd* until the thirteenth century, when *alqāb* had come to function differently among both Muslims and Jews, as the Maimonidean statements I quoted earlier attest.)[75]

As for prerogatives, there was one letter of the late 1030s in which Sela found an oblique reference to a function supposedly exercised by David b. Yiṣḥaq, an undated and fragmentary draft of a letter from the community of Fustat to an unknown recipient describing the affair of a certain Avraham, otherwise unidentified, who had been excommunicated and taken to prison by Fatimid agents (another instance of Jewish leaders calling upon the state to punish an offender). But, the Fustat community writes, "when his imprisonment became known to David b. Yiṣḥaq and Avraham al-Tustarī"—Ḥesed's younger brother, who was also a courtier—members of the Palestinian *yeshiva* (*ḥaverim*) assembled in David's *majlis* in Cairo to request that the ban be canceled.[76]

[74] T-S 13 J 14.20; ENA 4020.45. That the title *ha-sar ha-kabir ve-ha-rosh ha-addir* is in *sajʿ* further suggests that it was intended as an honorific. On the use of *sajʿ* in honorifics (as well as book titles), see *EI²*, s.v. "*sadjʿ*," third part: "In Arabic literature of the Islamic period" (T. Fahd, W. P. Heinrichs, and Afif Ben Abdesselem).

[75] Goitein, *Mediterranean Society*, 2:23; Cohen, *Jewish Self-Government*, 38–41.

[76] Sela, "Headship of the Jews," 262–63. T-S 13 J 35.3 + AIU VII A 23; see Gil's comments, *History of Palestine*, secs. 792, 881, and Goitein, *Palestinian Jewry*, 165 n. 96. Gil ingeniously suggests on the basis of T-S Ar. 54.93 that it was Avraham ibn Sughmār and that he was excommunicated for dallying with a Muslim prostitute.

On Sela's reading, the request to cancel the ban took place in David's *majlis* because as *ra'īs al-yahūd* he possessed the authority to decide on the cancellation of bans—this is the prerogative she finds mentioned in the letter. Yet this scenario is difficult to reconcile with the petition of investiture according to which the *ga'on* enjoyed the exclusive right to issue bans of excommunication. Sela resolved this conflict by arguing that the *ga'on* did indeed hold sole power to impose bans, but it was the *ra'īs al-yahūd* who decided on their cancellation, leaving the *ga'on* to attend to the halakhic niceties of lifting them.[77]

The letter—like most private letters—does not spell out important contextual details too well known to writers and recipient to merit mention. This presents challenges to the historian seeking to reconstruct those details. Still, it would be stretching the evidence to the breaking point to suggest that, since the *yeshiva*'s notables gathered in David's *majlis* to attend to the lifting of the ban, he possessed the power to lift it himself. It is more likely that the *yeshiva* officials gathered there—together with another Qaraite courtier, Abū Sa'd Ibrāhīm al-Tustarī—to beseech the courtiers' help in extracting Avraham from the Fatimid prison. And even if David did enjoy the prerogative of canceling bans, Sela's scenario reduces his authority to the nearly symbolic and comes perilously close to vitiating her argument for the headship of the Jews before the 1060s as a discernible office with significant prerogatives.

Sela's contention that Qaraites served as heads of the Jewish communities of Fatimid Egypt and Syria remains a pleasingly revisionist one for anyone accustomed to modern accounts of Rabbanite-Qaraite relations, according to which no Rabbanite, let alone the *ga'on* of the *yeshiva* of Jerusalem, would have allowed himself to come under the administrative authority of a Qaraite. This revisionist impulse is justified, but for other reasons. In fact Sela's argument reinforces the old theory of Rabbanite-Qaraite alienation by suggesting that the two camps required offices and institutions in order to be made to cooperate with each other. The larger context of Rabbanite-Qaraite relations suggests instead that the two groups cooperated voluntarily. In arguing that David b. Yiṣḥaq was "accepted as communal leader by all communities of Jews" *despite* the fact that he was a Qaraite, Sela grants him a formal office without defining the nature of his power and the reasons he was able to amass it.[78] In fact, the rabbinic leadership in Jerusalem and Fustat cultivated him as a patron precisely *because* he was a Qaraite.

[77] Sela, "Headship of the Jews." Her theory was intended to resolve the larger question of how Qaraite heads of the Jews could govern the Rabbanite community, making legal decisions for it and appointing its judges. She answered on analogy with a later period, when the Rabbanite office claimed administrative control over the Qaraites and Samaritans but granted them jurisdiction over their own courts and religious affairs. The inverse, she suggested, was true during the earlier decades.

[78] Ibid., 259.

Beginnings of the Office

A certain overreliance on the explanatory power of top-down rule, government edicts, and continuous offices also characterized the first stages of research on the offices of Jewish leadership in Egypt. A series of late nineteenth- and early twentieth-century Geniza scholars argued that the Fatimids established the headship of the Jews on their conquest of Egypt. The most important of these was Jacob Mann, who attempted to account for the origins of the office of *ra'īs al-yahūd* by relying on an Ottoman Jewish literary tradition according to which the office was founded in the year 976–77 (366 AH), when the Abbasid caliph al-Ṭā'iʿ gave his daughter in marriage "to the king of Egypt"; she, in turn, called for the establishment of a Jewish leader in Egypt on the model of the exilarch in Iraq.[79] The tradition first appeared in a responsum by the Egyptian Jewish jurist David ibn Abī Zimra (1479–1573) and assumed more elaborate form in a chronicle by the Egyptian Jewish historian Yosef al-Sambarī (1640–1703).[80] In fact, no such marriage ever took place between an Abbasid princess and a "king of Egypt," and the marriage is one of many details that give the tradition the flavor of a foundation legend.[81] A host of earlier Jewish foundation myths set after some dynastic change also depict the old ruler personally granting the Jews the authority to run their own affairs. In the first century, Flavius Josephus depicted Alexander of Macedon bowing before the high priest at the Jerusalem temple, which in Josephus' day the Romans had just destroyed. The epistle of Natan ha-Bavli in the tenth-century embellished the ceremony of the installation of the Jewish exilarch with lavish details in order to model it on an Abbasid court in fact now steeply in decline. Medieval Ashkenazi sources reported Charlemagne himself to have granted the Jews of the Rhineland a charter of settlement.[82] Like these foundation myths, the Ibn Abī Zimra–Sambarī account drew heavily on the topos of a direct relationship between the highest ruler of the land and his Jew-

[79] Mann, *Jews in Egypt and in Palestine*, 1:251–52; for a detailed account of the historiography before and after Mann, see Cohen, *Jewish Self-Government*, 3–40.

[80] Shimon Shtober, "The Establishment of the Ri'āsat al-Yahūd in Medieval Egypt as Portrayed in the Chronicle Divrey Yosef: Myth or History?" *Revue des études juives* 164 (2005): 33–54, with part of the passage in question translated to English, 36–37; Hebrew original in idem, ed., *Sefer divrey Yosef by Yosef ben Yitzhak Sambari: Eleven Hundred Years of Jewish History under Muslim Rule* (Jerusalem, 1994), 138–41; see also Cohen's English translation, *Jewish Self-Government*, 7–9.

[81] As David Neustadt (later Ayalon) pointed out, al-Ṭā'iʿ himself (974–91) married the daughter of the Buyid *amīr al-umarā'*; see Neustadt, "Problems Concerning the 'Negidut' in Egypt during the Middle Ages," Hebrew, *Zion* 4 (1938–39): 126–49, and Shtober, "Establishment of the Ri'āsat al-Yahūd," 40.

[82] Flavius Josephus, *Antiquities of the Jews*, 11.8.5; for Natan's account, see Ben-Sasson, "Structure, Goals, and Content of the Story of Nathan Ha-Babli," 137–96; on the Charlemagne legends, see Ivan Marcus, "History, Story, and Collective Memory: Narrativity in Early Ashkenazic Culture," in *The Midrashic Imagination: Jewish Exegesis, Thought, and History*, ed. Michael Fishbane (Albany, 1993): 255–79; for an analysis of other foundation myths, see Franklin, "Shoots of David," chap. 6.

ish subjects.[83] Characteristically, the account received its fullest elaboration only after the Ottomans had abolished the office, for foundation myths are responses to ruptures and crises of continuity.

Mann recognized the problems with taking this story at face value. But instead of treating it skeptically, he presumed it to contain a kernel of truth and, in an attempt to link Jewish self-government to history outside the Jewish community, proposed that the Fatimids had established the headship of the Jews shortly after their conquest of Egypt, as a political move designed to make Egyptian Jews less dependent upon their leaders in Baghdad (who according to Mann were Abbasid appointees). Like his contemporary Ginzberg, Mann presumed that the initiative for Jewish self-government came from the state. In relying on the Ottoman account, he also projected the office in its late form, already shaped by the centralized control of the Mamluk state, back onto the more diffuse political conditions of the Fatimid period.[84]

The first to cast Mann's theory into doubt was David Neustadt (later Ayalon), who pointed out that the Egyptian Jewish account of the office's origins was a concoction of various Muslim and Jewish literary motifs. But it was Goitein and Cohen who dealt the theory a crippling blow with the help of a vast body of new evidence they uncovered from the Geniza. They established that the office had arisen not at the command of a Fatimid caliphate eager to establish the Jews' independence from Baghdad in the 960s, but organically among a coterie of Egyptian Jewish notables a century later. Unlike Mann, they made no attempt to fit the documentary sources into the literary accounts of the office; they abandoned the notion that the impetus for the office's establishment came from outside the Jewish community; and they realized that the title *nagid* and the office of *ra'īs al-yahūd* took independent courses.[85]

[83] This is what Yerushalmi has called "the myth of the royal alliance" in *The Lisbon Massacre of 1506 and the Royal Image in the Shebet Yehuda* (Cincinnati, 1976): xii; idem, "*Servants of Kings and not Servants of Servants": Some Aspects of the Political History of the Jews*, Tenenbaum Family Lecture Series in Judaic Studies at Emory University (Atlanta, 2007); cf. Baron, *Social and Religious History*^{2}, 9:135; and cf. Bareket, "'Ve-aruḥato aruḥat tamid nitena lo me-et ha-melekh': Rosh ha-yehudim be-arṣaot ha-Islam be-hishtaqefut kefula" ("A regular allotment of food was given him by order of the king": A reexamination of the head of the Jews in Islamic lands), *Devarim* 3 (2000): 35–48.

[84] Proponents of this theory furnished a candidate for the first bearer of the title of head of the Jews: an otherwise unattested Palṭi'el b. Shefaṭya, mentioned in the Scroll of Aḥima'aṣ, a hagiographic account of a southern Italian family with descendants in North Africa, composed around 1054. The scroll described Palṭi'el as a courtier in the entourage of the Fatimid caliphs in Ifrīqiya and during their conquest of Egypt; it also granted him the title *nagid*, probably on analogy with Ibn 'Aṭā. The text is preserved in a unicum in Toledo, Spain, and was first published by Neubauer in *Mediaeval Jewish Chronicles*, 2:111–32; edited with introduction and English translation in Marcus Salzman, *The Chronicle of Ahimaaz*, Columbia University Oriental Studies 18 (New York, 1924); and reedited with annotations by Benjamin Klar, *Megillat Ahima'as*, 2d rev. ed. (Jerusalem, 1974). For an exhaustive analysis see Bernard Lewis, "Palṭiel: A Note," *Bulletin of the School of Oriental and African Studies* 30 (1967): 177–81.

[85] Neustadt, "Problems Concerning the 'Negidat;'" Goitein, "The Title and Office of the Nagid: A Re-Examination," *Jewish Quarterly Review* 53 (1962): 93–119; Cohen, *Jewish self-Government.*

Goitein argued that, during the richly documented decades prior to 1065, Fustat abounded with Jewish grandees who wielded authority both at the caliph's court and among the Jews, but not a single one of them acted as a principal, chief, sole, or central authority. The Jewish grandees of Fustat "used their influential position to protect or promote their brethren during this first century of Fatimid rule," but in no Geniza source "is it stated that these powerful men had any official standing in the community." For Goitein, the only official high position in the Jewish community was that of the Palestinian *ga'on*. In arguing against Mann's theory and taking a primarily inductive approach to the problem of Jewish leadership, however, Goitein still relied on the pyramidal model of Jewish self-government: anyone besides the *ga'on* who exercised power in the community, he argued, did so strictly on an unofficial basis.[86]

Cohen traced the evolution of the office of *ra'īs al-yahūd* as it took its first halting steps in Fustat in the final decades of the eleventh century and grew to maturity in the first decades of the twelfth. He vastly increased the documentary basis of Goitein's thesis; he detailed the steps by which Rabbanite notables in Fustat in the 1060s gradually amassed the office's prerogatives and only later solicited ratification for the position from the chancery in Cairo and, by the 1080s, independence from the Palestinian *ga'on*.

Cohen further explained why the 1060s had been the crucial turning point for the office's establishment by extrapolating from parallel developments within the Coptic church. In a move critical to Fatimid foreign policy, the military vizier Badr al-Jamālī, who ran the empire during the last quarter of the eleventh century, transferred the seat of the Coptic patriarchate from Alexandria to Cairo. Because the Copts controlled church appointments in Nubia and Abyssinia, bringing the Coptic patriarch to the capital helped the vizier exert tighter control over the southern borders of the empire. Though Cohen found no evidence that the vizier had intended to do the same with the Jews in Syria, he nonetheless tried to imagine how the Jews might have regarded the transfer of the patriarch to the capital. "Egyptian Jewry could not have been unaware of what was transpiring in the other segment of the non-Muslim community," Cohen wrote. "Quite conceivably, the Jewish *kātib*s [courtiers], along with Jews outside the halls of government, concluded that it was essential to have their own titular and administrative chief located in the Fatimid court, next to his Christian counterpart. At the very minimum, it seems reasonable to assume that at a time when the ruler of Egypt was pressing the head of the Egyptian Christian minority to present himself regularly at court, his Jewish counterpart would have been subject to the same demand,

[86] Goitein, "Title and Office of the Nagid"; 99–101; idem, *Mediterranean Society*, 2:29–30.

and for similar reasons."[87] Whether or not the Fatimids explicitly encouraged the Jews to install their own chief at court, the Jewish leaders of Fustat possessed other motives for doing so. Fustat fell into a protracted crisis between 1054 and 1072, a period plagued by low Niles, famine, and disease, dubbed in the medieval histories "the crisis [alternately: disaster] of al-Mustanṣir's reign." Circumstances were hardly propitious for regular contact between Egyptian Jews and the Jerusalem *yeshiva*. The Jewish notables of Fustat, who had earlier clamored for independence, now saw a chance to break away from Palestine.

Meanwhile, the *yeshiva* began moving farther away from Cairo. The Seljuks conquered Jerusalem in 1073, and the *yeshiva* escaped northward to Tyre, thereby leaving the Fatimid orbit altogether (Tyre was then under the control of a rebel Sunnī *qāḍī*, Ibn Abī ʿAqīl, who in 1070 began paying tribute to the Seljuks). Tyre remained an independent city-state until 1089 and the *yeshiva* stayed there even longer, until the Crusader conquests forced it eastward to Damascus. Meanwhile in the south, the Jewish leaders of Fustat, itching to escape the central control of the ever-receding *yeshiva*, sought ratification for their *raʾīs* from the Fatimid chancery. They were granted it, and the office was transformed from the product of a few strong leaders and propitious circumstances into a permanent feature of Egyptian Jewish life until it was abolished by the Ottomans. The Crusader conquests followed on the heels of its establishment and turned Egypt into the undisputed center of Jewish administrative life. By 1127, the very gaonate of Palestine would merge with the office of *raʾīs al-yahūd* and continue for centuries under both names.[88]

The Geniza has not yet yielded evidence that before the 1060s anyone other than the *gaʾon* exercised power over the Jewish community as defined by recognizable privileges attached to some official post. But while Goitein and Cohen convincingly answered the question of how a coterie of Rabbanite notables had created the office of *raʾīs al-yahūd*, they did not consider the role of the Qaraites, which was indispensable. A century of cooperative leadership had tilled the soil in which an office governing the tripartite Jewish community took root. Precisely because that cooperation was informal and voluntary, it invites the historian to widen the scope of the investigation to include all Jews, and not just those governed by a supposedly autonomous rabbinic leadership.

THE SHAPE OF JEWISH LEADERSHIP IN THE ELEVENTH CENTURY

Both substantively and methodologically, then, one cannot hope to explain how Jewish leadership evolved during the first century of Fatimid rule

[87] Cohen, *Jewish Self-Government*, 77.

[88] In Geniza letters starting in 1127, incumbents of the office use both titles; see ibid., 291. On the date of the Seljuk conquest of Jerusalem, see chap. 12, n. 16.

by searching the Geniza for a set of institutions. Nor can one explain Rabbanite-Qaraite cooperation this way. What shaped both phenomena was the loose, formal-yet-informal nature of politics in a society in which individual relationships were binding while relations among groups were informal and more fluid; where individual ties were durable and retained a more definite shape over time than ties among groups.

The shape of Jewish communal leadership in the eleventh century was not pyramidal. Sources of authority were multiple. Systems of leadership were continually renegotiated. Titles became inflated and finally useless and were retired, and new ones were introduced in their place. Prerogatives attached to an office and detached from it depending on the power of its incumbent and the number of rivals vying for it. Jewish leaders were connected to the Fatimid government not at a single point via the *ga'on*, but at multiple points—via the *ga'on*, the head of the Jewish congregations in Fustat, Jewish courtiers, and local Fatimid administrators. The Qaraites were prominent among the last two groups, and their presence suggests the possibility of rethinking the shape of the medieval Jewish community without presuming where its borders lay or where its members imagined them to lie.

PART II

RABBANITES, QARAITES, AND THE POLITICS OF LEADERSHIP

CHAPTER FOUR
QARAITES AND THE POLITICS OF POWERLESSNESS

The Qaraites of the late tenth century offer us wildly contradictory testimonies about their relationship to Rabbanites. Many authors of what was later enshrined as the "golden age" of Qaraite literature presented themselves to posterity as the weak and persecuted victims of rabbinic tormentors. They understate their own power and overstate that of the Rabbanites; yet they also betray a certain political shrewdness and an understanding of the role politics could play in determining the balance of power between the two parties. In cases where Qaraites couch their claims of Rabbanite oppression in social and institutional terms, a naively positivist reading might suggest that the first decades of Fatimid rule in Palestine were a period of Qaraite powerlessness. But since the Geniza permits us to reconstruct the wider context in which those polemics were written, another reading is possible. While the "golden age" authors were writing in Jerusalem, Qaraites in Fustat, Ramla, and Damascus were running Fatimid bureaus and administering entire provinces. The close political alliances between Qaraites and Rabbanites in the 1020s, in fact, had their roots in the second half of the tenth century, a period usually seen as one of bitter internecine strife.

"THEY STRUCK ME, BRUISED ME, AND STRIPPED MY MANTLE FROM ME"

One Qaraite author, Yefet b. ʿEli (Abu l-Ḥasan b. ʿAlī al-Baṣrī, d. ca. 1004), contributed much to the perception that the tenth century opened an ever-widening and increasingly unbridgeable rift between Qaraites and Rabbanites.[1]

[1] On the question of Yefet's dates, see Frank, *Search Scripture Well*, 14 n. 55, and Polliack, *Karaite Tradition of Arabic Bible Translation*, 37 n. 2, both with references to previous discussions.

Yefet was raised in Baṣra in Iraq, and like many others of his generation, migrated westward. That the goal of his migration was Jerusalem rather than Damascus, Ramla, or Fustat already signaled his separatism. The works he wrote there paint the Qaraites as a group of ascetics with special claims to religious expertise. He also became the first individual, named Jewish author to compose a commentary on every book of the Hebrew Bible, and in so doing, created a handbook of Qaraite opposition to rabbinic tradition. At times, Yefet refutes rabbinic biblical exegesis nearly point by point, presuming an audience familiar with rabbinic tradition. He also quotes the Talmud and the rabbinic tradition of paraphrastic Aramaic Bible translations (*targumim*). We can assume he possessed more than merely a passing familiarity with rabbinic learning.[2]

Yefet's commentary on Song of Songs is one such handbook-like work offered to his readers as a store of anti-Rabbanite argumentation. The lover's lyrical description of his beloved as "a lily among thorns" in Yefet's hands trumpets the Qaraites' righteousness and his belief in their role as harbingers of redemption. Salmon b. Yeroḥam's polemic *Wars of the Lord* (ca. 955) had called the entire Qaraite community "the congregation of the Lily" (*'adat ha-shoshana*); but Yefet developed that ideology along the lines of messianic prognostication, commenting (on Song of Songs 2:1) that while the earlier Qaraites were the narcissus that blossoms briefly in winter, the current generation were the lilies that flower in the spring of Israel's salvation. The commentary is, then, both a dialogue with the rabbinic exegetical tradition and a deliberate departure from it. Various rabbinic midrash collections and commentaries had understood the beloved's increasingly desperate pursuit of her lover (Song of Songs 4, 6, and 7) as personifying Israel's love of God; for Yefet, the lover is still God, but the beloved is not Israel but the Qaraites. Yefet follows the classical rabbis in reading the Song as an allegory of Jewish collective self-representation, but for him it represents the Qaraites alone.[3]

Still failing to find out where her lover has gone, the beloved runs miserably afoul of the watchmen over the walls of the city: "The watchmen making their rounds in the city found me," she says; "the guardians of the city walls struck me and bruised me and stripped my mantle from me" (5:7). The watchmen not only beat her; they are brutish and torpid enough to ask her, "What is thy

[2] Frank, *Search Scripture Well*, 145–64; idem, "Karaite Commentaries on the Song of Songs from Tenth-century Jerusalem," in *With Reverence for the Word: Medieval Scriptural Exegesis in Judaism, Christianity, and Islam*, ed. Jane Dammen McAuliffe et al. (Oxford, 2003), 51–69. On Yefet's familiarity with rabbinic literature, see Ofra Tirosh-Becker, "The Use of Rabbinic Sources in Karaite Writings," in Polliack, ed., *Karaite Judaism*, 319–38, with reference to previous studies.

[3] For Yefet on Song of Songs, see Frank, "Karaite Commentaries on the Song of Songs," 58; idem, *Search Scripture Well*, 17, 161–66; Salmon b. Yeroḥam in Israel Davidson, ed., *The Book of the Wars of the Lord: Containing the Polemics of the Karaite Salmon ben Yeruhim against Saadia Gaon* (New York, 1934), 37, line 47; English translation in Nemoy, *Karaite Anthology*, 73 (and see 341, note to line 12).

beloved more than another beloved?" (5:9). While the rabbinic tradition had read the watchmen as Persian Achaemenid officials ruling over the Israelites in exile (cf. Ezra 5), for Yefet, the watchmen were the Rabbanites.[4] Yefet thus takes the border that rabbinic tradition had placed between the Jews and the nations and, instead, places it between the Qaraites and the Rabbanites.

He also seizes the opportunity to polemicize against the *ge'onim* and exilarchs. "'The watchmen,'" he says, "refer to the rabbinic judges and scholars who go around the region collecting pledges," the form in which the Jews of Iraq, Iran, and elsewhere rendered their donations. These "rabbinic judges and scholars" seem to be the loyalists of the *yeshivot*; later he says the "watchmen of the walls" are "the exilarchs and *ge'onim* [*ru'asā' al-jawālīth wa-l-mathā'ib*] who ensure that the people observe their customs and inventions [*mawḍu'āt;* one might translate this as 'invented traditions'] and do not permit anyone to break with them." In both instances, Yefet engages the question of religious power directly, attributing to these "watchmen" "the power to command, to prohibit, and to scrutinize people's affairs."[5] He also engages it in a way that exceeds even the most adamant of Rabbanite apologists, presenting rabbinic authority as nearly absolute. Even *Sefer ha-qabbala* (1160–61), the triumphalist history of the unbroken succession of the rabbinate by Avraham ibn Dāwūd (d. ca. 1180), which aimed among other things at refuting Qaraism, admitted that some time between 960 and 990—precisely in Yefet's day—"the income of the [Babylonian] academies, which used to come from [all over the Mediterranean], was discontinued," and the links between the center and the peripheries were ruptured never to be repaired.[6] For Yefet, the *ge'onim* and exilarchs still received income from their followers and exercised "the power to command, to prohibit, and to scrutinize people's affairs."

Indeed, Yefet describes the beloved's encounter with the watchmen on their rounds in nearly inquisitorial terms. When the Rabbanite "watchmen" find the Qaraite seekers, they interrogate them "about their disagreement over festivals and customs." The Qaraites retort with another verse of the beloved (3:3): "Have *you* seen the one my soul loves?!" What had been an innocent question

[4] Frank, "Karaite Commentaries on the Song of Songs," 59 (at n. 79).

[5] I am grateful to Daniel Frank for kindly bringing this passage to my attention before he published it. Yefet b. 'Eli al-Baṣrī, *Commentary on Song of Songs* 5:7, BL Or. 2513.73b and 2 Firk. Heb.-Arab. 3869, edited in Frank, *Search Scripture Well*, 297–98 (with English translation on 162–63, from which I have deviated slightly; second manuscript number given there as I.13869); the latter manuscript also edited in Mann, *Texts and Studies*, 2:89–90 (but not attributed to Yefet). See also Frank, "Karaite Commentaries on the Song of Songs," 59 and Jean Joseph Léandre Bargès, *In Canticum canticorum commentarium arabicum, quod ex unico Bibliothecae nationalis parisiensis manuscripto codice in lucem edidit atque in linguam latinam transtulit* (Paris, 1884); this passage on 73–74. Rabbinic judges and scholars: *al-dayyānim wa-beney berav al-ḥaverim*. For pledges, Yefet uses the word *fasā'iq*, an Arabicized plural of the Aramaic *pisqā*.

[6] Cohen, *Sefer ha-qabbalah*, 63 (Hebrew), 46 (English). For more on the author and the chronicle, see below, chap. 5, 134–36, chap. 7, 231–35, and Epilogue, 353–54.

in the mouth of the beloved becomes an indictment of rabbinic negligence: if *you* haven't seen the one my soul loves, then I must find him myself. Since "*you* do not have knowledge of what God, may He be exalted, has commanded by way of obligations in His law or of what He has forbidden and permitted, then how is it possible for *us* not to investigate it and act according to what it contains? And when [the Rabbanites] heard this answer from [the Qaraite seekers]," Yefet continues, "they knew that [the Qaraites] had broken with their injunctions and prohibitions and laws." For Yefet, the Qaraites parted company from an oppressive rabbinic establishment (the verb he uses is *kharaja*, to depart—a common one among Arabic heresiographers describing religious schools breaking with the mainstream).[7]

And so the Rabbanite watchmen punish the Qaraites for their secession. The watchmen "hastened to strike [the Qaraites]," he continues, "so that they would not differ from them and spoil the entire people on their account. It is widely known that wherever the Qaraites have appeared in the lands of the exile, these things have befallen them, and that is why [the verse] says, 'They struck me and bruised me' [the Judeo-Arabic gloss on these words follows]. This should be interpreted literally: they lashed and imprisoned them, and exposed them to all manner of mockery. And this is the doing of the 'watchmen.'" With the charge of lashings and imprisonments, Yefet invites these lines to be understood as a representation of the world around him, adding historical ballast to an otherwise allegorical account of persecution. How seriously can we take his claims?

Lashing is indeed one of the punishments rabbinic sources prescribed against those who broke certain commandments, but Jewish religious authorities in the Middle Ages were restricted in the types of punishments they could mete out, and in the Islamic East, under both the Abbasids and the Fatimids, lashing and imprisonment were privileges of the state. The Persian master of Arabic letters ʿUthmān al-Jāḥiẓ (d. 869) had observed that, "since the [Nestorian] *katholikos* and the [Jewish] exilarch are not allowed [to impose] either imprisonment or flagellation within the Islamic realm, they can only impose fines and prohibit discourse [*taḥrīm al-kalām*]," that is, impose the ban of excommunication. Thus the Abbasids had strictly limited *dhimmī* powers of enforcement. As for the Fatimids, the extant list of prerogatives presented to the chancery on behalf of the Jerusalem *ga'on* in 1036 mentions the ban of excommunication, but nothing of lashings or imprisonment. Yefet, then, holds a more sanguine view of rabbinic authority than other sources permit us to do. In fact, the only way the Rabbanites could lash and imprison the Qaraites was to denounce them to the government—a scenario Yefet goes on to depict: the

[7] Most famously, this is how the name of the Muslim Kharijites was commonly understood; see also below, Epilogue, 351, citing Moshe ibn ʿEzra, who applies the epithet to the Qaraite Abu l-Faraj Hārūn.

Rabbanites "do all this to [the Qaraites]," he writes, "lest the latter spoil their community on their account. Perhaps they even have slandered them before the [Muslim] rulers so that they might kill them. These are the deeds of the 'watchmen of the walls.'" But even Yefet admits that he has no evidence for this claim ("perhaps").[8]

He goes on to embellish the claims of powerlessness and persecution in his gloss on "they took my mantle from me," which, he says, "refers to removing their veil, when [the Rabbanite leaders] insult them and do not permit the community to visit them on the occasion of a circumcision or a happy or sad occasion." The removal of one's mantle or veil is a mark of shame; similar allusions make frequent appearances in petitions from the poor, who describe their disgrace in begging for sustenance as an act of "uncovering the face."[9] This line suggests that the Rabbanites have robbed the Qaraites of their rightful place as custodians of the true biblical law and that they have done so through the sheer exertion of the power to regulate public behavior.

What polemical advantage might a Qaraite have found in the claim of being subjected to punishment, of powerlessness, and of having left the mainstream? Yefet's Iraqi predecessor al-Qirqisānī chose to put it the other way around, claiming that the Rabbanites had broken away from the true meaning of the law, while the Qaraites eventually restored it. This is the more rational position. But Yefet was following a different polemical tradition, echoing Salmon b. Yeroḥam, for whom "the Qaraite people of the book seceded from the authority of the rabbinical scholars." For Salmon, independence from religious leadership was such a paramount value that he claimed that the Qaraites had not only "left the jurisdiction [*ri'āsa*] of the Rabbanites" but even taken it upon themselves "not to have a leader [*rayyis*] in the time of exile, as God said, 'For they remained many days without prince or king'" (Hosea 3:4).[10] Yet in Salmon's

[8] ʿUthmān al-Jāḥiẓ, *Kitāb al-ḥayawān* (The animals), ed. A. M. Hārūn (Cairo, 1966), 4:2; see Mann, *The Responsa of the Babylonian Geonim as a Source of Jewish History* (New York, 1917), 335–36 and 360–61; and Gil, *History of Palestine*, sec. 757. The question of gaonic power to administer corporal punishment (and therefore corroboration of al-Jāḥiẓ's statement) is complicated by the fact that the *ge'onim* issued contradictory statements on the matter; in practice, Jewish authorities nearly everywhere depended on the state to enforce laws with anything heavier than the ban. See further Goitein, *Mediterranean Society*, 2:330, 551, and 599; idem, *Palestinian Jewry*, 350; and Baron, *Jewish Community*, 2:220–36. For parallels between the use of excommunication by Jewish authorities and Nestorian *katholikoi* of the seventh, eighth and ninth centuries, see Mann, *Responsa of the Babylonian Geonim*, 336–37; and cf. Goitein's plea for a reexamination of the question of the gaonic ban of excommunication in comparison with contemporary Nestorian methods, *Mediterranean Society*, 2:333. The privileges of the Palestinian *ga'on* are stated in Halper 354, verso.

[9] Cohen, *Poverty and Charity*, 41–44.

[10] Judeo-Arab. "wa-lidhālik kān ahl al-kitāb beney miqra' yish[merem] ṣ[uram] kharajū ʿan ri'āsat beney berav, wa-alzamū nafsahum an lā yakun lahum rayyis fī zamān al-jalūt, ka-qaw[l] allāh taʿā[lā] ki yamim rabbim yashvu yisra'el eyn melekh va-eyn sar." Salmon b. Yeroḥam, *Commentary on Psalms* (from MS 1 Firk. 556), in Pinsker, *Lickute kadmoniot*, appendix 2, 51 n. 2, and Mann, *Texts and Studies*, 2:84.

day, the Qaraites did indeed have a leader from the line of the *nesi'im*, whose Davidic ancestry represented nothing less than a claim to kingship. By Yefet's day, they also had courtiers in the service of prince and king. For both writers, the needs of rhetoric overrode those of verisimilitude. Rhetoric demanded that they speak in terms at once self-marginalizing and self-aggrandizing, as persecuted innovators. The more monolithically they pained Rabbanite power, the clearer the statement they made on behalf of Qaraite identity. (Reciprocally, rabbinic tradition would equate much anti-Rabbanism with Qaraism.)[11] Concrete events—excommunications, lashings, and secessions—served the Qaraite polemicists of the Jerusalem school as convenient hooks on which to hang broader polemical claims.

QARAITES AND THE KINGDOM OF ISHMAEL

Yefet's admission that the state played some role in Rabbanite-Qaraite conflict betrays a certain political sophistication, as does his insistence on Qaraite powerlessness. Other Qaraite authors agreed that the state had a role to play in the outcome of Israel's history, and repeatedly invoked the state's role in determining the balance of power between the Rabbanites and Qaraites. They were not, however, unanimous as to whether the state served the interests of the Qaraites or the Rabbanites. Individual commentators themselves even issued contradictory opinions on the matter.[12]

Al-Qūmisī set the standard for self-contradiction. In his commentary on Daniel, he praised the Muslims for allowing the Jews to resettle in Jerusalem after their banishment by the Romans; the Ishmaelites "assigned them a quarter in which many from among Israel settled, and now Israel comes from the four ends of the earth to Jerusalem to study and pray."[13] In the sermon discussed in chapter 2, he also encouraged his listeners to take advantage of the array of political forces by moving to Palestine, suggesting that the Muslims especially favored the Qaraites because both determined the months through empirical observation of the new moon. "Since the beginning of the exile," he said in a justly famous passage,

[11] Rustow, "Karaites Real and Imagined."

[12] Nor can one dismiss the contradictions as a function of audience: Many criticisms of the role of the state were conveyed in works written or copied in Arabic script and thus easily accessible to Muslims, while some of the most adulatory remarks were written in Hebrew for a Jewish readership. See the comments in Ben-Shammai, "The Attitude of Some Early Karaites towards Islam," in *Studies in Medieval Jewish History and Literature*, ed. Isadore Twersky (Cambridge, Mass., 1984), 7–8. His discussion focuses on Qaraite attitudes to Islam as a religion, while the present one is restricted to Qaraite attitudes toward the state.

[13] T-S 10 C 2.2, fol. 1v (on Daniel 11:32).

the Rabbanites were princes [*sarim*] and judges, in the days of the kingdom of Greece, the kingdom of the Romans and the Persian Magians, and those who sought the Torah could not open their mouths with the commandments of the Lord out of fear of the rabbis . . . until the arrival of the kingdom of Ishmael, since they always help the Qaraites to observe the Torah of Moses, and we must bless them [for it]. Now you are amidst the kingdom of Ishmael, and they favor those who observe the month according to the new moon. Why, then, do you fear the rabbis? . . . For by means of the kingdom of Ishmael God broke the rod of the rabbis from upon you.[14]

The key to interpreting this passage lies in the last sentence, usually omitted from modern citations of this section of al-Qūmisī's sermon. Ishmael, al-Qūmisī suggests, is nothing but an instrument in divine hands. This is the classic Deuteronomistic and Isaianic view that the nations other than Israel serve as a means to punish or reward God's chosen people. These points are made even more clearly in al-Qūmisī's other works.

Did al-Qūmisī really imagine that Ishmael loved the Qaraites so much? Elsewhere, in fact, he complained that Muslims oppressed the Jews and accused Islam of superficial monotheism and secret idolatry. In a prognostic commentary on the book of Daniel that Mann discovered in the Cambridge Geniza collections, al-Qūmisī outlines the history of Christian and Muslim rule over Israel. He first expresses awe at the extent of the Islamic state—"Who can recite the provinces of their dominion?"—but immediately after, on the verse "And the king shall do according to his will; and he shall exalt himself, and magnify himself above every god, and shall speak strange things against the God of gods; and he shall prosper till the indignation be accomplished; for that which is determined shall be done" (Daniel 11:36), al-Qūmisī has this to say: "Deceit will prosper in [Ishmael's] hand and his kingdom will endure 'until indignation is accomplished,' that is, until the end of exile. For nobody after [Ishmael] will hold dominion until the coming of the Messiah.'"[15] For al-Qūmisī, then, the Arab conquests were nothing more than a harbinger of the end, the final, brutal kingdom that announces the messianic fulfillment of time. This was in keeping with the wider ancient and medieval tradition of prognostication based on Daniel's prophecy of the four kingdoms, but al-Qūmisī was one of the first to update the chronology and introduce Ishmael, rather than Rome and Byzantium, as the "fourth kingdom" (Daniel 11:2), the final epoch. These contradictory opinions, then, only serve al-Qūmisī's larger argument that Islam is the instrument of God's providence toward Israel.[16]

[14] Daniel al-Qūmisī's sermon: Bodl. MS Heb. d 36.13–18, here fols. 17r–17v.

[15] T-S 10 C 2.1, fol. 2r. See also Ben-Shammai, "Attitude of Some Early Karaites," 11.

[16] For references, see ibid., 8, 10; on al-Qūmisī and the four empires, see Cohen, *Sefer ha-qabbalah*, 235 n. 62, 237–38. There is a vast bibliography on the four empires; the classic discussion is Joseph Ward Swain, "The Theory of the Four Monarchies: Opposition History under the Roman Empire,"

With that in mind, one can rethink al-Qūmisī's apparent claim that Muslims favored the Qaraites over the Rabbanites because they practiced lunar observation. He had a larger point to make about Ishmael, and it was not that Ishmael loved the Qaraites, but that the Jews in diaspora should be persuaded of the advantages of life in Palestine (you will escape the reach of the Iraqi *ge'onim*) and of lunar observation (the rulers will reward you for it). We cannot conclude from here that al-Qūmisī loved the state, that the state loved the Qaraites, that Muslims approved of Qaraite methods of calendation, or that they even knew of them. Al-Qūmisī offered this claim strictly in the service of his exegetical and rhetorical concerns, which overrode the needs of verisimilitude. Regarding the appearance of the new moon, al-Qūmisī is reported to have permitted the testimony of Muslims, whom he elsewhere excoriated as hypocrites and liars in religious matters. Such are the politics of persuasion: when one wishes to raise an issue to prominence above all the others, one makes do with strange bedfellows.[17]

Salmon b. Yeroḥam (ca. 955) and David b. Avraham al-Fāsī (late tenth century) also appeared friendly toward the government, expressing their gratitude to the Muslim conquerors for allowing the Jews access to Jerusalem and for their general patronage as rulers. Salmon historicized: "When the Byzantines—by the grace of the God of Israel—departed from [Jerusalem] and there appeared the reign of Ishmael, then they allowed the Israelites to have access [to it] and to live [there] and handed the courtyards of the Temple over to them; and there they recited prayer for many years."[18] Yet elsewhere, Salmon laments the condition of the Temple Mount, complaining that "As for Ishmael, there is no limit to their brutality and harshness." As particularly annoying, he singled out the verbal humiliations to which the Muslims of Khurasān subjected the Jews (Yefet would later complain of the same), but then confessed that nothing was more annoying than the Rabbanites: "The humiliation [that I endure] from my coreligionists," he wrote, "is more difficult for me than [what I suffer] from the nations [*goyim*], because the nations are the enemies of God and Israel, while these [Rabbanites] share with us both religion [*dīn*] and genealogy [*nasab*]." Salmon's complaint reflects what Freud termed "the narcissism of minor differences," wherein precisely those who are closest to one another—territorially, ideologically, genealogically—struggle

---

Classical Philology 35 (1940): 1–21; see also Arnaldo Momigliano, "The Origins of Universal History," *Annali della Scuola Normale Superiore di Pisa*, 3rd ser. 12 (1982): 533–60; David Flusser, "The Four Empires in the Fourth Sibyl and in the Book of Daniel," in idem, *Judaism and the Origins of Christianity* (Jerusalem, 1988), 317–44; and on al-Qūmisī's literary predecessors and context, Yosef Yahalom, "The Transition of Kingdoms in Eretz Israel (Palestine) as Conceived by Poets and Homilists" (Hebrew), *Shalem* 6 (1992): 1–22.

[17] Ben-Shammai, "Attitude of Some Early Karaites," 12 (citing al-Qirqisānī); and 12–14 (on hypocrisy and lies).

[18] Salmon b. Yeroḥam, commentary on Psalms 2:18, in Mann, *Texts and Studies*, 2:18.

most to differentiate themselves. But it also reflects more than this: a kind of polemical opportunism that turned the target of the moment into the worst possible offender.[19]

The historian must weigh individual statements of this kind against its authors' wider oeuvre. They must also be weighed on the balance of accumulating rhetorical tradition. Subsequent Qaraites served not only the argument itself but also the tradition of their teachers.[20] Thus Salmon's younger contemporary al-Fāsī delivered himself of screeds against the religion in whose name the Muslims conquered Jerusalem, but also wrote that "from the time when there arose the kingdom of Ishmael, the Israelites experienced a great peace, in that [Ishmael] protected them and they [the Israelites] lived in their shadow. Then they obtained the possibility of access to Jerusalem, to make their prayer in front of the Temple."[21] Note the language of patronage: dwelling in the "shadow" of a more powerful person is one of the standard tropes of requests for private aid, which suggests that Qaraites could also be quite content with their subjection as *dhimmī*s when it served them.

Yefet's contemporary Abu l-Surrī Sahl b. Maṣliaḥ also proffered a nearly messianic evaluation of the advent of Islamic rule, which had brought "his nation" permission to build places in Jerusalem for "reading and expounding and praying at any time and setting up night-watches."[22] Yet elsewhere, he decried Muslim rule and—like Yefet—accused the Rabbanites of siding with the state in seeking its intervention against the Qaraites. The Rabbanites, Sahl claimed, had imposed the ban on the Qaraites and turned the government against them; he does not accuse them of lashing or imprisoning the Qaraites, as Yefet had, but only of "making themselves mighty and exhibiting excessive pride and lording it over [the Qaraites] with anathema and ban of excommunication and [resort to] the non-Jewish government."[23]

Yefet was characteristically darker and more irascible, painting state power as a looming, evil presence that took the side of the Rabbanites in intracommunal conflicts. He called Islam a false religion "that nonetheless claims that its dominion [*dawla*] will endure" (he is no kinder to Christianity), and elsewhere decried the harsh measures imposed on *dhimmī*s, "such as wearing distinctive clothing [*ghiyār*] and the belt [*zunnār*] and the prohibition against

[19] For textual references, see Ben-Shammai, "Attitude of Some Early Karaites," 10 and 11 n. 32. Sigmund Freud, *Civilization and its Discontents*, in *The Standard Edition of the Complete Psychological Works of Sigmund Freud*, ed. and trans. James Strachey, 24 vols. (London, 1957), 21:114.

[20] This observation is indebted to Ben-Shammai, "Attitude of Some Early Karaites."

[21] Quoted in Chiesa, *Emergence of Hebrew Biblical Pointing*, 42.

[22] Sahl b. Maṣliaḥ's epistle; see Harkavy, *Me'assef niddaḥim: meqorot be-toldot Yisra'el u-ve-sifruto*, 199.

[23] Heb. "mitgaddelim u-mitge'im u-mitgabberim 'aleyhem be-nidduy u-ve-ḥerem u-ve-shilṭey ha-nokhrim." Sahl's epistle in Pinsker, *Lickute Kadmoniot*, 2:31. Mann connects this passage with Yefet's commentary on Song of Songs 5:7: *Texts and Studies*, 2:90 n. 117.

riding horses, and similar well known [statutes]. Their aim is to humiliate Israel."[24] The statutes of the Pact of ʿUmar, which offered Christians and by extension all *dhimmīs* protection only if they remained visibly subservient to their Muslim patrons, explicitly required them to wear the *zunnār*.[25] But Geniza evidence stresses precisely the opposite: except for the period of al-Ḥākim (996–1021), Jews hardly ever wore the *ghiyār*, and as Goitein emphasizes, among innumerable references in Geniza sources to clothing and dress during the Fatimid and early Ayyubid periods, "nowhere do we meet . . . any allusion to a specific Jewish attire. On the contrary, there is much indirect evidence that there was none."[26] But for Yefet, Islamic rule and its oppression serve an apocalyptic purpose. Like the Syrian border skirmishes with Byzantium, which hinted at the wars of Gog and Magog, they were a sign of the end.[27]

I am, then, doubtful of the possibility of reading any of these statements as reflecting some general attitude of Qaraites toward caliphs, caliphs toward Qaraites, or Qaraites and Rabbanites toward each other. Each statement was conditioned by its own literary and polemical context, and should be judged on rhetorical considerations and against other evidence. But I do not think that it would be unduly positivistic to suggest that these contradictory attitudes toward the kingdom of Ishmael nonetheless share a common denominator: each author chose to make his point, whatever it happened to be, by invoking the power of the state. They all reflect the awareness that the state could potentially play a role in internal Jewish conflicts and in empowering one group within the Jewish community over the other.

WERE THERE TOO MANY JEWISH COURTIERS UNDER THE FATIMIDS?

Qaraites in other precincts, too, understood well the role of the state in Jewish politics. In the first century or so of Fatimid rule in Egypt, a large number of Qaraite government functionaries (*kuttāb*; sing. *kātib*) served in the *dīwāns* (bureaus), at court, and in the provincial administration. Between the Fatimid conquest of Egypt in 969 and the loss of much of Syria to the First Crusade in

[24] Yefet on Psalms 5:11, quoted in Frank, *Search Scripture Well*, 208 n. 16; on Isaiah 47:9–10, translated in Ben-Shammai, "Attitude of Some Early Karaites," 16–17 (more generally on Yefet, see 15–20); I have slightly altered his translation. On the *ghiyār* and *zunnār*, see *EI*² s.vv. (Moshe Perlmann and A. S. Tritton).

[25] On the Pact, see below, n. 32.

[26] Goitein, *Mediterranean Society*, 2:286. See the additional works cited in Yaacov Lev, "Persecutions and Conversion to Islam in Eleventh-century Egypt," *Asian and African Studies* 22 (1988): 77 n. 20, who notes that the *ghiyār* "as prescribed by the law was rarely enforced in the period prior to al-Ḥākim's persecutions," i.e., the period of Yefet.

[27] See the passages quoted in Ankori, *Karaites in Byzantium*, 77–78, 88–89 n. 7, 93–95.

1100, roughly thirty Jews served in high positions, eleven of whom were Qaraites. This is one of the factors that lent relations between the groups its particular tenor of political charge, cooperation, and irresolution during this period.

Numerous modern historians have put forward the notion that there was a disproportionate number of *dhimmīs* among the Fatimid *kuttāb*. They explain this on a mixture of strategic and ideological considerations, holding that the Shīʿī dynasty was eager to offset the Sunnī majority over whom it ruled by sowing the ranks of its administration with Jews and Christians, who as a group were vulnerable, dependent on the high rulers, and therefore more likely to serve the caliphate loyally.[28] But if it was good strategy to appoint religious minorities to government posts, then appointing Christians, at least, was not a good strategy: while the majority of Muslims in Egypt and Syria were Sunnīs and may indeed have felt disenfranchised by Shīʿī rule, Christians of various churches probably outnumbered Sunnīs at the beginning of the Fatimid period.[29] During the entire two centuries of Fatimid rule in Egypt, moreover, more Ismāʿīlīs (some of them converted Jews and Christians) served the regime as viziers than members of any denomination of any religion; and more Sunnīs were appointed to the office than converted Christians and Jews combined.[30]

What these historians really seem to mean by a "disproportionate" number of Christians and Jews is not the number serving in office as compared to their numbers in the general population (after all, the Fatimid state was not a representative institution) but as compared with the number in office under other dynasties. But given how few Islamic dynasties there had been to this point and the vastly differing nature of the societies over whom they ruled, there is no

[28] See, for example, Stillman, *Jews of Arab Lands*, 50, perhaps on partial analogy with the analysis of medieval Iberia in Baron, *Social and Religious History*[2], 4:36–43; cf. Leila S. al-Imad, *The Fatimid Vizierate, 969–1172* (Berlin, 1990), 75–76; and Goitein, *Mediterranean Society*, 2:345, according to whom "non-Muslim minorities during the Fatimid and most of the Ayyubid periods were represented in the entourage of the rulers and the administration of the state in numbers out of all proportion to their sizes."

[29] On the proportion of Muslims in Fatimid Egypt, see I. M. Lapidus, "The Conversion of Egypt to Islam," *Israel Oriental Studies* 2 (1972): 248–62; Michael Brett, "The Spread of Islam in Egypt and North Africa," in idem, ed., *Northern Africa: Islam and Modernization* (London, 1973), 1–12; J. M. Bloom, "The Mosque of the Qarafa in Cairo," *Muqarnas* 4 (1987): 7–20; Yaacov Lev, *State and Society in Fatimid Egypt* (Leiden, 1991), 181–82, 185–89, 190; and el-Leithy, "Coptic Culture and Conversion," 26, who argues convincingly that the relationship between persecutory edicts and religious conversion was not a direct one and approaches the exercise of demographic estimates with welcome skepticism, noting that certain figures have a tendency to assume a life of their own. On the question of how deeply Ismaʿīlī Shīʿism penetrated the Egyptian populace under the Fatimids, see Lev, "The Fāṭimid Imposition of Ismāʿīlism on Egypt (358–86/969–96)," *Zeitschrift der Deutschen Morgenlandischen Gesellschaft* 138 (1988): 313–25; and Devin J. Stewart, "Popular Shiism in Medieval Egypt: Vestiges of Islamic Sectarian Polemics in Egyptian Arabic," *Studia Islamica* 84 (1996): 35–66.

[30] Al-Imad, *Fatimid Vizierate*, 71, 73; cf. ibid., 163–70; *EI*[2], s.v. "Fāṭimids" (Marius Canard); Paul E. Walker, *Exploring an Islamic Empire: Fatimid History and Its Sources* (London, 2002), 131–32, 139–51.

reason to regard the Fatimids as anomalous. Moreover, the employment of non-Muslims in the administration of Islamic Egypt long predated the Fatimids, extending back as far as the conquests of the 640s. There is also no reliable evidence that the Fatimids made political appointments on the basis of religious identity rather than administrative skill—except in the case of viziers, most (but not all) of whom became Ismāʿīlī Shīʿī (if they were not already) before assuming office.

More important in advancement through the ranks of the state were the specific skills and traditions of administration to which some non-Muslims were heir. Copts, for instance, played an important role in agrarian administration, and administrative knowledge was often passed down through generations of the same family.[31] Related to this is the question of the specific social networks from among whose ranks administrators were chosen. *Kuttāb* frequently appointed other *kuttāb*, and some non-Muslim administrators appointed other non-Muslim administrators to serve them. These men often had fostered professional or family relationships prior to their appointment at court, and one was more likely to appoint someone one trusted.

Chief among the skills required of *kuttāb* were a high degree of literacy and experience in managing people and handling large sums of money. Also helpful were social standing and knowledge of medicine. These were rare qualities in general, but characteristic of long-distance traders, financiers, scholars (including religious specialists), and of course physicians. Together with government bureaucrats, schoolteachers, and scribes, these were the basic groups of literate people in the medieval Near East; to practice one of these professions often meant to practice two or three. Among the thirty Jewish courtiers whose biographical details are known to us, all brought special skills to the post: ten were physicians, nine (from three families) were traders, financiers, or scions of mercantile families, and two were authors of erudite works in the field of religion.

The notion that *dhimmī*s were "disproportionately" represented among Fatimid *kuttāb* is a residue of medieval thought, particularly of medieval Sunnī historians who were eager to discredit the Fāṭimid dynasty as Shīʿī heretics and usurpers of the caliphal title. Many of them complained vociferously about what they saw as the Fatimids' undue reliance on *dhimmī*s. Because the Pact of ʿUmar offered *dhimmī*s protection only if they remained visibly subservient to their Muslim patrons, for *dhimmī* government officials to rule over Muslim subjects was, at least in theory, a violation of the very grounds on which the protected peoples were allowed to practice their own religions. Contrary to the exaggerated prescriptive power sometimes accorded to the Pact of ʿUmar in modern historiography, however, the writers who voiced their objections never

[31] Lev, *State and Society*, 190.

did so on the grounds of the Pact (which jurists enforced or ignored at their convenience).[32]

Many of the *dhimmī* officials singled out for abuse by the anti-Fatimid historians were Qaraites, though the writers who heaped abuse on them seem not to have known this. They were singled out not for their Qaraism but for their general prominence, which turned them into archetypal non-Muslim courtiers. The historian Ibn al-Muyassar (1231–78), for instance, quotes the invective poem of an eleventh-century Syrian ridiculing the courtier Abū Saʿd Avraham al-Tustarī (fl. ca. 1020–47), whom the Geniza documents show to have been a Qaraite:

> The Jews of this time have reached
> The pinnacle of their desires, for they rule.
> They have power and wealth,
> And have produced councilor and king.
> O people of Egypt! I advise you:
> Become Jews, for heaven itself has become Jewish.[33]

Similarly, two high-ranking Jews (one a convert to Islam) were lampooned as a holy trinity together with the caliph al-ʿAzīz (975–96) in a poem recorded by the historian al-Maqrīzī (1364–1442):

> Convert to Christianity, for Christianity is the religion of truth,
> As our era proves.
> For greatness and glory comes in three,
> And all others are nothing compared to them:
> Yaʿqūb the vizier, the Father; and
> Al-ʿAzīz, the Son; and Faḍl, the Holy Ghost.

[32] The text called by medieval legists the Pact of ʿUmar (*ʿahd* or *ʿaqd ʿUmar*, or *al-shurūṭ al-ʿumariyya*) claims to be a treaty drawn up between the Christian inhabitants of Syria and Muslim invaders in the seventh century, though most agree that it is pseudepigraphic. The earliest surviving version in treaty form dates to the ninth or tenth century: Mark R. Cohen, "What Was the Pact of ʿUmar? A Literary-Historical Study," *Jerusalem Studies in Arabic and Islam* 23 (1999): 109; idem, *Under Crescent and Cross*, 54–72. For an English translation of the version found in *Sirāj al-mulūk* of Abū Bakr Muḥammad b. al-Walīd al-Ṭurṭūshī (1059–1126), completed in Cairo in 1122 for the Fatimid vizier al-Maʾmūn b. al-Baṭāʾiḥī (1122–25), see Stillman, *Jews of Arab Lands*, 157–58.

[33] This poem is frequently cited without historical contextualization in medieval invective against *dhimmī*s and in modern accounts of it. Tāj al-Dīn Muḥammad b. Yūsuf Ibn Muyassar, *Akhbār Miṣr*, ed. Henri Massé (Cairo, 1919), 2. Also cited in the late fifteenth-century history of Abu l-Faḍl ʿAbd al-Raḥmān b. Abī Bakr al-Suyūṭī, *Ḥusn al-muḥāḍara fī akhbār Miṣr wa-l-Qāhira* (The finest discourse on the history of Egypt and Cairo), ed. Muḥammad Abu l-Faḍl Ibrāhīm, 2 vols. (Cairo, 1968), 2:153; and in modern times by Fischel, *Jews in the Economic and Political Life*, 89. Proof that the Tustarīs were Qaraites: T-S Ar. 30.278 (see below, chap. 11, p. 319); see also Gregor Schwarb, "Sahl b. al-Faḍl al-Tustarī's *Kitāb al-īmāʾ*," *Ginzei Qedem* 2 (2006): 63–67.

The vizier was Yaʿqūb ibn Killis, a Jewish convert to Islam to whom I will return shortly; Abu l-Futūḥ Faḍl ibn Ṣāliḥ was his squire (*ghulām*); and the fact that they were Jews (or had been) rather than Christians was apparently immaterial to the poet, whose aim was to ridicule the relative place of the caliph in the hierarchy.[34]

The great historian Ibn al-Athīr (1160–1233)—who served the Zengid rulers of Mosul and fought against the Crusaders with Saladin; in short, who was no friend of the Fatimids—likewise condemns the Fatimids for relying on *dhimmī*s. In his compendium of universal history, he has the following to say about al-ʿAzīz:

> It is said that he appointed the Christian ʿĪsā b. Nasṭūrus as his *kātib* and designated as his deputy in Syria a Jew by the name of Menashshe. The Christians and the Jews waxed proud because of these two and caused injury to the Muslims.
>
> Then the [Muslim] people of Fustat strengthened their resolve and wrote a petition [*qiṣṣa*] that they put into the hand of a doll that they made of paper. It read: "By Him who has strengthened the Jews through Menashshe and the Christians through ʿĪsā b. Nasṭūrus, and who has humbled the Muslims through you, will you not expose the wrong that has been done to me?"
>
> They placed this doll with the petition [*ruqʿa*] in its hand in al-ʿAzīz's path. When he saw it, he ordered it brought to him. After reading its contents and seeing the paper doll, he understood what was intended by this. So he arrested both of them. He confiscated 300,000 dinars from ʿĪsā and took a great sum from the Jew.[35]

Untangling the jumble of pronouns, the petition in the doll's hand says: God has allowed the Jewish and Christian subjects to become strong through their *kuttāb*, but he has also allowed the caliph to oppress the Muslims (this is not a complex theological statement but a passing acknowledgement of God's

[34] The poet was a certain Ḥasan b. Bishr al-Dimashqī of Fustat, author of numerous verses defaming courtiers; see Aḥmad b. ʿAlī al-Maqrīzī, *Ittiʿāẓ al-ḥunafāʾ bi-akhbār al-aʾimma al-Fāṭimiyyīn al-khulafāʾ*, ed. Jamāl al-dīn al-Shayyāl (Cairo, 1967–73), 1:298 (my thanks to Yaacov Lev for helping me locate this reference); cf. Gil, *History of Palestine*, sec. 561 (where the reference in Ibn Khallikān is incorrect). On Ibn Killis, see Lev, "The Fatimid Vizier Yaʿqūb ibn Killis and the Beginning of the Fatimid Administration in Egypt," *Der Islam* 58 (1981): 237–49; and the entry in Aḥmad b. Muḥammad ibn Khallikān, *Wafayāt al-aʿyān wa-anbāʾ abnāʾ al-zamān* (Death-notices of notables and reports on people of the age), 8 vols., ed. Iḥsān ʿAbbās (Beirut, 1969–72), 7:29–35. Abu l-Futūḥ Faḍl ibn Ṣāliḥ was also a physician, and was military commander under both al-ʿAzīz and al-Ḥākim (996–1021); al-ʿAzīz appointed him *al-muḥtasib fī wujūh al-amwāl* (supervisor of the fisc) in 993. Bianquis, *Damas et la Syrie sous la domination fatimide*, 126–30; Gil, *History of Palestine*, secs. 549, 561.

[35] ʿIzz al-Dīn Abu l-Ḥasan ʿAlī ibn al-Athīr, *al-Kāmil fil-tārīkh* (Compendium of history), vol. 9, ed. Carl Johan Tornberg (Leiden, 1863), 116–17. English translations in Bernard Lewis, *Islam: From the Prophet Muhammad to the Capture of Constantinople*, 2 vols. (Oxford, 1987 [1974]), 2:282, and in Stillman, *Jews of Arab Lands*, 200. See also Gil, *History of Palestine*, sec. 560.

responsibility for human actions). The doll—here a stand-in for the 'oppressed' Muslims of Egypt—asks the caliph to rectify the wrongs they have suffered. Ibn al-Athīr thus depicts the Muslim inhabitants of Fustat as powerless at the hands of the Jewish and Christian officials and the officials as partisans of their coreligionists. Such was the negligence of the Shīʿī caliphs, he suggests, that they allowed *dhimmīs* to run roughshod over the Muslim subjects of Egypt. Unable to approach the caliph directly, the Muslims voiced their complaint via a ruse: the note in the doll's hand, the text of which implies that while God himself had raised these courtiers to their lofty positions, the caliph alone had allowed them to disgrace the Muslims.

Ibn al-Athīr's use of Fatimid chancery terminology suggests that he deliberately omitted some details from this picture. He calls what the Muslims submitted via the doll a *qiṣṣa* (report) and then a *ruqʿa* (petition), terms that reflect some understanding of Fatimid administrative procedure. Ibn al-Athīr must also have known that anyone could submit a petition directly to the chancery, even in matters involving complaints about courtiers (actual petitions that complain about Jewish courtiers have survived in the Geniza; see chapter 11). Instead, he says the Muslims of Fustat were forced to seek redress via the ruse of the doll. Presumably he does this to heighten the sense that the Muslims had no other recourse, and thus the indignity they endured.[36] Ibn al-Athīr also implies that Muslims represented the majority of Egypt's population, or at any rate its most important segment, which further serves to augment the caliph's crime but contradicts what we know of Egypt's history during the caliphate of al-ʿAzīz. He thus achieves the rhetorical effect of making the Fatimids appear to be heretical and seditious, and the Sunnīs appear the victims of the Fatimids and their *dhimmī* retainers.

Muslim descriptions of *dhimmī* courtiers are frequently cited either out of context or in a context suggesting some putatively universal and timeless Muslim contempt for non-Muslims.[37] In fact these later condemnations provide valuable evidence of non-Muslim social and political networks in the tenth through twelfth centuries, evidence greatly augmented by documents from the Geniza.

Menashshe ibn al-Qazzāz

Comparison of chronicles and biographical dictionaries with Geniza fragments has shown that the Jewish official whom Ibn al-Athīr mentions simply as

[36] In Ibn al-Athīr's account, the caliph is immediately convinced by the justice of the Muslims' complaint and has his two officials punished by fines, but the late Mamluk–early Ottoman historian Ibn Iyās (1448–1524) claims the caliph sent both to their early and ignominious deaths on the gallows. He is probably merely imposing the topos of the deposed *dhimmī* official upon events that ended more peaceably. For the sources, see Gil, *History of Palestine*, sec. 560, and cf. Mark Cohen and Sasson Somekh, "In the Court of Yaʿqūb Ibn Killis: A Fragment from the Cairo Genizah," *Jewish Quarterly Review* 80 (1990), 286 n. 10.

[37] An exception is the justified skepticism of Lev, *State and Society*, 190–91.

"Menashshe" was a Qaraite Jew named Abū Sahl Menashshe b. Ibrāhīm ibn al-Qazzāz ("son of the silk merchant"), one of three Jews who held high appointments under al-ʿAzīz.[38]

Menashshe ibn al-Qazzāz rose to prominence in the bureaucracy under the vizier Abu l-Faraj Yaʿqūb b. Yūsuf ibn Killis (930–91), an Iraqi Rabbanite who together with his father left Baghdad ca. 940, part of the wave of literate traders and administrators who fled the capital in search of more propitious markets and courts. His family came to Ramla and Ibn Killis eventually moved to Egypt and Ifrīqiya, where he became an architect of the Fatimid military campaign against Abbasid Egypt in 969. By 967, Ibn Killis had rid himself of his impediment to high office by converting to Islam according to the Ismāʿīlī *madhhab* of the Fatimids; al-ʿAzīz appointed him vizier in 977 and in 979 granted him the title *al-wazīr al-ajall* (the illustrious vizier), and he served in this capacity until his death.

Ibn Killis maintained connections among the Jews even after his conversion, a fact attested in a record found in the Geniza of a learned session (*majlis*) held at court attended by both "Rabbanites and their adversaries" (*al-rabbanīn wa-mukhālifīhim*). One of the works under discussion was an Arabic translation (from the Hebrew) and transcription (from the Judeo-Arabic) of Seʿadya's prayer book (*Kitāb al-ṣalawāt wa-l-tasābīḥ* [The book of prayers and blessings]), which the vizier and many of those present "vilified, ridiculed, and scorned," humiliating not just the Rabbanites present but the Qaraites as well. Ibn Killis's Jewish connections are also attested in the fact that he appointed Menashshe ibn al-Qazzāz to oversee his properties in Syria.

After Ibn Killis's death, al-ʿAzīz appointed the Christian ʿĪsā b. Nasṭūrus as vizier and Menashshe ibn al-Qazzāz as military administrator (*kātib al-jaysh*); ʿĪsā, in turn, promoted Menashshe to the post of governor (*wālī*) in Syria, the arrangement reflected in Ibn al-Athīr's story about the doll. Menashshe now held the highest administrative post in Syria. It was by no means an easy one to fill. In the 980s, the Fatimids had not yet gained a firm hold over Syria. Local tribal dynasties resisted rule from Cairo, playing the Fatimids off against the Byzantines and destabilizing the empire at its eastern and northern edges—

[38] The family's name is noted in some Arabic sources as Ibn al-Farrār, a mistaken tradition owing to lack of diacritical points in manuscripts; see, e.g., Abū Shujāʿ Muḥammad b. al-Ḥusayn al-Rūdhrāwarī, *Dhayl tajārib al-umam* (Continuation of al-Miskawayh's "The experiences of nations"), ed. H. F. Amedroz and D. S. Margoliouth, *The Eclipse of the ʿAbbasid Caliphate*, 7 vols. (Oxford, 1920–21), 3:186; Abū Yaʿla Ḥamza b. Asad al-Tamīmī ibn al-Qalānisī, *Dhayl tārīkh Dimashq* (Continuation of the history of Damascus), ed. H. F. Amedroz (Beirut, 1908), 25, 33; Mann, *Jews in Egypt and in Palestine*, 1:19–22; Fischel, *Jews in the Economic and Political Life*, 62–64; Goitein, *Mediterranean Society*, 2:354 (my interpretation of the Geniza letter differs from his; see below); Gil, *History of Palestine*, sec. 560. The medieval biographical dictionaries and historiographic sources are silent as to Ibn al-Qazzāz's scholastic affiliation (as they are with the Tustarīs and David b. Yiṣḥaq); Gil is cautious on the matter. The evidence offered by Geniza documents makes it virtually certain that he was a Qaraite.

revolts that continued into the 1020s. Syria had remained beyond the imperial orbit ruled from Cairo, with its economy based on trade and settled urban life; it was the pastoral-nomadic fringe that the center could not control. Even the cities of Aleppo and Ḥims came under Fatimid rule only fleetingly and intermittently, and the local nomadic tribes established their own ruling dynasties—the Ḥamdānid (905–1016) and Mirdāsid (ca. 1009–80) *amīrs*—who thrived on perennial warfare between the Fatimids, Byzantines, and Aleppo, and served as a further cause of it. Political fragmentation in Syria continued far enough into the eleventh century to enable the region to be conquered by two forces from outside that would forever alter the fate of the region: the Seljuks and the Franks.[39]

During the 980s, the principal persons charged with controlling the chaos were Ibn Killis and Ibn al-Qazzāz. Medieval historiographic works describe tactical disagreements between the two over how to manage the Syrian tribes. As military commander in Damascus, Ibn al-Qazzāz was present locally, had a better feel for the territory, and tried to appease the warlords. Ibn Killis, principal agent of the government in Cairo and its military mastermind, wanted only to crush them: he advised al-ʿAzīz not to provoke the Byzantines and to be content with the Ḥamdānids as vassals, but to treat the Jarrāḥids—a Palestinian tribal dynasty of whom we will see more in chapter 7—without mercy.[40]

Ibn al-Qazzāz was thus a noteworthy and visible presence in the daily life of Fatimid Syria during this period, a fact that Geniza documents corroborate. This makes one suspect that Yefet's silence about him may be ideologically motivated. Ibn al-Qazzāz continued to play a role in the Jewish community until some time between 1015 and 1025, well after later chroniclers claimed he had been executed. Eventually, his son ʿAdaya would assume his post as *kātib al-jaysh* in Palestine, a fact that supports the idea that he left office honorably. Toward the end of Menashshe ibn al-Qazzāz's life, the Tustarī family rose at court, and in 1023, the Qaraite David b. Yiṣḥaq assumed a high post at court too. Thus beginning in ca. 980 there was an

[39] Bianquis, *Damas et la Syrie sous la domination fatimide*, 102–71; Cohen and Somekh, "In the Court of Yaʿqūb ibn Killis," 283–314; eidem, "Interreligious Majālis in Early Fatimid Egypt," in *The Majlis: Interreligious Encounters in Medieval Islam*, ed. Hava Lazarus-Yafeh, Mark Cohen, and Sasson Somekh, Studies in Arabic Language and Literature 4 (Wiesbaden, 1999): 128–36; and *EI*², s.v. "Ibn Killis" (Canard), "Ḥamdānids" (Canard) and "Mirdāsids" (Bianquis); and the literature cited in Bosworth, *The New Islamic Dynasties: A Chronological and Genealogical Manual*, rev. ed. (New York, 1996), 66–67 and 85–86. The Geniza record is ENA 3734.12–13 + ENA 2643.11–12 (quotation is from the first leaf, verso, line 2). The suggestion that the Fatimids usually appointed a Jew as *kātib al-jaysh*, in Bareket, *The Jewish Leadership in Fustat in the First Half of the Eleventh Century*, Hebrew (Tel Aviv, 1995), 27–28, requires further investigation.

[40] Ibn al-Qazzāz seems to have played some role in negotiating a truce after a tribal revolt in 983–88. For the welter of contradictory medieval historiographic information on the wars of the 980s and 990s, see Gil, *History of Palestine*, secs. 562–64; for Ibn Killis's role, see *EI*² s.v. "Ibn Killis."

unbroken succession of Qaraite patricians in government, and they acted solicitously towards both wings of the Jewish community. Though the Qaraite literary elite of Jerusalem omitted this fact from its depiction of the era, it was one of which the rabbinic elites were well aware and upon which they were quick to capitalize.[41]

Menashshe in Later Memory

Ibn al-Qazzāz's son took pains to have his father's military exploits recorded for a Jewish audience. A Hebrew panegyric ode preserved in the Geniza, written by an unknown author for ʿAdaya, states that Menashshe "subdued the sons of Kedar and Nebaioth / and brought them low; // the sons of Abdeel, Mibsam and also Mishma / were forced to flee and were decisively repelled."[42] This is a reference to Menashshe's battles against the Syrian Bedouin. The proper names the poet uses are all sons of Ishmael (Genesis 25:13), who via a standard typology allude to the nomadic tribes of Syria, called Ishmaelites in Genesis 37 and 39. That the panegyric offers the elder Ibn al-Qazzāz the lion's share of the glory for subduing the Bedouin not only tells us that his son paid the poet handsomely; it also confirms that the Jews of Syria were presumed to know of Menashshe's role in the Fatimid military campaigns.

[41] Bodl. MS Heb. e 108.70 is an undated deposition in which Menashshe's granddaughter Mu'ammala takes possession of the family properties in a village called Ṭūr Rubā (near Tyre) and in Tyre itself. The deed designates the latter residence "the palace (*armon*) of Ibn al-Qazzāz," not necessarily evidence that he was still alive (see the Ibn al-Qazzāz family tree in Gil, *History of Palestine*, sec. 561). Based on the anonymous paean to his son ʿAdaya cited below (T-S 32.4), on ʿAdaya's tenure in office, and on the continued existence of this estate, Mann (*Jews in Egypt and in Palestine*, 1:21) and Goitein (*Mediterranean Society*, 2:354) argue that Menashshe died of natural causes, pace the accounts of Ibn Iyās and Ibn Taghribirdī; but cf. Gil, *History of Palestine*, sec. 560n. Mann and Goitein are correct: Menashshe survived the reign of al-ʿAzīz and continued to serve in office under his successor, al-Ḥākim (996–1021), a fact missing from modern scholarship and the Arabic chronicles I have consulted but evident from a bifolium containing copies of poems by the Andalusī poet Yiṣḥaq ibn Khalfūn, a rubric of which explains that one of the poems was written "To Abū Sulaymān (David b. Bapshād) complaining about a delay in the answer to his panegyric for Menashshe b. Ibrāhīm ibn al-Qaz[z]āz" (I will return to the poem of complaint itself in chap. 5): Bodl. MS Heb. d 36.9, in Hebrew and Judeo-Arabic, verso. Since Ibn Khalfūn came to the eastern Mediterranean and acquired patrons there only after 1015, Menashshe must have died some time after then. For the *terminus ad quem*, see the paean to ʿAdaya, which dates to the early 1020s, and from which it is clear that Menashshe was no longer living (lines 28–30).

[42] T-S 32.4, lines 19–20; see Mann's comments, *Jews in Egypt and in Palestine*, 1:19–22. ʿAdaya's name is biblical (2 Kings 22:1, Ezra, Nehemiah 11:5, and 1 Chronicles 6:26), and among medieval Jews was best known as the patronymic of the sixth-century Arabian Jewish poet and comrade of Imru'al-Qays, al-Samaw'al ibn ʿĀdiyā, whose poetry had already been anthologized by al-Nifṭawayh (d. 935) when Menashshe chose this name for his son. (Mann's rendering of the name should be corrected accordingly, *Jews in Egypt and in Palestine*, 2:11, n. 1, based on T-S 13 J 13.27, line 9.) See also T-S 12.125v and T-S NS 320.17 (ʿAdaya b. Peraḥya and Peraḥya b. ʿAdaya; the fact that the two were probably relatives of one another and had the name through family tradition confirms its rarity). Cf. Goitein *Mediterranean Society*, 4:427 n. 486.

Ibn al-Qazzāz's years in Syria would be remembered as an era of unusual tranquility. Despite Menashshe's reputation as a warrior, the continuation of the ode suggests that his career was also a particularly peaceful period in the Jewish community.

For was not peace on his tongue?
  He sought good for the chosen people
Bringing gladness to the sons of Aaron and David alike,
  Gladdening the hearts of the children of the congregation of Levi,
Satisfying every hungering soul,
  Slaking every thirsty soul,
Clothing those who were naked with fear,
  Covering them with sets of clothing,
And showing generosity toward orphans and widows:
  Their souls were satisfied by his kindness.[43]

These lines depict Ibn al-Qazzāz performing the various patrician acts of helping the weak. The references to the sons of Aaron (in turn sons of Levi) and David are perhaps intended here typologically, suggesting that Menashshe used his wealth and rank to the good of all Israel, the priesthood and the kingship, the religious and the political spheres alike. The twofold reference also contains a hint of peaceful Rabbanite-Qaraite relations: "the sons of Aaron and David" might refer to all Israel, regardless of *madhhab*, or to Rabbanites and Qaraites specifically.

A later account supports the second reading. It is a letter written in 1039 by a pretender to the gaonate of Jerusalem, Natan b. Avraham (see chapter 11). In consolidating his position, Natan b. Avraham appealed pointedly and repeatedly to Qaraites for their support. Thus several months into his gaonate, Natan b. Avraham attempted to impress a certain Netan'el b. Rawḥ, a Qaraite notable in Fustat, with the legitimacy of his claims to office by narrating at great length a Purim service he had held at his *majlis* in Ramla earlier that month. It was attended, Natan b. Avraham trumpeted, by every Qaraite and Rabbanite notable in Palestine. Natan concluded his description by adding: "Everyone agreed that there had not been a Purim like this one since the days of Ibn al-Qazzāz."[44] The meaning of Natan's comparison was a double one, and it would likely not have been lost on his Qaraite correspondent: Qaraites and Rabbanites had not come together publicly in such a harmonious way since the late tenth century; and Natan b. Avraham—who claimed rule over

[43] T-S 32.4, lines 23–27.

[44] ENA 4020.6, in Hebrew and Judeo-Arabic. Gil reads the letter as referring to Ibn al-Qazzāz *père*, an interpretation with which I agree: to convey his meaning, Natan would have had to refer to a figure active longer before than Menashshe's son ʿAdaya.

all Israel, Rabbanite and Qaraite alike—was the new Ibn al-Qazzāz. If the phrase was meant to invoke any meaning at all, Menashshe's governorship must have been an era of amicable Rabbanite-Qaraite relations in Syria and Palestine, and his memory such in the collective Jewish imagination that invoking it fifty years later could conjure up the image of a leader of both *madhāhib*.

This again suggests that Yefet was choosing his facts selectively, and the omission is even more striking when one pauses to consider the footprint Menashshe ibn al-Qazzāz left in the corpus of eleventh-century Syrian poetry in Arabic. His reputation extended far enough beyond the Jewish community that the great Arabic poet and belletrist Abu l-ʿAlāʾ al-Maʿarrī (973–1058) used him as an archetypal Jewish official in one of his famous epigrams:

> As I live, they who seek protection will feel safe,
> But those who hate are merely angry and tyrannical.
> Therefore, O Quss, sign the order to pay the preacher [*khaṭīb*],
> And become overseer of our mosque, O Menashshe.[45]

Quss probably refers to Quss ibn Sāʿida, a sixth-century Arabian bishop whose eloquence was famous in medieval Arabic literature; that he is asked to supervise payment for the preacher in the mosque suggests that professional virtue counts for more than religious affiliation.[46] Similarly, Menashshe's administrative skills qualified him, according to the poem, to run Islamic religious institutions.[47]

Abu l-ʿAlāʾ may simply have wished to invoke Ibn al-Qazzāz as an administrative archetype, but he may also have written this epigram to defend Menashshe's reputation from the poison pen of Abu l-Qāsim al-Ḥusayn b. al-Ḥasan al-Wāsānī of Damascus (d. 1004), whom Menashshe had ousted from some public office. In revenge, al-Wāsānī composed three defamatory poems (*qaṣāʾid hijāʾ*), all of which are outrageously ribald attacks. In general, al-Wāsānī's vicious defamatory poems earned him the title "the ibn al-Rūmī of his age" (after the Abbasid poet, d. 895); the poems he wrote against Menashshe, and the bonds of enmity between the two men, were so well known that al-Wāsānī's literary reputation rested in part on them: they were among the first things the literary encyclopedist Yāqūt al-Ḥamawī chose to mention about him. One of

45 "La-ʿamrī laqad amina l-ʿāʾidhūna wa-ʿūnisha dhū bighḍatin fa-ʿtanash // fa-yā Qussu waqqiʿ bi-rizqi l-khaṭībi wa-nẓur bi-masjidinā yā Manash." R. A. Nicholson, *Studies in Islamic Poetry* (Cambridge, 1921): 284 (Arabic), 195, no. 306 (English; my translation differs), and see ibid., 195 n. 3; see Goitein, *Mediterranean Society*, 3:10 and 428 nn. 51–52.

46 Nicholson, *Studies in Islamic Poetry*, 195 n. 3.

47 Goitein raises the possibility that Menashshe was not the only Jew to be immortalized in Abu l-ʿAlāʾ's epigrams: *Mediterranean Society*, 3:10, and see below, chap. 9, 253.

the poems depicts Ibn al-Qazzāz as hopelessly enthralled with a female ape-harlot:[48]

One day Menashshe said to his ape,
Who had charming eyes and was enchanting,
After he had covered his teeth with perfume
And lavished them with musk
And lapped up some mellowed wine
Aging in an earthenware jug in the tavern
And a buffalo had just kissed her on the mouth
And she was still sated from kissing,
"Do you have any more kisses? Then here, take
Fifty red coins," and undid his money-belt.
She said to him, "Give them to me, and here you are, and
Show me a glittering shit, and hurry now."
So he kissed her, then said: "There is one more thing."
So she said to him, and honored him in doing so,
"What is it [now]?! Tell me. Didn't I just kiss your anus?
And caress its bowels and intestines?!
Didn't I offer a mouth that I [usually] withhold
To a toilet [and] make its flies fly away?
He told her, "You put your tongue in
My mouth!" So she replied angrily:
"O thousand pimps, son of a pimp and,
Indeed, husband of a thousand pimps!
You are not satisfied that I have kissed a rear
Underneath a moustache that is like a pubis?
Now you have become so lowly that you liken
My tongue to a jackal?!"

In insulting Ibn al-Qazzāz, al-Wāsānī combines various weapons in the arsenal of tenth-century Arabic invective: the accusations of being *abkhār* (having bad breath), of fornicating with animals, and of performing grotesque acts of various kinds.[49] To these, he adds an insult often reserved for Jews, who are likened to apes (while Christians are likened to pigs),

[48] Yāqūt al-Ḥamawī, *Muʿjam al-udabāʾ* (Compendium of literary authors) (Beirut, 1988), 9:233 ("fa-huwa fī ʿaṣrihi ka-bni l-rūmiyyi fī zamānihi"). All three poems are preserved in al-Thaʿālibī, *Yatīmat al-dahr fī maḥāsin ahl al-ʿaṣr* (ed. Shams al-Dīn), 1:410–12. Also mentioned in Gil, *History of Palestine*, sec. 560 (citing the 1896 Damascus edition).

[49] Personal communication with Sinan Antoon (May, 2005), to whom I am grateful for improving upon my English translation of the *qaṣīda*. See idem, "The Poetics of the Obscene: Ibn al-Ḥajjāj and *Sukhf*" (Ph.D. diss., Harvard University, 2006).

but takes the trope a step further by making Menashshe pay an ape for sex.[50]

Even if we hear nothing of him in Qaraite works, then, Menashshe ibn al-Qazzāz left a lasting imprint in the works of Rabbanites and Muslims alike.

THE POLITICS OF POWERLESSNESS

The presence of Jewish courtiers in Cairo would have profound effects on relationship between Rabbanite and Qaraite Jews over the hundred-year period treated in the rest of this book. But the Middle Ages did not bequeath to us complete surveys of *kuttāb* in the Fatimid administration. The ones I discuss here are known only from scattered references in Arabic literary sources or in Geniza documents. (There may be other Jewish *kuttāb* about whom we will never know because their main contacts were with the Babylonian and Qaraite congregations in Fustat and they never appear in the Arabic historiography.) Arabic sources, moreover, are silent as to these courtiers' *madhhab*, and we know they are Qaraites only because of references to them in the Geniza.

Although the sources offer much on the Qaraite *kuttāb*, they offer us next to nothing on how they interacted with the book-producing Qaraites of Jerusalem. This is disappointing: one would like to know whether members of the Qaraite literate elite, the religious specialists on the one hand and the administrative experts on the other, maintained any significant bonds, or any bonds at all. Did the *kuttāb* commission works from scholars? Did scholars petition the *kuttāb* for financial assistance or political protection? As far as I know, the earliest evidence that can answer these questions dates to two decades after Yefet, in 1026–27, when a Qaraite scholar of Jerusalem, Abu l-Faraj Hārūn b. al-Faraj, witnessed the betrothal contract of the Qaraite courtier David b. Yiṣḥaq.

But perhaps lack of evidence of any earlier contact between the two branches of the Qaraite elite represents not merely a disappointing gap in the historical record, but a silence that tells us something. The self-conception of the Qaraite scholars was still rooted in an ethos of asceticism and world-denying intellectualism that was at odds with the cosmopolitanism of the courtiers. The scholars thus portrayed themselves as an oppressed community of schismatics even after their fellow Qaraites had penetrated the upper rungs of the urban elite, and in their writings, betrayed no awareness of their coreligionists in govern-

[50] On the Jew as ape and the Christian as pig in medieval Islamic polemic, see Bernard Lewis, "The Qasida of Abu Ishaq against Joseph ibn Naghrella," in Lieberman and Hyman, *Salo Wittmayer Baron Jubilee Volume*, 659 n. 13, with references to earlier studies; also Shlomo Simonsohn, *The Jews in Sicily, vol. 1: 383–1300* (Leiden, 1997), doc. 24a. Nemeses other than Jews are also "aped" in medieval invective.

ment. Writers like Yefet and Sahl wore as a badge of honor precisely the persecution of which they complained. Self-marginalization, then, cuts both ways: Heretics come into being if their accusers have the power to define orthodoxy; but they, too, play a part in how that process is remembered by representing themselves as victims of the powerful. Religious schisms require a certain collusion of power and powerlessness.

It is also telling that evidence of Ibn al-Qazzāz comes not from Qaraites but Rabbanites—and that many of Yefet's works were found in the Geniza. While the ascetics of Jerusalem continued to practice the politics of powerlessness, in segments of the Jewish community unmentioned in Yefet's work, the late tenth century was an era of particularly friendly Rabbanite-Qaraite relations.

CHAPTER FIVE
"NOTHING BUT KINDNESS, BENEFIT, AND LOYALTY": QARAITES AND THE *GE'ONIM* OF BAGHDAD

Sefer ha-qabbala (The book of tradition, 1160–61) by Avraham ibn Dāwūd of Toledo (via Córdoba, d. 1180) is probably the single most influential medieval chronicle of Jewish history. For the period between the late tenth and twelfth centuries, it is also the only medieval account of rabbinic history. It was transmitted widely and left its mark even on Qaraite chroniclers—despite the fact that it is an anti-Qaraite polemic whose purpose was to demonstrate that Jewish law had been transmitted from God's revelation to Moses on Sinai via an unbroken chain of rabbinic discipleship up until Ibn Dāwūd's own time. Ibn Dāwūd was educated in Córdoba and witnessed the triumph of the kings of Castile and Aragón over much of Islamic al-Andalus. He was not only a champion of rabbinic Judaism; like many educated Jews of his period, he worked as a translator of Arabic texts into Latin, and he knew the basic assumptions of Christian historiosophy. The principle of *translatio imperii* is uncannily palpable throughout the work, and the idea lent itself particularly well to his aims.[1]

In the chronicle, Ibn Dāwūd describes the period between 960 and 990 as one of crisis for the Babylonian *ge'onim*, when "the income of the academies, which used to come from Iberia, the land of the Maghrib, Ifrīqiya, Egypt, and the land of Israel, was discontinued."[2] Given his work's purpose and message, this admission of crisis is significant. He then explains how rabbinic tradition overcame the crisis, via a tale about the capture at sea and ransom in separate ports of four great rabbinic scholars—a section dubbed "The Story of the Four Captives."[3]

The tale is a compression of the entire work's argument. The self-proclaimed caliph of Córdoba, the Umayyad ʿAbd al-Raḥman al-Nāṣir (912–61), sent a

[1] Cohen, *Sefer ha-qabbalah*, xiii–xiv (on the work's influence), xvi–xviii (on the author's formation), xxvii (on *translatio imperii*), and xli (on Clunaic propaganda and its influence on Ibn Dāwūd).

[2] Ibid., 46 (English), 63 (Hebrew).

[3] Cohen, "The Story of the Four Captives," *Proceedings of the American Academy of Jewish Research* 29 (1960): 55–123.

fleet of ships on a raid into Christian territory, says Ibn Dāwūd. The fleet went as far east as Palestine, and then swung north and east to the Byzantine-ruled Aegean, where it captured a ship bound from Bari carrying "four great scholars . . . on their way to a *kalla* convention," the biennial gathering of Talmud students at the Babylonian *yeshivot.* On board the ship, the captive sages refrained from revealing how learned they were so as not to increase the ransom their captors could demand for them from Jewish communities in port. Each sage was redeemed separately in precisely the lands from which the academies' income had stopped flowing: Moshe b. Ḥanokh and his son Ḥanokh in Córdoba, where the father was recognized for his great erudition and appointed leader of a rabbinic academy; Ḥushiʾel on the coast of Ifrīqiya, whence he proceeded to Qayrawān, became head of the rabbinic academy and begat one of the greatest Talmud commentators of the eleventh century, Ḥananʾel b. Ḥushiʾel (d. 1055–56); and Shemarya b. Elḥanan in Alexandria, whence he proceeded to Fustat and became head of an academy about which I will say more in chapter 6. "As for the fourth [captive]," admits Ibn Dāwūd in a moment of seeming verisimilitude meant to bring the quantity of captives to the eschatologically significant number four, "I do not know his name."[4]

Thus did the hand of divine providence act through the fleet's captain to transplant the mantle of Babylonian rabbinic tradition from a declining Baghdad to the Mediterranean basin. The outlying Jewish communities in Ifrīqiya, Egypt, and especially Iberia eclipsed the Iraqi center without breaking the chain of transmission; or they usurped its authority through divine sanction: it was God's will that the mantle of rabbinic learning pass from Baghdad to Córdoba. The tale exhibits Ibn Dāwūd's notoriously economical deployment of historical fact in the service of a myth whose decoding yields ultimate (rather than empirical) significance; that way, he can have his unbroken chain of tradition and his Iberian center of rabbinic dominance too.

In general, comparisons of *Sefer ha-qabbala* with documentary evidence yield interesting discrepancies.[5] Modern scholarship has therefore questioned the reliability of the account while somewhat reflexively conceding it a "kernel of truth": Baghdad declined, other centers replaced it. In this case, though, the "kernel of truth" turns out to be more a husk of truth housing an inner kernel of polemic. Baghdad's fiscal decline and the capture of four great sages are mere vehicles for the argument that through divine will, Iberia took the mantle of learning from the east. In fact the fiscal decline of the east was real, as

[4] Cohen, *Sefer ha-qabbalah*, 63–65 (Hebrew), 46–47 (English); idem, "Story of the Four Captives," 86–93. Ḥananʾel b. Ḥushiʾel was the teacher of Yiṣḥaq al-Fāsī (see chap. 1, 22) and composed a Talmud commentary that was indebted to the work of Hayya Gaʾon and an important channel in the diffusion of gaonic learning to the western Mediterranean and Europe.

[5] Cohen, *Sefer ha-qabbalah*, passim; see further chaps. 6 and 8 below.

was the migration westward that had caused it and resulted from it, even if the migrants had not been forcibly displaced from an intended destination, as the four captives were.

In the second half of the tenth century, the *ge'onim* reached deeply and insistently into the coffers of the Jewish communities beyond their immediate borders, intensifying their campaign for the money and loyalty of Jews in two centers of trade in particular: Egypt, the great entrepôt sitting astride the Mediterranean and Indian Ocean trades, and Ifrīqiya, commanding the triangular trade with Sicily and Egypt. Both were full of Iraqis, and they had come in various waves: with the Islamic expansion, in the tenth century, and again in the late tenth and early eleventh, when the ranks of Iraqis in Egypt were swelled by Maghribis whose forebears had first come west and then migrated eastward again and stopped where the Mediterranean ended. By the early eleventh century Egypt was so full of Maghribī Jews that one could scarcely enter a synagogue in Fustat without finding some, and though they constituted a distinct group and are referred to as Maghribīs in numerous eleventh-century letters, they never formed a separate *madhhab*.[6] Nor did they offer fealty exclusively to the academies of Baghdad, instead dividing their loyalties between Iraq and Palestine. But the Babylonian *ge'onim* felt they were still entitled to the loyalty of former easterners.

The Iraqi migration westward, then, both hastened the decline of the Baghdad *yeshivot* and facilitated the transfer westward of the Babylonian tradition, enabling the *ge'onim* to strengthen their network in the west. But while the story of the four captives hints at this, there were details of the gaonic campaign that Ibn Dāwūd refrained from mentioning: stiff competition from Jerusalem; the dual loyalties of many communities, who raised funds for both Jerusalem and Baghdad; and the role certain Qaraites played in collecting and conveying funds to Baghdad.

To be fair, Ibn Dāwūd can hardly have been expected to mention this last detail had he known of it: the purpose of his account was to refute Qaraism in the interests of a maximalist interpretation of rabbinic tradition and its continuity on Iberian soil. Indeed, we would not have known of it either had scattered hints of it not been preserved in Geniza correspondence. In this chapter, I will build a portrait of the networks of trade and transport as they intersected with the Babylonian gaonic campaigns for loyalty at the end of the tenth and beginning of the eleventh centuries; the connections between the great merchant houses of the period and the *ge'onim* of both east and west; connections between Rabbanite and Qaraite traders; and the Qaraites' connections with the *ge'onim*.

[6] See the observations of Avner Greif, "Reputation and Coalitions in Medieval Trade: Evidence on the Maghribi Traders," *Journal of Economic History* 49 (1989): 862.

THE GREAT MERCHANT HOUSES: A BABYLONIAN ORIENTATION?

Though the Geniza itself was not an archive, it preserved numerous smaller archives whose owners and their descendants deposited them there, among them the papers of several merchant clans spanning the stretch from 980 until the end of the eleventh century. In particular, it preserved papers from four merchant houses that traded on a scale far exceeding the average: the house of Ibn ʿAwkal (980s–ca. 1050); the house of al-Tustarī (ca. 990–1058); the al-Tāhirtī clan (ca. 1010–75); and the house of Nahray b. Nissim (1045–ca. 96). In a period when most long-distance business endeavors rarely exceeded a few hundred dinars and household expenditures per month averaged three or four, these firms routinely invested in merchandise worth at least several thousand dinars. The first two of those houses had origins in Persia or Iraq, and by the time their surviving papers begin to multiply, they had long since left the east. (The Tāhirtīs cannot be traced any farther back than their base in Qayrawān and their name, which points to the western Maghrib.)

The papers enable us to reconstruct the firms' networks, their market geographies and migrations; they also demonstrate that all of them were involved with the organized Jewish community, maintaining relationships with both Baghdad and Jerusalem. That dual loyalty hints at the central role long-distance trade played in gaonic campaigns and also in the scholastic rivalries of medieval Jewish communities. All four clans had bases in Egypt and did business principally in the markets there, in Ifrīqiya, in Sicily and in al-Andalus. Strangely, records of trade in Iraq and Syria are exceedingly rare, despite their involvement in the affairs of the *yeshivot.* Accidents of preservation permit us to connect the houses of al-Tustarī and Ibn ʿAwkal with the trade in the east: a single letter attests that the Tustarīs had banking agents in Baghdad, Tikrit, Aleppo, Damascus, and Tyre, and a letter has survived from Persia addressed to the Ibn ʿAwkals in Baghdad, an address otherwise unattested in their archive and suggesting that they had partners in Baghdad who forwarded mail to them in Fustat. Other than that, the direction of trade is westward from Egypt.[7]

[7] On the merchant houses and family partnerships, see Goitein, *Mediterranean Society*, 1:180–83 (Tāhirtīs); ibid., 1:154 and 3:37 (Nahray b. Nissim); ibid., index, s.vv. "Ibn ʿAwkal," "Tāhertī," "Nahray b. Nissim"; Goitein, "Jewish Trade in the Mediterranean at the Beginning of the Eleventh Century (from the Archives of the Ibn ʿAwkal Family)," Hebrew, *Tarbiẓ* 36 (1967): 366–95, 37 (1968): 48–77, 158–90; Stillman, "East-West Relations in the Islamic Mediterranean in the Early Eleventh Century: A Study of the Geniza Correspondence of the House of Ibn ʿAwkal" (Ph.D. diss., University of Pennsylvania, 1970); idem, "The Eleventh Century Merchant House of Ibn ʿAwkal (A Geniza Study)," *Journal of the Economic and Social History of the Orient* 16 (1973): 15–88; Greif, "Reputation and Coalitions" (esp. 862); Udovitch, "Scenes from Eleventh-century Family Life: Cousins and Partners—Nahray ben Nissim and Israel ben Natan," in *The Islamic World: From Classical to Modern Times*, ed. Charles Issawi, C. E. Bosworth, Roger Savory, and A. L. Udovitch (Princeton, 1989); Udovitch, *Further Letters from the Eleventh-Century Correspondence of Nahray ben*

The clans of Ibn ʿAwkal and al-Tustarī dominated the span of four decades between ca. 980 and 1020. The value of their shipments was unequaled during this period, amounting to thousands and sometimes tens of thousands of dinars. Though commodity diversification typifies traders of this period, they were exceptional in dealing in gemstones and luxury fabrics, items one could hope to sell only to rulers. That fact explains why both houses came to center their businesses on Cairo. By the third generation, the Tustarīs were connected to the Fatimid court through more than just trade, becoming bankers and administrators at court. This is a leap the Ibn ʿAwkal clan never duplicated, remaining instead bound up in mercantile activities, though of a very high order. The valuable cargoes in which both clans dealt also connected them with each other; they seem to have arranged for two of their children to marry one another. And both were threads in the net tying the *geʾonim* of Baghdad to the Mediterranean.[8]

Ibn ʿAwkal

The house of Ibn ʿAwkal moved to Ifrīqiya in the mid-tenth century together with the great migrant waves. From there they followed the Fatimids east to Egypt, where Yūsuf ibn ʿAwkal emerged as the center of a network of traders. Still, for decades the family maintained its ties with the east: after his move to Ifrīqiya, Ibn ʿAwkal's father Yaʿqūb returned to Baghdad to study with Sherira Gaʾon (968–1004) at Pumbedita, a decision that typified Qayrawān's intellectual dependence on Baghdad. There is also the letter addressed to Yūsuf and his father in Baghdad.

In tandem with his emergence in trade, Yūsuf ibn ʿAwkal began acting as one of the key point-men of the *geʾonim* of Baghdad. His mission was to cultivate the Babylonian loyalties of the Jewish communities of Fustat and Ifrīqiya, an endeavor in which his network in the central Mediterranean helped him: a

Nissim: Merchant, Banker and Scholar, Judaeo-Arabic Studies at Princeton University 5 (Princeton, 1992); and Jessica L. Goldberg, "The Geographies of Trade and Traders in the Eastern Mediterranean 1000–1150: A Geniza Study" (Ph.D. diss., Columbia University, 2005). On the Tustarīs' banking agents in Iraq and Syria, see ibid., 291, on the basis of MS Meunier; Goldberg hazards that correcting for the westerly bias of the Geniza, the Tustarīs "may well have done the majority of their business with Iraq." On Ibn ʿAwkal's address in Baghdad, see T-S Ar. 42.176, cited with analysis in ibid., 292 n. 102.

8 Ibid., 290–91. The marriage: Yūsuf b. Yaʿqūb ibn ʿAwkal's daughter married someone named Abū Naṣr, probably the middle son of the third Tustarī generation, Abū Naṣr Ḥesed, but the marriage contract calls the groom only by his *kunya*, so there is no way to identify him with certainty. Goitein, "Jewish Trade," 368; cf. Stillman, "East-West Relations," 51–52, and Gil, *Tustaris*, 60, who demurs, proposing instead that Ḥesed al-Tustarī was the son-in-law of the Qaraite Sahlawayh b. Ḥayyim (identifying him as the groom in T-S 12.621, the marriage contract of Sahlawayh's daughter Sarah); see Olszowy-Schlanger's objection, *Karaite Marriage Documents*, 330. On Ibn ʿAwkal and the Tustarīs, see also T-S 8 J 36.2, in Judeo-Arabic, recto, line 6.

cousin in Sūsa in Ifrīqiya, an agent in Qayrawān, more relatives in Sicily.[9] Ibn ʿAwkal's firm collected legal queries and donations (the two usually went together) from the Jews of Ifrīqiya and conveyed them to Fustat, where other partners in the network sent them on to the *yeshiva* of Pumbedita; in the reverse direction, they received responsa in quires in Fustat, had them copied (hence their survival in the Geniza), and carried them back to their original questioners in Ifrīqiya.[10] As Cohen puts it, Ibn ʿAwkal's "position within the Egyptian Jewish community represents one of the most concrete manifestations of the transplantation of Tunisian [i.e., Ifrīqiyan] Jewry's Babylonian orientation onto Egyptian soil."[11] Pumbedita eventually granted Yūsuf the honorific title *rosh kalla* ("head of the assembly" of students at the *kalla* convention), probably in recognition of his transport services.[12]

But Ibn ʿAwkal's network was tied to the Jerusalem *yeshiva* as well. He himself contributed money to it; his chief representative in Qayrawān, Abū ʿImrān Mūsā b. al-Majjānī, was responsible for sending it the donations collected in Ifrīqiya.[13] They were not alone among Maghribī traders who maintained dual allegiances in this period: the al-Tāhirtī brothers and the Berekhya brothers, to whom I will return shortly, also helped collect funds in Qayrawān and pass them on to both Baghdad and Jerusalem.[14] Multiple allegiances were not a peculiarity of the traders. Congregations in Sicily, Ifrīqiya, and Egypt are also attested as soliciting responsa from the *ge'onim* of Baghdad while donating money to the *yeshivot* in Jerusalem and Baghdad and earning titles anywhere they could.

Though Yūsuf Ibn ʿAwkal had earned the Babylonian title *rosh kalla* and recognition as a devoted follower of Pumbedita and facilitator of its operations, strangely, he never appears in the hierarchy of the Jewish community of Fustat itself. His connection with the Palestinian congregation in Fustat could be anticipated solely from the bias of the source sample, since his papers were found in the Geniza, and it is confirmed by a contribution he made to the Jerusalem *yeshiva* in the late 1020s. But his activities should have earned him not just titles from the *yeshivot* but some concrete role in the local congregations that would have tied him to their inner workings. Yet he appears in no such role.

Goitein tried to resolve the problem by asking whether Ibn ʿAwkal might have been a Qaraite: the clan disappears from the Geniza after his sons' generation,

9 Stillman, "East–West Relations," 49–50, citing ENA 2738.10; contra his n. 6 there (and idem, "Eleventh-Century Merchant House," 17 n. 4), a fragment with that shelf-mark does currently exist in the JTS library.

10 Goitein, "Three Letters from Qayrawan Addressed to Joseph ben Jacob ibn ʿAwkal," Hebrew, *Tarbiz* 34 (1965): 162–82.

11 Cohen, "Administrative Relations," 120.

12 T-S 13 J 8.14.

13 On Ibn ʿAwkal and the *yeshiva*, see further below and Gil, *History of Palestine*, sec. 816. Al-Majjānī: T-S 16.64. See also Gil, *In the Kingdom of Ishmael*, sec. 380 on Jewish requests to Ibn ʿAwkal to intercede with Fatimid government officials.

14 Goitein, *Mediterranean Society*, 3:19 at nn. 19–20.

except for two scattered traces: a grandson, Yaʿqūb b. Hillel, who served as proxy in the marriage of a Qaraite woman in Fustat around 1050, and a letter sent from Alexandria in 1076.[15] But a grandson's appearance on a Qaraite marriage contract cannot be taken to mean that the entire clan—or even the grandson—was Qaraite. Stillman resolved the question more convincingly by suggesting that the main branch of Ibn ʿAwkal's firm was not in Fustat but in Cairo, where he also maintained his primary residence, went to synagogue, and deposited the greater bulk of the papers related to his role in synagogue life.[16] If he is correct, the sixty-one Fustat papers are but a small part of the firm's total archive. Stillman's theory accords with Ibn ʿAwkal's role as a purveyor of gemstones whose chief clientele were occupants of the palace grounds.

Another striking absence is Yūsuf ibn ʿAwkal's near total lack of trade with the coastal Levant. Though that absence is typical of his generation of traders, his ties with the Jerusalem *yeshiva* might lead one to expect networks in Palestine. Jessica Goldberg notes that this absence underscores just how weak a market Jerusalem was: exchanges there ranged up to twenty dinars, but were usually worth less than ten, despite the special potential Jerusalem possessed as an emporium of pilgrims and during pilgrimage holidays.[17] The converse is true as well: even though the Ibn ʿAwkal firm lacked any significant economic interests in the Levant, they maintained communal ties with the *yeshiva* in Jerusalem, despite its weak market.

In fact this pattern fits with the wider context of Mediterranean Jewry's multiple loyalties, the possibility of working on behalf of Baghdad and contributing money to Jerusalem.[18] Not only that: the more Ibn ʿAwkal assumed the role of lynchpin in the diocesan system from Baghdad, the more he moved to the center of politics in the Palestinian community of Fustat. The centers competed over the house of al-Tustarī, as well, and in their case, that movement is even clearer: they appear as allies of Pumbedita in the first decade of the eleventh century, but by the third decade, were central players in the political life of the Jerusalem *yeshiva*.

Al-Tustarī

The house of al-Tustarī was founded by a family of Qaraites originally from Shushtar (in Arabic, Tustar), a town that had served as a trade entrepôt since

[15] Bodl. MS Heb. b 12.31, in Hebrew (Stillman, "East-West Relations," 56, assumes incorrectly that the bride was Rabbanite); CUL Or. 1080 5.14 (Alexandria, 1076). Goitein's suggestion: "Three Letters," 164. His notion that Qaraism is "a bridge to assimilation" (his euphemism for conversion to Islam) should be dismissed. See also T-S 13 J 8.14, the fund-raising report of the Jerusalem *yeshiva* in which Ibn ʿAwkal's contribution is listed together with those of the Qaraites (below, chap. 7, n. 41).

[16] Stillman, "East-West Relations," 58–60.

[17] Goldberg, "Geographies of Trade and Traders," 292–93; 389–90; 347.

[18] See above, chap. 3, 74–75.

Sasanian times; it was northeast of Baṣra on the Kārūn river in the medieval Persian province of Ahwāz. The first generation in trade, Yisra'el al-Tustarī, abandoned Ahwāz probably toward the end of the tenth century with his three sons, Abu l-Faḍl Sahl (in Hebrew: Yashar), Abū Yaʿqūb Yūsuf (in Hebrew: Yosef), and Abū Sahl Saʿīd (in Hebrew: Seʿadya). Like their fellow easterners they probably left for economic reasons, but unlike the Qaraite ascetics whose destination was Jerusalem, theirs was Fustat. A letter of 1026 shows Yisra'el's descendants in Fustat selling off their remaining assets in Ahwāz.[19]

Next to nothing is known about what kind of Qaraism the Tustarīs had practiced in Persia. But there are tantalizing hints. The Qaraite al-Qirqisānī in his heresiography of the Jews (937–38) singles out the Qaraites of Tustar as one among many Qaraite groups whose opinions on philosophical matters strayed from the correct path. Among "those who are said to be Qaraites," he writes, "are the Persians, such as the people of Tustar and those of their kind [*qawm*], who, despite their appearance and claims to study, find fault with anyone who engages in intellectual speculation by means of secular sciences, be it dialectics or philosophy."[20] He says this in a fragmentary chapter listing the incorrect opinions he has found among Qaraites; the problem with the "people of Tustar," according to him, was their outright rejection of rationalism and thus of the entire enterprise of philosophical theology. Al-Qirqisānī also notes that the Qaraites of Tustar were stricter than others in observing the Sabbath and other festivals, differences that for him fell within the normal range of error into which those following received opinion might stray. But his description of the "people of Tustar" as a group—*qawm*—does nothing but distinguish them from others based on al-Qirqisānī's evaluation of their beliefs. In the next chapter, al-Qirqisānī likewise enumerates the history of the various Jewish schools since the time of the Israelite monarchy (in his anachronistic formulation), and designates them with the term *afārīq* (sing. *firqa*), which connotes groups sharing some doctrinal position but otherwise unrelated. He also uses the term *farīq* to describe the Babylonian and Palestinian Rabbanites, a term that, like *firqa*, denotes simply a group that shares beliefs and behaviors.[21]

Al-Qirqisānī's description of the "people of Tustar," then, indicates nothing more than the fact that not all Qaraites agreed with one another and that some of the Qaraites who rejected philosophy happened to come from Tustar. I make this point because Gil has argued that the Qaraites of

[19] Goldberg, "Geographies of Trade and Traders," 291; the letter is T-S 13 J 25.18, Efrayim b. Saʿīd in Ahwāz to Sahl al-Tustarī and his brothers in Fustat, 4 March 1026. For scholarship on the Tustarī family from 1879 until 1981, see Gil, *Tustaris*, 16–18; for summaries in English, Rustow, "Rabbanite-Karaite Relations," 171–72, and Gil, *Jews in Islamic Countries*, sec. 369. See also Fischel, *Jews in the Economic and Political Life*, ix–xvi and 68–69.

[20] Al-Qirqisānī, *Kitāb al-anwār wa-l-marāqib*, Book I, 1:2 (4); Chiesa and Lockwood, *Yaqub al-Qirqisani on Jewish Sects and Christianity*, 93; Nemoy, "al-Qirqisānī's Account," 320.

[21] Al-Qirqisānī, *Kitāb al-anwār wa-l-marāqib*, Book I, 10:1 (48).

Tustar constituted their own subgroup within Qaraism whose doctrines and customs made them distinctive enough to earn special mention in al-Qirqisānī's heresiography. To support his point, he cites early eleventh-century Geniza fragments written by members of the Tustarī family containing a calendar that differs from other contemporaneous Jewish calendars; he also cites a contract dated according to two separate Qaraite calendars (as well as the Islamic and Rabbanite ones), claiming that the second of the Qaraite calendars is "without doubt" the Tustarī one, though there is no evidence that this is the case. Gil concludes that the Tustarī family belonged to a separate "movement" within Qaraism, superimposing al-Qirqisānī's discussion of the "people of Tustar" on the Tustarī family and presuming they share the same practices.[22] But while the Arabic toponym certainly indicates place of origin, one cannot presume that it denotes *madhhab*. Underlying Gil's equation of them is the theory that calendrical differences create hard-and-fast divisions between groups, but calendrical diversity being what it was in the tenth century, this is putting the theoretical cart before the empirical horse.[23] There is no evidence that the Tustarīs' contemporaries recognized them as a "sect," sociologically separate or otherwise. On the contrary: the bulk of evidence suggests that the Tustarīs were regarded simply as Jews. That much is clear from modern scholarship's protracted disagreement over whether they were Qaraites at all (resolved after nearly a century of labor only in 1969): the sources are silent on their scholastic affiliation, except for one document of 1040. (There, Abū Naṣr Ḥesed al-Tustarī is singled out as belonging to a separate group of Jews, by Rabbanites petitioning the Fatimid chancery to prevent him from mediating a conflict among Rabbanites, and they raised the issue of al-Tustarī's Qaraism only for political reasons.)[24] For the rest, the Tustarīs' appearances in Rabbanite documents indicate that no one ever questioned their loyalty to rabbinic institutions.

As for al-Qirqisānī, his subdivision of the Qaraites can be seen as satisfying the taxonomic urges of a heresiographer, but it does not indicate the existence of an organized group. Al-Qirqisānī is a committed exponent of the position that one is obligated to adopt whatever beliefs emerge from investigation and study, so he hardly lamented this widespread disagreement—or he lamented it only insofar as what caused it was the mistaken rejection of rationalism in favor of received opinion, and he criticized the beliefs of a very large number of his contemporaries on the same grounds.

[22] Gil, *Tustaris*, 59–63. The contract: T-S J 3.47 verso; the calendar fragments: T-S NS J 609, ENA 4010.35, and ENA 4196.15; Gil's wording: "zerem nifrad" (ibid., 61, 62). See also idem, *History of Palestine*, sec. 780, and the references to al-Qirqisāni in idem, *Tustaris*, 62 n. 91.

[23] See above, chap. 2, n. 62.

[24] T-S Ar. 30.278; see below, chap. 11, pp. 316–19.

The Tustarīs, too, did not deposit an entire archive into the Geniza, either because they did not pray in the Ben Ezra or because as courtiers, they kept their primary residence in Cairo (or for both reasons). Despite this, they appear in more than sixty Geniza documents before 1048. This is a remarkably large number of appearances in a short space of time: the largest corpus relating to a single merchant, that of Nahray b. Nissim, totals roughly four hundred documents, including incoming and (a few) outgoing letters, plus notes and accounts over a period of four decades; the next largest is the Fustat portion of the Ibn ʿAwkal archive, which totals about seventy papers over an even longer stretch of time. That we know anything at all about the Tustarīs beyond what the Arabic literary sources have preserved owes to the roles they played in Rabbanite affairs.[25]

Documents mentioning the Tustarīs fall into two categories: the correspondence of their Rabbanite trading partners and that of the rabbinic leaders of Baghdad and Jerusalem.

The mercantile correspondence tells us something qualitative about the alliances of trust and friendship that were the backbone of medieval trade networks, which extended across *madhāhib*. They are also on occasion explicit about the tenor of Rabbanite-Qaraite relations and about how contemporaries viewed those relations. An example dating to ca. 1010 connects the Tustarīs with the al-Tāhirtī clan. Mūsā b. Barhūn al-Tāhirtī writes from Qayrawān, in his own name and that of his younger brother Isḥāq, to the second-generation Tustarī brothers in Fustat, Sahl, Yūsuf, and Saʿīd, regarding a number of highly priced textiles.[26] The letter is a veritable catalogue of luxury clothing. Apart from describing silks and other fine stuffs, Mūsā, who had just returned from a stay in Fustat, thanks the Tustarīs for taking care of two of his brothers while they were in Egypt buying merchandise. His brothers, Mūsā explains, wrote to tell him of the Tustarīs' solicitude while he was there, "how kind you have been to them and how much care you have given to their affairs. They thanked God for this, my lord, in the presence of all those who know you and those who do not know you." Public expressions of gratitude toward benefactors

[25] On the number of Ibn ʿAwkal papers, see Gil, *In the Kingdom of Ishmael*, sec. 378. I am grateful to Abraham L. Udovitch for his estimate of the number of Nahray b. Nissim papers (personal communication, April 2007); about two hundred of these are now available on line through the Princeton Geniza Project. Goitein, *Mediterranean Society*, 2:345–46, notes the dearth of papers of Jewish government officials in the Geniza, and argues that because the Tustarīs were Qaraites, none of the documents preserved in the Geniza came from their archives. In fact a few documents probably did, perhaps because of their links with the Palestinian Rabbanite congregation.

[26] T-S 12.133, in Judeo-Arabic. My translation differs slightly from Goitein's. On the alternation between singular and plural pronouns Stillman notes: "It was customary to include in the signature of a letter the name of a younger brother or son who was being initiated into the family's business affairs or communal responsibilities." Stillman, "East-West Relations," 197.

(*shukr al-munʿim*) were understood by both Jews and Muslims as constituting a central obligation in political life. Publicizing the favor the Tustarīs had done for the Tāhirtī brothers served as partial repayment; it also expressed their intention to continue and strengthen the partnership.[27]

Mūsā al-Tāhirtī also expresses his longing for Sahl al-Tustarī in a way that suggests how invisible scholastic differences could seem: "Although I am now back with my family, I am extremely unhappy to be separated from you," he writes; "I ask God to multiply people like you in the *umma*, for you are its ornament." The word *umma* in Arabic specifically denotes a community sharing a common religion, and the fact that Mūsā al-Tāhirtī uses it suggests that he conceived of the bonds the two clans shared specifically in terms of religious community. Further on, Mūsā lets on that the al-Tāhirtī clan were not alone among Rabbanite traders in cultivating ties with them. Abū Zikrī Yehuda, one of the chief merchants of Qayrawān and someone closely connected to both the Tāhirtī clan and the Zīrid rulers of Ifrīqiya, had asked the Tustarīs to arrange some purchases for him in Egypt and sent his page (*ghulām*) to fetch the items. In Fustat, the Tustarīs had asked the *ghulām* a favor that they now worried exceeded the bounds of Abū Zikrī's generosity. Mūsā al-Tāhirtī took it upon himself to reassure al-Tustarī that "the *ghulām*, my lord, was not terribly inconvenienced," and in any case, Abū Zikrī would not have minded, for "the man seeks your friendship [*widād*] . . . and a connection with you [through marriage]; he wants to profit from your honor [*jāh*] and have your advice in his undertakings."[28] Abū Zikrī didn't mind, in other words, because he wanted Sahl al-Tustarī to feel indebted to him: informal favors could be parlayed into lasting bonds, including marital ones. Indeed, so great was his desire to strengthen the connection, Mūsā al-Tāhirtī explains, that if Abū Zikrī "had a son fit to serve you as an apprentice, he would have been honored by this" and sent him right away.[29]

What Mūsā al-Tāhirtī and Abū Zikrī expressed toward Sahl al-Tustarī was not unusual in a network of reciprocal benefit, mutual trust, and frequent favors exceeding the terms of formal partnerships; nor was it unusual in partnerships between Rabbanites and Qaraites. Mūsā al-Tāhirtī would, by 1022, be appointed *ḥaver* of the Jerusalem *yeshiva*, and his connection with the house of

[27] Goldberg, "Geographies of Trade and Traders," 95.

[28] On *jāh*—literally, "place," but by extension, social rank—see Goitein, *Mediterranean Society*, 5:254–60; Halper 397, in Judeo-Arabic, lines 5–7 (ca. 1070); ENA 4020.43, margin, line 1; Mottahedeh, *Loyalty and Leadership*, 152, 188.

[29] The twelfth-century Syrian *amīr* Usāma ibn Munqidh (1095–1188) tells a similar story in his *Kitāb al-iʿtibār*: a Frankish knight wished to repay his friendship by offering to take his fourteen-year-old son back to Europe with him as an apprentice. Horrified by the prospect that his son would be educated by barbarians, Usāma politely declined on the grounds that the boy's grandmother would not let him go. Usāmah ibn Munqidh, *An Arab-Syrian Gentleman and Warrior in the Period of the Crusades: Memoirs of Usāmah ibn-Munqidh (Kitāb al-Iʿtibār)*, trans. Philip Khuri Hitti (New York, 2000), 161.

Tustarī in no way compromised his rabbinic credentials. On the contrary: by that point the Jerusalem *yeshiva* was as eager as Abū Zikrī to strengthen its connections with the Tustarīs.[30]

Finally, before turning to business matters, Mūsā al-Tāhirtī wishes Sahl al-Tustarī to see his sons as his father "has seen you, namely, that they will become even more successful than you." His wish was fulfilled when two of Sahl's three sons rose to heights at the Fatimid court of which their father could only have dreamed.

Pumbedita and the Tustarīs

Not only did the traders regard the Tustarīs as part of the same *umma*; during the same period they were part of the network that the *ge'onim* of Pumbedita employed to convey their responsa to the Jews of Fustat and Qayrawān.

Based on the literary evidence of Rabbanite-Qaraite relations, it is nearly impossible to anticipate that Babylonian *ge'onim* might nurture professional ties with Qaraites. True, the Tustarīs were a mercantile link between the Mediterranean and the east. But neither the volume of their trade nor the social position they derived from it is sufficient to explain the warmth that Hayya b. Sherira, *ga'on* of Pumbedita (1004–38), expressed toward Abū Naṣr Ḥesed al-Tustarī, Sahl's middle son. Nor can it explain why that relationship outlasted the period of the Tustarīs' documented trading activities.

The earliest mention of the Tustarīs' connection to the *ge'onim* is in a letter addressed to Ibn ʿAwkal shortly after 1007 by the Berekhya brothers of Qayrawān, who were in charge of collecting the local community's donations to the Baghdad *yeshivot* and passing them on to Ibn ʿAwkal in Fustat, who forwarded them onward.[31] Apparently Ibn ʿAwkal had been playing point-man to Pumbedita in Fustat for some time, a role he may have inherited from his father, who had

[30] Rabbanite-Qaraite connections among long-distance traders are common. See, for instance, three documents from the archive of Nahray b. Nissim: (1) AIU XI 268, in Judeo-Arabic, a list of goods (verso, line 6). (2) Bodl. MS Heb. c 28.61, a letter of ca. 1065 by Yaʿaqov b. Yishmaʿʾel al-Andalusī in Sicily to Nahray b. Nissim mentioning the trading activities of a certain Abu l-Faraj b. Asad with Rabbanites (recto, lines 11 and following). (Note the debate between Goitein, *Mediterranean Society*, 1:338 and Gil, *In the Kingdom of Ishmael*, 3:576, note to line 11 and 1 sec.163; and Ben-Sasson et al., *The Jews of Sicily, 825–1068: Documents and Sources*, Hebrew, Oriens Iudaicus, series 1, vol. 1 [Jerusalem, 1991], 282, note to line 11, who argue with excessive skepticism that this Abu l-Faraj b. Asad was not Yeshuʿa b. Yehuda.) (3) CUL Or 1080 J 167, a letter of Mūsā b. Abi l-Ḥayy, Alexandria, to Nahray b. Nissim (ca. 1057) mentioning the Qaraite Yosef b. al-Nafūsī and attesting to business dealings between the two. Gil identifies the party in T-S NS J 198 d, line 17 as Qaraite, but al-Qārī admits of other meanings; the same may be true in JNUL $4^0$577.3.2 (verso, line 8), a letter of Nahray b. Nissim ca. 1067. See also (4) T-S NS 338.95 (Fustat, 22 October 1050); (5) T-S 12.424, line 5 (ca. 1040); (6) T-S 8 J 21.9, recto, left margin (ca. 1060); (7) T-S 13 J 1.18 (1078); and (8) PER H 22, line 20 (1137).

[31] T-S 12.175, in Judeo-Arabic; I have deviated slightly from Goitein's translation, *Mediterranean Society*, 5:281–82. Goitein dates the letter ibid., 1:145. For further letters of the Berekhya brothers, see references ibid., 430 n. 19.

studied there. But lately Ibn ʿAwkal had begun to slack off. Yosef b. Berekhya wrote (in his own name and that of his brother) to complain of a severed business relationship, failed professional obligations, and sadness and pain at what seemed to be the end of his friendship with Ibn ʿAwkal. In passing, he reveals the Tustarīs' role in gaonic logistics.

> I am writing to you, my lord, may God protect you from what is feared and allow you to meet with what brings happiness, at the end of the month of Av [July–August, when the ships departed from and arrived in Ifrīqiya], sound in body but with pain in my soul at the delay of your letters, your neglect of us, and your turning your mind from our affairs.
>
> All the caravans and ships have arrived, but I have seen neither a letter nor a commission from you. Instead, letters [from you] arrived for our friend Abū ʿImrān ibn al-Majjānī [Ibn ʿAwkal's representative in Qayrawān], may God preserve him, and in them no mention is made of us. . . .
>
> Most difficult of all, my lord, is what you mentioned to Abū ʿImrān in one of your previous letters: that you had received some pamphlets and letters from our lords [Sherira and Hayya, *ge'onim* of Pumbedita], and that you were about to send them off [to Qayrawān] with someone you trust, but then you neglected the matter and we did not hear [a word about it, and I do not] know what is to be done.[32]
>
> And were it not for the fact that God, may he be elevated and exalted, granted that a letter should arrive from my lord Hayya, may God make him great, via the Tustarīs, which he brought to Abū Ibrahīm Ismaʿīl b. Barhūn [al-Tāhirtī in Fustat], and which they copied worrying that it would get lost before he could bring it [to Ifrīqiya? the letter is interrupted by a large hole in the middle of the paper]. . . . This letter strengthened my heart and soothed my soul [another lacuna] that he mentioned that he had not received a letter from me for five years. I do not know how this could have happened—perhaps because of the vicissitudes of fate. But God shows mercy in every situation.

According to the letter, Ibn ʿAwkal had neglected to forward the responsa from Pumbedita to the Berekhya brothers in Qayrawān and severed the link between Iraq and Ifrīqiya. Hayya, aware of the problem, called upon the Tustarī brothers instead, who had the responsa transported from Baghdad to

[32] Our lords: *sādatinā*. Goitein reads this as referring to Sherira and Hayya (*Mediterranean Society*, 5:585 n. 44), rightly in my opinion given the use of the technical term *karārīs* (copybooks or quires). Cf. Paul Fenton, "A Mystical Treatise on Perfection, Providence and Prophecy from the Jewish Sufi Circle," in Frank, *Jews of Medieval Islam*, 302 at nn. 7–8. Hayya was already *ga'on* by the time this letter was written, since Sherira had abdicated in his son's favor some time earlier but continued to lead the *yeshiva* along with his son (Brody, *Geonim of Babylonia*, 51–52 and references in n. 74; see also ibid., 345); that he was already *ga'on* is evident also in the next paragraph of the letter, where he is the only one of the two *ge'onim* mentioned by name. Goitein dates this letter to some time after 1006–7 because Yaʿaqov b. Nissim, who preceded Yosef b. Berekhya as representative in Qayrawān for the *ge'onim* of Baghdad, died in the winter spanning those years.

Fustat and passed them on to the Ṭāhirtīs, who in turn had them copied in Fustat before sending them to the Berekhya brothers in Qayrawān. Hayya Ga'on evidently knew he could turn to the Tustarīs when his other mediators failed him.

The paradox of the Babylonian *ge'onim* turning to Qaraites for help in spreading their responsa—instruments of the campaign for Babylonian rabbinic dominance—forces one to rethink scholastic ideologies and their limits. The responsa may certainly have been symbols of gaonic hegemony, just as the queries and donations that brought them were symbols of fealty; but that fealty was not exclusive.

It is possible that this was not the first time Hayya had employed the Tustarīs' help. It was certainly not the last: thirty years later, in December 1037 or January 1038, he would write to a leader of the Iraqi community in Fustat who was in danger of being ousted from office urging him seek protection from a Tustarī of the third generation, Abū Naṣr Ḥesed.[33] Hayya's ties with al-Tustarī thus extended beyond the limits of the Iraqi congregation and its logistical needs, and it is likely that they exchanged additional letters in the intervening thirty years, letters that went the way of the Tustarī archive or that the Geniza may perhaps yet yield.

SURA AND THE QARAITES

Nor were these alliances with Qaraites specific to the *yeshiva* of Pumbedita. Shemu'el b. Ḥofni, *ga'on* of Sura (998–1013), also relied on Qaraite support in extending his reach into Egypt.

Like his counterpart Hayya of Pumbedita, Shemu'el b. Ḥofni maintained social and intellectual connections outside the narrow confines of the *yeshiva* and thus revived a perennially flagging Babylonian gaonic culture.[34] He is known to have debated the Jerusalem Qaraite halakhist and philosopher Abū Yaʿqūb Yūsuf b. Ibrāhīm al-Baṣīr (d. ca. 1040), although only the most fragmentary remains of their debates have survived.[35] His Qaraite contacts also

[33] Mosseri Ia 5 (L 2) (see chap. 11, 298–301).

[34] This is the principal argument of David E. Sklare, *Samuel ben Ḥofni Gaon and his Cultural World: Texts and Studies* (Leiden, 1996).

[35] Sklare has identified three tiny Geniza fragments—no more than mere corners of what were once proper sheets of paper—as a record of debates (*intizāʿāt*) between Yūsuf al-Baṣīr and Shemu'el b. Ḥofni on the *aviv*: ENA 4016.7–8 and ENA 4016.10, perhaps connected with a manuscript now in Jerusalem entitled *Muntazaʿāt* on calendrical differences between Rabbanites and Qaraites. See Sklare, *Samuel ben Ḥofni*, 241 n. 11, and on further connections between the two men, 238–42. On the career and work of Yūsuf al-Baṣīr, see idem, "Yūsuf al-Baṣīr: Theological Aspects of his Halakhic Works," in Frank, *Jews of Medieval Islam*, 249–70, and Sklare and Ben-Shammai, eds., *Judaeo-Arabic Manuscripts in the Firkovitch Collections: The Works of Yūsuf al-Baṣīr* (Jerusalem, 1997).

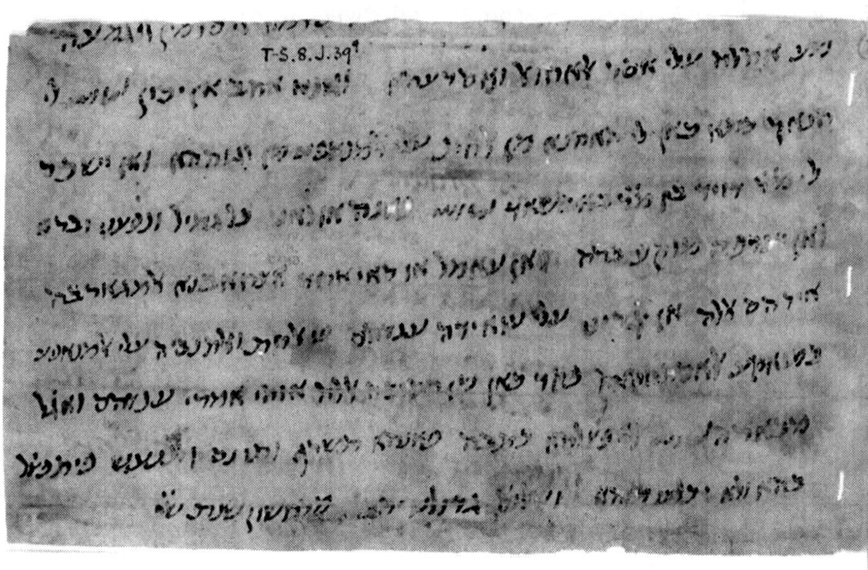

Fig. 3. A Qaraite's alliance with the *ga'on* of Sura: bottom segment of a letter from Shemu'el b. Ḥofni, *ga'on* of the Sura *yeshiva* in Baghdad, to an unknown correspondent in Fustat, thanking the Qaraite David b. Bapshād for his loyalty. In Judeo-Arabic and Arabic, 998. Cambridge University Library, T-S 8 J 39.9r.

included trusted allies to whom he could turn, much as Hayya turned to the Tustarīs.

In November of 998, while he still held the rank of *av bet din* or just after his appointment as *ga'on*, Shemu'el b. Ḥofni wrote to an unknown correspondent in Fustat—presumably some functionary of the *yeshiva*—for the purpose of cajoling the Maghribīs into increasing the frequency of their letters and (thus) their financial contributions (see fig. 3). "I would like to have there [in Fustat], may God be your support, something like what I have here [in Baghdad], [a means] to prod the notables to make contributions," he wrote. "If you have dealings with or see any of our colleagues [*aṣḥābina*] from the Maghrib, may God be their support, please do on my behalf as is your custom among them in prompting them and reminding them about contributing [to the *yeshiva*] according to their positions of merit. For it is among the punishments that God has visited upon me that He has weakened my position among them." But there was, he continued, one man in Fustat who had reliably and consistently supported him: Abū Sulaymān David b. Bapshād, son of a Persian Qaraite whose appearance in tenth-century book colophons suggests that he was a wealthy book collector and patron of Qaraite learning. "Please thank on my behalf my master David, the son of my master Bapshād, may God help him," he wrote, "since he has evinced toward me nothing but kindness and benefited me and been loyal to me [*innahu awlānī kull jamīl wa-nafaʿnī wa-barranī*]. Let him know of the esteem [in which I hold] his loyalty [*mawqiʿa birrihi*]."[36]

The expressions the *gaʾon* uses in describing his relationship with David b. Bapshād characterize the culture of personal ties in tenth- and eleventh-century Baghdad: acknowledgement and thanks in return for a favor bestowed (*jamīl*, which I have translated as kindness); a useful thing granted (*al-nafʿ*, benefit); and dutifulness or devotion (*al-birr*).[37] The implication is that the person in a position of power (here, the *gaʾon*) is duty-bound to acknowledge and reward the loyalty of someone who benefits him. The *gaʾon* and David b. Bapshād would both have considered their relationship as binding. The only thing missing from the *gaʾon*'s letter is the nature of the benefit David b. Bapshād bestowed upon him. Had he made a donation to the *yeshiva*, encouraged others to do the same, or served as financial intermediary for others' contributions? Qaraites are attested in all these roles in other Geniza documents. Ideological differences did not encumber the mutual loyalty the two men maintained; it is even possible that they strengthened them, that the *gaʾon* maintained alliances with Qaraites as part of his program to consolidate the power of the Babylonian academies. By the mid-1030s, Qaraite alliances would come to bolster the standing of rabbinic leaders among their followers, and though there is no evidence that this was the case as early as 998, the connection between David b. Bapshād and Shemuʾel b. Ḥofni may have entailed more than assistance with raising funds.

Support for this theory comes in the form of a treatise that Shemuʾel b. Ḥofni composed in response to queries from someone named Ibn Bapshād,

[36] T-S 8 J 39.9, in Judeo-Arabic. (*Birr* means both reverence and benefaction, a polarity I have attempted to render by translating it as loyalty.) On the basis of this letter, Goitein surmised that David b. Bapshād lived in Damascus, but the simpler reading is that the letter was addressed to Fustat. Goitein, "A Letter of the Gaon Samuel b. Ḥofni, Dated 998, and its Implications for the Biography of the Spanish Poet Isaac b. Khalfon," Hebrew, *Tarbiẓ* 49 (1979–80): 199–201. The colophons: Paul Kahle, *Masoreten des Westens*, 2 vols. (Hildesheim, 1967 [1927]), 1:71; Mann, *Texts and Studies*, 1: 164 n. 44b. Other descendants of Bapshād further suggest the family's connections among Fustat's Rabbanite-Qaraite mercantile elite, evidence that mitigates the uncertainty of Kahle's and Mann's identification of David b. Bapshād with the figures mentioned in the Firkovich colophons (even if Bapshād was a common name among Persians in this period). The poet Yiṣḥaq ibn Khalfūn wrote three encomia for an Abū Ayyūb Shelomo b. David, possibly the son of David b. Bapshād; see below. See also al-Khaṭīb al-Baghdādī, *Tārīkh Baghdād* (History of Baghdad) (Cairo, 1931), 7:307, for a certain Abū Saʿīd al-Ḥasan b. Dāwūd b. Babshād b. Dāwūd b. Sulaymān al-Miṣrī (d. 1 May 1048), whose father David (our David b. Bapshād?) had converted to Islam; it is possible that one son (al-Ḥasan) followed the father into Islam while the other (Shelomo) remained a Jew. A certain "daughter of Babshād," perhaps David's sister, deposited some money with Avraham b. Moshe al-Tāhirtī ca. 1050; Goitein, "Early Letters and Documents from the Collection of the Late David Kaufmann," Hebrew, *Tarbiẓ* 20 (1950), 197, 200; Gil, *Tustaris*, 37. See Gil, *History of Palestine*, sec. 927n.; Hayyim Schirmann, *New Poems from the Geniza*, Hebrew (Jerusalem: Israel Academy of Science and Humanities, 1965), 482; and Fleischer, *The Proverbs of Saʿīd b. Bābshād*, Hebrew (Jerusalem, 1990), 162–66 (on the author's relationship to David b. Bapshād).

[37] Mottahedeh, *Loyalty and Leadership*, chap. 2, esp. 72–95.

a treatise now lost but preserved in a library inventory.[38] One can only imagine what these queries might have contained: legal questions, theological ones, or both? If our David was the one who posed the queries that provoked the treatise, it would not push the limits of plausibility to imagine the *ga'on* answering him not out of zeal in defense of the faith, but out of affection for his friend and supporter.

A decade later, in July 1008, Shemu'el b. Ḥofnī continued to foster the connection. A second Judeo-Arabic letter, written by the *ga'on*'s son Abu l-ʿAlā' Yisra'el at his father's dictation, is addressed to one of the leaders of the Babylonian community in Fustat, probably Shemarya b. Elḥanan or Avraham b. Sahlān.[39] Abu l-ʿAlā' Yisra'el would assume the gaonate nine years later (he held it from 1017 until 1034), and as was the custom among the merchant houses, the father trained the son in correspondence and bequeathed to him his professional ties. The letter is a mere fragment, a strip of paper wider than it is long, containing the bottom eight lines of what was once a lengthier missive. Just before the tear, Yisra'el begins writing in his own voice and extends greetings to the children of his addressee, dating the letter at the bottom, then adding in the corner of the page, in the lower right margin, seemingly as an afterthought: "and greetings to our greatness and our light . . . Abū Sulaymān, the eminent elder, my master . . . son of my master and our teacher Babshād our elder, may God make both their strength eternal."[40] The two families maintained their connection to one another across generations as well as across the distance separating Baghdad and Fustat.

"Whose Clouds Pour Forth Crystal"

David b. Bapshād might have been a mere name in the correspondence of Shemu'el b. Ḥofni the number and strength of whose ties among Egyptian Rabbanites would have remained unknown were it not for a wandering Andalusian poet named Yiṣḥaq ibn Khalfūn who wrote no fewer than eight Hebrew poems for David b. Bapshād. Seven are encomia, and the eighth is a poem of complaint against Menashshe ibn al-Qazzāz (to whom direct complaints appear not to have availed).

[38] The work is called *Masā'il Ibn Bābshad*, loosely, "The difficulties raised by Ibn Bābshad," with the name spelled this way (the Persian *p* sound would have been rendered in Arabic as *b*, and vowel length is frequently mistaken in Geniza documents in Judeo-Arabic and in renderings of Persian into Arabic). Bodl. MS Heb. d 66.131–32 (131 verso, line 42). Gottheil mistakenly read Babshār; cf. Mann, *Texts and Studies*, 1:159 n. 76 and Sklare, *Samuel b. Ḥofni*, 31 n. 126.

[39] Following Gil's interpretation, *In the Kingdom of Ishmael*, 2:155.

[40] Mosseri IV 15.1 (L 21). Gil identifies the handwriting as that of Yisra'el b. Shemu'el. See Goitein, *Mediterranean Society*, 2:15; Gil, *In the Kingdom of Ishmael*, sec. 106 and n. 106; sec. 215 and n. 215.

David had probably sent Ibn Khalfūn to Ibn al-Qazzāz and arranged for his patronage, a fact that hints at the dense ties among Qaraite notables. It also increases the probability that Shemuʾel b. Ḥofni, who knew the Qaraites Yūsuf al-Baṣīr of Jerusalem and David b. Bapshād of Fusat, also knew of Menashshe ibn al-Qazzāz of Damascus. If this, in turn, is the case, then the Qaraites in Palestine were more than the mere victims of Yefet's "rabbinic judges and scholars who go around the region collecting pledges." They were also their trusted allies and supporters.

Ibn Khalfūn, for his part, cultivated Qaraite patrons but is best known for poems memorializing his childhood friendship with Shemuʾel ibn Naghrilla *ha-nagid*, the illustrious poet and talmudist of Granada (993–1056). Born to a Maghribī father in al-Andalus (possibly in Córdoba) ca. 985–90, Ibn Khalfūn set out for Qayrawān and points farther east in search of patrons some time between 1012 and 1015. In Qayrawān, he wrote two encomia for Avraham b. ʿAṭā, the leader of the Jewish community to whom Hayya Gaʾon granted the title *negid ha-gola* in 1015. He then found patrons further east among the Jews of Egypt and Syria and died ca. 1044.[41]

The *dīwān* of Shemuʾel ibn Naghrilla preserved Ibn Khalfūn's friendship poems but was printed for the first time only in 1879; Ibn Khalfūn's *dīwān* was gradually found among the remains of the Geniza.[42] Though the Ibn Naghrilla's poetry has more than made up for lost time, Ibn Khalfūn is still a forgotten poet. Not so in the eleventh and twelfth centuries, when his eastern *dīwān* circulated widely and was much beloved, to judge by contemporary testimonies. Half a century after Ibn Khalfūn's death, a Jewish scribe named ʿAlī wrote a Judeo-Arabic letter urgently begging a cantor in Damietta named Abū Isḥāq for a copy of Ibn Khalfūn's *dīwān*. "Either send it to me and I will copy it, or let my lord have it copied for me," ʿAlī urged his friend. "Please, oh please, since someone borrowed my copy . . . , was ashamed to return it, and took it with him to Yemen. Please my lord, do not neglect this matter under any circumstances!" One wonders (with Ann Brener in her study of the poet's work) whether the borrower somehow damaged ʿAlī's copy of the *dīwān* or had simply kept it for so long that he could not bring himself to give it back. The cantor of Damietta appears to have fulfilled ʿAlī's request to furnish him with a copy of the *dīwān*: of the

[41] On the poet, his life, his works, and the history of the modern reconstruction of his eastern *dīwān*, see Anne Brener, *Isaac ibn Khalfun: A Wandering Hebrew Poet of the Eleventh Century* (Leiden, 2003), and the earlier works cited there. The *dīwān* was published (on the basis of earlier editions) in Aaron Mirsky, *Itzhak ibn Khalfun: Poems*, Hebrew (Jerusalem, 1961); see also Giuliano Tamani, *La letteratura ebraica medievale (secoli X–XVIII)* (Brescia, 2004), 39 (who dates the poet's birth earlier).

[42] On the reception and publication of Shemuʾel ibn Naghrilla's poetry see Tamani, *La letteratura ebraica medievale*, 41.

eight copies that survived in the Geniza (all of them incomplete), one is written in ʿAlī's hand.[43]

When Ibn Khalfūn arrived in the east and began singing the praises of its powerful men, three of the twelve regular patrons he found were Qaraites. His eastern *dīwān* and its circulation belong, then, to the literary history of Rabbanite-Qaraite relations as much as the polemics of the tenth century. That a Rabbanite poet raised among the Andalusian elite wrote for Qaraite patrons suggests that the zealous anti-Qaraism of that elite was a phenomenon of the twelfth century but not the eleventh.[44]

Ibn Khalfūn's encomia call David b. Bapshād "the prince of the land" (*sar ha-adama*) and an "elder" (*zaqen*), neither of which suggests that he played a formal role either at court or in the Jewish community. One of Ibn Khalfūn's odes fills in some of the details merely outlined in Shemu'el b. Ḥofni's letter and sheds a bit more light on David b. Bapshād's role in the community:

> Unto David, the friend of my soul, shall I go to heal my heart from its sorrows.
> To the leader, generous-hearted, who made my people, his officers, into one people, whose clouds pour forth crystal and whose billows rain down the gold of Ophir.
> He is the elder of my people in knowledge, and though young in years puts the old ones to shame.
> Hence his God has made him a candle to light up their paths, just as He made a sun in His heavens, and, lo, even the far-away lands know of him, as though they were his neighbors.
> His name is great, his fame wide-spread, and who would not sing of him, were his image before him?
> A true gentleman, whose wisdom is his spear and whose inkwell and quill are his weapons.[45]

Even correcting for panegyric exaggeration, it is hard to imagine Ibn Khalfūn including the second line had David b. Bapshād done nothing to further the unity of the Jews, and it may be his activities on behalf of Sura that earned him this praise. Ibn Khalfūn found them worthy of praise and presumed that those who read or heard the poem would agree.

Though David b. Bapshād was loyal to Shemu'el b. Ḥofni, he was not always faithful to Ibn Khalfūn, who on at least one occasion had to prod him to pay:

[43] CUL Or. 1080 J 109; Brener, *Ibn Khalfun*, 25; Goitein, "Ibn Khalfun's Collection of Poems in 11th Century Egypt and Yemen," Hebrew, *Tarbiẓ* 29 (1959–60), 358.

[44] Cohen, *Sefer ha-qabbalah*, xvi–xlii; see further below, Epilogue.

[45] Bodl. MS Heb. d 36.10, recto (bottom) and verso (top), a bifolium on vellum from a copy of Ibn Khalfūn's *dīwān* containing panegyrics to Abu l-Faraj Yehoshuaʿ b. al-Qammūdī, Shemu'el b. al-Labdī, Abū Sulaymān David b. Bapshād, and others. I have deviated slightly from the translation in Brener, *Ibn Khalfun*, 137. Fleischer, *Proverbs of Saʿīd ben Babshad*, 165 n. 42, calls this poem Ibn Khalfūn's "only true [classical] *qaṣīda*" (cited in Brener, *Ibn Khalfun*, 85 n. 8; see her emendation there).

"The days of Purim are days of festivity," wrote the poet pointedly, "days of quiet, days of security / in which the rejected nation was saved from the hand of its enemy. / God saved it; therefore the days of Purim are for sending / tasty portions," the fragmentary last line being a reference to the custom of sending Purim gifts (and a reminder to the poem's recipient to pay).[46] The ode of complaint about Menashshe ibn al-Qazzāz is much longer and more extravagant:

> To whom can I turn, whither shall I go and upon whom vent my reproach?
> Do there yet remain in this country great men whose praises I can double?
> Are these not the great men of the land upon whom the dew gathers?
> Is this not he, to whom everyone in every town responds with dancing?
> My friend, don't argue with me and say: "Write the poem, and hope for reward."
> You sent me to a pleasant garden; but its choice fruits I found on the mountain peaks withering.
> I clung to the horn of the unicorn, but drowned in the deep.
> I ascended unto the skies, but my feet were pitched in the watery abyss.
> And this was what I said to my tortured heart: "Wretch, ask not for great things,
> Cease now, have no hope for his kindness; his favors—like a fleeting shadow—are dry husks.
> Wish not to visit his castles when his doors are locked in your face."
> He makes promises to you and commands: "Measure out, these are his portions."
> Do you not see that my verses, which once shone in the dark, are now dimmed?
> The poems I made from them and brought before them like virgins,
> Beautiful and strung together like beads—have they not been sullied like whores?
> Get thee to thy own place, have no hope in empty, useless words.
> God will be before you and with you: He, by whom all actions are weighed.[47]

Menashshe's failure to reward the poet for his efforts was so insulting, writes Ibn Khalfūn, that his poems ("virgins") had been defiled "like whores." The poet's only hope was to call upon the wrath of God for punishment—and to

[46] Bodl. MS Heb. d 36.9, verso (bottom); Brener, *Ibn Khalfun*, 149.

[47] Bodl. MS Heb. d 36.9, verso; Brener, *Ibn Khalfun*, 163 (I have altered her translation ever so slightly). The poem's rubric explains that it was written "To Abū Sulaymān [David b. Bapshād] complaining about a delay in the answer to his panegyric for Menashshe b. Ibrāhīm ibn al-Qazzāz." Ibn Khalfūn also wrote a poem to Menashshe's son ʿAdaya on the occasion of his failure to pay for services rendered: "My soul is bereaved of all hope and my heart bereft of expectation / Too exhausted am I to look towards my path, and my way is not paved. // My acquaintances keep me going on hopes long held out / Like the cumin plant whose owner says: 'Grow: You'll get watered tomorrow'" (T-S 8 K 14.2). For speculation on ʿAdaya's dissatisfaction, see Brener, *Ibn Khalfun*, 96.

complain to the powerful patron who referred Menashshe to him in the first place.

David b. Bapshād's ties to Menashshe b. al-Qazzāz hint at the former's place in a network of Qaraite notables spanning Syria and Egypt. There is more about that network in an undated letter from an anonymous Persian attesting to David b. Bapshād's ties to David b. Yiṣḥaq, the Qaraite courtier under al-Ẓāhir who would emerge, over the course of the 1020s, as one of the Jerusalem *yeshiva*'s staunchest supporters.[48] The letter suggests that David b. Bapshād's Rabbanite ties did not adversely affect his standing among the Qaraites of Syria and Egypt, who considered him "a trustworthy person"—not a meaningless characterization in a society in which good reputation translated into political capital. The letter also hints at the shift the Qaraite notables would make over the course of the early eleventh century, when they became the trusted allies of the Jerusalem *yeshiva*.[49]

"The Great Men of the Land upon Whom the Dew Gathers"

The alliance between the Babylonian *ge'onim* and the Qaraites of Egypt and Syria, first attested between 998 and 1008, renders in capsule form one of the basic conditions of Jewish communal life during the period: polemicize though they might against the Qaraites, rabbinic leaders fostered social and official relationships with them and relied upon them in matters pertaining to *yeshiva* business. Nor did the Qaraites balk at being used as instruments through which the *ge'onim* extended their network of followers.

That Qaraites and Rabbanites conducted both antagonistic intellectual exchanges and close social relationships with one another may seem less paradoxical when viewed in its total social context: a culture of personal loyalty in which the elite classes of Jewish society—"the great men of the land upon whom the dew gathers," as Ibn Khalfūn called them—maintained friendships that were not weakened by ideological differences and were perhaps even made stronger by them.

The *ge'onim* of Baghdad and Jerusalem, for their part, maintained considerably looser commitments to ideological niceties than one might expect, calling on Qaraites to help them with the logistics of institution building. Recogniz-

48 See chap. 7.

49 CUL Or 1080 J 146, in Hebrew; see Gil, *History of Palestine*, sec. 927. I deduce that the writer is a Qaraite of Persian origin from the facts that he notes the date "according to the observation of the new moon" (indeed 20 Sivan never fell on a Tuesday according to the Rabbanite calendar during the years when David b. Yiṣḥaq was active in public life, ca. 1020–55); that he spells Babshād with a *p* rather than a *b*; and that he writes David b. Yiṣḥaq's *kunya* Abu Naṣr (the first time) with a *sīn* rather than a *ṣād* and an *ā* rather than an *a*. Gil suggests that the writer lives in Ramla, presumably on the basis of the verb "to go up" to Jerusalem, the implied possibility of doing so easily, and its sizeable Qaraite population. My efforts to identify him further have not availed.

ing that the *ge'onim* campaigned for financial support already suggests that religious loyalties depended upon more than adherence to religious and legal dictates. The gaonic campaigns were linked to the fortunes of trade and its shifting centers, and also to traders. The *ge'onim* took advantage of the mercantile networks that Jewish migrants westward still kept in the east; this meant not distinguishing between the Qaraites and Rabbanites among those traders, whether or not they appealed to the Iraqi origins and Babylonian loyalties of the Rabbanites among them. In other words, if we admit that the gaonic project was tied to the world outside the *yeshivot*, we must also admit that it did not run on ideological considerations alone.

CHAPTER SIX
"UNDER THE AUTHORITY OF GOD AND ALL ISRAEL": QARAITES AND THE *GE'ONIM* OF JERUSALEM

Most of the evidence I presented in the previous chapter dates to the decade between 998 and 1008. Unfortunately after that one faces a void for slightly more than a decade. The dearth of Geniza sources may be related to the caliph al-Ḥākim's decrees against Christians and Jews (1007–19 and 1012–19 respectively), or simply to the fact that the Ben Ezra synagogue was rebuilt in 1025–39, the point from which people began depositing papers there. We know frustratingly little about the politics of the Jewish community in the interim.[1]

But when the documentary trickle swells to a stream with the start of the 1020s, a change is already discernable. The Iraqi *ge'onim* were no longer the only Rabbanite leaders cultivating alliances with the Qaraite grandees in Fustat and Cairo; they had now been joined by a vigorous Jerusalem gaonate, which continued to court the Qaraites of Egypt over the subsequent two decades. The Qaraites, in turn, become key players in Palestinian Rabbanite politics, a role they assumed with increasing frequency and effectiveness.

What happened in the meantime? Did something alert the Jerusalem *ge'onim* to the usefulness of the Qaraite courtiers? I have found no sources

[1] On al-Ḥākim's decrees, see Josef Van Ess, *Chiliastische Erwartungen und die Versuchung der Göttlichkeit: Der Kalif al-Hakim (386–411 H.)* (Heidelberg, 1977); Heinz Halm, "Der Treuhänder Gottes: Die Edikte des Kalifen al-Hakim," *Der Islam* 63 (1986): 11–72; Bianquis, *Damas et la Syrie sous la domination fatimide*, esp. 291–96; Paul Walker, "The Ismaili Da'wa in the Reign of the Fatimid Caliph al-Hakim," *Journal of the American Research Center in Egypt* 30 (1993): 160–82; and Ben-Sasson, "Geniza Evidence on the Events of 1019–20 in Damascus and Cairo," Hebrew, in Fleischer et al., *Mas'at Moshe*, 103–23. When the Ben Ezra was rebuilt is still unclear. The range I offer (following Goitein) attempts to account for contradictory evidence by using the dates as *termini post* and *ante quem*. Mann, *Jews in Egypt and in Palestine*, 2:375, dates it to 1025 following al-Maqrīzī, who in turn follows an inscription over the door of the building. Goitein, *Mediterranean Society*, 1:18 and 399 n. 44, extends the date probably in view of T-S Ar. 18(1).35+T-S 20.96+ENA 2738.1, which lists parts of the synagogue compound that were rebuilt between 1034 and 1039. See also ibid., 2:413, item 3, and Ben-Sasson, "The Medieval Period: The Tenth to Fourteenth Centuries," in *Fortifications and the Synagogue: The Fortress of Babylon and the Ben Ezra Synagogue, Cairo*, ed. Phyllis Lambert (Chicago, 1994), esp. 210–11.

that might answer that question directly, but two sets of documents suggest significant patterns of change. The first is a cluster of about a dozen letters pointing to a powerful faction of Jews in Fustat allied with both Baghdad and Jerusalem who were playing the two centers off against each other in an effort to establish an independent Jewish authority in Egypt. The second set is a pair of legal and administrative documents demonstrating the growing influence of Qaraites at the Fatimid court and their cooperation with the Rabbanite leadership in Jerusalem. Together, these sources suggest that when the Rabbanite faction in Fustat attempted open rebellion against the Jerusalem *ge'onim*, the latter acted swiftly and decisively in bringing Fustat to heel by realigning themselves with the Qaraites. One of the reasons they did so was to ensure that they had someone representing their interests before the Fatimid chancery.

THE REVOLT OF THE THIRD "CAPTIVE"

Ibn Dāwūd tells us that the fiscal crisis of the Babylonian *yeshivot* was resolved when four great Babylonian loyalists taken captive near Bari were brought to al-Andalus, Ifrīqiya, Egypt, and some fourth place. But it is strange that a century and a half after Ibn Dāwūd, the Egyptian "captive," Shemarya b. Elḥanan, still registered in the annals of rabbinic tradition as a link binding the Iraqi center to the Egyptian periphery. In fact he marked the beginning of the drive for Egyptian independence from Baghdad—and from Jerusalem.

It was hardly the only or the least of Ibn Dāwūd's creative inventions that Shemarya b. Elḥanan had been brought to Egypt by force (or accident, or providence): in fact he had been born there. In the mid-tenth century, Shemarya's father already held a number of titles in Fustat's Babylonian Jewish community.[2] Shemarya himself studied in Baghdad under Sherira Ga'on at Pumbedita; when he returned home to Fustat, he, too, rose within the Iraqi community, becoming, Ibn Dāwūd tells us, "head" in Fustat, though he does not tell us of what. The documents corroborate that by the last decade of the tenth century, Shemarya led the Babylonian congregation as his father had. He also founded his own academy, just like the other two named "captives." Letters addressed to Shemarya call him *rayyis* in one form or another: Ṣemaḥ b. Yiṣḥaq, *ga'on* of Sura (ca. 987–99), addresses him as *ra'īs al-yahūd* (head of the

[2] *Ha-rosh*: T-S Misc. 35.18 and T-S 12.851; *ha-rav ha-rosh*: T-S NS 298.25, T-S 20.35, T-S 12.193, T-S 16.134; *al-rayyis*: T-S 13 J 35.2, and cf. Bareket, *Fustat on the Nile*, 193 n. 8; *ha-rav ha-gadol she-haya'or doro ve-kitram ve-nizram*: T-S 16.68 (recto, line 9). Bareket attempts to reconcile Shemarya b. Elḥanan's having been born in Egypt with Ibn Dāwūd's claim that he was taken captive and ransomed there (ibid., 194), but given the high quotient of mythologization in Ibn Dāwūd's account there is no reason to presume its veracity.

Jews), perhaps merely because he recognized him as leader over the Babylonian congregation of Fustat, though the title also suggests that, at least in the mind of the *ga'on* of Sura, Shemarya led Fustat's entire Jewish community.[3]

Both Shemarya and his father, then, helped transplant the authority of the Babylonian *yeshivot* onto Egyptian soil. But Shemarya personified the problem of the ties between gaonic center and rabbinic periphery: the more powerfully he represented Baghdad, the more he threatened to throw off its authority.

The Rise and Fall of the Fustat *Midrash*

Shemarya b. Elḥanan was able to sustain the fragile balance between vassalage and outright independence, at least to the satisfaction of the *ge'onim*, partly through gestures of symbolic allegiance. During his tenure as leader in Fustat until his death in December 1011, he had the good sense to proclaim loyalty to his teacher Sherira Ga'on of Pumbedita and to his son and successor Hayya. When he established his own academy in Fustat, he refrained from calling it by the title *yeshiva*, and in deference to Baghdad and Jerusalem, called it instead a *midrash* (place of learning).[4] But he also arrogated titles and other formal phrases normally reserved for the *ge'onim*, such as the conventional epistolary preface containing blessings and greetings from the head of the *yeshiva* to his disciples.[5]

Shemarya was not quite as delicate with the prerogatives of the Jerusalem *ge'onim*. He adopted prerogatives that should by rights have been the *ga'on*'s, including the authority to issue responsa, and perplexingly, he did so with the tacit approval of the Jerusalem curia, who corresponded with him regularly, allowed him to bear the title *av bet din*, second-in-command of the *yeshiva*, and appointed his son Elḥanan to the Jerusalem *yeshiva*'s six-man governing board.[6]

To understand how the *ga'on* of Jerusalem could have allowed Shemarya to usurp his authority in so blatant a fashion, it helps to consider that the *ge'onim*

[3] Mosseri Ia 10.2 (L 279). Some eighty years later the title would come to indicate leadership over Fatimid Jewry in general, but it was not repeated until then and in the meantime did not represent a continuous office. See Cohen, "Administrative Relations," 126–27 n. 47, and above, chap. 3, n. 70; see also Goitein, "Shemarya b. Elḥanan; With Two New Autographs," Hebrew, *Tarbiẓ* 32 (1962–63): 266–72 and Bareket, *Fustat on the Nile*, 192–204.

[4] T-S 12.43, cited in Cohen, "Administrative Relations," 122 n. 26. Goitein connects the founding of the Fustat *midrash* with the establishment of al-Azhar: *Mediterranean Society*, 2:202.

[5] T-S 20.140, recto, lines 1–2; T-S 12.43, recto, line 1. Goitein, "Shemarya b. Elḥanan," 268.

[6] Responsa: T-S Misc. 35.17–18 and T-S 20.35, cited with references to previous discussions in Cohen, "Administrative Relations," 122 n. 28. Correspondence: T-S 16.68, in Hebrew, a letter from Shemu'el the Third to Shemarya b. Elḥanan; ibid., 122 n. 27 (see there also for Elḥanan's appointment to the board of governors); Mann, *Jews in Egypt and in Palestine*, 2:23–24. According to Gil, ca. 1000 the *ga'on* of the Jerusalem *yeshiva* was Shema'ya, a Maghribī; it is not known when Yoshiyyahu b. Aharon succeeded him. Gil, *History of Palestine*, secs. 855–56.

of both Baghdad and Jerusalem may have looked on Egyptian autonomy as consistent with loyalty to the center rather than as a victory for the other *yeshiva* or a threat to either. Still, one wonders how the Palestinian *ga'on* could have simply watched as Shemarya made successive bids for more prerogatives. One possibility is that since Fatimid rule over Egypt was but a generation old and over Syria was even newer, the Jerusalem *ga'on* still considered himself responsible only for Syria. He may not yet have expected ties of dependence from Egyptian Jewry, and therefore had no reason to mind when Shemarya cultivated those ties in his own name instead. Given the near total eclipse of information before the Fatimid conquests, one cannot assume that the Palestinian *yeshiva* had dominated Egypt continuously since Byzantine times. There is no evidence to confirm this. What evidence we do have suggests that in the late tenth century, the Jerusalem *ga'on* was not particularly disturbed when Shemarya assumed quasi-gaonic privileges in Fustat, either because he was weak or because he did not consider Fustat Jewry his to rule. The establishment of Fatimid rule in Egypt—its declaration of independence from Baghdad and the Abbasid realm—probably struck Shemarya as a propitious set of circumstances under which to assume greater autonomy in leading Egyptian Jewry. Or perhaps he assumed that the community expected this of him.

Whatever the reasons for this amicable sharing of powers, after three decades, Shemarya's son Elḥanan (dated documents: 994–1026) tipped the balance Shemarya had so delicately maintained by engineering Egyptian Jewry's secession from Babylonian and Palestinian authority.[7] Egyptian Jewry's era of relative autonomy then metamorphosed into full-scale secession.

"An Indescribably Humiliating Position"

Like his father, Elḥanan b. Shemarya had studied at Pumbedita in Baghdad under Sherira. Like his father, on his return to Fustat he continued to maintain close ties with both Sherira and Hayya; he also corresponded with the *ge'onim* of Sura, Ṣemaḥ b. Yiṣḥaq and his successor Shemu'el b. Ḥofni. And like his father, he served materially as a link between the Iraqi *yeshivot* and the Jews of Ifrīqiya. It may have been to him that the responsa of the Babylonian *ge'onim* were given to be copied in Fustat by the likes of Ibn ʿAwkal and Sahl al-Tustarī (see chapter 4) before they were sent on to Qayrawān.[8]

But around 1006, Elḥanan turned his attention to Syria, traveling there indefatigably. Perhaps he did this in order to pursue ties with the Jerusalem *yeshiva*; or perhaps it was in pursuit of grander designs to recenter Syrian

[7] On Elḥanan's dates, see Bareket, *Fustat on the Nile*, 209.

[8] See the sources cited in Cohen, "Administrative Relations," 122–23 nn. 31–32.

Jewry on Egypt. We know little of these trips, except that on one of them, between 1011 and 1013 or 1014, he was stranded in Damascus during the Fatimid attempt to crush one of the Jarrāḥid revolts. When he returned to Fustat, he found the Jews of Egypt suffering under al-Ḥākim's decrees.[9] Their agony became his opportunity. While in Damascus, he wrote to Jerusalem describing in a florid Hebrew the persecutions Jews were enduring in the capital, perhaps in order to play on the sympathies of his correspondents.[10]

On his return to Fustat, Elḥanan assumed the seat of chief justice of the Palestinian rabbinical court—a position his connections in Syria helped him maintain, since the provincial courts sent him documents to be validated. While sending documents to be validated was a routine part of business, it also expressed fealty, and so his validations offer us a glimpse of the formal and informal networks Elḥanan maintained. So does his titulature. When he validated a deed of 1019 drawn up in the Palestinian rabbinical court in Tyre, he still used the Babylonian title *rosh ha-seder she-le-khol Yisra'el*, which the exilarch in Iraq, Ḥizqiyyahu b. David (d. 1040), had granted him. But it was the last time he would express loyalty to Iraq, in a Palestinian legal document or anywhere else.[11] By about 1020, he became the leading representative of the *yeshiva* of Jerusalem in the Fatimid capital.[12]

It is possible that in turning toward Palestine and alienating the Iraqis, Elḥanan knew what he was doing. He may have made a conscious decision to forego his ties to Baghdad, at the time still nominally the Abbasid capital but de facto the protectorate of the Buwayhid *amīr*s, Imāmī Shīʿīs who made no secret of their contempt for their Ismāʿīlī rivals in the west. In view of the fact that the caliph in Cairo was an unpredictable ruler with a history of persecuting religious minorities, Elḥanan probably deemed it wise to avoid antagonizing him by keeping up ties in the east. The gamble of cutting his ties with Iraq paid off when, having become the leading Egyptian representative of the Palestinian *yeshiva* in Fustat, Elḥanan now attempted to procure recognition as head of the rabbinical court from the caliph himself—a power grab that set him on the road to being ousted from the good graces of the Palestinian *yeshiva* as well. He also usurped a few additional prerogatives from the *ga'on* of Jerusalem, including the closely guarded right to issue bans of excommunication, and then solicited—and received—donations for his father's *midrash* from Jews as far away as Acre and Damascus—as Cohen puts

[9] Bareket, *Fustat on the Nile*, 206–7.

[10] Bodl. MS Heb. a 3.21.

[11] MS PER 83.

[12] Bareket, *Fustat on the Nile*, 214 n. 120, with references to earlier literature. See also Gil's citation from T-S 8 J 7.13, in which a certain Ḥasan b. Saʿdān b. Aṣbagh had met with the caliph, who in turn mentioned that he had been brought a legal decision from Palestine approving all legal judgments and decisions as Elḥanan's exclusive prerogative. Gil identifies the fragment as written in Elḥanan's handwriting; *History of Palestine*, sec. 797.

it, "at the very back door of the [Jerusalem] *yeshiva*."[13] And, in the triumph of his career, he solicited—and received—an annual stipend for the *midrash* from al-Ḥākim, who had already granted one to the Jerusalem *yeshiva*.[14] This was too much for the Palestinian *ga'on*, Yoshiyyahu b. Aharon—but more was yet to come.

Even though Elḥanan b. Shemarya lacked the scholarly prestige of his father, he was successful (at least temporarily) in some of his more audacious designs on the Jewish community because the historical conditions were right—or rather, were highly unfavorable to Jewish institutional life. Even though Elḥanan's career spanned precisely the years of al-Ḥākim's anti-*dhimmī* edicts, including the wholesale destruction of synagogues and churches, he was nonetheless able to secure privileges from the caliph, including an investiture as chief judge and a stipend. The Jews of the realm must have understood that Elḥanan had the caliph's ear, and given the extraordinary instability of caliphal relations with *dhimmīs*, they must have welcomed a strong leadership close to the Fatimid court rather than in far-off Jerusalem.[15] This worked only to Elḥanan's advantage.

But within less than a month of al-Ḥākim's sudden demise or disappearance on February 13, 1021, Elḥanan took the final step that ended his career just short of what might have been its apex.[16] In chasing ever more official acknowledgement of his chiefdom of Egyptian Jewry, he attempted to blackmail Yoshiyyahu Ga'on into granting him the title his father had once held, *av bet din*, by threatening to block the *ga'on*'s ratification in office by the caliph. Since one could not be elected *ga'on* without first achieving the rank of *av bet din*, this move was a direct attempt to usurp the gaonate itself. Elḥanan knew that when the new caliph al-Ẓāhir (1021–36) ascended the throne, Yoshiyyahu would petition the chancery for confirmation as *ga'on*. Elḥanan also knew that Yoshiyyahu had no direct route to the chancery. And Elḥanan also knew that Yoshiyyahu knew that Elḥanan had connections at court, as evidenced by the confirmation he had received as judge and the stipend for the *midrash*. Elḥanan must have told Yoshiyyahu, then, that if he did not grant him the title he wanted, he would not facilitate his ratification; either way, Elḥanan was the next *ga'on*. His attempt at extortion was somehow foiled—whether by the *ga'on* himself or the *ga'on*'s supporters in Fustat we do not know.[17]

[13] Cohen, "Administrative Relations," 123. On the prerogatives that Elḥanan usurped, see P. Heid. P 910r, T-S 8 J 22.14, and T-S 16.134, cited in ibid., 123 nn. 33–34. On Syrian donations to the *midrash*, see T-S 18 J 4.5 and T-S 13 J 35.2, cited with reference to previous discussions in ibid., 123 n. 36. See also Goitein, *Mediterranean Society*, 2:202.

[14] Caliphal stipend for the *midrash*: T-S 18 J 4.5; for the *yeshiva*: T-S 13 J 26.16, both cited in Cohen, "Administrative Relations," 124 n. 37; but cf. Bareket, *Fustat on the Nile*, 208 at n. 93.

[15] Cohen, "Administrative Relations," 124.

[16] This paragraph is based on the interpretation put forward ibid., 124–27.

[17] Ibid., 127 n. 48.

The aftermath of Elḥanan's ambition appears in two additional letters. One is a poison-pen letter that Ḥizqiyyahu the Exilarch in Baghdad wrote to an Iraqi leader in Fustat in the month of Adar, 1021 (some time between 17 February and 17 March), claiming, among other things, that Elḥanan was disloyal, unlearned, and motivated only by the pursuit of power. The letter also discloses his attempt to blackmail the *ga'on*. "Does he not realize," the exilarch asks in dismay, "that his deeds are known in Aleppo, in Damascus, in Fustat, and in all of Palestine?"[18] In attacking Elḥanan's grandiose ambitions, the exilarch states that he "seeks leadership (Heb. *serara*), but it escapes him," a judgment that Cohen has pointed out paraphrases the talmudic dictum "He who chases greatness (Heb. *gedulla*), greatness escapes him."[19] The exilarch deliberately altered the talmudic phrase, Cohen argues convincingly, by inserting the word *serara*, which connotes administrative authority and is the precise Hebrew equivalent of the Arabic *ri'āsa*, "chiefdom." Was the exilarch referring again to the blackmail attempt, or to some new kind of *serara* after which Elḥanan was striving? The letter was written during a technical interregnum, since al-Ẓāhir was not proclaimed caliph until March 27, 1021; but al-Ḥākim's sister, Sitt al-Mulk, ruled the government de facto (and continued to do so until her death, probably by poison, two years later). Could Elḥanan have petitioned Sitt al-Mulk's chancery for something, either the same recognition as head of the rabbinical court in Fustat that he had received from her brother, or something more, formalization of the prerogatives he had accumulated, including those that threatened the very office of the Jerusalem *ga'on?*[20] Whatever it was that Elḥanan was seeking, the outcome was the same: the Jewish communal leadership in Jerusalem swiftly and decisively ostracized him and then assembled a new set of allies in the capital.

The last Geniza fragment that mentions Elḥanan's name shows him in a state of disgrace. Some time before Shelomo b. Yehuda acceded to the gaonate in

[18] P. Heid. P 910r, to Yehuda *rosh ha-seder* b. Avraham (February, 1021), lines 7–8 (blackmail) and 10–11 (quotation). See Goitein, *Mediterranean Society*, 2:562 n. 17; Cohen, "Administrative Relations," 125–26 and n. 40; Gil, *History of Palestine*, sec. 797 and n. 70; Bareket, *Fustat on the Nile*, 212–13.

[19] P. Heid. P 910r, lines 12–13; Babylonian Talmud, *'Eruvin* 13b; Cohen, "Administrative Relations," 125; on the connotations of the word *serara*, see Cohen, *Sefer ha-qabbalah*, 237.

[20] Cohen argues that the *serara* Elḥanan sought was authority over the Palestinian *ga'on* in the form of the title *ra'īs al-yahūd* ("Administrative Relations," 125–27). His article must therefore be seen as a partial revision of his earlier book, *Jewish Self-Government*, which argued that there was no headship of the Jews until the 1060s and no serious rival to the authority of the Jerusalem *yeshiva* until just before it moved north to Tyre in 1073. His article by contrast argues that there was an attempted breakaway by Egyptian Jewry as early as the 1020s in an attempt to establish a headship of the Jews. Still, what Elḥanan was trying to establish was not necessarily the same office that the leaders of the 1060s–80s eventually managed to institutionalize. On Sitt al-Mulk, see Delia Cortese and Simonetta Calderini, *Women and the Fatimids in the World of Islam* (Edinburgh, 2006), 124 at n. 77; *EI*² s.v. "Sitt al-Mulk" (Heinz Halm); and Lev, "The Fatimid Princess Sitt al-Mulk," *Journal of Semitic Studies* 32 (1987): 319–28. Sitt al-Mulk also possessed her own *dīwān* and received petitions there; see al-Musabbiḥī, *Akhbār Miṣr*, 111, cited in Lev, *State and Society*, 69.

1025, he wrote a letter to Fustat describing the annual pilgrimage convocation on the Mount of Olives in Jerusalem on Hoshaʿna Rabba, the largest public gathering of the Jewish liturgical calendar, and the public humiliation of Elḥanan b. Shemarya, forced to declare his loyalty to the Jerusalem *yeshiva*. The letter is fragmentary, but one can gather the tenor of events: "meanwhile," Shelomo b. Yehuda writes, "Elḥanan had arrived, but we chased him away, so that he found himself in an indescribably humiliating position. . . . Finally he testified before the assembly that he . . . to this *yeshiva*. And when. . . . Afterwards, we were friendly with him and called him up to the reading of the Torah."[21]

Around the time Yoshiyyahu Ga'on died in the spring of 1025 and Shelomo ha-Kohen b. Yehosef assumed the Jerusalem gaonate, followed after a very brief tenure by Shelomo b. Yehuda in the fall of that same year, Elḥanan abruptly vanishes from the Geniza. One of the first things the new Palestinian *ge'onim* did on assuming office was to put a speedy end to Elḥanan's career and thus all correspondence with him ceases.[22] Unlike Yoshiyyahu b. Aharon, the Palestinian *ge'onim* of the later 1020s would not tolerate an Egyptian secession. Even if holding onto Egyptian loyalists had not been important to them in its own right, they now had at least one good reason why it should be: access to the caliph. The *ge'onim* had averted Elḥanan b. Shemarya's power grab, but it taught them that they now needed to find a reliable route to the chancery to help them confirm their own positions and prevent others from usurping them.

ENTER THE QARAITES

Just before Elḥanan disappears, the volume of correspondence between the curia of the Palestinian *yeshiva* and the Qaraites of Fustat increases dramatically—even accounting for the general increase in extant rabbinic correspondence after 1025.

It is not merely the volume of correspondence that signals a change: the letters of the late 1020s reveal that both the rabbinic leadership and the Rabbanite laity knew there was a new Qaraite reservoir of political and fiscal power and began tapping it as needed (on the laity, see chapter 7). The Palestinian rabbinic leadership saw the Qaraites as potential political patrons and neutral mediators on their behalf—not despite their being Qaraites, but precisely

[21] T-S NS 320.42, in Arabic and Hebrew, lines 10–13, 16. Goitein dates the letter and makes the authorial attribution in "New Sources on the Palestinian Gaonate," 510–15, 529. Gil attributes it to Shelomo b. Yehuda's son Avraham, ca. 1045, but I follow Goitein's dating; see Gil, *History of Palestine*, secs. 796–800; Bareket, *Fustat on the Nile*, 207–15. Translation from Goitein, "New Sources on the Palestinian Gaonate," 509.

[22] Cohen, "Administrative Relations," 123–24.

because of their lack of affiliation with either the Babylonian or the Palestinian *yeshivot*.

How did they establish their connection to the Qaraite courtiers? How did they come to rely on them, and what led them to believe that the Qaraites would agree to play the role?

There are two significant pieces of documentary evidence that suggest answers to these questions. At first glance, they appear to be at cross-purposes with one another: in one, the Qaraites of Fustat attempt to free themselves from the administrative control of the Rabbanite leadership; in the other, they cooperate willingly with them. But on closer analysis, both these documents attest to a single development: the Qaraites' readiness to use their political power in the service of the *ga'on* of Jerusalem, including stamping out the embers of Rabbanite rebellion in Fustat if needed.

A Petition to al-Ḥākim's Chancery

The first document is a decree (*sijill*) from al-Ḥākim's chancery releasing the Qaraite community "of Fustat and elsewhere" from the supervision of a Rabbanite judge (see fig. 4).[23] The *sijill* alludes to legal differences between the two groups and divergences "over the permissible and the forbidden"; though it has been read as referring to food laws and specifically Rabbanite supervision of Qaraite butchers, the phrase should probably be read in more general terms. But it is also true that income from slaughterhouses was one means by which the high-ranking leaders of the Jewish community asserted their control over their underlings. Between June 1024 and March 1025, for instance, a communal official inheriting a ritual butcher and examiner post from his father in two slaughterhouses in Fustat was forced to give half his weekly income to a discretionary fund controlled by the *ga'on* Yoshiyyahu b. Aharon and a group of local Fustat notables allied with the *yeshiva*. Documents from other periods specify various kinds of taxes that butchers paid to some designated official of the community.[24] Whether or not the differences between Rabbanite and Qaraite methods of animal butchering were at stake, one deduces on the basis of this *sijill* that a certain Rabbanite judge of Fustat had

[23] T-S Misc. 20.92, in Arabic; see Khan, *Arabic Legal and Administrative Documents*, 440 (I have altered his translation). The word *sijill* derives from the Latin *sigillum* (seal, or in medieval usage, a document bearing one) via Byzantine Greek *sigillion* (treaty or edict) and Aramaic and Syriac *sigilion*; in Arabic it denotes a public or legal document in the form of either a letter or a scroll. See *EI*², s.v. "*sidjill*" (F. C. de Blois); J. E. Wansbrough, *Lingua Franca in the Mediterranean* (Richmond Surrey, 1996), 178.

[24] T-S 20.104; Goitein, *Mediterranean Society*, 2:227. The deceased father was David b. Shekhanya, on whom see below, chap. 7, 178–80. Rabbinic law holds that anyone unversed in the rabbinic laws of butchering animals can do so only under the supervision of someone who is versed in them (see Maimonides, *Mishne Torah*, Hilkhot sheḥiṭa, 4).

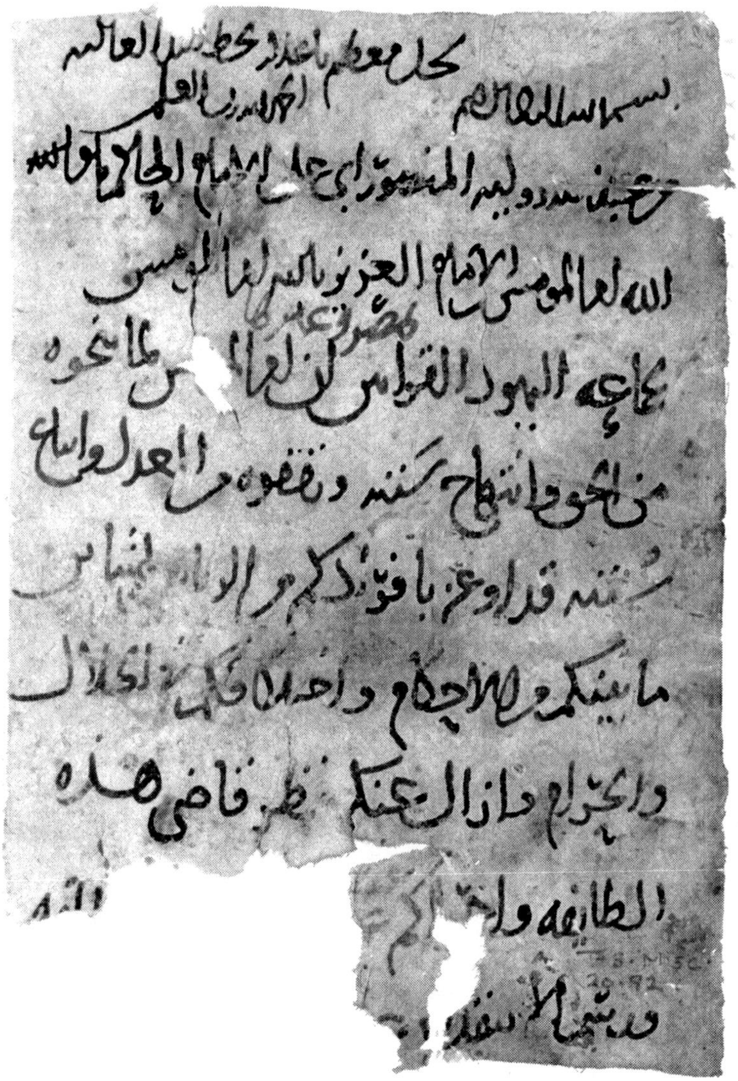

Fig. 4. The Qaraites' rise to power in Cairo: copy of a rescript granted by the Fatimid caliph al-Ḥākim to the Qaraites "of Fustat and elsewhere" exempting them from the supervision of the Rabbanite judge. In Arabic, ca. 1020. Cambridge University Library, T-S Misc. 20.92r.

managed to assert his dominance over the Qaraites, and they now fought back. It is highly probable that the judge in question, through whom this copy of the decree may have entered the Geniza, was Elḥanan b. Shemarya.

> A mighty *sijill* at the top of which [there is a caliphal motto, *ʿalāma*] in the writing of the exalted hand: praise be to God, lord of the universe.
>
> In the name of God, the merciful, the compassionate: from the slave of God and his deputy, al-Manṣūr Abū ʿAlī, the *imām* al-Ḥākim bi-Amr Allāh, Commander of the Faithful, son of the *imām* al-ʿAzīz bi-llāh, Commander of the Faithful, to the community of Qaraites [the following phrase is added above the line] in Fustat and elsewhere:
>
> On account of the righteous path that the Commander of the Faithful follows and the just course that he pursues, he has ordered your separation from the Rabbanites in consideration of the legal differences between you and your disparity over the permissible and the forbidden [*li-tabāyun mā baynakum min al-aḥkām wa-ikhtilāfikum fi l-ḥalāl wa-l-ḥarām*], and has removed from you the inspection of the judge of that group [*wa-azāla ʿankum naẓar qāḍī hādhihi l-ṭāʾifa*] and put you [the paper is torn]. . . . He has decreed that no attempt should be registered . . . [the document breaks off here].

The text is merely dispositive and contains neither a reference to the petition in response to which it was issued nor a narrative account of the circumstances that brought it about. But it is possible to piece together its context on the basis of circumstantial evidence.

Previous interpretations have presumed that the *sijill* came in response to clashes between Rabbanites and Qaraites, and the presumption of strife between the two groups made this seem the most likely explanation, as did the temptation of an analogy with two decrees of ca. 1030 and 1034 that separate Rabbanites and Qaraites in more sweeping language (see chapter 8). But there is no other evidence of clashes during this period, and explaining the decree by presuming them overlooks the problem of why the decree came about now rather than at any other point.

In fact the Fatimids were unconcerned with the internal dynamics of the *dhimmī* groups. With the exception of al-Ḥākim's persecutory edicts, the caliphs issued decrees only at the behest of the communities themselves. Initiative for administrative change had to come from the *dhimmī*s themselves, via petition. Later procedural manuals—particularly the vast compendium of the Mamluk chancery official al-Qalqashandī (1355–1418)—elaborate how the chanceries processed petitions. Subjects brought their written entreaties to the palace in Cairo and waited at one of its gates. A runner collected the petitions and handed them over to palace officials, who forwarded them to the caliph and his ministers. If the chancery endorsed a petition, it was returned to the party who had submitted it with the caliph's ratifying signature or motto (his *ʿalāma*). If he did not, it was forwarded to the chancery where a new decree was drawn up and ratified. Sometimes the petition was never returned at all. Petitioning for a rescript was therefore a business decisively facilitated by connections at court—by the presence of sympathetic courtiers who might see the petition through one of these processes. Having a *sijill* issued, then, depended on friends in high places.[25]

The surviving Fatimid decrees concerning the Jews—most of which date to the years between about 1000 and 1050—are either routine investitures of appointment or else address communal conflicts, Rabbanite-Qaraite or intra-Rabbanite.[26] This means that the Jews sought the intervention of the caliph's chancery in situations of political deadlock, when neither party was strong enough to impose its will upon the other by other means. This decree, likewise, suggests that while a Rabbanite faction of Fustat—or Elḥanan b. Shemarya himself—was powerful enough to impose its will on the Qaraites, the Qaraites now fought back, and were powerful enough to have a petition moved through the chancery. The difference between the Rabbanite thrust and the Qaraite riposte was one of method: the Rabbanite officials used their claims on the interpretation of Jewish law, while Qaraites resorted to the power of the state.

The Qaraites, however, had no monopoly on the latter method: Elḥanan b. Shemarya had also used petitions to al-Ḥākim as his chief means of establishing his control over the Jews of Fustat. In this case, however, he resorted to Jewish law, and the Qaraites trumped him in his strong suit.

We must exercise caution, though, before concluding that this *sijill* actually effected Qaraite "administrative independence" from the Rabbanites, let alone their "enfranchisement" in communal affairs.[27] Soon after, the Qaraites would throw their lot in with the *ga'on* of Jerusalem and his administrative control, a point to which I will return below. And in 1029, the Qaraites of Ramla would attempt to extricate themselves from the control of local Rabbanite meat market supervisors; this *sijill*, then, apparently never went into effect in Syria.[28] What is more, over the early 1030s, the Qaraites continued to seek independence from the Rabbanites in religious matters, struggles that resulted in the more sweeping edicts of ca. 1030 and 1034 that I just mentioned. This decree,

[25] al-Qalqashandī, *Ṣubḥ al-aʿshā*, 3:491–92; Stern, "Three Petitions," 187–88; Khan, *Arabic Legal and Administrative Documents*, 303–5 (also citing al-Maqrīzī). Cf. the page citation from al-Qalqashandī (3:529–30) in Stern, "Three Petitions," 207, and Khan, *Arabic Legal and Administrative Documents*, 303.

[26] See, e.g., CUL Or. 1080J 7 and T-S Misc. 20.92 (both treated below); cf. T-S Ar. 41.105 and T-S AS 182.291, from a conflict over liturgical innovations between factions of Rabbanites, thirteenth century.

[27] Cf. Khan, *Arabic Legal and Administrative Documents*, 440; Sela, "Head of the Rabbanite, Karaite and Samaritan Jews," 265, has gone even further in arguing that this decree "enfranchised" the Qaraites, who had been subject to sweeping Rabbanite administrative control under an office of the head of Fatimid Jewry, but now took power from them in a formalized and institutionalized way; cf. above, chap. 3.

[28] See the 1029 decree mentioned in the letter T-S 13 J 13.28+T-S AS 120.62.

then, cannot be taken as evidence that the Qaraites achieved administrative independence during the reign of al-Ḥākim. It does, however, shed light on shifting politics at the Fatimid court. It shows that during the reign of al-Ḥākim, Qaraites gained access to the palace in Cairo and enough power to have a decree sent through the chancery—the earliest Fatimid decree the Geniza has preserved regarding the Jews.

Who were these Qaraites? There are only two possibilities: members of the Tustarī family or David ha-Levi b. Yiṣḥaq.

The second generation of Tustarīs was already ensconced in Fustat by the first decade of the eleventh century. Letters datable to the 1010s show them trading with the al-Tāhirtī group in Qayrawān in the west and with others in Iraq, and dealing in textiles of all kinds, from simple Egyptian flax to wildly luxurious silks and brocades that only the wealthiest could afford to buy. By the same period, the two elder sons of the third generation, Abū Saʿd Ibrāhīm and Abū Naṣr Ḥesed, had already risen in the firm. The Egyptian historian al-Maqrīzī (1364–1442) affirms that during the period of al-Ḥākim (996–1021), "two Jewish brothers," Abū Saʿd Ibrāhīm al-Tustarī and Abū Naṣr Ḥesed, "achieved greatness, one dealing with merchandise and the other with currency exchange and imported merchandise from Iraq." He also notes that these Tustarī brothers rendered banking services to long-distance traders, and this tells us that they had already amassed both a great fortune and a reliable network of partners to distribute and collect funds. He further explains that it was al-Ẓāhir (1021–36) who "accepted Ibrāhīm b. Sahl al-Tustarī into his service to manage the purchasing of luxury goods"—a detail that implies that his formal connection with the court dated only to the period after the *sijill* was issued. But one must assume that that this formal connection was preceded by an informal one. The Tustarīs' connections in Cairo, then, most likely began before the third decade of the eleventh century with their trade in currency, gemstones, and fabrics, the consumers of which inhabited the palace grounds in Cairo. The brothers of the third generation then went on in the 1020s to develop a personal relationship with the caliph, and by the late 1030s were appointed to positions of rank at court.[29] David ha-Levi b. Yiṣḥaq, meanwhile, appears in 1023 as director of a bureau (*dīwān*) in the Fatimid administration (see chapter 7); his appointment, too, must have been preceded by a period of informal contacts at court. All these figures could well have seen to it that a petition submitted by their fellow Qaraites would turn into a decree.

While this petition was intended to effect Qaraite liberation from Rabbanite administrative control, it actually furnished the preconditions of Rabbanite

[29] I number the Tustarī generations differently from Gil, who has the sons of Yisra'el as first generation (see p. 364). On Tustarī trade with Ifrīqiya and Iraq, see above, chap. 5; MS Meunier; T-S 12.133; T-S 8 J 36.2; Fischel, *Jews in the Economic and Political Life*, 72–78; and Gil, *In the Kingdom of Ishmael*, sec. 369–75, citing (at sec. 372) al-Maqrīzī, *Khiṭaṭ*, where Ḥesed's name is garbled.

dependence on the Qaraites and of closer cooperation between the two groups by making it evident that the Qaraite courtiers had access to the chancery. Precisely at this point, this was information of use to the leadership of the Palestinian *yeshiva*, who were looking to quell Elḥanan b. Shemarya.

An Admonition from the Elders of the Community

The second piece of evidence from this period is a court document that shows Abū Yaʿqūb Yūsuf b. Yisraʾel al-Tustarī, the middle brother of the second generation, cooperating with the leadership of the Rabbanite community as presided over by the *gaʾon* of the Jerusalem *yeshiva*. While his nephews were working their connections at court to block the administrative power of one Rabbanite in Fustat, he submitted willingly to the administrative power of another in Jerusalem. This argues against presuming that administrative tensions between Rabbanites and Qaraites in this period were due to some state of permanent sectarian conflict.

The document is a fragmentary deposition from Fustat recording a dispute between a brother and a sister over the sister's right of inheritance.[30] According to Rabbanite (and some Qaraite) authorities, daughters could not inherit when they had brothers, and the sister was due no part of her father's estate.[31] According to Islamic law, however, she stood to inherit one-third of her father's estate and her brother two-thirds. Hoping for the better settlement, she brought the case before the chief Ismāʿīlī *qāḍī* in Cairo.[32] This pragmatic approach to justice is well documented among Jews during this period (and among both Copts and Jews under the Mamlūks), but Jewish communal authorities feared that allowing Jews to bring cases to the Islamic courts would undermine their own authority.[33] The Rabbanite communal leaders of Fustat

[30] T-S 13 J 30.3, in Hebrew. The document was cut for reuse and the surviving part was also reused a number of times: recto and verso are covered in interlinear Arabic writing both upside down and right side up relative to the Hebrew text.

[31] Some Qaraite legists allowed daughters with brothers the same share as in Islamic law, while others denied the daughter's right to inherit even in the absence of male heirs. The practice among Rabbanite Jews in the Fatimid and Ayyubid periods was more lenient to daughters than the law dictated, and various Geniza documents attest to daughters inheriting equal shares with their brothers (b. Bava batra 115b; Goitein, *Mediterranean Society*, 3:280–84; 2:395–98; and on this case, 3:331 and 599 n. 19). Mubāraka's brother may have wished to apply the stringent talmudic ruling, and out of fear that a rabbinical court would uphold it, she went outside the system. For a different interpretation, cf. Olszowy-Schlanger, *Karaite Marriage Documents*, 250 n. 19.

[32] Noel Coulson, *Succession in the Muslim Family* (Cambridge, 1971): 108–34, especially 114 and 108 n. 1. In the deposition the *qāḍī* is called *shofeṭ ha-shofeṭim* for the Arabic *qāḍī al-quḍāh*, a title the Fatimids had adopted formally in 999; see Adel Allouche, "The Establishment of Four Chief Judgeships in Fatimid Egypt," *Journal of the American Oriental Society* 105, no. 2 (1985): 317–20.

[33] See above, chap. 3, n. 12; below, chap. 8, n. 85; and a power of attorney from Tyre (1036–37) in which two sisters, who had inherited from their father in equal shares with their brother, grant him power to collect money owed on the estate. Since under Islamic law, the daughters would have been

therefore attempted to settle the sister's case preemptively by offering her the same inheritance she would have received in an Islamic court, despite the fact that under normal circumstances rabbinic law offered her nothing. The document demonstrates, then, not only that Jews were in the habit of shopping for justice, but also that the rabbinical courts had given up on controlling this habit and instead devised a system that probably only encouraged it. The document also demonstrates the precedence of rabbinic authority over rabbinic law: bringing rabbinic law into conformity with Islamic law, somewhat paradoxically, could help to preserve the rabbinical courts' authority and jurisdiction.

What remains of the deposition commences tantalizingly in the midst of the elders' admonitions to the girl (Mubāraka) not to seek redress in an Islamic court. They tried to tell her, they appear to be saying, that such practices are reprehensible and foment division and strife in the Jewish community, "and that they divide her from the congregation of Israel. But this Mubāraka neglected our words," they say, "and went to the chief *qāḍī*" of the Muslims. Meanwhile, the military police of the Fatimids (*rijjāla*) took Mubāraka's brother to the *qāḍī* to have him surrender her share, "and she mocked him," or perhaps gloated over his defeat (the wording is unclear). "She, for her part, is standing by her word and in her audacity is demanding her father's inheritance from her brother in a gentile court," it continues. "She has roughly five men supporting her, and they are hardly God-fearing. What we know of the matter we have written in our testimony in order to bring him [her brother] to [justice in] the *majlis* of our lord, head of the academy, may his Rock sustain him, to do what will bring him closer to his Rock."

And thus they ordered Mubāraka's brother to be remanded to the court of Yoshiyyahu b. Aharon Ga'on, who would presumably force him to surrender a third of his inheritance. Of the five signatures that still remain on the document, four are known from other documents as people involved in both Qaraite and Rabbanite affairs; their scholastic loyalty is impossible to determine.[34] The only one that belongs definitely to a Qaraite is that of Abū Yaʿqūb Yūsuf b.

entitled only to half-shares, they had gone to the trouble of preparing an equivalent power of attorney intended for Islamic courts lest the matter come before a Muslim *qāḍī* (Bodl. MS Heb. b 11.12). On the Mamlūk period, see el-Leithy, "Coptic Culture and Conversion."

[34] Also signing are Faraḥ b. Mu'ammal, whom the *ga'on* of Jerusalem Shelomo b. Yehuda would greet in a letter of 1029 along with the Tustarīs, David b. Yiṣḥaq, and some Rabbanites including the grandson of his predecessor Shelomo ha-Kohen b. Yehosef (T-S Misc. 35.15v); see also T-S 12.347 (addressed to him by the Qaraite scholar and *kātib* Ṭoviyya b. Moshe); Bodl. MS Heb. d 66.69 (addressed to him by Natan b. Avraham); and Yosef b. ʿAzarya, who signed a court copy of a Qaraite deed of betrothal in the 1060s (T-S 16.109). In his first treatment of this document, Gil asserts that all five witnesses were Qaraites (*Tustarīs*, 25), but later, he is more cautious and claims only two (*History of Palestine*, sec. 932). He further offers this document as evidence that the *ga'on* of the Palestinian *yeshiva* had jurisdiction over Qaraite Jews (Gil, *Tustarīs*, 25; *In the Kingdom of Ishmael*, sec. 371); cf. above, chap. 3.

Yisra'el al-Tustarī. Thus we see him actively working to help the *ga'on* maintain his authority over cases such as this one.

By their second generation in Egypt, then, the Tustarī family participated in the rabbinic legal and administrative system run by the Palestinian *yeshiva*. It even possible that al-Tustarī signed the document knowing of Elḥanan b. Shemarya's plans to usurp the power of the Jerusalem gaonate: he may have known that he could help curb Elḥanan's designs by allying himself with the Rabbanites of Jerusalem. What the caliphal edict could not achieve the Jerusalem *ga'on* perhaps could.

Qaraites at the Center of Rabbinic Politics

The *sijill* shows the Qaraite grandees in Cairo using their political muscle against the local Rabbanite leaders, while the deposition suggests a wider context in which Qaraites were willing to join forces with Rabbanites for the purposes of some common interest. Together, the documents demonstrate that in the early 1020s, the Qaraites of Fustat shifted their weight toward the Palestinian Rabbanites. The Palestinian Rabbanites, for their part, shifted in return toward the Qaraites even as they asserted their control over the Iraqi segment of the Rabbanite community in Fustat.

Thus when Shelomo ha-Kohen b. Yehosef acceded to the gaonate in the spring of 1025 and asked the notables of Fustat to solicit a caliphal appointment on his behalf—the letter I discussed in chapter 3 as the first stage in the process of gaonic ratification—the notables he addressed were a mixed group from all three congregations. This is the first appearance of Qaraites as brokers between the *ge'onim* of Jerusalem and the caliphs in Cairo. The letter is faded, especially at the beginning, where much of its ink has been rubbed off, and several addressees' names have vanished. Those that are still legible, though, suggest the ties this *ga'on* had cultivated among the notables of Fustat.

> Greetings to our master Yefet b. Ṭoviyya al-Nīlī . . . he mentioned you in [his] letter . . . and to David b. [Yiṣḥaq?] . . . [and to] Shelomo ibn Ḥakīm al-Fāsī, and to all abettors of truth and supporters of justice . . . my prayers day and night . . . the heads of the congregations, that is, the elders of both groups [*shetey ha-kittot*], the Palestinians, the Babylonians, [the Qaraite]s [?], their lords, their elders, and their sages . . . and the rest of the communities, their old and their young, may blessings and prayers be heard on your behalf and on behalf of those whom you hold dear and those who hold you dear, on behalf of them and on behalf of all Israel . . . the exalted, our lord, master David b. Yiṣḥaq, the mighty lord . . . in Hebrew in his name and in the name of his father. . . . [35]

[35] T-S 24.43, lines 1–10. I have used elements of both Goitein's and Gil's readings.

Of the three people whose names are still fully legible, two are Rabbanites, both members of the segment of the Palestinian rabbinic establishment that maintained ties with the Babylonian *yeshivot* in Baghdad—a sign that the Iraqis had not yet been fully ousted.[36] To the Qaraite courtier David b. Yiṣḥaq, the *ga'on* explains that he has written a separate letter in Hebrew that has alas not (yet?) been found among the Geniza papers.[37]

As the Palestinians' alliance with the Babylonians of Fustat broke down, they turned to the Qaraites in their stead. This explains why when Shelomo b. Yehuda acceded to the gaonate six months later, he wrote a letter offering lavish praise for the Qaraite *nasi* Ḥizqiyyahu b. David. In the same letter, he expressed repeatedly the fervent hope that he might return from Egypt to Palestine before Rosh ha-Shanah carrying "a writ from the government, may God defend it, to strengthen my hand from instigators of quarrels," by which I understand a rescript of appointment to defend himself from the incursions of Rabbanites in Fustat.[38] That is also why Shelomo b. Yehuda describes himself in a letter to Efrayim b. Shemarya (Abū Kathīr b. Maḥfūẓ al-Ghazzī), *ḥaver* of the Jerusalem *yeshiva* and head of the Palestinian congregation in Fustat (1020–47), as having led prayers for the Rabbanite and Qaraite communities of Ramla on alternate days: it was no secret that the caliph al-Ẓāhir had by now ratified two *ge'onim* in office through Qaraite mediation.[39]

The early 1020s, then, witnessed a tectonic realignment of the politics of the tripartite Jewish community. The Iraqis had overstepped their bounds; the Qaraites attempted to secede from their jurisdiction; the Jerusalem *ge'onim* would not allow the Iraqis to secede from theirs and used the Qaraites as a way

[36] On Yefet b. Ṭoviyya, see T-S 20.6 (1037, witnessing the marriage of Sahlān b. Avraham to Ester, granddaughter of the chief rabbinic judge of Sijilmāsa and daughter of Yosef b. ʿAmram; see Goitein, *Mediterranean Society*, 1:48 at n. 39 and 3:127–38) and T-S 8 J 4.1 (a contract drawn up between two merchants in 1028 at the Palestinian rabbinical court in Fustat). Shelomo b. al-Ḥakīm al-Fāsī was one of the seven *parnasim* of the Palestinian community in Fustat and the object of Hayya Ga'on's friendly inquiries in T-S 12.829 (a letter of 1007 addressed to two brothers in Fez who corresponded regularly with the *ge'onim* of Baghdad; see Mann, *Texts and Studies*, 1:113–15 and Goitein, *Mediterranean Society*, 3:430 n. 18); see also Bodl. MS Heb. a 2.4 (the marriage contract of Yefet b. Shelomo to Berakha b. Shemarya, perhaps the sister of Efrayim b. Shemarya); T-S 10 J 5.11 (from 1022, where his signature appears with those of Avraham b. Sahlān and Efrayim b. Shemarya among others). His signature is instantly recognizable because it is so sloppy, as if his hand shook terribly or he never learned to write Hebrew characters beyond what was required of him in primary school.

[37] Qaraites corresponded in Arabic and Judeo-Arabic as much as in Hebrew, but Jews from Tyre, whether Rabbanite or Qaraite, evince a marked preference for Hebrew. It may be David's geographic provenance that moved the *ga'on* to write in Hebrew, or else his presumption of Qaraite linguistic preference.

[38] T-S 13 J 17.17, in Hebrew, to an unknown person (possibly Efrayim b. Shemarya or Avraham b. Sahlān). The date Gil offers of ca. 1026 should be regarded as tentative but accords with what one can reconstruct of the context.

[39] ENA 2804.12–13. For Efrayim's full name, with *kunya*, patronymic, and toponymic *nisba*, see Bodl. MS Heb. b 13.54, address in Arabic on verso.

to extend their hand over Egypt. The Qaraites, for their part, had no objection to deeper involvement in the *yeshiva*'s affairs.

"If They Could Cast Their Net over Everyone . . ."

The gaonic turn toward the Qaraites did not entirely settle matters with the Iraqi contingent in Fustat. The Jerusalem *ge'onim* continued serving as the uncontested leaders of the Rabbanite Jews of the Fatimid realm while soliciting Qaraite involvement in rabbinic affairs. But the Iraqis were clamoring at the gates the entire time, poaching followers here and privileges there. Tensions and power struggles persisted into the early 1030s between members of the Iraqi- and Palestinian-rite congregations, replete with excommunications.

Thus Shelomo b. Yehuda complained bitterly in a letter of ca. 1030 about Hayya Ga'on's tireless campaigns to solicit donations for Pumbedita on his own turf in Fustat. The Iraqi leadership "are always sending letters about this matter," Shelomo b. Yehuda objects with palpable irritation, "and in this way they try to extend their borders. If they could only manage to cast their net over everyone [in their jurisdiction], all the better to increase their profit."[40] (In the Hebrew word for net, *reshet*, Shelomo b. Yehuda's addressee might have heard the word for gaonic jurisdiction, *reshut*; I have attempted to capture this echo in brackets.) Around the same time, Shelomo b. Yehuda tried to block the establishment of an Iraqi leader in Palestine by resorting to the tactic of petitioning the caliph, pleading with him not to let there be "two chiefs" in Palestine, for, as he wrote, "the *niʿma* bestowed [upon me] would then be no *niʿma* at all."[41]

That also explains why two *ge'onim* of Jerusalem, Shelomo ha-Kohen b. Yehosef and Shelomo b. Yehuda, granted Iraqi leaders the sorts of titles and positions that would bind them more closely to the Palestinian rabbinic network—to coopt them. Two heads of the Iraqi congregation in Fustat in this period, Avraham b. Sahlān (1016–ca. 1032) and his son Sahlān b. Avraham (1034–49), carried ordination both from Baghdad, as indicated by their title *alluf*, and from Shelomo ha-Kohen b. Yehosef and Shelomo b. Yehuda respectively, who called them by the Palestinian equivalent of that title, *ḥaver*.[42] In a letter of 1029, moreover, Shelomo b. Yehuda warned Efrayim b. Shemarya, head of the Palestinian congregation of Fustat, that he should make peace with Avraham b. Sahlān, now the head of the Babylonian congregation, "for these days are not like former days: for formerly you were your own authority, but now you

[40] T-S 13 J 14.8, in Hebrew, lines 23–28. Cf. the summary of the affair in Baron, *Social and Religious History*², 5:48. For further examples of Egyptian Jewry's loyalties toward Pumbedita during this period, see Cohen, "Administrative Relations," 129–30.

[41] ENA 4020.65; for a detailed discussion of this document, see chap. 3.

[42] Cohen, "Administrative Relations," 119.

have entered under the authority of God and the authority of [all] Israel."[43] Fustat used to be independent, the *ga'on* says, and each congregation did what it liked; but now it must be brought into the larger Jewish oecumene—of which I am head.

Also in 1029, Shelomo b. Yehuda traveled to Egypt for the special purpose of proclaiming a solemn excommunication against followers of the Babylonian-Iraqi rite for their methods of butchering animals. He describes the incident to his ally Efrayim b. Shemarya as follows. "Your letter arrived on the 24th of Sivan," he writes, "and on the 25th, on that very Monday, we gathered in the cemetery in a large group, and we brought out Torah scrolls and excommunicated every promulgator of sinful statutes and author of vanity and lies and those who foment quarrels between brothers in order to achieve their desires."[44] This is a telling formulation. The ban the *ga'on* declared against the Iraqis was worded against "those who promulgate false laws . . . in order to foment strife among Israel," a phraseology meant to imply that the Iraqis knowingly courted heresy.[45] There had always been various schools of thought and interpretations of usage in the complex questions of how to butcher an animal according to rabbinic law.[46] But the *ga'on* decided whether and when to make an issue of these differences. This also indicates that Rabbanites were no less vulnerable to being declared heretics than Qaraites were—it all depended on who was doing the excommunicating, when, and why. It all depended, in short, on questions of timing and power.

The tectonic realignment also explains why in May of that same year, Shelomo wrote to his son Avraham in Fustat urging caution and delicacy in mediating conflicts between the Rabbanites and Qaraites and warning him in no uncertain terms not to involve himself in their disputes. "In Fustat there is fighting between the Rabbanites and the Qaraites," he wrote, "and among the Rabbanites [themselves]. . . . Please, please, my son, be careful not to take part in that at all. Rather, write to me, and if you . . . write [to me] about it [telling me] what I can do. For the Jewish community [*umma*] today is ailing [and] needs special care, just as a sick person needs special care. I beseech God not to cause you anything that we will remember badly."[47]

Finally, it explains why Shelomo b. Yehuda, in presiding over the annual pilgrimage festival in Jerusalem on Hoshaʿna Rabba in 1029, refused to bend to a faction of Rabbanites who pressured him to excommunicate the Qaraites (see chapter 8). Mann explained the *ga'on*'s response as a result of his irenic

43 T-S Misc. 35.43, in Hebrew; verso, lines 3–4.

44 T-S 20.102, in Hebrew, lines 27–30.

45 Ibid., lines 33–34; cf. Isa. 10:1–2, "Those who write out evil writs and compose iniquitous documents to subvert the cause of the poor . . ."

46 For comments on the various usages and conflicts over them, see Goitein, *Mediterranean Society*, 2:225–27.

47 T-S 13 J 36.5, in Judeo-Arabic, written 7 May 1029, verso, lines 20–23.

personality. But it is no accident that he banned the Iraqis in Fustat the same year that he refused to excommunicate the Qaraites in Jerusalem. In the Palestinian Rabbanite political network, the latter had replaced the former.

If the Palestinian rabbinic leaders were in the vanguard of fostering friendships with the Qaraite grandees in Cairo, the rest of the Rabbanite Jews of the Egypt and Syria did not take long to follow. Over the course of the 1020s, the Qaraites received petitions from Jewish communities in every corner of the Fatimid empire, in a regular pattern of entreaty and aid that is the subject of the next chapter.

CHAPTER SEVEN
"GLORY OF THE TWO PARTIES": PETITIONS TO QARAITE COURTIERS

Over the course of the 1020s, Rabbanite individuals and congregations from all over the Fatimid realm began addressing petitions to the Qaraite courtiers in Cairo. Their entreaties attest to the fact that the Qaraites had become the principal link to the government not just for the Palestinian Rabbanite leadership, but for their followers.

About two dozen letters have survived from the quarter-century spanning the gaonate of Shelomo b. Yehuda (1025–51) in which Rabbanites from Tyre to Alexandria seek the patronage of the Qaraite grandees of Cairo, soliciting their help, thanking them for some generous deed, or publicly acknowledging their activities on behalf of the Jews. Every one of those letters is addressed to the Tustarīs of the second and third generations or to the courtier David ha-Levi b. Yiṣḥaq. They attest to a veritable awakening on the part of Fatimid Jewry over the course of the 1020s and their realization that the Qaraites offered them the surest route to government protection.

Two momentous clusters of events provide the context for this flurry of appeals on the part of the Jews of the Fatimid empire. The first was al-Ḥākim's persecutions of Christians and Jews. Though the Arabic chroniclers disagree over when the caliph first issued edicts concerning the *dhimma*, direct evidence comes in the form of a letter that Elḥanan b. Shemarya sent to the Jews of Jerusalem during his campaign in Syria between 1011 and 1013–14, in which he mentions the destruction of synagogues, desecration of Torah scrolls, and laws requiring Jews to wear black clothing and hang a wooden block from their necks (Christians were required to wear an enormous cross). Under the pressure of the edicts, many Jews and Christians converted to Islam—a detail Elḥanan's letter corroborates—though the caliph would later allow them to revert.[1] Churches and synagogues in Syria were destroyed as well: most famously, the Church of the Holy Sepulcher in Jerusalem, which sat at the city's

[1] Bodl. MS Heb. a 3.21, lines 34–35 (synagogues and scrolls), 37–38 (clothing and blocks), 40–41 (conversion); for a summary of the problem of dating in the Arabic accounts, see Gil, *History of Palestine*, secs. 568–76, with Elḥanan's letter discussed in sec. 572.

highest point, was reduced in 1009 to a heap of rubble. (That church's high dome had been rivaled only by the Dome of the Rock, which the Umayyads built in the 690s to eclipse it, but the Dome of the Rock itself collapsed in an earthquake on 4 September 1015.) By 1020, al-Ḥākim had repealed his decrees and received an enormous number of petitions from Christians requesting the return of churches that had been commandeered. Though no parallel petitions to the chancery have survived from Jews, the Geniza has preserved private petitions attesting that the Jews of the Fatimid empire concerned themselves with repossessing, restoring and rebuilding their synagogues during the early years of al-Ẓāhir's rule.[2]

But no sooner had the communities begun to return to normal life when Fatimid Palestine was consumed by another round of Bedouin revolts. The Jarrāḥids took Ramla and Tiberias in August 1024 and then moved south along the coast toward Egypt, attacking Ascalon, al-ʿArīsh, and al-Farāma and taking Ramla a second time in March 1025. The leader of the rebellion, al-Ḥasan b. al-Mufarrij b. Daghfal b. Jarrāh, divided the cities of Syria and Palestine in a pact with his allies Sinān and Ṣāliḥ b. Mirdās. Those caught in the crossfire suffered poverty and famine, blocked roads, lack of supplies, and plague. They also suffered extraordinary tax burdens, and their efforts to raise funds appear scattered in the Geniza correspondence dating to this five-year period. The revolt was finally quashed in May 1029.[3]

In the context of these two exigencies, the Qaraite courtiers—who had previously served as the Jerusalem curia's private channel to the chancery—came to occupy a central place in communal lives of Jewish congregations throughout Syria and Egypt. One must assume that news of these Qaraites' largesse spread all the more quickly because of the twin crises.

"WHO STANDS IN THE BREACH AND INTERCEDES ON ISRAEL'S BEHALF BEFORE THE CALIPH . . ."

Though it is frustratingly unclear precisely what position the Tustarīs occupied at the Fatimid court during the 1020s, al-Maqrīzī tells us that among the luxury goods Abu Saʿd Ibrāhīm al-Tustarī purveyed to al-Ẓāhir was one that would prove an extremely important sale: a slave-girl of Nubian, Abyssinian, or Sudanese origin named Raṣad, who became the caliph's concubine and in 1029 bore his only male heir, the future caliph al-Mustanṣir (1036–94). During al-Mustanṣir's caliphate, Raṣad would sustain her loyalty toward her former master and he would manage her considerable wealth, but she was

[2] Ibid., sec. 576.

[3] For an exhaustive treatment of the historiography on the Jarrāḥid revolts of 1024–29, see Bianquis, *Damas et la Syrie sous la domination fatimide*, 415–70.

unable to appoint him to any position until 1044, after the death of the vizier who had checked her power as regent, ʿAlī b. Aḥmad al-Jarjarāʾī. At that point Raṣad "ruled the state" (*ḥakamat ʿala l-dawla*, in the words of one historian from the thirteenth century), and Abū Saʿd became her *wāsiṭa* (proxy or chief administrator), head of her *dāwāwīn* and her chief of statecraft (in the words of another from the eleventh). His older brother Abū Naṣr Ḥesed was appointed to an official position in Palestine, though on the multiple occasions when Raṣad asked him to serve in her *dīwān* he refused. In any event, the brothers are not recorded in any official positions before al-Mustanṣir's caliphate.[4]

We know something more about David b. Yiṣḥaq during this period due to a fortuitous reference and an ingenious connection. The reference appears in a chronicle by the court historian al-Musabbiḥī (366–420/977–1030), of whose history of Egypt only a tiny fragment covering some of the period of 414–15 AH (1023–25) has survived, in a single manuscript now at the Escorial in Spain. There he notes that on 21 Jumādā 414 (10 September 1023), a certain David the Jew, "Dāwūd al-yahūdī," was appointed over some finances in the bureau of tax revenues (*dīwān al-kharāj*).[5] There were about twenty Fatimid *dawāwīn* in all, of which the *dīwān al-kharāj* was among the most important.[6] David b. Yiṣḥaq is not introduced in the text but simply referred to in a way that suggests that he might have appeared earlier in the chronicle and thus in other roles at court. The ingenious connection was made by Gil, who, in his determination to join the literary and documentary pieces of the puzzle of tenth- and eleventh-century Jewish history, connected this name with David b. Yiṣḥaq, who makes his first appearance in Geniza records in 1024. As evidence that David b. Yiṣḥaq served as a Fatimid *kātib*, this might appear thin, since he was surely not the only David the Jew inhabiting the Fatimid empire in the year 1023. But sources preserved in the Geniza offer ample evidence confirming Gil's hypothesis circumstantially, if not directly.[7]

Chief among these is a panegyric (see fig. 5) composed by a Rabbanite cantor named Abū Sulaymān David b. Shekhanya (d. 1024), who moved to Fustat some time before 1013 and secured for himself appointments as a cantor in the

[4] See most recently Cortese and Calderini, *Women and the Fatimids*, 110–11. It is still not known whether Raṣad was manumitted during al-Ẓāhir's lifetime (ibid., 45–46). The historians are Ibn al-Muyassar (ibid., 110) and al-Muʾayyad fi l-dīn al-Shīrāzī (111). See also Fischel, *Jews in the Economic and Political Life*, 78–79, with reference to sources; Gil, *Tustaris*, 38; idem, *History of Palestine*, sec. 598n. (citing Ibn al-Muyassar and al-Maqrīzī) and sec. 780; and Lev, *State and Society*, 42. On Abū Naṣr's appointment in Palestine, see below, chap. 11, 314–15.

[5] Al-Amīr al-Mukhtār ʿIzz al-Mulk Muḥammad b. ʿUbaydallāh b. Aḥmad al-Musabbiḥī, *al-Juzʾ al-arbaʿūn min Akhbār Miṣr* (The Fortieth Chapter of the History of Egypt), ed. Ayman Fuʾād Sayyid and Thierry Bianquis (Cairo, 1978), 12 (= 137v–138r of the Escorial manuscript).

[6] *EI*[2] s.v. *dīwān* (H. L. Gottschalk).

[7] Gil, *History of Palestine*, sec. 803n.

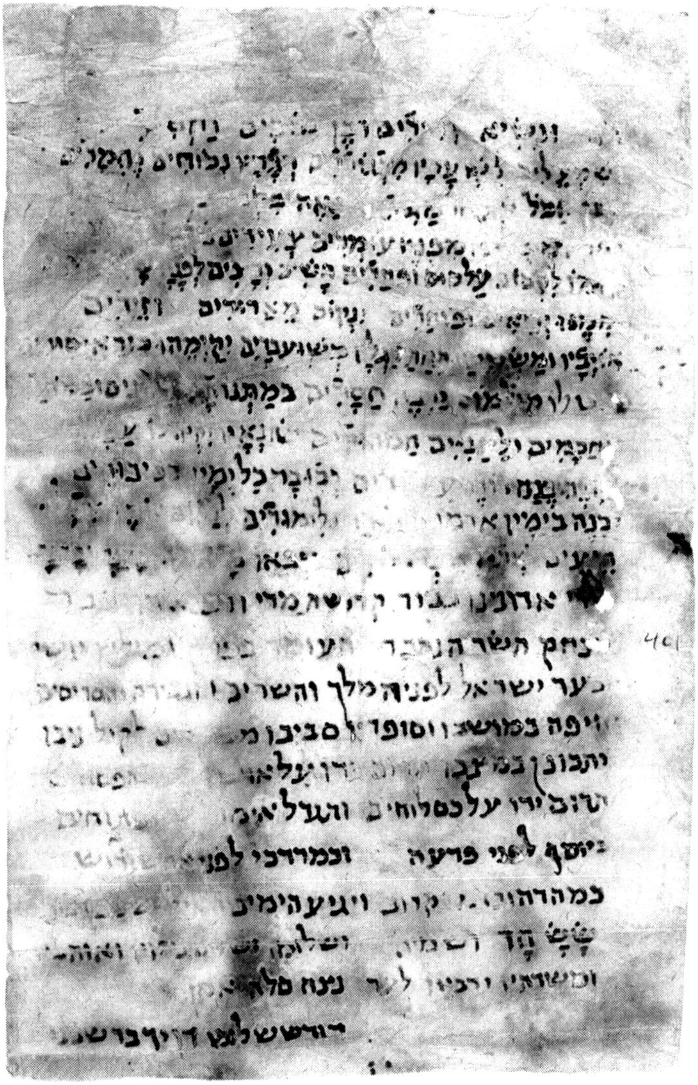

Fig. 5. Rabbanite praise for a Qaraite grandee: encomium for the Qaraite Abū Naṣr David ha-Levi b. Yiṣḥaq, a *kātib* in the Fatimid land tax bureau (*dīwān al-kharāj*), written by the Rabbanite cantor Abū Sulaymān David b. Shekhanya, Fustat. In Hebrew, ca. 1023–24. Center for Advanced Judaic Studies, University of Pennsylvania, Halper 401r.

Palestinian synagogue, a scribe in the Palestinian rabbinical court, and the overseer of two slaughterhouses.[8] Abū Sulaymān composed encomia for other Qaraites as well, including the Persian banker Sahlawayh b. Ḥayyim (fl. 1011–35), a banking partner of the Tustarīs.[9] Cantors were usually also poets and composed the texts they recited in synagogue, and though this one appears to be a proem introducing a longer letter that has not surfaced, it is also possible that it served as thanks for one of David's contributions to the Jewish community, on which more below.[10]

Here, what is interesting are the allusions the letter makes to David b. Yiṣḥaq's position at the court in Cairo and the shape his power assumed in the Jewish community during the early years of his appointment. It addresses him as "our lord, his honorable holiness, our master and teacher David b. Yiṣḥaq, the esteemed lord, who stands in the breach and intercedes on Israel's behalf before the caliph, the courtiers, the regent, and the eunuchs, and who holds court in his *majlis* surrounded by his *kuttāb* . . . like Joseph who stood before Pharaoh and Mordecai before Ahasueros." Like Joseph, David was "set over the whole land of Egypt" (Genesis 41:41), and like Mordecai in Persia (Esther), he was the archetypal court Jew, interceding with the ruler on behalf of his coreligionists. That the poet paints him in his *majlis* (*moshav* in the poet's calqued Hebrew) with a team of *kuttāb* (*soferim*) confirms Gil's identification.[11]

[8] On the poet, see Fleischer, "Rabbi Sakan—payyeṭan ereṣ-yisra'eli ba-me'a ha-'asirit," in *Studies in Geniza and Sepharadi Heritage Presented to Shelomo Dov Goitein on the Occasion of his Eightieth Birthday*, edited by Shelomo Morag and Issachar Ben-Ami, with the assistance of Norman A. Stillman, Hebrew (Jerusalem, 1981): 1–37; Bareket, *Fustat on the Nile*, 161–62; Goitein, *Mediterranean Society*, 2:138. Abū Sulaymān's father, Shekhanya, was also a liturgical poet, and sixteen of his poems have been identified so far.

[9] Mosseri II 246.2 (series B, P 46); on Sahlawayh b. Ḥayyim, see further Bodl. MS Heb. d 66.15 (verso, margin), where Ṣadaqa b. 'Ayyāsh asks Ḥesed ha-Tustarī to extend greetings to him; Goitein, *Letters of Medieval Jewish Traders* (Princeton, 1973), 311 n. 24, and idem, *Mediterranean Society*, 3:56 and 438–39 n. 33 (T-S 12.621, Bodl. MS Heb. e 108.70, and T-S Misc. 29.58a); Gil, *History of Palestine*, sec. 364 (DK 333); secs. 780 and 812 (T-S 13 J 8.14, recto, a list of donors to a joint Rabbanite-Qaraite collection for which David b. Shekhanya's ode may have served as thanks). An encomium to the Qaraite Abū Sa'd Ibrāhīm (Avraham) al-Tustarī was perhaps also authored by Abū Sulaymān (T-S 13 J 10.12): it begins by praising the second generation of Tustarīs, moves to Abū Naṣr Ḥesed and Abū Sa'd Ibrāhīm, and then focuses on the latter. It therefore probably dates to Abū Sa'd's rise at court in the 1020s. Mann reads this panegyric as a petition requesting support for needy people (Mann, *Jews in Egypt and in Palestine*, 1:81).

[10] On cantors, see Mann, *Jews in Egypt and in Palestine*, 2:269; Goitein, *Mediterranean Society*, 220–21.

[11] Halper 401. Cf. Gil, *History of Palestine*, sec. 803n., and Sela, "Headship of the Jews in Karaite Hands," 258, who interpret the word "queen" (*gevira*) as "regent" (in Hebrew the word means both) and take the poem as referring to al-Mustanṣir's mother. But the author of the encomium died before September, 1024, while the future caliph was born only in 1029; when the poem was composed, then, the future mother of al-Mustanṣir was not yet the regent but merely a concubine. On the date of the poet's death, see the Rabbanite marriage contract for Sibā' b. Avraham and Rayyisa b. Kathīr (T-S 10 J 2.2, Fustat, dated Thursday, 27 Tishri 1337 Sel. [1024]); David bar Shekhanya's son Yefet signs and

The first direct evidence of a regular pattern of entreaty to the Qaraites is dated late 1024, a year after David b. Yiṣḥaq's appointment to the *dīwān al-kharāj* and well into the Tustarīs' activities at court. The intercession of all three was called upon in a campaign to liberate the head of the Palestinian Jewish community in Fustat, Efrayim b. Shemarya, from prison.

As far as one can tell, Efrayim b. Shemarya had been imprisoned as a result of some slanderous plot, and one immediately wonders whether Elḥanan b. Shemarya (no relation) was the instigator: had Efrayim fallen victim to Elḥanan's malicious contrivances (see chapter 5)? Imprisonment could only come about as a result of an appeal to the government, and the same was true of prisoners' release. The caliph al-Ẓāhir had Efrayim freed after the intercession of personages both communal and governmental, a fact announced in an open letter from the curia of the Jerusalem *yeshiva* (still under the gaonate of Yoshiyyahu b. Aharon) to the Palestinian congregations of Fustat and Ramla.[12]

The letter is written on an unusually large piece of paper in a calligraphic hand, as befitted a piece of public correspondence. In rhyming couplets and strings of biblical quotations and allusions, it expresses gratitude to all those who had interceded on Efrayim's behalf, urging the congregations of Ramla and Fustat to thank various figures in the Fatimid government. The Fustat congregation probably knew the events intimately (those who did not were perhaps not meant to), so they are recounted in a way that frustrates the historian's efforts to ascertain precise details. But through the veil of oblique references emerge certain names and titles of those to whom praise is due: the caliph, the vizier, the governor of Palestine (Anūshtekīn al-Duzbarī), David b. Yiṣḥaq, who is lavished with even more praise than the previous three and called "our viceroy, our lord, our leader [*salarenu*], the distinguished lord, his honor and holiness, our master and teacher"; the three Tustarī brothers of the second generation, called by their Hebrew names (Yashar, Seʿadya, and Yosef); and finally and less precisely, all the other nobles and *kuttāb* who helped in the affair and the elders of "the two parties" (*shetey ha-pe'ot*), from which one understands that Efrayim's release was a bipartisan cause of the highest order.[13]

offers the blessing for the dead after his patronymic (see Bareket, *Fustat on the Nile*, 162 n. 165, and Fleischer, "Rabbi Sakan," 5 n. 8).

[12] T-S 18 J 4.26, in Hebrew. Gil dates this letter to the end of 1024; see his note to line 26. The letter was begun by Yoshiyyahu Ga'on who was evidently too ill to finish it, and completed by his successor-to-be Shelomo ha-Kohen b. Yehosef; Yoshiyyahu died in March 1025. Mann, *Jews in Egypt and in Palestine*, 1:120–22, proposes that the charges were brought against Efrayim by one of his rivals in the *yeshiva*, since the end of the letter makes a plea for an end of strife.

[13] On al-Duzbarī, see below. Gil ingeniously connects the Hebrew title given here, *ha-gevir ha-maṣliaḥ*, with his Arabic title, *al-amīr al-muẓaffar*, of which the Hebrew is a literal rendering: *History of Palestine*, 2:80, note to line 24. *Sālār*, leader, comes from the Persian word for commander and is frequent in Hebrew and Judeo-Arabic Geniza documents; see Mann, *Responsa of the Babylonian Geonim*, 158 n.

The letter ends with quotations from Isaiah that were laden with meaning given the exigency of Efrayim's imprisonment coupled with the generalized chaos of warfare: "Have we not enough with hatred from the gentiles, our enemies," it reads, "who demand our lives to the point where we are 'each devouring the flesh of his own kindred,' . . . 'Manasseh Ephraim's and Ephraim Manasseh's' [Isaiah 9:19]? Have we not enough with 'Aram from the east and Philistia from the west, who eat' us 'with greedy mouths' [Isaiah 9:11]?" This last allusion is a typological casting of the Bedouin as Aram, the tribal confederation that vied with the Israelite monarchy under King David and his successors for control of the land from Damascus south to Hammath; the Philistines, from the coast of Gaza, probably refer to the Fatimids, who would have sent their navies from Egypt. Manasseh and Ephraim (besides referring to the prisoner by name) may allude to the two wings of the Jewish community, Rabbanite and Qaraite, and thus to the possibility that ʿAdaya ibn al-Qazzāz, the Qaraite military governor of Palestine, had had a hand in Efrayim b. Shemarya's imprisonment. The allusions suggest together that the Jewish community was caught between the Bedouins on the one hand and the ravages of warfare on the other, and that resolving the problem of Efrayim's imprisonment would not hurt the cause of unity.[14]

Further testimony of David b. Yiṣḥaq's role in resolving the affair comes in a Hebrew letter of Efrayim b. Shemarya himself, probably also written in late 1024, thanking David b. Yiṣḥaq and other elders of Fustat whom he does not mention by name. The letter is a draft; it is full of false starts and infelicities, and hence is difficult to translate in its entirety (it also contains the sorts of spelling errors that show just how loose a grasp even the best-educated rabbinic leaders had of Hebrew orthography). But it is also full of metaphors that reflect the political vocabulary of patronage that we have seen thus far, only rendered in Hebrew: Efrayim calls David "the respected viceroy, elder of the generation" and compares him to a gushing spring, a fount of sustenance. The simile is deliberately chosen: a patron should not run dry, unless the client angers him with disloyalty. In petitions, flattery serves several functions: it honors the patron for past deeds and uses those deeds to convince him or her to do more by honoring the client's request. Thus Efrayim mentions David b. Yiṣḥaq's patronage, kindness, and benefactions and compares them with God's; he calls himself "your slave," invoking chancery protocol and establishing his relationship to David as one of subject to ruler. He goes on to write that he has

---

141, with references to earlier discussions, and Hirschberg, "The Salars and Negidim of Qayrawan," Hebrew, *Zion* 23–24 (1958–59): 166–73. The word *pe'a* in classical rabbinic literature means "corner" or "section," but in Geniza documents it means "party" or "group," a calque of the Arabic *fi'a*. See Goitein, *Mediterranean Society*, 2:534 n. 84 and 5:609 n. 39.

[14] Aram: 2 Samuel 8:5–12; 1 Kings 11:23–25; 1 and 2 Kings *passim*. Philistines: Judges and 1 and 2 Samuel passim. For more on ʿAdaya, see chap. 8 at n. 44.

"found favor with you and dwell among those who lodge in your shade," again a standard metaphor for patronage, and one that suggests that other people dwelled there with him—and that this was not the first of David b. Yiṣḥaq's generous acts toward the Rabbanites. Finally, he writes, "You command your minions //well// to read my petitions in my support," establishing that David's chief method of patronage was interceding with the government bureaucracy. The letter is a classic example of *shukr al-munʿim*, expression of thanks to a benefactor.[15]

Efrayim b. Shemarya's reliance on David b. Yiṣḥaq did, indeed, lead to ever greater appeals on behalf of the Jewish community—the next of them from the curia of the Jerusalem *yeshiva*.

"We Are Lacking in Everything, Naked, Grieving, and Poor"

On acceding to the gaonic office in March, 1025, the first thing Shelomo ha-Kohen b. Yehosef did was to solicit the notables in Fustat for an investiture from the chancery, a task in which David b. Yiṣḥaq served as main intercessor. The Tustarīs do not appear in the *gaʾon*'s covering letter, but it has survived in only a fragmentary state; but David b. Yiṣḥaq's name appears clearly (see chapter 6). The *gaʾon* happened to take office during a time of crushing hardship for Jerusalem's Jews—the Jarrāḥid campaign in Syria—and this explains why his petition was followed by a series of entreaties from the entire Jewish community of Jerusalem to the Qaraite notables.

At the start of the Jarrāḥid wars in 1024, the government levied a special tax upon the city's residents in order to raise revenue for the military campaign against the tribal rebels. The total tax amounted to the staggering sum of fifteen thousand dinars (three or four dinars could support the average family for a month), of which the Jews were responsible for six thousand. Half of the six thousand was to be paid by the Qaraites (possible evidence that they represented half the Jewish population of Jerusalem).[16]

Shelomo ha-Kohen b. Yehosef wrote to Efrayim b. Shemarya in Fustat to see about getting help with the tax payment. The letter is remarkable for its use of language that at times reproduces verbatim the stylized appeals found in letters written by poor people (or the professional scribes who helped them)

[15] T-S 12.273v, in Hebrew. The last line reads "ki teṣavve //ṭov// be-ḥelkha liqrot ketavay be-maʿonay"; *maʿon* in Hebrew means "refuge" or "dwelling place," but that definition is difficult to reconcile with the context and syntax here. The root *ʿ-w-n* in Arabic means to help or support; it seems that Efrayim intends the Arabic definition though he uses a Hebrew construction. On the letter, see Gil, *History of Palestine*, sec. 803n; Sela, "Headship of the Jews in Qaraite hands," 260 n. 16; see also Bareket, *Jewish Leadership in Fustat*, 250.

[16] Cf. Baron, *Social and Religious History*², 5:412 n. 73, who argues that Qaraites in Jerusalem were richer but not more numerous than Rabbanites, though it seems the wealthier ones were concentrated in Egypt. This tax should not be confused with the annual tax the Jews of Jerusalem were obliged to pay for the privilege of living there; see the manuscript Unidentified Firkovich.

asking for money from benefactors. "We have run out of everything we had," writes the *ga'on*, "and we are lacking in everything, naked, grieving and poor. No one has anything left in his house, not even his clothing or his household implements."[17] Although the *ga'on* does not single out the Qaraite grandees in his requests for assistance, he notes that "even the Qaraites" have been forced to borrow money to meet their share of the payment—a piece of rhetoric perhaps designed to play on the sympathies of the courtiers. Though nothing has surfaced on what became of this campaign, it is safe to assume that the Qaraite courtiers helped the Jerusalem community to meet this payment, since the next *ga'on* of Jerusalem, Shelomo b. Yehuda, urgently beseeched their aid in two later campaigns, when the Jews of Jerusalem were even more desperate.

"He Has Become a Wellspring of Our Generation": Tripoli

Right after this, the Qaraite courtiers began receiving solicitations from beyond the central axis of rabbinic administrative activities in Jerusalem and Fustat. By 1025 it was evidently known as far as Tripoli (Syria) that Abū Naṣr Ḥesed al-Tustarī could be relied upon to convince the caliph to issue decrees. It may also have been public knowledge that the *ga'on* Shelomo ha-Kohen b. Yehosef had been confirmed in office through the mediation of the Qaraite courtiers.

During the summer of Shelomo ha-Kohen b. Yehosef's brief tenure as *ga'on in* 1025, the Jews of Tripoli sent Abū Naṣr Ḥesed al-Tustarī an appeal, the first from the laity and the first from outside Jerusalem. Al-Ḥākim had turned the synagogue of Tripoli into a mosque. By 1025, synagogues in other places had been rebuilt or returned to the Jews, but the Jews of Tripoli were still unable to reappropriate their building from Muslim worshipers. Their only choice was to build a new one, but strictly speaking, this ran contrary to the Pact of ʿUmar, or at least one of its statutes more or less regularly enforced in this period. The congregation therefore wrote a Hebrew letter asking that one of their public buildings, which had also been commandeered by Fatimid bureaucrats, be returned to them for use as a synagogue.

The Hebrew, one should note, is hardly of an elevated variety (and also teems with Arabic usages; I have tried to render the awkwardness in translation), a fact that makes one ask why the Tripolitanians wrote in Hebrew at all.

[17] ENA 2804.8, in Hebrew; see Mann, *Jews in Egypt and in Palestine*, 1:160. Gil, who has developed an innovative technique for dating Geniza letters on the basis of *ʿalāmāt* (the mottoes with which rulers and communal leaders signed documents), dates this letter to the spring of 1025 since the address contains the *ʿalāma* of Shelomo ha-Kohen b. Yehosef (who served as *ga'on* from March 1025 until his death in August of that year). Although the events described in the letter bear a striking resemblance to those of 1029, including the Jews being forced to borrow money to pay the tax at exorbitant rates of interest, it probably describes events toward the beginning of the wars of 1024–29. Gil also derives from this letter the fact that the Jarrāḥids sacked Ramla for a second time in the spring of 1025.

They may have felt that their entreaties were more likely to reach the ears of the Qaraite grandee al-Tustarī if they couched them in a formal, biblicizing register, as with letters we saw earlier.[18] After ten lines of honorifics, they write:

> We, the congregation of Tripoli, all of us extend much peace to our lord the respected elder //and ask// the Lord our God, who hears the cry of the oppressed, to make him live long. We hereby inform his esteemed greatness that we are in great distress, without a place to pray. All the places of the house of Israel have returned to them, their synagogues, except for our city, since they had //turned// the synagogue into a mosque. We are asking our lord that he be kind to us in procuring an edict from the government to build for us from one of our destroyed places //in which the servants of the king are dwelling without paying rent// a synagogue like all the [other] places, and may we remind our lord // that// in this very year, the congregation of Jubayl built a synagogue, and not one of the gentiles said a word [about it], and we remind our lord that every year we pay a fee to the gentiles for our place, that . . . and it is not a fitting place in which to say the name [of God]. May your peace and blessings increase eternally, and may redemption be hastened.[19]

Just what the Tripolitanians wanted is slightly unclear: they seem to be asking to have a nonsynagogue building returned and to convert it into synagogue, but perhaps fearing that even this would be regarded as building a new place of worship, they point out that the Jews of Jubayl had very recently "built a synagogue, and not one of the gentiles said a word" about it. This same ambiguity was frequently played on by Jews and Christians under Fatimid rule: though in theory, the erection of *dhimmī* houses of worship was prohibited, in practice, it was permitted if the buildings were inconspicuous. That much is attested in another document mentioning a church or synagogue (*kanīsa*) that was ordered to be torn down not because it was new but because it was taller than a nearby mosque.[20]

Why Abū Naṣr Ḥesed al-Tustarī was singled out in this particular case is unclear; it suggests that his reputation as intercessor may have spread more rapidly

[18] ENA 4010.47, in Hebrew; recto and verso. See especially line 17, where they have *qahāl*, with a long vowel, on the basis of Arabic orthography; line 21, where they have the Hebrew *medina* for "city"; and line 22, where they use Arabic syntax (see Gil's note there). Gil suggests that the Rabbanites of Tripoli wrote in Hebrew for the same reasons those of Tyre did—a coastal preference for the language; but this explanation is weakened by their lack of facility with it.

[19] Mosque: *mirjaz*; see Gil, *History of Palestine*, 2:505 (note to line 22). Edict: *nishtevan*, borrowed from imperial Aramaic. See Ezra 4:7, 4:18, 4:23, and 5:5, where it indicates the official letter that Artaxerxes' governors send to him and his letter in reply; in 7:11, it indicates a letter sent by Artaxerxes containing a decree. The last phrase (*yeshaʿ yuḥash*) is the *ʿalāma* of Shelomo ha-Kohen b. Yehosef; Gil thus dates this letter to summer, 1025.

[20] Goitein, *Mediterranean Society*, 2:144, citing T-S 13 J 7.6 (lines 19–22).

than that of David b. Yiṣḥaq. An appeal from Ascalon the same summer was directed more generally to the "Qaraite elders" in Cairo.

Ascalon

The Jews of Ascalon were meanwhile busy with a second stage of the patron-client relationship: thanks for benefaction, offered with an eye toward strengthening the relationship. During the summer of 1025, the community wrote a Hebrew letter to the two Jewish communities of Fustat, the Palestinian and the Babylonian, to ask them to notify the courtly Qaraites (here unnamed)—who they hoped would notify the caliph—of the kindness of two Fatimid local governors. The letter asks that the proper thanks be conveyed to "the Qaraite elders" (*ziqney ha-qara'im*) and to the local governors themselves, in the hopes that having this done would encourage the officials to continue their favorable treatment of the Jews.[21]

After some flowery opening greetings, the Ascalonites write to "the two holy congregations of Fustat, and at their head the *ḥaverim*, cantors and respected and esteemed elders":

> With this letter we hereby . . . inform you that there has recently come to us a ruler over the city of Ascalon, and that he has been exceedingly kind with us. He has acted mercifully with us and never oppressed us in a single matter.
>
> We are asking your honors our lords that you intercede for us on his behalf to our elders the Qaraite elders [*sic*]. [Tell them] that a certain officer and the one known as Abū Ḥurayz, the elder of the city, both offer us respect and are good to us in everything we require. If they [the Qaraite elders] ask you, inform them that we told their praises to them [*sic*, i.e., you] so that they [the Qaraites] may encourage their [the officials'] kindness.

The letter suggests that the Qaraite courtiers were perceived as loyal allies and protectors of the Fustat Rabbanite congregations, or of their leaders, Avraham b. Sahlān and Efrayim b. Shemarya (who had already benefited from Qaraite largesse). The channel between these leaders in Fustat and the Qaraite courtiers was further understood to be operating without serious impediments—so much so that one even wonders how much interpretive weight to place on the conflation of pronouns in the letter. The Ascalonites mean to tell the Rabbanites of

[21] T-S 13 J 19.15, in Hebrew; see Gil, *History of Palestine*, secs. 305, 589. Shelomo ha-Kohen b. Yehosef's *'alāma* appears on line 28 and in the address on verso. Mann held that the Ascalon community writing here included both Rabbanites and Qaraites: Mann, *Jews in Egypt and in Palestine*, 1:169; cf. Gil, *History of Palestine*, sec. 305n, and Baron, *Social and Religious History*², 5:413 n. 75, 415 n. 82. Neither Mann nor Baron was yet aware of the identity of these Qaraite elders; Gil proposes that they were the Tustarīs, but David b. Yiṣḥaq is just as likely to have been among them and may have passed through Ascalon on frequent trips between Fustat and Tyre. In lines 19–20, only one of the Fatimid governors' names is given: "ha-yadua' Abū Ḥurayz, zaqen ha-medina" (cf. Gil's reading).

Fustat to "inform the Qaraites that we have praised the officials to you," but instead say "that we have praised the officials to them," meaning the Qaraites, as though anything they told the Rabbanite elders would immediately make its way back to the Qaraite courtiers. Though it was a mere slip of the pen, its repetition in the following sentence invites exegesis: "For you know, our lords, that we are a lowly trifle," they continued, "and that they [the Fatimid officials] are kind to us only because of them [the Qaraites], so that they [the officials] might find favor in your [the Qaraites'] eyes. Do not ignore that our eyes are turned toward you and toward your response to what we ask of you." By 1025, then, the Jews of Ascalon knew of the Qaraite courtiers and imagined that their future well-being depended upon them.

Did the advent of the Qaraite courtiers bring a concrete improvement in the lot of the Jews throughout the Fatimid realm, as this document might suggest? Since every adult still remembered the persecutions under al-Ḥākim, things certainly could not have gotten worse. Yet there had begun to form in the minds of various Jewish communities the perception that whatever improvements they noticed were due to Qaraite intervention.

REDEEMING CAPTIVES IN ALEXANDRIA

Nor were the communities of Syria alone in seeking the Qaraite courtiers' intervention. Captives of all faiths were a consequence of the ongoing skirmishes between competing Islamic polities and between the Fatimid and Byzantine empires, and kidnapping was a risk faced by anyone traveling by sea—and by those in port as well. Pirates and warriors took prisoners whose coreligionists they knew would pay fine sums to ransom them. For pirates, pressing for ransom was more lucrative than selling captives into slavery: the fee for a captive in the Arab ports of the Mediterranean—standardized to prevent further extortion—was 33 1/3 gold dinars, while slaves might be sold for less, particularly if they were very young or elderly. Victims were taken regardless of their religious affiliation, but at least under the Fatimids, they were ransomed by their coreligionists, not by the state. Communities in large port cities such as Alexandria were, then, frequently called upon to raise ransom money, and to do so quickly: kidnappers would announce the arrival of captives in port and await payment while threatening all manner of harm to the captives. Any delay might multiply the beatings, tortures, and sexual abuses to which they were subjected.[22]

The Alexandrian Jewish community repeatedly took up special collections for captives who came to port, but the community could give only so much.

[22] Goitein, *Mediterranean Society*, 1:327–32; Cohen, *Poverty and Charity*, 109–23.

They attempted to spread the burden by calling upon the wealthy of Fustat to donate as well; when the captives were of both *madhāhib*, they sent petitions separately to the Rabbanite and Qaraite congregations.

Thus in December, 1028, Efrayim b. Shemarya received an appeal from the two Rabbanite congregations of Alexandria regarding seven captives from Attalea on the southern coast of Asia Minor, four Rabbanites and three Qaraites.[23] The author of the appeal, Yehoshuaʿ ha-Kohen b. Yosef ha-Dayyan, writing in the name of "the two communities" of Alexandria (*shetey ha-qehillot*—the Palestinian and Babylonian Rabbanite congregations), mentions that he had sent a separate letter to the Qaraite congregation of Fustat, and also notes that he had had letters sent "from the Qaraites and Rabbanites [of Alexandria] to Tinnis, Damietta, and Ṣahrajt," in the Nile Delta.[24] In other cases, the Jewish communities of Egypt held collections to which Rabbanites and Qaraites contributed regardless of the *madhhab* of the captives.

David b. Yiṣḥaq and other Fustat nobles were mainstays of the special campaigns the Alexandrian community conducted, a fact attested in four letters. The first is an undated fragment (only the left side remains) from Alexandria thanking the Palestinian congregation of Fustat for its donations to a ransom campaign. The plight of the captives had been announced during synagogue services according to custom, they had been redeemed, and now the Alexandrians wrote to thank the congregation and its leaders: Efrayim b. Shemarya, the elders, cantors, and *parnasim* (social services officers). They also mention several private contributors, among them an Avraham b. . . . (his patronymic is effaced), possibly Abū Saʿd Avraham b. Sahl al-Tustarī, who donated fifty dinars; Efrayim b. Shemarya (now in a private capacity); and ". . . our master and teacher" David b. Yiṣḥaq. This suggests that the Qaraites sent their donations together with the funds the congregation had collected.[25]

On other occasions the community bypassed the special collections in synagogue and went directly to the major donors. A second letter of 1028 reports that two Byzantine Jewish captives had been taken aboard a ship and brought to Alexandria.[26] Their captors used a particularly effective method of extracting ransom: they asked to be directed to a wealthy Jewish local and sent the captive to

[23] Bodl. MS Heb. a 3.28, in Hebrew. The piece of paper is unusually large, as was common for public missives. See Mann, *Jews in Egypt and in Palestine*, 1:88–90; Ankori, *Karaites in Byzantium*, 46–49; and Olszowy-Schlanger, *Karaite Marriage Documents*, 46–47 n. 33. The captives were from Attalea, not Anatolia. Ultraviolet light permits the reconstruction of a few lacunae left in Cowley's edition but none of them alters the letter's meaning.

[24] On the Qaraite community of Tinnīs, see now Wilferd Madelung and Sabine Schmidtke, *Rational Theology in Interfaith Communication: Abu l-Ḥusayn al-Baṣrī's Muʿtazilī Theology among the Karaites in the Fāṭimid Age* (Leiden, 2006), 8 and 29 n. 22.

[25] ENA 2804.11 (accepting Gil's correction to line 25 but not to line 18). See the discussion in idem, *Tustaris*, 48 and 49 n. 64, and Sela, "Headship of the Jews in Karaite Hands," 260 n. 14.

[26] T-S 13 J 14.20, in Hebrew. Goitein dates the document to early 1029, *Mediterranean Society*, 1:453 n. 23. See also Joshua Starr, *The Jews in the Byzantine Empire*, 641–1204 (New York, 1970), 186.

him as a "gift." Faced with this "gift," the Jew was likely to offer a return "gift" of his own. The local patron chosen this time was the Rabbanite Netan'el ha-Kohen b. Elʿazar of Alexandria, who paid the captive's ransom at one-and-a-half times the normal rate—whereupon the pirates sent him another "gift," hoping to repeat their good fortune.[27] Unwilling to reward their insolence, he ransomed the second captive at the normal fee. The letter is torn at the top and so begins *in medias res*, but one can infer from what remains that a similar tactic had been attempted on "the chief [*rosh*], our master and teacher David ha-Levi, elder of the generation, the mighty lord, glory of the two parties, son of master Yiṣḥaq, may his resting place be in Eden," for whom the congregation had "prayed very much before our Lord in a [special] service of the entire congregation. . . . For they are as two lights in our land—and also in your city, may God preserve them and increase their favor and their honor."[28] The communities' troubles did not end there: immediately after, they received word of yet another shipment of captives from Attalea. The letter goes on to ask for donations toward this fresh shipment.

The third plea from Alexandria to David b. Yiṣḥaq is dated about a year later (December 1030 or January 1031).[29] The letter is torn and much of the right-hand side is missing, but the remaining half seems to indicate that yet another shipment of Byzantine captives had been deposited at the doorstep of the Alexandrians, who now write to him directly.

> . . . from the two congregations in Alexandria . . . services, and we pray for the life of our mighty one, who . . . may his days be lengthened, and may He who makes peace on high enfold you in His peace. The eternity of the Lord is a covenant of peace . . . heaped up in the treasure of the Lord of all creation. And he has become a wellspring of our generation . . . among Israel scattered to the four corners, and in particular to the residents of. . . . For may it be the will of God . . . , for he has kept watch over the religions of God, and . . . his great lordship, the mighty leader, his honor, greatness and holiness, our master and teacher David ha-Levi, may God preserve him, grant him encouragement, and redeem him from all his straits, and after . . . the son of his honor, greatness, and holiness Yiṣḥaq, may his memory be blessed and revived. . . . May God grant his mighty lordship great peace . . . and from his intimate friends and from the entirety of the two congregations . . . the synagogues of Palestine . . .

The two congregations are presumably the Palestinians and the Babylonians in Alexandria, and the elaborate dedication is even more abundantly strewn with

[27] On Netan'el, see T-S 13 J 34.3, in Hebrew.

[28] The letter also mentions prayers for David b. Yiṣḥaq on the Sabbath. Unlike the *khuṭba* in congregational mosques, where mention of the caliph was a political act indicating fealty to one imperial center or another, Jews reserved Sabbath prayers for grandees of all sorts. Goitein, *Mediterranean Society*, 5:298–99.

[29] ENA 4020.45, in Hebrew.

terms of flattery than was usual in letters seeking donations: "he has become a wellspring of our generation," a fixed source of aid upon whom they had come to rely consistently. This was in keeping with the pace David's generosity had kept with the Alexandrians' needs—and with what they were about to ask him:

> . . . to him to inform him that word reached us . . . from the land of Edom [Byzantium]. They brought three of them to the land of . . . healthy, and extremely difficult for the congregation . . . may its strength increase. And this captive came to us when . . . but almost the collection on his behalf and his clothing . . . and they trusted in the kindness of God and in the respected elder master Netan'el ha-Kohen b. Elʿazar, since there still remain in his company . . . We therefore beseech our mighty lord . . . as is his good custom, and that he send word to the elder . . . may he live forever, to send us thirty-three and one-third dinars . . . the elder rabbi Avraham b. ʿAllān . . .

As far as one can tell, three captives had been announced, all originally from Byzantium; they needed to be fed, clothed, and provided with transport home. Netan'el ha-Kohen was perhaps looking after two of them, and the Alexandrians petitioned David b. Yiṣḥaq for help redeeming the third.

The last letter is of a slightly different variety than the first three.[30] It is torn at the top and undated, but enough of the address remains to ascertain that it was written to David b. Yiṣḥaq directly, not by a captive but by a man from Alexandria who writes of his debt to the tax collectors (*baʿaley ha-mas*), probably a reference to the *jizya:* he had fled the tax collector and gone to Fustat to throw himself on the mercy of communal charity.[31] He addresses David as "his honor, greatness, and holiness David, the dear and respected, known as Abū Naṣr, the good elder, man of compassion, and man of peace, a bulwark of peace," followed by a string of messianic tidings and then his request—a variation on the standard format found in Arabic petitions to the chancery: "I hereby inform you, our lord the elder, in your glory, that I came from the land of Alexandria recently under great duress," he writes. "I owe a debt of fifteen dinars. I have left at home four daughters and two sons, hungry, naked, and lacking everything. The tax collectors are harassing them on my account, and I came here to request from [you], may you live, that I be redeemed from the debt that weighs upon me, so that I may return to my children. . . . And now, our lord the elder, you in every [the text is fragmentary here] . . . redeem captives and bring them to their land so that they may return to their dwelling places and be reunited with their children."

The reference to redeeming captives is metaphorical; the man sought to have had his *jizya* paid for him and possibly other debts as well. Though Mus-

[30] T-S 13 J 17.9, in Hebrew.

[31] Goitein, *Mediterranean Society*, 3:239 and 477 n. 104.

lim jurists discussed whether poor people should be excused from the *jizya*, Geniza documents like this one show that at least under the Fatimids and Ayyubids, not all were excused, and some relate beatings at the hands of the tax collector. (In some rural areas, meanwhile, collection attempts were never made.) By the twelfth century, the organized system of poor relief made *jizya* payments for the poor a line item in the community's budget, though the line between public and private charity was never as clear-cut here as in, for instance, early modern European communities.[32]

These four letters show that David b. Yiṣḥaq was known as a reliable (and deep-pocketed) contributor. It also shows that over the course of the late 1020s and early 1030s, he had become a mainstay, followed by Abū Naṣr Ḥesed al-Tustarī, whose brother Abū Saʿd appears nowhere by name in appeals from these years (though some are addressed to "the Qaraite elders" or "the Tustarī elders"). This may point to some decision by Abū Saʿd not to answer community appeals during the years of his rise at court. Was he too preoccupied with business to attend to community needs (such a division of labor between brothers is attested in this period, most famously in the case of Maimonides, whose brother was an India trader)? Or was he simply uninterested in looking after the welfare of his coreligionists?

Mainstays of the Jews of Jerusalem

Captive ransoming was an admittedly compelling cause with a long pedigree of rabbinic injunctions on its behalf, and a generous soul was unlikely to refuse it. It also involved small groups of people at a time (one Geniza letter attests to eighteen captives, but such numbers were rare). But David b. Yiṣḥaq did not limit himself to the singular, individual, local, and emergency acts of giving occasioned by captive appeals. Other appeals were more general, calling for aid to an entire Jewish community at a time.

In the spring of 1029, Palestine was suffering from protracted warfare and famine, as the Fatimid attempts to crush the Jarrāḥid revolt continued on into their fifth year. In December 1028, the governor of Palestine, Anūshtekīn al-Duzbarī, had begun his second serious offensive against the tribes, and the fighting continued for five months before al-Duzbarī defeated al-Ḥasan's ally Ṣāliḥ b. Mirdās on 12 May, 1029, impaled his head on a pike, and massacred his men as they fled south to the Arabian peninsula.[33]

Meanwhile, the residents of Palestine were struggling for their very survival. The roads were in disarray, the countryside was devastated, people were

[32] Cohen, *Poverty and Charity*, 137 (where this document is discussed and translated), 27, 40, 84, 198, and on towns and cities in which one could avoid paying the *jizya*, 137.

[33] See Bianquis, *Damas et la Syrie sous la domination fatimide*, 415–70; Gil, *History of Palestine*, secs. 580–93; *EI²*, s.v. "Djarrāḥids" (Canard).

starving and dying of plague. The pilgrims' caravans had been rerouted for season after season, further disrupting trade and the import of goods. Geniza documents offer intimate details about the day-to-day effects of the devastation that the narrative chronicles omit in favor of high politics. They also, of course, provide information primarily about how the Jewish community fared, although in this case it is perhaps safe to extrapolate those findings to the rest of the population. Rarely did the inhabitants of Palestine fare worse. The only people who managed to live well were those whose stipends came directly from the government in Cairo.[34]

In the spring of 1029, Shelomo b. Yehuda wrote a pair of letters to Fustat describing the dire situation in Jerusalem and asking for help from various leaders. He wrote the first letter on 7 May 1029, unbeknownst to him just five days before the decisive defeat of the Jarrāḥids, to his son Avraham, a *ḥaver* of the *yeshiva* then living in Fustat (see fig. 6).[35]

A number of Jerusalem's Jews had been forced to borrow money at exorbitant rates of interest and, unable to pay off the loans, were languishing in debtors' prison in Damascus. Debtors' prison was a particularly gruesome place: while a prison term in general meant paying the jailers and arranging food for oneself—thus, potentially, torture and starvation—debtors' prison included torture as a matter of course. "In addition to being flogged and beaten, the prisoner was put into the stocks," writes Goitein, "his joints wrenched, he would be chained with a nose ring like a bull, needles would be driven beneath his fingernails and into other sensitive parts of his body, and there is repeated mention of another instrument of torture (with a Persian name) not yet identified with certainty. Persons facing jail for any reason, for example, nonpayment of the poll tax, expected not to be unable to survive torture and life in prison in general."[36] This composite portrait drawn from Geniza documents includes practices from various times and places, so one should not imagine a single individual being subjected to all of them, but it is safe to assume that debtor's prison was an especially dreaded fate.

Among those who had been imprisoned were both Qaraites and Rabbanites, including the Qaraite *nasi* of Jerusalem. It is difficult to know how to interpret

[34] As Shelomo b. Yehuda complains of a certain *muftī*; see below.

[35] T-S 13 J 36.5, in Judeo-Arabic. Sela, "Headship of the Jews in Karaite Hands," 261 n. 19, tends toward the view that the Abū Naṣr mentioned here is David since the contemporaneous appeals for captive ransoming make him an obvious candidate to help the Jerusalem community, and he had been known to donate to the *yeshiva* in the past. I would add in support of her view that Shelomo b. Yehuda's subsequent letter about the same affair refers to the Tustarīs separately from whoever is meant by Abū Naṣr. The *ga'on* refers to David by his *kunya* alone and to Ḥesed and family by their collective *nisba*, al-Dasātira. Cf. Gil, *History of Palestine*, sec. 780. On the situation in Palestine, the Jews of Jerusalem, and the *ga'on*'s appeals during this period, see ibid., sec. 590 and 780.

[36] Goitein, *Mediterranean Society*, 2:373, on the basis of five Geniza documents (listed ibid., 609 n. 55), one of which he describes as "beyond imagination. Late," meaning, perhaps, from the early Ottoman period.

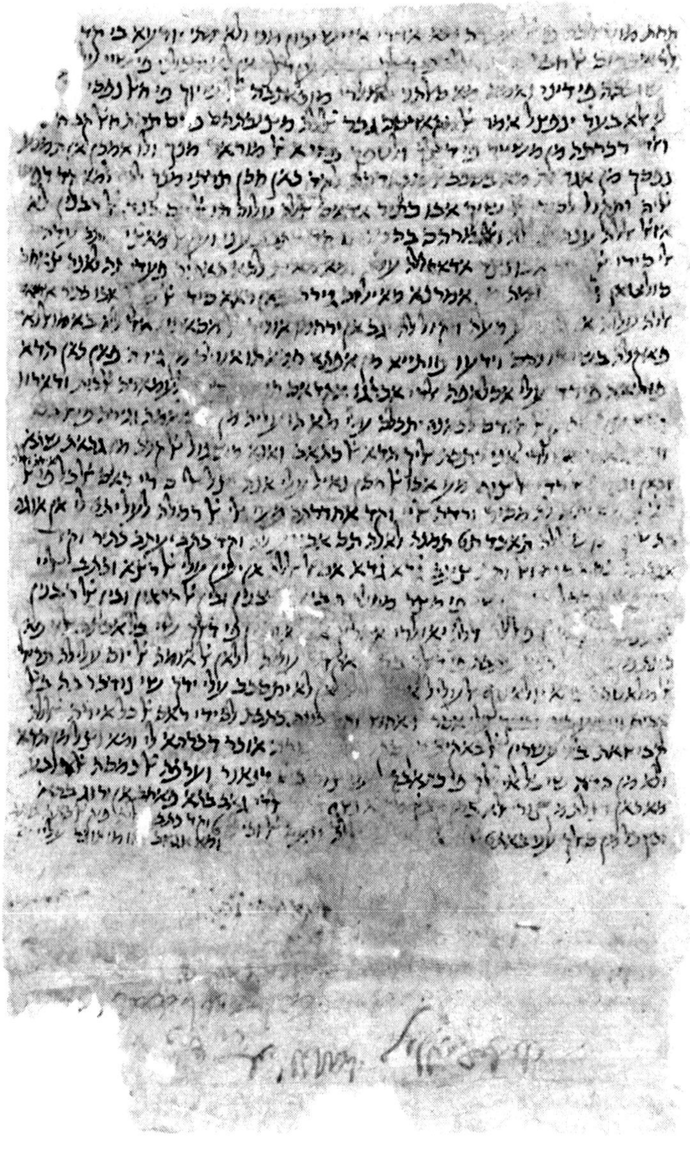

Fig. 6. A *ga'on* seeks Qaraite help: letter from Shelomo b. Yehuda to his son Avraham in Fustat, asking him to implore the Qaraite courtiers David b. Yiṣḥaq, Abū Naṣr Ḥesed al-Tustarī, and Abū Saʿd Ibrāhīm al-Tustarī for help paying the debt Jerusalem's Jews owe on a Fatimid military tax. He also urges his son not to take sides in a Rabbanite-Qaraite dispute. In Judeo-Arabic, May 7, 1029. Cambridge University Library, T-S 13 J 36.5v.

this fact: had even the local grandee gone into debt, a devastating turn of events for communal morale? Or had he gone there, as the letter hints, in solidarity with his flock? The Jews of Ramla, meanwhile, could not afford to pay their communal functionaries and were operating without a cantor or any other religious leader in their synagogue, a matter the *ga'on* tried to remedy by convincing the sons of his predecessor, Avraham and Eliyyahu ha-Kohen b. Shelomo (b. Yehosef), to serve without stipends. They refused to do so unless they could derive some income from the post, but, the *ga'on* explains, "there is no income to be had." The *ga'on* himself was also in straitened circumstances (the intimacy of writer and recipient, as usual, frustrates the historian's ability to ascertain the details, since many matters are passed over with only oblique references): "Know, my son, that I have come upon an insoluble situation," he wrote. "My situation is one of scarcity and impoverishment, with both of which you are familiar. I wonder how this difficult winter passed from upon me and I made it to the summer. What I have left from what is known to you [some amount of money?][37] is exceedingly little. If most of the weeds are in fine condition, most of the land has not been sown. A year ago I sold those small items of clothing along with what is known to you, whereas this year, there is nothing to be sold." The *ga'on* goes on to tell his son about those in Jerusalem who had been imprisoned for their debts: Mawhūb al-Baṣīr (the blind), Abu l-Faḍl and Mubārak ibn Ṣemaḥ. Others were wanted by the authorities. "And all my letter-writing on their behalf has accomplished nothing," he says. "This really shocked me: for whoever does not take part in their sorrow or show mercy to them, God will put him in their place [i.e., reduce them to poverty] and no one will say a single prayer for him, neither a 'merciful' nor a 'compassionate' [references to the attributes of God in the evening prayers]."

Shelomo then asks his son to contact Abū Kathīr, that is, Efrayim b. Shemarya, to have him put additional pressure on David b. Yiṣḥaq for donations—confirmation of my earlier suggestion that Efrayim's entreaties and letter of thanks to David either reflected or created a special relationship between the two men. The *ga'on* had written "several letters to my lord the elder Abū Naṣr [David b. Yiṣḥaq], may God make his high rank eternal," he wrote, "but I have seen no effect. I censured him, since he has power[38], and our affairs are his responsibility as much as anyone else's [*kāna yalzamuhu min amrinā mā yalzamu ghayruhu*]." The *ga'on* evidently perceived David's role vis-à-vis the Rabbanites of Jerusalem as one of moral obligation to use his power to help his coreligionists: because he has power in the Fatimid government, he is in a position to help free the imprisoned Jerusalemites; since he is

[37] Following Gil's suggestion, *History of Palestine*, 2:143, Hebrew translation, lines 20–21.
[38] *Li-annahu ṣāḥib sulṭān* (cf. Gil, *History of Palestine*, doc. 80, verso, lines 9–10, translation).

the highest among us in the government only he can see to it that the debt prisoners are released; and "our affairs are his responsibility as much as anyone else's," regardless of the fact that he is a Qaraite and we are Rabbanites.

The *ga'on* moreover assumed that Efrayim had better access to the Qaraite courtier and asked his son to contact him. "Perhaps my lord the leader Abū Kathīr [Efrayim b. Shemarya], may God make his high rank eternal, will see fit to meet with him and tell him that they should show some mercy on those poor people, for there is no one among us who exceeds him in wealth or rank," he wrote. Nor was this the avenue of first resort: he goes on to explain that the Jewish community of Jerusalem first attempted to circumvent the law regulating the use of income from religious trusts (*awqāf*) in order to bring themselves some relief. But a *muftī* in Jerusalem issued a legal opinion to the effect that once a religious endowment is dedicated for a particular purpose, its income may not be used for any other.[39] Finally, Shelomo entreats his son not to involve himself in the "fighting [in Fustat] between the Rabbanites and the Qaraites, and among the Rabbanites [themselves]," tensions about which we have no further details, though it is evident why Shelomo was at pains to advise his son not to alienate the Palestinian Rabbanite community from the Qaraite courtiers.

The Geniza has, as it happens, also preserved Shelomo's letter to Efrayim directly entreating him to pressure David for assistance.[40] The *ga'on* may even have written the letter in the same sitting. The upper right corner of the letter is torn away and the beginning is fragmentary, but the remainder contains valuable details about the channels the *ga'on* intended to utilize in saving his flock from starvation: "the lenders hardened their hearts toward the borrowers and the Bedouin, and the rest were caught and they oppressed them. . . . They asked to write a letter in their names from prison and they put their signatures on it, and it was sent via the *kātib*, the elder and noble Abū Naṣr, may God be his help." As far as one can tell, the imprisoned debtors were able to convey a petition to the government via David b. Yiṣḥaq. What became of it, however, was as much a mystery to the *ga'on* as it remains to us. Still awaiting a response to his last missives, the *ga'on* asked Efrayim b. Shemarya to change tack and contact the Tustarīs for help instead—not with the petition but with the debt relief directly.

> With him [David b. Yiṣḥaq] there were many [other] letters, and one of them was for you about the Tustarī elders, for the matter will not be solved except through them, because the debt is more than nine hundred dinars. "From

[39] T-S 13 J 36.5, verso, lines 12–15; see Gil's note to line 13 and idem, *Documents of the Jewish Pious Foundations*, doc 3.

[40] T-S Misc. 35.43; see Mann, *Texts and Studies*, 1:311, and Gil, *History of Palestine*, secs. 254n, 783n. The Abū Naṣr meant here is David b. Yiṣḥaq (see Shelomo b. Yehuda's letter to his son; in addition, there is no evidence that in this period Ḥesed al-Tustarī was already a *kātib*).

whence" can it possibly be paid—"from the threshing floor or from the winepress?" [2 Kings 6:27].

And our brethren //the Qaraites [he specifies above the line]//, after all that was sent to them from Fustat, have only eight-hundred dinars left. If they are thus, then what shall we say?

But the inhabitants of the Ṣelaʿ [the Qaraites] sent their entire donation to the *nesiʾim*, may God be their aid. And the party of the Rabbanites [*kat ha-rabbanim*] are expressing their displeasure with me, saying, we have been kind to you in not including you along with us, as the party of the Qaraites [*kat ha-qaraʾim*] did to the *nasi* [i.e., since we did not take you to prison with us].

Therefore, our dear one, it is fitting to be strong with them.

Even the Qaraites were having difficulty meeting their financial burdens, despite the donations they had received, says the *gaʾon*; they quickly parted with their money in order to contribute to the debt payments of their *nesiʾim*, perhaps including the one in prison. The *gaʾon* therefore urges Efrayim to seek help from the Tustarīs lest he be carted off to debtors' prison in Damascus.

The *gaʾon* does not address the Tustarīs directly, however. Strangely, he sends the letter via David b. Yiṣḥaq to Efrayim b. Shemarya, who was then expected to convey the request for financial help to the Tustarīs. This roundabout route is difficult to explain, though we will see it repeated again later: it may well be that petitions were more effectively submitted in person by those from those outside the Fatimid court.

Neither the *gaʾon* nor the recipients of these letters realized that relief was nigh. One assumes that when the war ended just days later, petitions to the government began once again to move through the proper channels in a less obstructed manner and the debt prisoners were released. Whether their debts were forgiven or paid off by the Fustat notables we do not know.

Two Campaigns on Behalf of Jerusalem's Jews

Finally, the Geniza has preserved evidence of two additional campaigns to help Jerusalem's Jews. The first attests to the growing enmeshment as the 1020s wore on of Qaraite notables in communal affairs—not merely the courtiers but the Qaraite elite in general. The second shows that Qaraites did not limit their generosity to emergency campaigns or bipartisan efforts to raise funds, but contributed directly to the Rabbanite *yeshiva* of Jerusalem—a fact even more difficult to anticipate than anything we have seen thus far.

The first document is a list of contributors to a massive campaign on behalf of the Jews of Jerusalem, and also a useful enumeration of most of the wealthy and powerful men of Jewish society in this period, Qaraite and Rabbanite alike. There are contributions from all over the Mediterranean, including Sicily and the Maghrib. My hunch is that this campaign was unrelated to the desperate pleas during the Jarrāḥid wars, since enlisting contributors from places across the Mediterranean would have taken more time than the Jerusalemites had to spare during the battle seasons of 1024 and 1029. Appeals for this new campaign, as well, were couched not only on the basis of need but of the sentimental attachment to Jerusalem.[41]

The list is penned in a sloppy hand (which Gil has identified as that of Efrayim b. Shemarya, writing in great haste) and is torn at the top and so begins *in medias res*. The very first contributor after the tear is David b. Yiṣḥaq, with the sum of twenty dinars. After him appear ten or eleven more people "from the aforementioned group"—aforementioned in a piece of the document no longer extant, but we can assume they are Qaraites—"may they be remembered and glorified and may their contribution be as a sacrifice and an offering," all of which rhymes in Hebrew.[42] The document then goes on to list about half as many contributors "from our chosen group, the Rabbanites, with a separate *suftaja*," and smaller contributions listed collectively as "a remaining sum from the God-fearing among the two groups, may their Rock be their aid."[43] Qaraites and Rabbanites had taken up separate collections for the campaign and remitted their donations in two separate payments, with the exception of Yūsuf ibn ʿAwkal, who remitted his together with his Qaraite trading partners; the "remaining sum" included contributions from members of both groups. Among the Qaraite contributors were ʿEzra bar Shemuʾel b. ʿEzra, a nobleman and associate of the Qaraite exilarch Ḥizqiyyahu and someone known for contributing to specifically Qaraite causes; Khalaf (Ḥalfon) b. Thaʿlab, a wealthy Qaraite of Tyre whose daughters would later have contracts drawn up at the rabbinical courts in both Fustat and Tyre; the Tustarī brothers of the third generation; and Sahlawayh b. Ḥayyim, the Persian Qaraite banker and trader for whom the Rabbanite cantor Abū Sulaymān composed a panegyric ode—possibly in order to honor him for his contribution to this campaign.[44]

As for the list of donors to the *yeshiva*, it dates from late 1028 and includes both the Qaraites David b. Yiṣḥaq as well as Ḥalfon b. Thaʿlab.[45] It is not only

[41] T-S 13 J 8.14, recto, in Hebrew.

[42] Ibid., lines 7–8: "Ha-kat ha-nizkeret yihyu le-shem u-le-tifʾeret ve-teraṣe nidvatam ke-qorban u-ke-qitoret." See next note.

[43] "From our chosen group": *mi-kat segullatenu* (on the word *kat*, see above, Introduction, n. 18). "From the God-fearing among the two groups": *u-min ḥareydey shetey ha-kittot ha-nishʾar*. *Suftaja* (the medieval Near Eastern bill of exchange, but unlike their European counterparts, payable on demand rather than on a specified date): *diyoqne*, an Aramaic-derived word usually used for *suftaja*; see Gil, *History of Palestine*, sec. 364 and Fischel, *Jews in the Economic and Political Life*, 17–21.

[44] ʿEzra b. Shemuʾel b. ʿEzra is also known as ʿEzra b. Yishmaʿʾel b. ʿEzra; see T-S 16.50 and Bodl. MS Heb. b 11.10, in Judeo-Arabic, a letter of 1044 in which he, the Tustarīs and other Qaraites are sent greetings by Moshe b. Yiṣḥaq, a Jerusalem Qaraite (on whom see Gil, *History of Palestine*, sec. 827 and the note to that section). On Khalaf (Ḥalfon) b. Thaʿlab, see chap. 10 at n. 18; on Ibn ʿAwkal, see chap. 5 at n. 7.

[45] Letter of Shelomo b. Yehuda, Jerusalem, to Avraham b. Sahlān, Fustat, in Hebrew, end of 1028 (December 29; Gil's dating). T-S 16.275+Halper 412, line 44 (in Gil's edition; line 12 in Mann, *Jews*

surprising that Qaraites would contribute to the Jerusalem *yeshiva*; it is also so accidental that their names were recorded at all that one wonders whether they perhaps made many more contributions of this kind. The list of names comes as part of a letter that Shelomo b. Yehuda wrote to defend himself from charges that he had improperly appropriated a large portion of the *yeshiva*'s income from abroad. He answers by detailing exhaustively whence and whither the money had traveled: David b. Yiṣḥaq had sent his donation in care of a certain Mevorakh ha-Sofer (another Jewish *kātib* in the government), but Mevorakh was forced to use the money for other purposes. Soldiers in one of the Fatimid army regiments were in the habit of extorting money from *kuttāb*, and Mevorakh had surrendered the donation to them.

Would it be exaggerated to claim that these two contributions add up to semiregular Qaraite contributions to the Rabbanite *yeshiva* in Jerusalem? Had the *ga'on* not written this letter to defend himself against accusations of irregular accounting, we would never have known of the Qaraite contributions, and there may have been numerous contributions of which no written proof has been preserved. There is also an undated draft of a letter from Efrayim b. Shemarya mentioning a contribution to the *yeshiva* "in the name of our mighty one, the lord, glorious elder of the generation [*avirenu ha-sar zeqan ha-dor ha-hadur*]"—and just then the letter breaks off; according to Bareket this title can refer to no one but David b. Yiṣḥaq, and I am inclined to agree.[46]

QUESTIONS OF LOYALTY

Why did these Qaraites contribute great sums of money to the upkeep and maintenance of the Jerusalem Rabbanite *yeshiva* if the meaning and purpose of Qaraism was to oppose the exclusive authority of the rabbis? The Qaraites also had an academy of their own to which they contributed (see chapter 2). What made them support the Rabbanites? Did it occur to them or disturb them that the *yeshiva* they were supporting was the very incarnation of what Qaraism disavowed?

Gil attempts to resolve the seeming contradiction by arguing that the *yeshiva* served as the main institutional representative of all the Jews in the Fatimid empire, with the *ga'on* as de facto head of all of Fatimid Jewry. On this theory, Qaraite notables contributed to the *yeshiva* because through it, they

---

in Egypt and in Palestine, 2:447). For the identification of David b. Yiṣḥaq, see ibid., 2: 446, and Gil, *History of Palestine*, sec. 865.

[46] T-S 13 J 16.20, in Hebrew. See Bareket, *The Jews of Egypt, 1007–1055: On the Basis of the Archive of Ephraim ben Shemarya* (Jerusalem, 1995), doc. 44, note to lines 26–27. See also T-S 12.374v, which is difficult to interpret but seems to refer to very large contributions made by Qaraites and Rabbanites ca. 1050.

contributed to the entire Jewish community of the empire. But as the document of investiture I discussed in chapter 3 states, the *ga'on* was head of the Rabbanites only. Sela takes the opposite approach, arguing that David b. Yiṣḥaq was head of the Jews (*ra'īs al-yahūd*) and thus institutionally obligated to contribute—an explanation that does not account for the other Qaraite contributions.

The solution can be found in Shelomo b. Yehuda's own reasoning. He himself says that an official position in the Jewish community is hardly required to induce an obligation to donate money: "our affairs are his responsibility as much as anyone else's," he writes, no more and no less. Were David's role any better defined, and had he occupied an official position, the *ga'on* would hardly have felt moved to remind him of those obligations. That "responsibility," rather, was dictated by a continually renegotiated and reaffirmed economy of patronage.

It seems, then, that when a Qaraite contributed money toward a key rabbinic institution of learning, he did not perceive himself as fraternizing with the enemy. The Qaraite leadership shared bonds of loyalty to other Jews that operated separately from questions of theological or legal differences. When they donated to the *yeshiva* and helped its leaders obtain rescripts from the chancery, they were apparently untroubled by any sense of conflict because the ideology that bound them to the *yeshiva* hierarchy was a shared one of obligation in communal leadership.

And what did the Rabbanites think of the fact that by the late 1020s, their survival as a community had become dependent on Qaraite largesse? All the voluminous Rabbanite correspondence, from communities as far removed from one another as Alexandria and Tripoli, demonstrates that they were aware of the centrality the Qaraite elders had assumed in their survival. To some, at least, this was probably just the way the world worked, by means of a power-sharing arrangement between Rabbanites and Qaraites, and we hear not a single rumble of complaint about it.

Yet it is clear that others were less content with the arrangement. Nor did the Palestinian Rabbanite leadership completely succeed in impressing its logic upon them. While up until 1029 the first noises of discontent are still undetectable in the Geniza papers, they exploded in a loud roar in late 1029 at the annual pilgrimage convocation in Jerusalem.

CHAPTER EIGHT
THE AFFAIR OF THE BAN OF EXCOMMUNICATION IN 1029

In autumn, 1029, a throng of Rabbanites attempted to have the Qaraites excommunicated en masse at the annual pilgrimage festival on the Mount of Olives in Jerusalem. The attempt failed because the *ga'on* opposed it and the elders of the *yeshiva* blocked it by calling on the local Fatimid governors.

The timing was significant. The assembly was probably the first pilgrimage convocation in years: the Jarraḥid wars of 1024–29 had stalled pilgrim traffic all over the region, and the difficulties holding festivals were only increased by the hardship imposed on Jerusalem's Jews by warfare, famine, plague, and the tax burden (see chapter 7). It is also unlikely that Jews had held festivals publicly during the previous decade or so. Al-Ḥākim had prohibited the Palm Sunday procession in Jerusalem in 1007 and the Epiphany procession in Cairo in 1009–10, and though there is no evidence that he also prohibited Jewish public assemblies during the years of his edicts, on December 31, 1011, a group of Muslims attacked the funeral cortège of a great Jewish cantor on its way from Fustat to the cemetery outside the town; twenty-three Jews were arrested and condemned to death by the *qāḍī* and governor of Fustat and released only after petitions to al-Ḥākim, who then found the Muslims guilty of perjury. Still, the risks must have been discouraging. The relief of finally holding the pilgrimage festival in the safety of an atmosphere free of war and persecution must have added to its momentousness in the eyes of those who attended.[1]

The assembly was fraught with tension for other reasons as well. The Jews of Egypt and Syria, having received the fiscal and political aid of the Qaraite courtiers in Cairo, were by now well aware that the Qaraites were indispens-

[1] On Christian processions, see *EI²*, s.v. "al-Ḥākim" (Canard) and on public celebration of non-Muslim festivals under the Fatimids, Lev, *State and Society*, 192–94. The incident of the funeral procession: *Megillat Miṣrayim*, the Cairo Purim scroll of 1012, Bodl. MS Heb. e 95.54+BL Or. 5560a+Mosseri I 85, another copy partially preserved in T-S 8 K 10. Shemarya b. Elḥanan may have died on the same day, but the scroll says the funeral was that of a certain Puṭi'el, whom Gil identifies as Palṭi'el he-ḥazzan b. Efrayim b. Ṭarasūn; *History of Palestine*, sec. 572n. See Cohen, *Under Crescent and Cross*, 184–85; Benjamin Hary, *Multiglossia in Judeo-Arabic* (Leiden, 1992), 123–25; Mann, *Jews in Egypt and in Palestine*, 2:30; Yerushalmi, *Zakhor*, 46–48.

able to the community—and to the leadership of the *yeshiva*. By the time the pilgrims assembled in 1029, the prominence of the Qaraites in Jewish communal politics emerged as a point of tension.

Ritual and ceremony were the channels of public protest closest at hand. The group who moved to excommunicate the Qaraites summoned up the traditional rabbinic condemnations as pretexts on which to register their objections to the new political arrangement—except that it was the *ga'on*'s exclusive prerogative to decree bans, and he was one of the Qaraites' staunchest allies.

It is rare that Geniza historians are liberated from history in fragments. The sources for the affair of the ban include a large and fairly coherent set of eyewitness accounts, most of them letters exchanged by the rabbinic curia, and several supporting documents, including chancery decrees and petitions. The sheer volume of correspondence itself suggests that the affair lingered in the minds of those present long after it ended, and indeed, the tensions, imprisonments, attempts at vengeance, and debates over the legitimacy of the ban lasted for an entire year.

The affair passed into Jewish historiographic tradition not via those letters but via a single paragraph in Avraham ibn Dāwūd's *Sefer ha-qabbala*. The letters demonstrate that Ibn Dāwūd's memorialization was a fiction, eloquent testimony to the author's propensity to convey triumphalist arguments in the guise of concrete events. His account has cast a long shadow over the historical memory of Qaraite-Rabbanite relations, but the documents show that his depiction of the Qaraites as forced to cower meekly before the indignity of the ban is far from the truth. The attempted excommunication was a response to Qaraite power rather than powerlessness, and the Qaraite response to it demonstrates that power serves as an effective shield against allegations of heresy.[2]

Taken together, the literary and documentary sources indicate three salient aspects of the events that, taken together, made it a singular turning point in the history of the Jewish community—far from the annual humiliation Ibn Dāwūd portrayed. First, its timing: the excommunication against the Qaraites was declared exactly once over the course of the eleventh century—not in 1029 but in 1038, for reasons manifestly political (see chapter 11). Here, the attempt emerged from one confluence of specific contingencies and was blocked in the context of another, a point that suggests the importance of considering the historical contexts in which accusations of heresy are lodged. Second, its futility: the Rabbanites knew not only of their leaders'

[2] Cohen, *Sefer ha-qabbalah*, xiii–xiv. See also the painting of the scene by John Frazer, based on Ibn Dāwūd plus selective use of the epistolary accounts cited below, at the Tower of David Museum, Jerusalem, reproduced in Eli Barnavi, ed., *A Historical Atlas of the Jewish People: From the Time of the Patriarchs to the Present* (New York, 1992), 89. Following Ibn Dāwūd, the caption there erroneously states that the Qaraites were "required to attend" the ceremony.

dependence on the Qaraite courtiers but also of Rabbanite-Qaraite alliances in trade and marriage (see chapters 9 and 10). Their insistence on the ban did nothing to change that dependence; paradoxically, via the chain of political reactions it unleashed, it deepened it. Third, what the affair of the ban revealed about the Jewish community's relationship to the Fatimid state: each side made ample use of its connections in government, via the courtiers in Cairo and the local bureaucracy in Palestine—but each also claimed that its victories in the affair were due not to those ties but to the justice of its cause in the eyes of God. The ban's memorialization as timeless, archetypal, and ideologically motivated, then, did not begin with Ibn Dāwūd, but with the near blindness of the participants in the affair to their own relationships to power. They passed silently over the links they themselves had forged in the Fatimid court and local administration—and for the most part, over the links they had forged with each other.

THE PILGRIMAGE FESTIVAL: INVIDIOUS DISTINCTIONS

The affair began on Hoshaʿna Rabba, the seventh day of Sukkot, when the ranks of pilgrims to Jerusalem were at their most swollen. Barring war, famine, and hostile decrees, Rabbanites from all over the Mediterranean and even from as far as Franco-Germany would convene on Jerusalem, and on the last day of the festival the curia of the Jerusalem *yeshiva* would exercise ritual functions that demanded for their effect a maximum number of worshipers: proclaiming the calendar for the upcoming year; soliciting financial contributions for the upkeep and maintenance of the *yeshiva*; distributing titles to those who had worked on the *yeshiva*'s behalf; confirming the positions of the *yeshiva*'s members; and declaring blessings and bans.[3]

Attending the pilgrimage festival was felt to be obligatory for anyone physically and economically capable of undertaking the journey. A letter from the Alexandrian trader Abū ʿImrān Mūsā b. Abī al-Ḥayy to the trade magnate Nahray b. Nissim in 1058–59 conveys this: "I arrived in Tyre and spent only five days doing business in the place and remained confined to bed for [some number larger than ten] days. God then bestowed health upon me and I departed for Jaffa and from there went up to Jerusalem, may God rebuild it. There as well, I did not do any business except on eight days, and I remained confined to bed for the entire month with chills and fever. And, by God, I was not able to ascend the Mount [of Olives] except by riding on a mount. My spirit

[3] Cf. Poznanski, "Ephraim ben Schemaria de Fostat et l'académie palestinienne," *Revue des études juives* 48 (1904), 153; Gil, *History of Palestine*, secs. 831–34. For a brief reference to the ceremony on Hoshaʿna Rabba and the confirmation of members of the *yeshiva* in their positions, see T-S NS 320.42.

was very discouraged."[4] The attendance of as many pilgrims as possible was, moreover, essential if the ceremony was to attain its full meaning, and while some shared Abū ʿImrān's hopes of effecting a few transactions during the festival, since traders regarded Jerusalem as "a weak city" the amount of business actually conducted there was negligible. As a mass assembly its meaning lay in transactions of a more symbolic sort. The climax of the ceremony came on Hoshaʿna Rabba, when the proclamations were made.[5]

The proclamations were redolent of the kinds of hierarchical distinctions that lent the rabbinic system and the assembly their meaning. Over the course of the tenth century, the Palestinian *yeshiva* in Tiberias and Jerusalem had used the calendrical proclamations to compete with the *yeshivot* in Baghdad, as during the great calendar controversy of 921–22.[6] The rhetoric and methods of the festival were at least in part a ritualized response to the ceremonials of the Iraqi *ge'onim*. Ben-Sasson has compared it with two of the assemblies at Baghdad: the investiture of the new *resh galuta* (or at least its baroque description in the account of Natan ha-Bavli ca. 950), and the *kalla* convocations, which brought Talmud scholars to Baghdad twice yearly for a month.[7] Each of these ceremonies iterated symbolic ties between the rabbinic centers and the outlying communities whose members had converged on them, and all three were pitched against one another in a competition for mass loyalties. The *yeshivot* also made frequent (and frequently shameless) use of titles for the same purpose, a fact that partly accounts for their proclamation at the festival itself.

After distributing the titles and honorifics, the *ga'on* proclaimed the blessings and bans. The honor of public blessing was reserved for the *ḥaverim* of the *yeshiva* and anyone who had contributed to it financially. In 1029, the contributors included not only Rabbanites but Qaraites—including the Fatimid *kātib* David b. Yiṣḥaq and the wealthy Ḥalfon b. Thaʿlab, both of whom had contributed less than a year earlier—and one must assume that they were publicly blessed as well.

[4] Bodl. MS Heb. d 75.20 (28 November 1062), in Judeo-Arabic. See Udovitch, "Formalism and Informalism," 66–72 (I have deviated slightly from his translation) and Goitein, *Mediterranean Society*, 4:126–27. The number of days in line 6 appears to contain two characters; Gil's reading of fifteen is possible.

[5] Letter of Yisra'el b. Natan to Nahray b. Nissim, ca. 1060, ENA NS 48.15, line 4: "li-annahu balad ḍaʿīf." See Goldberg, "Geographies of Trade and Traders," 346.

[6] A gaonic commentary states that the decision about intercalating the year was reached during the month of Av, but Geniza documents make it clear the senior curia confirmed the decision only during Tishri and announced it formally on Hoshaʿna Rabba. Goitein, "New Sources on the Palestinian Gaonate," 510–11, note to line 3; cf. Mann, *Texts and Studies*, 1:316 n. 11, and Gil, *History of Palestine*, sec. 784. On the calendar controversy, see above, chap. 1.

[7] Ben-Sasson, seminar presentation at the Center for Judaic Studies, University of Pennsylvania, October 1, 2003; see also idem, "Structure, Goals, and Content" and idem, "Varieties of Intercommunal Relations."

Immediately after the blessings, the *ga'on* solemnly pronounced the bans of excommunication in the presence of a Torah scroll.

The Double-Edged Sword of Excommunication[8]

Excommunication, in principle, was a form of social anathema used mainly against those who had committed infractions but refused to submit to penalties (including fines), or against anyone who had undergone punishment but still refused to comply with the law. Someone under a ban was barred from social contact with other Jews—not just members of his immediate local community, but (at least in theory) Jews everywhere—and depending on its severity, the ban could bar commercial contact as well.[9]

In the centuries most amply documented in the Geniza (ca. 1000–1250), the most common targets of excommunication fell into two categories: violators of rabbinic precepts and those who infringed indirectly on the authority of the leaders of the community. These included husbands who married a second wife without court permission (rabbinic law in Islamic lands permitted Jewish men a regulated form of polygamy, though its practice remained uncommon); litigants who resorted to Islamic courts instead of Jewish ones; defaulted debtors; renters in arrears; those who withheld tax monies from the communal coffers; and anyone who had failed to comply with a court decision or communal ruling. The set of infractions demonstrates that although the stated purpose of the ban was to enforce specific injunctions, it was used principally as a means of bolstering rabbinic authority itself and the rabbis' ability to regulate communal affairs.[10]

That is why, earlier in 1029, the *ga'on* of Jerusalem, Shelomo b. Yehuda, had traveled to Fustat to proclaim a solemn excommunication against followers of the Babylonian-Iraqi rite whose methods of butchering animals differed from the Palestinians'. He worded the ban against "those who promulgate false

[8] On this phrase see Yosef Kaplan, "The Social Functions of the Herem in the Portuguese Jewish Community of Amsterdam in the Seventeenth Century," in *Dutch Jewish History: Proceedings of the Symposium on the History of the Jews in the Netherlands*, ed. Jozeph Michman and Tirtsah Levie (Jerusalem, 1984), 120. This discussion follows his lines of analysis (115–21), though while he argues that excommunication in seventeenth- and eighteenth-century Amsterdam was double-edged because it subverted rabbinic authority by driving the excommunicated to the baptismal font (there is also Geniza evidence of conversion to Islam among excommunicated Jews), what interests me here is how unobserved excommunications of themselves weakened rabbinic authority.

[9] For a general description of types of bans of excommunication and their enforcement, see Baron, *Jewish Community*, 2:228–33, and cf. the introductory remarks of Katz, "Rabbinic Authority."

[10] Mann, *Responsa of the Babylonian Geonim*, 351–57 (the examples he cites on 363–64 refer to judicial imprecations); Goitein, *Mediterranean Society*, 2:331–33; Gil, *History of Palestine*, secs. 757–60; and Bareket, *Fustat on the Nile*, 66–68. See also T-S 16.213 (a late debtor; Goitein, *Mediterranean Society*, 1:259); T-S 13 J 21.31 (a statute for late tenants stipulating excommunication, Goitein, *Mediterranean Society*, 2:114–15, 421 no. 96); and Bodl. MS Heb. d 76.56 (excommunication of a polygamous husband).

laws . . . in order to foment strife among Israel," which offered a veneer of scholastic and ethical justification to an exercise in the sheer imposition of power, as the *ga'on* imposed his supracommunal authority over Iraqis who contemplating seceding from it.[11] The purpose of the ban, then, was to bind people more closely to rabbinic authority as a system of law and leadership.

There was therefore good reason to use the ban sparingly. Its force was vitiated without proper enforcement, and enforcing it depended on two things: the community's will to refrain from interacting with the banned party and making it known as widely as possible—particularly since the Jews of the Mediterranean orbit were so geographically mobile. Jews who had been excommunicated frequently attempted to escape the purview of the ban by fleeing to another town. The law caught up with some but certainly not all of them.[12] On Hosha'na Rabba the Jerusalem *ga'on* not only declared new bans but reiterated old ones to ensure that news of them was disseminated widely among the pilgrims.[13] Under ideal circumstances, a perfectly observed ban would excise the transgressor from the body of Israel until he repented, but a ban that went unobserved had the converse effect, acting not upon the transgressor but upon the rabbis who declared it and weakening their authority. Bans in fact tended to proliferate when rabbinic authority was weakest.

Rabbinic authorities even knew this. A provincial Egyptian *muqaddam* (local communal leader) complained in a letter to the chief Jewish judge of Cairo around 1100 that he had attempted to issue excommunications, but his community still refused to follow his dictates; in his remote outpost, he complained, he had limited access to books, and because of his lack of scholarly authority, he had been forced to overuse the ban as a means of communal control.[14] For that reason as well, use of the ban was carefully regulated, as even those outside the Jewish community knew. In chapter 3, I quoted the *Kitāb al-Ḥayawān* (The Animals) by al-Jāḥiẓ (d. 869), who described the Babylonian exilarch's power of excommunication (he calls it "the interdiction of discourse," *taḥrīm al-kalām*) and a similar instrument of punishment in the hands of the

[11] T.S 20.102.

[12] See, e.g., T-S 13 J 26.6v, a fragment of a letter about another polygamous husband who had been placed under a ban in Fustat and Dammūh for taking a second wife, and then fled to Qūṣ in Upper Egypt; see further Goitein, *Mediterranean Society*, 2:333, and Mann, *Responsa of the Babylonian Geonim*, 348.

[13] On the *ga'on*'s exclusive power to ban, see Halper 354 verso; Goitein, *Mediterranean Society*, 2:27–30; idem, *Palestinian Jewry*, 57–58; idem, "Rosh yeshivat ereṣ yisrae'el ke-rosh ha-yehudim ba-medina ha-faṭimit: mismakhim 'araviyim 'al ha-ge'onut ha-yisra'elit" (The head of the Palestinian *yeshiva* as the head of the Jews in the Fatimid empire: Arabic documents on the Palestinian gaonate), *Eretz-Israel* 10 (1971): 100–106; idem, "New Sources on the Palestinian Gaonate," 523–25; Cohen, *Jewish Self-Government*, 28–29, 206–7. When transgressions occurred outside Jerusalem, the *ga'on* would either go there or offer his signature to authorize the declaration of a ban; see T-S 10 J 29.5, in Judeo-Arabic, lines 8–12; cf. Gil, *History of Palestine*, sec. 757.

[14] T-S 16.154.

Nestorian *katholikos*. "The interdiction of discourse is not among the punishments found in their books," he wrote, referring to the Hebrew Bible and the New Testament. "But since the *katholikos* and the exilarch are not allowed [to impose] either imprisonment or flagellation within the Islamic realm, they can only impose fines and prohibit discourse."[15] Even if it was weaker than the alternatives, al-Jāḥiẓ still described excommunication as a prerogative of the highest *dhimmī* authorities. A responsum of Naṭronay b. Hilay, *ga'on* of Sura (857–64) and al-Jāḥiẓ's exact contemporary, stresses the importance of publicizing the ban: "Any community that sees this decree of banishment but does not excommunicate" the offender in question, he warned, the Lord's "wrath shall rest upon it."[16] A ban was thus only as good as the community's will to enforce it.

That the *ge'onim* themselves were aware of the dangers of overusing the ban is evident in a letter that Daniel b. ʿAzarya, *ga'on* of the Jerusalem *yeshiva* (1052–61), wrote to ʿEli b. ʿAmram, a *ḥaver* in Fustat, instructing him that there was no need to excommunicate a certain teacher whose "stature is less than what would necessitate writing a ban." The implication was that this teacher's public regard had already declined to the point where an excommunication would be "wasted" on him. Excommunication was, then, considered an appropriate measure only against those with a certain degree of social standing.[17] This helps to explain the controversy that the ban against the Qaraites provoked in 1029: the Palestinian *ga'on* opposed it, not just on the basis of his alliance with the Qaraite courtiers, but knowing, perhaps, that it could never be enforced. The throng who lobbied for its declaration, meanwhile, tacitly acknowledged the power the Qaraites held.

"Against the Eaters of Meat with Milk"

The *ga'on* had every reason for concern: the ban against the Qaraites was not quite the legal procedure of enforcement that it was supposed to be. That it was worded against them collectively already weakened its legal basis and its chances of being observed; everyone knew that Rabbanites and Qaraites in the Fatimid realm conducted regular professional and personal relations. The ban's aim was not to correct Qaraite religious behavior, but to achieve some

[15] Al-Jāḥiẓ, *Kitāb al-ḥayawān*, 4:2; see Ignaz Goldziher, "Renseignements de source musulmane sur la dignité de resch-galuta," *Revue des études juives* 8 (1884): 121–25; Mann, *Responsa of the Babylonian Geonim*, 360; Gil, *History of Palestine*, sec. 757.

[16] Cited in Baron, *Jewish Community*, 1:169, and paraphrased by Mann, *Responsa of the Babylonian Geonim*, 349. For similar language, see the responsum attributed to Naṭronay's immediate predecessor at Pumbedita, Palṭoy b. Abbaye (842–58), in Assaf, *ha-ʿOnashin aḥarey ḥatimat ha-Talmud*, 49 (no. 14), and his notes on 49–50.

[17] Judeo-Arab. *qadruh aqall mimmā yaḥtāj ilā kitāb bi-ḥaramih*. T-S Misc. 25.132r+T-S Misc. 25.139, second fragment, lines 4–5; cited in this connection in Gil, *History of Palestine*, sec. 757.

symbolic or ritual separation between the groups. It was equally problematic that the principal violation with which the Qaraites stood charged—challenging the rabbinic claim to exclusive authority in interpreting biblical law—was more general than the specific infractions that normally brought about a ban. Lest this lack of specificity seem an obstacle, the ban was couched, by a synecdoche that stood for an entire theological aberration, in terms of a specific infringement: eating meat with milk.[18]

Maledictions and the Social Order

The ban's special force was not limited to its manifest legal content. It also included the ritual setting. Excommunication was not merely a juridical statement but a performative utterance whose meaning lay in the circumstances of its declaration.

In his study of excommunication among medieval Latin Christians, Lester Little identifies four features of the act of banning: the political context in which an excommunication is declared; its ritual setting; the extrajuridical powers it possesses; and the authority of those who impose it. "The appropriate moment for pronouncing an excommunication," he notes, "was the moment of optimum public presence and attention," since this underscored that the ban was a communal endeavor, to be enacted and upheld by the collectivity: the divisions enacted through excommunication took on meaning only when they were divisions from the whole. That way the ban would also function as a warning to others. Although repeating the excommunication "would add nothing, at least of a juridical nature, to the original sentence," he adds, still, "the drama of cursing and clamoring was eminently repeatable, and for purposes other than juridical" ones.[19]

Little draws on the philosopher J. L. Austin's theory of speech acts, which distinguishes performative utterances as accomplishing the act they describe merely by being pronounced and understood as efficacious ("I hereby excommunicate you"). According to Austin's theory, such a statement must meet three "conditions of felicity": the procedure for pronouncing the utterance must be conventionally accepted; those uttering it and the circumstances in which they do so must be appropriate to the situation; and whoever utters it

[18] Tenth-century Qaraite Mourners of Zion refrained from eating the meat of cattle and sheep in Jerusalem but might have consumed milk and fowl together. Eating meat with milk is not explicitly proscribed in the Torah, but according to rabbinic interpretation, the prohibition is implicit in the injunction against boiling a goat kid in its mother's milk, and therefore counts as a biblical commandment and belongs to a category of infractions punishable by flagellation (*lav she-yesh bo maʿase*; the punishment is *malqut*). See Babylonian Talmud, *Pesaḥim* 47b, *Beṣa* 12a, and *Makkot* 21b. The thirty-nine lashes prescribed for violating biblical commandments were no longer part of the gaonic repertoire of punishments, although rabbinically ordained lashes had been devised as a substitute; but in place of lashes, the *ge'onim* usually resorted to excommunication.

[19] Lester K. Little, *Benedictine Maledictions: Liturgical Cursing in Romanesque France* (Ithaca, 1993), 50, 34.

must do it with the proper intent. If any of these conditions is not met, the statement makes no impact. The meaning of performative utterances, then, derives not just from their content but from the social context in which they are pronounced and the effects they bear on that context.[20]

"We Gathered in the Cemetery"

How might the Jews of the eleventh century have understood an excommunication?

It had been the practice since the late antiquity for Jews to declare excommunications—both juridical imprecations and punitive bans—in the presence of an open Torah scroll. Although by the Middle Ages Jews avoided using sacred objects in juridical contexts for fear of blasphemy, they continued to declare excommunications before an open scroll of the Law. Sometimes, the entire community would gather in a cemetery to declare a ban, though the setting added nothing of a legal nature to the ceremony; it was all performance and effect. Shelomo b. Yehuda explains that when he excommunicated the Iraqi congregation of Fustat, "we gathered in the cemetery in a large group, and we brought out Torah scrolls and excommunicated every promulgator of sinful statutes and author of vanity."[21]

Goitein interprets the graveside setting as part of the general phenomenon of using cemeteries as a locus of "public supplication in time of calamity." The purpose of the custom was to call upon the dead as witnesses (especially, he adds, since the excommunications were sometimes of dubious validity), and so the cemetery emphasized some of the ban's latent meanings. Inviting the ancestors implicitly drew upon the authority of ancestral tradition; it also expanded the collectivity from which the banned person was being excised to include all Israel, past, present, and future.[22] Gathering among the dead and attendant demons also threatened evil consequences to the banned party; and the presence of death served as metaphorical representation of the social death

[20] Ibid., 40, citing Wittgenstein, *Philosophical Investigations*; Austin, *How to Do Things with Words*; and idem, "Performative Utterances," in *The Philosophy of Language*, ed. Aloysius Martinich. See also S. J. Tambiah, "The Magical Power of Words," *Man* 3 (1968): 175–208.

[21] On the increasing reluctance to use sacred objects for judicial imprecations in the gaonic period, see Gideon Libson, "Gezerta and Ḥerem Setam in the Gaonic and Early Medieval Periods," Hebrew (Ph.D. diss., Hebrew University of Jerusalem, 1979), who argues that the reluctance was related to the gradual phasing out of oaths in favor of *gezerta* and *ḥerem setam* and motivated by the desire to place a fence around the injunction against taking the name of God in vain. Excommunication of the Iraqis: T-S 20.102, lines 28–29.

[22] G. K. Chesterton's paradoxical remarks on tradition capture something of the spirit of excommunication in a graveyard: "Tradition means giving votes to the most obscure of all classes, our ancestors. It is the democracy of the dead. Tradition refuses to submit to the small and arrogant oligarchy of those who merely happen to be walking about. All democrats object to men being disqualified by the accident of birth; tradition objects to their being disqualified by the accident of death." Chesterton, *Orthodoxy* (Garden City, 1959), 48. (Thanks to Patrick Allitt for bringing this passage to my attention.)

that the ban imposed. Though this detail of the ceremony remains undiscussed in the sources on 1029, the ritual gathering at the pilgrimage festivals on the Mount of Olives took place within sight of the largest Jewish cemetery in Jerusalem.[23]

Given that premodern literacy rates would have kept most Jews from access to the written polemics between Rabbanites and Qaraites, ritual was a good method for demarcating scholastic terrain.[24] In public, in the solemnity of a collective ceremony, rifts were made to appear clearly, if only for the duration of a prayer service.

THE FIRST RABBANITE RUMOR

The first letter in the series dates from late 1029 (October–November?), several weeks after the ceremony took place, and was written by Shelomo b. Yehuda, who had already been serving as *ga'on* for five years, to Efrayim b. Shemarya, head of the Palestinian Rabbanite community of Fustat. When the letter begins, we are already in the thick of things: throngs of Rabbanite pilgrims had ascended the Mount of Olives and a faction of them had begun pressuring their leaders to proclaim the ban.[25]

In the hubbub prior to the ceremony, "many of the common folk were provoking a quarrel," writes the *ga'on*. The pro-ban faction began spreading a rumor that the Qaraites had bribed the *ga'on* not to declare it, and "the defamers were saying to the people, 'The Qaraites have bribed this man so that the ban [against the eaters] of meat with milk will not be pronounced, and they say that he has assured them that he will not.'" In fact, the *ga'on* had no intention

[23] On banning in cemeteries: Goitein, *Mediterranean Society*, 5:185–86. Goitein's reading of the ritual appears in the final volume of this work, when he had begun to incorporating cultural anthropology into his work (an observation for which I am indebted to Harvey Goldberg). Classical rabbinic literature already expresses the link between excommunication and (social) death in deriving the Aramaic word *shamta*, "ban," from *sham mita*, "there is death there." See Babylonian Talmud, *Mo'ed Qaṭan* 17a. On the Jerusalem cemetery, see Dan Bahat, "The Physical Infrastructure," in Prawer and Ben-Shammai, *History of Jerusalem*, 98.

[24] On literacy rates, see above, chap. 1 at n. 4.

[25] T-S Misc. 35.11, in Hebrew. See Gil, *History of Palestine*, sec. 937. Ban [against the eaters] of meat with milk: *basar be-ḥalav setam*. Technically, the *ga'on* is misusing the legal terminology: the *ḥerem setam* was a judicial imprecation inviting punishment on anyone who made a false claim in court, but could be worded without explicitly naming the parties; this fact may account for the confusion here, since this ban would have been pronounced against unnamed "eaters of meat with milk." On the *ḥerem setam*, see Libson, "Gezerta and Ḥerem Setam"; idem, *Jewish and Islamic Law: A Comparative Study of Custom during the Geonic Period* (Cambridge, Mass., 2003), 104; and on its use as reflected in the Geniza, see Goitein, *Mediterranean Society* 2:340–41; cf. Gil, *History of Palestine*, sec. 758; and see n. 74 below. This letter partly parallels Mosseri VII 142 (L 210) and can be used to fill its lacunae. Gil attributes the second letter to Efrayim b. Shemarya on the basis of handwriting (*History of Palestine*, sec. 801 and 2:598–99) but the relationship between the two documents remains unclear (the second seems to have reported events narrated in the first using some of its wording).

of declaring the ban in any case, but that his detractors imagined him agreeing to this by order of the Qaraites is revealing.

Rumors spread fastest where they are most plausible, and indeed Shelomo b. Yehuda must have been widely perceived as a client of the Qaraites: he had probably asked the Qaraite courtiers to procure him his investiture when he acceded to office in 1025, as suggested by the letter of lavish praise for the Qaraite *nasi* Ḥizqiyyahu b. David.[26] Implied in the charge of bribery was the idea that the Qaraites' wealth gave them undue influence in Rabbanite affairs. In that sense, the Rabbanite "defamers" were not entirely wrong in imagining the Qaraites as blocking the ban with money and influence. But the rumor had him yielding to Qaraite wishes only after a bribe, as though preventing him from declaring it required extraordinary measures.

Similarly, his followers imagined him as willing to uphold tradition except in extraordinary circumstances, when offered a bribe. "'Tell him not to alter our tradition,'" the *ga'on* reported them as saying, "'and if he refuses [to comply], do not listen to him, and gather against him together.'" They defended tradition in the face of what they saw as his willingness to alter it; tradition required separation from the Qaraites (who opposed tradition). His followers thus imagined him as less deeply involved in politics than he really was, since he was swayed only by the promise of money; and they imagined the Qaraites as more corrupt than they really were in offering him a bribe rather than a fair political alliance. The rumor was therefore an indictment of gaonic dependence on Qaraite political standing and a discursive means of imagining his independence from it (if the bribe hadn't been offered, they thought, he would have declared the ban). Both these themes—his dependence on the Qaraites and his followers' unwillingness to accept it—would recur throughout the affair of the ban.[27]

The first Rabbanite rumor, then, forces us to rethink one point of scholarly consensus: that the presence of Qaraite grandees in the Fatimid administration ameliorated relations between members of the two *madhāhib* by preventing the Rabbanites from treating the Qaraites too harshly. In fact the *kātib* factor could have precisely the opposite effect: here, the Rabbanite crowd chafed under their leaders' dependence upon the Qaraites even as their leaders benefited from alliances with them.

Rabbanites and Qaraites "Saying Things That Aren't True"

As the provocateurs spread the rumor, the *ga'on* began to understand that the entire crowd was hungrily anticipating high drama. "After the sermon," he

[26] ENA 2804.12–13 (see also T-S 13 J 17.17); T-S 13 J 36.5.

[27] On gossip and rumor and their relationship to power, domination, and defiance, see J. C. Scott, *Domination and the Arts of Resistance: Hidden Transcripts* (New Haven, 1990), 142–52.

writes, "I was saying sweet words to the people for the sake of the contributions" to the *yeshiva*—as was his usual practice on Hoshaʿna Rabba—"but lo and behold, only a few people were making donations! These were the ones who had come in order to pray. The majority of those who had ascended the mountain had done so for the sake of the slander of the defamers and were talking insolently, gloating, and being impudent." (Josephus had noted something similar nearly a millennium earlier: "It was not the customary festival so much as indignation which drew the people in crowds" on pilgrimages.)[28]

Then the pilgrims directly accused the *gaʾon* of breaking with long-established rabbinic tradition. "You say in your sermons," they told him, "I accept rabbinic tradition as the rest of you." If you really do, they said, then " 'just as you have received the commandments and the customs, do not alter the custom of our forefathers. For if you alter it, everyone will follow and there will be Qaraites saying things that aren't true!' " Breaking the bonds of rabbinic custom (declaring the ban) was tantamount to Qaraism (which rejected rabbinic tradition); since they accused the *gaʾon* of the first, they also accused him of the second. And so he defended himself in his sermon by assuring his followers that he accepted rabbinic tradition just as the rest of them did. But the crowd was not appeased and warned him that if he failed to declare the ban, others would follow his example of compromise, and then the Qaraites would go around saying "things that aren't true," whatever that might mean.

Now, in this instance it was the Rabbanites who were "saying things that aren't true," spreading rumors about the bribe. What was the Rabbanite throng afraid the Qaraites would say to slander *them*? It was by now a hoary anti-Rabbanite accusation that the mere existence of internal dispute proved rabbinic tradition to be a human devisement, not transmitted from Sinai, and it may be that the crowd had heard Qaraites arguing this.[29] If you alter our traditions, they told the *gaʾon*, there will be yet another brick missing from the edifice at which the Qaraites have been chipping with their arguments for the mutability and human fabrication of rabbinic tradition. Don't preach to us about tradition, they told him; tradition dictates declaring the ban.

"It Is Not a Commandment that You Should Fight over It!"

At a certain point the fracas escalated to the point where the *gaʾon* washed his hands of the affair and allowed the Rabbanite throng to do as it chose. (The comparison with a certain first-century governor of Judea is not likely to have occurred to him or anyone else present.) "When I saw that no one was listening

[28] Flavius Josephus, *The Jewish War*, 2.42; cited in Steven Weitzman, "From Feasts into Mourning: The Violence of Early Jewish Festivals," *Journal of Religion* 79 (1999): 546.

[29] See, e.g., Salmon b. Yeroḥam in Israel Davidson, *Book of the Wars of the Lord*, 1:16, 2:7–11.

or paying attention," the *ga'on* wrote, "I stood on the [cantors'] chair and said, 'It is your choice. Do as you wish.'" What did his invitation to the throng to do as it wished really mean? Since the *ga'on* possessed the exclusive prerogative to declare bans, it can only be understood as a statement of despair.

The cantors' chair (*kisse' ha-ḥazzanim*) on which the *ga'on* was standing was the spot from which *ge'onim* customarily delivered their sermons on pilgrimage festivals and was also believed to occupy the exact site from which the Divine Presence had alighted in a verse from Ezekiel ("And the glory of the Lord went up from the midst of the city, and stood upon the mountain which is on the east side of the city," 11:23); both Rabbanites and Qaraites used the verse as the proof text for the sanctity of the Mount of Olives.[30] While the *ga'on* stood on the chair helplessly, the Third of the *yeshiva*, Ṭoviyya b. Dani'el, attempted to intervene, "speaking in their ears, saying, 'It is not a commandment that you should fight over it! Why should we concern ourselves with this dispute?!'"[31] Ṭoviyya thus attempted to convince the crowd not to raise a mere tradition (the ban) to the level of a religious obligation.

His admonitions precisely recapitulated the course of gaonic reaction against Qaraism over the previous two centuries. To the crowd, even a custom could not be altered lest all of rabbinic tradition come tumbling down with it. In this they echoed ninth- and tenth-century Rabbanite polemicists such as Naṭronay and Seʿadya, for whom rabbinic additions to Jewish law became unalterable biblical commandments.[32] Ṭoviyya, meanwhile, echoed his Iraqi contemporary Hayya b. Sherira of Pumbedita, who had ridiculed Seʿadya's maximalist claims as nothing but a slender "reed to ward off the heretic."[33] The eleventh-century leaders represented a new approach, one of a rabbinate unthreatened by cooperation with the Qaraites. The crowd still espoused the extreme arguments of the previous centuries.

But the throng ignored Ṭoviyya. "They did not listen to him," continues the *ga'on*, "and the people's quarrel on the mountain increased greatly." The breach between the instigators of the ban and their leaders was now beyond repair.

Government Intervention

At this point the elders of the synagogue intervened—the ten or so leaders responsible for supporting the head of the community in enforcing reli-

[30] For rabbinic and Qaraite texts attributing holiness to the site, see Gil, *History of Palestine*, sec. 831.

[31] Mann, *Texts and Studies*, 1:316 n. 8, and Gil, *History of Palestine*, sec. 937, identify this Third as Ṭoviyya b. Daniel.

[32] See above, chap. 1, n. 48.

[33] See above, chap. 2 at n. 67.

gious duties, attending the rabbinical court, and generally protecting public morality.[34] "They came with the governor of the city," explains the *ga'on*, "and said, 'Please rise and announce the order of the festivals of the Lord.'"

The elders, eager for the event to unfold without incident, seem to have invited the governor of Jerusalem, Abū Naṣr Fatḥ al-Qalʿī (known by his title Mubārak al-Dawla wa-Saʿīduha, Blessed and auspicious one of the realm).[35] The *ga'on* himself leaves open the question of who invited the governor—a particularly delicate question, since the leaders may have feared that calling for or even attracting government intervention could curb the Jews' freedom to worship publicly on pilgrimage festivals. (In another letter, Shelomo explained that the Jews of Jerusalem paid exorbitant sums for the privilege.)[36] But to control the throng, the elders were perfectly willing to align themselves with the governor. This step was only the beginning of Fatimid intervention in the affair that year.[37]

Under the watchful eye of the governor, the *ga'on* dutifully complied with the elders' request. "I stood up and announced [the calendar], as is the custom." The crowd, undeterred by the governor's presence, "cried: 'Declare the ban!'" The *ga'on* stood firm and "told them, 'I have already said that I shall not declare it!'"

Then three members of the *yeshiva*, all sons of *ge'onim*, took matters into their own hands.

The Priestly Brothers

The younger curia attempted to mollify the crowd with a ruse. The *ga'on* describes the two sons of his predecessor Shelomo ha-Kohen b. Yehosef, Yosef and Eliyyahu ha-Kohen b. Shelomo, and his own son Avraham, who was their cousin, as uttering the ban in such a way that it appeared to the throng that they had included the traditional excommunication formula against "the eaters of meat with milk."

It is not clear from the *ga'on*'s description how precisely this was done. "The two brothers, *ḥaverim* [of the *yeshiva*], may God keep them, stood up," he

[34] Goitein, *Mediterranean Society*, 2:58–60. Cf. idem, "Local Jewish Community," 144–45, where he points out, on the basis of T-S 13 J 30.5, that the elders were formally appointed.

[35] Bianquis, *Damas et la Syrie sous la domination fatimide*, 317 n. 2. I assume that al-Qalʿī still held this post in 1029.

[36] T-S 13 J 11.5, in Hebrew, Shelomo b. Yehuda to Sahlān b. Avraham, lines 12–17; see Gil's comments, *History of Palestine* secs. 249–51. T-S 13 J 33.6, in Hebrew, Shelomo b. Yehuda to Efrayim b. Shemarya, lines 6–15.

[37] On the question of communal autonomy and government intervention, see chap. 3. Previous treatments of this event have presumed that the governor arrived in order to enforce a pair of caliphal edicts promoting Rabbanite and Qaraite freedom of worship and assembly, but neither of those edicts had yet been issued. See below at nn. 66 and 80.

writes—adding, "my son was with them—and they declared it. But they [only?] appeased the crowd with their words: it [only] seemed to them that they had mentioned 'meat with milk.'" One imagines them mouthing the formula without actually declaring it in full voice, thereby rendering the utterance legally ineffective. The participation of the *ga'on*'s son is an essential detail, even though the *ga'on* appears to be obscuring his participation in the affair. Sons of *ge'onim* served as public spokesmen for the *yeshiva*, and in practice exercised their fathers' prerogatives. (That is why it is plansible that when the great rather than controversy erupted in 921–22, it was Aharon b. Me'ir who proclaimed the calendar, rather than his father, the *ga'on* Me'ir.) The *ga'on*'s son possessed the authority to excommunicate the Qaraites, but the *ga'on* was careful to note that he did not—to protect his son from punishment, to make it clear that no legally effective ban had been declared, or both.[38]

"Then," the *ga'on* continues, the younger curia "descended the mountain." But the fine distinction between utterance and nonutterance was lost on the Fatimid governor, who acted swiftly and decisively. Before the *ga'on* had even returned home, the governor of Jerusalem, al-Qalʿī, had sent word to the governor of Palestine, Abū Manṣūr Anushtekīn b. ʿAbdallāh al-Duzbarī (1023–ca. 1042, with interruptions), and his minions were in pursuit of the three young men. "I had not yet reached my house when there came soldiers of the governor of Palestine, [al-Duzbarī,] known as Muʿtazz al-Dawla, may God preserve him . . ." (the *ga'on*'s letter, which the millennium since it was written has not treated kindly, breaks off here). It was the second but not the last time leaders of the Jewish community would turn the power of the state against one another during the controversy over the ban.[39]

A subsequent letter relates how al-Duzbarī's men found the two brothers and carted them off to the prison in Damascus. The *ga'on*'s own son was spared punishment.[40]

[38] Cousins: CUL Or. 1080 J 45, recto; see Goitein, "New Sources on the Palestinian Gaonate," 511, 526; idem, *Palestinian Jewry*, 123, 171; Gil, *History of Palestine*, sec. 858; and cf. ibid., sec. 863, where he argues that the three youths were "stubbornly fanatic" in proclaiming the ban, but their motives may have been merely pragmatic in view of the need to appease the crowd. On Aharon b. Me'ir, cf. chap. 1, n. 28.

[39] For a list of medieval historiographic and biographical sources on al-Duzbarī, see Stern, *Fāṭimid Decrees*, 30 n. 1. For details of his career, and especially his repression of the Bedouin revolt, see Gil, *History of Palestine*, secs. 584–94, and Bianquis, *Damas et la Syrie sous la domination fatimide*, 424–523. Neither Mann, Goitein, nor Gil identifies this figure as al-Duzbarī; to the list of titles in Gil, *History of Palestine*, secs. 384 and 593 n. can be added *muʿtazz al-dawla*.

[40] ENA 4010.32, in Judeo-Arabic, recto, lines 5–8; ʿEli ha-Kohen b. Yeḥezqel (ʿAlī b. Ḥizqīl), the social services officer (*parnas*) of the Jerusalem Rabbanite community, to Efrayim b. Shemarya, late 1029 or early 1030. On the role of the *parnasim*, see Goitein, *Mediterranean Society*, 2:77–82. On the possibility that Avraham b. Shelomo b. Yehuda was spared because of his father's position, see ibid., 5:369, and Mann, *Texts and Studies*, 1:311.

Meanwhile a group of Qaraites exacted symbolic revenge for the ban, measure for measure, by returning to the Mount of Olives and breaking the cantors' chair. They were reported to have accompanied this act with the cry, "Let no Rabbanite come up to Jerusalem!'"[41]

The Qaraites would retaliate in a different idiom as well: diplomacy and politics. The brothers languished in prison for several months, without being fed and under the pressure of arranging payment for their jailers or facing torture.[42] They had also been kept in chains for some time. The *ga'on* had made efforts to have them freed and to that end, enlisted Sahlān b. Avraham, the leader of the Babylonian congregation in Fustat, to petition the administration in Cairo. It would have been a delicate matter for the *ga'on* to seek the help of the Qaraite courtiers now, though later we will see that they never held the affair of the ban against him; still, he says nothing of having contacted David b. Yiṣḥaq, who had freed Efrayim b. Shemarya from prison in 1024. And even if it was the elders of the *yeshiva* who had put the brothers in prison, we shall see that it was the Qaraites of Palestine who would keep them there.

In late 1029 or early 1030, the *ga'on* wrote again to Sahlān b. Avraham beseeching him more urgently for help. "You sought [intercession] before the caliph and the vizier, may they live eternally, in the matter of freeing the prisoners, may God bring them out into the light," he writes. "We were hoping for their release from darkness and shadows and for their bonds to be sundered, but lo and behold, edicts [*ketavim*] came from Damascus [saying] that they are still in prison, although their chains and yokes have been removed. But their jailers are punishing them daily, and they are ailing; may the King of Glory send his word, heal them, and take them out into the light, and may they [the rulers] come to see their righteousness." And in fact, they had been offered release, but on condition that they "swear by God and by the life of the caliph, may he live eternally, that they will never again be called by the title *ḥaver* and never serve the house of Israel in all of Palestine, in greater or lesser service, neither in law nor in any other matter." To this, the imprisoned brothers answered: "'We want to hear the words of this edict [*ha-peteq ha-ze*] from the mouth of its author and we will answer according to what . . ." (a small hole in the manuscript follows).[43]

[41] ENA 4010.32, recto, lines 12–13. Gil, *History of Palestine*, 2:135, suggests that the Fatimid authorities broke the chair, but cf. Goitein, *Mediterranean Society*, 5:369, whose interpretation fits better with other evidence.

[42] See above, chap. 7, 192.

[43] T-S 13 J 13.28+T-S AS 120.62, in Hebrew. The first fragment contains most of the letter, and the second only the lower left-hand corner; much ink has vanished from the first several words. My translation begins from line 5. Vizier: Heb. *rozen*; Mann, *Jews in Egypt and in Palestine*, 1:136 (Cohen, *Jewish Self-Government*, 188, notes that *rozen ha-zeman* was a title often accorded to Jewish courtiers,

The author of the edict was ʿAdaya b. Menashshe ibn al-Qazzāz, the Qaraite military governor of Palestine.[44] ʿAdaya probably worked closely with the governor of Palestine, Anushtekīn al-Duzbarī, who had sent soldiers after the brothers in the first place; but there is no evidence that ʿAdaya had put the brothers in prison in the first place. It is also impossible to know anything more about the relationship between the two governors, since ʿAdaya is absent from Muslim sources while al-Duzbarī appears only sporadically in Jewish ones. It may be that al-Duzbarī had delegated this Jewish affair to ʿAdaya, since he is the only Fatimid official about whom we hear for the rest of it. But ʿAdaya held no ideological animus against the *yeshiva*: three years earlier, he had signed a writ of agency for the betrothal of his sister-in-law—a daughter of David b. Yiṣḥaq—at the rabbinical court in Tyre. (On what Qaraites were doing having contracts drawn up in a rabbinical court, see chapter 9.)[45] Here, ʿAdaya intervened in the affair on the side of the Qaraites, but only because, as the writ goes on to suggest, they had petitioned him to help them benefit from the affair of the prisoners.

ʿAdaya's edict contained the set of injunctions that the Qaraites sought to impose on the Rabbanites, injunctions so harsh that the *gaʾon* complains that "even our overlords [the caliph, vizier, and local governors?] would not make conditions for their slaves as [the Qaraites] have done." (Here he echoes Salmon b. Yeroḥam, who had complained that the humiliation he suffered from the Rabbanites "is more difficult for me than [what I suffer] from the nations [*goyim*].")[46] "The essence" of the conditions, the *gaʾon* writes, "is that the ban

---

but here vizier is meant); see also Gil, *History of Palestine*, 2:166 n. 5, for *malkhut* as caliph. This is the first but not the last we will hear of al-Ẓāhir's vizier, Abu l-Qāsim ʿAlī b. Aḥmad al-Jarjaraʾī, who had served in high office under al-Ḥākim and had both of his hands and forearms cut off for malfeasance; al-Ẓāhir appointed him *wāsiṭa* and then *wazīr* (the second person to hold this title under the Fatimids; the first was Ibn Killis) and he continued to serve al-Mustanṣir until his death in 1045. A copy of the *sijill* appointing him *wazīr* (in Dhu l-Ḥijja 418/January 1028) appears in the twelfth-century history of Ibn al-Qalānisī (d. 1160): see Walker, *Exploring an Islamic Empire*, 46, 106–7 (and 214 nn. 14–16); who remarks (with irony?) that al-Jarjaraʾī "could not have personally held the *sijill* granting him the highest office in the government" or signed his own *ʿalāma* but instead had one of the *qāḍī*s do it for him. Gil, *History of Palestine*, sec 803n. (end) has al-Jarjaraʾī's appointment in 1027, but his calculation should be corrected to 1028.

44 Like his father, Abū Manṣūr ʿAdaya b. Menashshe ibn al-Qazzāz was a Fatimid *kātib*, and although the sources do not say explicitly what position he held, one can assume that he held his father's first post of military governor (*kātib al-jaysh*). An anonymous ode written to him during the early 1020s (T-S 32.4) supports this possibility, calling him "the glory of the entire land of Canaan" (*peʾer kelal araṣot kenaʿan*) and comparing him to Joab b. Zeruiah, King David's general (2 Samuel).

45 T-S AS 153.12+T-S 13 J 25.20 (see further chap. 10 at n. 28). ʿAdaya had married David b. Yiṣḥaq's other daughter some time before 1023: the anonymous panegyric refers to his wife merely as "a daughter of notables" (*bat gedolim*) without mentioning her father by name or title, and must therefore date to before David's government appointment in 1023. This would in turn date ʿAdaya's appointment, the panegyric, and the birth of ʿAdaya's two sons (mentioned in the poem) to the early 1020s at the latest.

46 See above, chap. 4, n. 19.

not be proclaimed again on the Mount of Olives; that the Qaraites separate out for themselves one shop in the market of the Jews to slaughter and sell meat without [Rabbanite] inspection or supervision," from which we learn that al-Ḥākim's edict (see chapter 5) was not in effect in Ramla, if it was still in effect at all; "that the rest of the butchers, if they have a pregnant ewe or cow, not sell it to one of the Jews," since consumption of pregnant animals was forbidden according to Qaraite but not Rabbanite law; "that if it is a holiday for [the Qaraites], the Rabbanites not come and try to desecrate it by opening their shops; that the rabbis not exercise authority over them; [and] that the imprisoned *ḥaverim* come neither to the Holy City nor to Ramla."[47]

The Qaraites, then, seized the opportunity to gain advantage over the Rabbanites by means of the local government in Palestine. The seven conditions fully preserved (a final one is partly effaced) all speak to Qaraite resentment of Rabbanite dominance in religious affairs. They also tell us that, like the Rabbanites, the Qaraites turned religious differences into insurmountable obstacles when it suited them to so, and it suited them to do so now because power was on their side.

The stipulations the Qaraites imposed had precisely the same goal as the Rabbanite ban for which they were intended as revenge: to free them from the dominance of the other group. The difference between the challenge and the riposte was one of method: the Rabbanites used the medium of religious ritual to escape from the web of Qaraite political power; the Qaraites exploited their governmental ties to escape from the web of Rabbanite religious authority. But having now abandoned the ceremonial excommunication for political maneuvering, the Rabbanites had inadvertently chosen the path of closer enmeshment with the Qaraites.

Trust in the Creator (but Send Letters to the Government)

The *ga'on* refused in no uncertain terms to heed the Qaraite stipulations. "I have already compromised as much as I can," he writes to Sahlān, and adds above the line, to make certain that his position is clear: "I will not agree to even one of their conditions, nor will the *ḥaverim*." He then expatiated upon the theme of all Israel's responsibility for one another—a theme that would resurface in his subsequent complaints about the Qaraites—but quickly followed these sentiments with a more pragmatic proposal: "Perhaps [the notables] will take letters for us to the government, may God defend it, in Ramla and Damascus, [asking] that they not force us to agree to this stipulation. And the letters that I have mentioned,

[47] On the Qaraite prohibition on consuming pregnant animals, see the tract cited in Gil, *History of Palestine*, sec. 930 and the additional references he offers there. "Not exercise authority": this reading is tentative; Heb. *[lo yihye davar] la-rabbanim 'aleyhem* (adopting Gil's reconstruction in brackets). The penultimate word is partly effaced, and Gil misreads it; Marmorstein reads it correctly.

and that our brothers have mentioned, do not seem disadvantageous. Time is short, for it is not hidden from you that the elders in Ramla and in Damascus . . ." (a large lacuna interrupts the sentence). And he follows this immediately with: "We rely upon the Lord our God."

The *ga'on*'s claim to place his trust solely "in the Creator" was not merely garden-variety piety. One of the chief complaints he would make about the Qaraites was their use of worldly power to serve their own interests rather than those of all Israel. At the same time, he reveals his willingness to ask for favors from the notables and play by the rules of politics. It is unclear, though, which notables he intends here. Although the word *sarim* usually denotes government officials, that he refers to those in Ramla and Damascus means that he still did not intend to involve David b. Yiṣḥaq and Ḥesed al-Tustarī. Logic points to the elders of the *yeshiva*, who had recruited the governor of Jerusalem to the ceremony in the first place: what they had set into motion they could also perhaps halt. The *ga'on* goes on to lament that his other attempts at advocacy had failed and that thus he had no choice but to go to Damascus himself, but he complained that he would not survive the cold Damascene winter. In the end, he did go to Damascus, but his trip yielded nothing.[48]

In closing, the *ga'on* complains of exhaustion, saying, "Because of my sins, I have become weak, and there is no strength left in me to write, nor to read that which I might ask to be written in my name." The letter is in the handwriting of a scribe.

Confrontation in Ramla

In a letter of 1030 to a correspondent in Fustat whose name has been lost, the *ga'on* described a meeting that was held in the "market of the Jews," the *majlis* in Ramla, to discuss the Qaraite demands and resolve the dispute before mediators.[49] There, the *ga'on* formally refused to meet the Qaraite demands.

[48] See ENA 4010.32, line 18 (cited above), where ʿEli b. Yeḥezqel speaks of the *rayyis* going down to Damascus and apologizes to Efrayim b. Shemarya for not having traveled with him himself, since he, too, had been ill. I assume that ʿEli b. Yeḥezqel wrote his letter after the one under discussion, even though he describes earlier events, including the arrest of the brothers. Cf. Goitein, *Mediterranean Society*, 5:369.

[49] T-S 13 J 19.16 and T-S 13 J 16.15, in Judeo-Arabic. The first document is written in the *ga'on*'s hand (Gil, *History of Palestine*, 2:170) and bears the folds characteristic of letters that were sent through the mails, while the second is a copy written in Fustat in the handwriting of a scribe; it lacks folds and also contains several corrections to the *ga'on*'s Judeo-Arabic, which is not clear in every place. Since the copy does not continue on verso but breaks off in the middle of the letter, it seems that it was copied as a model by an apprentice scribe. Gil identifies the writing as that of Ghālib ha-Kohen b. Moshe, the son-in-law of Efrayim b. Shemarya. See further Gil's comments, introduction to D. Z. Baneth, "A Letter from Shelomo b. Judah, Head of the Ge'on Yaʿaqov Academy in Jerusalem, to an Unknown Person in Fusṭāṭ [prepared for publication by M. Gil]," Hebrew, in *Studia orientalia memoriae D. H. Baneth dedicata*, ed. J. Blau et al. (Jerusalem, 1979), 1. See also Goitein, *Mediterranean Society*, 2:555 n. 43 (who calls this a "precious but difficult document"); cf. ibid., 5:610 n. 46, and see further

The Qaraite version of events was then presented to him and the other members of the *yeshiva* who were present, and the Qaraite elders were asked "that the matter be resolved without a stipulation [being placed] either upon or against" the Rabbanites. "I consented to this," says the *ga'on*, but the Qaraites refused. "Rather, they said, 'Our time has come! This is the day we have hoped for; we have lived to see it [Lamentations 2:16]!' " Again the Qaraites attempted to exploit their temporary advantage over the Rabbanites.[50]

It was then, writes the *ga'on*, that Fatimid agents entered the fray on the Qaraite side. He does not say who called them in or which authorities they were, but they were in all likelihood sent by al-Duzbarī or ʿAdaya at the Qaraites' request. The Fatimid agents "struck [with lashes] pitilessly," the *ga'on* writes; "both *kohanim* and scholars were struck," he writes, "and they were carried off," one assumes to the same prison where the brothers still languished, probably for refusing to heed the edict. "Israel was weeping and crying, but [the Qaraites] rejoiced until [the verse] was intoned to them: 'Israel was a laughingstock for you, though he was not caught among thieves [thus the *ga'on* protested the innocence of the scholars who were now arrested]; but whenever they spoke of him they shook their heads [in mockery, cf. Jeremiah 48:27].' "[51]

"Fallen Not to Rise Again Is Maiden Israel"

The *ga'on* then temporarily suspends his description of the meeting in Ramla to voice his complaints about the Qaraites and, in particular, the Qaraite elders of Jerusalem. First, he notes bitterly, though the Qaraites cannot agree with one another on a single point of law, they are unanimous in their hatred of the Rabbanites. "Would that those [Qaraite] elders saw us as making as great an effort in the interpretation of law as their followers, who differ from one another in school of law, each one forming his own *madhhab*. Yet if there is a dispute between them and the Rabbanites, they all agree with one voice to cut off their names from the land [Joshua 7:9; cf. Psalms 34:17] and they say, 'Fallen not to rise again [is maiden Israel]' [Amos 5:2; cf. Isaiah 24:20]."[52] What I have translated as "making an effort in the interpretation of law" is *mujtahidīn*

idem, "New Sources on the Palestinian Gaonate," 520 n. 30). Baneth's and Gil's Hebrew translations differ and neither is clear in every place; my departures are tentative. My narrative treats the events the *ga'on* describes in the order in which they occurred rather than in the order in which he describes them. The mediators may have been Abu l-Faḍl Mevorakh b. ʿEli, *rosh ha-qehillot*, and Abu l-Barakāt Netan'el ha-Kohen, to whom the *ga'on* had referred in his previous letter. Abu l-Faḍl Mevorakh b. ʿEli's daughter would eventually marry Natan b. Avraham, leader of the putsch against Shelomo b. Yehuda in 1038, but for the moment the two were still allied.

[50] T-S 13 J 19.16, recto, lines 1–3. Cf. the translations and comments of Baneth, "Letter from Shelomo b. Judah," 8, and Gil, ibid., 2.

[51] T-S 13 J 19.16, recto, lines 3–5. The verb *ḍarabu* (or possibly *ḍuribu*, "they were struck") in line 3 is the usual one used in Arabic for flagellation (see, e.g., the passage from al-Jāḥiẓ cited above, n. 15).

[52] T-S 13 J 19.16, recto, lines 5–8. "Saw us as making," etc.: *yā layt kānū . . . yajʿalūnā mujtahidīn mithl aṣḥābihim alladhīna hum mukhtalifīn al-madhāhib, kull wāḥid minhum ʿalā madhhab.*

in the *ga'on*'s Judeo-Arabic, a term he borrows from Islamic legal theory, in which it means exerting oneself in the search for the correct law. In both Qaraite and Islamic jurisprudence, *ijtihād* was the opposite of relying upon tradition, or *taqlīd*; about a century later Muslim jurists would begin to debate whether jurists could still depart from the legal methods and established rulings of their *madhāhib* or whether the "gates of *ijtihād*" had closed.[53] Qaraites, for their part, aimed to cut through centuries of accreted interpretation—what the Rabbanites called tradition. The *ga'on* responded pointedly: you say that the strength of your method consists in scholarly independence, and indeed it is as if every Qaraite has his own *madhhab*, yet you have no difficulty agreeing when it comes to despising the Rabbanites. In defining Qaraism as a barely controlled interpretive mayhem, the *ga'on* echoes no one so much as al-Qirqisānī; but he also points out that in their responses to the Rabbanites, the Qaraites exert noticeably less interpretive independence.

Next in his series of accusations, he excoriates the Qaraite elders for self-righteousness and willingness to break ranks with the rest of Israel. "My lord," he addresses his correspondent, "in my heart a fire burns [Isa. 25:5] because of the people who hastened to our calamity" in pressing their demands against the Rabbanites. "They see themselves as 'lilies' (*shoshanim*) and everyone else as 'thorns'; they consider themselves 'wise ones' (*maskilim*), but they disagree as to who among them is wise."[54] Here he echoes the tenth-century Jerusalem Qaraites, who styled themselves "lilies" and the rest of Israel "thorns" (after Song of Songs 2:2). Salmon b. Yeroḥam, in his polemic *Book of the Wars of the Lord* (ca. 955), had styled the Qaraite community "the congregation of the Lily" (*'adat ha-shoshana*), while al-Qūmisī had called them *maskilim* (after Daniel 11:33, 11:35, and 12:3).[55] Yefet b. 'Eli connected the two ideas and commented (on Song of Songs 2:1) that while the earlier *maskilim* had been like the narcissus that blossoms briefly in winter, the current generation of Qaraite *maskilim* were lilies flowering in the spring of Israel's salvation.[56] That the *ga'on* used the vocabulary of contemporary Qaraite polemics suggests that they circulated among Rabbanites as well, a possibility supported by copies preserved in the Geniza. It also suggests that some of the Qaraites of Jerusalem continued to

[53] See *EI*², s.v. *idjtihād* (Joseph Schacht and D. B. MacDonald); Wael B. Hallaq, "Was the Gate of Ijtihād closed?" *International Journal of Middle East Studies* 16 (1984): 3–41; idem, "On the Origins of the Controversy about the Existence of Mujtahids and the Gate of Ijtihad," *Studia Islamica* 63 (1986): 129–41. On *ijtihād* in the Rabbanite-Qaraite debate, see Diana Lobel, *Between Mysticism and Philosophy: Sufi Language of Religious Experience in Judah Ha-Levi's Kuzari* (Albany, 2000), 65–68.

[54] T-S 13 J 19.16, recto, lines 17–19.

[55] Salmon in Davidson, *Book of the Wars*, 37 l. 47; English translation in Nemoy, *Karaite Anthology*, 73 (and see 341, note to line 12). For the full connotations of *maskil*, see Ankori, *Karaites in Byzantium*, 420, where he quotes an eleventh-century Byzantine Qaraite use of the term, and n. 177; see also his citation at 211 n. 14 of al-Qūmisī's commentary to Dan. 11:35 (incorrectly cited as 11:36).

[56] Frank, "Karaite Commentaries on the Song of Songs," 58; see idem, *Search Scripture Well*, 163–65.

shape their self-understanding with the tools provided by Yefet in his extremism. Significantly, we hear none of this coming from Fustat.

In response, the *ga'on* attacks the Qaraites' lack of fellow-feeling, turning the epithets against them by complaining that they merely demonstrate their refusal to act in the interests of all Israel. "They should be ashamed," he writes: "which of us is obligated to his followers concerning the many laws of Israel that are not written, we or they?"[57] We are the ones who spend our time in apprenticeship of the oral tradition, he argues, and thus attend to the needs of the collectivity—a hint that he equated dedication to tradition with the obligations of leadership. The Qaraites, in his complaints about them, were not only pure legal and exegetical individualists; they used their power strictly to their own ends. "But when one mentions this to them, they feel ashamed and say, 'It is not so. If God, may He be exalted, gave us a high position in the service of power [*fī khidmat sulṭān*], it was so that our followers might attain their wishes over others."[58] Here we can be sure that the *ga'on* was referring only to the Qaraites of Jerusalem: the Qaraite courtiers in Cairo had acted manifestly on behalf of the collectivity and more specifically on behalf of the *ga'on* himself. In response to those who persisted in depicting themselves as a community apart from the rest of Israel, he drops a short citation from Ecclesiastes (7:15–18) warning against attributing worldly success to divine favor (he cites just a few words since the rest would have been known to his reader): "[Sometimes a righteous man perishes in spite of his righteousness, and sometimes a wicked one endures in spite of his wickedness. So do not be excessively righteous or excessively wise, or you might be disappointed, and do not be excessively wicked or excessively foolish, or you might die before your time.] It is best to grasp one without letting go of the other."[59]

Finally, the *ga'on* returns to the accusation of hypocrisy: "They have marked us with the status of one whose prayer God does not accept," he complains—Qaraites prayed from the psalter, while much of the Rabbanite prayer book was postbiblical—"but if to them we appear thus, why should they procreate with us or marry us? This should be forbidden to them!"[60]

Evidence of Qaraites marrying Rabbanites has been preserved from eleventh-century Fustat, Ascalon, and Tyre. Jurists on both sides approved of the practice (see chapters 9 and 10), nor did the *ga'on* object to it: "As for me, God knows what I would have said to our people when I heard them say, 'We want

[57] T-S 13 J 19.16, recto, lines 19–20.

[58] Ibid., lines 21–22. Cf. below, chap. 12, 339.

[59] Ibid., line 23.

[60] T-S 13 J 19.16, recto, lines 23–25. Line 25, *yuṣāhirūnā*: Baneth, "Letter of Shelomo b. Judah," 11 n. 31, suggests that this means specifically to marry Rabbanite women; cf. Goitein, *Mediterranean Society* 5:610 n. 46. On the polemics exchanged by Rabbanites and Qaraites over the status of the book of Psalms, see Uriel Simon, *Four Approaches to the Book of Psalms: From Saadiah Gaon to Abraham Ibn Ezra*, trans. Lenn J. Schramm (Albany, 1992 [1982]), esp. chap. 2.

to separate from those people because of the enmity they show toward us,'" presumably a reference to the excommunication attempt. "I would have said: My brothers, this thing is not good between us. We have found that the house of Judah did not refrain from marrying even the tribes that were worshipping idolatrously. They are our brothers."[61] Even when the tribes of the northern kingdom of Israel were prostrating themselves to Baal, he argues, they still married from among the daughters of Judah; how can we refuse the Qaraites ours?

As for his comparison to Judah and Israel, this was another tested weapon in the Rabbanite-Qaraite polemical arsenal, with each side vying for the role of Judah. Al-Qirqisānī had traced the rise of the various Jewish schools back to "the time when Jeroboam committed the aforementioned acts [maintaining idolatrous shrines etc.] and dissent arose among the children of Israel, and similar practices were planted in their midst, one generation inheriting them from the other." For al-Qirqisānī, Qaraites were the true descendants of Judah while the Rabbanites had followed the straying path of the tribes of Israel.[62] Salmon b. Yeroḥam ended his lengthy anti-Rabbanite polemic with a fervent prayer for the day when God would "restore the glory of the tents of Judah and Israel as of old; may they become one."[63] The *ga'on*, for his part, echoed a passage from the Mishnah, the rabbinic code of law of ca. 200 CE, which had proclaimed that even though the schools of Hillel and Shammai disagreed over principles of marriage law and ritual purity, they refrained neither from marrying each other's women nor from eating each other's food.[64]

In this segment of the letter, the *ga'on* demonstrates that his alliances with the Qaraites hardly emerged from personal or theological sympathy. On the contrary: to him, they were guilty of all manner of failings the most grave of which was excluding themselves from catholic Israel. Contrary to the imaginings of his followers on the Mount of Olives, his alliances with the Qaraites of Cairo were purely political.

"They Trusted in Their Courtiers and Kuttāb . . . *but We Call on the Name of the Lord our God"*

By the end of the meeting in Ramla in spring 1030, the brothers languishing in prison had been joined there by more Rabbanite scholars, the Qaraites continued to press their demands, and the *ga'on* still refused to meet them. But somewhere around line ten of the *ga'on*'s letter, it becomes evident that the crisis

[61] T-S 13 J 19.16, recto, lines 25–30.

[62] al-Qirqisānī, *Kitāb al-anwār wa-l-marāqib*, Book I, 1:6–14; Chiesa and Lockwood, *Ya'qūb al-Qirqisānī on Jewish Sects and Christianity*, 99–100; Nemoy, "Al-Qirqisānī's Account of the Jewish Sects and Christianity," 324–25 (where the passage is truncated); idem, *Karaite Anthology*, 45–53.

[63] Salmon in Davidson, *Book of the Wars*, 131. Cf. Baron, *Social and Religious History*², 5:285.

[64] Mishnah *Yevamot* 1:4.

had broken and that the Rabbanites had somehow succeeded in blocking the Qaraite demands. He alludes to the circumstances only briefly: "'Blessed is the Lord, God of our fathers, who put it into the mind of' our lord 'the king' [cf. Ezra 7:27], may he live forever, and into the mind of our lord the vizier, may God save him, to speak on our behalf and to seek what is good for us, may His name be elevated for all eternity."[65] By order of the caliph and the vizier, the Rabbanite brothers were freed. What had happened in the mean time?

The answer lies in a decree that al-Ẓāhir issued to the governor of Palestine, al-Duzbarī, ordering him not to show partiality in his treatment of "the two parties." The edict has survived only in a Judeo-Arabic copy of the (lost) Arabic original issued to the governor and the Jews in tandem, and it states plainly that it came in response to a petition from the *ga'on*'s party. It also makes reference to a previous *sijill*, probably the document of appointment that Shelomo b. Yehuda received on his accession in 1025.[66]

> To His Majesty, Commander of the Faithful:
>
> A petition [*ruqʿa*] [was submitted] in the name of the community of the Rabbanite Jews [*jamāʿat al-yahūd al-rabbānīn*] asking that they be treated according to the most high *sijill* issued on their behalf, namely, that their *ḥaverim* should be able to fulfill the requirements of their religious practices and their ancient customs [*furūḍ diyānatihim* (*sic*) *wa-sālif sunanihim*] in their synagogues and to serve their communities in Jerusalem, Ramla, and other places; and that those who interfere with them should be stopped, as this is not compatible with the justice of the government; and that they [the interferers] should not be given a free hand to do what is not in accordance with established usage; and that they should not be disturbed on their holidays and in particular while they hold their services on them; and that those among their adversaries who do such things should be checked.
>
> Therefore the Commander of the Faithful has ordered that decrees [*kutub manshūra*][67] should be issued to the effect that each group [*ṭā'ifa*] of the two Jewish groups, the Rabbanites and the Qaraites,[68] should not interfere with one another; and all who belong to one of these two schools [*kull man yatamadhhab hādhayn al-madhhabayn*] should be allowed to conduct themselves according to

[65] T-S 13 J 19.16, recto, lines 12–15.

[66] T-S 13 J 7.29, in Judeo-Arabic, undated. Gil dates it speculatively to 1034; previous scholars had dated it to some time after 1026. Since its contents suggest that it was submitted to the chancery in response to the events described here I date it to ca. 1030. Goitein's readings are correct in lines 2, 3, 20 and 25 (1, 2, and 19 and 24 according to his numbering); Gil's are correct in lines 7, 11, 32, 34, and 35. I have largely followed Goitein's English translation.

[67] On the term *manshūr*, see Stern, *Fāṭimid Decrees*, 85–90, and Khan, *Arabic Legal and Administrative Documents*, 448–49; for *sijill manshūr*, see below, p. 228; on *sijill maftūḥ*, see Wansbrough, *Lingua Franca in the Mediterranean*, 178.

[68] The text is awkward here: *kull ṭā'ifa min al-ṭā'ifatayn min al-rabbānīn wa-l-qarrā'iyyīn min al-yahūd*. The intermediate phrase (*min al-rabbānīn wa-l-qarrā'iyyīn*) was probably added as an afterthought in further specification and incorporated into the copy.

the customs taught in their religious schools [*diyānātihim*] without the harassment of one of the two parties [*al-ṭāʾifatayn*] against the other.

In particular the Qaraites should not harass the leaders of the Rabbanites by exiling them from the districts of Jerusalem and Ramla, and the merchants of the two parties should conduct themselves according to their customs with regard to transactions of buying and selling or abstaining from such according to their wishes on the days of their feasts.

Each of the groups [*al-ṭāʾifatayn*] shall beware of acting against the provisions of this order. Let everyone know that he who disobeys and trespasses will receive heavy punishment, which will check him and deter others.

The caliph thereby made into law everything the Rabbanites had requested to counter the Qaraite demands. One wonders who shepherded this edict through the chancery. In his letter, the *gaʾon* had accused the Qaraites of "trusting in their courtiers and *kuttāb* and wealthy ones and those close to the government," while the Rabbanites "'call on the name of the Lord our God' [Ps. 20:8]." But he passes silently over the fact that the Rabbanite camp had procured Fatimid intercession on its own behalf.

As a result of this decree, the deadlock between the two sides ended. Only by appealing to the state could either side impose its will on the other.

The Second Rabbanite Rumor

Though the affair had drawn to a close, the Rabbanites made one last attempt to wreak vengeance on the Qaraites.

Some Rabbanites in Jerusalem had spread another rumor saying that the Qaraites had burnt three Rabbanite figures in effigy on Purim.[69] It was a time-honored tradition, at least among Rabbanites, to burn effigies of one's enemies on Purim, a carnivalesque holiday involving the obligatory consumption of alcohol and the inversion of social roles.[70] The *gaʾon* does not say whom

[69] T-S 13 J 19.16, lines 30–31: *wa-la-qadʾ ashnaʿū aṣḥābunā annahum ṣawwarū fī l-fūr 3 ashkhāṣ wa-annahum ʾaḥraqūhum*. From the language of the document, it is undecidable whether "our followers" is nominative or accusative (*aṣḥābunā* or *aṣḥābanā*) and therefore whether it is the subject or object of the verb—in other words, whether the Rabbanites slandered the Qaraites or the other way around. Although in classical Arabic, the verb would be singular at the beginning of this sentence—*ashnaʿa* rather than *ashnaʿū*—in Judeo-Arabic, verbs commonly appear in the plural before a plural subject. Hence the contradiction between Goitein's, Baneth's, and Blau's version of events, in which the Rabbanites are the slanderers, and Gil's, where they are slandered; I follow the majority opinion. Gil, *History of Palestine*, sec. 937; idem in Baneth, "Letter from Shelomo b. Judah," 2; Goitein, *Mediterranean Society*, 5:369; and Blau's review of Gil, *History of Palestine*, in *Tarbiẓ* 57 (1987–88): 131, note to page 172 line 30, where he corrects Gil's reading of this line and maintains based on context (and following Baneth) that "our followers" is the subject.

[70] See Elliott Horowitz, *Reckless Rites: Purim and the Legacy of Jewish Violence* (Princeton, 2006), and the articles collected in *Poetics Today* 15 (1994) under the title *Purim and the Cultural Poetics of Judaism*, ed. Daniel Boyarin.

the effigies were supposed to have represented according to the rumor, but since there were three of them, Goitein ingeniously connects them with the Rabbanite leaders who had (not) pronounced the ban on the Mount of Olives.[71]

To find out whether the Qaraites had done such a thing, the *ga'on* called upon the diplomacy of two elders, Abu l-Barakāt Netan'el ha-Kohen and Abū ʿAlī Muḥsin b. Ḥusayn. "Shaykh Abu l-Barakāt," the *ga'on* writes, "may blessing come to him, called in those who had declared [the libel] and they denied [having uttered] it. He denounced them and said to them: 'If this is the nature of your testimony, surely you will bring destruction upon the world.'"[72] Realizing that the Rabbanite slanderers were lying, he advised the *ga'on* to punish them. "And then came his colleague Abū ʿAlī Muḥsin, may he be remembered well"—he was the scion of a Rabbanite trading family from the northern Syrian coast, *parnas* in the Palestinian Rabbanite community in Fustat, and representative of the merchants there—"and he told me and told the elders [what had transpired] and advised me that I had no way out of this libel but to announce an excommunication on whoever did what was said and on whoever spread slander of nonexistent things in order to endanger people."[73] To prevent an explosive Qaraite response and punish to the libelers for giving false testimony, then, the elders recommended declaring another ban. The *ga'on* complied.[74]

"It was done on a fast day in the *majlis* in the Jewish market" in Ramla.[75] "The group assembled and I said before them what I could: 'Is the sin of Peor such a small thing to us' [Josh. 22:17; cf. Num. 25:1–9] and what was done against us, so that now the affair will continue because of us, and we will renew the dispute?" The three who renewed the ban on Hoshaʿna Rabba have already suffered imprisonment, he reminded his followers; is that not enough, or should we risk provoking more strife? "If we are not bound by any decree [i.e., hostile stipulations]," he added, "then we should not exact retribution on them for what they inflicted upon us."

71 Goitein, *Mediterranean Society*, 5:369; cf. Gil, *History of Palestine*, sec. 937 n. 21, and Baneth, "Letter from Shelomo b. Judah," 12 (subheading).

72 T-S 13 J 19.16, recto, lines 31–32.

73 On Abū ʿAlī Muḥsin, see Goitein, "New Sources on the Palestinian Gaonate," 518–20.

74 It is possible that the kind of ban being suggested here is not a ban of excommunication but a *ḥerem setam*, or judicial imprecation, designed to force litigants to tell the truth; see Libson, "Gezerta and Ḥerem Setam." On the distinction between this and the ban of excommunication see Goitein, *Mediterranean Society*, 2:331, where he notes that in reality the difference is not always clear, since rabbinic authorities did not scrupulously maintain the distinction either in terminology or in legal practice. Thus Shelomo b. Yehuda calls the ban of excommunication against the Qaraites "basar be-ḥalav setam" (see n. 25 above).

75 Gil assumes that this *majlis* is a meeting place in the *yeshiva* in Jerusalem, but cf. Blau, review of Gil, *History of Palestine*, 172, line 36; Goitein, *Mediterranean Society*, 2:165–66; and Brody, *Geonim of Babylonia*, 285–86 with reference to earlier literature.

The assembly answered: "Cast the ban and cast the ban! Behold, we are suffering mightily from the terrible thing they have said, even though it happened against our will." We opposed the libel, they told him, but we were made to suffer for it. "[Cast the ban] lest a decree [*ḥujja*] be issued against us [saying] that this happened because of us!" The page is torn here; after a lacuna, the *ga'on* continues on verso: as the crowd demanded, "we cast the ban and we ended [the affair], but it troubled many of them, since they knew that they were [the ones] bringing this about."

The affair of the ban had now come full circle. On the Mount of Olives, the Rabbanites had spread rumors about the Qaraites; so they did now. On the Mount of Olives, the crowd had demanded the ban; so they did now, only now they demanded it against Rabbanites. The Rabbanite throng had finally been convinced of the prudence of avoiding further confrontation, but it had taken imprisonments, decrees, and the intervention of the governor of Jerusalem (al-Qalʿī), the governor of Palestine (al-Duzbarī), the military governor of Palestine (ʿAdaya ibn al-Qazzāz), the vizier (al-Jarjaraʾī), and the caliph's chancery to convince them of this.

ECHOES INTO THE FUTURE

For much of the run of holidays the following autumn, it seemed that the controversy would repeat itself. "Most of those who made the pilgrimage came only for the sake of the dispute," the *ga'on* wrote to Efrayim b. Shemarya in Fustat some time after the festival in 1030 (see fig. 7), "and to seek to be separated from the other group [*kat*], so that they might not mingle with them in any matter." This time, the Rabbanite throng went even further than they had the previous year, imputing Qaraite sympathies not just to the *ga'on* but to anyone who opposed the ban. "They waged war with any person who did not listen to them and defamed him [and said] that he is one of them and made him 'the butt of gossip in every language and of ridicule from all people' [Ezekiel 36:3]."[76]

Yet the festival unfolded without incident, for one reason: the governor's men attended in a state of high alert. "On the first day of the festival," the *ga'on* explains, "the people were hardly hearing or listening to the words of the

[76] Bodl. MS Heb. c 13.23, in Hebrew, recto, lines 12–15 (verso contains trials of the pen in Arabic). Cf., again, Flavius Josephus, above, n. 28. See Mann, *Jews in Egypt and in Palestine*, 1:139; Gil, *History of Palestine*, sec. 833; and Bareket, *Fustat on the Nile*, 152. Gil dates this letter to ca. 1035 (Bareket, *Jews of Egypt*, doc. 35, follows him), likely because line 17 mentions Anushtekīn al-Duzbarī, whom Gil assumes was responsible for protecting the Qaraites only after the edict of 1034 (Qaraite synagogue in Cairo, G 13+G 15; see below, n. 80); but the affair of the ban would have fallen within al-Duzbarī's jurisdiction even without a formal decree. Though the events the letter describes are strikingly similar to those of autumn 1029, the high alert of the government figures (lines 17–19) suggests that the festival had gone awry previously. The letter probably dates to 1030.

Fig. 7. The end of the excommunication controversy: letter of Shelomo b. Yehuda to Efrayim b. Shemarya, head of the Palestinian congregation in Fustat, describing the holidays of the year following the affair of the ban against the Qaraites. The festival unfolded without incident in the presence of the Fatimid governor Fatḥ al-Qalʿī, who had been called in at the request of the Jews. In Hebrew, probably late 1030. University of Oxford, Bodleian Library, MS Heb. c 13.23.

preacher, until an edict came from the government and the military governor [*amīr al-juyūsh*, that is, al-Duzbarī] to the governor of Ramla to warn [us] not to declare the ban, and [to inform us] that anyone who contravened [the order] would be harmed." Al-Duzbarī, singled out in the decree of 1030 as in charge of enforcing the peace among the Jews, drafted an edict ordering the governor of Ramla (the provincial seat of Palestine) to warn the Rabbanites not to excommunicate the Qaraites on penalty of lashes and imprisonment. Al-Duzbarī also "wrote to the governor of Jerusalem [ordering him] to come up to the mountain on Hoshaʿna Rabba with instruments of punishment, and [adding that] anyone who uttered the excommunication should be flogged and sent to prison." The governor of Jerusalem, al-Qalʿī, ascended the Mount of Olives to supervise the festival proceedings, just as he had the year before—only this time he came prepared with lashes and chains in hand.[77]

Al-Duzbarī set this chain of decrees in motion in the first place at the behest of the Jews, but the *gaʾon* registers neither protest against the government's meddling in his community's affairs nor resentment against the elders or the Qaraites for bringing it in. His silence suggests that al-Duzbarī was merely enforcing the edict of 1030, and that inviting state intervention was a normal part of Jewish affairs under the Fatimids.[78]

But for the moment, the *gaʾon* opposed any further attempts to use the government as a means of regulating internal Jewish conflicts. "Before the ordained ones were imprisoned," he now reported himself saying to his followers to persuade them against the wisdom of the ban, "did not the [Rabbanite and Qaraite] people of Ramla separate themselves from one another, since they eat [meat] without inspection? Why should we renew [the ban]?"[79] The people of Ramla now kept separate butcher stalls, perhaps in compliance with an edict; we can achieve the same results as the ban and separate ourselves when necessary without government intervention and without imprisonments, he argued. I also hear in his statement the implication that the onus is on the Qaraites to petition the government: Why should we be the ones to vie for separation? Let them do it and let them assume the attendant risks.

And indeed, within a few years the Qaraites petitioned the caliph, or so one assumes on the basis of an edict (*sijill manshūr*) issued by the chancery on 11 Jumadā I, 425 AH (3 April 1034) threatening measures against anyone "interfering with the Qaraites in their synagogue." The edict is addressed to al-Duzbarī (here called *amīr al-juyūsh*) and the local governors, ordering them

[77] Bodl. MS Heb. c 13.23, recto, lines 15–20. Edict: *patshegen* (e.g., Esther 4:8); government: *malkhut*; military governor: *negid ha-maḥanot*, a calque translation of the Arabic *amīr al-juyūsh*; see Mann, *Jews in Egypt and in Palestine*, 1:136. The title is also referred to in a later document as *baʿal ha-maḥanot* (T-S 13 J 15.23, in Hebrew and Judeo-Arabic, ʿEli ha-Kohen b. Yeḥezqel to Evyatar ha-Kohen b. Eliyahu, April, 1071, recto line 28).

[78] T-S 13 J 7.29 (above, n. 66).

[79] Bodl. MS Heb. c 13.23, recto, lines 26–27 and right margin, lines 1–2. Ramla: *Ḥula*.

to protect both groups of Jews in keeping with the government's mandate to protect its *dhimmīs*. It further orders that the followers of each group (*ṭā'ifa*) "should be permitted to live according to their own *madhhab*" and "to buy and sell as they follow or neglect to do so according to their will and their choice on the days of their festivals." The stipulations closely parallel the conditions stated in the edict that ʿAdaya ibn al-Qazzāz had issued in 1030 while the brothers were still in prison. This can only mean that once ʿAdaya did issue the edict in the end. The Rabbanites then blocked it by appealing to the caliph, and now the Qaraites followed suit and sent their conditions to the Fatimid chancery in Cairo.

The decree notes that it was copied in the *dīwān al-inshā'*, and indeed it is markedly different from the other hundreds of documents cited in this book: its fifty rows are so widely spaced that they occupy a sheet of paper no fewer than eight meters long—not including the missing beginning section. It is also the only original document I quote in this book that was preserved outside the Geniza: it survived in the archives of the Qaraite synagogue in Cairo. I assume that the chancery made additional copies and issued them to one or more of the Rabbanite congregations as well, and it may be that a Judeo-Arabic copy made by Rabbanites still lurks among the Geniza papers.[80]

But despite his reluctance to involve the government further, the *ga'on* would soon petition the chancery himself on the occasion of the threat to his office by the head of the Iraqi congregation in Ramla, Yūsuf al-Sijilmāsī, who himself had petitioned the caliph for recognition as the leader of the Iraqi congregations of Palestine—in other words, who had tried to secede from the jurisdiction of the Palestinian *yeshiva*. With his counterpetition (preserved in the Judeo-Arabic copy discussed in chapter 3), the *ga'on* held the Iraqis off until his death in 1051.[81]

In the end, the ban was not declared in 1030. "By the mercy of the Merciful One," writes the *ga'on*, "there is peace here, and no one was harmed, and blessed be God, and all the people ascended for [Shemini] ʿAṣeret," the day after Hoshaʿna Rabba, and conducted the festival as usual.[82]

[80] Qaraite synagogue in Cairo (G 13+G 15). Gil's reading of the date as 425 AH is correct (*History of Palestine*, sec. 783). Gottheil misread the year as 415 AH and Stern, Goitein, and Richards followed him; Mann and Goitein therefore supposed that this decree was the *reason* the authorities intervened in 1029 while war in Palestine had accounted for the five-year delay in its enforcement, but in fact the Rabbanites themselves invited the authorities to intervene in 1029, and this Qaraite decree came in response to immediate events that the Geniza has not yet yielded. *Sijill mashhūr*: line 41 (see above, n. 67); the date: lines 46–47; *amīr al-juyūsh*: line 33; protecting the two groups of Jews in accordance with the *dhimma*: line 35–36; *madhhab*: lines 6–7; buying and selling: lines 8–13.

[81] ENA 4020.65 (see chap. 3 for full analysis), an undated Judeo-Arabic copy. The original petition probably dated to the early 1030s.

[82] Bodl. MS Heb. c 13.23, recto, margin, lines 21–27. Peace here: *aval be-raḥamey raḥum halom shalom*. The nonstandard usage of the word "*halom*" (in biblical Hebrew, "hither" rather than "here") seems to be occasioned by the rhyme the *ga'on* has chosen.

The *ga'on* had convinced his followers to relinquish their attachment to the ban—but not by illuminating its political risks. Instead, he castigated them for their own sins. "'Ephraim is addicted to images—let him be' [Hosea 4:17]," he wrote in an undated letter: the masses may make their demands, but the Qaraites should not be excommunicated because what they do "is not one of the [infractions] for which lashes . . . // they forbid //" (the letter is fragmentary). In the new eleventh-century spirit of rebuking his followers for ninth- and tenth-century zealotry, he objects that his flock had gone too far against the Qaraites.[83]

And why, he adds, should we trouble ourselves with the sins of others when our own are great enough? For Qaraites who commit what rabbinic law deems sins, "there should suffice for us the curses written [in the Torah]: 'Cursed be he who does not uphold [the terms of this Torah and observe them, Deut. 27:26].' [This means that] everyone who . . . does not uphold [these commandments] will enter into a curse. Should we excommunicate everyone who desecrates God's sabbaths?! But the majority desecrate [the sabbath]!! Who is he who keeps the sabbath as ordained?! And [should we excommunicate] everyone who desecrates the festivals of the Lord?! But [the Qaraites] say that we are the ones who desecrate [it]!"[84] In a remarkable moment of religious pluralism, the *ga'on* argues that to the Qaraites, we are sabbath and festival desecrators as much as they are to us. We have our interpretation of biblical law, he says, and they have theirs. God will judge the Qaraites; we should mind our own transgressions.

But there were not merely transgressions at issue. At issue were the limits of the *ga'on*'s jurisdiction, and about this he had no illusions.

> [Should we excommunicate] everyone who pursues cases in Islamic courts, and who takes inheritances according to their [Islamic] laws?! But many people who have a legal case go to Islamic courts! [Should we excommunicate] those who spread gossip?! But most [engage] in gossip! [Should we excommunicate] anyone who performs magic?! But many—both men and women—do it! And [eating] meat with milk is included [among these transgressions]. "That is why a curse consumes the earth" [Isaiah 24:6]. But as for those who [merely] seek a quarrel, it seems to them that with the mention of [the ban against the eaters of] "meat with milk" the Torah will be upheld. Let us not mention our own evil deeds, our enormous guilt, the abominations and disgraces on our own part. Are there no commandments left for us to uphold except the mention of "meat with milk," which has caused us these troubles?![85]

[83] T-S 13 J 33.12, in Hebrew, recto, lines 3–5. The top and upper left portions are missing and this makes it impossible to determine with certainty who is referring to whom. Mann, *Texts and Studies*, 2:63–64, has the *ga'on* relating Qaraite accusations against the Rabbanites, but since he spends the bulk of the letter complaining about his own followers' intransigence toward the Qaraites, it is more likely that he is citing Rabbanite accusations against them.

[84] T-S 13 J 33.12, recto, lines 5–7.

[85] Ibid., lines 7–13. Jews pursued cases in Islamic courts when they had something to gain from it, as in inheritance cases in which women stood to inherit according to Islamic but not Jewish law; see

The *ga'on* exhibits a startling realism here: he knew that the sword of excommunication bore a double edge and balked at overusing it. Yet as he often did, here he invoked the righteousness of his cause only to reveal the politics behind it. He closes by objecting again to inviting government interference—"people have nearly been destroyed and the hand of the government has entered into [our affairs] and troubled itself on our account"—but his objection was not that inviting state intervention diminished Jewish communal autonomy, nor that it diminished his own authority, nor even that it turned his flock against itself. Rather, it was that "the government has troubled itself on our account," and by making trouble for it, one diminishes one's political capital and thus one's potential to make effective use of the government when necessary. And with that, he goes on to thank a certain *negid ha-gola*—most likely Avraham b. ʿAṭā of Qayrawān—and a certain faithful envoy (*shaliaḥ ne'eman*, possibly one of the traders with Ifrīqiya) for interceding with the government on behalf of the Rabbanites and against "the deceivers" (perhaps those who spread the rumor of the burnt effigies on Purim). That the *ga'on* had called on contacts as far away as Ifrīqiya suggests a roundabout route to the chancery in Cairo—via the Zirid governors of Ifrīqiya. He would take the same route during the affair of the gaonic schism of 1038–42 (see chapter 11), and there as here, the reason for it seems clear: the direct route via the Qaraite courtiers was unavailable to him, since they were busy ferrying petitions through the chancery on behalf of the Qaraites.[86]

Shelomo b. Yehuda avoided a second excommunication affair, and this is the last we hear of the ban against the Qaraites until 1038. But he did not succeed in stamping out extremism in the Rabbanite camp. The excommunication he worked so hard to avoid would go down in history as an event attended not by government agents with whips and chains at the ready to punish anyone who uttered it, but by tiny, cowering flocks of Qaraites helpless to defend themselves from the charges.

Ibn Dāwūd's Depiction of the Excommunication Ceremony

Of the various medieval authors who describe the ascent of the Jews to the Mount of Olives on pilgrimage holidays and on Hoshaʿna Rabba in particular,

---

Goitein, *Mediterranean Society*, 2:395–407; Gil, *History of Palestine*, sec. 274; and above, chap. 3, n. 12, and chap. 6, n. 33. Both men and women: an allusion to the talmudic dictum associating magical practices with women; see Babylonian Talmud, *Sanhedrin* 67a.

[86] Line 13. Nearly been destroyed: Heb. *ve-kim'aṭ qaṭ hayu nefashot ovedot*. The expression *kimʿaṭ qaṭ* is a *hapax legomenon* in the Hebrew Bible (Ezek. 16:47) and means "almost," while in medieval Hebrew poetry it means "hardly anything," perhaps under the influence of Arabic *qaṭ*, "not at all" (Sáenz-Badillos, *History of the Hebrew Language*, 238). The biblical Hebrew meaning is the one intended in this context. The *ga'on* uses it the same way in a letter to Efrayim b. Shemarya ca. 1040, where he writes, "[kimʿa]ṭ qaṭ hayu son'eyhem aved[u]m," "their enemies have almost destroyed them" (Bodl. MS Heb. c 50.21, line 28).

Ibn Dāwūd is the only one who mentions the excommunication of the Qaraites as part of the ceremony.[87] For that reason, most historians of the subject have relied on his description.

Ibn Dāwūd composed *Sefer ha-qabbala* two or three generations after the Crusaders had put an end to the Jewish community of Jerusalem and with it to the public convocations on the Mount of Olives. Although Jewish pilgrims did continue to reach Jerusalem during his lifetime, under Crusader rule they went there on private pilgrimages only. To the mere handful of Jews they found in the city—four according to Binyamin of Tudela in 1170, only one according to Petaḥya of Regensburg a few years later—the gatherings were at best a distant memory transmitted to them in childhood by their elders.[88] Ibn Dāwūd therefore reconstructs the ceremony on the basis of his *Tendenz* rather than of eyewitness accounts. The liberties he takes render his account more valuable as a record of twelfth-century anti-Qaraite polemic than as a reliable rendering of events.[89]

His description falls in his conclusion to the work, where he sharpens his claims against the Qaraites by arguing that they fell outside the recognized succession of Jewish tradition, the consensus (*ijmāʿ*) of believers comprised of the Rabbanite majority. First, he repeats the claim that ʿAnan b. David was nothing but an embittered renegade pupil of one of the Babylonian *geʾonim*: "The fact is that the evil ʿAnan and his son Shaʾul, may the name of the wicked rot, were disciples of Rav Yehuday [Gaʾon], but broke with him and his tradition for no reason whatsoever other than the envy that overcame them. Hence they cannot possibly say, 'Thus have we received on the testimony of so-and-so [who received it] from the prophets.' Instead, they fabricate things out of their own hearts."[90] Next, he argues that Qaraite legal rulings are counterfeit since they derive from human argumentation rather than divine dispensation. Neither of these arguments was new. But then he adds a claim of his own: the Qaraites are "disqualified [from religious legitimacy] by the sheer meagerness of their number" (*baṭelim be-miʿuṭam*). Even if one were to forgive their illegiti-

[87] There is also a short description of the ceremony in al-Bīrūnī, *al-Athār al-bāqiya ʿan al-qurūn al-khāliya* (Sachau, *Chronologie orientalischer Völker*, 277; idem, *Chronology of Ancient Nations*, 270); a corrupt manuscript tradition has garbled the Hebrew name of the Mount of Olives, but the gist of the description is that the Jews assemble there on the "festival of the congregation" (*ʿīd al-jamʿ*, Hoshaʿna Rabba). See also the interpolation to the midrash on Ecclesiastes preserved in a fifteenth-century manuscript (JTS MIC. 5592/2), cited in Mark Hirshman, "The Priest's Gate and Elijah b. Menaḥem's Pilgrimage," Hebrew, *Tarbiẓ* 55 (1986): 217–26 and idem, "'R. Elijah Interpreted the Verse Concerning Pilgrims' (Shir Rabba 2, 14, 7): Another Medieval Interpolation and Again R. Elijah," Hebrew, *Tarbiẓ* 60 (1991): 275–76.

[88] On the Jewish population of Crusader Jerusalem see Joshua Prawer, *The History of the Jews in the Latin Kingdom of Jerusalem* (Oxford, 1988): 46–49; 128–68 (on Jewish pilgrims); 169–250 (on travel accounts).

[89] Cf. Cohen, *Sefer ha-qabbalah*, xv.

[90] Ibn Dāwūd, ibid., 67 (Hebrew), 91–92 (English, from which my translation differs slightly).

mate origins and antitraditionalist methods, says Ibn Dāwūd, their error is demonstrable *eo ipso* from their lack of a widespread following.

This last piece of argumentation was decidedly mendacious. It had first appeared in Augustine, according to whom the very fact that the Jews were a scattered remnant proved that God no longer favored them. Ibn Dāwūd even offered an exaggeratedly paltry representation of Qaraite demography in the closing section of his work, claiming that they had effectively ceased to exist "except in one city in the Maghrib, in the desert, called Warjlān, a handful of them in Egypt, and a handful in Palestine." Further on, he claimed that his own Iberian peninsula had been fully emptied of Qaraites.[91]

Immediately following the section on comparative demographics, Ibn Dāwūd launches into his description of the ritual excommunication on the Mount of Olives. The juxtaposition is not accidental: his rendering of the scene derives its effect from the claim of Rabbanite numerical supremacy and therefore of divine favor. "When the Jews used to celebrate the festival of Tabernacles on the Mount of Olives," he writes, "they would encamp on the mountain in groups and greet each other warmly. The heretics [*minim*] would encamp 'before them like two little flocks of goats' [1 Kings 20:27]. Then the Rabbanites would take out a scroll of the Torah and pronounce a ban on the heretics right to their faces, while the latter remained silent like 'dumb dogs' [Isaiah 56:10]."[92]

Several dramatic embellishments invite closer examination. None of the eyewitness accounts mentions so much as a single Qaraite at any of the ceremonies, and there is no reliable evidence that Qaraites "encamped" before the Rabbanites on Hoshaʿna Rabba. (Qaraites did ascend the Mount of Olives to offer up private prayers at various times of the liturgical year.)[93] The Qaraites thus never attended the yearly ceremony in which they were excommunicated "right to their faces." But taking this liberty allows Ibn Dāwūd to concretize his argument by borrowing the simile of the "two little flocks of goats" from 1 Kings.

[91] Ibn Dāwūd, ibid., 68 (Hebrew), 93 (English, from which I have deviated slightly for reasons of syntax and consistency in transliteration). On Qaraites in Warjlān and other medieval Saharan communities, see H. Z. (J. W.) Hirschberg, *A History of the Jews in North Africa*, vol. 1: *From Antiquity to the Sixteenth Century* (Leiden, 1974), 160–63.

[92] Ibn Dāwūd in Cohen, *Sefer ha-qabbalah*, 68 (Hebrew), 94 (English).

[93] See Sahl b. Maṣliah, *Sefer ha-miṣvot*, in Harkavy, *Me'assef niddaḥim* 1 no. 13, 198, 203; Fleischer, "Pilgrims' Prayer at the Gates of Jerusalem," Hebrew, in Friedman, Fleischer, and Kraemer, *Mas'at Moshe*, 298–327; Ben-Shammai, "A Unique Lamentation on Jerusalem by the Qaraite Author Yeshuaʿ b. Yehuda," Hebrew, ibid., 93–102; Hirschberg, "Concerning the Mount of Olives in the Gaonic Period," *Bulletin of the Jewish Palestine Exploration Society* 13 (1947): 156–64; Gil, "Immigration and Pilgrimage in the Early Arab Period (634–1099)," Hebrew, *Cathedra* 8 (1978): 124–33, with responses by Safrai, Grossman, and Ben-Shammai; T-S 10 J 9.19 and Gil, *History of Palestine*, secs. 831–34; the memorial list in Mann, *Texts and Studies*, 2:260 lines 50–54; Prawer, *History of the Jews in the Latin Kingdom*, 138; Elchanan Reiner, "Pilgrims and Pilgrimage to Ereṣ Yisra'el, 1099–1517," Hebrew (Ph.D. diss., Hebrew University, 1988); and Y. Rozenson, "'Be-ʿalot ʿam laḥog be-shalosh peʿamim': ʿal ʿaliyya le-regel le-har ha-zeytim ba-piyyuṭ ha-ereṣ-yisra'eli ha-qadum," *Sinai* 117 (1997): 176–85.

It is not the most obvious one he might have chosen. In 1 Kings, it is not heretics who encamp like little flocks of goats, but rather the Israelites, the heroes of the tale, standing in their sparseness against the mighty force of the Arameans, whom they could not possibly hope to defeat without divine intervention. But the Israelites vanquish the Arameans because God delivers them into their hands. In the biblical narrative, the victory serves as evidence of God's favor. By conjuring up this passage, then, Ibn Dāwūd raises the question of divine providence. But according to him, it works in the reverse manner of 1 Kings, where God sides with the weak. For Ibn Dāwūd, God sides with the mighty. The difference between Ibn Dāwūd's theology and the biblical one reflects one of the innovations of his work: the application of triumphalist historicism to Rabbanite polemic. (The existence of the Qaraite political class in the Fatimid empire might have disproved Ibn Dāwūd's belief that worldly success is evidence of divine favor, and indeed they go unmentioned in his chronicle.)

But the Qaraites are not only weak in numbers according to Ibn Dāwūd; they are silent in the face of humiliating treatment. They are "dumb dogs," who in Isaiah "have lost their bark." These Isaianic dogs have a long pedigree in Jewish polemic, starting with Isaiah's indictment of the postexilic Israelite leadership. In the Rabbanite-Qaraite debate, they made their first appearance on the Qaraite side and quickly became a standard indictment of rabbinic authority. An anonymous Qaraite halakhist warned his fellow Jerusalemites against consuming meat and wine "even while the city of your holy mount lies destroyed, without an altar and without your priests; dumb and blind dogs are watching you; and menstruating women, ritually impure men, lepers, and uncircumcised Christians enter the shrine of the elevated ʿOfel,"[94] where the "dumb and blind dogs" probably refer to the negligent watchmen and guardians of the flock, the Rabbanite Jews. Al-Qūmisī, in his commentary on Hosea (5:1), also compared Rabbanite leaders to inattentive watchmen, although he did not call them dumb dogs.[95] Yefet b. ʿEli's commentary on Song of Songs is filled with attacks on the Rabbanites as negligent watchmen (see chapter 4), and the Byzantine Qaraite Yehuda Hadassi shot the same arrow at the Rabbanites only twelve years before Ibn Dāwūd shot it back.[96]

[94] JTS Schechter Geniza, 17r–18v; see Gil, *History of Palestine*, sec. 930; cf. citations ibid., sec. 837.

[95] Dani'el b. Moshe al-Qūmisī, *Pitron sheneym-ʿasar* (Commentary on the Twelve Minor Prophets), ed. Israel Markon (Jerusalem, 1948), 8. Cf. Qūmisī's epistle, Mann, "Tract by an Early Ḳaraite Settler," 280.

[96] On Yefet, see Frank, "Karaite Commentaries on the Song of Songs," and above, chap. 4. Yehuda Hadassi, *Eshkol ha-kofer* (The cluster of henna blossoms), alph. 123, cited in Wieder, *Judean Scrolls and Karaism*, 203 n. 2 and 260–61 n. 3. Cohen suggests that Ibn Dāwūd knew Hadassi's work or that both drew on some earlier common source; see *Sefer ha-qabbalah*, 160–61.

Ibn Dāwūd uses the simile of the dumb dogs to much the same effect as his adversaries, but now the Qaraites are the negligent guardians of the flock of Israel. At first blush, it seems that the simile is meant only to reflect the Qaraites in their cowering failure to defend themselves against the ban (manifest proof of their error). But toward the end of his work, Ibn Dāwūd reapplies the verse in claiming that the Qaraites "never did anything of benefit for Israel, nor produced a book demonstrating the cogency of the Torah or a work of general knowledge or even a single poem, hymn, or verse of consolation. 'They are all dumb dogs who cannot even bark.' If one of them finally did produce a book, he reviled, blasphemed, and spoke insolently against Heaven." With this Ibn Dāwūd gives away what bothers him most about the Qaraites, even more than their passivity: their failure as leaders, since implicit in the failure of leadership is their readiness to break ranks with the rest of Israel.

Ibn Dāwūd's characterization of the Qaraites' passivity notwithstanding, they had not only attempted to have the excommunication ceremony outlawed but also used their government connections to the advantage of the Rabbanites.[97] This points to a second liberty Ibn Dāwūd takes in his description: he implies that the ban excommunicating them was issued annually "when the Jews used to celebrate the festival of Tabernacles on the Mount of Olives," that is, for the entire period during which they did so. But the evidence at our disposal indicates that after 1029 the ban was made illegal, and that in the period leading up to the Crusades it was declared only in 1038. On both these occasions, its declaration was opposed not only by the Qaraites but by the Rabbanite leadership itself.

Ibn Dāwūd construes the Rabbanite ban as evidence of Qaraite defeat. But the actual circumstances of its proclamation hardly paint a picture of a Rabbanism militant.

"TO BE SEPARATED FROM THE OTHER GROUP, SO THAT THEY MIGHT NOT MINGLE WITH THEM IN ANY MATTER"

The three factions involved in the affair—the Rabbanite laity, the Rabbanite leaders, and the Qaraite laity and leadership—each practiced a different form of communal politics. Their differences emerged in the compacted arena of the pilgrimage festival as on a proscenium.

The Rabbanite instigators of the ban still adhered to the old congregational style of Jewish communal politics (what Goitein called the "ecumenical" model), according to which one pledged one's loyalty to one of the two rabbinic centers in Jerusalem and Baghdad. The Rabbanite leadership, by contrast, had

[97] Cf. Cohen, *Sefer ha-qabbalah*, 94, note to lines 44–45.

already moved toward a politics of the regional Jewish community, regardless of rite or *madhhab*, in which the tripartite community acted increasingly as one transscholastic bloc. Qaraite participation was essential to this new model.

For the Rabbanite laity, there was the rub. Because the leaders who propounded the new model accepted scholastic differences, their followers opposed them by policing those differences. They were vexed at now being expected to join ranks with the Qaraites, and perhaps even more vexed that their leaders were beholden to the Qaraites. The new rabbinic realpolitik turned into an occasion for declaring heresy: the followers agitated for the excommunication as a reaction against their leaders' alliance with the Qaraites. But because the leaders invited the state to intervene, the excommunication could not stick.

The first Rabbanite rumor allowed the *ga'on*'s followers to imagine his authority as based solely on internal rabbinic sources such as his place in the *yeshiva* hierarchy, his commitment to tradition, and his defense of rabbinic authority. But the ground was shifting under their very feet. The ban heeded a logic of rabbinic ideals and their expression in ritual. Rabbinic politics heeded a different logic: that of utility and compromise with strange bedfellows. The authority of Jewish communal leaders owed as much to connections at court and beyond as to traditional genealogies of rabbinic learning.

As for the Qaraites, they responded by setting a chain of edicts in motion, drawing on sources of governmental power not only to punish the instigators of the ban but to throw off the authority of rabbinic leaders. The Rabbanite laity could not win at this game. Both the Rabbanite and the Qaraite leaders had experience obtaining government edicts, and the leaders fought one another through by means of the state. Government decrees were now the language of Jewish politics. In the process of fighting the Rabbanites, the Qaraites only further demonstrated how indispensable they were to the Jewish community's functioning.

The tensions of the late 1020s and 1030s were strictly a local matter, centered on Jerusalem, the historical locus of the extreme versions of Qaraite anti-Rabbanism. In Jerusalem, agitation for the ban served as a barometer of the limits of transscholastic cooperation. The wider landscape of the eastern Mediterranean—and the wider history of the eleventh century—attest to forms of Rabbanite-Qaraite cooperation in the context of which the Rabbanite insistence on the ban at Jerusalem was exceptional, an occasion of heretication whose immediate causes lay in the changing shape of power in the Jewish community. Those more prevalent forms of cooperation form the subject of Part 3.

PART III

SCHOLASTIC LOYALTY AND ITS LIMITS

CHAPTER NINE
RABBANITE-QARAITE MARRIAGES

The events in Jerusalem and Ramla in 1029–30 failed to alter one aspect of community life in the Fatimid territory: as the *ga'on* Shelomo b. Yehuda had himself remarked, Qaraites were in the habit of taking the Rabbanites' daughters in marriage. The converse was also true.

The first direct evidence of the practice emerged from the Geniza collections in 1901, when Solomon Schechter published the contract for the marriage in 1082 of the daughter of a Qaraite notable to David b. Dani'el, a Rabbanite aspirant to the office of *ra'īs al-yahūd* and son of a *ga'on* of the Jerusalem *yeshiva*. Given the near vacuum of supporting documents in which the discovery appeared, it remained not merely surprising but practically inexplicable that the stipulations the contract contained protected the religious observances of both husband and wife: the son of a *ga'on* had agreed to allow his wife to desecrate rabbinic feasts and fasts when her Qaraite tradition required it of her. Though Schechter did not know this, the marriage represented a broader trend: it had been arranged by a group of Rabbanite notables in Fustat who chose a Qaraite bride for one of their young and ambitious members in order to strengthen his claims to the office of *ra'īs al-yahūd*.[1]

The Geniza has meanwhile yielded evidence of Rabbanite-Qaraite couples in Egypt and Syria scattered over the eleventh and twelfth centuries. These remain some of the best surviving evidence of how the rank and file regarded scholastic loyalty. The marriages were not stories of star-crossed lovers. Betrothals were hard work, the results of neither romantic love nor individual choice but agreements contracted between families and entire communities on considerations of formal friendship, business partnership, and social station. As Amitav Ghosh has put it, it was "a culture where marital negotiations can

[1] T-S 24.1; Solomon Schechter, "Genizah Specimens: A Marriage Settlement," *Jewish Quarterly Review*, o.s. 13 (1901): 218–21; translated and discussed below, chap. 12, 335–37. That Qaraites and Rabbanites married one another in Fatimid times had been known to nineteenth-century historians on the basis of references in medieval literary works (see Löw, cited ibid., 218).

cast the whole weight of a family's honour upon the scales of public judgement."[2] In the decision to contract alliances with the other *madhhab*, the bride and groom were mere strands in a web that extended well beyond them. Jews throughout the Fatimid empire were aware of the practice. Jurists on both sides sanctioned the marriages as valid, approved the religious practices the contracts stipulated, and pledged to enforce the stipulations with the power vested in their court systems.

How did families choose spouses for their children? What kinds of negotiations did they conduct before contracting a marriage? How did they determine the religious stipulations their marriage contracts would contain? What led some to maintain loyalty to their own school and others to transfer to their spouse's? And which set of practices did the couple teach their children? The documents that have survived answer many, of not all, of these questions.

MARRIAGE STRATEGIES

Betrothal decisions usually belonged to the women of the family, but as Goitein notes, the reasoning behind their decisions rarely reaches us via the Geniza. He observes two general patterns governing the selection of mates. One was to fall back on endogamy, particularly first-cousin marriage, on which the twelfth-century India trader Avraham ben Yijū had this to say: "the son of my brother has more rights to [my daughter] than strangers." In such marriages couples possessed the advantage of knowing their future partners and in-laws.[3]

But we have much more detail about the other kind of marriages, the ones through which families extended themselves geographically or upward in the social hierarchy. Exogamous marriages had the potential to increase a family's symbolic capital, expand its social network, and strengthen it in other ways too. Merchants used these marriages to move into a market or shift their operations into new terrain. They also used them in the opposite way, once they had moved to a new base and sought to maintain a foothold in the old one. It is endemic to the evidence that there is more information about exogamy: the Geniza speaks most volubly about the literate, the geographically mobile, and the ambitious, all of whom, sometimes for different reasons, communicated in writing.[4]

That is not to say that marriages were always instruments of the parents' designs. Legally, after the age of twelve girls could no longer be betrothed without their consent, though in practice, when they married as teenagers

[2] Amitav Ghosh, *In an Antique Land: History in the Guise of a Traveler's Tale* (New York, 1993), 317.

[3] T-S 12.337, quoted in Goitein, *Mediterranean Society*, 3:56.

[4] Ibid., 3:55–61.

their fathers (in some cases, their maternal uncles) served as their legal proxies in contracting their betrothals, while mothers, aunts, and grandmothers may have arranged the match. One imagines that some girls protested their family's choices, though one hears nothing of this, but betrothals could be legally dissolved at the behest of the bride (except according to certain authorities who also asked for the groom's repudiation as well). Exceptionally, a virgin bride could negotiate and contract her own marriage. Older women, divorcées, and widows did so regularly.[5]

After the initial negotiations, families discussed the terms of the betrothal proper, including the groom's marriage gift to the bride, the settlement terms should the marriage end in divorce or death, the dowry and its appraisal, and detailed stipulations regarding the couple's circumstances while married, such as whether the husband could take a second wife or a maidservant without his wife's approval, where the couple would live, and which of their older kin (or children from previous marriages) could live with them. Marriage being a contractual arrangement, all kinds of personal preferences were subject to bargaining and were stipulated explicitly in written agreements attached to the betrothal document or contained in the marriage contract (*ketubba*, pl. *ketubbot*).

When Rabbanites married Qaraites, neither partner was expected to relinquish his or her religious customs for the sake of the marriage. These too, formed the subject of negotiation between the families. To understand the clauses themselves, it helps to know something about the differing forms and requirements of the *ketubba* in each legal school.

The Rabbanite *ketubba* outlines the formal basis of the marriage partnership, including its material conditions and terms of its dissolution, but it says little about what will actually transpire concretely between the couple during the marriage. The Qaraite version, in contrast, details the formal elements of the partnership but also includes clauses specifying how husband and wife should comport themselves toward one another, particularly in the area of religious observance. This is true regardless of whether a Qaraite married another Qaraite or a Rabbanite: the Qaraite *ketubba* regularly lists distinctive areas of religious custom, even if the bride and groom shared them. The clauses enjoining the observance of specific laws therefore read as guides to Qaraite practice, safeguards of custom, and statements of distinctiveness. Nonetheless, they did not follow a stereotyped formula. They were points over which the families and couples deliberated, bargained, and finally had to agree. When one of the partners was Rabbanite, then, the Qaraite contract merely adapted the usual set of religious stipulations according to the families' and couples' negotiations. If the couple used a Rabbanite *ketubba*, they imported the feature of religious clauses

5 Ibid., 3:65–79. On child marriage (exceptional in the world of the Geniza), see Friedman, "On Marital Age, Violence and Mutuality in the Genizah Documents," in Reif, *Cambridge Genizah Collections*, 160–77.

from the Qaraite formulary. The stipulations about religious observance differ in all the extant Rabbanite-Qaraite marriage contracts.[6]

Though the stipulations did not adhere to precise formulae, there was a basic set of practices around which they revolved: whether the couple could engage in sexual intercourse on the Sabbath (forbidden for Qaraites as labor and potentially leading to ritual impurity, recommended for Rabbanites, for whom the Sabbath functioned in practice as a time set aside for fulfillment of conjugal duties); whether they could benefit from the use of light on Friday evenings (Qaraites: burning a fire, therefore forbidden; Rabbanites: if not igniting the fire, permitted); how to manage differences between the Rabbanite and Qaraite calendars; and details of animal butchering and consumption.[7] The stipulations spoke to the practical areas of difference in Rabbanites' and Qaraites' observance of Jewish law—about what they found important to preserve—but also about the possibilities of cohabitation: when there was some motive for living together harmoniously, Rabbanite and Qaraite did so. Conversely, when harmonious relations collapsed (as on the Mount of Olives in 1029), the causes were more than differences in religious practice and belief.

Legal Reciprocity

The *ketubbot*, then, open a window (even if not as wide a window as letters do) onto the possibilities of mutual recognition among Rabbanites and Qaraites. Understanding their form—and the work of the lower court functionaries who wrote them and sanctioned the marriages—opens an even wider window. In point of legal practice, the schools did not patrol their borders rigorously. Legal practice was flexible on the ground—as it had to be in order to remain adaptable to a range of situations.

Further evidence of this flexibility lies in the fact that Qaraite law mandates the use of marriage contracts at all. This is odd at first glance, since the Hebrew Bible does not mention *ketubbot*. Rabbinic law requires them on analogy with the biblical law of divorce, which requires a writ (though the custom of writing *ketubbot* is older than its hermeneutical justifications in the Talmud). Nor can anyone find the origins of the Qaraite *ketubba* with certainty. The

[6] On religious stipulations in Qaraite marriage contracts, see Olszowy-Schlanger, *Karaite Marriage Documents*, 247–55. Like her, I avoid using the term "mixed" for these couples, since it suggests either ontological differences or differences on the grounds of "identity." The contracts demonstrate that such differences were not presumed as given but subject to negotiation. Qaraite marriage contracts stipulate that the couple should avoid appealing to Muslim courts (something rabbinic authorities also forbade), but that clause is represented in only one of the contracts discussed below. According to Olszowy-Schlanger, the clause developed as a reaction against Babylonian rabbinic contracts for transactions other than marriage, which contain a clause claiming their validity in any court, including non-Jewish ones.

[7] For more on religious differences between Rabbanites and Qaraites, see above, chap. 1, 26–27.

most convincing hypotheses locate them in the same ancient Babylonian Jewish tradition that gave rise to rabbinic law, or else in rabbinic practice itself. Regardless, the Qaraite *ketubba* is the best proof that the Qaraites were not the biblical literalists they have sometimes been imagined to be. They, too, developed a body of postbiblical tradition; it was only the rabbinic monopoly on the postbiblical to which they objected.[8]

That the Qaraites required written contracts for both betrothal and marriage speaks to their commonalities with rabbinic law. So does the wording of the Qaraite *ketubba*, which is markedly similar to that of the Rabbanite version, with one important difference: Qaraite legal documents are in Hebrew (the biblical tongue) while Rabbanite ones are in Aramaic (the idiom of the rabbis). But the biblicizing register of Qaraite *ketubbot* is only a superficial difference. Divorce documents, *giṭṭin*, are biblically mandated, and here the Qaraite and Rabbanite formulae differ considerably. The marriage documents, in both cases postbiblical practices, are remarkably similar.[9]

One of the first decisions the couple and their families had to make was which language and formulary their marriage contract would use. There was a standard mode of deciding: contracts nearly always followed the bride's *madhhab*, a Qaraite contract in Hebrew for a Qaraite bride, a Rabbanite contract in Aramaic for a Rabbanite one—with the religious clauses imported and written in Hebrew.[10] Beyond those basic differences, however, the very form of the contracts shows that Rabbanite and Qaraite court clerks—the standing armies of the legal schools—regarded one another as occupying places along a continuum of juridical validity. The marriages speak to legal reciprocity not only among the couples and their families but also in the specialized area of the courts.

HOW REPRESENTATIVE IS THE SURVIVING EVIDENCE?

Geniza documents have yielded thirteen cases of Rabbanite-Qaraite marriage dated between 1009 to 1135.[11] More than half the documents are from

[8] Olszowy-Schlanger, "Karaite *Ketubbot* from the Cairo Geniza and the Origins of the Karaite Legal Formulae Tradition," Hebrew, *Teʿuda* 15 (1999): 127–44; Friedman, "On the Relationship of the Karaite and the Palestinian Rabbanite Marriage Contracts from the Geniza," Hebrew, *Teʿuda* 15 (1999): 145–57. Olszowy-Schlanger argues that the Qaraite marriage contract was, in fact, essentially borrowed from the Rabbanite one—both the practice of using a *ketubba* and its general content; *Karaite Marriage Documents*, passim.

[9] Olszowy-Schlanger, "La lettre de divorce caraïte et sa place dans les relations entre caraïtes et rabbanites au moyen age: Une étude de manuscrits de la Geniza du Caire," *Revue des études juives* 155 (1996): 337–62.

[10] The one known exception is the Rabbanite contract of David b. Dani'el (T-S 24.1), which follows the groom's *madhhab*; see chap. 12 at n. 36.

[11] Some are undated but likely fall into this range. The documents are Antonin 637 (Rabbanite *ketubba*, Qaraite groom, Tyre, 1011–47); CUL Add. 3430 (Qaraite *ketubba*, possibly Rabbanite groom,

Fustat, a disproportion typical of Geniza documents in general. Eight brides are Rabbanite and five are Qaraite. This is not a large number of cases compared with the corpus of four hundred marriage documents Goitein used for his volume on the family and the fifty-eight known Qaraite marriage documents from the period.[12] But the evidence should not be viewed in crudely numerical terms, for several reasons.

First, Geniza evidence represents a relatively small sample of the document production among Jews in the medieval Near East, and its texts were discarded unsystematically. This makes any statistical argumentation unscientific at best.

Second, the dowry amounts and other evidence of social status suggest that the couples came from every stratum of Jewish society. This contradicts Goitein's claim that Rabbanite-Qaraite alliances "prevailed between the members of the high bourgeoisie belonging to the two denominations."[13] Goitein presumed that religious ideology held little import for the upper classes, while the poor were less cosmopolitan, more parochial, and more endogamous. While it is true that the poor traveled less and thus had less recourse to the advantages of marriage with partners from faraway places, they, too, recognized the value of other kinds of exogamy, including marrying their children into other clans and schools. Conversely, the rich were hardly immune to attractions of ideological commitment. The range of economic strata to which these Rabbanite-Qaraite couples belong suggests that their marriages may

Jerusalem, January 1028); T-S 12.621 (Qaraite *ketubba*, possibly Rabbanite groom, Fustat, 1030s–40s); ENA NS 18.37 (Qaraite *ketubba*, Rabbanite groom, Fustat, 1030s); T-S Misc. 35.13 (Rabbanite *ketubba*, Qaraite groom, Fustat, 1052); T-S 24.1 (Rabbanite *ketubba*, Qaraite bride, Fustat, 1082); T-S 13 J 6.33 (marriage agreement, Rabbanite bride, Qaraite groom, Fustat, late eleventh century); Bodl. MS Heb. e 98.60 (Rabbanite court document containing copy of a Rabbanite *ketubba*, Qaraite groom, bride probably Rabbanite, Ascalon–Fustat, 1100; see further chap. 12, n.44); Bodl. MS Heb. a 3.42 (Qaraite *ketubba*, Rabbanite groom, Fustat, 1117); T-S 8.223 (Rabbanite *ketubba*, Qaraite groom, Fustat, 1128–35); ENA 2728.2a (premarital contract, Rabbanite bride, Qaraite groom, Fustat, undated); Mosseri II 195 (L 197) (undated letter of a Jew in Cairo, possibly Rabbanite, to his brother-in-law in the Maghrib seeking the return of his Qaraite wife); ENA 3787.10 (Rabbanite wife, Qaraite husband, but groom seems to have been Rabbanite at the time of his marriage; Damascus-Fustat, undated). See also Bodl. MS Heb. d 65.26+ENA NS 3.24+Bodl. MS Heb. b 3.28+T-S 12.128 (Rabbanite marriage contract, Tinnīs, Egypt late tenth–early eleventh century), whose groom Poznanski and Friedman have argued may be Qaraite since his name, Mevasser b. Yiṣḥaq, appears in the colophon of a biblical codex from Ramla, 1013, in the Firkovich collections. Both his name and patronymic were too common in the eleventh century for this identification to be certain. Friedman, *Jewish Marriage in Palestine: A Cairo Genizah Study*, 2 vols. (Tel-Aviv: Tel-Aviv University, 1980), 2:2–3 and n. 3, and Poznanski, "The Beginning of the Karaite Settlement in Jerusalem," Hebrew, *Jerusalem* 10 (1913), 115. But Norman Golb, "The Topography of the Jews of Medieval Egypt: VI: Places of Settlement of the Jews of Medieval Egypt," *Journal of Near Eastern Studies* 33 (1974), 143, s.v. "Tinnīs," refers to Qaraites; see Halper 393 recto, line 55.

[12] Goitein, *Mediterranean Society*, 3:364–422; on the total number of Qaraite marriage documents, see below, n. 22.

[13] Goitein, *Mediterranean Society*, 2:7.

have been broadly representative of social practice, embracing households ranging from the wealthy to the average and unimportant.

Third, evidence of these marriages extends beyond the *ketubbot* themselves. In addition to the thirteen marriages, there are two formularies for Rabbanite-Qaraite marriages—templates that court scribes kept on hand to facilitate drawing up such *ketubbot* when needed—one from Ramla (1009) and one from Fustat (1036).[14] Their existence indicates that the marriages were frequent enough to warrant codification in formularies, as well as meeting with the approval of the judges and scribes responsible for contracting them. They can therefore be considered a reliable gauge of the practice's acceptance.

Formularies

The formulary from Ramla treats the marriage of Qaraite brides to Rabbanite grooms; it was thus probably produced to be kept on hand in a Qaraite court. A small pamphlet, it contains formulae for both marriage and divorce documents according to Qaraite practice.[15] Such formularies, produced by scribes for the benefit of other courts or for their own reference, are relatively common in the Geniza. This is one of nine Qaraite formularies for marriage and betrothal and one of six for divorce found in the Geniza collections thus far.[16] Here, the Judeo-Arabic instructions regarding divorce dictate that under normal circumstances, "Two people must testify for the purposes of the divorce document and present it to [the wife] in the presence of two witnesses," but "according to the Rabbanites, she [the wife] must acknowledge" its receipt.[17] The formulary thereby instructs Qaraite court functionaries in how to make a divorce valid according to rabbinic law. The court must have had a reasonable expectation of seeing more than isolated cases.[18]

The second formulary, composed in Fustat in 1036, offers formulae for marriages according to the Qaraite school (see fig. 8). It was also drawn up for Qaraite brides who married Rabbanite grooms, but it is not immediately clear

[14] T-S Misc. 35.10 and Bodl. MS Heb. d. 66.49v–50r.

[15] T-S Misc. 35.10. What has been preserved of the pamphlet comprises two quires of two bifolia each and two single leaves, or twenty small pages in all, but their order is unclear. As the leaves are currently bound in the volume at Cambridge, Gil's edition has the first quire as fragments 6 and 5, then the two leaves in the order in which they are currently bound, and the second quire as leaves 1 and 2.

[16] On the number of Qaraite formularies in the Geniza see Olszowy-Schlanger, "Karaite Legal Documents," in Polliack, *Karaite Judaism*, 260. The other divorce formularies are listed ibid., 260, n. 25.

[17] T-S Misc. 35.10, fourth fragment (first single leaf), recto, lines 4–7 (in Gil's edition, 2:549, segment 3). See Gil's comments, *History of Palestine*, sec. 932n.

[18] That the Qaraite formula acknowledged the difference between rabbinic and Qaraite divorce practices as early as 1009 is significant in light of Maimonides' later ruling; see Olszowy-Schlanger, "Lettre de divorce"; below, chap. 12, 345.

Fig. 8. Rabbanite-Qaraite marriages: Qaraite formulary in Hebrew setting out the wording of marriage contracts for Rabbanite-Qaraite couples. The Judeo-Arabic instructions specify: "This is the wording of the *ketubba* of Fustat for the Qaraites," suggesting that the formulary was kept on hand in a Rabbanite court. In Hebrew and Judeo-Arabic, Fustat, 1036. Bodleian Library, MS Heb. d 66 49v–50r.

whether it was intended for use in a Rabbanite or Qaraite court. Its Judeo-Arabic superscription explains, "This is the wording of the *ketubba* of Fustat for the Qaraites," which can be read as instructing a Rabbanite court that saw enough Qaraite brides to keep the formulary on hand. This interpretation finds support in the fact that Qaraites frequently had their documents drawn up in rabbinical courts (see chapter 10). Rabbanite scribes would also have kept Qaraite formularies on hand for guidance in how to write negotiated stipulations into hybrid marriage contracts that otherwise followed the Rabbanite formulary. One must remember, as well, that this formulary survived in the Geniza of the Ben Ezra synagogue, just a few paces away from where the scribes of the Palestinian rabbinical court of Fustat did their work.[19]

The instructions on the formulary offer a model for the couple's religious stipulations: if the Rabbanite husband infringes upon his wife's Qaraite

[19] The formulary of Fustat, 1036: Bodl. MS Heb. d 66. 49v–50r. On Qaraites having contracts drawn up in rabbinical courts, see, e.g., the writ of agency from Tyre, 1026–27: T-S AS 153.12 + T-S 13 J 25.20 (see chap. 10 at n. 28 for a detailed discussion); and a power of attorney from al-Mahdiyya, 1073: T-S 20.187.

susceptibilities, she has grounds to request and be granted a divorce. "And she will have this [right of] request over him in any place she desires."[20]

The formularies indicate that the number of surviving composite contracts may be only a part of the total for Egypt and Syria over the long eleventh century. References to Rabbanite-Qaraite marriages in other sources confirm this: while only one contract for a Rabbanite-Qaraite couple has survived from Jerusalem (dated 1028), in 1030 the *ga'on* of Jerusalem complained of unions of this type in a manner suggesting that they were a repeated occurrence.[21]

Provenance

The substantial number of Qaraite legal documents preserved in the Geniza casts further light on the problem of Rabbanite-Qaraite marriages. Of the corpus of fifty-six Qaraite marriage documents from the Geniza, only four pertain to such unions. Fifty-two, on the face of it, have no business among Rabbanite papers. They include signed and witnessed documents kept in the couple's possession; draft documents reused by the court; and copies of the documents kept in court archives. Some of them contain writing exercises on verso.[22]

There are several possible routes by which these documents might have arrived in the Geniza. Some were probably deposited there once the marriage had ended through either death or divorce. Others may have passed into the possession of the Qaraite couple's heirs, and a family member in a subsequent generation married into the Palestinian Rabbanite community or transferred to it outright, bringing his or her family documents into the Geniza. Qaraites may also have deposited their papers there directly. Finally, the *ketubbot* of

20 Bodl. MS Heb. d 66. 49v–50r, lines 20–23.

21 CUL Add. 3430; for the complaint, see above, chap. 8, 221.

22 These fifty-six include the fifty-seven in Olszowy-Schlanger, *Karaite Marriage Documents*, minus two from the Firkovich collections (2 Firk. Heb. A 717r and 2 Firk. Heb. A 506+2 Firk. Heb. A 2222), since Firkovich probably did not acquire single-page documents from the Geniza, plus one I identified in the Russian National Library: Antonin B 627, Rayyisa b. Yehuda and Aharon b. Samīḥ ha-Kohen; agent of the bride is Yeshaʿya b. Namer. The four for Rabbanite-Qaraite couples are T-S Misc 35.10; Bodl. MS Heb. d 66.49v–50r; Bodl. MS Heb. a 3.42; ENA NS 18.37. It should be noted, though, that there is a slight possibility that some of the thirty-six of Olszowy-Schlanger's documents from the Taylor-Schechter collection came from the Dār Simḥa synagogue of the Qaraites in Fustat. Schechter, who brought what was left of the Geniza to Cambridge in 1897, wrote of having visited "genizas" rather than "the geniza" or "a geniza" in Cairo; Ben-Sasson and Ben-Shammai argue that he acquired manuscripts from the *geniza* of Dār Simḥa. But even an overly cautious minimum of twenty Qaraite legal documents from the Ben Ezra Geniza is enough to warrant consideration of how they arrived there. See Ben-Sasson, "Firkovich's Second Collection: Remarks on Historical and Halakhic Material," Hebrew, *Jewish Studies* 31 (1991): 59–60; Zeev Elkin and Ben-Sasson, "Abraham Firkovich and the Cairo Genizas in the Light of His Personal Archive," Hebrew, *Pe'amim* 90 (2002): 51–95; Ben-Shammai, "Scholarly Study of Karaism," in Polliack, *Karaite Judaism*, 14 and 14 n. 17. Sklare has identified an additional seventy-six *ketubbot* in the second Firkovich collection under the classmark RNL Heb. II K, almost all from Ottoman or post-Ottoman Cairo: Sklare, "A Guide to Collections of Karaite Manuscripts," in Polliack, *Karaite Judaism*, 907.

both schools tended to be written on large, expensive sheets of parchment likely to be reused. Once the marriage had ended, the parties could write on the back or else sell the parchment as writing material, sometimes after cutting it into smaller pieces. This possibility suggests merely that Rabbanites and Qaraites frequented the same stationery merchants on the buying and selling ends, but it cannot be ruled out that Rabbanite scribes kept old Qaraite contracts on hand as models (much as they kept formularies). Even the Qaraite marriage and betrothal documents in which neither member of the couple is Rabbanite, then, may represent channels of Rabbanite-Qaraite contact.[23]

Finally, there may be more Rabbanite-Qaraite marriages than we realize at present even among the hundreds of marriage documents known to date that follow both the Rabbanite and the Qaraite formularies. When marriage documents include stipulations about the religious conduct of both bride and groom, we can determine the religious affiliations of each. But occasionally one partner to a marriage leaves behind his or her former customs so completely that no evidence of the couple's differing origins appears in the contract. Identifying the couple beyond mere names in such cases depends upon the luck of corroborating documents and prosopographic matches. Additional couples, whose affiliations will come to light only in the course of further research, may lurk amidst the known corpus of marriage documents.

"ONE HUNDRED DINARS TO THE POOR OF THE QARAITES AND THE RABBANITES IN EQUAL SHARES"

The contracts do not always make themselves entirely clear in what they require of the couple. Some contracts appear to stipulate equal obligations of bride and groom in allowing for one another's legal practices; others do not; still others leave ambiguities that one suspects resulted from unresolved negotiations.

One contract, dated August 1117, records the remarriage of the Rabbanite physician Yaḥyā b. Avraham and the Qaraite Rayyisa b. Seʿadya. It was the bride's third marriage but her second to the same man: after being widowed, she married Yaḥyā, was divorced, and then married him a second time.[24] Their contract from their first marriage has not (yet?) surfaced.

The couple's marriage(s) represented the union of two families from Fustat's patrician class. As a physician, Yaḥyā was among the most educated of the elite, though the sum he brought to the marriage indicates that he was not as well off as Rayyisa; the dowry she brought to the marriage totaled 719 dinars,

[23] Goitein, *Mediterranean Society*, 3:96–97; Olszowy-Schlanger, *Karaite Marriage Documents*, 29–31.

[24] Bodl. MS Heb. a 3.42, in Hebrew, dated Elul 1428 Sel. (August 1117); see Olszowy-Schlanger, *Karaite Marriage Documents*, 477–78.

a staggeringly large sum. Her wealth probably represented some combination of her family's holdings and what she had inherited from her first husband (Qaraite law allowed women to inherit from their husbands if the marriage produced offspring; she had a daughter). The couple had their *ketubba* drawn up in a Qaraite court, as usual following the bride's school.

The scribe they found was unusually gifted and produced a calligraphic *ketubba* with sumptuous decorations, a rarity in this period: the document's borders contain a latticework of micrographic biblical verses on which traces of gold and blue ink are still visible.[25] The bride's trousseau list, too, is elaborate: among the items it includes are gold, silver, pearls, linen, silk, and a bridal trunk inlaid with tortoiseshell, ivory, and silver.

The couple's religious stipulations cover the three usual areas of difference: the Sabbath, the calendar, and food. They also include other points over which the couple had negotiated: among these, once he moves into her home, she cannot charge him rent. At first glance, the document appears to enjoin the Rabbanite Yaḥyā to take up his wife's Qaraite ways, but on closer scrutiny, her stipulations are nearly symmetrical to his.

> And our elder, dear Yaḥyā stipulated, according to his will and resolve, that he would come into the covenant of the Lord, blessed be His name, and that he would not profane against his aforementioned wife the festivals of the Lord according to the sighting of the moon, and that he would not light the Sabbath candles against her [custom], and not coerce her [to contravene her laws of] eating and drinking, and that all the time she is with him he would not take another wife or concubine and would not [the clause is interrupted by a lacuna] . . . except according to her wish and agreement, and that her daughter would remain with her in her house at his expense and be supported by him until she is married.
>
> If he breaks one of these conditions he will have to pay one hundred dinars to the poor of the Qaraites and the poor of the Rabbanites in equal shares.
>
> And this Rayyisa accepted in favor of her aforementioned husband not to profane against him the festivals of our brethren the Rabbanites all the time she is with him, to take care of his food and drink and not to take from him the rent of the house in which they currently live.
>
> They both took it upon themselves to be together with full resolve, willingness and honesty, and to behave according to the custom of the Qaraites who observe the holy festivals according to the sighting of the moon and the finding of the barley crop in the land of Israel, and not to appeal to gentile courts to change the laws of the Torah.

There is a tension in this document between its Qaraite framework and the specific stipulations the couple has negotiated. On the one hand, Yaḥyā is said

[25] The top and part of the bottom of the contract and the right and left margins have decayed. Micrography is still preserved on the left. For a description of the latticework, see ibid., 472.

to "come into the covenant of the Lord," here meaning that he will not profane his wife's Qaraite festivals, break her Sabbath rules, or contravene her food laws. He alone is required to pay one hundred dinars to the Qaraite and Rabbanite poor if he breaks the stipulations. (The punishment fit the crime: should he fail to observe a judicious compromise between his Rabbanite ways and his wife's Qaraite ones, his charitable donation would succeed.) The stipulations conclude by stating that the couple would "behave according to the custom of the Qaraites" with regard to festivals. Thus it appears that Yaḥyā had fully accepted Qaraism.

But the rest of the stipulations show this to be a mere artifact of where the document was drawn up, a Qaraite court. Rayyisa is equally enjoined to avoid desecrating her husband's Rabbanite festivals, having "accepted in favor of her aforementioned husband not to profane against him the festivals of our brethren the Rabbanites." In fact both partners agreed to observe both sets of holidays. Nor could he could force her to eat parts of the animal prohibited by the Qaraites, while she had to ensure that he could observe Rabbanite food laws, including buying meat from Rabbanite butchers and not serving him meat and dairy together. As is the way of contracts, this one leaves some room for interpretation, but the basic impression is one of symmetry despite what appears to be a Qaraite legal framework. If the contract does not spell this out clearly, it is probably because it was the couple's second marriage and they already had a history of living together despite their differences.

Other contracts suggest that brides held advantages in negotiating religious stipulations. The formulary for the rabbinical court written in Fustat in 1036 specifies that the groom "will not force her to profane the festivals of the Lord of Hosts, according to the sighting of the moon and the finding of the barley crop in the land of Israel, because she is from the Qaraites and belongs to their custom."[26] My impression is that the bride's religious practices took precedence when the marriage was contracted according to her *madhhab*. Similarly, a Qaraite man who married a Rabbanite bride in 1052 in Fustat "with a Rabbanite marriage contract" (as the contract itself notes) specified that "I have taken it upon myself not to desecrate before her the festivals of the Lord as observed by the Rabbanites."[27] Scribes appear, then, to have used the contracts as a means of safeguarding the bride's customs while at the same time including the results of the families' deliberations.

But those deliberations did not always protect the bride's customs. A fragment of a rabbinical court record from Fustat dating to 1128–35—probably what remains of a prenuptial contract—shows a Qaraite groom yielding to Rabbanite law in not compelling his wife to eat meat slaughtered by Qaraites,

[26] Bodl. MS Heb. d 66.49v–50.

[27] T-S Misc. 35.13, in Aramaic and Hebrew, probably a draft, written on a very small piece of vellum (lines 4, 10–11); Yosef b. Avraham the Qaraite and Sara b. Efrayim the Rabbanite.

but the Rabbanite bride yielding to Qaraite law in refraining from sexual relations on the Sabbath and not desecrating Qaraite festivals.[28] This last stipulation required that she observe two sets of holidays, a burden not placed on him, at least explicitly.

One couple seems to have extended the pursuit of equality and symmetry to their very choice of court system: they conducted their premarital negotiations in a rabbinical court while contracting the marriage itself according to the Qaraite formulary. In an undated draft from a Rabbanite court in Fustat, the Rabbanite Abū ʿAlī Yefet ha-Kohen and his Qaraite fiancée Sitt al-Yumn, known as Nājiya, stipulated not to transgress each other's practices in calendation and food (and perhaps other matters as well, but the contract is fragmentary). Any violation, says the contract, will result in a fine of thirty dinars to be divided evenly "between the [poor of the] two parties (*al-ṭāʾifatayn*)." Then the couple went to a Qaraite court to contract the betrothal and the marriage. By doing so, they ensured that the stipulations would be enforced by both court systems. Or perhaps the groom had some other business to conduct in the rabbinical court; one tried to effect as many legal transactions as possible in one sitting to negotiate a lower price with the court clerk (single legal documents frequently cover multiple transactions).[29]

Fines for breach of contract were a source of revenue for the community chest. Breaking labor contracts and other agreements, delaying repayment of debts, and failing to appear in court could all result in fines. But it is unclear whether fines levied on marital contracts could have yielded much revenue for the community. Maimonides writes in a responsum that it was extremely difficult to prove breach of contract in cases involving domestic arrangements, and nearly impossible to collect those fines. Grooms may have promised to pay large fines with little expectation of ever having to make good on them, as in the case of Yaḥyā's hundred dinars. But even if these fines were collected only

[28] T-S 8.223r, written and signed by the court clerk Ḥalfon b. Menashshe. The date preserved is Thursday, 7 Kislev, 14?? of the Seleucid era, hence between 1088 and 1188; Ḥalfon produced dated documents between 1100 and 1138, and 7 Kislev fell on a Thursday during twelve years of his tenure, the last of them in 1135; the document says "reshutey de-adonenu," a phrase reserved for the *gaʾon*, thus dating the document after 1127, when *geʾonim* reigned in Cairo; this yields a date range of 1127–35—more precisely 1128, 1132, or 1135. Confirming that is the signature on verso of Natan ha-Kohen b. Shelomo the *ḥaver*, a refugee from the Crusades in Palestine (see Weiss, "Legal Documents," 1080) whose dated documents fall between 1127 and 1137.

[29] ENA 2728.2a; my thanks to Mark Cohen for allowing me access to Goitein's unpublished edition of this document, since made publicly available. The document is torn on the left side; the preserved sections read: "It was decided before us, we the court . . . the *rayyis* Abū ʿAlī b. R. Yefet ha-Kohen . . . ha-Kohen the mighty lord, may the spirit of the Lord rest upon him . . . ha-Kohen son of our teacher [. . .]m [ha-]Kohen the elder . . . [Sitt al-] Yumn, known as Nājiya, that she shall not transgress before hi[m] . . . the intercalation, and that he shall not transgress before her the festiva[ls of . . .] and likewise, in the case of food not to (?) . . . between the two parties, the party of the . . . thirty dinars of gold." For the insight that one grouped transactions into single documents in court, I am grateful to Judith Olszowy-Schlanger (personal communication, August 2007).

in part, they would have made a large difference in the lives of those who lived from the communal coffers: a fine as small as ten dinars could buy two thousand loaves of bread, enough to feed all the poor Jews of Fustat for three days. Though the difficulty of collecting fines might have emboldened a groom of limited means to promise a higher fine than he could afford, the court's willingness to enforce it even in part might cause him to think twice about infringing upon his wife's religious susceptibilities. He also might have hesitated if her family was well connected.[30]

In any event, the clauses earmarking the fines for poor Rabbanites and Qaraites in equal shares are manifestly written to suggest that fairness, equity, balance, and negotiation were meant to be the principal considerations in contracting the marriages.

QUESTIONS OF LOYALTY

While for some, the differences between Rabbanite and Qaraite practice were dearly enough held to warrant negotiation, others maintained no particular attachment to their *madhhab*.

A prenuptial agreement drawn up in a rabbinical court in Fustat in the late eleventh century details stipulations for the eventual marriage of the Qaraite trader Abū Saʿīd Dāwūd b. Abū Naṣr Ben Shaʿyā and his betrothed, the unnamed daughter of a Rabbanite elder called ʿAmram.[31] Both were children of important dynasties: their fathers are titled "the exalted elder," *al-shaykh al-jalīl*, and the groom's family, the Ben Shaʿya clan, was one of the most illustrious mercantile dynasties of the late eleventh century, successors to the houses of Tustarī, Ibn ʿAwkal, al-Tāhirtī, and Nahray b. Nissim.[32]

The contract contains no religious stipulations whatsoever. It specifies that Abū Saʿīd must not force his wife to leave the house of her mother (apparently

[30] Goitein, *Mediterranean Society*, 2:110; M. A. Friedman, *Jewish Polygyny: New Sources from the Cairo Geniza*, Hebrew (Jerusalem, 1986), 69; Maimonides, *Responsa quae exstant ab ipso Arabice scripta ex schedis Cairensibus et libris tam manu scriptis quam impressis, ed. Jehoshua Blau*, 2d rev. ed., 4 vols. (Jerusalem, 1986), no. 88, 1:138–44, cited in Cohen, *Poverty and Charity*, 225 n. 135; see there for the price of loaves and the number of poor. That contracts stipulate that fines were to be divided equally between the two communities suggests that the communities ran separate social services, at least during this period. That makes it all the more noteworthy that Qaraites appeared on the poverty lists of the Rabbanite community. Cf. below, n. 44.

[31] T-S 13 J 6.33, in Aramaic (see Goitein, *Mediterranean Society* 2:110, 545 n. 36; 5:386, 610 n. 48); Friedman dates this contract to the late eleventh century.

[32] The Ben Shaʿyā dynasty is worthy of an in-depth study based on both Arabic literary sources and Geniza documents. Meanwhile, see Mann, *Jews in Egypt and in Palestine*, 1:215–17, 2:264–69; Goitein, *Mediterranean Society*, 1:243, 2:356–57 and 605 n. 6, 3:428 nn. 44–47; 4:237; 5:219; 5:568 n. 11; idem, *Letters*, 89–95; idem, "A Maghrebi Living in Cairo Implores his Karaite Wife to Return to Him," *Jewish Quarterly Review* 73 (1982): 138–45; Gil, *History of Palestine*, docs. 514 and 517; idem, *In the Kingdom of Ishmael*, doc. 688; and below, chap. 12, 341–44.

a divorcée), that he must not force her to have sexual intercourse with him at any time, and that he may take neither a second wife nor a concubine; but there are no clauses pertaining to matters of religious or ritual conduct in the couple's home. Nor does it seem that Ben Shaʿyā planned to take on his wife's Rabbanite practices: only the polygamy clause specifies a penalty of one hundred dinars to the poor of the Rabbanites and the Qaraites. It is fitting, then, that like Ibn al-Qazzāz before him, Ben Shaʿyā's name was immortalized in one of epigrams of the great Arab poet Abu l-ʿAlāʾ al-Maʿarrī (973–1058) promoting what one should perhaps call religious indifference:

> If a person refrains from injuring me,
> Then he will have bounty and protection his entire life.
> If he wants, let him learn the book of Moses,
> Or if he likes, let him become a client of Shaʿyā.

More important than the larger social commitments of clientage and belonging to a religion, says the poet, is one's personal loyalty.[33]

A similar indifference to religious commitment appears in a betrothal contract from a Qaraite court in Fustat, ca. 1030–40, in which the Rabbanite groom [?] b. Manṣūr (the contract is torn at the top and shredded on the left side, so his first name has been lost) performs a full-scale migration to the Qaraite *madhhab* of his bride, Karīma b. Ḥasan.[34] The contract contains all the usual clauses safeguarding the bride's Qaraite practices, but no reciprocal clauses requiring her to respect his Rabbanite ones, stating instead that "he has come with her to the religion of the Lord which is the rite of the Qaraites . . . as it is written: 'Therefore a man shall leave his father and his mother to cleave unto his wife' [Gen. 2:24]." This is the only complete account we have of a Rabbanite groom becoming a Qaraite for the sake of marriage.

Why did [?] b. Manṣūr choose to cross over to Qaraism? Neither bride nor groom appears in other texts, and since the document is a betrothal rather than a marriage contract, it lacks a trousseau list that would disclose his bride's social standing. But the names of the witnesses fill this gap. One, Moshe b. Sibāʿ, was an associate of David b. Yiṣḥaq, possibly a *kātib* and almost certainly a trader. He is known from two other documents that reveal his connections to both schools: they were drawn up in Rabbanite courts, but one involved Qaraite parties only.[35] It is likely that, like Moshe b. Sibāʿ, [?] b. Manṣūr maintained

[33] *Idha l-insānu kaffa l-sharra ʿanni / fa-suqyā fi l-ḥayāti lahu wa-ruʾyā // Wa-yadrusu in arāda kitāba Mūsā / wa-yuḍmiru in aḥabba walāʾa Shaʿyā*. Nicholson, *Studies in Islamic Poetry*, no. 309, 284 (Arabic), and cf. his English translation, 196, from which I have departed. Goitein, *Mediterranean Society*, 3:10, cites the poem and identifies this Shaʿyā as a member of the family in question.

[34] ENA NS 18.37.

[35] On Moshe b. Sibāʿ, see also chap. 10 at n. 17. Moshe b. Sibāʿ's son Sibāʿ b. Moshe and his grandsons Efrayim and Menashshe b. Sibāʿ appear in the colophon of a biblical codex that they were given

connections in both communities. Another witness, Sahlawayh b. Ḥayyim, also sustained strong ties in both camps. A banking partner of the Tustarīs and a wealthy member of the mercantile elite in both Fustat and Tyre, he had donated money to the Rabbanite *yeshiva* of Jerusalem in the campaign of 1028, and the Rabbanite cantor David bar Shekhanya had written an encomium for him.[36] Another witness, a certain Manṣūr b. Moshe, is perhaps the groom's father, and if that is the case, he may have appointed one of his trading partners to witness his son's betrothal. Our Rabbanite groom [?] b. Manṣūr, on contracting this betrothal, solidified his bonds with a diverse milieu of some economic heft. The decision to join his betrothed in "the religion of the Lord which is the rite of the Qaraites" suggests extensive prior contact with the group, perhaps also a desire to be accepted by them, and certainly the strength of the bride's family. The most likely possibility is that his choices of *madhhab* and bride were conditioned by business considerations—either his own or his father's—and ambition.

Thus decisions to marry exogamously resulted from a diverse mixture of arrangements and motives. Some, out of loyalty to their clan and community of origin, retained their customs, but for the sake of domestic harmony also adopted their spouse's. Others, rather than adopt some of the customs of the other *madhhab* for the sake of marriage, transferred to it outright.

Questions of Motive

These marriages intimate a world in which the categories "Rabbanite" and "Qaraite" were neither mutually exclusive nor immutable. Some joined the other school for the sake of a harmonious marriage; others did so on micropolitical considerations, as when Efrayim b. Shemarya's congregants, offended by his autocratic behavior, migrated to the Iraqi synagogues and the Qaraite *majālis*.[37] Others did so out of a desire to benefit from the social capital (*jāh*) of their new clan. The case of a Qaraite man from Damascus named Yosef repre-

by or purchased from a certain Shelemo b. Mevasser b. Sahl al-ʿAnī. T-S K 6.148; see Olszowy-Schlanger, *Karaite Marriage Documents*, 481.

[36] On the donation, see T-S 13 J 8.14 (above, chap. 7, 196–97). The encomium: Mosseri II 246.2 (series B, P 46). Sahlawayh's children were more firmly connected with the Qaraite community: one of his sons, Ḥayyim b. Sahlawayh, married a granddaughter of Menashshe b. al-Qazzāz, as mentioned in the inheritance deed Bodl. MS Heb. e 108.70; a second son, ʿEli, donated a Bible codex to the Qaraite congregation of Fustat, 2 Firk. Heb. B 180. See Olszowy-Schlanger, *Karaite Marriage Documents*, 305, where she also cites a Bible codex that his son Ḥayyim purchased in Jerusalem in 1057, 2 Firk. Heb. B 34.1. Ḥayyim's daughter, Ḥusn, married Abu l-Ḥasan Jābir, *wakīl al-tujjār* in the Egyptian port of Tinnīs; their marriage is recorded in T-S AS 145.307r + T-S Misc. 29.58a recto. There is a debate as to whether Sahlawayh b. Ḥayyim's other daughter Sara married Abū Naṣr Ḥesed al-Tustarī, since the latter was perhaps married to a daughter of Yūsuf ibn ʿAwkal; see above, chap. 5, n. 8.

[37] See Introduction, pp. xxvi–xxvii

sents a fourth possibility: adopting a *madhhab* in order to benefit from its social services.

Yosef first enters the stage of recorded history having abandoned his wife and their four children and surfaced in Egypt after three years as a Rabbanite. His wife had perhaps waited for him, or else made efforts to find him, and the news finally reached her that he was in Egypt. She appealed to the Jewish community of Damascus to return him. They, in turn, sent an open letter to the Jewish community of Fustat inquiring about him.[38] The letter is a narrow strip written in Hebrew in the hand of a professional scribe, and was meant to be displayed publicly.

> There is a woman [here] who has been "a widow in [her husband's] lifetime" for more than three years now. We have heard that her husband is in Egypt. His name is Yosef, and with him is another man also named Yosef. He is a young man with reddish hair, and his distinguishing characteristic is that he was a Qaraite, one who does not acknowledge the words of our sages, and now has become a Rabbanite. She is an *'aguna* [see below] with four children who are dying of starvation. In your kindness, if he is there, tell him to return to his wife. And if he has left, or you have heard that he is verifiably deceased, please send her a letter here in Damascus [to that effect].

Since her husband could not be confirmed deceased—and would not send her divorce papers—she remained an *'aguna*, a "tied woman" who could not remarry. Left to fend for herself and her children, she threw herself on the mercy of the community. The expression "a widow in [her husband's] lifetime" (*bi-almanut ḥayut*, 2 Samuel 20:3) was a standard feature of appeals on behalf of poor women with absent or missing husbands. So were references to children "dying of starvation," not necessarily hyperbolic rhetoric.[39]

Why did Yosef become a Rabbanite? The letter is unrevealing as to his motive, but there are clues in the concurrence of his geographic and religious migration. Such a concurrence is common among religious converts during this period. In eighty or so cases that I have studied from Geniza documents spanning the years 1006–1234, all those who converted (in some cases, reverted) to Judaism eventually found their way to Fustat. That explains the accident of their stories having been preserved in the Geniza, but it also suggests the possibility of some meaningful connection between their becoming Jews and their migrating there. The conspicuous abundance of converts among recipients of charity has been understood to indicate that converts were forced to give up their homes and possessions, and so came to Fustat to live off the

[38] ENA 3787.10.

[39] See Cohen, *Poverty and Charity*, 143, discussing this document, and the other documents he cites there at nn. 19–20.

community chest. But one might equally suppose that conversion did not precede or cause their economic hardship but the other way around.[40] Many probably became Jewish in order to benefit from the public charity of the Jewish community in Fustat. Organized Jewish communities, particularly Fustat's, offered the promise of alms and other forms of material and social support to those who were destitute, and conversion to Judaism served as a way of qualifying for the social services of the Jewish community. In some cases, it may have served as a means of urbanization for rural Christians and Muslims.[41] A surprising abundance of female converts suggests that the community chest substituted for husbands in providing them with economic support; conversion may have served unmarried women as a means of material sustenance. That is not to suggest that one can recover converts' motives with any degree of certainty (even where they are stated explicitly in the first person). But their motives are a question worthy of speculation, and there is no reason to presume that they were ideological rather than pragmatic.

Though we still do not know why our Qaraite Yosef left his family in Damascus, it is possible that he came to Fustat to live off the community chest.[42] Strictly speaking, however, there was no need for him to become a Rabbanite in order to receive Rabbanite charity. Charity lists drawn up by the Palestinian Rabbanite community in Fustat include Qaraites—distinguished as such—as recipients of food and money. A charity list dating from ca. 1040–60 contains the names of a certain Abu l-ʿAlāʾ the Qaraite and another Ibrāhīm al-Ghazzī b. Hārūn the Qaraite; Mawhūb the Qaraite appears on a charity list of ca. 1070.[43] There may well be more Qaraites lurking in the lists who are not labeled as such. These poor Qaraites offset the impression that all the Qaraites in Egypt were wealthy and Rabbanites depended upon them for succor; in fact the poor Qaraites of Fustat also turned to Rabbanite charity in the face of need and hardship.[44] (They may have turned to Qaraite grandees for private charity or to a Qaraite community chest, but the sources are unrevealing on this

[40] Cf. Goitein, *Mediterranean Society*, 2:311; Cohen, *Poverty and Charity*, 26, 125.

[41] The usual objection to the possibility of Muslim converts to Judaism is the prohibition of apostasy by Islamic states. But all one needed to do was stay off the state's radar, and the poorer one was the easier this was to do.

[42] This possibility was first suggested by Friedman, "Qara'(im)=ben(ey) miqra'; baʿal(ey) miqra'," 297.

[43] T-S NS J 179, verso, lines 3 and 10; T-S K 15.96, folio c, left-hand page, line 1. I am grateful to Mark Cohen for making available to me his unpublished editions of these documents.

[44] Qaraite orphans also appear on charity lists from the first half of the twelfth century, but the fact that this was after the creation of the office of *raʾīs al-yahūd* means there may have been a single community chest that attended to the needs of both Rabbanites and Qaraites. The following are all translated into English in Cohen, *The Voice of the Poor in the Middle Ages: An Anthology of Documents from the Cairo Geniza* (Princeton, 2005). From ca. 1107: T-S K 15.5 (recto line 16); T-S K 15.15 (recto, right column, line 15); T-S K 15.39 (recto, right column, line 3); T-S K 15.50 (recto, right column, line 14). From ca. 1100–40: T-S Misc. 8.9 (verso, right column, line 9); T-S NS J 41 (recto, column 1, line 15); and T-S J 1.4 (verso, left side, line 6).

point.) But while Yosef did not have to become a Rabbanite in order to receive Rabbanite charity, he may well have become Rabbanite in order to facilitate his transition to the Jewish community in Fustat. The facts of his dislocation and his religious transformation accord with what we find in cases of conversion, and confirm that transfer between congregations was effected with ease.

"I Will Go and Return to my First Husband, for Then I Fared Better than Now"

Some transferred out of conviction, others from pragmatic motives; still others did so for each motive seriatim. This was the case with a pair of Rabbanites from Toledo who became Qaraites, migrated to Jerusalem, and then were forced to become Rabbanites again. They effected the first transfer for ideological reasons and at great risk to their personal fortunes, and the second one for the sake of convenience.

Their story is contained in a letter sent in 1057 by fellow immigrants from Toledo to Jerusalem, Shimʿon and Shaʾul al-Ṭulayṭulī, a father and son who had already been in Palestine for some time.[45] The father was old, sick, and nearly blind, so despite what the letter's return address reports, its author was the son, Shaʾul, who often took it upon himself to help other Andalusī immigrants settle in Palestine. In his informal role as communal leader, he kept abreast of goings-on among them, and now wrote to his sister, Ballūṭa, in Toledo to update her as to the fate of Toledans in the west. Several of Ballūṭa's letters had gone unanswered, he explains, because he was unaware they had arrived and hadn't looked for them on account of the "confusion in the west" (*tashwīsh al-gharb*), probably the Hilālī invasions of Ifrīqiya, which stalled the flow of mails. Though the interrupted communication was a source of pain to both brother and sister, it is a gift to the historian: Shaʾul provides Ballūṭa with several years' worth of news about Toledans in the east, and us with a complete narrative account of their travails.

A new group of Toledan immigrants had recently found their way to Jerusalem after a particularly trying journey, he tells us, during which they had been taken captive, brought against their will to Rūm (Christian Iberia or Byzantium), and finally ransomed in Ramla. Among them were a certain Ibrāhīm b. Fadānj and his wife, who after a terrible journey arrived in Ramla only to become the butt of gossip among the other Toledan immigrants there. The

[45] T-S 13 J 9.4, in Judeo-Arabic, dated Ḥeshvan 4418 (October 1057). I discuss this letter in comparison with geographically and religiously migrating Iberians from the fifteenth and eighteenth centuries in Rustow, "Karaites Real and Imagined." Ben-Shammai, "Between Ananites and Karaites," 29 n. 53, speculates that these immigrants may have been Ananites before they left Toledo, but I read the reference to their having been married in a rabbinical court as proof that they were Rabbanites before they emigrated.

source of gossip: Ibn Fadānj and his wife had originally been Rabbanites, but while still in Toledo had switched over to Qaraism—probably the reason they had emigrated to Palestine in the first place, since proximity to the site of the Temple and mourning for its destruction were Qaraite religious duties of the highest order. Conviction, then, appears to have brought them from Rabbanism to Qaraism and from Toledo to Jerusalem. Their migration can also be understood in the context of the western European pilgrimages to the Holy Land of the eleventh century.[46]

That Ibn Fadānj and his wife had defected to Qaraism was hardly the problem for the Toledan women of Ramla, who seem to have been Rabbanites. Rather, Ibn Fadānj's marriage to his wife was, technically speaking, forbidden according to Qaraite law, for his brother was also married to her sister. Under Rabbanite law, the marriage would have been permitted; but Qaraite law considered the marriage consanguineous: early Qaraite jurists had forbidden such marriages on the basis of Genesis 2:24 (in which husband and wife become one flesh, and thus kin) and Leviticus 18:16 ("You shall not uncover the nakedness of your brother's wife: it is your brother's nakedness"). The degree of legitimate legal analogy, called *rikkuv* in later Qaraite sources, was theoretically infinite, as was the number of forbidden marriage partners.[47] The Toledan women therefore began publicizing the family's history among the Qaraites of Ramla (an indication that the channels of gossip between Rabbanite and Qaraite women were open): they "saw fit to spread rumors about them among the Qaraites," al-Ṭulayṭulī writes, "[saying] that his wife should be forbidden to him [in marriage]." Ibn Fadānj and his wife, then, found themselves in the uncomfortable position of wanting to live among the Qaraites of Palestine but finding them perhaps more zealous than they had expected. "And the news reached me," al-Ṭulayṭulī writes.

Al-Ṭulayṭulī himself was a Rabbanite who repeatedly refers to the Qaraites as "they" and ridicules the stringency of Qaraite law, but he wasted no time in protecting his charges and seeing to it that the Qaraites would accept them. Scholastic self-interest did not prevent him from helping Ibn Fadānj join the Qaraites; in this case, what moved him was the fellow-feeling of one Andalusī for another. Local origin trumped scholastic affiliation. Al-Ṭulayṭulī silenced the Toledan women: "I approached them, and this threw them into turmoil. I prohibited anyone from making their affair known, for I knew that [Ibn Fadānj] was leaning toward the Qaraites." Meanwhile, Ibn Fadānj and his wife remained betwixt and between.

They also remained perilously close to the net of gossip in Ramla but evaded it long enough to move to Jerusalem along with their four children and join the

[46] On eleventh-century Christian pilgrims from western Europe to Palestine and the eastern Mediterranean in general, see Gil, *History of Palestine*, secs. 723–27.

[47] Olszowy-Schlanger, "Early Karaite Family Law," 283.

Qaraite community there. But after two years, the matter of their forbidden marriage caught up with them. "When they arrived in Jerusalem, they went up to Samaritiké [the Qaraite neighborhood], and they sojourned with [the Qaraites] and joined their community [literally, became a part of them, *ṣārū minhum*] and made their living among them. And [the Qaraites] put them up in their homes and treated them well. [But] after they had stayed with them for about two years, the matter [of Ibn Fadānj's marriage] was made known to the Qaraite elders, and they said that he could continue to live with his wife, but that she was forbidden to him according to their [the Qaraites'] school of law [*ʿalā madhhabihim*]. But they wanted to separate."[48]

Previous scholars have argued that the Qaraite elders allowed the couple to remain married but ruled that Ibn Fadānj's wife was sexually forbidden to him. But the plain sense of the letter is that the elders made an allowance for the couple in spite of the theoretical prohibition of their marriage. That interpretation also accords better with the historical circumstances: one of these Qaraite elders was probably Yeshuʿa b. Yehuda, who had recently overturned the *rikkuv* laws.[49] The couple, for their part, rejected such leniency, and duly offered to divorce one another.

"When I learned of this," al-Ṭulayṭulī writes, "I raised a [legal] objection against them [the Qaraite elders] and there was a dispute between us because of them." Al-Ṭulayṭulī leapt to the protection of these poor immigrants; the thought of the Ibn Fadānj family being broken apart already having survived migration and captivity understandably upset him. So he pointed out to the head of the Qaraite community in Jerusalem, a man whose name he records only as Yaʿqūb, that by the very same prohibition of consanguineous marriage, "'your wife is forbidden to you according to your own religion and your

[48] On Samaritiké, see Ben-Shammai, "The Karaites," in Prawer and Ben-Shammai, *History of Jerusalem*, 204–8.

[49] While the tenth-century Qaraite *nasi* Shelomo b. David b. Boʿaz and the early eleventh-century jurist Yūsuf al-Baṣīr had objected to the prohibition, it was not until Yeshuʿa b. Yehuda made a sustained argument against it in his *Sefer ha-yashar* that this type of marriage began to be permitted. Ibid., 281–83; see also 284 n. 34 for the suggestion that Yeshuʿa abrogated the law because he himself had married a relative by marriage several times removed, a fact reported in Sahl b. al-Faḍl al-Tustarī's *Maqāla fi l- ʿarayot* (Treatise on prohibited sexual relations); Mann, *Texts and Studies*, 2:40, and on the author see now Schwarb, "Sahl b. al-Fadl al-Tustarī's *Kitāb al-īmāʾ*," 62–71. The suggestion that the elder named further on in the letter is Yeshuʿa himself cannot be sustained since the letter refers to him as Yaʿaqov. See also Nemoy, "Two Controversial Points in the Karaite Law of Incest," *Hebrew Union College Annual* 49 (1978): 247–65. Cf. Gil, *History of Palestine*, sec. 931, and *EI²*, s.v. "Ḳaraites" (Nemoy), which popularized the view that Yeshuʿa abrogated the *rikkuv* laws because they had rendered Qaraite endogamy so difficult as to threaten the survival of the community; and Nemoy, *Karaite Anthology*, 124–25 (claiming erroneously that Qaraites lived in "small communities, each more or less self-sufficient and comparatively limited in contact with the others"). For another possible case of such a marriage among Qaraites from roughly the same period, see T-S 20.187 and T-S 28.6 C, cited in Goitein, *Mediterranean Society*, 3:434 n. 83 and discussed in this connection in Benjamin Hary and Marina Rustow, "Karaites at the Rabbinical Court: A Legal Deed from Mahdiyya Dated 1073," *Ginzei Qedem*, n.s. 2 (2006): 17–18.

madhhab, since you are two brothers who have taken two sisters [in marriage], and this is forbidden among the Qaraites!'" Yaʿqūb immediately followed suit and divorced his own wife: "when he heard this from me," says al-Ṭulayṭulī, "he left her and was separated from her."

It is unclear from al-Ṭulayṭulī's tone whether he found this turn of events as farcical as it might seem to us. In any case, in view of his failure to convince the chief Qaraite to act sympathetically toward his new charges, it seemed they would indeed divorce. So al-Ṭulayṭulī had recourse to the head of the rabbinical court in Jerusalem in order to find a loophole by which Ibn Fadānj's wife might nonetheless receive some means of financial support. "I consulted with our lord the *av bet din* on account of the poor captive [feminine, i.e. Ibn Fadānj's wife], and he sent word to the Qaraites, saying that [Ibn Fadānj] should divorce her only according to the *madhhab* according to which he had married her. And her *ketubba* was written by the Rabbanites, so [Ibn Fadānj] should pay her marriage payment and then divorce her." Since the contract that governed Ibn Fadānj's marriage was still a Rabbanite one—they had been married in Toledo in a rabbinical court—she was entitled to the full amount of compensation specified if they drew up Rabbanite divorce papers. Al-Ṭulayṭulī and the *av bet din* agreed on the matter: their principal goal was to help Ibn Fadānj and his wife become better Qaraites by helping him to divorce her, not to solve their problem by convincing them to become Rabbanites.

In the midst of al-Ṭulayṭulī's negotiations on the couple's behalf, they put an end to their own predicament by re-joining the Rabbanite community, according to which their marriage was permitted. "I had not ceased acting indulgently in the matter," al-Ṭulayṭulī writes, "when the Rabbanites accepted him and he went down to [live] among them with his wife and their children, Abū Zikrī, Yūsuf, Mūsā, and Ḥulwa. They put them up in their houses, among the Rabbanites, and they treated them kindly and they lacked nothing, even though they had [at first] not been willing to accept them since they had been Rabbanites but became Qaraites, and they had sojourned among them [the Qaraites] for two years. When I saw what they wanted to do to the poor woman, to separate her from her husband and have the children remain 'orphans in his [their father's] lifetime'—and it was a time of hardship and famine—I acted in their affair in a manner for which God will reward me." The desire of the Toledan couple to preserve their marriage now trumped the religious ideology that had brought them to Jerusalem in the first place. Although the Rabbanites of Jerusalem at first objected to their Qaraite past, eventually they accepted them into the community.

As for al-Ṭulayṭulī, he dismisses and disparages the strict Qaraite regulations of kinship and marriage and can't help but notice that the Qaraites themselves don't observe them. "For they have a rule about the prohibition of two sisters [even] after the death [of one of them] for which no jurist today can find a reason, except to say that this was the tradition of ʿAnan, the founder and ancestor of the Qaraites [*hākadhā istasanna ʿAnan rayyisuhum wa-qadmon al-qarrāʾiyyīn*], and they are being perplexed by fictitious things [i.e., added prohibitions] upon which one cannot rely [*yabhatū bi-shibāhin lā muʿawwil ʿalayhā*]." Those rules might cause even the staunchest Qaraites to defect to the Rabbanites, he comments. "For when they saw that Ibn Fadānj had left them and returned to the Rabbanites, as in the saying 'I will go and return to my first husband, for then I fared better than now' [Hosea 2:9], they permitted Yaʿqūb's marriage lest he, too, leave them in order to stay with his wife. But they made him swear that he would refrain from intercourse with her, 'something I never commanded and that never occurred to me' [Jeremiah 7:31]."

Via the verse from Jeremiah, al-Ṭulayṭulī derides the Qaraite laws of *rikkuv* as contrary to the spirit of biblical law; via the verse from Hosea, he derides Ibn Fadānj's fickle religious commitments. He objected to two things: Ibn Fadānj's allowing convenience to trump religious loyalty; and the Qaraites' allowing their cultivation of membership to trump the dictates of their own laws.

Ibn Fadānj and his family, then, switched schools of law not once but twice: the first time out of conviction and the second time out of convenience. Al-Ṭulayṭulī, for his part, acted on considerations of a geographic bond, not a scholastic one. He did not seem to mind whether Ibn Fadānj and his wife chose Qaraism or Rabbanism. His only mandate was that of helping his fellow Andalusīs. Even in Jerusalem, which was full of religious pilgrims, loyalty to one's place of origin outweighed scholastic loyalty—or perhaps especially in a Jerusalem full of immigrants and pilgrims from far-off places. That in itself is enough to suggest that questions of heresy and orthodoxy do not resolve themselves in a vacuum. Religious zeal is not a default position, but requires a particular confluence of circumstances in order to flourish. The Toledan women, too, accused Ibn Fadānj and his wife of incorrect religious praxis out of hostility to them as newcomers. The leaders of both communities were decidedly less zealous and more pragmatic in their approach to resolving the problem. This accords with the kind of pragmatism the contracts reflect in negotiations over marriage partners and married life.

Parents and Children

When Rabbanites and Qaraites married one another, which rite did their children follow? Surprisingly, the extant marriage contracts make no provisions for how the couple's children were to be raised. This is significant given that the contracts stipulate both outward and intimate aspects of the couple's shared life, including which nights of the week were appropriate or inappropriate for sexual relations. Though the standard religious clauses in Qaraite marriage documents have nothing to say on the matter of children, why should the hybrid contracts, which reflected the couple's negotiations, be silent? Was any mention of offspring omitted out of fear of the evil eye? Did child rearing, like the contract itself, follow the wife's custom, and was the children's *madhhab* thus evident to all? Or should we interpret the silence as a sign of some greater latitude: did the children learn to practice according to both schools, and did they not always make a choice? The Geniza has yielded no evidence of the religious loyalties of such children, and this, too, may be significant: it suggests either that they became so well integrated into the *madhhab* they chose that no further reference was made to their origins, or that the fringes of scholastic belonging remained genuinely unregulated.

There is, however, some circumstantial evidence that casts light obliquely on the question: the letters of Ṭoviyya b. Moshe, a Byzantine Qaraite scholar who married a Christian woman who had converted to Judaism. Ṭoviyya b. Moshe, called "the translator" (Heb. *ha-maʿatiq*), had migrated to Fatimid Palestine some time before 1040 to study at the feet of the masters, including Yeshuʿa b. Yehuda, at the Qaraite academy in Jerusalem and translated major works of Qaraite literature from Arabic into Hebrew for the consumption of Byzantine and other non-Arabic-speaking Qaraites. While living in Palestine, he was also appointed administrator (*wakīl*) of a set of government compounds, possibly by Abū Naṣr Ḥesed al-Tustarī. Thus he was another member of the book-producing classes doubling as a government functionary.[50]

At some point, Ṭoviyya's wife left him with their daughter for Egypt and reverted to Christianity (no reference is made to a divorce)—again an example of the confluence of geographic and doctrinal dislocation. He stayed in Palestine. This is lucky for us, since the geographic removal of daughter from father occasioned one of the letters that constitute our only written evidence of their family's drama. In it, he queries his daughter on how she construed her religious affiliation.[51]

He writes in an exceptionally good humor. As a government administrator, he was living high on the hog. (This was far from the case in his subsequent letters, where he complains of neglect by his patrons.) His good fortune did not, however, stop him from heaping bitter invective upon his former wife, whom he accuses of leaving him for the sake of greed. In the days before his government appointment, when he was merely a scholar and translator, it seems his income was not commensurate with her expectations; one can only

[50] Ankori, *Karaites in Byzantium*, passim; idem, "The Correspondence of Tobias ben Moses the Karaite of Constantinople," in *Essays on Jewish Life and Thought Presented in Honor of Salo Wittmayer Baron*, ed. Joseph L. Blau (New York, 1959): 1–59; Gil, *History of Palestine*, secs. 938–39; and on the letters, Benjamin Outhwaite, "Karaite Epistolary Hebrew: The Letters of Ṭoviyyah ben Moshe," in Khan, *Exegesis and Grammar* 195–234. The order of events is unclear: did Ṭoviyya's wife convert to Judaism before marrying him or only upon returning to him?

[51] CUL Or 1080 J 21, in Judeo-Arabic; see Gil, *History of Palestine*, sec. 939, who dates the letter to 1040 or 1041. Gil identifies the letter's author as Ṭoviyya b. Moshe on the basis of the letter's content and its handwriting; cf. Goitein, *Mediterranean Society* 5:47–48, 518.

imagine the history of mutual recrimination that led Ṭoviyya to tell his daughter that it was her mother's greed that had made her "an orphan in my lifetime," fatherless and dependent upon the charity of others—from which we catch another glimpse of the attractions of Fustat for unmarried women. In his suddenly improved material circumstances, Ṭoviyya wrote to his daughter to win her back, in part by bragging of his good fortune, and knowing that she would convey the news to her mother.

Ṭoviyya then promised to send his daughter money contingent on one factor: that she express unwavering loyalty toward the Judaism of her father.

> I am writing to you, my daughter, from Jerusalem, may God keep it, with three [days] remaining in the month of Rajab [according to the Islamic calendar; he does not record the year]. Part of what I have to tell you, my daughter, is what I think about your affairs. A fire [burns] in my heart because of you. God stands between me and the one who harmed you and made you an orphan in my lifetime. You, my daughter, must depend on people's kindness because of the deeds of your mother. I beseech God, may He be exalted, not to forgive her the sin by which, because of her greed, she destroyed you. God will set you right from her account.
>
> Know, my daughter, that I have sworn a solemn oath not to send you anything as long as I am uncertain about your status and do not know what to do about your situation. God knows that I have no consternation or worry other than for you. Nay, my health and my affairs are well, and my clothes do not hold me for happiness and good fortune.
>
> Had I sought nothing but worldly gain, then I could regard myself today as a great success [*la-kunt al-yawm fī bāb kabīr*], for I have become the administrator of the government compounds in Palestine, for an ample salary and a good . . . [income?]. Your maternal aunt has seen me, and her husband has too, and also Abu l-Faḍl. At my disposal are men, commandment and prohibition, and I am powerful. God has made me happier than I had been before. So good fortune has been mine and misfortune your mother's, God be praised.
>
> And now, my daughter,[52] I do not know with whom you are. I do not know whether you are with the Jews, who are the stock of your father, or the stock of your mother, the non-Jews. But this I wish you to know: even if [the Christians] wanted to sell you to me, my own daughter, I would buy you and rescue you from their hands. What else could I do?

It seems that the girl had written to her father asking him for money. At first, he seems to make helping her contingent on her decision to remain with "the Jews, who are the stock of your father," saying that he had "sworn a solemn oath not to send you anything as long as I am uncertain about your status." While this might seem like an unadorned attempt to manipulate her

52 The text reads only *yā* here; the author intended *yā bintī*.

loyalties, we must assume that Ṭoviyya genuinely believed in the wisdom of choosing Judaism together with his financial assistance. But at the end of the letter, he appears to retract this, offering to help her unconditionally, even if it meant "ransoming" her from her Christian "captors." Admittedly, from her point of view, whatever he was offering her may not have been a real choice: declare your Judaism and I will help you, or remain a Christian and I will rescue you from the Christians. But the letter suggests, at least, that there were choices to be made about one's religious loyalty.

"Let me inform you," he closed, "that after [the festival of] Shavuʿot, I am leaving for Byzantium, for my native land and my family. Let me know first what your intentions are so that I can decide what to do about your situation, *in shāʾ allāh*." What the girl's decision was we cannot know with certainty. A later letter reports to an unknown correspondent that someone had returned to him, to Judaism, to Jerusalem—it is unclear whether his wife, his daughter, or both (he refers to "daughters of Edom"). He even quotes the same verse from Hosea that al-Ṭulayṭulī had quoted, "I will go and return to my first husband [for then I fared better than now]," though it is still unclear how literally he intended this.[53] The letter Ṭoviyya sent to his daughter in Egypt made its way to the Geniza, a fact that suggests that she may have joined the Jewish community of Fustat.

If children of Jewish and Christian parentage were perceived as having choices of where to affiliate, one imagines that the progeny of Rabbanite-Qaraite marriages might have had similar decisions before them.

MADHĀHIB AND THEIR MEANINGS

Medieval Jews based their decisions to join or abandon a *madhhab* on a wide range of factors, including material and social considerations and ideological commitments. Modern presumptions of individual interiority might make it seem that pragmatic motives smack of cynicism, but the sources suggest that religion was performed and enacted in various social and material contexts that, in turn, had a hand in determining its character.

Rabbanite-Qaraite marriages attest to webs of alliances among future relatives rather than mutual antagonism between their respective communities. The noncoercion clauses indicate, as well, that religious differences did not lead inevitably or necessarily to social conflict: if couples could live under the same roof while observing their feasts and fasts on separate days, so could communities in the same towns and cities. Even the malicious gossip of the

[53] DK 166+T-S AS 153.82, in Hebrew, recto, lines 20–22. I depart from Gil's interpretation of the letter, *History of Palestine*, sec. 939.

Rabbanite women of Ramla about Ibn Fadānj and his wife was directed at their failure to abide by the fine points of Qaraite jurisprudence, which suggests that though the women were Rabbanites they understood these matters.

The noncoercion clauses also suggest a degree of scholastic reciprocity according to which both sets of customs were recognized as equally valid. Those clauses were the work of court clerks who lent their imprimatur to the marriages, combining elements of the Rabbanite and Qaraite legal formularies in such a way as to suggest their recognition of the validity of both. One of those clerks is the subject of the next chapter.

CHAPTER TEN
IN THE COURTS: LEGAL RECIPROCITY

Contracts, writs of agency, depositions, certificates, and other court records are frustrating artifacts because they seem to offer so very little information in proportion to the number of words they use. With luck they preserve dates, maybe some names, but unless those names also appear in other texts, they remain mere names. Other than that, one seems to be faced with a template repeated more or less verbatim in scores of similar documents—many lines of text to formalize but a single moment in time.

But legal documents also represent not merely product but process. Scribes used what worked, and they knew what worked by coming to know what had worked in the past. Legal documents record the progressive formalization of juridical language in response to the search for maximum efficacy. They also attest to repeated contact between clients and the scribes, clerks, and judges who wrote for them, and between scribes, clerks, and judges and the high courts that validated and ratified what they wrote. Validations—judges' certification of witnesses' signatures—ensured that the documents would be accepted as valid in any Jewish court; they also enabled judges to check each other's work. Many judges validated signatures of witnesses in faraway courts because they recognized them.[1] Documents appear to be frozen, but they are records of time, process, contact, and the accumulation of expertise.[2]

Writing was a technique restricted to a small number of people, and it constituted at least one-third of a clerk's claim to professional skill. The other two-thirds lay in his ability to create effective juridical instruments by translating real situations into formal terms, and in his ordination by some central authority. "One gets the impression," Goitein comments, "that it was not so much the contents of the law applied as the authority administering it which gave the parties the feeling that they were judged according to 'the Law of the Torah.'" The contents of proceedings remained in large measure based on

[1] On validations, see Goitein, *Mediterranean Society*, 2:336–37.

[2] On form as evidence of process in documentary sources, see Wansbrough, *Lingua Franca in the Mediterranean*, esp. chap. 2.

"customary law," the body of juridical instruments that developed in the course of repeated transactions. The hierarchy of the central system of court appointments offered customary law its veneer of sanctity. The *ge'onim* even knew this. One Babylonian *ga'on* writes in a responsum that although "our sages have said that one should not send *suftajas*," bills of exchange, "we see that people actually use them; therefore, we admit them in court, since otherwise commerce would come to a standstill, and we give judgment exactly in accordance with the law of the merchants." Rabbinic law did not restrict itself to mandating behavior; it also lent its authority to existing customs. Writing effective documents required standardization and authorization, but individual cases required flexibility, and those two elements stood in tension with one another.[3]

In point of practice, neither the Babylonian Rabbanite, the Palestinian Rabbanite, nor the Qaraite legal formulary was perfectly formalized, despite the distinctive labels they bore. They remained ranges of formulae, and contracts exhibited variety within those general frameworks.[4] Judges and court clerks retained the flexibility to use what came to hand. The experienced ones knew how to manipulate a range of phrases in order to achieve maximum efficacy—defined, in this case, as maximum enforceability. A contract's efficacy depended on certain key words and constructions, but for the rest, those who wrote them did the best they could with the means at their disposal, attempting to effect real and legally binding transactions through the use of mere language.

In a sense, then, legal documents were the art of making something out of nothing through the magic of writing. But what was the something one was making? Were court clerks in fact the standing armies of the central academies that ordained them? Or were they committed solely to creating a set of enforceable obligations between two parties? Did any part of their work consist of staking out the borders between legal schools? The *ge'onim* composed formularies that they hoped would serve as handbooks for court clerks; the *ge'onim* also possessed the power to appoint provincial judges and scribes. But was a clerk's practice really an index of his adherence to a particular school of law or of the control of the central institutions over the courts?

THE WORLD OF THE COURT CLERK

Court functionaries were not only centrally authorized but also creatures of their locale. They were appointed from above by the *ge'onim*, but a gaonic

[3] Goitein, *Mediterranean Society*, 2:327 (on the *suftaja*, see ibid., 1:242–45); the responsum is quoted ibid., 2:328.

[4] The insight belongs to Friedman, *Jewish Marriage in Palestine*, 2:36, who applies it to the Palestinian Rabbanite formulae.

appointment was never enough to offer them legitimacy, as in the case of the provincial judge in the Egyptian Delta ca. 1100 who resorted to overusing the ban of excommunication to make his authority felt. The respect and cooperation of the local community were essential.[5]

Jews often developed personal relationships with court functionaries in their town or congregation, particularly if they were merchants and had frequent or repeated need of their services. There was no separate class of notaries, since one had to have contracts validated before a court anyway; besides, writing contracts required so much specialized knowledge—including facility with Judeo-Arabic, Hebrew, and Aramaic—that by the time one knew what was necessary to write them, one was already more than a notary. Instead, judges themselves drew up documents, or their assistants doubled as court clerks (in Fustat, they often doubled as cantors as well). In towns of small or middling size, judges and court clerks were the community's leaders.[6]

The close bond between the local community and its court also meant that the clerk was of the community, and the documents he wrote reflected both his habits and his clients' needs. Rabbanite-Qaraite marriages required rabbinic judges to master clauses borrowed from the Qaraite marriage formulary (see chapter 9); so, too, scribes in mixed communities were called upon to master the Qaraite formulary and draw up contracts in accordance with Qaraite specifications.

Such was the case with Yosef ha-Kohen b. Yaʿaqov, chief judge, court clerk, and de facto leader of the Jewish community in Tyre between ca. 1011 and 1047. In Tyre, Rabbanites and Qaraites mingled closely.[7] Yosef ha-Kohen b. Yaʿaqov served both Rabbanite and Qaraite clients, and his corpus of contracts attests to his pragmatism and flexibility in writing them. Watching him at work permits us to understand the decisions he made and the criteria on the basis of which he made them.

A HETEROGENEOUS CITY

For much of the eleventh century, Tyre was the wealthiest of the chain of port cities on the eastern Mediterranean littoral. It was a city of middling size, "on the sea, or rather in the sea," as al-Maqdisī described it ca. 990. Like Venice after 1846, Tyre was attached to the mainland via a causeway, its umbilical cord. Its water came from an overhead aqueduct; a single gate gave onto the causeway; three city walls barricaded it from the sea; and the harbor was

[5] Chap. 8, n. 14
[6] Goitein, *Mediterranean Society*, 2:214–17; 3:311–12, 320.
[7] Olszowy-Schlanger, *Karaite Marriage Documents*, 358.

chained closed at night.[8] Its Jewish community was wealthy enough to survive the Jarrāḥid depredations unaffected, while cities farther inland, such as Jerusalem and Ramla, complained bitterly of financial distress. When the Jewish communities of Tripoli, Ascalon, Alexandria, and Jerusalem all petitioned David b. Yiṣḥaq for assistance, Tyre did not do so, despite the fact that he was a son of the city.

Tyre's significance in the landscape of the Jewish Levant is best illustrated by the following anecdote. During the Jarrāḥid wars of 1024–29, when all of Palestine was in desperate economic circumstances, a Rabbanite cantor from Baghdad named Rawḥ ha-Kohen b. Pinḥas, apparently heedless of war, traveled across the Syrian desert to make a pilgrimage to Jerusalem. On what would have been his return voyage, he was caught in the fighting between the Fatimid armies and the Jarrāḥids, who took him captive and robbed him of all his possessions.[9] When he was ransomed—by whom we are not told—the Jerusalem community mobilized a collection for his return journey to Baghdad, according to the usual custom, but the congregation came up short, having themselves been reduced to begging for aid from the diaspora (see chapter 7). The chief of the Jerusalem rabbinical court, Ṣadoq ha-Levi b. Levi, had to turn the Iraqi cantor away and refer him instead to Fustat, and to that end, issued him a letter of introduction to Efrayim b. Shemarya. Fustat was well out of the way of his route from Jerusalem to Baghdad. But, Ṣadoq pleaded, no other avenue lay open to his ill-fated charge: "in all of Palestine no community remains that can help, with the exception of Tyre alone." Since the cantor had just spent the winter in Tyre, imposing upon its benefactors for food, shelter, and clothing, it was decided that he would collect money in Fustat instead. The Geniza documents have not disclosed whether Rawḥ b. Pinḥas finally returned to Baghdad, but his story illustrates Tyre's position as a beacon among towns on the Mediterranean coast. Its economic abundance rivaled that of Fustat despite its size.

David b. Yiṣḥaq continued to keep a house in Tyre even after he had been summoned to Cairo, and traveled there frequently; both his daughters continued to live there.[10] He was only one of several wealthy Qaraites who maintained a base in Tyre. Among the others was the long-distance trader and banker Sahlawayh b. Ḥayyim, who also had a base in Fustat. That both made significant contributions to the Jerusalem *yeshiva* is typical of the porous

[8] al-Muqaddasī, *Aḥsan al-taqāsīm*, 163–64; idem, *The Best Divisions for Knowledge of the Regions: Aḥsan al-taqāsīm fī maʿrifat al-aqālīm*, trans. Basil Collins (London, 2001), 150.

[9] ENA 4020.48, in Hebrew. Heb. *nitpas be-redato be-reshet ha-ʿaravim ve-nivzaz ve-nilqaḥ kol asher lo akh niṣal be-nafsho va-tehi lo li-shlal*, "he was taken on his departure from Jerusalem in a net of Bedouins, and he was robbed, and all that he had was taken; but he escaped with his life, which was his booty" (lines 27–28; on the last phrase, cf. Jeremiah 21:9, 38:2, 39:18, 45:5).

[10] See below and Olszowy-Schlanger, *Karaite Marriage Documents*, 57, citing the letter of Shemuʿel b. Moshe, T-S 13 J 18.1+T-S 10 J 12.25.

boundaries between Tyre's Rabbanites and Qaraites. The family of Menashshe ibn al-Qazzāz also maintained a large compound in Tyre as well as property in Ṭūr Rūbā, a town nearby.[11]

The traders of Tyre were in continual communication with the mercantile elite of Fustat. Despite the fact that Tyre was neither as cosmopolitan as Fustat nor an administrative center like Ramla, a map showing trade partnerships and marriage alliances would be heavily inked at the arc between Tyre and Fustat. This fact partly explains the quantity of documents related to Tyre preserved in the Geniza. The other explanation lies in the Jerusalem *yeshiva*'s relationship to the city: it spent two decades there in exile before relocating to Damascus and finally Fustat, and probably carried its archives on each successive move.[12]

The corpus of documents from Tyre attests that its rabbinical court was one through which Qaraites passed with some regularity. It is unknown whether the Qaraites had a court of their own in Tyre; the one Qaraite *ketubba* that might have come from such a court could equally have come from a Rabbanite one, as we shall see.[13] If they did not have a court, the extraordinary wealth and geographic mobility of the Qaraites who used the rabbinical court suggest that had doing so been important to them, they could have gone to Qaraite courts elsewhere or established one themselves. Their frequency in the rabbinical court calls for another explanation.

A Flexible Scribe

Yosef ha-Kohen b. Yaʿaqov of Tyre followed his father into the scribal profession, or so we learn from the titles after his patronymic. Some time between 1019 and 1026, Yosef was appointed to the rank of *ḥaver*, a position that authorized him to work in the rabbinical court in exchange for a salary funded by taxes, fines, and donations to the community chest. By 1037 at the latest, he had been promoted to Fourth of the *yeshiva*. It is unknown whether he ever advanced beyond this rank, and no documents bearing his name have been found that definitively postdate that year. He was, in the end, a communal servant of middling rank in a Jewish community of middling size, a mere functionary in a city that housed a disproportionate number of wealthy international traders. Yet his court permits an excellent vantage point from which to survey Tyre's overlapping social, kinship, and trade networks.[14] Of what must have been a more voluminous output over the course of nearly two decades, nine

[11] Bodl. MS Heb. e 108.70, lines 13–15.

[12] Goitein *Mediterranean Society*, 2:214. Tyre also housed a Fatimid mint; Walker, *Exploring an Islamic Empire*, 98 and 210 n. 6.

[13] T-S 20.2; see below, n. 38.

[14] On the value of mediocre figures as connectors in social network problems, see Malcolm Gladwell, *The Tipping Point: How Little Things Can Make a Big Difference* (New York, 2000), chap. 2.

documents have surfaced that he wrote, witnessed, or both.[15] The first three show him as an assistant; subsequent ones show him writing documents, running the court, and finally passing the operation on to his own apprentice.

Three of these documents offer a glimpse of the network of Rabbanites and Qaraites in Tyre and Fustat. The earliest of these dates to 24 November 1019, before Yosef's appointment as *ḥaver* of the Jerusalem *yeshiva*. It is the testimony of a certain Dara b. Shelomo, daughter of Shelomo b. Rabīʿa, a Rabbanite of Fustat, confirming that she had collected her entire inheritance from her father's estate from his executor in Fustat. Her husband was a trader and a merchants' representative (*wakīl al-tujjār*) in Tyre, Khalaf b. Moshe b. Aharon, known as Ibn Abī Qīda, and he had most likely been his father-in-law's trading partner. The larger port cities had one or more *wukkalāʾ al-tujjār* and their jurisdictions were determined by their cities of origin or their family connections. Ibn Abī Qīda probably oversaw shipments to Fustat.[16] One of the witnesses to Dara's testimony is Moshe b. Sibāʿ, whom we met on the betrothal contract of the Rabbanite [?] b. Manṣūr to a Qaraite bride whose *madhhab* he joined.[17] It is one of several documents connecting Yosef's court to the legal world of the Qaraites, and not only attests to Fustat–Tyre connections but hints at Rabbanite-Qaraite ones. The testimony was later sent to Fustat where it was validated by Elḥanan b. Shemarya, still head of the rabbinical court and on the cusp of permanently alienating the Babylonian and Palestinian *geʾonim* with his bid for leadership of Egypt's Jews (see chapter 6).

The second document is a letter Yosef b. Yaʿaqov sent some time between 1036 and 1047 to an unknown recipient in Fustat, probably Efrayim b. Shemarya, head of the Palestinian rabbinical court, to inform him of the death of Ḥalfon (Khalaf) b. Thaʿlab, an important and wealthy Qaraite in Tyre and one of the Qaraites who had donated money to the Jerusalem *yeshiva* in 1028.[18] Before his death, Ḥalfon b. Thaʿlab had arranged for the betrothal of his two daughters, Sitān and Sara, and designated Sitān's fiancé, Ṣedaqa b. ʿEzra, as executor of his estate. The fragment, alas, breaks off here, but we learn more of the affair from the second letter, in which Yosef's successor, Shemu'el b. Moshe,

[15] Cf. Friedman, *Jewish Marriage in Palestine*, 2:35 n. 3, with references to earlier literature on Yosef's documentary output; and Gil, *History of Palestine*, sec. 299.

[16] PER H 83 (Friedman, *Jewish Marriage in Palestine*, 2:35 n. 3, should be corrected accordingly). This document calls Shelomo b. Rabīʿa "Shelomo b. Dani'el, known as Ben [or Ibn] Rabui." Gil first matched the two names, *History of Palestine*, doc. 272, n. to l. 3. Yosef wrote two documents for Shelomo ibn Rabīʿa while he was still alive: one in 1011 appointing him as his son-in-law Ibn Abī Qīda's proxy to collect a debt in Fustat (T-S 13 J 33.5); and a second in 1011–12, appointing him as court-appointed proxy (*apoṭropos*) to receive the inheritance of four orphaned children in Tyre (T-S NS 321.4). On the *wakīl al-tujjār*, see Goitein, *Mediterranean Society*, 1:186–92; Udovitch, "Merchants and Amīrs," 65; and Roxani Eleni Margariti, *Aden and the Indian Ocean Trade: 150 Years in the Life of a Medieval Arabian Port* (Chapel Hill, 2007), chap. 6, especially 178–81.

[17] ENA NS 18.37. See above, chap. 9, 253–54.

[18] T-S 10 J 27.7.

evidently eager to prove his worthiness for the judgeship he has just assumed, writes to Efrayim b. Shemarya in unusually flowery language informing him that Sitān and Sara had appointed Abū Saʿd al-Tustarī as their proxy to sell a sumptuous golden garment from their father's estate. Shemu'el b. Moshe explains to Efrayim b. Shemarya that he had written the power of attorney in question—not the only power of attorney written in a rabbinical court for a Qaraite.[19] The golden garment was currently in al-Tustarī's possession. It may well have been a ceremonial garment that Ḥalfon had received together with a government title, though nowhere does his name appear adjacent to one.[20] In any case the sisters probably reasoned that an expensive item required the market of the capital. Shemu'el b. Moshe asks Efrayim to see to it that once the garment was sold, its proceeds be divided between the daughters. The contract, he explains, bears the signatures of Ibn Abī Qīda and three others. The rabbinical court in Fustat, then, knew that the court in Tyre wrote documents for Qaraites and was perfectly willing to validate and enforce them.[21]

Money, a Contract, and Sexual Intercourse

Three additional documents in Yosef's output attest that Qaraites passed through his court regularly and ultimately affected his rendering of contracts.

The first is a very large and ornate Rabbanite contract that Yosef wrote, signed, and dated November 28, 1023, recording the marriage of Raḥel b. [?] the Cantor b. Avraham (the parchment is torn where her father's name was written) to a certain Natan b. Shelomo, originally from Safed, now residing in Tyre. Raḥel's dowry totaled forty-some-odd and one-third dinars (the last digit is effaced), a sizeable but not enormous sum. The signatures of witnesses have been torn away.[22]

[19] T-S 10 J 12.25+T-S 13 J 18.1 (for additional powers of attorney written for Qaraites in rabbinical courts, see below, n. 47 and chap. 9, n. 19). Three additional letters of Shemu'el b. Moshe have been identified: Mosseri II 181 (L 183), addressed to Yaʿaqov b. Yosef, head of the rabbinical court in Aleppo; T-S 13 J 22.25, the left half of a letter to Efrayim b. Shemarya about another debt collection matter (Gil, *History of Palestine* 2:501, and Goitein, *Mediterranean Society*, 3:306 and 495 n. 147 differ in their interpretations of what little remains of this letter); and T-S 13 J 26.3, a letter to ʿEli b. ʿAmram (Efrayim b. Shemarya's successor) acknowledging a donation to be conveyed to the leper colony in Tiberias (on the lepers, see Gil, *History of Palestine*, sec. 296).

[20] T-S 13 J 8.14, line 3: *ha-zaqen*; T-S 16.275+Halper 412, line 41: *rav*; T-S 10 J 27.7, line 9: no title. The latter document would have been most likely to reveal a title since it dates to just after his death.

[21] In the same letter, Shemu'el b. Moshe also disposes of the case of a Rabbanite woman from Tyre named Nāʿima b. Moshe b. Ḥusayn al-Dulūkī (her *nisba* suggests origins in Doliche, on the Byzantine-Syrian frontier; Goitein, *Mediterranean Society*, 2:545 n. 37). Some people in Fustat owed Nāʿima debts on her son-in-law's and father's estates, and through Shemu'el she requested that her debtors be warned to repay her on pain of excommunication and that the matter be announced in the synagogues of Fustat. She indicated that the payments could be transported to Tyre with David b. Yiṣḥaq or a second party whose first name is effaced.

[22] JNUL Heb. 4⁰577.4.98.

This is the only rabbinic marriage contract not merely in Yosef's oeuvre but known to exist in which the following line appears: "And he brought her into his home and performed complete marriage [*qiddushin*] by means of money, a contract, and sexual intercourse [*be-khesef u-vi-shṭar u-ve-*[*vi'a*]." (The last word is interrupted by a tear in the left margin of the parchment.)[23] That phrase is instantly recognizable to anyone who has studied rabbinic literature: it is quotation from the mishnaic laws of marriage, which state that a woman "is acquired [in marriage] by means of money, a contract, and sexual intercourse [*be-khesef bi-shṭar u-ve-vi'a*]."[24] The plain meaning of the mishnaic law is unclear: is a marriage valid and binding only when effected through the combination of some guarantee of financial support for the bride ("money"), a written contract, and consummation through sexual intercourse, or can it be effected by one of these methods alone? The Palestinian Talmud offers the second interpretation and all subsequent rabbinic law follows it in allowing unions to be effected by the written document only: the *ketubba*.[25]

Despite this, the rabbinic *ketubba* itself never actually quotes the mishnaic law on which its justification is based. The reason seems evident enough: post-mishnaic rabbinic law considers the marriage contract the sole instrument for effecting a valid marriage, and quoting a statute in which the contract seems to be only one-third of the package would only undermine the legal force of the contract itself.

Perhaps oddly, however, the Qaraite *ketubba* does quote that law—oddly because the Qaraites did not recognize mishnaic law as binding. Qaraite law does, however, require all three elements in order to effect a legal marriage, and Qaraite marriage contracts thus mandatorily contain the following clause, in the groom's voice: "I shall introduce her into my home and perform complete *qiddushin* [legal marriage] by means of the bride-price, a contract, and sexual intercourse [*be-mohar bi-khtav u-ve-vi'a*]." The sole departures from the text of the Mishnah are the substitutions of "money" (*kesef*) with the biblical word for bride-price (*mohar*) and the Aramaic-derived "contract" (*sheṭar*) with its biblical Hebrew equivalent, *ketav*. All this is in keeping with the Qaraite insistence upon biblicizing Hebrew over rabbinic Aramaic and with the Qaraite adoption of neobiblical legal practices such as bride-price. Qaraite marriage contracts, then, unlike Rabbanite ones, paraphrase the Mishnah.[26]

23 Ibid., line 17.

24 Mishnah, *Qiddushin* 1:1.

25 R. Ḥiyya in Palestinian Talmud, *Qiddushin* 1:1, 58b. See Friedman's notes on manuscript variants of this *mishna* (*u-vi-shṭar* rather than *bi-shṭar*) and on scholarly speculation as to the original intent of the law; *Jewish Marriage in Palestine*, 1:202 nn. 34–36.

26 For details of the Qaraite bride-price, see Olszowy-Schlanger, *Karaite Marriage Documents*, chap. 12; on the choice of Hebrew over Aramaic in Qaraite legal tradition, ibid., chap. 5. Qaraites are on record as having read the Mishnah at least as early as the tenth century: Tirosh-Becker, "Use of Rabbinic Sources," in Polliack, *Karaite Judaism*, 319–38, with references to her earlier publications on the subject.

Why, then, does Yosef b. Yaʿaqov include the mishnaic phrase in this rabbinic *ketubba*? The most convincing answer is that he borrowed it from the Qaraite formulary. Just a few years later, in 1026–27, he would write up documents for the betrothal of Qaraites according to the Qaraite formulary, and he evidently knew that formulary well enough to use it when he wanted to. Even for a Rabbanite marriage, Yosef b. Yaʿaqov utilizes a hybrid legal formula, suggesting that the Qaraite formulary had influenced his drafting of Rabbanite contracts.[27]

A Qaraite Betrothal Document

Yosef's Qaraite document, the contract of 1026–27, is a writ of agency that he prepared for the betrothal of a Qaraite woman in Tyre (see fig. 9). This is odd, since in most cases, couples used the courts run by the bride's *madhhab*; why didn't they have the writ drafted in a Qaraite court? It is even stranger when one considers that the bride was the daughter of David b. Yiṣḥaq, who worked in Cairo and could have had the contract drawn up there. More important than the scholastic affiliation of the court drawing up the contract, apparently, was the style according to which it was drawn up, so that a Qaraite document drawn up by a Rabbanite scribe would suffice. And so Yosef b. Yaʿaqov, having mastered the Qaraite formulary, dutifully prepared a Qaraite contract not only in Hebrew but in monumental Hebrew letters, a regular feature of Qaraite marriage and betrothal documents but not a regular feature of Rabbanite ones.[28]

[27] Olszowy-Schlanger and Friedman agree that this contract represents some mixing of legal formularies but disagree as to the direction of influence. In general, Olszowy-Schlanger believes that the Qaraite marriage contract is nothing but a modified translation into biblicizing Hebrew of the Babylonian Rabbanite *ketubba*, while Friedman argues that the Qaraite formula was a reworking of the Palestinian rabbinic tradition, not the Babylonian one (Olszowy-Schlanger, "Karaite *Ketubbot*," and Friedman, "On the Relationship"). But in discussing Tyre, while Friedman still holds that the similarities between its one known Rabbanite *ketubba* and Qaraite *ketubbot* in general are due to Palestinian Rabbanite influence on the Qaraite formulary, Olszowy-Schlanger holds that in this particular case, the Qaraite tradition itself influenced the rendering of the Palestinian Rabbanite formula. Friedman admits that the Palestinian Rabbanite tradition to which he refers is "in this case . . . known to us from only one document" (*Jewish Marriage in Palestine*, 1:203–4); Olszowy-Schlanger suggests that precisely because the 1023 contract is the sole witness to Rabbanite use of that phrase, "it is more likely that the opposite is the case, and that the appearance of this formula . . . actually reflects Karaite influence" on the Tyrean Rabbanite tradition—and on Yosef in particular (*Karaite Marriage Documents*, 183–84). Examination of Yosef's corpus has convinced me that she is correct.

[28] T-S AS 153.12 (part of top)+T-S 13 J 25.20 (bottom). Goitein, *Mediterranean Society*, 3:57 and 439 n. 39, missed the top fragment (in discussing the bottom one he seems unaware that David b. Yiṣḥaq, whose *kunya* is revealed only in line 6, is the Qaraite notable in question; cf. Olszowy-Schlanger, *Karaite Marriage Documents*, 56 n. 95), but he is the only one who has transliterated the name of the betrothed correctly. The top half of the writ is tattered, including the line containing its date, but one can recognize the Hebrew word "and seven." The date cannot be 4777=1016, since Joseph had not yet been appointed *ḥaver*, and 4797=1036 is too late, since he had probably been appointed Fourth by then. The document probably dates from 4787=1026–27. Cf. Gil, "Palestine during the First Muslim Period (634–1099): Additions, Notes, Corrections," Hebrew, *Teʿuda* 7 (1991): 324–25.

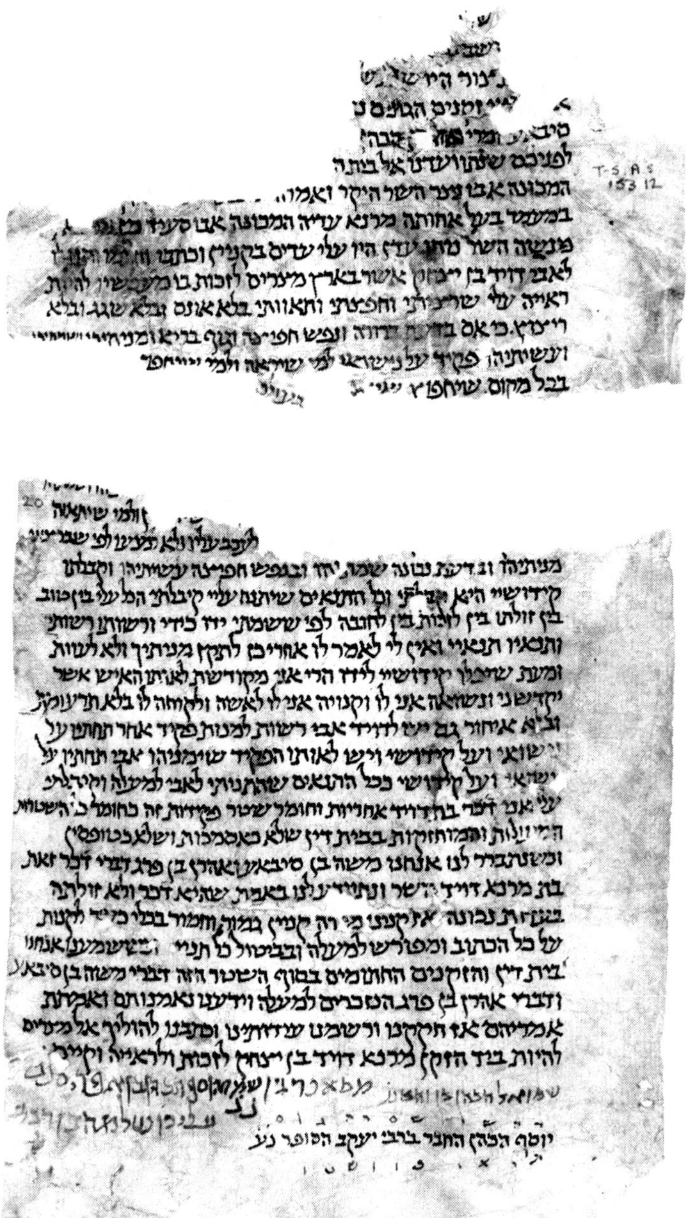

Fig. 9. A Qaraite marriage document written by a Rabbanite scribe: deed for the betrothal of Dhukhr, daughter of the Qaraite courtier David b. Yiṣḥaq, written according to the Qaraite formulary by the rabbinic judge Yosef ha-Kohen b. Yaʿaqov. Witnessing is the Fatimid governor ʿAdaya b. Menashshe ibn al-Qazzāz; one of the two agents for the betrothal is the Qaraite linguist Abu l-Faraj Hārūn b. al-Faraj. In Hebrew, Tyre, 1026–27. Cambridge University Library, T-S AS 153.12 + T-S 13 J 25.20.

The contract is a writ of appointment for the bride's agent, a type of document particular to the Qaraite method of contracting betrothals.[29] At the stage of arranging the marriage, the bride would designate a legal agent, often but not necessarily her father, who served as "proxy" even in her presence during the marriage ceremony. For couples living in the same city, the appointment was simply noted in the betrothal deed or the marriage contract, but when the groom lived elsewhere, the agent actually contracted the betrothal for her. In those cases, a separate deed was necessary to record the appointment.[30] In this case, David b. Yiṣḥaq's daughter, Dhukhr, was in Tyre and granted her father the legal right to betroth her to someone in Fustat or to appoint a secondary agent to do so. Any man he, his proxy, or his proxy's proxy chose for her would become her legal husband. Her writ of agency is one of only two such deeds discovered so far in the Geniza.[31]

But there was a further complication. Since David b. Yiṣḥaq was not physically present in Tyre to accept the appointment as his daughter's agent, he had to appoint two subagents in Tyre to accept the agency on his behalf. Each transfer of agency required its own witnesses, thereby multiplying the cast of characters involved in contracting the betrothal. That serves our purposes nicely, since the longer the list of proxies and witnesses, the better we can reconstruct the overlapping social networks of Rabbanites and Qaraites at Yosef's rabbinical court.

One witness was ʿEli, the brother of Dara and the son of Shelomo b. Rabīʿa, the Rabbanite of Fustat whom we met above. A second signatory was the Qaraite military governor of Palestine, ʿAdaya b. Menashshe ibn al-Qazzāz, who happened to be married to David b. Yiṣḥaq's other daughter; his father-in-law had apparently had him summoned from his offices in Ramla. Though the contract shows ʿAdaya submitting to the authority of the Palestinian *yeshiva*, three years later he would require several of its members to relinquish their positions in it (see chapter 8). Though this seems paradoxical, in fact there were two independent networks of authority operating here: the *yeshiva* and its provincial courts and the government and its provincial administration. Politics and contingencies dictated which of these networks he served at any given moment, and when his father-in-law requested it of him, he appeared at the rabbinical court.

[29] Olszowy-Schlanger, *Karaite Marriage Documents*, 212–17, and cf. Gil, "Palestine during the First Muslim Period: Additions, Notes, Corrections," 124.

[30] On the relationship between the proxy in Qaraite law and the *walī* in Islamic law, see ibid., 124, and cf. Friedman *Jewish Marriage in Palestine*, 1:231; Goitein, *Mediterranean Society*, 3:104; Olszowy-Schlanger, *Karaite Marriage Documents*, 215–17 and 300–301; and T-S 18 J 1.10, an Islamic marriage contract of 1028–36 possibly kept on hand for reference in a Jewish court, as evidenced by the Jewish court document written on verso (the deathbed declaration of Maymūn b. Khalfa, 1072).

[31] On the other, see below, n. 34.

Finally, one of the two proxies appointed was a certain Aharon b. Faraj, probably the Qaraite linguist Abu l-Faraj Hārūn b. al-Faraj of Jerusalem. The biographical sources support this identification: Ibn al-Hītī's chronicle says that he began studying with Yūsuf al-Baṣīr in Jerusalem as early as 1002 and outlived his teacher, who died ca. 1040, while Ṭoviyya b. Moshe, the Byzantine Qaraite translator, mentions him in a letter of ca. 1048.[32] In 1026, the year he signed the contract, he completed his work *al-Kitāb al-mushtamil ʿala l-uṣūl wa-l-fuṣūl fī l-lugha l-ʿibrāniyya* (The comprehensive book of general principles and particular rules of the Hebrew language).[33] By now he was teaching alongside his master at the Qaraite academy in Jerusalem, and he would have had to travel to the port of Ascalon or Jaffa to reach Tyre. While several decades earlier Yefet b. ʿEli had complained about the powerlessness of the Qaraites and the "Rabbanite judges and scholars" who oppressed them, Abu l-Faraj Hārūn submitted to the authority of the rabbinical court of Tyre together with David b. Yiṣḥaq's other proxy, ʿAdaya ibn al-Qazzāz.

It was a role Abu l-Faraj Hārūn was to repeat once more in his lifetime: a certain Aharon b. Yehoshuaʿ (the usual Hebrew equivalent of al-Faraj; both names indicate redemption) appeared as witness in a second Qaraite proxy appointment of ca. 1040–47 (the only other Qaraite proxy appointment preserved in the Geniza).[34] The bride was Amat al-ʿAzīz, the daughter of the Qaraite *nasi* Ḥizqiyyahu of Jerusalem; the groom was Yefet (Ḥasan) b. Ibrāhīm al-Tustarī of Fustat, the son of the courtier Abū Saʿd Ibrāhīm al-Tustarī. After his father's assassination in 1047 (and after his marriage), Yefet rose at the Fatimid court and by 1064 converted to Islam and was appointed superintendent of the fisc (*ṣāḥib bayt al-māl*). Amat al-ʿAzīz had appointed her father the *nasi* to contract

[32] To the best of my knowledge, no one has yet made this identification. The document (T-S AS 153.12, line 4) calls him Aha[ro]n ha-Kohen (and subsequently only Aharon b. Faraj), and while none of the other medieval sources refers to him as a Kohen, Arabic works frequently dropped Kohen and Levi from men's names (I am grateful to Daniel Frank for pointing this out). The letter of Ṭoviyya: T-S 12.347, in Hebrew, line 23: "Were it not for the fact that the elder Abu l-Faraj Aharon, may his Rock preserve him, sends on occasion to ask after me, I would not know good from evil." (The entire letter is a tour-de-force of self-pity.)

[33] This work is currently being prepared for publication by Aharon Maman. Abu l-Faraj Hārūn also prepared a shorter version of the same work called *al-Kitāb al-kāfī* (The sufficient book). See Gil, *History of Palestine*, sec. 938 and Geoffrey Khan, "'Abū al-Faraj Hārūn and the Early Karaite Grammatical Tradition," *Journal of Jewish Studies* 48 (1997): 314–44, both with reference to previous studies; and Khan et al., *Karaite Tradition of Hebrew Grammatical Thought*. See also Hartwig Hirschfeld, "An Unknown Grammatical Work by Abul-Faraj Harun," *Jewish Quarterly Review (n.s.)* 13 (1922–23): 1–7; Khan, "The Early Karaite Grammatical Tradition," in *Jewish Studies at the Turn of the Twentieth Century: Proceedings of the 6th EAJS Congress, Toledo, July 1998*, ed. Judit Targarona Borrás and Angel Sáenz-Badillos (Leiden, 1999), 1:73.

[34] T-S 16.50. See Olszowy-Schlanger, *Karaite Marriage Documents*, 213. The document is undated, but based on the biographies of the people mentioned can be placed between 1040 and 1047. The original was written at a Qaraite court in Jerusalem; the preserved copy is from Fustat. On the groom, see the references in Fischel, *Jews in the Economic and Political Life*, 87 n. 3. Olszowy-Schlanger identified the witness in this contract as the famous grammarian (*Karaite Marriage Documents*, 51).

the betrothal, but unable or unwilling to travel from Jerusalem to Fustat, he delegated the role to a wealthy Qaraite named ʿEzra b. Yishmaʿʾel (Shemuʾel) b. ʿEzra, whom we met briefly when he contributed to the Jerusalem *yeshiva* in 1028.[35] Abu l-Faraj Hārūn served as witness to that subappointment.

To the combination of social status and noble ancestry represented by these two betrothals, Abu l-Faraj Hārūn added the endorsement of scholarly achievement. Who, in the end, became Dhukhr's betrothed is a secret that Geniza documents have not disclosed. The Geniza has, however, disclosed that Yosef, for his part, knew how to write a Qaraite document, and that Qaraites made use of his court, even for internal Qaraite matters. He obliged them by writing documents according to the Qaraite formulary and taught his successor how to do so: a betrothal contract of April 2, 1051, the only known case of a Qaraite groom appointing a proxy, is the deed for the betrothal of a certain Yamān b. David of Fustat to Shela b. ʿAmram al-Qirqisānī of Tyre, drawn up at the Qaraite court in Fustat and signed by the groom's proxy, Shelomo b. ʿAdaya ibn al-Qazzāz (grandson of Menashshe b. al-Qazzāz on one side and of David ha-Levi b. Yiṣḥaq on the other). The deed for the groom's proxy appointment was written and witnessed at the rabbinical court in Tyre by Yosef's successor Shemuʾel b. Moshe, who then sent it to the Qaraite court in Fustat, where the *nasi* David b. Ṣemaḥ validated it and copied it into the deed of betrothal. The writ of agency has not itself survived in the Geniza, but oddly, the betrothal contract written at the Qaraite court has.[36] Thus while Dhukhr's writ of agency was validated at the Qaraite court in Fustat, but survived in the Rabbanite Geniza (how did it find its way there?), her Qaraite marriage contract did not; and while Shela's writ of agency from the rabbinical court in Tyre has not been found among the Geniza documents, his betrothal contract from the Qaraite court has—even though it bears only the most tenuous relationship to the Rabbanites: the name of the court scribe Shemuʾel b. Moshe, which had been copied into it. The deeds endured crossed destinies after they had outlived their use as functioning legal documents; but in their lifetimes, so to speak, each was recognized as valid and binding.

A Rabbanite-Qaraite Marriage

The final document preserved from Yosef b. Yaʿaqov's oeuvre is a hybrid *ketubba* written for a Rabbanite bride and a Qaraite groom.[37] The parchment is fragmentary and the section containing the date and place has been torn away; the document is partly the work of an apprentice, which may place it some time

[35] On ʿEzra b. Yishmaʿʾel b. ʿEzra, see T-S 13 J 8.14 and chap. 7, n. 44.

[36] Mosseri Ia 2 (A 2).

[37] Antonin 637. Friedman identifies the formulary as from Tyre and the handwriting as that of Yosef b. Yaʿaqov. For confirmation, see Olszowy-Schlanger, *Karaite Marriage Documents*, 357–58.

after Yosef was appointed *ḥaver*. What remains is the bottom section, written on recto and verso in square script in Aramaic, according to the Rabbanite formula and in keeping with the tradition of following the bride's *madhhab*.

The Rabbanite bride, Dalāl b. Yaḥya of Tyre, brought to the marriage a modest dowry consisting only of clothing and linens totaling nine and one-third dinars. Her father's name is mentioned with neither titles nor honorifics, confirming the humble station of her family. The groom was a Qaraite of Tyre named Mevorakh b. Yefet, all other traces of whom are absent save one: his signature on a Qaraite marriage contract written in Tyre on which one of the other witnesses is Rabbanite.[38] As for Mevorakh b. Yefet's own marriage contract, the two witnesses who have signed it are both Rabbanite.[39]

This hybrid marriage contract exhibits one anomaly: two separate versions are written on the front and back of the parchment. Because the writing on the front of the document is much larger than that on the back, more text of the document has been preserved on the verso. The text common to both sides exhibits slight differences that serve as clues to its mysterious doubling: the same dowry items are appraised on one side at 8 Fatimid dinars and on the other at 9 1/3. The families of the bride and groom must have haggled over the dowry's appraisal and had the document redrawn to reflect the higher amount. The corrected version of the text is in Yosef b. Yaʿaqov's writing, which is not only smaller but more practiced; the first version is probably the work of a disciple, who also exhibits a preference for Judeo-Arabic terms, while Yosef corrects them using the Aramaic and Hebrew ones and also improves the grammar. It seems that Yosef did not even allow the young scribe to try a second draft, and to satisfy the couple, their families, and the court, he redid the work.[40]

The stipulations about the couple's religious observance also differ from each other on front and back. The student's text reads, "We effected a valid

[38] T-S 20.2, for the marriage of the Qaraites Sitt al-Ahl and Mevorakh b. Shemu'el. This contract is definitely from Tyre: to the arguments of Olszowy-Schlanger, *Karaite Marriage Documents*, 357–58, can be added the fact that the agent, ʿEli b. Shelomo, was also from Tyre (see T-S AS 153.12+T-S 13 J 25.20, above, n. 28). It was either drawn up at the rabbinical court in Tyre or furnishes evidence that there was a Qaraite court there.

[39] They are ʿOvadya ha-Kohen, whose patronymic has not been preserved, and Yiftaḥ ha-Kohen b. Yosef b. ʿAmram, who signed a second marriage contract, also Rabbanite (T-S NS 262.41). He may have been the son of Yosef ha-Kohen b. Yiftaḥ, mentioned in a letter sent to Tinnīs, Egypt, since Yiftaḥ was an extremely rare name (according to Friedman, *Jewish Marriage in Palestine*, 2:295). The letter is from ʿOvadya ha-Kohen b. Yiṣḥaq to his cousin Abū Zikrī Yaḥyā ha-Kohen b. Yosef b. Yiftaḥ, Tinnīs, who had asked ʿOvadya for some books; unable to procure them, he sent what he had on hand, "three parts [quires?] of an Iraqi prayerbook, and R. Seʿadya's commentary (*maʿānī*) on Job and Proverbs" (recto, right margin). Bodl. MS Heb. d 66.58, in Hebrew and Judeo-Arabic. See also Goitein, *Jewish Education in Muslim Countries, Based on Records from the Cairo Geniza*, Hebrew (Jerusalem, 1962), 137–38, no. 15; idem, *Mediterranean Society*, 2:124.

[40] Friedman, *Jewish Marriage in Palestine*, 2:288–89. Cf. Goitein, *Mediterranean Society*, 3:159 and 461 n. 88. The disciple uses the Arabic *niṣf* for "half," while Yosef uses the Aramaic *pelag*; the disciple renders "five" as *khams* (in the wrong gender), while Yosef uses the Hebrew *ḥamisha*.

acquisition [*qinyan*] with a suitable instrument from Mevorakh b. Yefet, the groom"—this was the standard rabbinic method of enacting the transaction—"[stipulating] that he not alter the law of the Rabbanites with all their festivals and their fasts and all of their [other] laws. And [the bride] shall conduct herself with him according to his law. And this Dalāl b. Yaḥyā shall not desecrate his law in his presence." The Qaraite groom is enjoined "not to alter" rabbinic law, meaning to refrain from desecrating it; the Rabbanite bride is enjoined to observe Qaraite law along with her husband and not to desecrate it in front of him. At first glance, these seem to be symmetrical stipulations, but in fact, the Qaraite groom is nowhere mandated to observe rabbinic law. In other words, double observance is incumbent upon the Rabbanite bride alone, who is both to retain her Rabbanite custom and to adopt the Qaraite one. There is no converse stipulation that the groom, as a Qaraite, must adopt the ways of the Rabbanites—merely that he must not violate rabbinic law in her presence. The wording at the end is also awkward.

In the second version of the contract, the lack of reciprocity has been redressed. "We effected a valid acquisition [*qinyan*] from him [stipulating] that he not desecrate her festivals in her presence, and that he conduct himself with her as she conducts herself with him." The clauses have been made reciprocal largely through elimination of detail. This is strange, since except for these lines, the second version of the contract is more detailed in all its clauses. When the bride's family had the dowry appraisal corrected, they must have renegotiated the religious stipulations so as not to disadvantage their daughter unduly. Or perhaps when Yosef intervened in the work of his student, he corrected the first set of clauses and the burden they placed on the Rabbanite bride; or perhaps he eliminated the original details in the interests of saving time and parchment.

A Scribe at Work

Thirty years of experience writing out deeds had given Yosef b. Yaʿaqov an intimate familiarity with their wording that allowed him to be flexible with them, to feel his way through the phrases and explore their breadth as he wrote them down. To such a scribe, legal formulae were not rigid dictates to be set down verbatim but iterations of a language with its own latitude and range, and the differences between the Qaraite Hebrew and Rabbanite Aramaic marriage contracts were perhaps cosmetic: though they were written in different languages and represented different traditions, their meanings were roughly the same and he knew this. His adeptness at writing both, and the two deeds in which he mixes them, suggest that for him, those traditions were connected to one another. He was perfectly willing to raise a fuss when his student failed to uphold the standards of the guild, correcting his grammar and other details; but he also appears uninterested in drawing a priori distinctions between the

Rabbanite and Qaraite formulae. He was, in that sense, the kind of chief judge one would expect of a city like Tyre, where Jews did not draw their boundaries too sharply.

That gives the clear distinctions that are customary in the study of religion, between Rabbanite law and Qaraite law, for example, a somewhat artificial feel. Neither of those abstractions captures in fine hues the lived experience of Jews in a place like Tyre. Rather than "law," then, one should speak perhaps of legal practice, or better yet, of people engaged in a series of decisions as to how best to practice.

Questions of Influence

Qaraite influence on Rabbanite scribal practice in Tyre extended beyond Yosef's court, too. This is evident from the anomalous way in which court documents from Tyre are dated.

Quite apart from the complications attending the differences between Rabbanite and Qaraite calendar determinations, legal documents of different schools use different dating systems for the year. Babylonian Rabbanite documents are dated, following an ancient tradition, according to the Seleucid calendar (which begins with the reign of Seleucus I in Babylon, an event Jews and other Babylonians marked in spring, 311 BCE, though the Macedonian court marked it in autumn 312 BCE).[41] Qaraite documents use the same Seleucid calendar as the Babylonian Rabbanites. Palestinian Rabbanite documents, by contrast, usually record the number of years since the creation (*anno mundi*, traditionally dated to 3761 BCE) or else since the Roman destruction of the Temple in Jerusalem (rendered alternately as 67, 68, 69, or 70 CE; the latter figure is the accurate one). The one exception to this is Palestinian-style contracts from Tyre, which record the date according to the Seleucid era.[42]

Does this practice indicate Babylonian rabbinic influence on the Palestinian Rabbanite custom of Tyre?[43] If so, one would be hard pressed to explain why no other Palestinian Jewish communities, as far as anyone knows, used Seleucid-era dating in their marriage contracts—even communities in cities that housed large Babylonian-Iraqi populations and maintained direct ties with Baghdad, such as Fustat and Ramla. A more likely explanation, then, is Qaraite influence on the Palestinian Rabbanite usage of Tyre.[44] In support of this hypothesis is the fact that all the legal documents and even

[41] Elias J. Bickerman, "Notes on Seleucid and Parthian Chronology," *Berytus* 8 (1943): 73–84.

[42] Olszowy-Schlanger, *Karaite Marriage Documents*, 161.

[43] Olszowy-Schlanger herself suggests that this is the case (e.g., ibid., 210, 240–41).

[44] The Qaraite custom of recording the year according to the Seleucid era may ultimately derive from Babylonian rabbinic tradition as well (ibid., 161), but the number of other influences of the Qaraite formulary in Tyre lead one to believe that the Babylonian influence was not direct but mediated through the Qaraites.

some letters known to have emanated from Tyre are in Hebrew, with the exception of Aramaic marriage contracts. While in itself this does not point to Qaraite influence, it does suggest a shared interest in the biblical tongue and a common degree of independence from rabbinic traditions of document production.[45]

The deeds drawn up in Tyre were upheld in Jerusalem and Fustat by judges and *ge'onim* who must have simply understood and accepted that in Tyre, rabbinic judges did things differently.

QARAITES AT RABBINICAL COURTS

Some degree of legal reciprocity is attested in other cities as well. In chapter 6, I discussed the case of the woman remanded to the court of Yoshiyyahu Ga'on in Jerusalem, in which Yosef al-Tustarī served as witness.[46] Four additional cases suggest that Qaraites conducted legal business in rabbinical courts elsewhere, too.

The first is from Ifrīqiya and dates to the late eleventh century. Abū Saʿd Yiṣḥaq b. Khalaf ibn ʿAllūn (d. 1073–74), a Qaraite *kātib* who had served as the Fatimid minister of taxation (*ʿāmil*) in Jerusalem until roughly 1060, had a rabbinical court in al-Mahdiyya draw up a power of attorney in 1073. Having been deposed from his post, Ibn ʿAllūn seems to have resided in Alexandria; it is possible that he remained persona non grata in Cairo and was reluctant to return there out of fear for his safety. Thus in the power of attorney he authorized a proxy in Ifrīqiya, a certain Ḥassūn b. Abi l-Faraj al-Mahdawī about whom nothing further is known, to collect some items he had left in care of his sister-in-law in Fustat. Though al-Mahdawī was farther from Fustat than Ibn ʿAllūn was, he may have been traveling that way, and in any case, Ibn ʿAllūn may have taken pains to avoid the capital. But al-Mahdawī failed to collect the items and Ibn Allūn died shortly thereafter. His widow, Nājiya b. Sulaymān b. Hiba, then had the same rabbinical court in al-Mahdiyya draw up a second power of attorney appointing a different agent to collect the items, a certain Abū Sahl Menashshe b. Mūsā the Qaraite (identified as such in the contract). Whether Ibn ʿAllūn's wife Nājiya was herself a Qaraite cannot be known with certainty; nor is anything known about the scholastic affiliation of al-Mahdawī. That the second agent was a Qaraite suggests at the very least that Nājiya maintained ties among Qaraites while continuing to have legal deeds executed

[45] Olszowy-Schlanger points out that medieval Jews themselves, Qaraite and Rabbanite alike—among them Sahl b. Maṣliaḥ and Maimonides—admitted the possibility of Qaraite influence on Palestinian custom (ibid., 268–69 n. 16), but they may have had ulterior motives for making the claim.

[46] Chap. 6, 169–71.

in the rabbinic system, and that the Qaraite proxy felt himself bound by the Rabbanite contract.[47]

The second case appears in an undated, torn, and badly effaced Rabbanite marriage contract of monumental size enjoining the bride to make regular use of the *miqve* (ritual bath). Rabbanite women were required to perform regular ritual ablutions following their menstrual periods while Qaraites were not. The stipulation might be read to mean that the bride was a Qaraite, but in fact the contract follows the Rabbanite custom, which usually indicates that the bride is a Rabbanite. Besides, the usual set of religious stipulations for hybrid contracts is absent in this one. Why would the contract contain only this stipulation? The likely answer is that the bride was a Rabbanite influenced by Qaraite practice. This possibility is corroborated by a responsum that Maimonides wrote on the subject in which he notes that the Qaraites had so profoundly influenced Rabbanite women that special efforts needed to be made to see to it that they perform their ablutions. That a Rabbanite *ketubba* included this religious stipulation suggests, in turn, that the Qaraite practice of including religious stipulations in marriage contracts had infiltrated rabbinic *ketubbot*—as though while the couple avoided lapsing into hybrid legal practices, the court would gladly embrace them.[48]

The third case of legal reciprocity dates from the latter part of the eleventh century, and concerns a Qaraite merchant from Jerusalem, a certain Yefet b. Meshullam, who obtained a certificate from a rabbinical court licensing him to sell an enormous quantity of cheese.[49]

Wine, cheese, and meat were closely regulated by rabbinic authorities because of the complex set of rules governing their fitness for consumption in rabbinic law (*kashrut*).[50] I have already mentioned some of the tension that attached to the sale of meat and the supervision of slaughterhouses, a lucrative

[47] The first contract: T-S 20.187; the second contract: T-S 28.6 C; both in Aramaic and Judeo-Arabic. Abū Sa'd Iṣḥāq b. Khalaf b. 'Allūn appears in three additional documents: two letters of 'Eli ha-Kohen b. Yeḥezq'el (T-S 8 J 21.24 and Bodl. MS Heb. c 28.43) and the fragment T-S 8.14, where he is described as Qaraite. For a detailed treatment, see Hary and Rustow, "Karaites at the Rabbinical Court."

[48] T-S 24.8; Goitein dates it to the thirteenth century (*Mediterranean Society*, 3:408, no. 233). Maimonides, *Responsa*, no. 320 (to Yūsuf b. Jābir of the Iraqi community), 2:588–89. See also the sources cited in Olszowy-Schlanger, *Karaite Marriage Documents*, 268–69 n. 16, and Friedman, "Menstrual Impurity and Sectarianism in the Writings of the Geonim and of Moses and Abraham Maimonides," Hebrew, *Maimonidean Studies* 1 (1990): 1–21.

[49] T-S 10 J 6.14. The document was signed by two people so far unattested in the Geniza, a fact in keeping with their having worked in one of the lesser-known Palestinian rabbinical courts. Goitein, *Mediterranean Society*, 1:124, notes that a third, Aharon ha-Kohen b. 'Amram, also signed a document written in Fustat in 1100 (Mosseri VII 209 [L 276]). Gil (*History of Palestine*, sec. 930) speculates that the latter's son (named 'Amram after his grandfather) was married to the *ga'on* Evyatar ha-Kohen b. Eliyyahu's daughter, and that is possible if Goitein's dating is correct. For the suggestion that this document came from Acre, see Goitein, *Palestinian Jewry*, 4 n. 7.

[50] I have benefited enormously from an exchange with David Freidenreich about religious regulations related to wine, meat, and cheese (March–April 2005).

enterprise and an important communal function.[51] The tension was due not merely to the differences between the two *madhāhib* over the details of animal slaughter and consumption; control of the supervision process was a broader technique that rabbinic authorities used to gain a firmer hold over the food market and partake of its economic benefits.

The complexity of wine revolved around the rabbinic requirement to attest to the religious observance and general probity of its manufacturers, handlers, and sellers. The earliest rabbinic laws regulating the consumption of wine and meat prepared by non-Jews (pagans in the Mishnah and the Tosefta, both products of Roman Palestine) paralleled one another because their authors presumed that pagans would dedicate either meat or wine to their deities; the purposes of these laws were to make it as difficult as possible for Jews to commit idolatry even indirectly or inadvertently.[52] The rabbinic restrictions regarding commerce in wine on pagan holidays were more stringent than those regarding meat, but later rabbinic law added stringencies to the laws of butchering by insisting that anyone unversed in those laws could not butcher animals without the supervision of someone who was.[53]

The probity of Qaraites in handling wine was questioned only rarely: the Geniza has preserved a much faded and undated fragment of a Rabbanite responsum prohibiting Qaraite wine, though in the late twelfth and early thirteenth centuries, both Maimonides and his son Avraham permitted the use of Qaraite wine by Rabbanites. That the question was asked points to new uncertainties about the status of Qaraites in rabbinic food laws, uncertainties whose circumstances still require investigation, though Avraham's responsum admits that "most of the time, [the Qaraites] buy their wine from Rabbanites."[54]

As for cheese, its complexity had nothing to do with the differing Rabbanite and Qaraite prohibitions on consuming meat and milk together. Even though most of rabbinic literature assumes that cheese is made with rennet derived from the stomach lining of either a calf or a kid, rennet is so attenuated an animal by-product that it is not considered to be meat. The key rabbinic requirement, rather, was that the animal providing the rennet be slaughtered properly according to rabbinic law. If the cheese was made with rennet from an animal that had not been slaughtered according to rabbinic law or by someone not versed in that law, the cheese was not kosher. Qaraite law, by contrast, ruled that the rennet's origin was irrelevant.[55]

[51] See chap. 6, 164, 174; chap. 8, 217.

[52] Mishnah and Tosefta, *Ḥullin* 1 and 2.

[53] Maimonides, *Mishne Torah*, Hilkhot Sheḥiṭa 4.

[54] T-S 6 J 2.17, cited in Goitein, *Mediterranean Society*, 5:608–9 n. 34; Bodl. MS Heb. d 66.84, an autograph responsum by Avraham Maimonides. (My thanks to Mark Cohen for making his then-unpublished edition available to me.)

[55] In Islamic law, too, the problem of cheese revolves around how the animal from which rennet is taken is slaughtered and by whom (the "infidel rennet" problem, as Michael Cook has called it):

In practice, cheese was much more widely consumed than meat. In terms of protein per price, it was more economical—two-and-a-half kilograms of cheese went for the same price as a single chicken—and it was also more readily available. It was a staple of the Mediterranean diet, the most important food after bread, and an object of brisk trade. It was generally made from sheep's milk, in the main sheep-raising areas such as Sicily, the hinterlands of Qayrawān in Ifrīqiya, Crete, Byzantium, and Palestine.[56] From those places, traders imported cheese to other regions; both Egypt and India are attested as importing foreign cheese, even though there were cheesemaking businesses in the villages of Egypt, and one presumes in India as well. Since rabbinical authorities closely supervised the manufacture, transport, and sale of cheese because of the complexities attached to its *kashrut*—and probably because of its potential profits—cheese is relatively well attested in the Geniza in the form of the certificates rabbinical courts issued to merchants certifying the fitness of the product they intended to sell.[57]

And so, when Yefet b. Meshullam the Qaraite acquired about seventy-five kilograms of cheese from Rabbanite cheesemakers in Palestine with the intent of selling it in Egypt to Rabbanite customers, he applied for certification from a Syrian rabbinical court (perhaps in Acre, whose hinterland was a center of cheese manufacture), and was granted it. It is hardly remarkable to find commercial ventures in which Qaraites traded Rabbanite-manufactured products: in the mercantile networks such alliances are well represented. And while it might seem peculiar that this particular Qaraite was trading in a foodstuff over which Rabbanite and Qaraite law disagreed and then going to the trouble to have it certified, in fact certification was merely one of the transaction costs that Yefet b. Meshullam, like all other cheesemongers, assumed in the course of business. In having the document drawn up, Yefet recognized the authority of the rabbinical court, at least for business purposes.

The scribe therefore wrote a document containing two separate clauses. The first contained the usual statement about the fitness of the cheese for Rabbanite consumption, a standard element of cheese certificates regardless of the

---

Qaraite and Islamic law permit it, while rabbinic law prohibits it. See Cook, "Magian Cheese: An Archaic Problem in Islamic Law," *Bulletin of the School of Oriental and African Studies* 47 (1984), 465.

56 On the Mediterranean cheese trade, see Goitein, *Mediterranean Society*, 4:251–52, and Nadia Zeldes and Miriam Frenkel, "The Sicilian Trade: Jewish Merchants in the Mediterranean in the Twelfth and Thirteenth Centuries," in *Gli ebrei in Sicilia dal tardoantico al medioevo: Studi in onore di Monsignor Benedetto Rocco*, ed. Nicolò Bucaria (Palermo, 1998), 254–55.

57 Goitein, *Mediterranean Society*, 4:10, 251–52. See also ibid., 1:46 (on imports from Sicily, Crete, and Byzantium—or Christian lands in general?); 1:126 (production and import from Palestine); 1:367, sec. 27 (a partnership in cheesemaking); 1:428 n. 66 (local types of cheese); 2:251 (a certificate for a cheese merchant in Alexandria with ninety-five molds from Sicily); idem, *Letters of Medieval Jewish Traders*, 196 (cheese sent to India); Gil, *History of Palestine*, sec. 315 (cheese from Hebron imported to Egypt); and Eliyahu Ashtor, *Histoire des prix et des salaires dans l'Orient médiéval*, Monnaie, prix, conjoncture 8 (Paris, 1969), index, s.v. *fromage*.

purveyor for whom they were written. It reads: "I hereby notify our masters in the land of Egypt that one Yefet bar Meshullam, who is from the Qaraite group [*kat*] who [live] in Samaritiké, came and bought thirty *raṭl*s of cheese of Rabbanite manufacture, and they are kosher and it is permitted for Rabbanites to buy them."[58] The scribe was careful to note Yefet's religious affiliation and his origin in the Qaraite neighborhood of Jerusalem.

The second clause has nothing to do with cheese. It is a rider designed to resolve the differences between legal methods of acquisition (*qinyan*) in rabbinic and Qaraite law. For Rabbanites, *qinyan* was effected through symbolic barter, in practice by "exchanging" the object being acquired for some other object of little value, usually a kerchief (*sudar*; hence *qinyan sudar*, "acquisition via the kerchief"). Qaraites effected *qinyan* without an intermediate object, from hand to hand (*qinyan yad le-yad*). The second clause is designed to obviate the potential conflict between Yefet's method of *qinyan* and that of his Rabbanite buyers. To do this, the court devised the legal fiction of assuming ownership of the cheese by entering into a commercial partnership with Yefet b. Meshullam. "We have allowed [his customers to] purchase from him only after we acquired [the cheese] from his hands according to their [the Qaraites'] method of *qinyan*, which is hand-to-hand, and we have made him swear by oath on the holy Torah," apparently a judicial imprecation to ensure that he was telling the truth about having acquired the cheese from reputable Rabbanite sources. "And their number is three hundred and thirty-nine molds."[59] The rabbinic authorities who drew up and signed this document did so in order to protect the Qaraite merchant, and at his behest. The legal fiction they devised should not be read as evidence of hostility or mistrust, but as an attempt to help him sell his cheese to Rabbanites.[60]

[58] *Raṭl*s: for a discussion of which measurement is intended, see Goitein, *Palestinian Jewry*, 4 n. 6, and following him Gil, *History of Palestine*, sec. 347n. Of Rabbanite manufacture: this phrase is partially effaced along a fold but clearly reads *mi-ma'ase ha-rabbanim*. See Goitein, *Palestinian Jewry*, 4, and cf. Gil, *History of Palestine*, 2:564, doc. 309, and secs. 596, 832, 935, and 930, who claims incorrectly that the cheese was made by Qaraites on the Mount of Olives, and Ben-Shammai, "Karaites," 217n. The last word on line 1 should be Miṣ[r].

[59] Molds: *tefusim*. Cheese molds usually had the name of the importer stamped in them; see Goitein, *Mediterranean Society*, 4:251. Compare with T-S AS 147.24, a cheese certificate issued in Alexandria in 1214, which an Alexandrian Rabbanite cheesemonger asked the rabbinical court to write for him after the Sicilian merchant from whom he bought his wares had appeared before them and declared that his own cheese was kosher. No judicial imprecation was administered, and since the rabbinical court did not serve as intermediary to the transaction, the method of acquisition was not specified.

[60] Two pieces of evidence attest to later doubts about the kashrut of Qaraite foodstuffs: a Rabbanite statement that in testimonies about the kashrut of meat, a freed slave is more trustworthy than a Qaraite (CUL Or 1080J 110, sec. 4, cited in Goitein, *Mediterranean Society*, 5:609 n. 34 and 1:136) and a letter denouncing Rabbanite merchants from Cairo as having eaten in the houses of Samaritans, Qaraites, and *ḥurrāsīn* (BL Or. 5566 D 24+T-S 10 J 16.8; see Goitein, *Mediterranean Society*, 1:424 n. 99, and for an explanation of the term, 1:115).

The fourth case of legal reciprocity appears in a letter addressed to Aharon ibn Ṣaghīr (ben Ṣaʿir), the head of the Qaraite community of Cairo in the mid-fourteenth century and probably a descendant of the Ben Shaʿyā dynasty. A group of Qaraites traveled from Cairo to Jerusalem to make pilgrimages to holy sites. Among them were a woman named Rivqa, who hoped to be married in the holy city, and her two suitors, Ibrāhīm and Sulaymān. The elders traveling with them decided she should marry Ibrāhīm, but she protested in favor of Sulaymān, whereupon Ibrāhīm became so angry that he swore he would kill one of the two. The elders sent word to Rivqa's father in Cairo asking what to do. He replied that the choice of suitors belonged to his daughter. The first suitor, Ibrāhīm, remained unreasonable, so the elders decided to put the matter off until the group's return to Cairo. Then the second suitor, Sulaymān, also lost his reason and had "one of the Rabbanites" forge a marriage contract for him and Rivqa containing the "signatures" of the Qaraite elders themselves. The contract fooled no one. The mistake this Rabbanite made was forging the signatures, while the contract he wrote was so convincing that his fellow Rabbanites came to the Qaraite elders and asked them, "How can you write someone a *ketubba* . . . [the edge of the page is torn and a word is missing] to keep him from his betrothed?!" The Rabbanite forger was placed under a temporary ban and Rivqa, perhaps in view of both her suitors' unreason, decided to marry neither of them. The story suggests that the forger knew how to write a convincing Qaraite marriage contract, even if he could not convincingly fake signatures.[61]

LEGAL RECIPROCITY

The principal function of the court system was not to reinforce the central authority of the *yeshivot*; it was to write documents that would be upheld in other courts of law. Though courts also administered justice, adjudication of cases constituted only a small proportion of the work brought before them. Most of it was document production. The day-to-day workings of provincial courts speak to the flexibility of legal authorities in facilitating legal transactions and the lived degree of interchange and reciprocal recognition between the schools of law. The documents that clerks wrote did not represent a series of ideological statements designed to uphold the central authority of the institution that had ordained them but a series of pragmatic decisions made under the pressure of producing legally binding documents.

Those documents attest to the fact that Rabbanites and Qaraites were perfectly capable of devising methods of coexistence and cooperation

[61] JNUL $4^0$577.3.11. Descendants of Ben Shaʿyā: Goitein, *Mediterranean Society*, 3:11.

when it suited them to do so. Couples with different customs found ways of living under the same roof, sometimes by taking on the feasts, fasts, and laws of two *madhāhib*. Judges in rabbinical courts from Jerusalem, Fustat, and the provinces honored Qaraite contracts as legally binding, learned how to write them, and adopted elements of them when it suited their purpose.

All this touches on two questions. First, what is "heresy"? Both of the judges of the rabbinical court in Tyre wrote contracts for Qaraites according to the Qaraite formulary, and one of them also imported elements of that formulary into his Rabbanite contracts. Yet instead of being accused of heresy, he functioned in his capacity as judge until his death, sending his work on to Fustat for validation and encountering neither questions nor opposition to his practices. This suggests that heresy is a category whose imposition depends on contingencies, and that histories of heresy should examine not merely the beliefs and practices called heretical but the circumstances under which the label is imposed. Here, the label is noticeably absent.

Second, what is a "community"? The historiographic consensus about the medieval Jewish community holds that law is central to its creation: it is the area of life that created a stable boundary between Jews and others or between segments of the Jewish community itself. The theory of Jewish judicial autonomy is based on the notion that administering justice according to its own religious canons gives a community structure and order. But law itself was permeable, subject to influence, and adapted practices from other legal traditions.[62] This suggests that one cannot presume that a community's boundaries fell neatly in line with its scholastic affiliations. During the events that form the subject of Part 4, this was a presumption that the Jews of the Fatimid empire themselves were less and less inclined to make.

[62] Libson, *Jewish and Islamic Law*, passim.

PART IV

THE ORIGINS OF TERRITORIAL GOVERNANCE

CHAPTER ELEVEN
AVIGNON IN RAMLA: THE SCHISM OF 1038–42

After the excommunication affair of 1029–30, the rabbinic community's relationship toward the Qaraites changed. Before, high-ranking members of the Jerusalem *yeshiva* hierarchy (and their followers) had solicited the help of Qaraites in emergencies. Now they began to do so for the sake of their own bids for leadership and campaigns for political legitimacy within the Jewish community itself. Rabbinic leaders—especially those who sought to bypass the recognized rules for promotion through the *yeshiva*'s ranks—now assumed that they could not hope to achieve high positions without Qaraite support. They may initially have sought alliances with the Qaraites with an eye on the Fatimid chancery. But soon those alliances came to include large numbers of Qaraites outside Cairo and took on a life of their own.

Relations between the Rabbanite laity and leadership also improved. Rabbinic leaders made renewed efforts to bring Rabbanite and Qaraite worshipers together, either to avert crises or in the interests of their own personal ambition, and the Rabbanite laity began to accept the new relationship to the Qaraites in a way it had not yet done in 1029. In that sense, the excommunication affair of 1029 was a crisis that doubled as a node of social and political transformation.

The Rabbanite leadership, however, engaged in bitter internecine struggles whose net effect was to transform the Qaraites into kingmakers. In 1038, this new stage of tensions engendered its own excommunication affair, though one different from the first. The fault line underlying the events of 1029 healed, but in its place a new one opened up between two camps within the Rabbanite hierarchy.

Finally, the Iraqis in Fustat and elsewhere sought to strengthen their alliances with the Qaraites. In response to competition with the Jerusalem leadership over Qaraite support, the Iraqi *ge'onim* now encouraged their followers in Fustat to seek the support of local Qaraites as well.

Three years after the end of the excommunication affair, the Rabbanites and Qaraites joined together in Ramla in a ritual setting that inverted the excommunication drama of four years earlier. The occasion was an earthquake that shook Palestine on December 5, 1033.[1]

Yūsuf al-Sijilmāsī, the head of the Iraqi community of Ramla, had a dream warning him about impending disaster.[2] He notified his coreligionists of the dire events in his dream in the following testimony.

> Yūsuf al-Sijilmāsī the judge, while he was in Jerusalem, had a dream that he was walking in the old cemetery in Ramla, where he came upon three men standing with three Torah scrolls on which there were black [cloths]. He walked away from them and passed them. But then he turned back to them and greeted them, saying, "Who are you?" They told him, "We are Moses, Aaron, and Samuel." He fell in prostration. Trembling and fright overcame him.
>
> Then they said to him, "Arise and go down to Ramla, and tell them to declare a decree of twelve days, and to repent unto God before great afflictions befall them."
>
> So he woke up, got dressed, and went to pray in the Bāb Yahūda [in Jerusalem]. His father overtook him and prayed with him. And when they completed their prayers, Yūsuf told his father about the dream he had had. The latter said to him: "Why, I had exactly the same dream!" And he swore to him with an oath [that it was true].
>
> They went together to the *ga'on*, Shelomo [b. Yehuda], Head of the Yeshiva, and told him about the dream, and he said to them, "Why, I had exactly the same dream three nights ago!"
>
> And Yūsuf the judge went down to Ramla and sat in the Palestinian synagogue and made an announcement to all who were there, telling them about the dream. He ordered them to conduct a fast on Mondays and Thursdays. And he sent Bishr the cantor to a "mourner" from among our friends the Qaraites [*li-aṣḥābinā al-qarrā'iyyīn*] and he told them about the dream.
>
> After this, God saved them from what happened in Ramla. We beseech God for favorable consequences. And He will do so in His benevolence and granting of success [or reconciliation: *tawfīq*].[3]

[1] Gil, *History of Palestine*, sec. 595, on the basis of a letter of Shelomo b. Ṣemaḥ and Naṣir Khusraw's account (whose date of five days later he dismisses).

[2] Treatises on the interpretation of dreams have been preserved in the Geniza. See, for example: T-S Ar. 51.38a, T-S Ar. 51.39, T-S Ar. 51.40, T-S Ar. 51.41, T-S Ar. 52.212; see Colin F. Baker and Meira Polliack, *Arabic and Judaeo-Arabic Manuscripts in the Cambridge Genizah Collections: Arabic Old Series (T-S Ar. 1a-54)*, Cambridge University Library Genizah Series 12 (Cambridge, 2001), 520, 530. See also the mini-treatise on dream interpretation in the Babylonian Talmud, *Berakhot* 55a–57b.

[3] T-S 13 J 13.13r+T-S 13 J 27.5r, in Judeo-Arabic. On verso is a letter from ca. 1053 sent by Yefet b. David b. Shekhanya, son of the *payyeṭan* discussed in chap. 7, 178–80, to Dani'el b. ʿAzarya. On Yūsuf al-Sijilmāsī, see Hirschberg, "Links between the Jews of the Maghreb and Palestine in the Period of

Because the three Jewish congregations in Ramla—the Babylonians, the Palestinians, and the Qaraites—joined together in penitential fasting, Yūsuf's testimony tells us, they survived the earthquake unharmed. Once the crisis had passed, they drafted an open letter to be read aloud in all the congregations of Fustat publicizing Ramla's deliverance from danger. The message of the letter was clear: communal solidarity and repentance had averted the crisis. The letter inverted the excommunication ceremony by announcing that the three congregations had cooperated for this common purpose.

But al-Sijilmāsī's aims in drafting the letter were not innocent. Yusūf al-Sijilmāsī was the Iraqi leader who had attempted to secede from the authority of the Jerusalem *ga'on* but a few years earlier. To check his designs, Shelomo b. Yehuda had submitted a petition to the caliph detailing the exchange of benefactions and loyalty that legitimated his office, complaining that if al-Sijilmāsī was allowed "to split apart what has been bestowed upon" him, "the *ni'ma* bestowed [upon me] would then be no *ni'ma* at all."[4] The dream testimony served political functions. Publicly, it was a statement of reconciliation [*tawfīq*] with the *ga'on*. But it also placed al-Sijilmāsī in a role equal to or more important than the *ga'on*'s, and so continued to serve his designs at leadership. Finally, it was an attempt to reach out to the Qaraites of Ramla. That way al-Sijilmāsī could capitalize on the tensions between the Palestinian *yeshiva* and the Qaraites in the wake of the excommunication affair and cultivate his own alliances with them. One presumes that he did this to further his designs on leadership prerogatives the *ga'on* had not allowed him: befriending the Qaraites might mean access to the chancery and the possibility of the caliph confirming his prerogatives against the *ga'on*'s.

Still, the Rabbanites and Qaraites of Ramla had joined together in public prayer for the first time, but not the last. Paradoxically, the excommunication crisis of 1029–30 fostered conditions in which Qaraites and Rabbanites could now do so. Something had shifted at the *majlis* in Ramla: over the course of the 1030s, they would come together with increasing ease and frequency.

Shelomo b. Yehuda's Rescript of Investiture

In 1036, when al-Mustanṣir became caliph, Shelomo b. Yehuda sought reconfirmation in office via his supporters in Cairo. It is impossible to know whether this time they were Qaraites or Rabbanites: what has been preserved

---

the Geonim," Hebrew, *Eretz-Israel* 5 (1958): 217; on his title, see Ben-Sasson, *Emergence of the Local Jewish Community*, 321–22.

[4] ENA 4020.65 (see chap. 3 for full analysis), an undated Judeo-Arabic copy. There, Yūsuf al-Sijilmāsī is called Ibn al-Sijilmāsī. In practice, toponymic *nisba*s shifted from father to son and back: Yūsuf's father (who appears in the testimony about the dream) was probably from Sijilmāsa himself, and the son was known both as Ibn al-Sijilmāsī and al-Sijilmāsī.

is the draft of their petition informing the Fatimid chancery of the prerogatives he had exercised over the years of his gaonate (see fig. 10).[5]

The draft is undated. Nor does the reverse side (recto as currently catalogued) offer much help: it contains an unrelated document (such reuses are common), a Hebrew testimony from the Palestinian rabbinical court of Fustat declaring that two brothers from Aleppo had collected a deposit that their father had left with Efrayim b. Shemarya, chief judge of the court (dated documents: 1020–47). That gives us our *termini post* and *ante quem*, but the only way to date the petition more precisely is from its contents and circumstances.

The petition's contents offer two clues to its dating. First, it is written in the form of a testimony by witnesses who attest to "whatever they know and understand and are able to testify [regarding the leadership] of the *ṭā'ifa* known as the Rabbanite Jews," that is, all the *ga'on*'s existing prerogatives (rendering legal decisions, authorizing marriages and divorces, enforcing religious law, imposing and canceling the ban, writing responsa, expounding lessons, appointing cantors to pray in synagogues and butchers inside and outside the markets, making appointments and dismissals of all kinds including those of *ḥaverim* and judges, and supervising the *parnasim* and the court trustees). That sounds like the confirmation of an existing leader, not the appointment of a new one. This puts us at some juncture after the *ga'on*'s initial appointment in autumn 1025.

There is a second clue. Goitein assumed that the document referred to Shelomo b. Yehuda because of the date range of the testimony on recto. But that does not exclude the two previous *ge'onim*, who came into office ca. 1020 and 1025. Since there are no names on the document—or so Goitein thought—it could refer to any of the three. In fact the document contains three words that Goitein could not discern to his satisfaction, but with the help of a high resolution photograph it is now possible to read them (they are in italics here, while the reconstruction of the words missing from the right margin is Goitein's): "All this," the draft says, meaning the list of prerogatives just named, "is within the competence of the head of all [the Rabbanite Jews in every] period and time, on whose leadership the entire collectivity is agreed, namely, [the leader wh]ose position is called head of the *yeshiva, and ibn Yahūda has been appointed to it*."[6] Ibn Yahūda can be no one but Shelomo b. Yehuda. The *ga'on*'s supporters, asked to enumerate his prerogatives, state his title—*ra's al-mathība*, the Arabic title of the *ga'on*—and the fact that he had already been appointed to the office. The caliph had merely to return the document as a confirmation of investiture.

[5] Halper 354, verso (see chap. 3, 93–94).

[6] Ibid., line 13: *qullidahu ibn Yahūda* or, possibly, *qalladahu ibn Yahūda*. Compare the shape of the first two letters of *Yahūda* with the second and third letters of *minhum*, line 2; cf. Goitein, *Palestinian Jewry*, 57 n. 17, and idem, "New Sources on the Palestinian Gaonate," 525 n. 44.

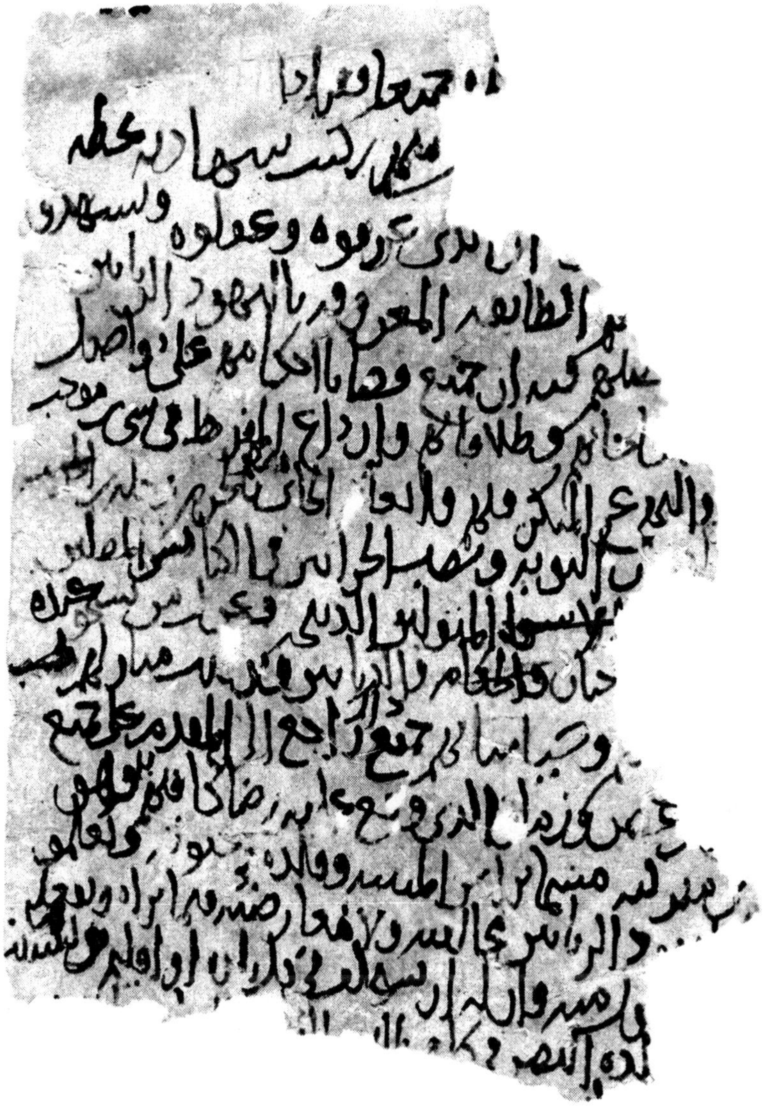

Fig. 10. A *ga'on*'s supporters petition the caliph: draft of a petition from the Cairo supporters of Shelomo b. Yehuda requesting a rescript of investiture from the newly anointed Fatimid caliph al-Mustanṣir (1036–94). The petition testifies to all of the prerogatives the *ga'on* has enjoyed, including the exclusive right to issue bans of excommunication, and notes that he bears the title head of the *yeshiva* (*ra's al-mathība*). In Arabic, 1036. Center for Advanced Judaic Studies, Halper 354, verso.

That brings us firmly within the range of his gaonate, when he had already been serving in office. The historical circumstances during this period point to two junctures at which he might have sought a confirmation of investiture: the conflict with Yūsuf al-Sijilmāsī in the early 1030s and al-Mustanṣir's succession in 1036. But since we have a copy of the petition he wrote in response to the threat from al-Sijilmāsī, the most likely possibility is the investiture of the new caliph in 1036.[7]

As for who the followers were who submitted the petition, the circumstantial evidence points to the Qaraite courtiers.

The Mother of Al-Mustanṣir

Al-Mustanṣir (1036–94) became caliph at the age of only seven, and his reign would last nearly sixty years, longer than that of any caliph in the dynasty—or in the entire Islamic Middle Ages.[8] The caliph's mother, Raṣad, had been Abū Saʿd al-Tustarī's slave. He sold or gave her to the caliph al-Ẓāhir; she gave birth to the future caliph in 1029. With barely concealed contempt, the medieval narrative histories describe Raṣad (usually called Umm, the mother of, al-Mustanṣir) as the mastermind behind the throne during al-Mustanṣir's minority and as locked in rivalry with the vizier, al-Jarjarāʾī, who had been appointed under al-Ẓāhir. Raṣad took over the government on al-Jarjarāʾī's death in 1044, and at that point, made Abū Saʿd al-Tustarī head of her *dīwāns*.[9]

Despite the Tustarī brothers' lack of official appointments when the caliph ascended the throne, Tustarī support became the object of intense competition between the various Jewish leaders of Egypt and Syria immediately in 1036. The accession of a caliph so closely linked to the Tustarīs had the effect of strengthening both Palestinian and Iraqi alliances with the Qaraite elite—although Geniza documents report much about Abū Naṣr Ḥesed and hardly anything about Abū Saʿd. The Tustarī family already had a long history of involvement in Rabbanite affairs when Abū Saʿd penetrated the inner circle of the caliphate in 1036. But after that point, he nearly disappears from the Geniza sources. Was he merely preoccupied with affairs at court? Or did his position somehow preclude protecting the Jews? Abū Naṣr Ḥesed, meanwhile,

[7] ENA 4020.65.

[8] Al-Bīrūnī mentions a "theory of the astrologers that," with few exceptions, "none of the caliphs of Islam and the other kings of the Muslims reigns longer than twenty-four years." Al-Bīrūnī, *al-Athār al-bāqiya ʿan al-qurūn al-khāliya*, in Sachau, *Chronologie orientalischer Völker*, 132 (Arabic); idem, *Chronology of Ancient Nations*, 129 (English).

[9] The attitude of the sources is reflected in *EI*² s.v. "al-Mustanṣir bi'llāh, Abū Tamīm Maʿadd b. ʿAlī al-Ẓāhir" (H. A. R. Gibb and Paul Kraus), who call Umm al-Mustanṣir "the evil genius of al-Mustanṣir's reign." For a more balanced view, see Lev, *State and Society*, 42–43; and Cortese and Calderini, *Women and the Fatimids*, 110–11.

moved to the center of Rabbanite politics. But whereas before, the Rabbanites had contacted him in emergencies, after 1036, he lurked in the background of rabbinic power struggles as patron and kingmaker.

SOLICITUDE (AL-ʿINĀYA)

The first we hear of this is a gaonic missive from Baghdad.

When Hayya bar Sherira had acceded to the gaonate of Pumbedita on his father's abdication in 1004, he was already in his mid-sixties and could recall three generations of *geʾonim* (Seʿadya himself might have held the tiny Hayya on his knee).[10] Hayya had maintained direct contact with the Tustarī brothers of the second generation since the first years of his tenure as *gaʾon*, sending them responsa that they forwarded to the elder al-Tāhirtī brother, who had them copied before sending them to Qayrawān and al-Andalus.[11] Thirty years later, Hayya still held office, only by now he was ninety-nine years old and his links with the Tustarīs extended to the third generation, and to Abū Naṣr Ḥesed in particular.

Notoriously conservative in intellectual matters, Hayya could hardly be accused of sympathy for Qaraism—or even for works beyond the canon of traditional rabbinic literature. Even the rationalism of Seʿadya or of Hayya's contemporary Shemu'el b. Ḥofnī seemed too much for him, and he was outspoken about the dangers of philosophy and the paramount importance of focusing one's studies on the Talmud.[12] Hayya also seems to have harbored a certain anxiety about the potential effects of Qaraite arguments upon the practices of ordinary Jews. In a responsum on the permissibility of blowing rams' horns (*shofarot*) on Rosh ha-Shana, he included a discussion of halakhic methodology that amounts to a defense of the maximalist view of tradition. On the practice in question, he wrote:

> It is a tradition, handed down, transferred and transmitted from fathers to sons for consecutive generations of Israel, from the time of the prophets to the present. . . . It is the words of the many that attest to every *mishnah* and every part of the Talmud [*gemara*] that they have been faithfully handed down as tradition from the mouths of the prophets, [and that they are] the law as handed down from Moses at Sinai. And the greatest proof [that this is the correct ruling]

[10] Ibn Dāwūd claims that Hayya Ga'on lived to the age of ninety-nine and died on the last day of Passover, 1349 Sel., 4798; Cohen, *Sefer ha-qabbalah*, 43 (Heb.), 58–59 (Eng.). The same claim can be found in an interpolation in the so-called Damascus manuscript of the Epistle of Rav Sherira Ga'on; on that basis the year of Hayya's birth is assumed to be 939. Seʿadya died three years later. For details and references, see Gil, *In the Kingdom of Ishmael*, sec. 228.

[11] T-S 12.175.

[12] Brody, *Geonim of Babylonia*, 298–99.

is: go out and see what the people do in practice—and that is the chief support. Only then do we examine everything that has been said in the Mishnah and the Talmud on that matter and what can be derived from them. If it can be explained as we wish, good and well; but if it contains something that cannot be explained as we wish and cannot be supported by proof, this does not alter the chief ruling [which is based on tradition].[13]

Lest it be said that Hayya's openness toward popular custom and consensus indicated a general liberalism, matters were precisely the reverse. His invocation of popular practice as a source of rabbinic law was probably pitched against Qaraism, in two ways. First, by bridging the gap between textually mandated law and popular practice, he addressed the problem of internal rabbinic dissent—disagreement between the two Talmuds, within the Talmuds themselves, and between the Talmud and popular practice. Qaraites argued that the abundance of disagreement in rabbinic tradition proved it to be a human product and not divinely revealed; Hayya bound the written and behavioral sources of law into a seamless whole and thus claimed that rabbinic law, not merely in texts but as practiced, partook of revelation.[14] Second, Hayya's appeal to popular practice entailed something like an appeal to consensus (*ijmāʿ*), and invoking consensus may have served him—as it would Ibn Dāwūd more than a century later—as a polemic against Qaraism: since Qaraite jurists represented the minority of Jewish legal authorities, they were excluded from *ijmāʿ*. Hayya should not, then, be misunderstood as preferring political expediency to religious ideology.

Yet he continued until the end of his life to call upon the services of Abū Naṣr Ḥesed al-Tustarī. Now, instead of logistical support for the *yeshiva*, Hayya asked al-Tustarī to offer protection to one of Hayya's appointees in Egypt.

A faction wished to overthrow the head of the Iraqi community of Fustat, Sahlān b. Avraham, who had been serving as head of the Iraqi community of Fustat for about three years, since 1034. In December 1037 or January 1038, only a few months before Hayya's death, he wrote to Sahlān to discuss with him of rumors of the plot against him and to advise him on how to conduct

[13] Benjamin Manasseh Lewin, *Oṣar ha-geʾonim: The Responsa of the Babylonian Geonim and Their Commentaries according to the Order of the Talmud* (Jerusalem, 1928), *Rosh ha-shana*, 61; cited in Libson, *Jewish and Islamic Law*, 20, and in idem, "Halakha and Reality in the Gaonic Period: *Taqqanah*, *Minhag*, Tradition and Consensus: Some Observations," in Frank, *Jews of Medieval Islam*, 79; see Libson's references to earlier discussions in n. 6, particularly that of Ben-Sasson (and see next note, below), and cf. Hirschberg, *History of the Jews in North Africa*, 1:159–60. I have combined elements of each of Libson's translations. Hayya's call to "go out and see what the people are doing" is a quotation from several *amoraʾim* in the Babylonian Talmud who use popular practice as a basis for deciding law.

[14] So I understand the interpretations of Libson, "Halakha and Reality," 79 n. 7; idem, *Jewish and Islamic Law*, 20. Ben-Sasson, *Emergence of the Local Jewish Community*, 48–49, suggests that this ruling contains an anti-Qaraite polemic.

himself toward his supporters and detractors.[15] Hayya speaks the language of patronage relationships fluently. He notes the ties of loyalty that bound Sahlān to him and his obligation (*ʿahd*) toward his protégé. That obligation demanded that he supervise affairs in Fustat from afar, despite his extraordinarily advanced age and apparently failing health. He writes, dictating to a scribe:

> I am writing—may God lengthen the days of our much esteemed one, delight of our soul, //the *ḥaver,*// *ra's al-kull*, deputy of the academy [*segan ha-yeshiva*], *rosh ha-seder*—from Baghdad[16] . . . of Ṭevet, 1349 Sel. [1037–38; the precise day is effaced].
>
> I thank God for my soundness of mind, but were I to go into a description of what ails me by way of persistent weakness—life has become loathsome to me because of bouts of illness—my explanation would wax prolix indeed. Therefore I say only: blessed be the Lord in all His deeds. And I beseech Him to bring about a favorable ending and a constructive result, for it is He who bestows this.
>
> My heart verily longs for you, my lord, may God preserve your glory. . . .
>
> Be aware, my lord, that mere days ago I received an open letter from the people of the Iraqi synagogue addressed to no one in particular, saying that a faction [*qawm*] has risen up against you, and that some of them have written briefs [against you]. This filled me with consternation. I do not know how the affair unfolded.
>
> There also arrived . . . a letter addressed to me from to Sulaymān b. Mevorakh, who mentioned that he was in Baghdad [the text is effaced] . . . the honored elder Efrayim, known as Ibn al-ʿAkkī, may God preserve his glory, was with him, and his distress waxed //because of him//. And he told me that the man known as Naṣr is inciting them to bring a case against you and to write briefs [against you], and this magnified my distress. He mentioned that this did not avail them in . . . the synagogue, may God help them, and that most of the community supports you. This pleased me. May God in his compassion make you successful.

None of the three personalities the *ga'on* mentions in this paragraph—Sulaymān b. Mevorakh, Efrayim ibn al-ʿAkkī, or "the man known as Naṣr"—is known from other Geniza documents. Evidently they were all members of the Iraqi synagogue in Fustat; that also explains their general absence from documents

[15] Mosseri Ia 5 (L 2), in Judeo-Arabic. See Gil, *In the Kingdom of Ishmael*, sec. 106, end of last paragraph; idem, *History of Palestine*, sec. 764. On Sahlān b. Avraham, see Bareket, "Sahlan b. Abraham," Hebrew, *Tarbiẓ* 52 (1983): 17–40.

[16] Three characters have been preserved here (*aleph*, *lamed*, and *samekh*, equivalent to the Arabic *alif, lām, sīn*). Gil reads [*min dār*] *al-sa*[*lām*] (Gil, *In the Kingdom of Ishmael*, 2, doc. 41, line 2); more likely is [*min madīnat*] *al-sa*[*lām*], the name conferred on Baghdad by its founder, the Abbasid caliph al-Manṣūr, and reproduced on government items of the period such as coins and weights. See *EI*², s.v. "Baghdād" (A. A. Duri).

from the Geniza. As far as one can tell, Naṣr was one of those fomenting rebellion against Sahlān's leadership; Sulaymān b. Mevorakh and Efrayim ibn al-ʿAkkī supported Sahlān, and when Naṣr tried to incite them to oppose his leadership, they informed Hayya of the brewing plot. The *ga'on* continues:

> [. . . Sulaymān b. Mevorakh told me] to whom we should write among those who have sincere intentions toward you [*munāṣiḥika*] so that we can thank them, and to whom we should write among your adversaries so that we can make peace between you and them.
>
> And he also mentioned to me //that// Abu l-ʿAlāʾ al-Mubārak, the son of master Avraham al-Ṣippori . . . and that he is one of the instigators against you. Therefore please inform me, may God help you, of his reputation [*dhikr*], and who he is, whether he is Iraqi or Syrian [i.e., which congregation he claims], and how to address him, and I will turn my attention toward this.

Abu l-ʿAlāʾal-Mubārak ibn al-Ṣippori—or Mevorakh b. Avraham—is as unknown to us as he was to the *ga'on*; this is the only Geniza document I know that mentions him. Hayya asks Sahlān for three pieces of information about him: his reputation; his rank ("how to address him"); and what kind of loyalty he was likely to offer the *ga'on* should he intervene ("whether he is Iraqi or Syrian"). The *ga'on* then states his intended course of action:

> I shall write to the honorable esteemed Shaykh Abū Naṣr master Faḍl [Ḥesed], son of master Sahl [al-Tustarī], may God make His aid to him eternal, and ask him to tell me about the situation with all its facts, and to direct his solicitude [*ʿināya*] toward you. May God come to your aid and remove from you all trouble and distress, and direct toward you peaceful designs. And I have strong expectations of this.

The Arabic term Hayya uses here, *ʿināya* (concern, attention, or solicitude), conjures up the technical term for divine providence in works of medieval Arabic philosophy, *al-ʿināya al-ilāhiyya*; in the Sufi lexicon, *al-ʿināya* means divine benefaction or generosity. Like *niʿma*, it is a concept with divine-human origins and human-human consequences perhaps best translated as patronage. Also like *niʿma*, it is a form of benefaction in exchange for which one was obligated to render loyalty. Hayya thus introduces a theme that would recur in Rabbanite references to Ḥesed throughout the late 1030s and 1040s: his ascent as general patron of the Jewish leadership.

It is also clear from Hayya's letter that he trusted Ḥesed to offer a neutral and even-handed account of the conflict. Hayya tells Sahlān that he is seeking Ḥesed's version of what happened between him and his opponents in Fustat; he expected Sahlān to share his faith in Ḥesed's account. Only then does the *ga'on* ask Sahlān to "write a letter of explanation in several copies," an account he expected would conform to Ḥesed's.

In the middle of writing his letter—as often happens in Geniza correspondence—Hayya received the letter from Sahlān containing his version of events. After reading it, Hayya simply reiterates:

> I will write to the honorable esteemed shaykh Abū Naṣr [al-Tustarī], may God sustain his aid to him, that he inform me . . . [of] the essence of the matter, and he will direct his solicitude [*ʿināya*] toward you. I will beseech God to be a helper and protector, "and your enemies will cower before you, and you shall trample their backs" [Deut. 33:29].

Hayya's letter adumbrates Ḥesed al-Tustarī's place as protector of the Jewish community during the decade prior to his assassination in 1049 or 1050. Nine months later, before the holidays in the fall of 1038, an associate of Sahlān's wrote to him to congratulate him on his recent marriage and on the resolution of the crisis in the Iraqi community of Fustat. By now, news of Ḥesed's patronage was widely known; in the course of its circulation it had grown from "solicitude" to wholesale deliverance of the Jews.

That associate was Daniʾel b. ʿAzarya, a descendant of the Davidic line with his own leadership ambitions to which I will return in chapter 12. He writes to Sahlān b. Avraham in Fustat on September 12, 1038:

> Your letters arrived, and I read them, and I was reassured by what they informed me of your wellbeing. I thanked the God of Israel and I asked Him to make your wellbeing eternal. You mentioned what happened with the faction [*al-qawm*] whose methods are infamous. After that, I read the letters of our lord the esteemed Abu l-Faraj Daniʾel b. Ḥasan, may the Merciful One preserve him, in which he mentioned matters that made me most distressed. I was very glad that God granted their resolution through my lord the esteemed, honorable Abū Naṣr [al-Tustarī], may God lengthen his days, may God always appoint him a deliverer [*moshiaʿ*] and preserve his wealth and his standing for the sake of the collectivity [*al-kāffa*].[17]

If the messianic weight with which Daniʾel b. ʿAzarya freighted Ḥesed's honorifics seems excessive, he also referred more pragmatically to the obligation of the Jews' man at court: to preserve his own power for the sake of its benefit to the Jewish community. Whether Ḥesed saw his own mission that way is less clear, as we shall see. But when Daniʾel campaigned for the gaonic chair

[17] T-S 13 J 25.3, in Hebrew. The date of the document is partly effaced: "Tuesday, 11 Tishri. . . ." Gil notes that 11 Tishri fell on a Tuesday in 1035, 1038, and 1039, but as Goitein had reasoned previously, the end of the letter congratulates Sahlān on his marriage, the contract for which bears the date September 9, 1037. That coupled with its references to the affair of December 1037–January 1038 makes this letter most likely to date from 1038. Gil, *History of Palestine*, 2, doc. 344, note to page 1, line 3; Goitein, "Daniʾel ben ʿAzarya, nasiʾ ve-gaʾon: berurim u-mismakhim ḥadashim," *Shalem* 2 (1975–76): 45–46 (reprinted in idem, *Palestinian Jewry*). See also Gil, *In the Kingdom of Ishmael*, sec. 83 n.

thirteen years later, Qaraite solicitude would prove instrumental to his success.

THE GAONIC SCHISM OF 1038–42

The centrality of the Qaraites in rabbinic politics may still have been known only among the high-ranking leaders. But it became clear to all in the late 1030s, when the Qaraites emerged as a weighty force in rabbinic political battles. Three times over the subsequent decades, alliances with them would prove decisive to rabbinic campaigns for office.

The first incident was the case of the pretender to the Palestinian gaonate Natan b. Avraham, who successfully manipulated Qaraite support in order to usurp the gaonic chair from Shelomo b. Yehuda in 1038–42.

The rival gaonate of Ramla is one of the better-known and better-documented affairs the Geniza has added to the annals of medieval Jewish history. It is also among the more sordid ones. For precisely four years, from Hoshaʿna Rabba in 1038 until the same festival in 1042, two men claimed the Palestinian gaonate for themselves and exercised its various prerogatives: Shelomo b. Yehuda, the reigning *ga'on* in Jerusalem, and his rival Natan b. Avraham, whose power base was in Ramla. Their followers vied for control of the main synagogue in Ramla and for the right to proclaim the name of their *ga'on* during Sabbath services just as the caliph's name was pronounced in the congregational mosques. As a result of the fighting, the synagogue remained closed for more than two years. The affair came to involve Jewish communities as far west as Qayrawān and as far north as Damascus and Tripoli, and government officials including the Zirid amīr of Ifrīqiya and the Fatimid vizier al-Jarjarāʾī in Cairo. It was also a dispute that both sides knew could be resolved only by means of the Qaraites—a knowledge that was shared, this time, by both the notables and the nameless masses.

"Only a Syrian Can Accede to This Office"

Historians over the course of the twentieth century have tried to work out the wider significance of the conflict. Mann, who first discovered many of the letters written in the thick of it, understood it primarily in terms of the personal ambition of a pretender from outside the *yeshiva*. In fact, the dynamics were nearly the reverse: the pretender, Natan b. Avraham, descended from a Palestinian gaonic clan (his mother's brother had been *av bet din* of the Jerusalem academy) and the reigning *ga'on*, Shelomo b. Yehuda, was an outsider from Fez in the far Maghrib, whose opponents harped on his foreign origins: several of the letters refer to him not by *kunya* or title but, contemptuously, as "the man from Fez" (al-Fāsī).[18] Natan himself was not above exploiting his Palestinian origins for political gain: one of his detractors disclosed in a letter to the *nagid* of Qayrawān, Yaʿaqov b. ʿAmram, that Natan "finds it unacceptable that someone should be appointed to the gaonate who is a Maghribī; only a Syrian can accede to this office."[19]

But Natan's nativist claims were entirely disingenuous, since a long sojourn abroad merely added to his stature, just as Shelomo's outsider status enhanced his. Natan was intellectually a son of Qayrawān as much as genealogically he was Syrian: he had studied in Qayrawān with the master of the academy there, Ḥushiʾel b. Elḥanan (d. 1027), one of the "four captives" in Ibn Dāwūd's account.[20] Everyone knew that both Seʿadya and Shemuʾel b. Ḥofni had been educated outside the *yeshivot* whose gaonate they assumed; Shelomo b. Yehuda, likewise, had sent his son to study in Baghdad with Hayya b. Sherira, and like Hayya, Ḥushiʾel was of the stature to warrant travel in pursuit of learning. Natan and everyone else, then, knew of his ties to Qayrawān and knew how to understand them. By disclosing Natan's nativist arguments to the *nagid*, his detractor was implying Natan's disloyalty to Qayrawān and attempting to embarrass him in front of his teachers.

Shelomo b. Yehuda, meanwhile, deployed his lack of dynastic connection within *yeshiva* clans to rhetorical effect: in the absence of nepotism, divine providence had caused his election to office. He reminded Efrayim b. Shemarya in Fustat: "I was neither appointed on the strength of my father nor named [*gaʾon*] because of my family . . . but rather by the will of God."[21] It was not the first time Shelomo b. Yehuda claimed to have achieved something "with God's help" precisely when he had brought it about through political means. (He may not have distinguished between the two if he held God to be the ultimate bestower of *niʿma*.)[22]

[18] CUL Or 1080 J 45, in Judeo-Arabic. See Mann, *Texts and Studies*, 1:323–45; idem, *Jews in Egypt and in Palestine*, 1: 141–51; 2:159–74, 352–54, and 447–50; Goitein, *Mediterranean Society*, 2:16; Mark R. Cohen, "New Light on the Conflict over the Palestinian Gaonate, 1038–42, and on Daniel b. ʿAzarya: A Pair of Letters to the Nagid of Qayrawan," *Association for Jewish Studies Review* 1 (1976): 1–37, who was the first to discover the involvement of the Qayrawānī Jews and widen the question of the schism's significance beyond mere personal rivalries (see 2 n. 1 for a list of previous publications, including Mann's, and additional unpublished documents); Gil, *History of Palestine*, secs. 870–84, who summarizes the events and the epistolary sources; Ben-Sasson, *Emergence of the Local Jewish Community*, 368–72; and Gil, *In the Kingdom of Ishmael*, sec. 48, who discusses it in light of other gaonic and exilarchic schisms of the tenth and eleventh centuries.

[19] ENA 3765.10 recto+T-S 18 J 4.16 verso, in Judeo-Arabic, letter from Shemarya b. Maṣliaḥ in Fustat to Yaʿaqov b. ʿAmram, *nagid* of Qayrawān (lines 14–16).

[20] Gil, *History of Palestine*, sec. 881, also claims that Natan had come to Fustat from Qayrawān armed with letters of recommendation from the *nagid* to give him an entrée into the Fatimid court. I find no evidence to that effect in the sources he cites in the footnote there.

[21] In a letter to Efrayim b. Shemarya, in Hebrew: Bodl. MS Heb. c 50.21 (lines 12–13).

[22] See T-S 13 J 19.16, above, chap. 8, 218–26.

Previous scholarship has overlooked the Qaraites' role in the gaonic schism. Their role illuminates important aspects of the conflict, however, and the conflict, in turn, illuminates qualitative shifts in the Qaraites' embroilment in *yeshiva* politics.

THE RETURN OF NATAN B. AVRAHAM

Some time during the first decade of the eleventh century, Natan left Palestine and headed west to Ifrīqiya to collect debts owed on his father's estate. He stayed in Qayrawān for more than twenty years, becoming a disciple there and developing a network of ties that would serve him on his return to the east.

Having finished with the west—or having grown too ambitious to stay—Natan moved to Fustat during the mid-1030s (at the latest, in the spring of 1038). There he pursued trade deals in a desultory fashion (his correspondence contains some details about tar and gypsum, both materials used in construction) but kept busy multiplying and strengthening his ties and testing the waters of rabbinic politics. He was not a very successful trader. By 1038 he had lost all his money and was deeply in debt, at which point he set out northward for Jerusalem, bereft of means but full of larger designs.

It is unclear precisely when Natan became aware of the Qaraite factor in gaonic politics. It is clear, however, that by his stay in Fustat he already knew of Ḥesed al-Tustarī and of the importance of having the Qaraite grandees on one's side. Evidence comes in a letter he wrote in 1038 to his trade associate Abū Yūsuf Elʿazar b. Ismāʿīl in Qūṣ on the Nile.[23] Qūṣ was the major trade entrepôt of Upper Egypt, the gateway to the India trade, and sat astride the Egyptian pilgrimage route to Mecca; it was an eight-day journey by boat from Cairo and slightly longer by caravan from the Red Sea port of Qusayr on the way from India or Aden.[24] Elʿazar had asked Natan for some prices, and he dutifully reported them in the margins of the letter, writing them backwards to keep the information from Elʿazar's competitors in Qūṣ. Natan also gave Elʿazar news of the scandal of Avraham b. David ibn Sughmār's dalliance with a Muslim prostitute and his imprisonment by Fatimid agents. Ibn Sughmār had been in prison for a month and a half; after a lacuna, we learn that "the

[23] T-S Ar. 54.93. See the comments of Goitein, *Mediterranean Society*, 1:387 (appendix D, no. 85); idem, *Palestinian Jewry*, 112 n. 77; Gil, *History of Palestine*, secs. 871, 881.

[24] Jean-Claude Garcin, *Un centre musulman de la Haute-Egypte médiévale, Qus* (Cairo, 1976), 3, 9–10, 98–100. Naṣīr Khusraw passed through Qūṣ on his return voyage from Mecca to Cairo in 1050: W. M. Thackston, *Naser-e Khosraw's Book of Travels=(Safarnama)*, Persian heritage series 36 (Albany, 1986), 63–64. Goitein notes that letters from Fustat could take as long as seven weeks to reach Qūṣ, but the journey in the opposite direction with the current was far faster (Goitein, *Mediterranean Society* 1:290). Indeed, Natan expresses horror that Elʿazar has received none of his letters, despite the fact that he dispatched two to him every Monday.

shaykh Abū Naṣr al-Dustarī" had been involved in attempts to have Ibn Sughmār released, but no longer "thought it permissible to speak" about the matter.[25] The fact that Abū Naṣr Ḥesed al-Tustarī was the contact of first resort for liaisons with the government must not have escaped Natan b. Avraham's notice. Even before his proclamation as anti-*ga'on*, Natan recognized that his status in the community depended upon winning Ḥesed's support, and throughout the affair, he would stay abreast of Ḥesed's fortunes in government.

It took Natan about six months after his arrival in Palestine to mount his war on Shelomo b. Yehuda's reign.[26] When he got to Jerusalem, he convinced the elders of the rabbinic academy to have him appointed *av bet din*, a position his maternal uncle had held, even though he was not next in line for succession. This was a breach in the strictly hierarchical rules for advancement through the academic ranks, since it meant passing over Ṭoviyya b. Dani'el the Third.[27] This breach in *yeshiva* protocol did not please Shelomo b. Yehuda, but he allowed it to happen. He would later regret the lapse of vigilance.[28] Once Natan had been installed as *av bet din*, he began amassing a motley faction of followers arrayed against the reigning *ga'on*, many of them in Ramla.

Ga'on and Anti-*Ga'on* on the Mount of Olives

The conflict erupted on October 23, 1038—as in 1029, during the yearly pilgrimage to the Mount of Olives. We have accounts of the week's events from both camps, although in significant ways they do not square with each other.

Shelomo b. Yehuda informs us that even before the festival, the elders of Ramla had begun to complain to him about this upstart newcomer who was now *av bet din*. They wrote to the *ga'on* in Jerusalem with an urgent plea for intervention: "The man to whom you granted a title and a bit of authority has now extended his hand over everything," they told him. "Come quickly."[29] The *ga'on* went down to Ramla via Damascus.

A follower of Natan's meanwhile wrote to an unknown recipient (in a letter of which only the middle section has been preserved) that the *ga'on* arrived in Ramla with his son carrying an edict (*tawqī'*) that Gil speculates was a reconfirmation in office from local officials—a likely possibility, since he had come from Damascus.[30] It is unclear, though, why a local edict would have availed

[25] See chap. 3, n. 76.
[26] Gil, *History of Palestine*, sec. 872.
[27] On Ṭoviyya's brief role in the excommunication affair of 1029, see chap. 8, n. 31.
[28] Cohen, "New Light," 4–6.
[29] T-S 16.261, in Hebrew, letter of Shelomo b. Yehuda to Shelomo b. 'Eli in Tripoli.
[30] CUL Or 1080 J 45.

the *ga'on*, who had been granted one by the central government just two years earlier. He probably thought at this point that the affair would remain a local one, and opted to treat it as a matter of provincial Syrian politics.

In time for Hoshaʿna Rabba, the *ga'on*, his son Avraham, and one of the sons of the previous *ga'on*, Yosef ha-Kohen b. Shelomo, made it back to Jerusalem and ascended the Mount of Olives. During the ceremony, Avraham declared the calendar for the upcoming year. Then, according to Natan's party's account, someone (it is not clear who, though it is seems Avraham is meant) "excommunicated all those who desecrate the Lord's festivals as they have been passed down through tradition." It was evident to all who the targets of the ban were: the Qaraites, though Natan's follower notes that this was an excommunication formula "normally unheard of." The usual formulation was "against the eaters of meat with milk," the subject of the controversy in 1029–30.[31]

Why would Avraham have renewed the excommunication against the Qaraites? Was he attempting to relive the drama of nine years earlier, to win favor with the more zealous camp by proclaiming the ban? Was he shoring up his own bid to succeed his father in the gaonic office by exercising one of its cherished prerogatives, the right to issue excommunications? Or was he attacking the Qaraites in an attempt to defend his father's office? The latter seems likely if the targets of the ban were not the Qaraites but Natan and his cultivation of them. If this was his strategy, it backfired horribly. Instead of winning over the zealots, the *ga'on* and his son alienated a good part of the crowd on the mountain that day, sending them straight over to the camp of Natan b. Avraham. Natan's follower, meanwhile, hastened to report on the event. "Their purpose was only to renew dissension among Israel, to multiply evil and to extol themselves. They were successful in this as long as people believed them to be pious, but now God has exposed their utter lack of piety. A great fracas ensued on the mountain, and no one took pleasure in the pilgrimage. Israel was greatly vexed."

After the ceremony, Natan's followers descended the Mount of Olives and repaired to a private house, where they proclaimed Natan *ga'on*. On that day, he began to sign his correspondence with elaborate and florid titles of office, none of which were rightfully his to use. He also claimed several key prerogatives: appointing judges, declaring excommunications, issuing responsa, and dispensing titles to his followers. (Some of those titles are unattested anywhere else in the Geniza and were of his own idiosyncratic devising.) He also strived to accumulate the authority of the office in other ways, including delivering sermons at Sabbath services and cultivating a far-reaching network of supporters, the crucial armature without which he could not have functioned securely in office for as long as he did.

[31] On sons of *ge'onim* making public pronouncements for their fathers, see above, chap. 1, n. 28.

Undeterred by this temporary setback, the next day, on Shemini Aṣeret, Avraham ascended the mountain again and proclaimed the ban a second time, this time using the traditional formula, "against the eaters of meat with milk." "And now, O Israel," wrote Natan's follower, "is the sin of Peor such a small thing to us [Josh. 22:17; cf. Numbers 25:1–9]? Is what has already happened between the two [gaonic] factions [*al-ṭāʾifatayn*] not enough, so that now they have renewed this strife?" He chastised Shelomo b. Yehuda's camp evidently unaware that he was using precisely the same biblical verse with which Shelomo b. Yehuda himself had chastised the Rabbanite throng for demanding the ban against the Qaraites in 1029, warning them not to continue the dispute.[32] The context suggests that by the "factions," Natan's follower meant the two Rabbanite camps.

This letter is the only account we have of the festivities in which the excommunication is mentioned; Shelomo b. Yehuda's own description passes over that detail in silence. Natan's followers wasted no time in reporting the matter to their supporters in Fustat. For Natan to emerge as a champion of peace with the Qaraites, Shelomo b. Yehuda had to become their archantagonist.

"BLESSED BE THE LORD WHO HAS UNITED THE TWO PARTIES BY YOUR HAND"

Several months after these events, on the eve of Purim in February 1039, Natan assembled several hundred people in the *majlis* in Ramla for a prayer service and a ceremonial reading from the Book of Esther. But this was not the standard Purim fare. The congregation was composed of Rabbanites and Qaraites together—a fact the anti-*gaʾon* wasted no time in reporting to his Qaraite patrons in Cairo in a set of transparently grandiose letters.

The first was a missive to a prominent Qaraite in Fustat named ʿAlī Abu l-Barakāt (Berakha) ibn Rawḥ.[33] Natan had known Abu l-Barakāt from his stay in Fustat; he had sent him a letter immediately upon his departure for Palestine from the coastal town of Damietta, whence he would set out for the port of Tinnīs and thence to Ascalon and Jerusalem. The letter reads as something like a parody of Ibn Khalfūn's elegies on leaving his patrons (see chapter 5): Natan laments, "We parted and my eyes brimmed with tears, and my separation from you filled me with grief." And yet in the same letter, Natan also addresses Abu l-Barakāt as "my disciple" (*talmidenu*). In light of Abu l-Barakāt's nobility, the fact that he was a Qaraite, and the ambitions Natan harbored en route to Palestine, it is difficult not to see his mixing of the roles of client and

32 T-S 13 J 19.16 (above, chap. 8, 225).
33 T-S 8 J 20.1.

patron as the first clue that something was amiss in his cultivation of this man, that he was manipulating the conventions of loyalty rather than participating in them sincerely.

The second letter confirms this suspicion.[34] Writing in February 1039, Natan describes his Purim celebration as an unparalleled triumph in the annals of Jewish leadership. The letter suggests that Natan's designs extended even beyond the role of the *ga'on* and that he would have liked to achieve dominion over the Qaraites as well. In any case, he united the two groups only in order to extend his hand over that much greater an empire.

> Natan, Head of the Yeshiva of the Splendor of Jacob, son of Rabbi Avraham, of blessed memory.
>
> To our dear, estimable, and esteemed master, Berakha our student, the wise and learned, punctilious in the commandments of the God of Israel—may the Holy One preserve him and may the Creator guard him—son of master Rawḥ, may his resting place be in Eden:
>
> Your Hebrew letter arrived, may God preserve your glory, in which you mention that you had previously sent us a letter with a second letter attached [to it], sent to you by the Cherished One of the Academy [*ḥemdat ha-yeshiva*], which had come from the Maghrib. Indeed it arrived.

Natan was apparently dispensing titles to followers as far away as Qayrawān—in this case to Shemu'el b. Avraham al-Tāhirtī, scion of the trading clan that had previously conveyed responsa and donations between Pumbedita and Qayrawān.[35] Natan was not only using his old Qayrawān connections to his full advantage; he was also encroaching on the heart of the existing network of merchant supporters of the *yeshivot* in Baghdad.

Natan asks the Cherished One to "write to the Maghribīs" to circulate the information that one of his opponents in Fustat had been neutralized. He instructs him "to inform them of the baseness of the one who writes letters in Fustat, I mean //the boy// ben Me'ir, and that he [ben Me'ir] was excommunicated in Fustat, and excommunicated in Acre //and in Ramla//, and that his own father excommunicated him upon reading the letter." The "boy ben Me'ir" was Shelomo *he-ḥaver* b. Me'ir *rosh ha-seder*, a grandson of Seʿadya's antagonist in the great calendar dispute of 921–22.[36] Shelomo b. Me'ir had appar-

[34] ENA 4020.6, in Hebrew and Judeo-Arabic; see also a third letter Natan wrote to him, T-S 13 J 31.1, in Hebrew.

[35] Bareket, *Fustat on the Nile*, 95 n. 75 and references to previous literature; T-S 13 J 5.1; ENA 2747.16; T-S AS 149.180; ENA 2735.4; Mann, *Jews in Egypt and in Palestine*, 1:278 n. 6; 2:313, 374; Gil, *History of Palestine*, index, s.v. "*ḥemdat ha-yeshiva*"; Bareket, *Jewish Leadership in Fustat*, 74 n. 52; 77 n. 74; 113 n. 97.

[36] Gil, *History of Palestine*, sec. 851. See also Bareket, *Fustat on the Nile*, 146 n. 91, who offers corroboration that Shelomo the *ḥaver* ben Me'ir turned against Shelomo b. Yehuda and "came to terms with the group of conspirators," that is, Natan b. Avraham's camp (against Gil's reading, *History of*

ently been writing letters to Qayrawān in support of Shelomo b. Yehuda and against Natan b. Avraham, so the latter excommunicated him in Fustat, Acre, and Ramla—but not, as Gil points out, in Jerusalem, an omission I take to mean that the holy city was a stronghold of support for Shelomo b. Yehuda.[37]

> He [the Cherished One] should also mention [in his letters] the gathering of the people of Damascus and their prayers for us as Head of the Yeshiva, [and mention that they wrote] a document on Sunday [supporting us] witnessed by four hundred men, and that they will continue to sign as witnesses.
>
> As for that [Purim] evening of ours, may God bring such events about for you repeatedly in years to come and grant you the merit to build His Temple—as they [*sic*] performed miracles for our ancestors in those days, so may He do for us[38]—a better evening has never been witnessed. There assembled in the *majlis* about four hundred men, and in the adjoining room even more than these. There was not a single Rabbanite or Qaraite who did not attend. It was an excellent thing the likes of which has not been seen. There were perhaps thirty candelabra with more than two hundred candles and about thirty lamps and twenty lanterns, and the whole world was illuminated. And gentiles were in attendance, and the scroll [of Esther] was read from thirty scrolls in expert readings.
>
> [He adds above the line—as if to make his meaning very clear:] //Not a soul remained in the Babylonian synagogue, and only about twenty in the Palestinian, and at the house of the man from Fez [Shelomo b. Yehuda, who had evidently been reduced to holding prayer services in his home], fewer than ten.//
>
> In attendance there were perhaps two hundred Qaraites, every notable among them. The learned Qaraites came out among the people, and the people rejoiced at the unanimity of the affair and at the presence of the two parties [*al-ṭāʾifatayn*] together. And I prayed for the two parties together, and people departed rejoicing. And everyone agreed //that// there had not been a Purim like this one since the days of [Menashshe] ibn al-Qazzāz.[39]
>
> And it was a good thing, the two communities [*al-jamāʿatayn*] saying with one voice, "Blessed be the Lord who has united the two parties [*al-ṭāʾifatayn*] by your hand and in your *majlis*!" And the people's joy was great.

Natan is of course writing to a Qaraite, and is therefore interested in representing himself as commanding as much Qaraite support as possible. But even correcting for self-serving exaggeration, the vision is arresting: the man claiming the highest rabbinic office in the Fatimid realm is at pains to emphasize the presence of Qaraites in his house of worship. As for the comparison with Ibn

Palestine, sec. 851), interpreting T-S 13 J 31.7, a letter of Shelomo b. Yehuda to Efrayim b. Shemarya, only the right half of which has been found.

37 Gil, *History of Palestine*, doc. 183, note to line 9 (page 314).

38 A conflation of various lines from the Purim liturgy; see Maimonides, *Mishne Torah*, Seder ha-tefilla, 24 and ibid., Hilkhot megilla, 1:3.

39 See above, chap. 4, n. 44.

al-Qazzāz, its meaning would have been clear to Natan's Qaraite correspondent: Qaraites and Rabbanites were returning to an era of harmonious unity; and Natan, like Ibn al-Qazzāz, claimed dominion over all the Jews of Syria and Egypt, Qaraite and Rabbanite. The political vocabulary of rabbinic Palestine was such that a gaonic contender could compare himself to a long-deceased Qaraite official to enhance his own stature.

Several months later, in July 1039, Natan wrote a letter to Abu l-Barakāt's brother, Netan'el ha-Levi ibn Rawḥ, to whom he granted the title *nezer ha-yeshiva* (Diadem of the Academy), a title otherwise unattested in the Geniza.[40] The letter opens with twenty-seven lines of greetings, honorifics, and flowery Hebrew expressions—an excess of praise even by medieval epistolary standards—and the content (far outweighed by the honorifics) consists of Natan's thanks to Netan'el for his support, whether moral or fiscal we do not know. Again, the vision is arresting: a self-styled *ga'on* dispenses titles and rank flattery to a Qaraite because he believes his security in office depends upon it.

THE QAYRAWĀN PLAN

How did Shelomo b. Yehuda respond to Natan's cultivation of the Qaraites? In one of his letters to Efrayim b. Shemarya, he directed a lengthy invective against his rival and complained bitterly of his use of the Qaraites in Cairo. His complaints offer a parodic catalogue of the repertoire of symbols from which a gaonic usurper might have chosen.

First, Shelomo says, Natan "rides around on his donkey all day long," evidently modeling himself after the Muslim *ʿulamāʾ*, for whom riding on donkeys was both a privilege and a symbol of social status.[41] "He goes from gate to gate," he continues, "and beseeches [people], 'Help me, oh help me, and I shall respond to your queries.' " If Natan was going to be a *ga'on*, then he needed to act the part and issue responsa; but, the *ga'on* complained, he makes a mockery of the office by reducing it to a bare calculus of responsa for donations. "He has made a laughing stock of piety."

It was not merely Natan's reduction of the gaonic office to charlatanry that bothered Shelomo b. Yehuda. More gravely, he was aware that Natan knew how to conjure the loyalty of two politically unpredictable kinds of people: the Qaraites and the *ʿayyārūn*, underemployed young men whom the seminomadic

[40] T-S 13 J 31.1. The indexes of the works of Goitein, Gil, and Bareket and a search in the Princeton Geniza Project database revealed similar titles—*nezer ha-nesi'ut*, *nezer ha-sarim*, *nezer ha-ḥakhamim*, and *nezer ha-maskilim* (the latter is attested as a judge's title during the twelfth century; Goitein, *Mediterranean Society*, 2: 513, item 16)—but this is the only instance I have found of *nezer ha-yeshiva*. Netan'el he-Levi b. Rawḥ signed a Qaraite *ketubba* probably from Fustat: ENA 4020.38v.

[41] Not because he was styling himself a messiah: cf. Zechariah 9:9 and Isaiah 21:7.

fringes of Syria and northern Iraq rendered particularly likely to form bands that might metamorphose into roving militias.[42] It may well be that the Jarrāḥid wars of the 1030s saw unusual numbers of these young men at large in Jerusalem and Ramla. We see hints of this in the *ga'on*'s complaint that Natan "has gathered around him the thorns from among the people and turned them into great elders." Here, Shelomo b. Yehuda borrows a bit of rhetoric from the Qaraites, who, as he wrote in 1030, "see themselves as 'lilies' and everyone else as 'thorns'": now that the "thorns" threw their weight behind his rival, he himself became a lily. His rival, meanwhile, repaid the loyalty of the thorns with titles.

Shelomo then complains that Natan has exploited the support of the Qaraites. "Many of those from the other party [*ṭā'ifa*] are helping him secretly," he writes, "but acting as though they are on my side. Woe betide the times that call for such measures!" The *ga'on* refused to stoop to his rival's level, since he relied upon no one but the Almighty in His grace—except, of course, when he relied upon the elders of Qayrawān. And with that, he asks Efrayim b. Shemarya to send some missives he has written to Qayrawān to win over the Qayrawānī Jews and to enlist the support of their communal leader.

How the Qayrawān subplot unfolded is well understood thanks to Cohen. Since reports in the east had it that Natan enjoyed the backing of the elders of Qayrawān, two of Shelomo b. Yehuda's Fustat supporters dispensed twin appeals to the *nagid* of Qayrawān, Yaʿaqov b. ʿAmram.[43] One attempted to sway him and his followers back to their camp. The other asked him to write letters to Fustat, in his name and those of the elders, repudiating their support for the usurper. The letters also set in motion a remarkably indirect chain of requests: the *ga'on*'s followers in Fustat asked the *nagid* to petition the Zirid *amīr* of Qayrawān, al-Muʿizz ibn Bādīs (r. 1016–62), to write a letter to the Fatimid vizier al-Jarjarā'ī in Cairo asking him to have al-Mustanṣir's chancery issue a rescript confirming Shelomo b. Yehuda in office.[44]

[42] Also called *aḥdāth* in the sources. See Cohen, "New Light," 15–16; Claude Cahen, *Mouvements populaires et autonomisme urbain dans l'Asie musulmane du moyen âge* (Leiden, 1959); Lev, "The Fatimids and the Aḥdāth of Damascus, 386/996–411/1021," *Welt des Orients* 13 (1982): 98–106; and Ben-Sasson, "Geniza Evidence on the Events of 1019–1020," the latter with reference to a letter of Sahlān b. Avraham had written two decades earlier, ENA 2727.52. If Hayya's advice to Sahlān refers to an actual conflict between the youth and the established elders of Fustat, and those youth were indeed comporting themselves like *aḥdāth*, then this would contradict Cahen's assertion that the *aḥdāth* were found in Syria and Iraq but not in Egypt. The entire matter requires investigation.

[43] For an account of the Qayrawān subplot, see Cohen, "New Light." Drafts of the letters have been preserved, back to front on the same sheet of paper, but it was cut in half at some point, with one half currently in Cambridge and the other in New York. First letter: ENA 3765.10 verso+T-S 18 J 4.16 recto, in Hebrew, an unknown writer in Fustat to Yaʿaqov b. ʿAmram in Qayrawān. Gil identifies the handwriting as that of Avraham b. David ibn Sughmār. Second letter: ENA 3765.10 recto+T-S 18 J 4.16 verso, from Shemarya b. Maṣliaḥ in Fustat, to Yaʿaqov b. ʿAmram, *nagid* of Qayrawān.

[44] The letter attesting to the scheme, which dates to ca. 1040, thus represents the latest evidence known of friendly relations between the Zirid *amīr*s of Ifrīqiya (972–1148) and their Fatimid benefactors. Cohen, "New Light," 16–17.

It was far from unusual to invoke exogenous political ties to help resolve internal rabbinic disputes. Hayya Ga'on had instructed Sahlān b. Avraham in Fustat to secure Tustarī protection against his detractors. Numerous Palestinian *ge'onim* had invited the state to throw its weight behind them. It was a regular part of Jewish politics under the Fatimids to use the state—and the Qaraites—against one's enemies in times of conflict. One can also understand Shelomo b. Yehuda's efforts to involve the Jews of Qayrawān in what was essentially just a local dispute: communities farther west comprised the network of support that lent the Babylonian gaonate its vitality for two centuries; why should Jerusalem behave differently?

But Shelomo b. Yehuda's resort to the *nagid* of Qayrawān was, from another perspective, perplexing. If the *ga'on* was seeking a caliphal rescript confirming himself in office, why did he not simply go through the regular channels, the Fustat notables and the Qaraite courtiers? David b. Yiṣḥaq and Ḥesed and Abū Saʿd al-Tustarī had all supported him in the past. The indirect route he chose is even more perplexing when one considers that he had been reconfirmed in office only two years before Natan's putsch began. It seems that Shelomo b. Yehuda took pains to avoid seeking Qaraite help, telling Efrayim b. Shemarya that he refused to rely on those in power while asking his supporters to enlist government help up to the highest echelons—but in Ifrīqiya. In another letter, he told Efrayim, "It is not fitting for me to write [petitions] to receive aid on the basis of the power [*serara*] of others—far be it from me."[45] Scruples of this kind had never stopped him before. Why, in the thick of the controversy in 1040, did the *ga'on* avoid a direct Qaraite route to the Fatimid chancery?

The answer is that it was closed to him, for two reasons. First, Natan b. Avraham had monopolized Qaraite patronage; and he was more successful in mobilizing Qaraite support, it seems, because he understood the need to cultivate not only the grandees but others as well. It may also be that the *ga'on* refused to lodge his petition via the Qaraites precisely because Natan had politicked among them so shamelessly. Second, when the *ga'on*'s son publicly excommunicated the Qaraites in 1038, he must have ruined the *ga'on*'s chances of seeking their support. Shelomo b. Yehuda could not ask the Tustarīs for a rescript confirming him in office because by now they had good reason to begrudge him one.

The circuitous route to the chancery was required not only for these reasons. If the *ga'on* suspected that the Qaraites were supporting Natan "secretly," he could only be referring to those who had supported him in the past, including the Tustarīs. Abū Saʿd al-Tustarī was the right-hand man of the regent, Umm al-Mustanṣir; the official whom the *ga'on* now wished to present his peti-

[45] T-S 13 J 23.1, in Hebrew, line 22. I take his reference to "the other faction" (*ha-kat ha-aḥeret*) in line 24 to mean Natan's followers (not the Qaraites).

tion to the caliph (still only a boy of ten) was the armless al-Jarjarā'ī, her archrival and the administration's most forceful check on her power.[46] By aiming for al-Jarjarā'ī, the *ga'on* in effect pitted two factions of the Fatimid court against one another.

The Qayrawān plan, then, was intended to solve the problem of access to the Fatimid court in the absence of Qaraite support. Ben-Sasson has argued that the rival gaonates and the Qayrawān plan are quintessential examples of the power the peripheries held to dictate affairs in the gaonic centers, and this schism was indeed a barometer of the new gaonic politics of the eleventh century, which played themselves out increasingly in Qayrawān, Palermo, Fustat, and Ramla and less in Jerusalem and Baghdad. But it was also a barometer of the degree to which Qaraite support had become instrumental in rabbinic leaders' claims to office—and in the competition of the Palestinian and Babylonian *yeshivot* for the loyalties of the periphery.

The Typology of the Rabbinate according to Ibn Sughmār

The Babylonian *yeshivot* were currently in the process of collapse and would close precisely during the years of the schism. When Hayya b. Sherira died in 1038, his position had been filled by the exilarch, Ḥizqiyyahu b. David; when the *ga'on* of Sura died shortly thereafter, he was not replaced. Just as the *yeshivot* were in crisis, they began to be invoked repeatedly by both sides. This is typical of the *yeshivot*, which achieved the pinnacle of their literary apotheosis only posthumously. It was also typical of particularly bitter political conflicts among medieval Jews to resort to argumentation from history.

In Shelomo b. Yehuda's camp, Gil has noted that the same sheet of paper that contains the two draft letters to the *nagid* of Qayrawān also contains an Aramaic passage in the handwriting of Ibn Sughmār—the same Ibn Sughmār who had been excommunicated and imprisoned for dallying with a Muslim prostitute, and who now opposed Natan's designs on the gaonate.[47] That passage is a section of the epistle of Sherira bar Ḥananya, *ga'on* of Pumbedita, written in Baghdad in 963 and sent to the Jews of Qayrawān to answer their queries about the succession of the Babylonian *ge'onim*. For medieval Jews, appeals to typology—patterns of history deployed with a teleological, even prescriptive, message—were extraordinarily powerful pieces of rhetoric, as Ibn Sughmār must have known. As in Ibn Dāwūd's chronicle, they were particularly useful when used to counter the polemical claims of competing groups by establishing chains of apostolic succession; but the Rabbanite-Qaraite debate had no monopoly on them.

46 Armless: see above, chap. 8, n. 43.

47 ENA 1490.7 verso; see *History of Palestine* (English only), 713 n. 154.

The section of the epistle that Ibn Sughmār copied for the benefit of the *nagid* of Qayrawān and his followers—who must have known the work well—described a gaonic schism at Pumbedita in the 820s, one that was resolved peacefully, says Sherira, when Yosef bar Ḥiyya recused the office and contented himself with the position of *av bet din*, allowing Avraham bar Sherira to reign unchallenged.[48] The message Ibn Sughmār sent to Qayrawān was clear: like Yosef bar Ḥiyya, Natan should step down from the gaonate and be content with his former title; like Avraham bar Sherira, Shelomo b. Yehuda should be allowed to reign as *ga'on* to the end of his days. Three years later when the dispute was resolved, this is what happened.

Natan's side, too, related the schism to an ancient one: that of the exilarchal house at the time of Bustanay in the eighth century. They did this when, at the height of the schism, Dani'el b. ʿAzarya, the scion of the Babylonian exilarchal house (*nasi*) and a descendant of Bustanay, arrived in Palestine. The *nasi* cast his weight behind Shelomo b. Yehuda, and in revenge, Natan's followers in the Iraqi congregation of Fustat—and Sahlān b. Avraham in particular—copied out a long composition that Natan claimed to have received from his teachers in Qayrawān casting aspersions on the exilarchal line from which Dani'el descended. Though the pamphlet besmirched the credentials of the newly arrived *nasi*, it must have been aimed at the *ga'on*, too. And it could not have been accidental that all this happened as the *yeshivot* of Baghdad closed: as Iraqis like Dani'el b. ʿAzarya moved west, it must have become clear to many that the future of the gaonate now lay, at least temporarily, in Palestine.[49]

The Sheep Herd the Shepherd

Understanding the Qaraite role in the gaonic schism of 1038–42 not only illuminates the reasons behind the Qayrawān episode. It also explains a puzzle attending the next subplot in the affair, when the schism finally entered the Fatimid court in Cairo.

In the thick of the controversy, Natan was watching the career of Ḥesed al-Tustarī closely. In 1040, he wrote a letter informing someone in Fustat that Ḥesed had just been named chief administrator to the military commander of Palestine, Anushtekīn al-Duzbarī. It is from Natan that we learn of Ḥesed's appointment. The way he describes it speaks to his eagerness for Qaraite patronage. (All that has been preserved of the letter are the last few lines of the first page and the first few lines of the second.[50])

[48] In Lewin, *Epistle of Rav Sherira Ga'on*, the parallel is with the "French" recension, 110–11.

[49] BL Or. 5552 D+T-S 12.504+ENA 4012+T-S NS 298.6. See Gil, *In the Kingdom of Ishmael*, sec. 47, 48, 122, and idem, *History of Palestine*, sec. 870, 879; Franklin, "Shoots of David," 184–86.

[50] T-S AS 157.232r+T-S AS 157.231r (in that order), in Judeo-Arabic. The fragments preserve continuous passages since Natan flipped the paper over and upside down before continuing to write. Gil

. . . and ensnaring him in the verdict . . . in great peril. And he drafted letters . . . that are enclosed in this letter. [Natan has enclosed letters of support, and asks his correspondent:] May you satisfy [us], O cherished one [*ḥemdat libbenu*, not an official title], by delivering them to him [?] and to Shaykh Abū Naṣr ibn al-Tustarī, may his Rock preserve him. He was appointed a *kātib* of the commander [of the armies, *amīr al-juyūsh*]. And he is our patron [*wa-huwa murāʿī lanā*], heeding what we direct his way [*mumtathil mā nukhāṭibuhu fīhi*]. It behooves you to write a letter to him, O cherished one, may the Merciful One preserve you, congratulating him for what has come to pass, and conveying to him our gratitude, for he has accomplished . . . all that he has found in his path. . . .

The language Natan uses here is telling: what I have translated as "patron" is the word *murāʿī* in Judeo-Arabic, from the verb meaning "to tend," as a shepherd tends a flock (the verb is the same in Hebrew). *Riʿāya*, "patronage," is a near-technical term conveying a formal relationship between patrons and their charges. But, Natan notes, he "heeds what we direct his way," working in our service, not the other way round. Again, something was amiss in Natan's cultivation of his patrons. The other side of the patronage relationship bears noting as well: this letter confirms Shelomo b. Yehuda's suspicion that Ḥesed had taken Natan's side in the conflict.[51]

Natan was quick to convey the news that his camp's powerful Qaraite ally had just been made more powerful. Ḥesed's appointment brought him out of Cairo and into Ramla, the administrative capital of *jund filasṭīn*, al-Duzbarī's base of operations, and Natan's prime locus of support. Natan therefore urged his followers in Fustat to write him letters of congratulation. For the rest of the affair, Natan's camp would benefit from Ḥesed's presence in Ramla. Even Ḥizqiyyahu b. David, exilarch in Baghdad and now *gaʾon* of Pumbedita, wrote to Fustat to congratulate Ḥesed on his appointment: in an undated letter he extends his felicitations to a certain Abū Naṣr, describing him as God's instrument of redemption: "Do not cease praying for the exalted *shaykh* Abū Naṣr, may God make his help eternal, and always mention him in the blessings in your synagogues, because God has 'made him as a covenant of the people, a light of the nations, to open blind eyes, to bring prisoners out of the dungeon, and those that sit in darkness out of the prison-house' [Isa. 42:6–7]."[52]

---

identifies the handwriting as Natan b. Avraham's. See brief discussions in Gil, *Tustaris*, 38–39, and in idem, *History of Palestine*, secs. 780 and 882.

[51] Mottahedeh, *Loyalty and Leadership*, 120–22, emphasizes the passivity of the sheep; here, they are not passive.

[52] T-S Misc. 35.40, in Judeo-Arabic; page 3, lines 5–8. Goitein and Gil identify Abū Naṣr as Ḥesed, Sela as David b. Yiṣhaq; see Sela, "Headship of the Jews in Karaite Hands," n. 19.

The Petitions

We find confirmation of Ḥesed al-Tustarī's defection from Shelomo b. Yehuda's side—and David b. Yiṣḥaq's unsuccessful mediation in the affair—in drafts of a petition that the *ga'on*'s supporters wrote for submission to the chancery in Cairo in the spring or summer of 1040 (see fig. 11).[53]

Given the Qayrawān plan and its circuitous route to the chancery, filing a petition directly must have been a measure of last resort. The *ga'on*'s followers must have feared that all else would fail, though unbeknownst to them, the Qayrawān plan ultimately bore fruit. In turning to the chancery directly, they produced no fewer than eight drafts of their petition, and these reveal a thought process at work as the petitioners grope and search for the correct phrase and the most effective way of presenting their request.

The first seven drafts are written in Judeo-Arabic in an awkward hand. The final draft, however, is in a practiced calligraphic Arabic, a fact that suggests that whoever wrote the drafts was more fluent in the Arabic than the Hebrew alphabet. (The Judeo-Arabic drafts, moreover, are in the same hand that copied Shelomo b. Yehuda's petition invoking the caliph's *niʿma* against Yūsuf al-Sijilmāsī.[54] My attempts to identify the writer—a supporter of Shelomo b. Yehuda, probably in Fustat-Cairo—have not availed.) The final draft reads as follows:

> The slaves of our master, the community of *dhimmī*s, the Rabbanite Jews.
>
> In the name of God, the compassionate, the merciful:
>
> God's prayers and blessings, His increasing benefactions and most excellent salutations to our lord and master the Imām al-Mustanṣir bi-llāh, Commander of the Faithful, and blessings enduring until Judgment Day to his pure ancestors, the rightly guided Imāms.
>
> On account of their having two leaders, a disturbance arose among the slaves of our lord and master, the Imām al-Mustanṣir bi-llāh, Commander of the Faithful, the prayers of God be upon him. Each party [*ṭā'ifa*] attempted to gain the upper hand by putting forward its own leader over that of the other and to obligate the other party [*ṭā'ifa*] to accept him and to enter into what is not permitted to them in their religious convictions [*fī adyānihim*]. They raised the matter before the Glorious Presence, may God make his rule eternal, and made the matter known to him.

[53] T-S Ar. 30.278, in Judeo-Arabic: six drafts of a petition to al-Mustanṣir from the followers of Shelomo b. Yehuda; Bodl. MS Heb. b 18.21, in Judeo-Arabic and Arabic: seventh and eighth drafts of the same petition. (All of Gil's corrections to Stern's edition of the Judeo-Arabic text should be accepted except one: on recto [Stern's verso], line 2, the official in question is not titled *muntakhab al-dawla*, as Gil reads, but either *muwaffaq al-dawla*, as Stern reads, or *muwaththaq al-dawla*. In the Arabic text, all of Stern's readings are preferable to Gil's.) Stern speculates that Natan's followers also issued an appeal to al-Mustanṣir seeking confirmation of their *ga'on*: Stern, "Petition to the Fāṭimid Caliph al-Mustanṣir," 209).

[54] ENA 4020.65 (see fig. 2) as Gil also notes, *History of Palestine*, sec. 779; for his identification of the copyist, see chap. 3, n. 60.

Fig. 11. During an internal Rabbanite dispute, a Qaraite is accused of heresy: eight drafts of a petition to the Fatimid caliph al-Mustanṣir from Shelomo b. Yehuda's party during the gaonic schism of 1038–42. The fourth draft complains that the Qaraite courtier Abū Naṣr Ḥesed al-Tustarī had "used force over" the Rabbanite faction in question, with "government authority and policemen, and expelled them from their synagogue." It then asks the caliph to prevent al-Tustarī from interfering in their affairs "since he does not share their religious practice," that is, since he is a Qaraite. The subsequent drafts omit this clause. Judeo-Arabic and Arabic, 1040. Cambridge University Library, T-S Arabic 30.278 r and v and Bodleian Library, MS Heb. b 18.21 r and v.

Then the exalted order, may God increase its efficacy, went forth to Dāwūd ibn Isḥaq [*sic*] to arrange the affairs of the collectivity [*al-kāffa*]. But Dāwūd ibn Isḥaq did not do anything of the sort, and failed in his obligation toward them. And the affair has become prolonged between the two parties until this time, and their synagogue [in Fustat] has been closed and they remain unsettled in their affairs.

Lately, a faction [*qawm*] from among them went and behaved overbearingly toward the others, opened the synagogue for themselves and for him whose appointment to office they prefer. They overpowered the slaves with policemen[55] and required of them what is not permissible for them according to their religious convictions [*fī adyānihim*] and threatened imprisonment and all kinds of terrible things.

The slaves humbly beseech God, may He be exalted, and the Glorious Presence, may God perpetuate his reign, to issue an exalted order, may it always prevail, for equality between them and to permit them their religious convictions just as others are so permitted, and to be allowed to follow their religious convictions like the others and to avert trouble.

Three things had happened. The Qaraite courtier David b. Yiṣḥaq—until now, absent from the affair—had been asked to mediate the conflict and had failed. The synagogue in Fustat had been closed due to the conflict, it seems in November 1039. Natan's party had enlisted the authorities to reopen it, apparently only for members of their group. The *ga'on*'s party thus asked the caliph to do three things: to have the Fustat synagogue reopened for them too; to protect them from the intimidating behavior of Natan's followers; and to handle the conflict directly rather than through the Qaraite grandees.

The final draft of the petition mentions only David b. Yiṣḥaq's attempt at mediation (to which I will return shortly). But one of the draft copies discloses that a supporter of Natan's father-in-law, Abu l-Mand, who was chief of the shipyard in Cairo and so operated close to the palace complex, had asked Ḥesed al-Tustarī (here called by his Arabic name, Faḍl) to intervene, with disastrous effects for the *ga'on*'s party. The fourth draft reads:

During this past week, Faḍl b. Sahl al-Tustarī took the side of some of them and helped them against the others. He opened the synagogue for them and enabled them to mention their leader [in prayer and announce his name as *ga'on*]. And he used force over the others by means of government authority and policemen, and expelled them from their synagogue, and forced them to change their religious practice [*dīnahum*]. He attributed this to a man known as Abu l-Mand, administrator of the shipyard. The slaves remained scattered and overpowered under the hand of this al-Dustarī [Tustarī], for he intimidated them with his

[55] Arab. *rijjāla*. (Stern and others interpret this to mean Fatimid agents, and subsequent references to local authorities confirm this interpretation.

prestige and his wealth and his awe-inspiring demeanor *(bi-l-jāh wa-l-māl wa-l-hayba aẓīma).* This has prevented the slaves from appearing before the Presence. May it please the Presence to grant the slaves the favor of preventing this al-Dustarī from wronging them and interfering in their affairs //since he does not share their religious practice [*idh laysa huwa min dīnihim*]//.

S. M. Stern, who first published the petition, pointed out that this final remark, "added as an afterthought between the lines in draft 4, is as unfair as it is human. The Rabbanite Jews [had] freely approached the Tustarīs for help and enjoyed their protection, and the *ga'on* Solomon b. Judah himself had occasion to thank them for their intervention on previous occasions. Now that Faḍl al-Tustarī took the part of his adversary, Solomon's supporters suddenly remembered that Faḍl was a Qaraite and had no business interfering in a quarrel among the Rabbanites."[56] The conflict over the gaonate and Ḥesed's support for the usurper now became a set of circumstances provoking an accusation of heresy against someone whose beliefs and behavior might have inspired it earlier or later, only it was political factors that finally brought it about now. Just as the rival gaonate was the reason the Qaraites were excommunicated on the Mount of Olives in 1038, so it was the reason that Ḥesed was now suddenly remembered "not to share religious practices" with the Rabbanites—the only evidence in the entire Geniza of his Qaraism (and the clue that enabled Stern finally to resolve the debate over whether Ḥesed was a Rabbanite or a Qaraite).

But just as the power of the accusers can make the accusation of heresy adhere permanently, so, too, can the power of someone accused of heresy repel it. Ḥesed al-Tustarī's power in government prevented the accusation from amounting to anything: the *ga'on*'s party questioned the wisdom of attacking one of the caliph's courtiers in a petition to the caliph, and in the final draft of the petition, they omitted the paragraph about Ḥesed.

Returning to the final draft of the petition, then, it becomes clearer why David b. Yiṣḥaq's mediation had failed. It is significant that thus far in the conflict we have heard nothing of David, and it may well be that he was trying to stay out of it. Ḥesed was in Ramla, and as local governor, could not avoid being drawn in. David was still in Cairo, and his geographic distance also allowed him to remain neutral as a mediator. But a year later, in 1041, we learn that he had in fact taken Natan's side.

In 1041, David b. Yiṣḥaq was asked to carry forward a second petition to the chancery, this one also involving a closed synagogue, this time probably in Ramla.[57] That petition offers some details of what had happened in the interim:

[56] Stern, "Petition to the Fāṭimid Caliph al-Mustanṣir," 211.

[57] CUL Or. 1080 J 7, in Arabic: draft of a petition to the caliph in the margins of a letter written in the hand of Efrayim b. Shemarya, January, 1041. I have altered Khan's translation slightly.

In the name of God, the merciful, the compassionate.

The slaves report their case to the Noble Presence, may God increase his nobility, as follows.

When their leader [*rayyis*] and their *ḥaverim* had suffered harm for two years the Glorious Presence, may God make his rule eternal, charitably issued a mighty decree, on account of which the harm done to them ceased, until a man called Nāthān ibn Ibrāhīm arrived from the west, claiming the place of the head of our *yeshiva* [*ra's mathībatinā*], which he [Shelomo b. Yehuda] has headed for sixteen years. [The *ga'on*] resisted him and his *ḥaverim* and did not recognize him. Prior to this, he had been recognized and been in office for sixteen years.

Then he went and brought the local authorities [*wulāt al-bilād*] and they opened doors until [the writer then crosses out the last phrase]. One month ago, he came to Egypt and asked for help from our colleagues [*aṣḥābinā*; again the word is crossed out] the Qaraites. He won over one of the family relations [of the Qaraites] who could help him acquire the money to shower honors on the *amīr*. This was because the *amīr* Munjiz al-Dawla ordered their synagogue to be closed months ago, [the place] where they used to worship, read the Torah, and pray for the commander of the faithful, the peace of God be upon him. When they took their case before the Glorious Presence, he assigned their affair to the slave of our lord, Dāwūd ibn Isḥaq, but he was preoccupied with his illness and his travels, and he caused the slaves to fear one another. The situation of the slaves has become desperate and serious.

The slaves request the charity to be done to them of issuing an exalted command to one of the Muslim servants of the government to open their synagogue and permit them to pursue their lives as is their custom and to restrain the hand of those who treat them overbearingly.

David's preoccupation and illness were probably mere excuses the petitioners offered in order to avoid attacking him personally, much as they left Ḥesed's intimidating behavior out of the first petition: they admitted immediately thereafter that "he caused the slaves to fear one another"—probably by taking Natan's side.

Who, then, was the Qaraite this petition mentions, the one whom Natan approached for help and whose relatives helped him "shower honors on" the *amīr* (I assume this means they bribed him)? It could not have been David b. Yiṣḥaq himself, for he is introduced in the next sentence as having been asked to mediate in the conflict. It may have been one of the brothers Berakha or Netan'el ibn Rawḥ of Fustat, to whom Natan so elaborately described his triumphant Purim of 1039. It may have been Abū Sa'd al-Tustarī. Or it may have been his brother closer to home: Ḥesed al-Tustarī, who as chief administrator to the military governor of Palestine was now based in Ramla. And thus Natan b. Avraham, too, found a way of deploying government power against his enemies without directly approaching the chancery in Cairo.

The End of the Affair

After four years of schism, Natan was finally deposed and demoted to *av bet din*, and Shelomo b. Yehuda was reinstated in office. The crisis ended under circumstances that we know about from three documents. The first is a letter that Shelomo b. Yehuda wrote to his supporters in Fustat, presumably at the end of 1042, in which he expresses his gratitude toward the governor of Jerusalem, the elders of the city, the governor of Ramla (possibly Anushtekīn al-Duzbarī), the caliph, the vizier (al-Jarjarā'ī), an otherwise unknown Jewish notable named Mawhūb b. Yefet, and David b. Yiṣḥaq.[58] Which of these individuals was finally responsible for ending the schism in Shelomo's favor is a matter of speculation. One is tempted to imagine that he was well served by al-Jarjarā'ī's rivalry with the Tustarīs, who are noticeably absent from the list.

The second document is a letter that Shelomo b. Yehuda wrote to Efrayim b. Shemarya on November 29, 1042, in which he expresses lofty praise and undying gratitude to Ḥesed al-Tustarī for having seen to it that the synagogue (whether in Fustat or Ramla we do not know) was reopened.[59] Why was Ḥesed suddenly helping the *ga'on*'s party again? It seems that some combination of the Qayrawān scheme and the petitions to the chancery had borne fruit and convinced Ḥesed to reopen the synagogue.

The third document is an agreement drawn up at the rabbinical court in Jerusalem, probably in late 1042 or early 1043, between Shelomo b. Yehuda and Natan b. Avraham whose terms lean in Shelomo's favor, except for one item: the creation of a board of five overseers to regulate the affairs of the *yeshiva*, including the *ga'on* and the *av bet din*, i.e., Natan.[60] Shelomo later complained about this curtailment of his powers, saying, "I have the title but not the power of my office."[61] This is one of those statements that linger in the mind: it points to the constant danger that one's title and one's power could become unlinked. Natan usurped the title of *ga'on*, and through his own efforts won some of its prerogatives. Shelomo held the title by official appointment, but feared (and, in fact, risked) losing its power. It was one of the first signs of a weakened gaonate in Jerusalem, a weakening that would progress

[58] T-S 13 J 15.11, in Hebrew. Gil speculates that the recipient of this letter may have been Avraham ha-Kohen b. Yiṣḥaq ibn Furāt. On the identities of the parties mentioned (lines 11–15), see Stern, "Petition to the Fāṭimid Caliph al-Mustanṣir," 213 n. 2.

[59] T-S NS 321.2, in Hebrew. A second letter may be connected to this: PER H 135, in Hebrew, ca. 1043, draft of a letter from Efrayim b. Shemarya to Shelomo b. Yehuda, in which Efrayim asks Shelomo to write a letter to Ḥesed thanking him for his part in bringing peace (verso, lines 12–16).

[60] Gottheil-Worrell 43, in Judeo-Arabic and Hebrew. (For the date of the document see Goitein, *Mediterranean Society*, 2:200.)

[61] T-S 12.217, in Hebrew, line 21. In part following Mann, Gil dates the letter to 1029, but see Cohen, "New Light," 2 n. 1, following Goitein, *Mediterranean Society*, 2: 14, who demonstrates convincingly that the letter was written later and pertains to the denouement of the schism.

over the course of the next three decades until the Jerusalem academy splintered and moved to Tyre, making way for the emergence of the office of *ra'īs al-yahūd* in Fustat.[62]

As for the Qaraite courtiers, over the course of the 1040s we hear precious little of Ḥesed al-Tustarī's intervention in the affairs of the *yeshiva*, although private individuals continued to send petitions to him. David b. Yiṣḥaq plays a slightly greater role. He would also outlive the Tustarī brothers, who were both assassinated (Abū Sa'd in October 1047 on the orders of his rival, the vizier Yūsuf al-Fallāḥī, whom the caliph's mother then had killed in June 1048; and Abū Naṣr in 1049 or 1050); David died of natural causes in 1055.[63]

Over the course of the 1030s, the Rabbanite leadership turned from cultivating the support of Qaraite grandees alone to cultivating the Qaraite laity as well, as an indirect result of the affair of the ban of 1029–30. They continued to do so for a half-century. This changed the balance of power in the Jewish community, laying the groundwork for the establishment of an administrative office that ruled officially over all the Jews in the Fatimid caliphate, Qaraite and Rabbanite alike. During the late tenth century and early eleventh centuries, putting the Qaraites under the administrative aegis of a Rabbanite leader had been a matter of protracted tension, as attested in Yefet b. 'Eli's complaints and the caliphal edicts until 1030. By the mid-eleventh century, matters were different. They changed because of the increasingly central role the Qaraites played as power brokers among the Rabbanite leadership.

[62] On the arc of decline and the factors that contributed to it, see Cohen, *Jewish Self-Government*, 80–84.

[63] On the brothers' assassination, see Fischel, *Jews in the Economic and Political Life*, 86–87; Gil, *Tustaris*, 41–42, and the medieval sources cited in both places. Only six documents mentioning Ḥesed or David have been preserved that can be dated (even speculatively) to the 1040s. Most are requests from private petitioners (Rabbanite or Qaraite) or communal leaders in Syria. This might be explained by the fact that Ḥesed moved with his appointment in Ramla away from Egypt and thus farther from the Ben Ezra Geniza; the requests to him from this period are Syrian, not Egyptian. In some, it impossible to determine whether the Abū Naṣr referred to is Ḥesed or David. They are: T-S 10 J 27.7; T-S 13 J 18.1+T-S 10 J 12.25; T-S 12.222 (ca. 1050), in Hebrew, letter from Hillel b. Yeshu'a of Tiberias, requesting David's aid for the leper colony there; T-S K 6.189 (undated), in Judeo-Arabic, letter from Yehuda b. Yosef b. Ḥānī al-Andalusī to Ḥesed; T-S 8.106 (undated), in Judeo-Arabic, letter from a Damascene Qaraite to a Qaraite leader in Fustat accompanying a petition to Ḥesed al-Tustarī (Goitein dates the document to ca. 1000, likely too early; Gil's speculative dating of 1040 is more likely correct given that Ḥesed was appointed to Ramla around that time, and the letter came from Damascus); and Bodl. MS Heb. d 65.40, a dirge on the death of both brothers, on which see Mann, *Jews in Egypt and in Palestine*, 1:82 and Gil, *In the Kingdom of Ishmael*, sec. 371.

CHAPTER TWELVE
THE TRIPARTITE COMMUNITY AND THE FIRST CRUSADE

In the midst of the gaonic schism, during the summer of 1039, the attention of both factions had been briefly diverted by the arrival from al-Mahdiyya of Daniʾel b. ʿAzarya, a scion of the Davidic house (*nasi*) from Baghdad. It was like Davidic dynasts to wander from place to place: the symbolism they wielded drew on making dramatic entrances and being received as harbingers of redemption.[1] Daniʾel b. ʿAzarya was one of a new generation of Iraqi Rabbanite leaders who transplanted themselves onto Egyptian and Syrian soil in the mid-eleventh century and began to play a central role in the affairs of the *yeshiva*. For them, inviting Qaraite participation in Rabbanite communal affairs was a natural and normal part of Jewish political life.

Daniʾel b. ʿAzarya was born in Baghdad to the line of David b. Zakkay, an exilarch in Baghdad in the 930s with whom Seʿadya had come into characteristically dramatic conflict.[2] Daniʾel b. ʿAzarya migrated west to Fustat in the 1030s and remained in Egypt for about seven years, having decided, like other *nesiʾim* of the period, to throw his lot in with the west rather than returning to Baghdad. This proved to be a perspicacious decision. During Daniʾel's stay in Egypt, both of the *yeshivot* in Baghdad foundered. His brother-in-law ʿAzarya ha-Kohen, the grandson of Shemuʾel b. Ḥofni, briefly headed Sura (1034–37; the common name is coincidental and the only relation the two bore was that ʿAzarya had married Daniʾel's sister); then a certain Yiṣḥaq ha-Kohen headed the *yeshiva* for another two years at most, after which Sura was left without a

[1] Franklin, "Shoots of David," especially 54–98, and idem, "Cultivating Roots." On Daniʾel b. ʿAzarya, see Goitein, "New Sources on Daniʾel b. ʿAzarya"; Fleischer, "Qavim ḥadashim li-dmuto shel rav Daniʾel ben ʿAzarya, nasiʾve-gaʾon," *Shalem* 1 (1974): 53–74 (on the encomium BL Or. 5557 K 8); Gil, *History of Palestine*, secs. 885–96; and Franklin, "Shoots of David," 181–86.

[2] The conflict between Seʿadya and David b. Zakkai is reported in Natan ha-Bavli's composition about the *yeshivot* and the exilarchate in Baghdad in the tenth century (see above, chap. 1, n. 2, and chap. 3, n. 3); see Brody, *Geonim of Babylonia*, 26–30 and Ellis Rivkin, "The Saadia–David Ben Zakkai Conflict: A Structural Analysis," in *Studies and Essays in Honor of Abraham A. Neuman, President, Dropsie College for Hebrew and Cognate Learning, Philadelphia*, ed. Bernard D. Weinryb, Meir Ben-Horin, and Solomon Zeitlin (Philadelphia, 1962), 388–423.

ga'on. In 1038, Hayya died and Pumbedita appointed as its *ga'on* the exilarch Ḥizqiyyahu b. David (a distant cousin of Dani'el's) in the absence of other suitable candidates. Ḥizqiyyahu himself died in 1040, the year that Jewish historiography marks as the end of the "gaonic period," though the office was revived in the twelfth century (perhaps even the late eleventh) and persisted until after the Mongol conquests in the thirteenth.[3]

Dani'el's move west, then, coincided with the beginning of the apotheosis of Baghdad in the medieval Jewish imagination—its transformation from a sacred center in actual space into a piece of rhetoric in the service of rabbinic authority. Baghdad's centrality in all subsequent discourse surrounding rabbinic political legitimacy depended in part upon its inaccessibility: the collapse of its *yeshivot* and the continuing migration westward of its rabbinic class. One effect of the disappearance of the Babylonian center and the rupture of the tradition it represented was that Babylonian *nesi'im* outside Iraq made claims, in increasing proliferation, to Davidic genealogy, claims that bore both political overtones (invoking ancient Israelite kingship) and messianic ones (see, e.g., Isa. 9:7, 11:1; Jer. 23:5).

The eastern Mediterranean, by contrast, was still vital, if not stable. In the 1050s, Ifrīqiya was invaded by Hilālīs from Egypt and in 1061, the Normans embarked on their thirty-year conquest of Sicily, interrupting the triangular trade with Egypt. Though the central Mediterranean was in chaos, in the east a new influx of Maghribīs from one side and Iraqis from the other added to Fustat's importance as an arena for rabbinic conflicts. All this set the stage for a total reorganization of Jewish communal life, one in which Dani'el b. ʿAzarya and his son David b. Dani'el were chief actors. They were concrete manifestations of the final stages of the process that had begun in the late ninth and early tenth centuries: the Iraqi center's penetration of the Mediterranean basin.

ENTER THE NESI'IM

The local community greeted Dani'el b. ʿAzarya's arrival in Fustat with the excitement worthy of his Davidic ancestry. We hear of this in one of the letters Shelomo b. Yehuda's supporters wrote to the *nagid* of Qayrawān during the conflict of 1038–42: just as Dani'el supported the *ga'on*, the *ga'on*'s faction had an interest in Dani'el's ability to capture the attention of the masses. "Out of God's great goodness and compassion upon us in these times," says the letter,

[3] Gil, *History of Palestine*, sec. 886; Brody, *Ge'onim of Babylonia*, 345; Gil, *In the Kingdom of Ishmael*, sec. 222. On the gaonic revival of twelfth-century Baghdad, see ibid., secs. 261–68, and above, chap. 1, 12, and chap. 3, n. 2.

"He has brought us a son of King David . . . who has raised up the banner of our teachers [and] interpreted what we have forgotten."[4]

Dani'el b. ʿAzarya's seven years in Fustat elapsed in much the same way as Natan b. Avraham's stay there: in trading on a small scale, building political connections, and harboring larger designs. Dani'el's correspondence mentions shipments of silk, olive oil, wood, and indigo; he seems to have shuttled between Fustat and Tyre, along a route intensively plied by Rabbanite and Qaraite traders.[5]

In Fustat, Dani'el joined his nephew Abū Saʿd Yoshiyyahu b. ʿAzarya, the child of his sister and the penultimate *ga'on* of Sura, ʿAzarya ha-Kohen b. Yisra'el b. Shemu'el b. Ḥofni. Yoshiyyahu, too, was part of the generation of Iraqis who filled the Mediterranean communities with a palpable sense of continuity with the gaonate of Baghdad now in eclipse. He had also left Baghdad in the 1030s, but unlike his uncle he headed northwest, describing an arc along the Euphrates; after an unusually difficult series of travails in Aleppo and al-Maʿarra (where the famous Arabic poet Abu l-ʿAlā' was "doubly imprisoned," *rahnu l-maḥbisayn*, by seclusion and blindness), Yoshiyyahu arrived in Tripoli and set sail for Egypt.[6] But while Yoshiyyahu stayed in Fustat (where he would emerge much later as a kingmaker in Jewish politics), Dani'el b. ʿAzarya had designs on Jerusalem. He did not stay long in Fustat, but moved west to al-Mahdiyya and then east again to Palestine, and in 1051 set his sights on the Jerusalem gaonate. Baghdad's gaonate was closed, and he may have sensed that Jerusalem's would succeed it.

THE CONFLICT OVER THE GAONATE IN 1051

Shelomo b. Yehuda died in 1051, already in his eighties and having served as *ga'on* for more than a quarter century, in spite of all attempts on his office and jurisdiction. According to the agreement of 1042, Natan b. Avraham was *av bet din* and next in line for succession. But Shelomo b. Yehuda had outfoxed his rival by means of longevity, surviving him by six years. When he died, the *av bet din* was Yosef ha-Kohen b. Shelomo, son of Shelomo b. Yehuda's predecessor Shelomo ha-Kohen b. Yehosef, who had served as *ga'on* for six months in 1025.[7]

[4] ENA 3765.10 verso, lines 15–19 (see the entire passage, 14–29). Cohen, "New Light," 24 (English translation).

[5] Gil, *History of Palestine*, sec. 887; on trade between the two cities, see chap. 10, 269–70.

[6] Ibid., sec. 887. For Abu l-ʿAlā''s biography—despite the poet's seclusion, full of intriguing connections with Fatimid politics, as the two poems quoted above (chap. 4, 130, and chap. 9, 253) suggest—see *EI*², s.v. "al- Maʿarrī, Abu l-ʿAlā' Aḥmad b. ʿAbd Allāh b. Sulaymān" (P. Smoor), with full references to medieval and modern sources.

[7] Gil, *History of Palestine*, sec. 886 (Gil dates Natan's death to 1045).

Dani'el b. ʿAzarya now stepped to the fore and began to fight Yosef ha-Kohen for the gaonate. The question was whether a Babylonian newcomer could win enough support to wrest the Palestinian gaonate from its rightful heir. Shelomo b. Yehuda had been a Maghribī and helped broaden the Jerusalem gaonate beyond its entrenched Palestinian families; he had brought Egypt under his rule and kept it, and both he and his rival Natan b. Avraham had mobilized Qaraite support at critical junctures. Dani'el b. ʿAzarya used all these tactics and also enlisted the genealogical claims of the Iraqi exilarchate as a new and potent factor in Jewish politics.

This was not how spectators to the conflict interpreted matters. Instead, both sides did what medieval Jews usually did in such situations: they rummaged through the stockpiles of tradition to arm themselves with typological weaponry. The battle of gaonic succession quickly assumed the character of an age-old war between Davidic kingship (in the person of Dani'el) and priestly lineage (Yosef ha-Kohen). The battle between kingship and priesthood lasted for nearly a year and a half, from April, 1051, until September, 1052, at the end of which Dani'el emerged victorious. It was exceedingly rare that a rabbinic leader united in a single person the titles of *nasi* and *ga'on*, and it had happened only three times in recorded history: with Mar Zuṭra, a Babylonian exilarch who had migrated to Palestine and assumed the leadership of the academy in Tiberias in the sixth century; and the brothers Yehoshafaṭ and Ṣemaḥ b. Yoshiyyahu, the Ananite *nesi'im* who had held the gaonate of Tiberias (862–93).[8] Dani'el served as *ga'on* of Jerusalem until his death in 1062.

Daniel b. ʿAzarya as Usurper

Dani'el's election to the gaonate left smoldering resentments and a permanent feud between houses. More than thirty years later, in 1094, Yosef ha-Kohen's nephew Evyatar ha-Kohen b. Eliyyahu would attack Dani'el b. ʿAzarya's rise to office by claiming, among other things, that he had secured the gaonate with the help of the Qaraites and the Fatimid court. Evyatar did so as part of a lengthy poetic character assassination against Daniel's son, David b. Dani'el. Evyatar composed it in the form of a scroll announcing his deliverance from evil, after his reinstatement as *ga'on* of the Jerusalem academy-in-exile in Tyre and Damascus (he served two terms, 1083–93, 1094–1112).[9]

[8] Ibid., secs. 729, 885; above, chaps. 1, 33–34, and 2, 55, 60. On Daniel's own theories about the superiority of the Davidic over the priestly line, see ENA 3765.5, his letter to one of the Maghribīs, December, 1051.

[9] T-S 10 K 7.1 and T-S 12.729 (*Megillat Evyatar*), in Hebrew. The first fragment is a copy of the whole Megilla; Gil surmises that the copyist was Yehuda Halevi. See "The Scroll of Evyatar as a Source for the History of the Struggles of the Yeshiva of Jerusalem during the Second Half of the Eleventh Century—A New Reading of the Scroll," Hebrew, in *Jerusalem in the Middle Ages: Selected Papers*, ed. B. Z. Kedar (Jerusalem, 1979), 39–40; idem, *History of Palestine*, 3:391, and Cohen's rebuttal,

"In the days of the two *ge'onim*, Yosef ha-Kohen and Eliyyahu ha-Kohen," Evyatar wrote of the rivalry of 1051–52, referring to the sons of Shelomo ha-Kohen b. Yehosef—his uncle and father—as rightful heirs of their father's gaonic chair, "Dani'el b. ʿAzarya arose against them from Iraq and received support from the Party of the Calamity [*kat ha-ṣelaʿ*], and others along with them, and the hand of the government (*reshut*). And great evils came to pass, and tribulations were set over them." The Party of the Calamity referred to the Qaraites (via a pun on the Jerusalem neighborhood, Ṣelaʿ ha-elef, in which they had settled in the tenth century); the reference to "others along with them" suggests that Rabbanites, too, had supported Dani'el b. ʿAzarya's ascent to the gaonate.[10] Were Evyatar's accusations correct—had Dani'el b. ʿAzarya won his position through a combination of Qaraite, Rabbanite, and Fatimid help?

We look in vain for documentary evidence of connections between Dani'el and the Qaraite grandees of Fustat. In the small part of Daniel's otherwise voluminous correspondence that dates to the period before he acceded to office, he mentions only one Qaraite: the representative of the merchants (*wakīl al-tujjār*) in the Egyptian port of Tinnīs, Abu l-Ḥasan Jābir b. Azhar, to whom he sent some funds in anticipation of a shipment of merchandise during his stay in Fustat in the 1040s.[11] But that contact was in the usual course of business, and can hardly compare with the veritable campaign that Natan b. Avraham had waged among the Qaraite nobility in Fustat in the 1030s. It is possible that Dani'el fostered connections with Qaraite courtiers—David ha-Levi b. Yiṣḥaq (who died in 1055) would have been a likely candidate—and used them to seek a rescript of appointment from the Fatimid chancery. But the documentary sources are unyielding on the question.

Evyatar's accusations against Dani'el yield more information about the 1090s, when they were leveled. For the real battle Evyatar was fighting was not against the long-deceased Dani'el b. ʿAzarya but against his son, David b. Dani'el, whom Evyatar regarded as an evil usurper who had achieved the office

Jewish Self-Government, 178–79 n. 1. The second copy is later and incompletely preserved. See further Mann, *Jews in Egypt and in Palestine*, 1:178, 274–75; Cohen, *Jewish Self-Government*, 189; and Gil, *History of Palestine*, secs. 889–91.

[10] On Qaraites and the neighborhood identified with the biblical Ṣelaʿ ha-elef, see Mann, *Jews in Egypt and in Palestine*, 1:274–75.

[11] T-S 13 J 26.2, in Judeo-Arabic. The letter is cut, torn, or folded at the top and so begins *in medias res*; Abu l-Ḥasan Jābir b. Azhar is mentioned in the first full line of what remains. The latter's marriage contract has also been preserved in fragmentary form in the Geniza, possible further evidence of the connections he maintained with the Rabbanites of the Palestinian *yeshiva*; T-S AS 145.307 recto +T-S Misc. 29.58a recto. His bride was Ḥusn b. Ḥayyim, the granddaughter of Sahlawayh b. Ḥayyim, the banker of Fustat, who was still alive when the marriage was contracted in the 1030s or 1040s.

of *raʾīs al-yahūd* with Qaraite help.[12] He launched his polemic against the Qaraites in the context of a political struggle—here as elsewhere, religious ideology was called upon in the service of political opportunism.

DAVID B. DANIʾEL'S BID FOR OFFICE

When Daniʾel b. ʿAzarya died in 1062, the gaonate reverted peacefully to the brother of the candidate he had ousted, Eliyyahu ha-Kohen b. Shelomo b. Yehosef (Yosef ha-Kohen's brother and Evyatar's father), thereby remaining within the group of old families from whom the Jerusalem *geʾonim* had traditionally been chosen. The Palestinian gaonate was still in Jerusalem. But during Eliyyahu's tenure in office (1062–83), the Jewish leadership in the eastern Mediterranean split into two centers, Tyre and Fustat. The cities had been closely linked for decades by trade, kinship, and rabbinic administrative connections, but now they pulled asunder, due in part to Eliyyahu's weakness as *gaʾon*. During the first two years of Eliyyahu's reign (1062–64), he awarded the title of *nagid* to the Rabbanite physician and Fatimid courtier Yehuda b. Seʿadya, partly in a bid to shore up his own waning support in Fustat.[13] The tactic backfired: eventually the Rabbanite patricians of Fustat would use the legitimacy that Eliyyahu had granted them to supplant Eliyyahu's own rule over Egypt. But a decade of crisis and anarchy in Egypt prevented Yehuda b. Seʿadya from exercising his power independently from the gaonic center in Jerusalem, and this afforded Eliyyahu and the gaonic office some temporary stability.

Meanwhile, the Egyptian and Syrian spheres of the Fatimid empire pulled asunder for their own reasons. The 1060s were an era of administrative and economic chaos dubbed by the medieval chronicles "the [years of] calamity during al-Mustanṣir's reign" (*al-shidda al-mustanṣiriyya*).[14] Nilometer readings were perilously low, crops were paltry, people starved, plagues struck. The Turcomans pushed westward into Iraq and Syria, taking over parts of the Abbasid and Fatimid realms and filling them with a network of their own Seljuk *amīr*s. The Seljuks soon began strengthening their hold on Syria. The Fatimid vizier Badr al-Jamālī fought to keep Damascus (1060–68), but in 1069, a bout of fighting between the eastern and Maghribī factions of the Fatimid army turned into such a severe conflagration that the Umayyad mosque of Damascus burned down.[15] The Seljuk Atsīz finally occupied Damascus in 1076 and entered Cairo itself in 1077. The Fatimid realm was in peril.

[12] On David b. Daniʾel, see Cohen, *Jewish Self-Government*, 178–212, and Franklin, "Shoots of David," 186–95.

[13] Cohen, *Jewish Self-Government*, 162.

[14] See Lev, *State and Society*, 43–46; Walker, *Exploring an Islamic Empire*, 62–64.

[15] Ibid., 65; *EI*², s.v. "Fāṭimids" (Marius Canard).

Meanwhile, Atsīz besieged Jerusalem from the summer of 1073 until 1077, and then held it for more than twenty years.[16] When the siege broke, in response to a rebellion Atsīz began killing the city's inhabitants. The *yeshiva* decamped to Tyre, never to return to Jerusalem.[17] The arrangement was temporary—after less than two decades, the *yeshiva* pulled up its stakes again and abandoned Tyre for Damascus—but the shift northward further severed the gaonate from its Egyptian base of support. Between Tyre and Fustat there now lay a chasm that would grow only vaster as the century waned.

As early as 1070, Tyre had begun attracting scholars from all over a Syria threatened by Fatimid-Seljuk warfare, and the city became something of a refuge for religious groups seeking shelter from the chaos—or taking advantage of the opportunity to put some geographic distance between themselves and the Fatimid court. In 1070, a local Sunnī *qāḍī*, ʿAbdallāh b. ʿAlī b. Abī ʿAqīl, began paying tribute to the advancing Turcoman princes of Iraq and Syria, thus transforming Tyre into an independent city-state to which Jewish and Muslim scholars alike were drawn. The city's independence from the Fatimid imperial reach northward and the Seljuk encroachments from the east in turn attracted the chief Shāfiʿī scholar of Syria, Abu l-Fatḥ Naṣr b. Ibrāhīm al-Maqdisī al-Nābulusī (d. 1096), who fled Jerusalem after the siege of 1073–77.[18] Gil's suggestion that *yeshiva* officials traded with Ibn Abī ʿAqīl would partly explain the decision to move to Tyre; the heavily inked arc of contacts between the Jewish elite (Rabbanite and Qaraite) in Tyre and Fustat perhaps accounts for it as well: Fustat was too close to the vortex of Fatimid calamity, and Tyre was the next best thing to Fustat.[19]

As much as Tyre had seemed a logical place for the *yeshiva* to go after Jerusalem, it did not stay there long. Neither did the Sunnī *qāḍī* Abu l-Fatḥ, who held on to his semi-independent principality only until 1089, when a rebellious Fatimid general (known only by his military titles *munīr al-dawla al-juyūshī* and *naṣīr al-dawla al-juyūshī*) staged a general revolt against Fatimid rule in the

[16] The date usually offered for the Seljuk conquest of Jerusalem is 1071, but on the basis of Geniza sources Gil argues that Jerusalem did not fall to the Seljuks until roughly two years after the battle of Manzikert, that is, in the summer of 1073. See Gil, *History of Palestine*, secs. 603–4, citing T-S Misc. 36.174; idem, "Scroll of Evyatar," 43; and Prawer, *History of the Jews in the Latin Kingdom*, 8 n. 17.

[17] Ibid., 8–9. The precise year the *yeshiva* arrived in Tyre is not known, but it was up and running by 1079 at the latest. Circumstantial evidence points to 1077 as the year it left Jerusalem.

[18] Goitein, *Mediterranean Society* 2:201 and 562 n. 14. Both Ibn Abī ʿAqīl and al-Nābulusī later moved to Damascus (Gil cites the latter's Damascene death in his timeline: *History of Palestine* [English], p. 861). See also Cohen, *Jewish Self-Government*, 81–84; Gil, "Scroll of Evyatar," cited ibid., 82 n. 6; on the Jewish leadership's assessment of the turmoil in Tyre, see ibid., 111 n. 54; and for an account of the generalized chaos in the period of Seljuk and Crusader invasions, including the rise of various chiliastic movements, Prawer, *Jews in the Latin Kingdom*, 6–18.

[19] Gil, "Scroll of Evyatar," 45–46, 72, adduces other possible reasons for the *yeshiva*'s decision. See also Cohen, *Jewish Self-Government*, 82–83, who asks why the *ga'on*, "chartered by the Fatimid government upon his accession," would move to "a city that had renounced Fatimid suzerainty" rather than to Cairo.

coastal cities of Palestine, from Jubayl in the north to Acre farther south, including Beirut, Sidon, and Tyre in between. In July of that same year, the Fatimids quashed the rebellion, but then Tyre's governor, al-Katīla, also attempted to throw off Fatimid rule and held Tyre until autumn 1097. The *yeshiva* escaped the chaos for Damascus some time before 1093.[20]

While all these leaders had come to Tyre to establish their circles beyond the reach of the Fatimid court, moving away from the court proved disastrous for Eliyyahu and the Palestinian *yeshiva.* When Eliyyahu left Jerusalem, he may have anticipated a greater degree of political independence in Tyre—not from the Fatimids, upon whom the *yeshiva* continued to depend for edicts and decrees, but from his fellow Rabbanites, since Fustat was home to the energetic faction of leaders one of whom Eliyyahu himself had named *nagid.* But by avoiding the faction in Fustat and moving north, Eliyyahu created the conditions for his own irrelevance.

And thus with Eliyyahu Ga'on far removed in Tyre, the faction in Fustat made its move. Some time before 1079, the younger brother of the *nagid* Yehuda b. Seʿadya, Abu l-Faḍl Mevorakh b. Seʿadya, chief judge of the Jewish community of Fustat, declared himself head of the Jews in the Fatimid empire, *ra'īs al-yahūd.* A year later, he began appointing judges further afield in Egypt, arrogating the *ga'on*'s powers. By 1080, there were effectively two heads of Fatimid Jewry: Mevorakh b. Seʿadya, *ra'īs al-yahūd* in Fustat, and Eliyyahu ha-Kohen, *ga'on* of the *yeshiva*-in-exile in Tyre.[21] The bifurcation of the Jewish leadership precisely paralleled the splintering Fatimid empire, beset by Turcomans in Egypt and Seljuks in Syria and soon to be halved by the Franks. The Fatimids now held only the thinnest coastal strip—Ascalon, Beirut, Tyre, Sidon, and Acre—and would eventually see most of those cities transformed into Crusader principalities. The Jews shifted both north and south, unaware that their future lay not in Tyre or Damascus but in Egypt alone.

It was now, around 1080, that Dani'el b. ʿAzarya's son David entered the stage in Fustat and made his bid for power, successfully wresting the headship of the Jews from Mevorakh b. Seʿadya. He also attempted to oust the newly anointed Evyatar from the gaonate in Tyre, at least according to Evyatar himself. If this is so, David's campaign would have marked an attempt to reunite Fatimid Jewry under a single chief, an attempt for which he can hardly be blamed, though this was not how Evyatar viewed the matter. Indeed, Evyatar corroborates that the upstart aimed to continue his father's dual role as *nasi* and *ga'on*, while adding to both titles that of *ra'īs al-yahūd.*

There is a certain disjunction between Evyatar's polemical description of events in his scroll and what the documentary sources convey. Evyatar's

20 A business letter reports that in 1094, there were only three Qaraites still left in Tyre (ENA 1822 A 44–45).

21 Cohen, *Jewish Self-Government*, 157–77.

narrative casts the events in truly typological fashion, pitting the aptly named David, representative of kingship, against Evyatar ha-Kohen's own priestly line of Aaron. He paints father and son perfectly symmetrically: just as David now aimed to wrest the gaonic chair from Evyatar, thirty years earlier in 1051, David's father Daniʾel had done the same to Evyatar's uncle Yosef ha-Kohen.

In Evyatar's account, David b. Daniʾel embarked on a premeditated campaign for control over all of Fatimid Jewry. In Fustat, he ousted Mevorakh b. Seʿadya as *raʾīs al-yahūd*, forcing him into exile in Alexandria. He brought Egypt under his rule by taxing its Jews and then began working his way northward up the coast, bringing Ascalon, Caesarea, and Haifa under his control as well. Then in 1093, Evyatar tells us, he drove both Evyatar and the *av bet din* of Tyre into exile from their *yeshiva*-in-exile, and proceeded to rule as *raʾīs al-yahūd* until 1094, when Mevorakh b. Seʿadya was restored in Fustat and Evyatar in Tyre. In that year, Evyatar declared a feast to celebrate his liberation from the evil oppressors—a Second Purim—and publicized the miracle of his deliverance from David b. Daniʾel by composing his scroll, modeled on the biblical book of Esther, to be read aloud in all the synagogues under his jurisdiction.[22] For a remarkably long stretch of years, from the late tenth century until the sixteenth, Jews instituted Second Purims to celebrate their deliverance from more recent and local catastrophes than Esther and Mordecai's salvation of the Jews from Ahasueros and Haman of Persia. In the classically medieval manner of mapping biblical history onto the lived present and the recent past, Evyatar's scroll announced itself as "a publicization of the miracle" (*pirsumey nisa*), the talmudic phrase associated with the injunction to celebrate the original festival of Purim.[23]

Evyatar probably did not invent his scroll from whole cloth, as Cohen points out. Those who heard the story read aloud in synagogue would not have stood for outright fabrication, at least if the narrative was to serve its intended purpose of celebrating his reinstatement as *gaʾon*. But the Geniza documents paint a more nuanced picture of David b. Daniʾel's rise to power.

From *Nasi to Rosh Gola*

In fact David pursued his aspirations to high office in a more gradual fashion. Between 1082 and 1089, documents call him merely *nasi*, or "Davidic dynast," which is after all what he was. Only beginning in 1085 was he called *rayyis*, leader—not yet *raʾīs al-yahūd*—although he seems to have exercised Mevorakh's prerogatives already and had indeed usurped his office. Then in

22 T-S 10 K 7.1, in Hebrew. For analyses of the scroll's agenda and rhetoric, see Gil, "Scroll of Evyatar," and Cohen, *Jewish Self-Government*, 180–85.

23 On Second Purims, see the discussions cited above, chap. 8, n. 1. Unlike the Purims studied in Yerushalmi, *Zakhor*, Evyatar's does not seem to have been celebrated annually.

1090 or 1091, David appears with the title *rosh ha-gola*, head of the diaspora or exilarch—a title that was meant to convey the status and privileges of the *ra'īs al-yahūd*. That a leader from the venerable line of exilarchs in Iraq was now the Egyptian *rosh ha-gola* stood as yet another symbol of how the Iraqi center had transplanted itself onto Egyptian soil, but it was a transformation that had come about over the course of decades.[24]

Evyatar also claims that he was forced to quit the *yeshiva* early in his reign, when David b. Dani'el made it known in Tyre that he had been proclaimed *rosh ha-gola* and demanded that Tyre submit to his authority. In fact, Evyatar went into exile as late as 1093, ten years after assuming office—a detail he leaves deliberately fuzzy in his scroll in order to amplify the injury David inflicted on him and provoke even deeper outrage in his listeners. And why, in fact, was Evyatar forced to quit the *yeshiva*? Because it had escaped the chaos attendant on al-Katīla's revolt (1089–97) and took a year to reconstitute itself in Damascus and open for business. David b. Dani'el was the villain in the scroll meant to celebrate Evyatar's reinauguration as *ga'on*—and the reopening of the *yeshiva*—in Damascus in 1094, but pace Evyatar, he was probably innocent of designs on the gaonate. That was not because he revered the *yeshiva* and wished to preserve its regular succession of *ge'onim*. On the contrary: in his letters, David b. Dani'el disparaged it as an irrelevant institution, even though his father had served at its head.[25]

There is, however, one detail of David's biography on which Evyatar and the Geniza documents agree: his marriage, for political purposes, to the daughter of a Fustat grandee.

David b. Dani'el's Marriage

When Dani'el b. 'Azarya died in 1062, his son was only four years old. David b. Dani'el, his mother, and his elder brother Shemu'el left Jerusalem before or after the Seljuk siege of 1073. Significantly for David's formation, they went to Damascus rather than accompanying the rabbinic leadership to Tyre, and Shemu'el became a leader of a congregation there. According to Evyatar, David left Damascus for Egypt in about 1078, when he was twenty years old.[26]

[24] Cohen, *Jewish Self-Government*, 190–96. I depart from Cohen here on the meaning of the title *rayyis*: he argues that here it "must stand for the title head of the Jews" (196), but cf. ibid., 166–68. As he points out, the only evidence that David held this office as early as 1082 is Megillat Evyatar's assertion that he forced Mevorakh to flee Fustat; there is nothing to suggest that he had received a confirmation in office from the Fatimid chancery.

[25] Gil, *History of Palestine*, sec. 908.

[26] On the question of when David left Syria and arrived in Egypt, see Cohen, *Jewish Self-Government*, 186 n. 18, and compare Gil, *History of Palestine*, sec. 902. On his biography and career, see ibid., secs. 903–15.

His first stop was Damīra on the eastern side of the Nile Delta, where there was a community of Damascene Jews. A notable from among them took David in as one of his own, providing him with a tutor and his daughter's hand in marriage. After two years, his father-in-law sent him off from Damīra to Fustat in exilarchal style, with a chariot and runners, expecting that like other *nesi'im*, he would be greeted as a harbinger of redemption.[27] Among those who acknowledged David's royal claims in Fustat were the *ra'īs al-yahūd* Mevorakh b. Seʿadya and his own first cousin, the now aging Yoshiyyahu b. ʿAzarya. The two men cannot but have felt some duty to attend to David out of loyalty to his deceased father.

Then, Evyatar tells us, David turned on his patrons. He divorced the daughter of the Damascene notable, broke his ties with his other patrons in Damīra, and conspired to have Mevorakh ousted as head of the Jews. To add insult to injury, he married the daughter of a Fustat grandee (otherwise unidentified) and proceeded to work his way up the Mediterranean coast, bringing city after city under his iron-fisted rule, until finally he reached the *yeshiva* in Tyre.[28] Thus far Evyatar, whose chronology would have David's arrival in Fustat in 1081 and his marriage in 1082.

On this detail, the documentary evidence shows that Evyatar was not so far from the truth, though on every other detail, he exaggerated for polemical purposes: David's marriage contract has survived in the Geniza, and it is dated 23 Shevat 1393 Sel. (January 25, 1082). The young woman David married was a certain Nāshiya, daughter of a Qaraite *kātib* named Moshe ha-Kohen b. Aharon.[29]

It would be all too easy to accept the polemical message of Megillat Evyatar and understand David b. Dani'el as a shrewd, ambitious, and scheming young man who dropped his Rabbanite wife in order to contract a more strategic marriage to a Qaraite—to interpret his marriage in the same vein as Natan b. Avraham's alliances with Qaraite grandees in the 1030s. But the marriage took place entirely with the approbation of David's Damascene benefactors in Damīra—including his erstwhile father-in-law. The nobles of Damīra collected 120 dinars on David's behalf so that he could send his first wife money along with her divorce papers, as Evyatar himself notes; and it was Yoshiyyahu

[27] Megillat Evyatar, pp. 2–3. On Damīra (Damiga in the manuscript), see Cohen, *Jewish Self-Government*, 181 n. 4; on the symbolism of the chariot and runners in exilarchal investitures, see ibid., 187 n. 21.

[28] Megillat Evyatar, p. 3 (marriage to the grandee's daughter: line 9).

[29] The bride's name was Nāshiya (in literary Arabic, Nāshi'a, but the *hamza* is colloquialized), not Nāsia, as Schechter had it (and following him Olszowy-Schlanger, *Karaite Marriage Documents*, 373). The name means "young woman," an assurance against infant mortality (an explanation I owe to Ramzi Rouighi). The name is also attested in the divorce document T-S 8 J 12.2, dated 3 Ḥeshvan 1488 Seleucid (September 28, 1177), Fustat (Goitein mistakenly has the bride's name as Geveret ʿAlamot, the Hebrew translation of Sitt al-Banāt; *Mediterranean Society*, 2:136).

b. ʿAzarya, David's cousin and scion of the *geʾonim* of Sura, who arranged his marriage. The contract sanctifying David's union bears the signature of the presiding judge: Shelomo ha-Kohen b. Yosef (II), president of the high court of the Jerusalem *yeshiva* in Fustat (1077–98)—Evyatar's first cousin and grandson of the Palestinian *gaʾon* of 1025.[30]

David b. Daniel's marriage to a Qaraite took place, then, with the full approbation of the Syrians in Damīra and the Palestinian rabbinic establishment in both Tyre and Fustat. It enjoyed the support of the Palestinian *yeshiva* and the Palestinian high court of Fustat—and even of David's ex-in-laws. Evyatar chose David for the role of villain because the rest of the rabbinic establishment had abandoned him in David's favor.

But why did Evyatar pass over in silence the fact that David b. Daniʾel—son of the Jerusalem *gaʾon*, scion of the Babylonian exilarchal house, aspiring head of the Jews of the Fatimid empire—had divorced his Rabbanite wife to marry a high-born Qaraite? This must have been known to all who heard the scroll, and it would have been so easy for Evyatar to use it against him. And why did he harp on Daniʾel b. ʿAzarya's Qaraite connections instead of seizing the opportunity to attack David's?

The answer to the first question lies in the second. Evyatar avoided expressing direct criticism of David's Qaraite connections and instead, veiled it in typological rhetoric about his father—though even then, the most direct criticism he seems to have been able to get away with was to say that "Daniel b. ʿAzarya rose up . . . strengthened by the Party of the Calamity and others along with them, and the hand of the government."[31] Even this was sanctimonious: every *gaʾon* of the entire eleventh century had come to power "by the hand of the government," and to deny this came close to vitiating history. But like the accusation of consorting with heretics, that of resorting to government intervention was leveled selectively. Gaining power through the hand of the government was either something one did or failed to do, but if one failed to do so, he could always accuse others of it to besmirch their character. As for David's Qaraite connection, Evyatar veiled his criticism with good reason. By the 1090s, one could no longer criticize a communal leader for his alliance with Qaraites. A distant and deceased *gaʾon* of forty years past, perhaps; a currently reigning exilarch, no. Evyatar himself even revealed that David had been declared *rosh gola* in 1093 in Tyre—right under his nose, so to speak—in an assembly on the eve of Rosh ha-Shana in a gathering that included

[30] See Goitein, *Mediterranean Society*, 2:512, no. 11 for other documents written at his court. The year Shelomo ha-Kohen II was appointed judge, he composed a Hebrew panegyric for the caliph al-Mustanṣir and the vizier Badr al-Jamālī (T-S Misc. 36.174). Gil's assertion that "the relationship between the two cousins, Solomon and Abiathar, was marred for some reason" (*History of Palestine*, sec. 904) is anachronistic: as early as 1082, there was no reason for Shelomo ha-Kohen II not to support the union.

[31] Megillat Evyatar, p. 2, line 9.

Qaraites.[32] By staging the ceremony, David may have deliberately tried to re-create Natan b. Avraham's Purim of 1039; the fact that he chose Rosh ha-Shana left Evyatar free to choose Purim for his own celebration.[33] Evyatar knew that David b. Dani'el had the support of Qaraites, and also perhaps suspected that it was futile to try to win Qaraite adherents himself given David's unassailable claims on their loyalty. His only hope was to downplay the importance of the Qaraites themselves by leaving them out of the story of David b. Dani'el in his scroll. Hence the affiliation of David's bride was passed over in silence—as were the concessions to her religious customs that David made in their marriage contract.

The Marriage Contract

Nāshiya's father, the Qaraite Moshe ha-Kohen b. Aharon, held an appointment in the Fatimid government, though of what sort one cannot know. In the documents he is variously styled *sanī al-dawla*, "exalted one of the realm" (a Fatimid title); *ha-sar ha-addir*, "the mighty prince," a Hebrew title that had been granted to David b. Yiṣḥaq fifty years earlier and thus suggests a connection with the Jewish community; and *rozen ha-zeman*, "the ruler of the age," the title he is granted in Evyatar's scroll and one attested for other Jews who were Fatimid *kuttāb*.[34]

The couple's marriage contract, written in Aramaic, follows the traditional rabbinic formula. This is unusual, since contracts for marriages between Rabbanites and Qaraites normally followed the bride's custom. Schechter, who first published the contract in 1901, surmised that this exception was made in view of David's exalted lineage and high station; but Schechter and most subsequent scholars were also unaware of the larger context that had led to the

[32] Ibid., p. 4, lines 1–3.

[33] On the Purim of 1039, see chap. 11, 308–309.

[34] *Sanī al-dawla*: T-S 12.104, the marriage contract for Moshe ha-Kohen's other daughter, Sitt al-Ḥusn, to another high Jewish communal functionary, Abū 'Imrān Mūsā b. Yefet, *tif'eret ha-qahal*, possibly also a Rabbanite (the couple had their marriage contract drawn up at a rabbinical court). The title *sanī al-dawla* does not tell us what Moshe ha-Kohen's position was, though compound titles in *dawla* were caliphal prerogatives and thus lofty. *Ha-sar ha-addir*: T-S 24.45 + T-S NS J 86 (the contract from the now widowed Sitt al-Ḥusn's second marriage to her first cousin, Menashshe, two fragmentary strips of a large parchment) and T-S 8 K 22.2 (a Qaraite memorial list). All are noted in Olszowy-Schlanger, *Karaite Marriage Documents*, 373, but cf. Goitein, "Three Trousseaux of Jewish Brides from the Fatimid Period," *Association for Jewish Studies Review* 2 (1977), 102. Moshe ha-Kohen's will was also preserved in the Geniza: T-S 8 J 21.14+T-S 8 J 8.12. Several other officials bore this title: see Bodl. MS Heb. a 3.22, a letter of thanks to a certain Shelomo *ha-sar ha-addir ha-qarui*, *sanī al-dawla wa-amīnuhā*. See also the fragmentary Judeo-Arabic theological work *al-Uṣūl al-Muhadhdhabiyya* by Yashar b. Ḥesed al-Tustarī, composed on the instruction of a later official called *al-qāḍī al-ra'īs* (the chief judge) al-Muhadhdhab *sanī al-dawla*, 2 Firk, Heb.-Arab. 3951, discussed in Ben-Shammai, "Major Trends in Karaite Philosophy and Polemics in the Tenth and Eleventh Centuries," in Polliack, *Karaite Judaism*, 358–59.

marriage. The contract probably followed the rabbinic rite because the marriage had been arranged by the Palestinian rabbinate in Tyre and Fustat. By using the Palestinian Rabbanite rite, as well, David may have meant to demonstrate his loyalty to Palestinian rather than Babylonian custom, despite his lineage. This, too, is significant, given the persistent temptation to assume that by the late eleventh century, the Babylonian triumph over the Jews of the Mediterranean was complete.

Nāshiya's father, for his part, contributed an astonishingly large dowry to the marriage—between eight and nine hundred dinars. He also offered through the marriage his support for David's claims to represent the Qaraites in addition to both segments of the Rabbanites—and offered him a connection with the Fatimid court. This may have been "the hand of the government" of which Evyatar accused him. As for the interests of his father-in-law, Gil rightly points out that the Qaraites supported the exilarchal family, having long ago subsumed ʿAnan b. David's branch into their own genealogy. Moshe ha-Kohen recognized, then, that as a Davidic dynast, David had meaningful claims on some position of leadership over all the Jews.[35]

Although most of the contract follows the Palestinian Rabbanite custom, there is one section that is borrowed from the Qaraite marriage formulary: the clauses stipulating how groom and bride must accommodate each other's religious differences. The contract (torn at the top left but otherwise complete except for small holes in the parchment) reads:

> . . . [On this] twenty-third day of the month of Shevaṭ of the year 1393 according to the calendar of documents [the Seleucid year], in Fustat, which is situated in the land of Egypt, his honor, greatness, and holiness, our master and teacher, our *nasi* David the Nasi, Nasi of the Diaspora of all [Israel], son of Daniʾel . . . , the great Gaʾon of the Yeshiva of the Splendor of Jacob [the title refers to his father], blessed be the memory of the holy and pure, said to this honorable Nāshiya the virgin bride, daughter of his honor, greatness, and holiness, our master and teacher, our lord, our leader, Moshe ha-Kohen, banner of the Jews and the strength and joy of their glory, son of his honor, greatness and holiness, our master and teacher Aharon ha-Kohen, may his resting place be in Eden: "Be my wife according to the law of Moses and Israel. And I will serve, sustain, cherish, and trust you just as [the men of Israel] serve and sustain, cherish, and trust their wives in truth. And this honorable Nāshiya shall be to me as my wife."
>
> Our *nasi*, our David, has also taken it upon himself that if, heaven forefend, this Nāshiya should die without children, they shall allocate her dowry to her father's

[35] Cf. Cohen, *Jewish Self-Government*, 188–89. Cohen rightly argues against interpreting the affair of David b. Daniʾel as a primordial battle between *geʾonim* and exilarchs. Qaraite opposition to the *geʾonim* was not one of Moshe ha-Kohen's motives for marrying his daughter to David, since though he was an exilarch his father had been a *gaʾon*. Rather, as Cohen also suggests, the Qaraites were as impressed by Davidic lineage as the Rabbanites were.

house, as is the custom of the rabbis of the land of Israel, and according to the saying . . .

He further took upon himself not to force this Nāshiya, his wife, to sit with him by the light of a Sabbath candle, nor to eat the fat tail, nor to desecrate her festivals, on condition that she observe with him his festivals.[36]

David was required to respect his wife's customs by allowing her to excuse herself from using light on the Sabbath and from eating the part of the sheep forbidden to Qaraites; she would have to observe the fast days and festivals according to the Rabbanite calendar, but he had to allow her to observe the Qaraite ones as well.

The effect of the marriage was to secure David b. Dani'el's claim to the office of *ra'īs al-yahūd* with threefold symbolic stature. As an Iraqi exilarch, as the son of a Palestinian *ga'on*, and now as the son-in-law of a Qaraite *kātib*, he combined in his person the tripartite Jewish community.

Polemics in the Scroll of Evyatar

There are two central motifs in the Scroll of Evyatar that served the purposes of demigrating the legitimacy of David b. Dani'el. Evyatar pursued the theme of the contest between priesthood and kingship for pages and pages, citing various talmudic and midrashic texts in his support and casting aspersions on the Davidic line as far back as the idolatrous kings of biblical Judah: Ahaz, Manasseh, Amon, and Jehoiachin. In doing so, he meant to attack the exilarchate and the entire house of David. Since the Qaraites put as much stock in Davidic lineage as Rabbanites did, Evyatar's attack on the Davidic line served the dual purpose of undermining David b. Dani'el's exilarchal claims and negating the legitimacy of the Qaraite support that had gotten him there.

The second theme on which Evyatar harps is the calendar. He defends his own authority as *ga'on* by insisting on the exclusive right of the Palestinian *ge'onim* to determine the calendar, their monopoly on the secret of the intercalary month (*sod ha-'ibbur*), and their right to sanctify the New Year formally by announcing it at the annual pilgrimage festivals (which after the Seljuk conquest had relocated from Jerusalem to Haifa). Evyatar's decision to elaborate on this theme suggested that no outsider from Babylonia—neither Dani'el nor David—could possibly hope to head the Jews legitimately, and both were disqualified from office. Here Evyatar resorted to a tried-and-true medieval rhetorical technique: the argument from the unbroken continuity of tradition. Palestinian *ge'onim* had been passed the secret of intercalation in a chain of tradition stretching back to Moses himself, the argument ran, and Evyatar was

[36] T-S 24.1, in Aramaic, Hebrew, and Judeo-Arabic.

a Palestinian *ga'on*. The calendar constituted his principal claim to office and defense of the special status of the Palestinian *yeshiva*.[37]

I would like to pause here to consider what it might have meant for a Palestinian *ga'on*, in the year 1094, to claim the exclusive right to intercalation. The historiographic tradition claims that Seʿadya won the battle over this prerogative against Ben Me'ir in 921–22 and silenced the Palestinians' claims. It seems that matters were not so settled. If in the tenth century, the Palestinians acquiesced to the Babylonian calculation for the sake of peace within the community, in the absence of peace at the end of the eleventh, that acquiescence came undone. Or perhaps the Seʿadya–Ben Me'ir controversy had settled nothing.

How would Evyatar's contemporaries have seen matters? Did the Jews of the Fatimid empire in 1094 still believe in the supremacy of Palestine over Babylonia in calendation? Was this the calendar controversy of 921–22 in a different key, or some more general episode of Babylonian–Palestinian infighting about gaonic prerogatives?

Had Evyatar wished only to cast aspersions on the Babylonian usurper, he might have chosen to focus on any number of other gaonic privileges, including the ones that David and his predecessors as *ra'īs al-yahūd* had by now successfully poached: appointing judges and declaring the ban. Even though these were only communal and administrative privileges, it would not have been difficult to imbue them with meaning and trace their authority back through tradition. Evyatar's choice was significant: there were those within David's very own household who had no need for the "secret of intercalation"—those who determined the date of the New Year via empirical observation. By harping on the exclusive legitimacy of the Palestinians in calendation, he meant to imply that Babylonians were as illegitimate as the Qaraites. The calendar differences between Qaraites and Rabbanites had been felt by many. They were pressed into service as reasons for strife when there was strife to be fomented, and polemicists had by now thoroughly polarized them along scholastic lines. Rabbanite and Qaraite scholars alike had devised retroactive theories about the rabbinic discovery of the "secret of intercalation" as early as the fourth century CE (Evyatar traced it all the way back to the third day of creation). The calendar was prime material for polemic; and any eleventh-century synagogue-goer would have heard Evyatar's polemic not only as anti-Babylonian but as anti-Qaraite.

By harping on the exclusive access of the Palestinian *ge'onim* to the secret of the intercalary month, then, Evyatar felled two polemical birds with one stone: David's Babylonian outsider status and his Qaraite ties. Seʿadya had polemicized against the Qaraites and the Palestinian Rabbanites in ways that

[37] Cohen, *Jewish Self-Government*, 183–84; Gil, *History of Palestine*, sec. 915.

seemed to equate them; Evyatar now opposed his Palestinian Rabbanite force of good against the arrayed Babylonian and Qaraite forces of evil. But Evyatar's polemics only served to marginalize him, effectively cutting off the Palestinian *yeshiva*-in-exile from the center of Jewish leadership in Fustat.

Tandem Crises of Succession

In 1094, the caliph al-Mustanṣir died and there ensued a struggle for the caliphate between the heir apparent, Nizār, and the caliph's younger son, al-Mustaʿlī, who eventually succeeded him.

In an ill-fated plot to block his brother's accession, Nizār retreated to Alexandria. When he arrived, Mevorakh b. Seʿadya was also there in exile from Fustat, having amassed a large following among Alexandria's Jews. There is no way to know whether the two men met. More important is the fact that Mevorakh had access to news of what was happening in Cairo, where not only was the succession of the caliphate in crisis; as the vizier Badr al-Jamālī, who ruled the government de facto, lay dying, a secession struggle broke out over his post as well. The party loyal to Badr al-Jamālī's son and eventual heir, al-Afḍal, was led by the governor of Alexandria, Nāṣir al-Dawla Aftakīn. As Cohen has pointed out, the timing of al-Afḍal's succession as vizier, David b. Daniʾel's ouster as *raʾīs al-yahūd*, and Mevorakh b. Seʿadya's reinstatement "cannot be dismissed as pure coincidence." Evyatar offers confirmation in noting that Mevorakh owed his reinstatement to a certain "lord" (*adon*). Indeed, Mevorakh had been Badr al-Jamālī's physician and "counselor since his days of youth," as a letter from the Geniza put it. Mevorakh, too, affirms his connection to al-Afḍal when he complains that during his second term, "service to the ruler" (*khidmat al-sulṭān*) stole time from his communal duties. His "service to the ruler" is probably precisely what restored him to his office, just as David b. Daniʾel's connection with the court had won him his.[38]

When Evyatar reassumed the gaonate in Damascus in 1094 and Mevorakh b. Seʿadya the headship of the Jews in Fustat, one thing was certain: although David b. Daniʾel had lost the battle, the type of leadership he represented had already won the war. By the end of the eleventh century, the tripartite community of Jews in Egypt and Syria had been fully united under the aegis of a single administrative office. The *gaʾon* of the Jerusalem *yeshiva* had never been able to unite the three communities officially under his rule, but with a century of cooperation behind them, Babylonian Rabbanites, Palestinian

[38] Cohen, *Jewish Self-Government*, 213–27 (quotation on 219). Counselor to Badr al-Jamālī (*yoʿeṣ la-melekh haya mi-neʿurav*), al-Afḍal's love for him: CUL Add. 3335 (quoted ibid., 219–20; Neubauer, *Mediaeval Jewish Chronicles*, 36). *Khidmat al-sulṭān*: T-S 13 J 28.10, line 15 (quoted in Cohen, *Jewish Self-Government*, 220).

Rabbanites, and Qaraites were now able to forge a territorial office that united the three *madhāhib* into one community.

"THE FIRST AND MOST PERFECT INSTANCE AFTER THE COMPASSION OF HEAVEN"

The tumultuous decades of political fragmentation at the beginning of the second Fatimid century facilitated the Frankish conquests in Syria. In 1098–99, the first crusading armies from Europe—exhausted after a three-year journey and depleted in ranks—nonetheless succeeded in capturing Antioch, Acre, Caesarea and Jerusalem. Though the *yeshiva* had left Tyre around 1093, the rest of the Jewish community would not desert the city until it was seized by Crusader armies in July, 1124. Damascus, where the *yeshiva* was now encamped, was besieged by Crusaders in 1111.[39] That same year, Mevorakh b. Seʿadya died of plague and the headship of the Jews passed to his son and chosen successor, Abu l-Bayān Moshe b. Mevorakh, who died in 1126–27 and did not pass the office to his own son.[40] With most of the Syrian coast and some of the inland areas under Frankish rule—and with the office of head of the Jews firmly established in Fustat—the *yeshiva*, too, pulled up its stakes and moved to Fustat some time before 1127. That year, there acceded to the gaonate of the Jerusalem *yeshiva* in Fustat the first incumbent of the office also to bear the title of *raʾīs al-yahūd*: Maṣliaḥ ha-Kohen b. Shelomo b. Eliyyahu (1127–39)—Evyatar's nephew, who now combined the gaonate with the office his uncle had worked so hard to supplant.[41]

Meanwhile, the tripartite Jewish community in Egypt responded to the refugee crisis brought about by the Frankish invasion of Palestine, ransoming captives and rescuing Torah scrolls and books, among other places from the Qaraite synagogue in Jerusalem.

Several Geniza letters have survived attesting to the Frankish conquest of Palestine. One Rabbanite letter mentions the burning of a synagogue during or after the siege of Jerusalem in the summer of 1099, an incident also mentioned in the Arabic chronicles, which say the Jews were gathered into a synagogue and burned alive; but the Latin chronicles say that most of the Jews were taken captive. Other letters confirm that possibility.[42]

39 Prawer, *Jews in the Latin Kingdom*, 9 (with references to earlier literature); Gil, *History of Palestine*, sec. 916. The sources say that the *yeshiva* was in Ḥadrakh, after Zech. 9:1 ("the land of Hadrakh and Damascus"), but medieval Jews probably interpreted the phrase as a hendiadys. Gil confirms that Ḥadrakh was in Damascus rather than outside it.

40 Cohen, *Jewish Self-Government*, 274.

41 On the reasoning behind this decision, see Cohen, *Jewish Self-Government*, 285–86.

42 T-S AS 146.3; Gil, *History of Palestine*, sec. 943.

But by far the most extensive of them is a letter written by Qaraites from Ascalon who had fled to Egypt (probably Alexandria) in 1099, preserved in two separate fragments.[43] The Qaraites wrote in April 1100 and intended their letter to be read aloud to the congregations of Egypt (or only Fustat?)—Rabbanite and Qaraite—to induce people to donate money on behalf of Jews taken captive by the Franks or stranded in Ascalon. The Franks had routed the Fatimid army outside Ascalon itself; the Jews must have feared that Ascalon would fall within days (the Franks did not capture it until 1153). The letter emphasizes insistently that the community had ransomed absolutely all the captives it could, drawing on a donation sent from Fustat and on the support of a Qaraite grandee of the Ben Shaʿyā clan—but they needed more help.

> We received the letter of your excellencies, our lords, the illustrious *shaykh*s, may God prolong your lives and make permanent your strong, high, and exalted position, and crush those who envy you and your enemies.
>
> The letter [we received] contained instructions concerning the *suftaja* attached to it, which was destined for our brothers the captives from Jerusalem. We have received the sum from the person charged with the payment, which our community much appreciated and valued highly. We regarded it as large, not as compared with your usual generosity but in consideration of your present troubles. We were particularly impressed by this donation because you acted immediately, without delay. . . .
>
> We thanked God the exalted for giving us the opportunity to induce you to fulfill this pious deed and for allowing you to take a share in it with us. We spent the money on ransom for some of the captives after duly considering the instructions contained in your letter, namely, to send what was available to those who had already been ransomed.

The judgment being made here reflected a standard dilemma in captive crises: whether to spend funds redeeming prisoners of war or offering food, shelter, and clothing to captives who had already been ransomed but whose cities, towns, and homes had been destroyed.

> News still reaches us continuously that, of those who were redeemed from the Franks [*al-Ifranj*] and remained in Ascalon, some are in danger of dying from want of food and clothing, and from exhaustion. Others remained in

[43] T-S 10 J 5.6+T-S 20.113, in Hebrew and Judeo-Arabic. The first fragment contains the first surviving section of the letter (on verso as currently bound) and the final section of the main part, with additions and signatures. My translation begins from line 6 of the first fragment; I have relied in the main on the translation in Goitein, *Mediterranean Society*, 5:372–79, with some alterations. The letter's origin in the Qaraite community is now beyond dispute, as is the fact that it attests to a joint Rabbanite-Qaraite collection; for too cautious a summary of the question, see Prawer, *Jews in the Latin Kingdom*, 27 n. 29.

captivity, and of these, some were killed with all manner of torture out of sheer lust for murder before the eyes of others who were spared.

We did not hear of a single Jew in such danger without exerting ourselves to do all that was in our power to save him. God, may He be exalted, has granted opportunities for relief and deliverance to individual refugees, of which the first and most perfect instance—after the compassion of heaven—was the presence in Ascalon of the honorable elder Abu l-Faḍl Sahl b. Yūshaʿ b. Shaʿyā, may God preserve him, who has dealings with the government [*mutaṣarrif maʿa al-sulṭān*], may God bestow glorious victories upon it. His hand [i.e., influence and patronage] is spread over Alexandria and his word is heeded. He negotiated and exerted himself [to overcome] this disaster [*talaṭṭafa wa-taṣaddara fī hādhihi l-nawba*] in ways it would be lengthy to describe. He could not ransom some people and leave others.

The government connections of Abu l-Faḍl ibn Shaʿyā, scion of the dynasty of Qaraite traders, bankers, and *kuttāb*, must have lived in Fustat or Cairo. What, then, was he doing in Ascalon during the winter of 1099–1100, when the entire Palestinian coast was falling to the Franks? Marrying the daughter of a Rabbanite government official (with the lofty title *thiqat al-malik*, Trust[ed one] of the Sovereign), Sitt al-Dalāl b. ʿUlla, whom he had divorced some time earlier; and redeeming captives. In his marriage contract, he bears the exalted Hebrew title *sar bet yisraʾel*, prince of the Jews.[44]

"In the end," the letter continues, "all those who could be bought from them," meaning the Franks, "were liberated, and only a few whom they kept remained in their hands, including a boy of about eight years of age, and a man known as Abū Saʿd, the son of [Sahl b. Faḍl] al-Tustarī's wife. It is reported that the Franks urged the latter to embrace Christianity of his own free will and promised to treat him well, but he said to them, 'How can a Kohen become a Christian and [then] be left in peace by those who have already disbursed a large sum on his behalf?' "

This Tustarī was the stepson of Abū Faḍl Sahl b. Faḍl al-Tustarī, the son of Abū Naṣr Ḥesed al-Tustarī and a philosopher, whom the *ḥadīth* scholar of Seville Abū Bakr Muḥammad Ibn al-ʿArabī (1076–1148) had met as a young student during a stay in Jerusalem and described in a much later reminiscence as "a leading scholar" and "erudite." His stepson steadfastly refused to buy his release by converting to Christianity.[45] Both he and the eight-year-old boy "still remain in their hands," together with another group "who were

[44] The contract for the second marriage has been preserved, and it quotes the first contract as well: Bodl. MS Heb. e 98.60, in Judeo-Arabic, Hebrew, and Aramaic. Friedman, *Jewish Polygyny*, 341–42, argues that Ibn Shaʿyā divorced Sitt al-Dalāl, married another woman, and then took Sitt al-Dalāl back as an additional wife.

[45] Gil, *Tustaris*, 65–66; idem, *History of Palestine*, sec. 947. The passage (T-S 20.113, recto, line 19 [line 31 in Gil's edition]) is torn along a fold and much text has been destroyed. The amount of space would seem to indicate that two separate people are being discussed, the eight-year-old boy and the

taken to Antioch." But those who remain in captivity, the letter continues, "are few—not counting those who abjured their faith because they lost patience, since ransoming them was impossible, and because they despaired of ever being permitted to go free. We were not informed, praise be to God the exalted, that the accursed ones who are called Franks violated or raped women, as others do." It is unclear whether these "others" who did rape their female captives were pirates, Seljuks, or—as Goitein once suggested—the Crusaders who killed and forcibly converted Jews in Mainz, Worms, and Speyer in 1096.[46]

> Now, among those who have reached safety are some who escaped on the second and third days following the battle [of Jerusalem] and left with the governor who was granted safe conduct, and others who, having been caught by the Franks, remained in their hands for some time and escaped in the end; these are but few. The majority consists of those who were bought free. To our sorrow, some of them ended their lives in all kinds of suffering and affliction. The privations that they had to endure caused some of them to leave for this land [Egypt] without provisions or protection against the cold, and they died on the way. Others perished at sea; and still others, after having arrived here safely, were exposed to a change of climate, having arrived at the height of the plague, and a number of them died. At that time, we reported the arrival of each group.
>
> But when the aforementioned honored elder [Ben Shaʿyā] arrived, he brought a group of [refugees], that is, most of those who had reached Ascalon. He passed the Sabbath and celebrated Passover with them on the way, in the manner required by such circumstances. He contracted a private loan for the sum needed to pay the camel drivers and for their maintenance on the way, as well as for the caravan guards and other expenses, after having already spent other sums of money that he did not charge to the community.

Celebrating Passover "in the manner required by such circumstances" is a reference to the obligation to share the unleavened "bread of affliction" with the poor—all the more so if they were refugees from captivity.

The letter then goes on to describe the fate of the synagogue and community libraries:

> All this is in addition to the money that was borrowed and spent in order to buy back two hundred and thirty Bible codices, one hundred other volumes,

son of al-Tustarī's wife. For the quotation from Ibn al-ʿArabī, see Schwarb, "Sahl b. al-Faḍl al-Tustarī's *Kitāb al-īmāʾ*," 69.

[46] Cf. Goitein, "Geniza Sources for the Crusader Period: A Survey," in *Outremer: Studies in the History of the Crusading Kingdom of Jerusalem Presented to Joshua Prawer*, ed. B. Z. Kedar et al. (Jerusalem, 1982), 312; idem, *Mediterranean Society*, 5:612 n. 84; and the citations in both places.

and eight Torah scrolls. All these are communal property and are now in Ascalon.

After having disbursed on different occasions about five hundred dinars for the actual ransom of the individuals, for maintenance of some of them, and for the ransom of the communal property, as mentioned above, the community remained in debt for the sum of two hundred and some odd dinars. This is in addition to what has been spent on behalf of those who have been arriving steadily from the beginning until now, on medical potions and treatment, maintenance, and, insofar as possible, clothing. If it could be calculated how much this has cost over such a long period, the sum would indeed be enormous. . . .

But all the money we have spent to meet this emergency, from the beginning until now, is but insignificant and negligible with respect to its magnitude and the intensity of the sorrow it has entailed.

There is good reason to believe that one of the books Ben Shaʿyā helped the community ransom was the masoretic manuscript that would later become known as the Aleppo Codex, the Tāj, written in Tiberias in the early tenth century by *baʿaley miqraʾ*, annotated with vowels and cantillation marks by Aharon b. Asher, and given by a certain Yisraʾel b. Simḥa of Baṣra to the Qaraite community of Jerusalem, where it was cared for by the Qaraite *nesiʾim* Yoshiyyahu and Ḥizqiyyahu b. Shelomo until they moved to Fustat at mid-century. Thus the Tāj, which had been kept and cared for by the Qaraite community of Jerusalem for nearly two centuries, may have been rescued by a joint Rabbanite-Qaraite venture. If so, it passed into Rabbanite hands not, as Abraham Firkovich might have believed, via Rabbanite appropriation of Qaraite cultural patrimony, but because by the year 1100, Rabbanites and Qaraites shared a long history of joint communal endeavors and the Jewish community of Fustat to which it was taken was a united one.[47]

Maimonides would meet the Tāj when he arrived in Fustat and acknowledge it as the authoritative version of the biblical text. He would also accede to the leadership of the united Jewish community, in part on the strength of a captive-ransoming campaign he helped organize soon after his arrival. He held the title of *raʾīs al-yahūd* from 1171 until 1177 and again from ca. 1195 until his death in 1204, while serving as physician to Saladin's vizier, al-Qāḍī al-Fāḍil (d. 1200), and then to Saladin's son al-Afḍal. His long interregnum as *raʾīs al-yahūd* signaled yet more political conflict, this time with a certain Sar Shalom ha-Levi, who came from the family

[47] Goitein, "Contemporary Letters on the Capture of Jerusalem by the Crusaders," *Journal of Jewish Studies* 3 (1952): 168; see the sources cited in Olszowy-Schlanger, *Karaite Marriage Documents*, 148 nn. 21–22, and the discussion of the colophon in Ben-Shammai, "Heʿarot le-gilgulav shel Keter Aram-Ṣova," to appear in the forthcoming volume *Ḥalab: ha-ʿir ve-ha-qehilla* (Aleppo: the city and the community), ed. Yom Tov Assis, Miriam Frenkel, and Yaron Harel.

that had traditionally held the office and temporarily ousted the brilliant outsider from Córdoba.[48]

Maimonides was the first to rule in a responsum that the Qaraite bill of divorce (*geṭ*) was ineffective according to Rabbanite law, though he never outlawed marriages between Rabbanites and Qaraites. Some have argued that this was a de facto prohibition of Rabbanite-Qaraite marriage, since rabbinic law considers an improperly divorced woman's children to be bastards (*mamzerim*) and unmarriageable except by other *mamzerim*, to the *n*th generation. Indeed today, rabbinic marriage law presumes that all Qaraites are possibly (*safeq*) *mamzerim*. But this has nothing to do with what Maimonides wrote, even if later jurists interpreted it that way. Maimonides ruled that if a woman is divorced with a Qaraite *geṭ*, "she is still tied to her husband and is still indubitably married *until he has a geṭ written for her by a Jew according to rabbinic law, with Rabbanite witnesses*" (my emphasis). He never extended the logic of this ruling to render all Qaraites *safeq mamzerim*; rather, as soon as the woman's husband granted her a rabbinic *geṭ*, she was properly divorced and her subsequent children would not be *mamzerim*. The law's effect would have been to promote the use of the rabbinic *geṭ* among Qaraites—a ruling that the united Jewish community of Egypt would not have found difficult to enact and enforce, under his aegis or Sar Shalom ha-Levi's, since the Rabbanite *raʾīs al-yahūd* controlled all court appointments, even among Qaraites. A Jewish court would have treated a woman who had divorced according to Qaraite law and then wished to marry a Rabbanite in the same fashion as any *ʿaguna* (a woman whose husband was missing but not confirmed dead): it would have attempted to find her husband and convince or pressure him to grant her proper rabbinic divorce papers. Maimonides' prohibition cannot be read for historical purposes, then, as a de facto ban on Rabbanite-Qaraite marriage, which is explicitly allowed in his ruling (with either a Rabbanite or a Qaraite marriage contract). The first to introduce the question of those marriages' validity was Yosef Qaro (1488–1575), author of the first code of Jewish law to supersede that of Maimonides, the *Shulḥan ʿArukh* (1565). Qaro came from an Iberian Jewish milieu that at the time of his birth had probably been devoid of Qaraites for three hundred years; for more than a century before the *Shulḥan ʿArukh*, Iberian Christian polemicists had railed against the genealogical "impurity" of New Christian converts and insisted on their own *limpieza de sangre*. But even Qaro's prohibition of "hybrid" Rabbanite-Qaraite marriages does not constitute evidence that they ceased.[49]

[48] On Maimonides and the Tāj, see above, chap. 2, 45; as *raʾīs al-yahūd*, Goitein, *Mediterranean Society*, 2:32–33; on the captive-ransoming campaign, Cohen, *Poverty and Charity*, 118, 121–23.

[49] See Maimonides, *Responsa*, 2:628–29 (no. 341); Baron, *Social and Religious History*², 5:275 (and ibid., 273–75, for evidence that Rabbanite-Qaraite marriages continued even after Maimonides'

The Ottomans abolished the office of *ra'īs al-yahūd* in the sixteenth century, but the Jewish community of Egypt continued to comprise both Rabbanites and Qaraites until the late twentieth century. And in his Cairo trilogy, the Egyptian novelist Najīb Maḥfūẓ would celebrate the inhabitants of the Qaraite Jewish quarter, the *ḥārat al-Yahūd al-Qarrā'īn*, as "the quintessential traditional Cairenes."[50]

ruling); cf. Assaf, "Le-toldot ha-qara'im be-arṣot ha-mizraḥ," 184 (repr.); Olszowy-Schlanger, "Lettre de divorce," 339.

[50] There is a sizeable diaspora of Egyptian Qaraites today, most of them living in Israel and the United States. See Joel Beinin, *The Dispersion of Egyptian Jewry: Culture, Politics, and the Formation of a Modern Diaspora* (Berkeley, 1998), 39–44 (the Maḥfūẓ quotation on 39). See also ibid., 81–82, on the Qaraite Dāwūd Ḥosnī (1870–1937), the father of the Egyptian art song (*dawr*), many of whose compositions were performed by the legendary Umm Kulthūm; and 179–203, on Qaraite emigration from Egypt to the San Francisco Bay area. On modern Egyptian Qaraite demographics, see Gudrun Krämer, *The Jews in Modern Egypt, 1914–1952* (Seattle, 1989), 24–26, and Michael M. Laskier, *The Jews of Egypt, 1920–1970: In the Midst of Zionism, Anti-Semitism, and the Middle East Conflict* (New York, 1992), 4–7, 293.

EPILOGUE
TOWARD A HISTORY OF JEWISH HERESY

Every heretic, wrote Georges Duby, first becomes one in the eyes of others. He added that one should not consider "orthodoxy" and "heresy" as "two provinces on opposite sides of a river, divided by a definite border. Instead it is more a question of two poles, between which wide margins extend, enormous areas of indifference perhaps, sometimes of neutrality, at any rate undefined and changing fringes."[1] When do indifference and neutrality give way to accusations of heresy?

Accusations of Heresy and Their Context

Over the course of the eleventh century, the Rabbanites of the Fatimid empire made hostile use of the discursive distinction between themselves and the Qaraites on a total of four occasions. The first was the Rabbanite attempt to excommunicate the Qaraites in 1029 as "eaters of meat with milk." The Qaraites and the *ga'on* blocked the attempt via the local administration in Palestine and the central one in Cairo; the Rabbanites who proclaimed the excommunication were jailed; the ban went unobserved.

The second occasion was the start of the schism of 1038–42, when the *ga'on*'s men excommunicated the Qaraites as "those who desecrate the Lord's festivals as they have been passed down through tradition." Or at least that is what they were reported to have said according to the supporters of the rival claimant to the chair, who hastened to report the matter to correspondents in Fustat and did so with a great deal of sanctimony. The excommunication resulted not in the Qaraites being placed under a ban, but in the Qaraite courtier Abū Naṣr Ḥesed al-Tustarī's support for the pretender, who wrote flattering letters to Qaraite grandees throughout the length of his tenure.

On the third occasion, as part of the same schism two years later, the *ga'on*'s supporters submitted a petition to the chancery in a draft of which they complained that al-Tustarī had taken "the side of some of them and helped them

[1] Duby, "Conclusion," in *Hérésies et sociétés dans l'Europe préindustrielle: 11e–18e siècles: Communications et débats du colloque de Royaumont: 27–30 mai 1962*, ed. Jacques Le Goff (Paris, 1968): 399; English translation, "Heresies and Societies in Preindustrial Europe between the 11th and 18th Centuries," in Georges Duby, *Love and Marriage in the Middle Ages*, trans. Jane Dunnett (Chicago, 1994), 187.

against the others" by "using force" to "expel them from their synagogue," in the course of their complaints pointing out that al-Tustarī did not share their religious practices ("*laysa huwa min dīnihim*") and should therefore "be prevented from wronging them and interfering in their affairs." The petitioners saw fit to mention that al-Tustarī was a Qaraite only because he had sided with the other Rabbanite camp, but they left him out of the final draft of their petition. Instead, they noted that the Qaraite *kātib* David ha-Levi b. Yiṣḥaq had "failed in his obligation" to mediate between the two sides—but said nothing of his religious practices. The accusation of heresy was withdrawn and failed to bear consequences because of power the Qaraites held.

Finally, in 1094, Evyatar Ga'on complained that Dani'el b. ʿAzarya had attained the gaonate through "support from the Party of the Calamity [*kat ha-ṣelaʿ*] . . . and the hand of the government." Here again, the polemic (and the accusation of inviting the government to meddle in the Jewish community's affairs) appeared in the context of a political struggle.

In all four cases, invoking one's enemies as Qaraites, with the accusation of heresy either stated or implied, served political battles whose main causes and effects lay beyond the Rabbanite-Qaraite debate over principles. In each case, the label did not adhere to its targets because they held enough power to repel it. Heresies, then, are declared under particular circumstances, as a result of irritants and provocations of which those doing the declaring may not even be fully conscious. Rabbanites accused Qaraites of heresy to challenge or restrict the power they wielded in the Jewish community; Qaraites complained of rabbinic oppression when they had something to gain by representing themselves as marginalized and oppressed. The moments in which heresy was declared were, then, discreet and contingent, even if religious invective thrived on the illusion of continuity among them. But only a specific and rare confluence of circumstances could produce an accusation of heresy that bore social consequences; social circumstances create heresies, not necessarily the other way round.

The history of heresy, then, encompasses not merely the ideas or practices ascribed to heretics, but the set of human circumstances that cause the label to be attached to them. There is no such thing as an "inevitably heretical" belief because beliefs do not become heretical unless people with the power to make them so exercise that power. The taint of heresy is not endemic to particular beliefs or practices but depends on who believes or performs them, where, how, and who disapproves.

Thus the anti-Qaraite zeal of various eleventh- and twelfth-century Iberian Jewish courtiers, Ibn Dāwūd among them, should not be generalized beyond their time and place. Their opinions about Qaraism and their histories of it took shape in an institutional and ideological context in which rabbinic authorities turned the state's powers of enforcement against dissenters on more than one occasion. In contrast, one searches the eastern Mediterranean in vain for evidence of some similar suppression of the Qaraites.

Rabbanite-Qaraite relations on the Iberian peninsula were a special case in part because Jews in Christian Iberia exercised capital jurisdiction, an anomaly in the entire history of the Jews (other jurists rationalized their powerlessness by claiming that capital punishment could be meted out only as long as the Temple was still in existence). According to Baron, this anomaly was an aftereffect of Islamic rule in al-Andalus: the rulers had granted the Christian population the right to execute heretics and could not deny it to the Jews, and Jewish leaders continued to benefit from the arrangement under Christian rule as well. Their zeal to punish heretics only increased as Christian forces pressed southward and the Almoravids and Almohads pressed northward.[2]

"Of Those Heretics It Is Said, 'May the Name of the Wicked Rot' "[3]

The story of the Qaraite linguist Abu l-Faraj Hārūn b. al-Faraj, whom I introduced in chapter 10 via his signature on a pair of Qaraite writs of agency from 1026–27 and ca. 1040–47, serves as a microcosm of the contrast between east and west.[4] In the decades between the two signatures, his treatise *Kitāb al-mushtamil ʿala l-uṣūl wa-l-fuṣūl fi l-lugha l-ʿIbrāniyya* (The comprehensive book about the roots and branches of the Hebrew language, 1026) would be copied in Jerusalem by a scholar named Yaʿaqov of León (or: ha-Levi), "the pilgrim-scribe" (*al-ḥājj al-sofer*), and brought back to the Iberian peninsula. The manuscript's traversal of the Mediterranean signaled its removal from a world in which Rabbanites and Qaraites mingled easily to one in which they did not. Iberian Rabbanite linguists and biblical exegetes admitted the work's value, read the *Mushtamil* and cited it, but they avoided mentioning its author by name for fear of infecting their work with a semblance of Qaraite sympathy.

Thus the Rabbanite physician and grammarian Abu l-Walīd Yona ibn Janāḥ (ca. 990–1050) quoted the book, but referred to its author as "a certain Jerusalemite whom I will not mention by name" (*rajulun muqaddasīyyun lā usammīhi*, a statement of contempt rather than ignorance of authorship). The exegete Abū Zakariyyā Yaḥya (Yehuda b. Shemu'el) ibn Balʿam of Seville (late eleventh–early twelfth century) similarly cited Abu l-Faraj Hārūn as "the Jerusalem grammarian" (*ha-medaqdeq ha-yerushalmi* or *ha-medaqdeq she-haya be-vet ha-miqdash*). Though Moshe ibn ʿEzra (1060–1139) openly named him "the master Abu l-Faraj Hārūn, the Jerusalemite, the Qaraite" (*al-shaykh Abu l-Faraj Hārūn al-maqdisiyyu l-qarrāʾ*), in a second passage, he branded him "a defector from our school of law" (*al-khārijiyyu min madhhabinā*). His nephew Avraham

[2] See the citations in chap. 3, n. 13 and Baron, *Social and Religious History*², 5:45–46.
[3] Ibn Dāwūd in Cohen, *Sefer ha-qabbalah*, 74 (Hebrew), 103 (English).
[4] Above, chap. 10, nn. 276–78.

ibn ʿEzra of Tudela (1089–1164), in his Hebrew commentaries to the Bible, made copious use of Qaraite works, including the *Mushtamil* (which he cited in his *Mozney leshon ha-qodesh*, composed in Rome in the 1140s), but he refused to cite its author by name, and appended introductions to some of his commentaries that made his anti-Qaraism perfectly clear.[5]

The Iberian peninsula in the eleventh and twelfth centuries was home to a living tradition of rabbinic persecution of Qaraites; Rabbanite courtiers carried out attacks against them with the help of the rulers whose courts they served.[6] The first we hear of this comes from Abū Ibrāhīm Ismāʿīl (Shemu'el) ibn Naghrilla (993–1056), talmudist, poet, and *wazīr* of the Zīrid city-state of Granada (whom I have mentioned as a childhood friend of the poet Ibn Khalfūn and early recipient of the title *nagid*). Ibn Naghrilla is reported to have boasted that there had never been "any Qaraism [*minut*, literally, heresy] among [Iberian Jewry] except in a number of villages bordering the land of Edom [Christian-ruled Iberia]. These people are reported to have secret sectarian leanings, but they deny this. Our ancestors flogged some of them . . . and they died as a consequence of the punishment."[7]

The invocation of flogging is significant, though one cannot be sure whether it reflects Ibn Naghrilla's period or the earlier one he describes, that of his "ancestors." In either case it signals the administration of active sanctions in the form of corporal punishment (and on occasion, apparently, death) against Ibe-

[5] S. L. Skoss, *The Arabic Commentary of Ali ben Suleiman the Karaite on the Book of Genesis* (Philadelphia, 1928), 13–14; *Kitāb al-lumaʿ: Le livre des parterres fleuris. Grammaire hébraïque en arabe d'Abou'l-Walid Merwan ibn Djanah de Cordoue*, ed. Joseph Derenbourg (Paris 1886), 322, cited in Khan, "Abu al-Faraj Harun," 315 n. 10; Moshe ibn ʿEzra, *Kitāb al-muḥāḍara wa-l-mudhākara* (The book of discussion and conversation, ca. 1138), ed. Abraham S. Halkin, *Liber discussionis et commemorationis: Poetica Hebraica* (Jerusalem, 1975), 246; Khan, Gallego, and Olszowy-Schlanger, *Karaite Tradition of Hebrew Grammatical Thought*, xxxi–xxxii; Simon, *Four Approaches to the Book of Psalms*, 202–16. On the pilgrim-scribe's town of origin, cf. Gil, *History of Palestine*, sec. 829. Ankori assumed that Avraham ibn ʿEzra thought the Jerusalem grammarian was a Rabbanite (*Karaites in Byzantium*, 185–86 n. 64), but this is unlikely in view of his uncle's knowledge that he was a Qaraite.

[6] On Qaraites (and Ananites) in medieval Iberia, see Baron, *Social and Religious History*², 5:271 and the sources cited ibid., 412 n. 72; Baer, *History of the Jews in Christian Spain*, 1:65, 77 (based on al-Bargelonī and Ibn Dāwūd and taking their reports at face value); Cohen, *Sefer ha-qabbalah*, xlvi–l, 159–65; Daniel J. Lasker, "Karaism in Twelfth-Century Spain," *Journal of Jewish Thought and Philosophy* 1–2 (1992): 179–95; Ben-Shammai, "Between Ananites and Karaites," passim, esp. 25 and 28–29 n. 51 (but cf. chap. 9, n. 45); and the additional works cited in Frank, "Study of Medieval Karaism, 1989–1999," 11–12. Baron claims, based on Ibn Dāwūd, that Qaraites were eradicated on the Iberian peninsula by 1178, a claim that is difficult to refute given the exiguous amount of information that has been preserved about them after that point.

[7] Yehuda b. Barzillay al-Bargeloni, *Sefer ha-ʿIttim*, ed. J. Schorr (Cracow, 1903), 267, cited in Cohen, *Sefer ha-qabbalah*, xlvii, n. 12, who also had difficulty making sense of the two words in ellipsis. On the Zīrids of Granada, see *EI*², s.v. "Zīrids" (Amin Tibi). Among Iberian authors, *minut* was the epithet of choice for Qaraism; for further references, see Cohen, *Sefer ha-qabbalah*, xxxviii n. 110, and Gil and Fleischer, *Judah Halevi and His Circle: Fifty-Five Geniza Documents*, Hebrew (Jerusalem, 2001), 183 n. 46. Petaḥya of Regensburg uses the same term for Qaraites in eastern Europe ca. 1180: see Harviainen, "Karaites in Eastern Europe," 636.

rian Jews accused of heresy. This, in turn, reflects the altogether exceptional combination of the powers of enforcement granted the Iberian Jewish communities by the states ruling over them and their use of that power in defense of the faith.

Ibn Naghrilla's words were recorded in a work of Yehuda b. Barzillay al-Bargeloni (late eleventh century), an Iberian compiler of Babylonian gaonic responsa and, like Ibn Dāwūd, a self-styled heir to the Babylonian rabbinic tradition. Both authors' works circulated widely and eventually the Jewish tradition forgot the more irenic episodes of Rabbanite-Qaraite relations in the east, which never again witnessed the zealotry of Seʿadya. While Seʿadya's polemical campaign against the Qaraites failed to bear long-term consequences because it was quickly followed by the events narrated in this book, the Iberian one during the era of the *reconquista* altered the landscape of Judaism.

Why were Iberian Jews so zealous in defense of the rabbinic tradition? Qaraite Judaism represented a particular kind of threat to a courtier class that feared that any successful attack on rabbinic tradition and its exclusive legitimacy would render Judaism and the Jews vulnerable to the attacks of Christians and Muslims. The stakes were not low. War wedged the Jews between the anvil of Islam and the hammer of Christianity. As the Almoravids (1085–1147) and Almohads (1147–1269) overtook Muslim al-Andalus from the south, the kings of León, Castile, and Aragón fought back by pushing southward and taking over more Muslim territory. The most famous defense of Judaism against these flanking opponents came at the height of the chaos, the treatise *Kitāb al-radd wa-l-dalīl fi l-dīn al-dhalīl* (Refutation and proof regarding the humble faith, known as the *Kuzari*) of Yehuda Halevi of Toledo (1085–1141), and it is in large measure an anti-Qaraite argument. The author confessed in a letter preserved in the Geniza that "the reason for writing it was a challenge by one the followers of heresy [*minut*] living in the land of the Rūm [here, Christian Iberia] who questioned me concerning certain problems." Indeed the work is a defense of unbroken rabbinic tradition in terms even more sweeping than Seʿadya's.[8]

But it was not merely theological problems that were at stake. One of the effects of the *reconquista* was to empower the Jews by granting them administrative appointments in the newly conquered Christian territories. Christian

[8] Yehuda Halevi, *Kitāb al-radd wa-l-dalīl fi l-dīn al-dhalīl (al-Kitāb al-Khazarī)*, ed. D. Z. Baneth and Haggai Ben-Shammai (Jerusalem, 1977); Halevi, *The Kuzari=Kitab al Khazari: An Argument for the Faith of Israel*, trans. Hartwig Hirschfeld (New York, 1964). The letter: ENA NS 1.5 L 41, in Judeo-Arabic (recto, margin, lines 3–4). "The land of the Rūm" might refer to any Christian territory, but Goitein argues convincingly that Halevi referred to Christian Iberia; Goitein, "Autographs of Yehuda Halevi," Hebrew, *Tarbiẓ* 25 (1956), 393–412. On the relationship between Seʿadya's criticism of Qaraite thought and Halevi's, see Lobel, *Between Mysticism and Philosophy*, 59–68; see also Lasker, "Judah Halevi and Karaism," in *From Ancient Israel to Modern Judaism; Intellect in Quest of Understanding. Essays in Honor of Marvin Fox*, ed. Jacob Neusner et al., 4 vols. (Atlanta, 1989), 3:111–25.

rulers found that Jewish courtiers who had served under the Muslims possessed the skills—and knowledge of the enemy—that made them linguistically and diplomatically useful without the drawbacks of their actually being Muslim. Jews given positions in Christian courts used their power to protect their coreligionists from war and to resettle Jewish refugees. The courtiers wielded increasing power during the late eleventh and twelfth centuries, particularly in Castile under Alfonso VI, Alfonso VII, and Alfonso VIII.[9]

Looking back over this history at its culmination stood Ibn Dāwūd of Toledo (ca. 1100–80) who portrayed the excommunication of the Qaraites in Jerusalem as an annual event before which they submitted like sheep or cowered like dogs, depending on which of his two descriptions one prefers. Throughout his chronicle, he makes much of the extirpation of Iberian Qaraism by the Rabbanite courtier class. He tells us that, ca. 1090, Yosef ibn Ferrizuel "Cidellus," the physician to Alfonso VI, King of León (1065–1109) and Castile (1072–1109), "drove [the Qaraites] out of all the strongholds of Castile except for one, which he granted them, since he did not want to put them to death, seeing as capital punishment was not administered at the time. But after his death, the heretics erupted again, until the reign of the King Don Alfonso [VII] son of Raimund, King of Kings, the Imperator. In his reign there arose *nesi'im* who pursued the ways of their fathers and suppressed the heretics" again—meaning, one presumes, not just by concentrating them in one place but by having them killed.[10]

Ibn Ferrizuel continued, then, where Ibn Naghrilla's ancestors had left off, and the *nesi'im* took over from him, in an unbroken tradition of the extirpation of Qaraism. Though in the passage just cited Ibn Dāwūd does not specify the nexus between the suppression of Jewish heresy and the power of the state, in the one immediately following, he makes perfectly clear that the king and the military forces of León and Castile had played a role in routing out the Qaraites and adds another link to the chain of tradition: Yehuda b. ʿEzra, the *almoxarife* (revenue-collector) of Alfonso VII (1126–57).

The Jews first suffered during the wars of Alfonso VI against the Almoravids, Ibn Dāwūd writes. But then by means of the strong arm of Yehuda b. ʿEzra, they proceeded to uproot the Qaraite heresy from their midst: in Ibn Dāwūd's providentially dialectical history, God wreaks calamity on the Jews only when he has also planted the seeds of redemption. The Almoravids, he recounts, "having wiped out every remnant of the Jews from Tangiers to al-Mahdiyya . . . , tried to do the same thing in all of the cities of the Ishmaelite kingdom in Spain." So the Jews fled northward. But "some were taken captive

[9] On the appointment of Jewish courtiers with experience in administration under Iberian Muslim rulers to office under Christian ones, see Baron, *Social and Religious History*², 4:36–43.

[10] Ibn Dāwūd in Cohen, *Sefer ha-qabbalah*, 69 (Hebrew), 95 (English, which I have altered slightly).

by the Christians, to whom they willingly indentured themselves on condition that they be rescued from Muslim territory." It was then, he tells us, that God, "who prepares the remedy before afflictions,"

> put it into the heart of King Alfonso [VII] the Imperator to appoint our master and teacher, the rabbi, the *nasi*, Yehuda b. ʿEzra over [the newly conquered] Calatrava and to place all the royal provisions in his charge. The latter's forefathers had been among the leaders of Granada, holders of high office and men of influence in every generation [as far back as] the reign of Bādīs b. Ḥabbūs, the king of the Berbers, and his father, King Ḥ abbūs.

Both were Zīrid *amīrs*; Ḥabbūs (1019–38) had appointed Ibn Naghrilla as his vizier, and Bādīs (1038–73) came to depend on him even more. In keeping with this illustrious tradition of using court appointments to help one's coreligionists,

> Yehuda b. ʿEzra supervised the passage of the [Jewish] refugees [to Christian territory], released those bound in chains and let the oppressed go free by breaking their yoke and undoing their bonds. . . . When the entire nation had finished passing over [the border to Christian lands] by means of his help, the king sent for [Yehuda b. ʿEzra] and appointed him lord of all his household and ruler over all his possessions. *He [then] requested of the King to forbid the heretics to open their mouths throughout the land of Castile, and the King commanded that this be done.* Accordingly, the heretics were suppressed and have not been able to raise their heads any longer. Indeed, they are dwindling steadily.[11]

Thus did Yehuda b. ʿEzra use the state as an instrument of orthodoxy—not *religio instrumentum regni* but *regnum instrumentum religionis.*[12]

Lest we imagine that Ibn Dāwūd's zeal against Qaraism moved him to exaggerate the account of its extirpation, other sources confirm it. Maimonides, who fled his native Córdoba during the Almohad invasion, wrote in his commentary on the Mishnah (which he began writing in exile in Fez, in 1160–61) that the Jewish laws prescribing the execution of heretics "are being applied in all western lands with respect to many individuals."[13] In 1177–78, in the northern city of Carrión, Yosef Alfacar, later appointed royal physician to Alfonso IX, King of León (1188–1230), punished Qaraites who had compelled Rabbanites

[11] Ibid., 70–72 (Hebrew), 96–99 (English); my emphasis. See also Baer, *History of the Jews in Christian Spain*, 1:50–51.

[12] A formulation for which I am indebted to Piero Capelli. On Yehuda b. ʿEzra, see ibid., 1:77.

[13] Maimonides, *Commentary on the Mishnah*, Ḥullin 1:2, quoted in Baron, *Social and Religious History*^{2}, 5:45.

to conform publicly to Qaraite Sabbath prohibitions—a sign that the Qaraites were still vital, even if the Rabbanite courtiers in the end used their power more successfully in the conflict.[14]

The triumphalist narrative of Rabbanite supremacy over Qaraism is, then, a product of a particular set of power relations on the Iberian peninsula, where the courtiers were Rabbanite rather than Qaraite. To be sure, some eastern Qaraites of the tenth century, in response to Seʿadya, represented the Qaraites as having seceded from the main body of the Jewish people, as when Yefet b. ʿEli argued that the rabbis had instituted a fixed calendar by fiat in the second or third century, or Salmon b. Yeroḥam (ca. 955) described "the Qaraite people of the book" as having "seceded from the authority of the rabbinical scholars."[15] But this linear conception was immediately replaced in the east by a very different kind of relationship; and the eastern polemics were pitched in philosophical terms. The Iberian ones, in contrast, were pitched in political and historiographic ones and reflected a struggle against heresy waged not merely in the pages of learned works but on the ground.

What matters, then, is not just who does the accusing and when but how much power they have to make the accusation stick. In light of this, how heresy is regulated in a religion that lacks a church, ecclesiastical councils, and other institutionalized mechanisms for deciding upon matters of correct doctrine and behavior may be a *question mal posée*. The important differences between heresy in Islam and Judaism on the one hand and Christianity on the other lie not in the mechanisms they use to define it, but whether they possess the power and institutions to punish heretics—that is, in how successfully each religion utilizes violence.

In practice, then, the historical problem at stake is the relationship between religion and power. The church and various Muslim authorities resorted to state power in certain contexts; Jews did more rarely. In Aragón and Castile, Jewish leaders exercised the maximum degree of authority and not coincidentally, Qaraism was wiped out there long before the Jews were expelled in 1492.[16] In Fatimid Egypt and Syria, by contrast, in the second quarter of the eleventh century, it was not the heretics who were punished but those suspected of persecuting them, as in 1029, when Yosef and Eliyyahu ha-Kohen b. Shelomo were taken to prison merely for having appeared to utter the ban. Excommunicating the Qaraites had itself become a religious error punishable by the state.

[14] Cohen, *Sefer ha-qabbalah*, xlvii–xlix.

[15] See above, chap. 4, n. 10.

[16] Baer, *History of the Jews in Christian Spain*, 1:93 (the death penalty for those who sought exemption from the authority of the *aljama*, thirteenth century); 1:95 (the Qaraites driven out of Castile by the Jewish *aljama* with the help of the state; see the sources he cites at 1:390–91, n. 45); cf. Baron, *Jewish Community*, 2:221–24. The role of the state and the *aljama* (and not just of rabbinic thinkers or the Jewish courtier class) in driving Qaraism out of in Iberia deserves a thorough investigation.

In the east, the contest for power between Rabbanites and Qaraites endured longer because the structure of the Jewish community was not as tightly pyramidal as in the Iberian states and both sides could enlist the state in their service. But since the number of documentary sources that survive from the Jewish communities of the eleventh- and twelfth-century Iberian peninsula is tiny, we cannot know. Perhaps Iberia had its own irenic episodes, too, and perhaps the Qaraites dominated at times, a possibility hinted at in the story of Yosef Alfacar, under whom the Qaraites apparently compelled the Rabbanites to conform publicly to their Sabbath prohibitions.

Yet it was the version of Rabbanite-Qaraite relations preserved in the Iberian literary sources that triumphed in the Jewish historical tradition, while the eastern one lay buried in the Ben Ezra Geniza for eight centuries.[17] Comparing them helps bring into sharper relief the triangular relationship between the Rabbanite and Qaraite leadership and the state with which they negotiated for legitimacy. Tracking the role of power in that triangle and its transfer and exercise makes it possible to understand the history of medieval Jews with fresh eyes, free from the polemics of medieval authors and similarly free from the teleological presumption that rabbinic Judaism was bound for triumph beginning in late antiquity.

[17] Cf. Ben-Sasson, "Al-Andalus: The So-Called 'Golden Age' of Spanish Jewry—A Critical View," in *The Jews of Europe in the Middle Ages (Tenth to Fifteenth Centuries): Proceedings of the International Symposium Held at Speyer, 20–25 October 2002*, ed. Christoph Cluse (Turnhout, 2004): 123–37, who argues that the myth of the "golden age" of Iberian Jewry was an effect of the long afterlife of the historical works of Moshe ibn ʿEzra and Avraham ibn Dāwūd.

GLOSSARY

Terms in Judeo-Arabic often bear meanings not reflected in Arabic dictionaries. Some of these are now given in Joshua Blau, *A Dictionary of Judaeo-Arabic Texts* (Jerusalem, 2006).

ARABIC AND JUDEO-ARABIC TERMS

ʿalāma	cipher or signature (used by caliphs on official documents and by Jewish leaders on their correspondence)
amīr	lord, commander
dhimmī	member of a non-Muslim religious group to which Islamic law grants protection and religious freedom in exchange for acknowledging the domination of Muslims; also *ahl al-dhimma*, "protected people"
dīn (pl. *adyān*)	(1) religion; (2) religious practice or conviction
dīwān (pl. *dawāwīn*)	(1) government bureau; (2) collection of poetry
dīwān al-kharāj	land-tax bureau
diyāna (pl. *diyānāt*)	(1) religious practice; (2) way of practicing religion, school
fatwā (pl. *fatāwā*)	nonbinding legal opinion, responsum
ḥadīth	oral tradition ascribed to the prophet Muḥammad or concerning him
ism	given name
jizya	head tax levied on *dhimmī*s
kanīs	synagogue; congregation
kanīsa	place of worship (of any religious community)
kātib (pl. *kuttāb*)	courtier; government functionary or bureaucrat
kunya (pl. *kunā*)	Arabic by-name (for men, beginning with Abū; for women, beginning with Umm)
laqab (pl. *alqāb*)	formal title
madhhab (pl. *madhāhib*)	school of law; community of interpretation
majlis (pl. *majālis*)	(1) place of meeting; (2) scholarly session; (3) place of worship, congregation (Qaraites only)
muftī	jurist, writer of *fatāwā* (q.v.)
muqaddam	official, leader, or appointed executive of a Jewish community

muʿtazilī (pl. *muʿtazila*)	follower of a system of philosophical theology (principally Islamic but also Jewish and Christian) characterized by rational speculation, belief in free will, and the negation of divine attributes
niʿma	benefaction—strictly as bestowed by God, more loosely as bestowed by a human patron—requiring in exchange loyalty and expression of gratitude
qāḍī	judge
raʾīs	leader
raʾīs al-yahūd (pl. *ruʾasāʾ al-yahūd*)	head of the Jews, an office that developed in Fustat over the last decades of the eleventh century. By the thirteenth, *ruʾasāʾ al-yahūd* were consistently granted the title *nagid* (q.v.)
raʾs al-kull	see *alluf*
raʾs al-mathība	see *gaʾon*
rayyis	see *raʾīs*
ṣāḥib (pl. *aṣḥāb*)	friend, colleague, associate
sijill (pl. *sijillāt*)	caliphal decree
suftaja	bill of exchange, letter of credit, used to avoid the risk of transporting money; involved paying a fee and penalties for delay in payment. Issued by and drawn upon a bank or a *wakīl al-tujjār* (q.v.)
sulṭān	(1) power, dominion; (2) ruler; (3) with definite article: the government, the authorities
ṭāʾifa (dual *ṭāʾifatān*, *ṭāʾifatayn*; pl. *ṭawāʾif*)	group, party
Tāj	the "crown" (Heb. *ha-Keter*), the medieval name for the tenth-century biblical manuscript later known as the Aleppo Codex
wālī	governor
wakīl (pl. *wukalāʾ*)	representative, administrator
wakīl al-tujjār (pl. *wukalāʾ al-tujjār*)	merchants' representative
waqf	pious foundation established for specific beneficiaries such as religious institutions, congregations, and the poor
wazīr	vizier: chief administrator and minister to the caliph

HEBREW AND ARAMAIC TERMS

alluf	scholar appointed by one of the Babylonian *yeshivot* to serve as judge or leader
av bet din	head of the court; also vice-*gaʾon* of the *yeshiva*
aviv	the barley crop; for Qaraites and some Rabbanites, the state of the ripening *aviv* determined the intercalation of the year
baʿaley miqraʾ	"experts in Scripture"; Masoretes; later also Qaraites

ga'on (pl. *ge'onim*)	head of the *yeshiva* (in Arabic, *ra's al-mathība*); full title: *rosh yeshivat ge'on Ya'aqov*
gemara	see Talmud
geniza	storage chamber for disused written material in Hebrew script; sometimes also library; also used for material in other scripts. When capitalized, the Cairo Geniza or Ben Ezra Geniza, the lumber-room of the Palestinian Rabbanite synagogue in Fustat
halakha	Jewish law
ḥaver (pl. *ḥaverim*)	the Palestinian *yeshiva*'s equivalent of *alluf* (q.v.)
Hosha'na Rabba	seventh day of Sukkot (q.v.) and a day of pilgrimage
kat (pl. *kittot*)	group, party
ketubba (pl. *ketubbot*)	marriage contract; also the monetary sum representing the divorce settlement as specified in the contract
kohen (pl. *kohanim*)	descendant of the caste of priests of the Temple and of the tribe of Levi via the line of Aaron
levi	descendant of the tribe of Levi not via the line of Aaron
malkhut	government, the state
masora	system of critical and diacritical notes on the text of the Hebrew Bible
megilla	scroll, roll-book; work modeled on the Book of Esther
midrash	(1) rabbinic interpretation of the Bible, either in homiletic form or as exegesis of legal passages; (2) *bet midrash*, rabbinic college
min	heretic
minut	heresy
Mishnah	rabbinic code of law in Hebrew, redacted in Palestine ca. 200
nagid (pl. *negidim*)	"prince," leader; in the eleventh century, a rare title the *ge'onim* granted to communal leaders who were usually also courtiers; see also *ra'īs al-yahūd*
nasi (pl. *nesi'im*)	"prince," leader, and descendant of the house of David; under Roman rule, the patriarch invested with leadership over the Jews of Palestine; in the Middle Ages, a member of the Babylonian exilarchal family (both Rabbanites and Qaraites had *nesi'im*)
parnas (pl. *parnasim*)	lower community official responsible for the synagogue's maintenance, administration, and finances, including social services and poor relief
piyyuṭ	liturgical poem or poetry
Purim	Jewish festival in early spring commemorating the events described in the Book of Esther
reshut	gaonic jurisdiction, especially for the purposes of taxation
rosh	see *ra'īs*
rosh gola	"leader of the dispersion," exilarch; Aramaic: *resh galuta*; Arabic: *ra's al-jālūt*

rosh kalla	see *alluf*
Rosh ha-Shana	autumn New Year festival
serara	authority, administrative power
Shavu'ot	Jewish festival in early summer
Shemini 'Aṣeret	day after Sukkot (q.v.), observed as eighth day of festival in diaspora
Sukkot	Feast of Tabernacles, seven-day Jewish festival in autumn (eight days in diaspora)
Talmud	rabbinic compendium of traditions and legal discussions, structured as a commentary to the Mishnah (q.v.) and quoting named transmitters; the Palestinian Talmud was redacted in the late fourth century and the Babylonian Talmud by the seventh
targum (pl. *targumim*)	Aramaic Bible translations of most of the books of the Hebrew Bible, often periphrastic, redacted over the course of a millennium beginning at the latest in the first century
Torah	the first five books of the Hebrew Bible (the Pentateuch)
yeshiva (pl. *yeshivot*)	central Jewish institution of learning, which doubled as an administrative center and a high court of justice. In the period under discussion, there were two in Baghdad and a third in Jerusalem (which moved eventually to Tyre, Damascus, and Fustat)

GUIDE TO PLACES AND PEOPLE

PLACES[1]

Iraq and Iran

As a geographic and administrative designation, Iraq dates back to the Arab conquests of the 630s. In the tenth and eleventh centuries, the name strictly referred to an area that encompassed the administrative district around Baghdad, one much smaller than the modern country of the same name, but in popular usage, it included both Iraq proper and the area north of it between the Euphrates and the Tigris, called the Jazīra. Iran extended farther north and east than the modern country.

In Hebrew, Jews called Iraq by its biblical name, Bavel. This is conventionally rendered Babylonia in English, despite the anachronism (the Babylonian kingdom fell in 539 BCE). In Judeo-Arabic, the congregations loyal to the *ge'onim* in Iraq called themselves *kanīsat al-ʿirāqiyyīn*, "the synagogue of the Iraqis," which I have sometimes rendered "Babylonian synagogue" in order to emphasize the sense of continuity, palpable for medieval Jews, with ancient Iran and Mesopotamia.

Syria and Palestine

In medieval texts in both Arabic and Judeo-Arabic, Syria is called *al-Shām*. Where precisely its boundaries lay fluctuated as much in the minds of its Fatimid governors as in the minds of their Jewish subjects.

Medieval geographers said that al-Shām included the land between the Euphrates River and the Mediterranean Sea north to the Taurus Mountains and south to the desert region below the Dead Sea or the Gulf of ʿAqaba. In practice, the southern region appears in the historical record as a thoroughfare for local nomads and pilgrims to Mecca, and the other land-boundaries were contested for most of the period of Fatimid rule. For the Fatimids, Syria constituted one larger administrative district, with the exception of northern and eastern fringes not under caliphal control. Palestine was a subdistrict of Syria.

Palestine (*jund filasṭīn*) was governed from Ramla. The name is originally biblical, and in the Bible refers only to the southern coast around Ascalon; but it was adopted by the Romans and then the Umayyads, Abbasids, and Fatimids to refer to a larger territory.

The Jews unvaryingly referred to the eastern Mediterranean littoral in Judeo-Arabic as al-Shām, but they used the term to mean at least two different things. Sometimes they meant al-Shām in the sense given above, but sometimes the context makes it evident that they intended only the coastal region of *jund Filasṭīn*. My translations use Syria and Palestine accordingly.

[1] See al-Muqaddasī, *Aḥsan al-taqāsīm*, Eng. trans. al-Muqaddasī, *Best Divisions*; see further the other medieval works in M. J. De Goeje, ed., *Bibliotheca Geographorum Arabicorum*, 8 vols. (Leiden, 1967 [1870–94]) and the digest in Guy Le Strange, *The Lands of the Eastern Caliphate* (Cambridge, 1905).

Outside Syria (in Fustat, for instance), congregations that followed the *ga'on* of Jerusalem called themselves *kanīsat al-shāmiyyīn*, "the synagogue of the Syrians." I render this "Palestinian-rite synagogue" to conjure up the association with the Palestinian Talmud and the Palestinian Jewish community of the Roman and Byzantine periods, again palpable for Jews.

In Hebrew, Jews referred to the region including Jerusalem and Ramla (but not coterminous with *jund filasṭīn*) as *ereṣ Yisra'el* (the land of the people Israel; in medieval Hebrew the second word is not a geographic entity but the name of a group of people).

Egypt and Points West

Arabic and Judeo-Arabic sources from the Geniza call Egypt Miṣr, but they also use that term for Fustat, and it is not always clear from context which one a writer intends. (Likewise, Siqiliyya, Sicily, refers either to the entire island or to its capital, Palermo.) Ifrīqiya is an Arabization of the Latin name Africa and encompasses the old Roman district (modern Tunisia and northwest Libya) and part of Numidia (northeastern Algeria).

The Maghrib is "the west," both in the specific sense of Ifrīqiya and the vaguer one of the sweep of territory to the west of Egypt as far as the Atlantic coast. The expression "far Maghrib" refers more or less to modern-day Morocco but sometimes includes al-Andalus, the part of the Iberian peninsula ruled by Muslims, which shrank over the course of the late eleventh, twelfth, and thirteenth centuries.

Cities

Cities and towns familiar to English-speaking readers appear with English names (e.g., Jerusalem, Aleppo, Tyre). Unfamiliar names appear in technical transliteration (e.g., Qūṣ), but without the definite article (Qayrawān, not al-Qayrawān, which is cumbersome). Fustat has been rendered as a familiar place name (not al-Fusṭāṭ).

Under the Fatimids and Ayyubids, Fustat was a city separate from Cairo, and was where most of the population lived. The northern walled city of Cairo (al-Qāhira) was the royal compound.

PEOPLE

Fatimid Caliphs in Egypt[2]

al-Muʿizz	953–75
al-ʿAzīz	975–96
al-Ḥākim	996–1021
al-Ẓāhir	1021–36
al-Mustanṣir	1036–94
al-Mustaʿlī	1094–1101
al-ʿĀmir	1101–30
al-Ḥāfiẓ	1131–49
al-Ẓāfir	1149–54
al-Fā'iz	1154–60
al-ʿĀḍid	1160–71

[2] I use the title "caliph" rather than "caliph-imām," and I refer to caliphs by the shortest possible form of their regnal titles. For their given names, patronymics, *kunā*, and full titles, see Bosworth, *New Islamic Dynasties*, 63–65.

Ge'onim of Iraq and Palestine in the Tenth and Eleventh Centuries (as far as they are known)[3]

The *Yeshiva* of Pumbedita in Baghdad

Ḥananya b. Yehuda	938–43
Aharon b. Yosef	943–60
Neḥemya b. Kohen-Ṣedeq	960–68
Sherira b. Ḥananya	968–1004
Hayya[4] b. Sherira	ca. 1004–38

The *Yeshiva* of Sura in Baghdad

Seʿadya b. Yosef al-Fayyūmī	928–42
Ṣemaḥ b. Yiṣḥaq	after 987–before 998
Shemu'el ha-Kohen b. Ḥofni	before 998–1013
Dosa b. Seʿadya	1013–17
Yisra'el ha-Kohen b. Shemu'el (b. Ḥofni)	1017–33
ʿAzarya ha-Kohen	1033–37
Yiṣḥaq ha-Kohen	1037–after 1038

The *Yeshiva* of Ereṣ Yisra'el

In Tiberias	
Ṣemaḥ and Yehoshafaṭ b. Yoshiyyahu (*nasi'im*)	862–93
Aharon b. Moshe	893–910
Yiṣḥaq	910–12
Me'ir	912–26
Avraham b. Aharon	926–33
In Tiberias or Jerusalem	
Aharon ha-Kohen	933–?
Yosef ha-Kohen b. ʿEzrun	ca. 950?
ʿEzrun	ca. 955–85?
In Jerusalem	
Shemu'el	ca. 989?
Shemaʿya	ca. 1000?
Yoshiyyahu b. Aharon	after 1000–March 1025
Shelomo ha-Kohen b. Yehosef	March 1025–August 1025
Shelomo b. Yehuda al-Fāsī	1025–51
Dani'el b. ʿAzarya	1051–62
Eliyyahu ha-Kohen b. Shelomo b. Yehosef	1062–ca. 1073
In Tyre	
Eliyyahu ha-Kohen b. Shelomo b. Yehosef	ca. 1077–83
Evyatar ha-Kohen b. Eliyyahu b. Shelomo b. Yehosef	1083–93
In Damascus	
Evyatar ha-Kohen b. Eliyyahu b. Shelomo b. Yehosef	1094–1112
Shelomo ha-Kohen b. Eliyyahu b. Shelomo b. Yehosef	1112–?
In Fustat	
Maṣliaḥ ha-Kohen b. Shelomo b. Eliyyahu	ca. 1127–39

[3] The list of Iraqi *ge'onim* is taken from Brody, *Geonim of Babylonia*, 341–45, with one modification taken from Sklare, *Samuel b. Ḥofni*, 10. The Palestinian *ge'onim* follow the dates set out by Gil, *History of Palestine*, secs. 852–55 et passim.

[4] On the proper vocalization of the *ga'on*'s name (rendered Hai in older scholarship), see Shemu'el Morag, "On the Form and Etymology of Hai Ga'on's Name," Hebrew, *Tarbiẓ* 31 (1961): 188–90.

TUSTARI FAMILY TREE[5]

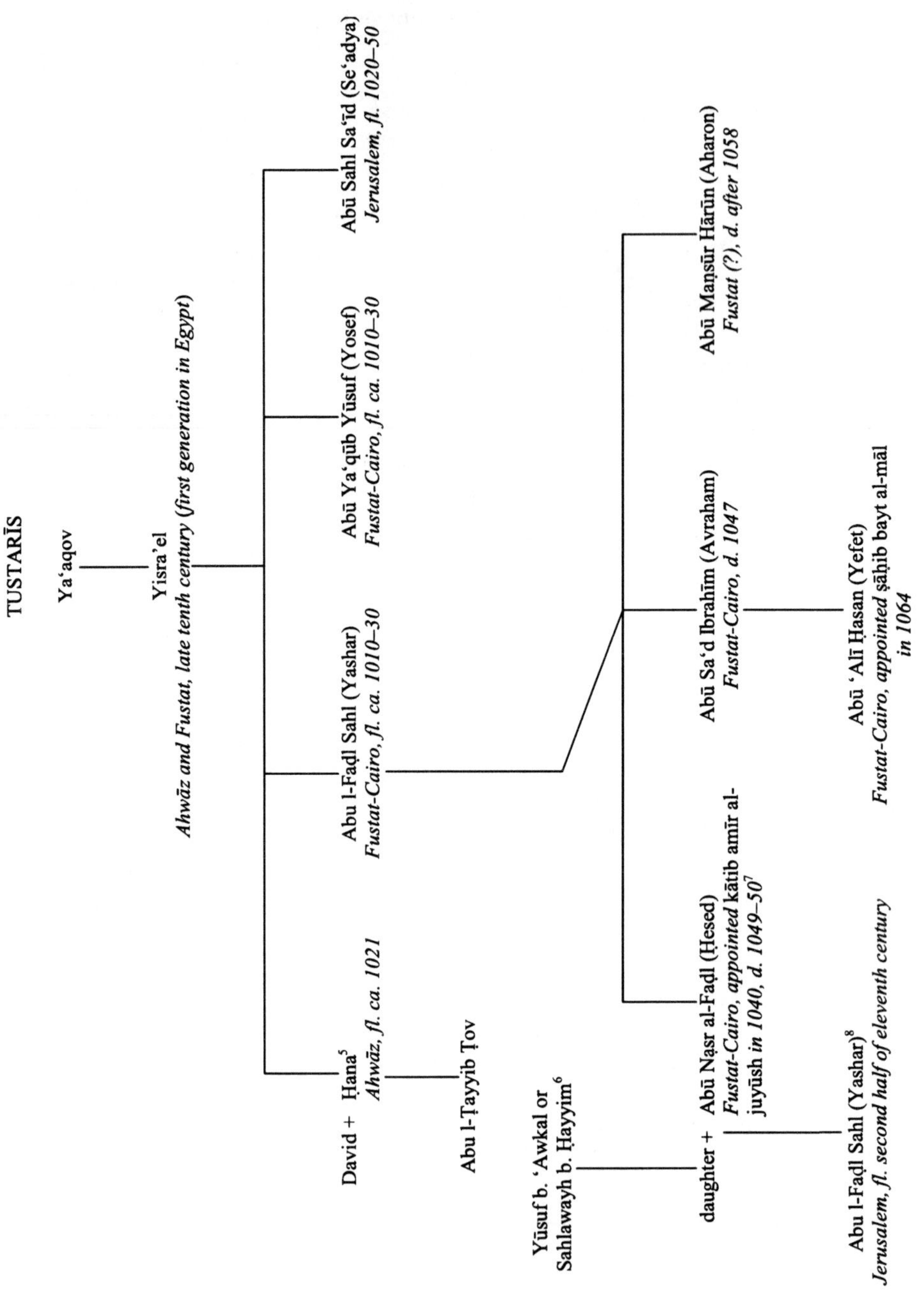

[5] After Gil, *Tustaris*, 116 et passim, with one difference (see n. 7, below).

[6] See chap. 5, n. 8.

[7] See Madelung and Schmidtke, *Rational Theology*, 10 n. 18; 10–12, and 63–107; Schwarb, "Sahl b. al-Fadl al-Tustarī's *Kitāb al-īmā*," and cf. Gil, *Tustaris*, 116, and idem, *History of Palestine*, sec. 940.

MANUSCRIPT SOURCES

This is a list of manuscript sources arranged alphabetically by city and then by collection according to shelfmark. Also listed are the editions I have consulted and the notes in this book where each manuscript is cited. Some non-Geniza manuscripts are also noted.

I have marked some of the editions below as available on-line through the Princeton Geniza Project (www.princeton.edu/~geniza/). This corpus now includes hundreds of otherwise unpublished editions, as well as editions Goitein published but then corrected in his own article offprints, in addition to published material. I have listed the Princeton Geniza Project edition only when it is unpublished elsewhere.

I have cited all manuscripts as they are currently known in the libraries in question (with the exception of manuscripts in Heidelberg and St. Petersburg, which I was not able to visit in person and cited following the conventions of previous researchers). Where the current nomenclature differs from how scholars have cited these manuscripts in the past, I have noted the change.

BUDAPEST: HUNGARIAN ACADEMY OF SCIENCES, DAVID KAUFFMAN COLLECTION

DK 166+T-S AS 153.82
Gil, *History of Palestine*, doc. 296
9 n. 53

DK 333
Gil, *History of Palestine*, doc. 463
7 n. 9

CAIRO: ARCHIVES OF THE QARAITE SYNAGOGUE, CAIRO

For a description of the documents in this collection, see D. S. Richards, "Arabic Documents from the Karaite Community in Cairo," *Journal of the Economic and Social History of the Orient* 15 (1972): 105–62; and Sklare, "Guide to Collections of Karaite Manuscripts," 903. An incomplete set of photographs of the archival documents (rescripts and real-estate transactions) described by Richards can be found at the Institute for the Microfilmed Hebrew Manuscript at the Jewish National and University Library in Jerusalem and consulted on request from the librarians.

G 13+G 15
Richard J. H. Gottheil, "A Decree in Favour of the Karaites of Cairo Dated 1024," in *Festschrift zu Ehren des Dr. A Harkavy*, ed. Baron D. von Günzburg and Israel Markon (St. Petersburg, 1908), 115–25
Stern, *Fāṭimid Decrees*, 23–26 (on the basis of Gottheil's edition)

See corrections in Richards, "Arabic Documents from the Karaite Community in Cairo," 107 (cited as no. 15), and Gil, *History of Palestine*, sec. 783n.
8 nn. 76, 80

CAMBRIDGE: CAMBRIDGE UNIVERSITY LIBRARY

Oriental Collection (acquired separately from the Taylor-Schechter collection)

Or. 1080 5.14
Gil, *In the Kingdom of Ishmael*, doc. 844
5 n. 15

Or. 1080 J 7
Gil, *History of Palestine*, doc. 196
Khan, *Arabic Legal and Administrative Documents*, doc. 73
Bareket, *Jews of Egypt*, 161–66
6 n. 26; 11 n. 57

Or. 1080 J 21
Goitein, "Mikhtavim me-Ereṣ Yisra'el mi-tequfat ha-ṣalbanim," *Yerushalayim: Meḥqerey Ereṣ Yisra'el* 2–5 (1955): 68–69 (cited incorrectly as Or. 1080 [14])
Goitein, "Parents and Children: A Geniza Study on the Medieval Jewish Family," *Gratz College Annual of Jewish Studies* 4 (1975): 56–57 (corrected edition with English translation)
Goitein, *Palestinian Jewry*, 276–77
Gil, *History of Palestine*, doc. 293
9 n. 51

Or. 1080 J 45
Gil, *History of Palestine*, doc. 182
8 n. 38; 11 nn. 18, 30

Or. 1080 J 109
Goitein, "Ibn Khalfun's Collection of Poems in 11th Century Egypt and Yemen," Hebrew, *Tarbiẓ* 29 (1959–60), 357–58 (partial edition only)
5 n. 43

Or. 1080 J 110
Shtober, "Questions Posed to R. Abraham b. Maimonides," Hebrew, *Shenaton ha-mishpat ha-ivri* 14–15 (1988–89): 270–72 (partial edition only)
10 n. 60

Or. 1080 J 146
Gil, *History of Palestine*, doc. 288
Rustow, "Rabbanite-Karaite Relations," 168 (English translation only)
5 n. 49

Or. 1080 J 167
Gil, *In the Kingdom of Ishmael*, doc. 448
5 n. 30

Additional Collection (acquired before Schechter's visit to Cairo in 1897)

Add. 3335
A. Neubauer, "Egyptian Fragments II," *Jewish Quarterly Review*, o.s. 9 (1896): 24–38 (no shelf-mark cited)
12 n. 38

Add. 3430
Goitein, "Three Trousseaux of Jewish Brides from the Fatimid Period," 81–86
Goitein, *Palestinian Jewry*, 193–99
Goitein, *Mediterranean Society*, 4:314–16 (English translation only)
Gil, *History of Palestine*, doc. 305
Olszowy-Schlanger, *Karaite Marriage Documents*, doc. 39
9 nn. 11, 21

Taylor-Schechter Genizah Collection
(N.B.—The Word "Box" has now been Omitted from all Shelfmarks)

Old series: T-S A–K (formerly in boxes, now in binders)

T-S J 1.4
Unpublished
Cohen, *Voice of the Poor*, doc. 64 (English translation only)
9 n. 44

T-S J 3.47 (formerly T-S 13 J 32)
Assaf, "Seridim min ha-geniza," in *Sefer Klausner: Me'assef le-madda' u-le-sifrut yafa mugash le-Professor Yosef Klausner le-yovel ha-shishim*, ed. N. H. Torczyner, A. A. Kabak, E. Tcherikover, and B. Shohetman (Tel Aviv, 1937), 230
See Gil, *Tustaris*, 63 n. 92
5 n. 22

T-S K 6.148
Unpublished
See Olszowy-Schlanger, *Karaite Marriage Documents*, 481
9 n. 35

T-S K 6.189
Gil, *History of Palestine*, doc. 289
See also Mann, *Jews in Egypt and in Palestine*, 2:79; Goitein, *Mediterranean Society*, 1:451 n. 69
11 n. 63

T-S K 15.5
Unpublished
Cohen, *Voice of the Poor*, doc. 60 (English translation only)
9 n. 44

T-S K 15.15
Unpublished
Cohen, *Voice of the Poor*, doc. 61 (English translation only)
9 n. 44

T-S K 15.39
Unpublished
Cohen, *Voice of the Poor*, doc. 62 (English translation only)
9 n. 44

T-S K 15.50
Unpublished
Cohen, *Voice of the Poor*, doc. 63 (English translation only)
9 n. 44

T-S K 15.96
Unpublished
9 n. 43

Old series: T-S number A–K

T-S 6 J 2.17
Unpublished
See Goitein, *Mediterranean Society*, 5:608–9 n. 34
10 n. 54

T-S 6 Ja 1
Gil, *In the Kingdom of Ishmael*, doc. 7
1 n. 29

T-S 8 G 7.1
Mann, *Jews in Egypt and in Palestine*, 2:41–2 (doc. 13)
Gil, *In the Kingdom of Ishmael*, doc. 3
Stern, *Calendar and Community*, 277–83, with English translation and photographic reproduction (see his comments, ibid., 184–86)
1 n. 26

T-S 8 J 4.1
Mann, *Jews in Egypt and in Palestine*, 2:98 (partial edition only)
Goitein's edition available on-line through the Princeton Geniza Project
6 n. 36

T-S 8 J 7.13
Unpublished
See Gil, *History of Palestine*, sec. 797
6 n. 12

T-S 8 J 8.12: see T-S 8 J 21.14

T-S 8 J 12.2
Goitein's edition available on-line through the Princeton Geniza Project
12 n. 29

T-S 8 J 20.1
Mann, *Jews in Egypt and in Palestine*, 2:169–70
Gil, *History of Palestine*, doc. 180
11 n. 33

T-S 8 J 20.12
Gil, *History of Palestine*, doc. 297
1 n. 63

T-S 8 J 21.9
Gil, *In the Kingdom of Ishmael*, doc. 717
5 n. 30

T-S 8 J 21.14+T-S 8 J 8.12
Joseph Rivlin, *Inheritance and Wills in Jewish Law*, Hebrew (Ramat Gan, 1999), docs. 18 and 19
12 n. 34

T-S 8 J 21.24
Gil, *History of Palestine*, doc. 449
10 n. 47

T-S 8 J 22.14
Goitein, "The Communal Activities of Elhanan b. Shemarya," Hebrew, in *Joshua Finkel Festschrift: In Honor of Joshua Finkel*, ed. S. B. Hoenig and L. D. Stitskin (New York, 1974), 121, 126
6 n. 13

T-S 8 J 36.2
Gil, *Tustaris*, doc. 1
Gil, *In the Kingdom of Ishmael*, doc. 154
5 n. 8; 6 n. 29

T-S 8 J 39.9
Goitein, "Letter of the Gaon Samuel b. Ḥofni," 199–200
Gil, *In the Kingdom of Ishmael*, doc. 48
5 n. 36; fig. 3

T-S 8 K 10
Mann, *Jews in Egypt and in Palestine*, 2:432–36
8 n. 1

T-S 8 K 14.2
H. N. Bialik and Y. H. Ravnitsky, eds., *Shirey Shelomo b. Yehuda ibn Gavirol*, 5 vols. (Tel Aviv, 1927), 5:7–15
Mirsky, *Itzhak ibn Khalfun*, no. 35
Brener, *Ibn Khalfun*, 121 (English translation)
5 n. 47

T-S 8 K 22.2
Mann, *Jews in Egypt and in Palestine*, 2:210–11 (partial edition)
Full document unpublished
12 n. 34

T-S 10 C 2.1
Jacob Mann, "Early Ḳaraite Bible Commentaries," *Jewish Quarterly Review* 12 (1922): 473–79 (cited incorrectly as T-S 10 C 2)
4 n. 15

T-S 10 C 2.2
Mann, "Tract by an Early Ḳaraite Settler," 517–21 (English translation, 521–26; cited incorrectly as T-S 10 G 2)
Ben-Shammai, "Fragments of Daniel al-Qūmisī's Commentary on the Book of Daniel," 275–78
2 n. 43; 4 n. 13

T-S 10 J 2.2
Unpublished
7 n. 11

T-S 10 J 5.6+T-S 20.113
Goitein, "New Sources on the Fate of the Jews During the Crusaders' Conquest of Jerusalem," *Zion* 17 (1952): 136–40 (second fragment only)
Goitein, "Contemporary Letters on the Capture of Jerusalem," 162–77 (English translation)
Goitein, *Palestinian Jewry*, 240–50
Gil, *History of Palestine*, doc. 577
Goitein, *Mediterranean Society*, 5:372–79 (English translation)
12 n. 43

T-S 10 J 5.11
Mann, *Jews in Egypt and in Palestine*, 2:97 (partial edition)
Bareket, *Jewish Leadership in Fustat*, 205–7 (partial edition)
Full document unpublished
6 n. 36

T-S 10 J 6.14
Goitein, *Palestinian Jewry*, 4 (partial edition)
Gil, *History of Palestine*, doc. 309
Stefan C. Reif, *Why Medieval Hebrew Studies? An Inaugural Lecture Given in the University of Cambridge, 11 November 1999* (Cambridge, 2001), plate 2 (facsimile)
10 n. 49

T-S 10 J 9.19
Gil, *History of Palestine*, doc. 290
8 n. 93

T-S 10 J 12.25: see T-S 13 J 18.1

T-S 10 J 16.8: see BL Or. 5566 D 24

T-S 10 J 27.7
Mann, *Jews in Egypt and in Palestine*, 2:79 n. 1
Gil, *History of Palestine*, doc. 277
10 nn. 18, 20; 11 n. 63

T-S 10 J 29.5
Goitein, *Palestinian Jewry*, 172–73 (lines 12–22 only)
Gil, *History of Palestine*, doc. 445
8 n. 13

T-S 10 J 29.13
Gil, *History of Palestine*, doc. 205
Introduction n. 14

T-S 10 K 7.1 and **T-S 12.729** (*Megillat Evyatar*)
Solomon Schechter, *Saadyana: Geniza Fragments of Writings of R. Saadya Gaon and Others* (Cambridge, 1903), 86–104 (first shelf-mark); 83, 105–6 (second shelf-mark)
Gil, "Scroll of Evyatar as a Source," 81–106
Gil, *History of Palestine*, doc. 559
Facsimile of first fragment in Gil, "The Jewish Community," in Prawer and Ben-Shammai, *History of Jerusalem*, 187
12 nn. 9, 22

T-S 13 J 1.18
Goitein's edition available on-line through the Princeton Geniza Project (and see also idem, *Mediterranean Society*, 2:512, item 10, 3:498 n. 15)
5 n. 30

T-S 13 J 5.1
Mann, *Jews in Egypt and in Palestine*, 2:98 (partial edition only)
Bareket, "Books of Records of the Jerusalemite Court from the Cairo Genizah in the First Half of the Eleventh Century," Hebrew, *Hebrew Union College Annual* 69 (1998): 31–37
11 n. 35

T-S 13 J 6.33
Goitein, *Mediterranean Society*, 3:151 (partial English translation only)
Friedman, *Jewish Polygyny*, 70 (with facsimile, plate 6)
9 nn. 11, 31

T-S 13 J 7.6
Gil, *History of Palestine*, doc. 404
7 n. 20

T-S 13 J 7.29
Goitein, "A Caliph's Decree in Favour of the Rabbinite [*sic*] Jews of Palestine," *Journal of Jewish Studies* 5 (1954): 123
Stern, *Fāṭimid Decrees*, 32–33 (in Arabic transliteration)
Gil, *History of Palestine*, doc. 310
Stillman, *Jews of Arab Lands*, 198–99 (English translation only)
8 nn. 66, 78

T-S 13 J 8.14
Gil, *History of Palestine*, doc. 326
See Goitein, *Mediterranean Society*, 2:427, item 4, and idem, *Palestinian Jewry*, 291 n. 30
5 nn. 12, 15; 7 nn. 9, 41–43; 9 n. 36; 10 nn. 20, 35

T-S 13 J 9.4
Assaf, *Meqorot u-meḥqarim*, 1:108–10 (with Hebrew translation by Ashtor and Baneth)
Ashtor, "Documentos españoles de la Genizah," *Sefarad* 24 (1964): 49–53 (with Spanish translation, 54–59)
Gil, *History of Palestine*, doc. 457
3 n. 72; 9 n. 45

T-S 13 J 10.12
Mann, *Jews in Egypt and in Palestine*, 2:75–77
7 n. 9

T-S 13 J 11.5
Mann, *Jews in Egypt and in Palestine*, 2:186
Gil, *History of Palestine*, doc. 105
Stillman, *Jews of Arab Lands*, 192–93 (English translation)
8 n. 36

T-S 13 J 13.13r+T-S 13 J 27.5r
Gil, "Maʿase be-ḥalom niflaʾ u-ve-misrat ṣibbur ba ba-yamim," in Morag, *Studies in Geniza and Sepharadi Heritage*, 69–70
Gil, *History of Palestine*, doc. 313
See Mann, *Jews in Egypt and in Palestine*, 2:219 (first fragment); Goitein, *Palestinian Jewry*, 132, 158 (first fragment)
11 n. 3

T-S 13 J 13.14
Mann, *Jews in Egypt and in Palestine*, 2:132–34
Gil, *History of Palestine*, doc. 53
1 n. 31

T-S 13 J 13.27
Gil, "The Jews in Sicily under Muslim Rule in the Light of the Geniza Documents," *Italia Judaica: Atti del Convegno internazionale, Bari 18–22 maggio 1981* (Rome, 1983), 107–12 (with facsimile, 134–35)
Ben-Sasson, *Jews of Sicily*, doc. 6
Gil, *In the Kingdom of Ishmael*, doc. 238
4 n. 42

T-S 13 J 13.28+T-S AS 120.62
A. Marmorstein, "Solomon Ben Judah and Some of His Contemporaries," *Jewish Quarterly Review* 8 (1917): 21–23 n. 30 (first fragment only)
Mann, *Jews in Egypt and in Palestine*, 2:152–55
Gil, *History of Palestine*, doc. 90

See also Mann's corrections to Marmorstein's readings, "A Note on 'Solomon Ben Judah and Some of His Contemporaries,'" *Jewish Quarterly Review* 9 (1918–19): 417–21
6 n. 28; 8 n. 43

T-S 13 J 14.8
Mann, *Jews in Egypt and in Palestine*, 2:125–26 (incorrectly listed as T-S 13 J 14.18)
Gil, *History of Palestine*, doc. 106
6 n. 40

T-S 13 J 14.20
Mann, *Jews in Egypt and in Palestine*, 2:87
Mann's edition, corrected on the basis of comparison with original document, available on-line through the Princeton Geniza Project
3 n. 74; 7 n. 26

T-S 13 J 15.1
Mann, *Jews in Egypt and Palestine*, 2:124–25
Gil, *History of Palestine*, doc. 82
1 n. 65

T-S 13 J 15.11
Mann, *Jews in Egypt and in Palestine*, 2:166–67
Gil, *History of Palestine*, doc. 132
11 n. 58

T-S 13 J 15.23
Mann, *Jews in Egypt and in Palestine*, 2:222–23
Mann, *Texts and Studies*, 349–52, with facsimile on 716
Gil, *History of Palestine*, doc. 455
8 n. 77

T-S 13 J 16.15
Mann, *Jews in Egypt and in Palestine*, 1:146 (partial)
Baneth, "Letter from Shelomo b. Judah," 1–16
Gil, *History of Palestine*, doc. 92
1 n. 45; 3 n. 13; 8 n. 49

T-S 13 J 16.20
Bareket, *Jews of Egypt*, doc. 44
7 n. 46

T-S 13 J 17.9
Sela, "Headship of the Jews in Karaite Hands," 280–81
Bareket, "'Thou Shalt Surely Open thy Hand to thy Poor and Needy Brother: Letters Requesting Financial Aid from the Geniza," Hebrew, *Teʿuda* 16–17 (2001), 367
7 n. 30

T-S 13 J 17.17
Mann, "Note on 'Solomon b. Judah,'" 415
Gil, *History of Palestine*, doc. 64
1 n. 65; 6 n. 38; 8 n. 26

T-S 13 J 18.1 + T-S 10 J 12.25
Mann, *Jews in Egypt and in Palestine*, 2:77–78 (first fragment only, mistakenly attributed to Shelomo b. Yehuda)
Assaf, "Old Deeds from Eretz-Israel and Egypt," Hebrew, *Yerushalayim: meḥqerey Ereṣ Yisraʾel* 33 (1952): 109 (second fragment only)

Gil, *History of Palestine*, doc. 278; see also idem, *Tustaris*, 36 n. 48 (where he notes the join)
10 nn. 10, 19; 11 n. 63

T-S 13 J 19.15
Mann, *Jews in Egypt and in Palestine*, 2:198–99
Gil, *History of Palestine*, doc. 314
7 n. 21

T-S 13 J 19.16
Mann, *Jews in Egypt and in Palestine*, 1:146 (partial)
Baneth, "Letter from Shelomo b. Judah," 1–16 (with facsimile after page 179)
Gil, *History of Palestine*, doc. 92
1 n. 45; 3 n. 13; 8 nn. 49, 50, 51, 52, 54, 57, 60, 61, 65, 72; 11 nn. 22, 32

T-S 13 J 21.31
Gil, *Documents*, 411–12
8 n. 10

T-S 13 J 22.25
Gil, *History of Palestine*, doc. 282
10 n. 19

T-S 13 J 23.1
Mann, *Jews in Egypt and in Palestine*, 2:161–62
Gil, *History of Palestine*, doc. 126
11 n. 45

T-S 13 J 25.3
Goitein, "Dani'el ben 'Azarya, nasi've-ga'on," 45–48
Goitein, *Palestinian Jewry*, 135–47
Gil, *History of Palestine*, doc. 344
11 n. 17

T-S 13 J 25.18
Gil, *In the Kingdom of Ishmael*, doc. 178
5 n. 19

T-S 13 J 25.20: see T-S AS 153.12

T-S 13 J 26.1
Gil, *History of Palestine*, doc. 88
Introduction n. 18

T-S 13 J 26.2
Gil, *History of Palestine*, doc. 345
12 n. 11

T-S 13 J 26.3
Mann, *Jews in Egypt and in Palestine*, 2:195–96
Gil, *History of Palestine*, doc. 283
10 n. 19

T-S 13 J 26.6v
Friedman, *Jewish Polygyny*, 267–69
8 n. 12

T-S 13 J 26.16
Mann, *Jews in Egypt and in Palestine*, 2:69–70
Gil, *History of Palestine*, doc. 36
6 n. 14

T-S 13 J 27.5r: see T-S 13 J 13.13r

T-S 13 J 28.10
Unpublished
12 n. 38

T-S 13 J 30.3
Mann, *Jews in Egypt and in Palestine*, 2:173
Gil, *History of Palestine*, doc. 44
See also Gil, *Tustaris*, 25 and Olszowy-Schlanger, *Karaite Marriage Documents*, 250 n. 19
3 n. 12; 6 n. 30

T-S 13 J 30.5
Goitein, "The Local Jewish Community in the Light of the Cairo Geniza Records," 155–58
Goitein, *Palestinian Jewry*, 110–11
8 n. 34

T-S 13 J 31.1
Mann, *Jews in Egypt and in Palestine*, 2:167–68
Gil, *History of Palestine*, doc. 186
11 n. 34, 40

T-S 13 J 31.7
Mann, *Jews in Egypt and in Palestine*, 2:150–51
Gil, *History of Palestine*, doc. 129
11 n. 36

T-S 13 J 32: see T-S J 3.47v

T-S 13 J 33.5
Goitein, "The Medieval Glass Industry as Reflected in the Cairo Geniza," *Readings in Glass History* 2 (1973): 18–26 (English translation only)
Gil, *History of Palestine*, doc. 268, with references to earlier publications
10 n. 16

T-S 13 J 33.6
Gil, *History of Palestine*, doc. 109
8 n. 36

T-S 13 J 33.12
Mann, *Jews in Egypt and in Palestine*, 2:155–57
Gil, *History of Palestine*, doc. 121
3 n. 12; 8 nn. 83–86

T-S 13 J 34.3
Mann, *Jews in Egypt and in Palestine*, 2:344–45
7 n. 27

T-S 13 J 35.2
Goitein, "Communal Activities of Elhanan b. Shemarya," 134 (partial; cited incorrectly as T-S 13 J 35 F2.2)
Gil, *History of Palestine*, doc. 317
6 nn. 2, 13

T-S 13 J 35.3+AIU VII A 23
Gil, *History of Palestine*, doc. 177
3 n. 76

T-S 13 J 36.5
Goitein, "Le-toldot ha-ge'onut be-ereṣ yisra'el," *Shalem* 1 (1974): 36–44
Goitein, *Palestinian Jewry*, 97–103
Gil, *History of Palestine*, doc. 80
6 n. 47; 7 nn. 35, 39; 8 n. 26; fig. 6

T-S 18 J 1.6
Bareket, *Jewish Leadership*, doc. 16 (with facsimile)
3 n. 13

T-S 18 J 1.10
Khan, *Arabic Legal and Administrative Documents*, doc. 32 (Arabic side only)
Golb, "Legal Documents from the Cairo Genizah," *Jewish Social Studies* 20 (1958): 41–42 (Judeo-Arabic side only)
Gil, *In the Kingdom of Ishmael*, doc. 565 (Judeo-Arabic side only)
10 n. 30

T-S 18 J 4.5
Mann, *Jews in Egypt and in Palest*ine, 2:39–40 (partial)
Abramson, *In the Centers and the Peripheries*, 175–79
6 nn. 13–14

T-S 18 J 4.16 recto: see ENA 3765.10 verso

T-S 18 J 4.16 verso: see ENA 3765.10 recto

T-S 18 J 4.26
Mann, *Jews in Egypt and in Palestine*, 2:139–41
Gil, *History of Palestine*, doc. 47
7 n. 12

Old series: T-S Ar. (Arabic and Judeo-Arabic, formerly in boxes, now in binders)

T-S Ar. 18(1).35+T-S 20.96+ENA 2738.1
Goitein, "The Synagogue Building and Its Furnishings According to the Records of the Cairo Geniza," Hebrew, *Eretz-Israel* 7 (1964), 83–87
Gil, *Documents*, doc. 3
6 n. 1

T-S Ar. 30.278
Stern, "Petition to the Fāṭimid Caliph al-Mustanṣir," 214–16
Gil, *History of Palestine*, doc. 197
4 n. 33; 5 n. 24; 11 n. 53; fig. 11

T-S Ar. 32.17
Allony, "'Elī ben Yehuda Hannazīr," 97–104 (with facsimile)
2 n. 32

T-S Ar. 41.105
Khan, *Arabic Legal and Administrative Documents*, doc. 65
6 n. 26

T-S Ar. 42.158
Stern, "Three Petitions," 174–75
Khan, *Arabic Legal and Administrative Documents*, doc. 74
3 n. 25

T-S Ar. 42.176
Unpublished; see Baker and Polliack, *Arabic and Judaeo-Arabic Manuscripts*, 385
5 n. 7

T-S Ar. 51.38a
Unpublished; see Baker and Polliack, *Arabic and Judaeo-Arabic Manuscripts*, 520
11 n. 2

T-S Ar. 51.39
Unpublished; Baker and Polliack, *Arabic and Judaeo-Arabic Manuscripts*, 520
11 n. 2

T-S Ar. 51.40
Unpublished; Baker and Polliack, *Arabic and Judaeo-Arabic Manuscripts*, 520
11 n. 2

T-S Ar. 51.41
Unpublished; Baker and Polliack, *Arabic and Judaeo-Arabic Manuscripts*, 520
11 n. 2

T-S Ar. 51.107
Stern, "Three Petitions," 182–84
Khan, *Arabic Legal and Administrative Documents*, doc. 85
3 n. 27

T-S Ar. 52.212
Unpublished; Baker and Polliack, *Arabic and Judaeo-Arabic Manuscripts*, 530
11 n. 2

T-S Ar. 54.93
Gil, *History of Palestine*, doc. 176
3 n. 76; 11 n. 23

Old series: T-S Misc. (including material formerly in boxes, now in binders; documents formerly numbered Loan 1–209 are now divided between Misc. 35 and Misc. 36)

T-S Misc. 8.9
Unpublished
Cohen, *Voice of the Poor*, doc. 59 (English translation only)
9 n. 44

T-S Misc. 20.92
Khan, *Arabic Legal and Administrative Documents*, doc. 115
6 nn. 23, 26; 10n. 51; fig. 4

T-S Misc. 25.132r+T-S Misc. 25.139
Goitein, *Palestinian Jewry*, 183–85
Gil, *History of Palestine*, doc. 370
8 n. 17

T-S Misc. 25.139: see T-S Misc. 25.132r

T-S Misc. 28.231+ENA 2804.16
Gil, *History of Palestine*, doc. 111
Introduction n. 18

T-S Misc. 29.58a recto: see T–A AS 145.307r

T-S Misc. 35.10
Mann, *Jews in Egypt and in Palestine*, 2:168–70 (partial: marriage formulae only)
Gil, *History of Palestine*, 2 doc. 303

Olszowy-Schlanger, *Karaite Marriage Documents*, doc. 47 (partial: marriage and betrothal formulae only)
9 nn. 14, 15, 17, 22

T-S Misc. 35.11
Mann, *Text and Studies*, 1:315–16
Gil, *History of Palestine*, doc. 85
Facsimile in Gil, "The Jewish Community," in Prawer and Ben-Shammai, *History of Jerusalem*, 179
3 n. 13; 8 n. 25

T-S Misc. 35.13
Mann, *Texts and Studies*, 2:170–71
9 nn. 11, 27

T-S Misc. 35.15
Gil, *History of Palestine*, doc. 210
6 n. 34

T-S Misc. 35.17–18
Assaf, *Responsa Geonica*, Hebrew (Jerusalem, 1942), 114–16
Mann, "The Responsa of the Babylonian Geonim As a Source of Jewish History," *Jewish Quarterly Review* 8 (1918): 341–45
6 n. 6

T-S Misc. 35.40
Mann, *Texts and Studies*, 1:181–84
Gil, *In the Kingdom of Ishmael*, docs. 68 and 69
11 n. 52

T-S Misc. 35.43
Mann, *Texts and Studies*, 1:317–20 (partial edition only)
Gil, *History of Palestine*, doc. 84
1 n. 65; 6 n. 43; 7 n. 40

T-S Misc. 36.174
Julius H. Greenstone, "The Turkoman Defeat at Cairo," *American Journal of Semitic Languages and Literatures* 22 (1905–6): 159–63
12 n. 16, 30

Old series: T-S number (originally between glass, now in binders)

T-S 8.14
Unpublished
See Goitein, *Mediterranean Society*, 2:610 n. 20; Hary and Rustow, "Karaites at the Rabbinical Court," 14–15
10 n. 47

T-S 8.106
J. Eliash, "New Information on 11th Century Palestine," Hebrew, *Sefunot* 2 (1957–58): 20–21
Goitein, "Petitions to the Fatimid Caliphs," 30–38 (partial edition only)
Gil, *History of Palestine*, doc. 291
See also Khan, "The Medieval Karaite Transcriptions of Hebrew into Arabic Script," *Israel Oriental Studies* 12 (1992): 159 n. 15; and Gil, *History of Palestine*, sec. 937
11 n. 63

T-S 8.223
Weiss, "Legal Documents Written by the Court Clerk Halfon ben Manasse (dated 1100–1138): A Study in the Diplomatics of the Cairo Geniza" (Ph.D. diss., University of Pennsylvania, 1976), doc. 27

See also Goitein, *Mediterranean Society*, 3:392, item 16
9 n. 11, 28

T-S 12.43
Abramson, *In the Centers and the Peripheries*, 170–71
Goitein, "Shemarya b. Elḥanan," 270–72
See also Cohen, "Administrative Relations," 122 n. 26
6 nn. 4, 5

T-S 12.104
Weiss, "Legal Documents," doc. 38
12 n. 34

T-S 12.125v
Unpublished
4 n. 42

T-S 12.128: see Bodl. MS Heb. d 65.26

T-S 12.133
Goitein, *Letters of Medieval Jewish Traders*, 74–79 (English translation)
Gil, *Tustaris*, 69–75, with facsimile (see his discussion on 26, 31–34, and 39)
Gil, *In the Kingdom of Ishmael*, doc. 128
See also Mann, *Jews in Egypt and in Palestine*, 1:122 n. 1; Goitein, *Mediterranean Society*, 4:411, 5:239, 572, 609 n. 36; Ben-Sasson, *Emergence of the Local Jewish Community*, 159 (cited incorrectly as T-S 12.33); Ben-Sasson, "Communal Leaders in North Africa—Figure and Image: Literary Composition as an Historical Source," Hebrew, *Pe'amim* 26 (1986), 134; and Scheiber, *Geniza Studies*, 168
5 n. 26; 6 n. 29

T-S 12.138
Mann, *Texts and Studies*, 2:131
1 n. 67

T-S 12.147
Gil, *History of Palestine*, doc. 302
See also Goitein, *Mediterranean Society*, 1:425 n. 1, 426 n. 21
1 n. 22

T-S 12.175
Goitein, "Three Letters," 170–72
Revised edition, made on the basis of Goitein's corrections, available on-line through the Princeton Geniza Project
Goitein, *Mediterranean Society* 5:281–82 (English translation)
5 n. 31; 11 n. 11

T-S 12.193
Unpublished
6 n. 2

T-S 12.217
Mann, *Jews in Egypt and in Palestine*, 2:145–46
Gil, *History of Palestine*, doc. 86
3 n. 45; 11 n. 61

T-S 12.222
Gil, *History of Palestine*, doc. 251
11 n. 63

T-S 12.273 verso
Bareket, *Jews of Egypt*, doc. 30
7 n. 15

T-S 12.337
Unpublished
9 n. 3

T-S 12.347
Mann, *Texts and Studies*, 1:383–84
Ankori, "Correspondence of Tobias ben Moses," 31–34
Gil, *History of Palestine*, doc. 295
6 n. 34; 10 n. 32

T-S 12.374v
Goitein, *Palestinian Jewry*, 218
See Goitein, *Mediterranean Society*, 2:472–73 (item 6)
7 n. 46

T-S 12.424
Gil, *In the Kingdom of Ishmael*, doc. 655
5 n. 30

T-S 12.504: see BL Or 5552 D

T-S 12.621
Olszowy-Schlanger, *Karaite Marriage Documents*, doc. 20
5 n. 8; 7 n. 9; 9 n. 11

T-S 12.729: See T-S **10** K **7.1**

T-S 12.829
Mann, *Texts and Studies*, 1:123–26, with facsimile 1:691–92
6 n. 36

T-S 12.851
Mann, *Responsa of the Babylonian Geonim*, 8:341–45
Gil, *In the Kingdom of Ishmael*, doc. 18
6 n. 2

T-S 16.50
Olszowy-Schlanger, *Karaite Marriage Documents*, doc. 4 (with facsimile, plate 3)
7 n. 44; 10 n. 34

T-S 16.64
Goitein, "Additional Material from the Ibn ʿAwkal Archives on the Mediterranean Trade around 1000," *Tarbiẓ* 38 (1969): 22–26
Stillman, "East-West Relations," 226–37 (no. 37; English translation only)
Gil, *In the Kingdom of Ishmael*, doc. 145
5 n. 13

T-S 16.68r
Mann, *Jews in Egypt and in Palestine*, 2:23–24
Gil, *History of Palestine*, doc. 18
6 nn. 2, 6

T-S 16.109
Olszowy-Schlanger, *Karaite Marriage Documents*, doc. 1 (with facsimile, plate 1)
6 n. 34

T-S 16.134
Abramson, *In the Centers and the Peripheries*, 116
Bareket, *Jews of Egypt*, 173–77
6 n. 2, 13

T-S 16.154
Unpublished
See Goitein, *Mediterranean Society*, 2:74–5, 333, 538 n. 29, 593 n. 41, 600 n. 30
8 n. 14; 10 n. 5

T-S 16.171r
Mann, *Texts and Studies*, 2:196–200
See also Olszowy-Schlanger, *Karaite Marriage Documents*, 49
1 n. 62; 3 n. 39

T-S 16.213
Unpublished
8 n. 10

T-S 16.261
Mann, *Texts and Studies*, 1:337–40
Gil, *History of Palestine*, doc. 127
11 n. 29

T-S 16.275+Halper 412
Mann, *Jews in Egypt and in Palestine*, 2:141–42, 446–47
Gil, *History of Palestine*, doc. 76
7 n. 45; 10 n. 20

T-S 20.2
Olszowy-Schlanger, *Karaite Marriage Documents*, doc. 29
10 nn. 13, 38

T-S 20.6
Mann, *Jews in Egypt and in Palestine*, 2:103 (partial)
Simha Assaf, "Old Genizah Documents from Palestine, Egypt and North Africa," Hebrew, *Tarbiẓ* 9 (1938): 30–32
6 n. 36

T-S 20.35
Louis Ginzberg, Alexander Marx, and Israel Davidson, *Ginzey Schechter: Genizah Studies in Memory of Dr. Solomon Schechter*, 3 vols. (New York, 1928), 2:261–69 (cited incorrectly as T-S 35.20)
6 nn. 2, 6

T-S 20.96: see T-S Ar. 18(1).35

T-S 20.102
Schechter, *Saadyana*, 111–13
Gil, *History of Palestine*, doc. 79
1 n. 33; 6 nn. 44–45; 8 nn. 11, 21

T-S 20.104
Goitein, *Palestinian Jewry*, 87–90
Gil, *History of Palestine*, doc. 319
6 n. 24

T-S 20.113: see T-S 10 J 5.6

T-S 20.140
Goitein, "Shemarya b. Elḥanan," 269–70
Goitein's corrected edition available on-line through the Princeton Geniza Project
6 n. 5

T-S 20.187
Hary and Rustow, "Karaites at the Rabbinical Court," 21–24
9 nn. 19, 49; 10 n. 47

T-S 24.1
Schechter, "Genizah Specimens," 220–21 (partial: omits dowry list; shelfmark cited incorrectly as T-S 241)
Asher Gulak, *Oṣar ha-sheṭarot ha-nehugim be-Yisra'el* (Jerusalem, 1926), 33–34
High-resolution digital image available on-line at www.lib.cam.ac.uk/Taylor-Schechter/exhibition.html
See also Goitein, *Mediterranean Society*, 3:456 n. 95
9 nn. 1, 10, 11; 12 n. 36

T-S 24.8
Unpublished
10 n. 48

T-S 24.43
Goitein, "New Sources on the Palestinian Gaonate," 531–32 (doc. 2, with English translation and commentary, 517–23, and facsimile, 534–35)
Goitein, *Palestinian Jewry*, 73–75 (facsimiles, 75–76)
Gil, *History of Palestine*, doc. 51
3 n. 52, 54; 6 n. 35; fig. 1

T-S 24.45+T-S NS J 86
Olszowy-Schlanger, *Karaite Marriage Documents*, doc. 33 (with facsimile, plate 11)
12 n. 34

T-S 28.6 C
Goitein's edition available on-line through the Princeton Geniza Project
Frenkel, "*Compassionate and Benevolent*", doc. 41
9 n. 49; 10 n. 47

T-S 32.4
Mann, *Jews in Egypt and in Palestine*, 2:11–13
3 n. 43; 4 nn. 41–43; 8 n. 44

New Series (sorted since 1954 and divided into NS number and NS J number; the latter is documentary material mainly in Judeo-Arabic)

T-S NS 262.41
Unpublished (cited in Friedman, *Jewish Marriage in Palestine*, 2:295)
10 n. 39

T-S NS 298.6: see BL Or. 5552 D

T-S NS 298.25
Unpublished
6 n. 2

T-S NS 312.82
Gil, *History of Palestine*, doc. 3
1 n. 67

T-S NS 320.17
Unpublished
4 n. 42

T-S NS 320.42
Goitein, "New Sources on the Palestinian Gaonate," 529 (doc. 3, shelf-mark listed incorrectly as T-S 320.16; with facsimile, 530, and English translation 508–10)
Gil, *History of Palestine*, doc. 141 (with substantially different readings)
6 n. 21; 8 n. 3

T-S NS 320.45
Goitein, "New Sources on the Palestinian Gaonate," 536 (doc. 4, with English translation, 526–27, and facsimile, 537)
Goitein, *Palestinian Jewry*, 77–78
Gil, *History of Palestine*, doc. 315
3 n. 58

T-S NS 321.2
Gil, *History of Palestine*, doc. 133
11 n. 59

T-S NS 321.4
Gil, *History of Palestine*, doc. 269
10 n. 16

T-S NS 338.95
Gil, *In the Kingdom of Ishmael*, doc. 500
5 n. 30

T-S NS J 41
Cohen, *Voice of the Poor*, doc. 58 (English translation only)
9 n. 44

T-S NS J 86: see T-S 24.45

T-S NS J 179
Eliyahu Ashtor, "Yediʿot ʿal ha-yehudim bi-ṣfon Ereṣ Yisraʾel ba-meʾa ha-aḥat ʿesre u-va-maḥaṣit ha-rishona shel ha-meʾa ha-sheteym ʿesre" in *Zer li-gvurot: qoveṣ meḥqarim ba-Miqraʾ, bi-ydiʿat ha-areṣ, bi-lshon u-ve-sifrut talmudit mugash le-Zalman Shazar nesiʾ ha-medina be-yom huladeto ha-83*, ed. Bentsion Lurie (Jerusalem, 1973), 505–9
9 n. 43

T-S NS J 198
Gil, *In the Kingdom of Ishmael*, doc. 291
Goitein, "Bankers' Accounts from the Eleventh Century AD," *Journal of the Economic and Social History of the Orient* 9 (1966): 43–51 (English translation)
5 n. 30

T-S NS J 609
Gil, *Tustaris*, 92
5 n. 22

Additional Series (sorted in 1974)

T-S AS 120.62: see T-S 13 J 13.28

T-S AS 145.307r+T-S Misc. 29.58a recto
Olszowy-Schlanger, *Karaite Marriage Documents*, doc. 8
9 n. 36; 12 n. 11

T-S AS 146.3
Goitein, *Palestinian Jewry*, 254–56
Goitein, "Geniza Sources for the Crusader Period," 309–12 (English translation only, with commentary)
12 n. 42

T-S AS 147.24
Miriam Frenkel and Nadia Zeldes, "The Sicilian Trade—Jewish Merchants in the Mediterranean in the Twelfth and Thirteenth Centuries," Hebrew, *Michael* 14 (1997): 132–33 (partial edition)

Goitein, *Mediterranean Society*, 2:251 (English translation only)
10 n. 59

T-S AS 149.180
Bareket, *Jews of Egypt*, 143–45
11 n. 35

T-S AS 153.12+T-S 13 J 25.20
Assaf, "Old Deeds from Eretz-Israel and Egypt," 106–7 (second fragment only)
Gil, *History of Palestine*, doc. 272 (second fragment only)
Gil, "Palestine during the First Muslim Period (634–1099): Additions, Notes, Corrections," 324–25
See also Friedman, *Jewish Marriage in Palestine*, 1:218 n. 5 (where he notes the join) and Goitein, *Mediterranean Society* 3:57 and 439 n. 39 (second fragment only)
8 n. 45; 9 n. 19; 10 nn. 28, 32, 38; fig. 9

T-S AS 153.82: see DK 166

T-S AS 157.231r: see T-S AS 157.232r

T-S AS 157.232r+T-S AS 157.231r
Gil, *Tustaris*, doc. 6 (with facsimile)
11 n. 50

T-S AS 182.291
Khan, *Arabic Legal and Administrative Documents*, doc. 66
6 n. 26

Jacques Mosseri Collection (Private Collection, formerly in Paris, in Cambridge as of 2006)

Numbers here are as given in *Catalogue de la collection Jack Mosseri, edité par l'Institut de Manuscrits Microfilmés Hébraïques avec le concours de nombreux specialistes* (Jerusalem, 1990), with old call-numbers in parentheses.

Mosseri I 85 (H 8): see Bodl. MS Heb. e 95.54

Mosseri Ia 2 (A 2)
Mann, *Jews in Egypt and in Palestine*, 2:455–57
Gil, *History of Palestine*, doc. 307
Olszowy-Schlanger, *Karaite Marriage Documents*, doc. 13
10 n. 36

Mosseri Ia 5 (L 2)
E. D. Chapira, "Lettre du Gaon Hai," *Revue des études juives* 82 (1926), 327
Gil, *In the Kingdom of Ishmael*, doc. 41
See also Mann, *Texts and Studies*, 1:118–19
5 n. 33; 11 n. 15

Mosseri Ia 10.2 (L 279)
E. D. Chapira, "Mikhtav me-ha-ga'on R. Ṣemaḥ Ṣedeq bar Yiṣḥaq le-R. Elḥanan b. Shemarya mi-Miṣrayim," *Ginzei Qedem* o.s. 3 (1925): 3–13
See the correction to the address in Cohen, "Administrative Relations," 126–27 n. 47
3 n. 73; 6 n. 3

Mosseri II 181 (L 183)
Mann, *Jews in Egypt and in Palestine*, 2:437–38
Gil, *History of Palestine*, doc. 281
10 n. 19

Mosseri II 195 (L 197)
Goitein, "Maghrebi Living in Cairo," 144–45
9 n. 11

Mosseri II 246.2 (series B, P 46)
Unpublished
See Gil, *History of Palestine*, sec. 812n.
7 n. 9; 9 n. 36

Mosseri IV 15.1 (L 21)
Mann, *Texts and Studies*, 1:163–64 (facsimile on 704)
Gil, *In the Kingdom of Ishmael*, doc. 55 (shelf-mark given there as IV 15)
5 n. 40

Mosseri VII 142 (L 210)
Gil, *History of Palestine*, doc. 327
8 n. 25

Mosseri VII 200 (L 268)
Frenkel, "*Compassionate and Benevolent*", doc. 20
See Goitein, *Mediterranean Society*, 2:561 n. 7
1 n. 64

Mosseri VII 209 (L 276)
Unpublished
See Goitein, *Palestinian Jewry*, 4 n. 7
10 n. 49

CAMBRIDGE: WESTMINSTER COLLEGE

West. Coll. Bib. 6.52: see Unknown Locations: MS Levi

HEIDELBERG: PAPYRUSSAMMLUNG DER UNIVERSITÄT HEIDELBERG

P. Heid. P 910
For bibliography until 1964, see Shaul Shaked, *A Tentative Bibliography of Geniza Documents, Prepared under the Direction of D. H. Baneth and S. D. Goitein* (Paris, 1964), 165
Abramson, *In the Centers and the Peripheries*, 110–12
Gil, *History of Palestine*, doc. 27 (cited as MS Heidelberg Heb 10; see there for references to previous publications and discussions)
6 nn. 13, 18, 19

JERUSALEM: JEWISH NATIONAL AND UNIVERSITY LIBRARY

JNUL $4^0$577.3.2
Eli (Eliyahu) Ashtor (Strauss), "Documents for the Economic and Social History of the Jews in the Near East," Hebrew, *Zion* 7 (1942): 152–53
Gil, *History of Palestine*, doc. 508b
5 n. 30

JNUL $4^0$577.3.11
Avinoam Yellin's edition, cited in Goitein, *Mediterranean Society*, 3:442, was not available to me. I consulted the manuscript only.
10 n. 61

JNUL Heb. 4^{0}577.4.98
This document has been missing from the library's collection since about 1970.
Friedman, *Jewish Marriage in Palestine*, doc. 2 (edited from a photograph)
See ibid., 2:37 n. 4
10 n. 22

LEIDEN: BIBLIOTHEEK DER RIJKSUNIVERSITEIT (NON-GENIZA)

Cod. Or. 4760 (Warner 22)
Pinsker, *Lickute kadmoniot*, appendix 10, 87–92 (partial edition)
1 n. 30

LONDON: BRITISH LIBRARY (FORMERLY BRITISH MUSEUM)

BL Or. 2402 (non-Geniza)
G. Margoliouth, "Ibn al-Hiti's Chronicle of the Karaite Doctors," 429–43
1 n. 61

BL Or. 2513 (non-Geniza)
4 n. 5 (see there for publication information)

BL Or. 2563 (non-Geniza)
Unpublished
See Ben-Shammai, "Qeṭaʿ ḥadash"
1 n. 30

BL Or. 2564 (non-Geniza)
Unpublished
See Ben-Shammai, "Qeṭaʿ ḥadash"
1 n. 30

BL Or. 2577 (non-Geniza)
Unpublished
See Ben-Shammai, "Qeṭaʿ ḥadash"
1 n. 30

BL Or. 5552 D+T-S 12.504+ENA 4012+T-S NS 298.6
Gil, *In the Kingdom of Ishmael*, doc. 2 (see there for references to earlier publications)
11 n. 49

BL Or. 5557 K 8
Mann, *Jews in Egypt and in Palestine*, 2:220 (partial)
See Fleischer, "Qavim ḥadashim li-dmuto shel rav Daniʾel ben ʿAzarya," 53–74
12 n. 1

BL Or. 5560a: see Bodl. MS Heb. e 95.54

BL Or. 5566 D 24+T-S 10 J 16.8
Goitein, *The Yemenites: History, Communal Organization, Spiritual Life (Selected Studies)*, Hebrew (Jerusalem, 1983), 67–72
10 n. 60

NEW YORK: THE LIBRARY OF THE JEWISH THEOLOGICAL SEMINARY OF AMERICA

JTS Schechter Geniza, 17r–18v
Unpublished
2 n. 20; 8 n. 94

Elkan Nathan Adler Collection

ENA 2 B (formerly ENA 2556)
Gil, *In the Kingdom of Ishmael*, doc. 198
See there for Goitein's previous partial publication
3 n. 40

ENA 1490.7 verso
Gil, "Palestine during the First Muslim Period (634–1099): Additions, Notes, Corrections," 281–345, doc. 192a
11 n. 47

ENA 1822 A 44–45
Gil, *History of Palestine*, doc. 557
12 n. 20

ENA 2556: see ENA 2 B

ENA 2727.52
Ben-Sasson, "Yehudim mul meʾoraʿot 1019–1020," 118–21
11 n. 42

ENA 2728.2a
Goitein's edition available on-line through the Princeton Geniza Project
9 nn. 11, 29

ENA 2735.4
Unpublished
See Bareket, *Jewish Leadership in Fustat*, 256
11 n. 35

ENA 2738.1: see **T-S** Ar. 18(1).35

ENA 2738.10
Unpublished
5 n. 9

ENA 2739.18
Gil, *History of Palestine*, doc. 383
Introduction n. 18

ENA 2747.16
Unpublished
See Bareket, *Jewish Leadership in Fustat*, 256
11 n. 35

ENA 2804.8
Mann, *Jews in Egypt and in Palestine*, 2:179–80
Gil, *History of Palestine*, 2, doc. 49
7 n. 17

ENA 2804.11
Mann *Jews in Egypt and in Palestine*, 2:89–90 (listed incorrectly as MS Adler 2804.7)

Frenkel, "*Compassionate and Benevolent*", doc. 10
See Gil, *Documents*, 111 n. 116
7 n. 25

ENA 2804.12–13
Mann, *Jews in Egypt and in Palestine*, 2:142–45 (listed incorrectly as ENA 2804.8)
Gil, *History of Palestine*, doc. 75.
6 n. 39; 8 n. 26

ENA 2804.16: see T-S Misc. 28.231

ENA 3734.12–13+ENA 2643.11–12
First and last leaf only in Cohen and Somekh, "In the Court of Yaʿqūb ibn Killis," 290–91, 303–4 (facsimiles on 311–14)
Others unpublished
4 n. 39

ENA 3765.5
Mann, *Jews in Egypt and in Palestine*, 2:215–16 (incorrectly listed as ENA 3765.1)
Gil, *History of Palestine*, doc. 365
12 n. 8

ENA 3765.10 recto+T-S 18 J 4.16 verso
Mann, *Jews in Egypt and in Palestine*, 2:354 (second fragment only)
Cohen, "New Light," 28–30 (with facsimiles)
Gil, *History of Palestine*, doc. 192
11 nn. 19, 43

ENA 3765.10 verso+T-S 18 J 4.16 recto
Mann, *Jews in Egypt and in Palestine*, 2:352–54 (second fragment only)
Cohen, "New Light," 21–23 (with facsimiles)
Gil, *History of Palestine*, doc. 191
11 n. 43; 12 n. 4

ENA 3787.10
Friedman, "Qaraʾ(im)=ben(ey) miqraʾ; baʿal(ey) miqraʾ," 297
See also Bareket, *Jewish Leadership in Fustat*, 20, 71
9 nn. 11, 38

ENA 4010.32
Gil, *History of Palestine*, doc. 433
8 nn. 40, 41, 48

ENA 4010.35
Gil, *Tustaris*, 86
5 n. 22

ENA 4010.47
Mann, *Jews in Egypt and in Palestine*, 2:72–73 (recto)
Gil, *History of Palestine*, doc. 284 (verso)
7 n. 18

ENA 4012: see BL Or. 5552 D

ENA 4016.7–8
See Sklare, *Samuel b. Ḥofni*, 241 n. 11
Unpublished
5 n. 35

ENA 4016.10
See Sklare, *Samuel b. Ḥofni*, 241 n. 11

Unpublished
5 n. 35

ENA 4020.6
Mann, *Jews in Egypt and in Palestine*, 2:172–3
Gil, *History of Palestine*, doc. 183
Rustow et al., *Scripture and Schism*, 81 (facsimile only)
4 n. 44; 11 n. 34

ENA 4020.38
Gil, *History of Palestine*, doc. 308
Olszowy-Schlanger, *Karaite Marriage Documents*, doc. 43
2 n. 20, 11 n. 40

ENA 4020.43
Udovitch's edition available on-line through the Princeton Geniza Project
Gil, *In the Kingdom of Ishmael*, doc. 504
5 n. 28

ENA 4020.45
Mann, *Jews in Egypt and in Palestine*, 2:91 (doc. 17; shelf-mark not listed there)
Corrected edition available on-line through the Princeton Geniza Project
Frenkel, "*Compassionate and Benevolent*", doc. 11
3 n. 74, 7 n. 29

ENA 4020.48
Mann, *Jews in Egypt and in Palestine*, 2:182–84
Gil, *History of Palestine*, doc. 212.
10 n. 9

ENA 4020.65 (formerly MS Adler 109)
Goitein, "Congregation versus Community," 291–304, with a facsimile between pages 291 and 292
See revised interpretation in Goitein, "Petitions to the Fatimid Caliphs from the Cairo Geniza," *Jewish Quarterly Review* 45 (1954): 30–38
Gil, *History of Palestine*, doc. 312
3 nn. 60, 62; 6 n. 41; 8 n. 81; 11 nn. 4, 7, 54; fig. 2

ENA 4196.15
Gil, *Tustaris*, 88–89
5 n. 22

ENA NS 1.5 L 41
Goitein, "Autographs of Yehuda Halevi," 408–12
Gil and Fleischer, *Judah Halevi and His Circle*, doc. 19 (with facsimile)
Goitein, *Mediterranean Society*, 5:465 (English translation only)
Epilogue n. 8

ENA NS 3.24: see Bodl. MS Heb. d 65.26

ENA NS 18.37
Olszowy-Schlanger, *Karaite Marriage Documents*, doc. 57
Rustow et al., *Scripture and Schism*, 79 (facsimile only)
9 nn. 11, 22, 34; 10 n. 17

ENA NS 48.15 (formerly Misc. 15)
Gil, *History of Palestine*, doc. 477 (cited as JTS Geniza Misc. 15)
8 n. 5

OXFORD: UNIVERSITY OF OXFORD, BODLEIAN LIBRARY

Bodl. MS Heb. a 2.4
Poznanski, "Ephraim b. Schemaria de Fostat et l'académie palestinienne," 173–75
Goitein's edition available on-line through the Princeton Geniza Project
Bareket, *Jewish Leadership in Fustat*, 251, 254, 260
6 n. 36

Bodl. MS Heb. a 3.21
Mann, *Jews in Egypt and in Palestine*, 2:39
Gil, *History of Palestine*, doc. 26
6 n. 10; 7 n. 1

Bodl. MS Heb. a 3.22
Mann, *Jews in Egypt and in Palestine*, 2:268–69
12 n. 34

Bodl. MS Heb. a 3.28
A. Cowley, "Bodleian Geniza Fragments," *Jewish Quarterly Review*, o.s. 19 (1906–7): 250–56
7 n. 23

Bodl. MS Heb. a 3.42
Mann, *Texts and Studies* 2:177–80 (partial edition, without Judeo-Arabic trousseau list)
Friedman, *Jewish Polygyny*, 66–68 (with facsimile)
Olszowy-Schlanger, *Karaite Marriage Documents*, doc. 56
9 nn. 11, 22, 24

Bodl. MS Heb. b 3.28: see Bodl. MS Heb. d 65.26

Bodl. MS Heb. b 11.10
Eliash, "New Information on 11th Century Palestine," 17–18
Gil, *History of Palestine*, doc. 301
1 n. 22; 7 n. 44

Bodl. MS Heb. b 11.12
Gil, *History of Palestine*, doc. 274 (see there for reference to Assaf's earlier publication)
3 n. 12; 6 n. 33

Bodl. MS Heb. b 12.31
Olszowy-Schlanger, *Karaite Marriage Documents*, doc. 42
5 n. 15

Bodl. MS Heb. b 13.54
Gil, *History of Palestine*, doc. 207
Introduction n. 14; 6 n. 39

Bodl. MS Heb. b 18.21
Stern, "Petition to the Fāṭimid Caliph al-Mustanṣir," 220–21 (Stern designates recto as now bound in the volume as verso and vice versa)
Gil, *History of Palestine*, doc. 197
11 n. 53; fig. 11

Bodl. MS Heb. c 13.22: see Unknown Locations: MS Levi

Bodl. MS Heb. c 13.23
Poznanski, "Ephraim ben Schemaria," 172–73
Gil, *History of Palestine*, doc. 122
8 nn. 76, 77, 79, 82; fig. 7

Bodl. MS Heb. c 28.15
Gil, *History of Palestine*, doc. 89
Introduction n. 18

Bodl. MS Heb. c 28.23
Goitein, "New Documents from the Cairo Geniza," 719
2 n. 18

Bodl. MS Heb. c 28.43
Gil, *History of Palestine*, doc. 450
10 n. 47

Bodl. MS Heb. c 28.61
Murad Michaeli, "The Archive of Nahray b. Nissim: Merchant and Communal Leader in Egypt in the Eleventh Century," Hebrew (Ph.D. diss., Hebrew University, 1967), doc. 190
Gil, "Jews in Sicily," 126
Ben-Sasson, *Jews of Sicily*, doc. 65
Gil, *In the Kingdom of Ishmael*, doc. 576
5 n. 30

Bodl. MS Heb. c 50.21
Mann, *Jews in Egypt and in Palestine*, 2:162–63
Gil, *History of Palestine*, doc. 128
8 n. 86; 11 n. 21

Bodl. MS Heb. d 36.9–10
Mann, *Jews in Egypt and in Palestine*, 2:16–19
Mirsky, *Itzhak ibn Khalfun*, nos. 14–20
Brener, *Ibn Khalfun*, 137, 149, 163 (English translations only)
4 n. 41; 5 nn. 45, 46, 47

Bodl. MS Heb. d 36.13–18
Mann, "Tract by an Early Ḳaraite Settler," 273–98
Nemoy, "The Pseudo-Qumisian Sermon to the Karaites," 49–105 (Hebrew text reprinted with English translation)
1 nn. 46, 52, 53; 4 n. 14

Bodl. MS Heb. d 65.9
Simha Assaf, "Letters from Kairwan and Alexandria to R. Joseph ibn Ukal," Hebrew, *Tarbiẓ* 20 (1948–49): 177–90
Stillman, *Jews of Arab Lands*, 183–85 (English translation only)
Gil, *In the Kingdom of Ishmael*, doc. 148
See Cohen, *Jewish Self-Government*, 30 n. 86
3 n. 40

Bodl. MS Heb. d 65.26+ENA NS 3.24+Bodl. MS Heb. b 3.28+T-S 12.128
Assaf, "Old Genizah Documents," 24–25 (two fragments only)
Friedman, *Jewish Marriage in Palestine*, doc. 1
9 n. 11

Bodl. MS Heb. d 65.40
Mann, *Jews in Egypt and in Palestine*, 2:79–80 (incorrectly cited as Bodl. MS Heb. d 65.65)
11 n. 63

Bodl. MS Heb. d 66.15
Goitein's edition available on-line through the Princeton Geniza Project
Goitein, *Letters of Medieval Jewish Traders*, 307–11 (English translation only)
Gil, *Tustaris*, 80–85, doc. 4
Gil, *In the Kingdom of Ishmael*, doc. 158

Ben-Sasson, *Sicily*, doc. 57
Bareket, *Jewish Leadership in Fustat*, 253
7 n. 9

Bodl. MS Heb. d 66.49v–50r
Mann, *Texts and Studies*, 2:171–73
Olszowy-Schlanger, *Karaite Marriage Documents*, doc. 52
9 nn. 14, 19, 20, 22, 26; fig. 8

Bodl. MS Heb. d 66.58
Unpublished
10 n. 39

Bodl. MS Heb. d 66.69
Mann, *Jews in Egypt and in Palestine*, 2:173
Gil, *History of Palestine*, doc. 184
6 n. 34

Bodl. MS Heb. d 66.84
Cohen's edition available on-line through the Princeton Geniza Project
10 n. 54

Bodl. MS Heb. d 66.131–32
Richard J. H. Gottheil, "Tit Bits from the Geniza," in *Jewish Studies in Memory of Israel Abrahams*, ed. George Alexander Kohut (New York, 1927), 156
Nehemya Allony, *The Jewish Library in the Middle Ages: Book Lists from the Cairo Genizah*, Hebrew, ed. Miriam Frenkel and Haggai Ben-Shammai (Jerusalem, 2006), doc. 46
5 n. 38

Bodl. MS Heb. d 74.31
A. Guillaume, "Further Documents on the Ben Meir Controversy," *Jewish Quarterly Review*, n.s. 5 (1915): 553–54
3 n. 3

Bodl. MS Heb. d 75.20
Gil, *In the Kingdom of Ishmael*, doc. 449
Udovitch, "Formalism and Informalism," 66–72 (English translation only)
8 n. 4

Bodl. MS Heb. d 76.56
Friedman, *Jewish Polygyny*, 244–45
Gil, *History of Palestine* doc. 148
8 n. 10

Bodl. MS Heb. e 95.54+BL Or. 5560a+Mosseri I 85 (H 8)
Mann, *Jews in Egypt and in Palestine*, 1:30–32, 2:31–35 (first two fragments); third in idem, "A Second Supplement to 'The Jews in Egypt and in Palestine under the Fāṭimid Caliphs,'" *Hebrew Union College Annual* 3 (1926): 258–62
Gil, *History of Palestine*, doc. 19 (second fragment only)
8 n. 1

Bodl. MS Heb. e 98.60
Friedman, *Jewish Marriage in Palestine*, doc. 52
Gil, *History of Palestine*, doc. 594
See Goitein, *Palestinian Jewry*, 236, and Friedman's corrections, *Jewish Polygyny*, 341 n. 2
9 n. 11; 12 n. 44

Bodl. MS Heb. e 108.70
Gil, *History of Palestine*, doc. 16

See also Goitein, *Mediterranean Society*, 2:604 n. 42
4 n. 41; 7 n. 9; 10 n. 11

Bodl. MS Heb. f 56.82–83
Gil, *In the Kingdom of Ishmael*, doc. 6
1 n. 29

Bodl. MS Neubauer 356 (non-Geniza)
Halkin, *Divulgatio mysteriorum*
1 n. 34

PARIS: ARCHIVES OF THE LIBRARY OF THE ALLIANCE ISRAÉLITE UNIVERSELLE

AIU VII A 23: see **T-S** 13 **J** 35.3

AIU XI 268
Gil, *In the Kingdom of Ishmael*, doc. 279
5 n. 30

PARIS: JACQUES MOSSERI COLLECTION:

See under Cambridge

PHILADELPHIA: LIBRARY OF THE CENTER FOR ADVANCED JUDAIC STUDIES

Former Dropsie College, now part of the University of Pennsylvania. Shelf-marks are formerly Dropsie, now Halper, as catalogued in Ben-Zion Halper, *Descriptive Catalogue of Genizah Fragments in Philadelphia* (Philadelphia, 1924). High-resolution images of all documents available on-line at http://sceti.library.upenn.edu/genizah/.

Halper 332
Gil, *In the Kingdom of Ishmael*, doc. 5
1 n. 29

Halper 354
Goitein, *Palestinian Jewry*, 57, with facsimile and Hebrew translation of verso
Goitein, "New Sources on the Palestinian Gaonate," 524–25 (doc. 3, verso only, English translation)
1 n. 64; 3 n. 57; 4 n. 8; 8 n. 13; 11 nn. 5, 6 (Goitein's reading emended); fig. 10

Halper 393
Goitein's edition available on-line through the Princeton Geniza Project
9 n. 11

Halper 397
Gil, *History of Palestine*, doc. 451
5 n. 28

Halper 401
Unpublished
See Gil, *History of Palestine*, sec. 803 n.
7 n. 11; fig. 5

Halper 412: see T-S 16.275

ST. PETERSBURG: NATIONAL LIBRARY OF RUSSIA (RNL)

The RNL collections were recently renamed: the first Firkovich collection (1 Firk.) is now RNL Yevr. 1, the second Firkovich collection (2 Firk.) is divided among RNL Yevr. 2, RNL Yevr.-Arab. 1 and RNL Yevr.-Arab. 2 (not to be confused with RNL Arab.-Yevr.); and the Antonin collection is RNL Yevr. 3. See Sklare, "Guide to Collections of Karaite Manuscripts," 905–9. I have not used the new nomenclature below. It is unclear whether any of the Firkovich manuscript derive from the Ben Ezra Geniza.

Antonin Collection

Antonin B 627
Unpublished
9 n. 22

Antonin 637
Simha Assaf, *Formulary of Hai Gaon*, *Tarbiẓ* 1, no. 3 (supplement) (1930): 55–58
Friedman, *Jewish Marriage in Palestine*, doc. 30
9 n. 11; 10 n. 37

Firkovich Collections

1 Firk. Heb. B 19a (Leningrad Codex)
2 n. 19

2 Firk. Cod. 223
Colophon: Kahle, *Masoreten des Westens*, 1:67; Mann, *Texts and Studies*, 2:134–35
1 n. 62

2 Firk. Heb. A 506+2 Firk. Heb. A 2222
Olszowy-Schlanger, *Karaite Marriage Documents*, doc. 55
9 n. 22

2 Firk. Heb. A 717r
Olszowy-Schlanger, *Karaite Marriage Documents*, doc. 46
9 n. 22

2 Firk. Heb. A 2222: see 2 Firk. Heb. A 506

2 Firk. Heb. B 34.1
Colophon: Kahle, *Masoreten des Westens*, 1:74–77
See Olszowy-Schlanger, *Karaite Marriage Documents*, 305
9 n. 36

2 Firk. Heb. B 180
Marginal note cited in Olszowy-Schlanger, *Karaite Marriage Documents*, 305
9 n. 36

2 Firk. Heb.-Arab. 3869
4 n. 5 (see there for publication information)

2 Firk. Heb.-Arab. 3951
See Ben-Shammai, "Major Trends," 358–59.
12 n. 34

Unidentified shelfmark
Albert Harkavy, "Mikhtav mi-Yerushalayim mi-ketav yad asher be-Petersburg," *Oṣar tov* (1878): 77–81

Mann, *Jews in Egypt and in Palestine*, 2:189–91
Gil, *History of Palestine*, doc. 420
7 n. 16

VIENNA: ÖSTERREICHISCHE NATIONALBIBLIOTHEK, PAPYRUSSAMMLUNG UND PAPYRUSMUSEUM, PAPYRUSSAMMLUNG ERZHERZOG RAINER

PER H 22
Goitein's previously published edition, with corrections from his personal offprint, available on-line through the Princeton Geniza Project
5 n. 30

PER H 83
Assaf, "Old Genizah Documents," 197–99
Gil, *History of Palestine*, doc. 271
10 n. 16

PER H 135
D. H. Müller and D. Kaufmann, "Der Brief eines aegyptischen Rabbi an den Gaon [Salomo] Ben Jehuda," *Mittheilungen aus der Sammlung der Papyrus Erzherzog Rainer* 5 (1892): 127
Gil, *History of Palestine*, doc. 334
11 n. 59

WASHINGTON, DC: SMITHSONIAN INSTITUTION, FREER GALLERY OF ART

Numbered in Richard J. H. Gottheil and William Hoyt Worrell, *Fragments from the Cairo Genizah in the Freer Collection* (New York, 1927).

Gottheil-Worrell 35
Gottheil and Worrell, *Fragments*, doc. 35 (with English translation and facsimile)
Gil, *In the Kingdom of Ishmael*, doc. 743
3 n. 35

Gottheil-Worrell 43
Gottheil and Worrell, *Fragments*, doc. 43 (with English translation and facsimile)
Gil, *History of Palestine*, doc. 199
11 n. 60

UNKNOWN LOCATIONS

MS Meunier
Gil, *In the Kingdom of Ishmael*, doc. 127 (see there for previous publications)
5 n. 7

MS Levi (formerly in the possession of Israel Levi, chief Rabbi of France)+West. Coll. Bib. 6.52+Bodl. MS Heb. c 13.22
Gil, *In the Kingdom of Ishmael*, doc. 8
1 n. 29

BIBLIOGRAPHY

Abramson, Sheraga. *In the Centers and the Peripheries during the Geonic Period: The History of the Geonim and Exilarchs in Palestine and Babylonia and the Sages of Egypt and North Africa, based on Geniza Documents*. Hebrew. Jerusalem: Rav Kook Institute, 1965.

Adler, Marcus Nathan. *The Itinerary of Benjamin of Tudela: Critical Text, Translation and Commentary*. London: Oxford University Press, 1907.

Alexander, Elizabeth Shanks. *Transmitting Mishnah: The Shaping Influence of Oral Tradition*. Cambridge: Cambridge University Press, 2006.

Algamil, Yosef. *Sefer ha-miṣvot le-rav Levi b. Yefet ha-Levi ha-mekhune Abu Saʿid*. 5 vols. Ashdod: Makhon Tifʾeret Yosef le-ḥeqer ha-yahadut ha-qaraʾit, 2004.

Allony, Nehemya. "ʿElī ben Yehuda Hannazir and His Treatise '*Kitāb uṣūl al-lugha al-ʿibrāniyya*.'" Hebrew. *Lĕšonénu* 34 (1969–70): 75–105, 187–209.

——. *The Jewish Library in the Middle Ages: Book Lists from the Cairo Genizah*. Hebrew. Edited by Miriam Frenkel and Haggai Ben-Shammai. Jerusalem: Ben-Zvi Institute, 2006.

Allouche, Adel. "The Establishment of Four Chief Judgeships in Fatimid Egypt." *Journal of the American Oriental Society* 105 (1985): 317–20.

Ankori, Zvi. "The Correspondence of Tobias ben Moses the Karaite of Constantinople." In *Essays on Jewish Life and Thought: Presented in Honor of Salo Wittmayer Baron*, edited by Joseph L. Blau, 1–59. New York: Columbia University Press, 1959.

——. "Ibn al-Hītī and the Chronology of Joseph al-Baṣīr the Karaite." *Journal of Jewish Studies* 8 (1957): 71–81.

——. *Karaites in Byzantium: The Formative Years, 970–1100*. Columbia Studies in the Social Sciences 597. New York: Columbia University Press, 1959.

Antoon, Sinan. "The Poetics of the Obscene: Ibn al-Ḥajjāj and Sukhf." Ph.D. diss., Harvard University, 2006.

Ashtiany, Julia. *ʿAbbasid Belles-Lettres*. Cambridge History of Arabic Literature. Cambridge: Cambridge University Press, 1990.

Ashtor, Eliyahu. "Documentos españoles de la Genizah." *Sefarad* 24 (1964): 41–80.

——. *Histoire des prix et des salaires dans l'Orient médiéval*. Monnaie, prix, conjoncture 8. Paris: S.E.V.P.E.N., 1969.

——. "Un mouvement migratoire au haut moyen age: Migrations de l'Irak vers les pays méditerranéens." *Annales: Economies, sociétés, civilizations* 27 (1972): 185–214.

——. "Yediʿot ʿal ha-yehudim bi-ṣfon Ereṣ Yisraʾel ba-meʾa ha-aḥat ʿesre u-va-maḥaṣit ha-rishona shel ha-meʾa ha-sheteym ʿesre" (The Jews in northern Palestine in the eleventh and first half of the twelfth century). In *Zer li-gvurot: qoveṣ meḥqarim ba-Miqraʾ, bi-ydiʿat ha-areṣ, bi-lshon u-ve-sifrut talmudit mugash le-Rav Zalman Shazar, nesi ha-medina be-yom huladeto ha-83*, edited by Bentsion Lurie, 489–509. Jerusalem: Kiryat Sefer, 1973.

Ashtor (Strauss), Eli (Eliyahu). "Documents for the Economic and Social History of the Jews in the Near East." Hebrew. *Zion* 7 (1942): 140–55.

Assaf, Simḥa. *Formulary of Hai Gaon*. Hebrew. *Tarbiẓ* 1, no. 3 (supplement) (1930).

——. "Le-toldot ha-qaraʾim be-arṣot ha-mizraḥ." *Zion* 1 (1935–36): 208–51.

——. "Letters from Kairwan and Alexandria to R. Joseph ibn Ukal." Hebrew. *Tarbiẓ* 20 (1948–49): 177–90.

——. "Old Deeds from Eretz-Israel and Egypt." Hebrew. *Yerushalayim: meḥqerey Ereṣ Yisra'el* 3 (1952): 104–17.
——. "Old Genizah Documents from Palestine, Egypt and North Africa." Hebrew. *Tarbiẓ* 9 (1937–38): 11–34, 196–221.
——. *ha-ʿOnashin aḥarey ḥatimat ha-talmud: ḥomer le-toldot ha-mishpaṭ ha-ʿivri* (Punishments after the close of the Talmud: Material toward the history of Jewish law). Jerusalem,1922.
——. *Responsa Geonica ex fragmentis Cantabrigiensibus*. Hebrew. Jerusalem: Meḳiẓe Nirdamim, 1942.
——. "Seridim min ha-geniza." In *Sefer Klausner: me'assef le-maddaʿ u-le-sifrut yafa mugash le-Professor Yosef Klausner le-yovel ha-shishim*. Edited by N. H. Torczyner, A. A. Kabak, E. Tcherikover, and B. Shohetman, 226–34. Tel Aviv, 1937.
——. *Tequfat ha-ge'onim ve-sifrutah* (The gaonic period and its literature). Edited by Mordecai Margaliot. Jerusalem: Rav Kook Institute, 1976.
Astren, Fred. *Karaite Judaism and Historical Understanding*. Studies in Comparative Religion. Columbia: University of South Carolina Press, 2004.
Baer, Yitzhak F. *A History of the Jews in Christian Spain*. Translated by Louis Schoffman. 2 vols. Philadelphia: Jewish Publication Society of America, 1961 [1945, 1959].
——. "ha-Yesodot ve-ha-hatḥalot shel irgun ha-qehillot bimey ha-benayim." *Zion* 15 (1950): 1–41.
Bahat, Dan. "The Physical Infrastructure." In *The History of Jerusalem: The Early Muslim Period*, 638–1099, edited by Joshua Prawer and Haggai Ben-Shammai. 38–100. Jerusalem: Yad Izhak Ben-Zvi and New York University Press, 1996.
Baker, Colin F., and Meira Polliack. *Arabic and Judaeo-Arabic Manuscripts in the Cambridge Genizah Collections: Arabic Old Series (T-S Ar. 1a–54)*. Cambridge University Library Genizah Series 12. Cambridge: Cambridge University Press, 2001.
Balog, Paul. "Pious Invocations Probably Used as Titles of Office or as Honorific Titles in Umayyad and Abbasid Times." In *Studies in Memory of Gaston Wiet*, edited by M. Rosen-Ayalon, 61–68. Jerusalem, 1977.
Baneth, D. Z. "A Letter from Shelomo b. Judah, Head of the Ge'on Yaʿaqov Academy in Jerusalem, to an Unknown Person in Fusṭāṭ [prepared for publication by M. Gil]." Hebrew. In *Studia orientalia memoriae D. H. Baneth dedicata*, 1–16, edited by J. Blau, S. Pines, M. J. Kister, and S. Shaked. Jerusalem: Magnes Press, 1979.
——, ed. *Mose ben Maimon: Epistulae*. Jerusalem: Magnes Press, Hebrew University, 1985 [1946].
Bareket, Elinoar. "Abraham ha-kohen b. Isaac ibn Furat." Hebrew. *Hebrew Union College Annual* 70–71 (1999–2000): 1–19.
——. "Books of Records of the Jerusalemite Court from the Cairo Genizah in the First Half of the Eleventh Century." Hebrew. *Hebrew Union College Annual* 69 (1998): 1–55.
——. *Fustat on the Nile: The Jewish Elite in Medieval Egypt*. The Medieval Mediterranean 24. Leiden: Brill, 1999.
——. *The Jewish Leadership in Fustat in the First Half of the Eleventh Century*. Hebrew. Tel Aviv: Diaspora Research Institute, Tel Aviv University, 1995.
——. *The Jews of Egypt, 1007–1055: On the Basis of the Archive of Ephraim ben Shemarya*. Hebrew. Jerusalem: Ben-Zvi Institute, 1995.
——. "Rais al-Yahud in Egypt under the Fatimids: A Reconsideration." Hebrew. *Zemanim* 64 (1998): 34–42.
——. "Sahlan b. Abraham." Hebrew. *Tarbiẓ* 52 (1983): 17–40.
——. "'Thou Shalt Surely Open thy Hand to thy Poor and Needy Brother: Letters Requesting Financial Aid from the Geniza." Hebrew. *Teʿuda* 16–17 (2001): 359–89.
——. "'Ve-aruḥato aruḥat tamid nitena lo me-et ha-melekh': rosh ha-yehudim be-arṣot ha-Islam be-hishtaqefut kefula" ("A regular allotment of food was given him by order of the king": a reexamination of the head of the Jews in Islamic lands). *Devarim* 3 (2000): 35–48.
Bargès, Jean Joseph Léandre, ed. *In Canticum canticorum commentarium arabicum, quod ex unico Bibliothecae nationalis parisiensis manuscripto codice in lucem edidit atque in linguam latinam transtulit*. Paris: Ernest Leroux, 1884.
Barnavi, Eli, ed. *A Historical Atlas of the Jewish People: From the Time of the Patriarchs to the Present*. New York: Knopf, 1992.

Baron, Salo Wittmayer. *The Jewish Community: Its History and Structure to the American Revolution.* 3 vols. Philadelphia: Jewish Publication Society, 1942.
——. *A Social and Religious History of the Jews.* 2d ed., 17 vols. Vols. 4 and 5. New York: Columbia University Press, 1957.
Baumgarten, Albert I. *The Flourishing of Jewish Sects in the Maccabean Era: An Interpretation.* Supplements to the Journal for the Study of Judaism 55. Leiden: Brill, 1997.
Beinin, Joel. *The Dispersion of Egyptian Jewry: Culture, Politics, and the Formation of a Modern Diaspora.* Berkeley: University of California Press, 1998.
Beit-Arié, Malachi. *Hebrew Manuscripts of East and West: Towards a Comparative Codicology.* The Panizzi Lectures 1992. London: The British Library, 1993.
Ben-Sasson, Haim Hillel. "The Karaite Community of Jerusalem in the Tenth–Eleventh Centuries." *Shalem* 2 (1976): 1–18.
Ben-Sasson, Menahem. "Al-Andalus: The So-Called 'Golden Age' of Spanish Jewry—A Critical View." In *The Jews of Europe in the Middle Ages (Tenth to Fifteenth Centuries): Proceedings of the International Symposium Held at Speyer, 20–25 October 2002*, edited by Christoph Cluse, 123–37. Turnhout: Brepols, 2004.
——. "Communal Leaders in North Africa—Figure and Image: Literary Composition as an Historical Source." Hebrew. *Pe'amim* 26 (1986): 132–62.
——. *The Emergence of the Local Jewish Community in the Muslim World: Qayrawan*, 800–1057. Hebrew. 2d rev. ed. Jerusalem: Magnes Press, 1997.
——. "The Emergence of the Qayrawan Jewish Community and Its Importance as a Maghrebi Community." *Judeo-Arabic Studies* (1997): 1–14.
——. "Firkovich's Second Collection: Remarks on Historical and Halakhic Material." Hebrew. *Jewish Studies* 31 (1991): 47–67.
——. "Fragmentary Letters from the Geniza: Concerning the Ties of the Babylonian Academies with the West." Hebrew. *Tarbiẓ* 56 (1987): 171–209.
——. "Geniza Evidence on the Events of 1019–1020 in Damascus and Cairo." Hebrew. In *Mas'at Moshe: Studies in Jewish and Islamic Culture Presented to Moshe Gil*, edited by Ezra Fleischer, Mordechai A. Friedman, and Joel Kraemer, 103–23. Jerusalem: Bialik Institute, 1998.
——. "The Jews of the Maghreb and Their Relations with Eretz Israel in the Ninth through Eleventh Centuries." Hebrew. *Shalem* 5 (1987): 31–82.
——. "Maghrib-Mashriq Ties from the Ninth to the Eleventh Centuries." Hebrew. *Pe'amim* 38 (1989): 35–48.
——. "The Medieval Period: The Tenth to Fourteenth Centuries." In *Fortifications and the Synagogue: The Fortress of Babylon and the Ben Ezra Synagogue, Cairo*, edited by Phyllis Lambert, 201–23. Chicago: University of Chicago Press, 1994.
——. "Religious Leadership in Islamic Lands: Forms of Leadership and Sources of Authority." In *Jewish Religious Leadership: Image and Reality*, edited by Jack Wertheimer, 1: 177–210. New York: Jewish Theological Seminary, 2004.
——. "The Structure, Goals, and Content of the Story of Nathan Ha-Babli." Hebrew. In *Culture and Society in Medieval Jewry: Studies Dedicated to the Memory of Haim Hillel Ben-Sasson*, edited by Menahem Ben-Sasson, Roberto Bonfil, and Joseph Hacker, 137–96. Jerusalem: Zalman Shazar Center, 1989.
——. "Varieties of Inter-Communal Relations in the Geonic Period." In *The Jews of Medieval Islam: Community, Society, and Identity*, edited by Daniel Frank, 17–31. Leiden: Brill, 1995.
Ben-Sasson, Menahem, Nadia Zeldes, and Miriam Frenkel. *The Jews of Sicily, 825–1068: Documents and Sources.* Hebrew. Oriens Iudaicus, Series 1, Volume 1. Jerusalem: Ben-Zvi Institute, 1991.
Ben-Shammai, Haggai. "The Attitude of Some Early Karaites towards Islam." In *Studies in Medieval Jewish History and Literature*, edited by Isadore Twersky, 1–40. Cambridge: Harvard University Press, 1984.
——. "Between Ananites and Karaites: Observations on Early Medieval Jewish Sectarianism." In *Studies in Muslim-Jewish Relations*, edited by Ronald L. Nettler, 19–29. Chur: Harwood Academic Publishers in cooperation with the Oxford Centre for Postgraduate Hebrew Studies, 1993.
——. "Fragments of Daniel al-Qūmisī's Commentary on the Book of Daniel as a Historical Source." *Henoch* 13 (1991): 259–81.

——. "The Karaite Controversy: Scripture and Tradition in Early Karaism." In *Religionsgespräche im Mittelalter*, edited by Bernard Lewis and Friedrich Niewöhner, 11–26. Wiesbaden: Harrassowitz, 1992.
——. "The Karaites." In *The History of Jerusalem: The Early Muslim Period, 638–1099*, edited by Joshua Prawer and Haggai Ben-Shammai, 201–24. Jerusalem: Yad Izhak Ben-Zvi and New York University Press, 1996.
——. "Major Trends in Karaite Philosophy and Polemics in the Tenth and Eleventh Centuries." In *Karaite Judaism: A Guide to its History and Literary Sources*, edited by Meira Polliack, Handbuch der Orientalistik, pt. 1: Nahe und Mittlere Osten, 73, 339–62. Leiden: Brill, 2003.
——. "Qeṭaʿ ḥadash me-ha-maqor ha-ʿaravi shel Sefer ha-miṣvot le-Levi ben Yefet ha-qaraʾi." *Shenaton ha-mishpaṭ ha-ʿIvri* 11–12 (1985): 99–133.
——. "The Scholarly Study of Karaism in the Nineteenth and Twentieth Centuries." In *Karaite Judaism: A Guide to its History and Literary Sources*, edited by Meira Polliack, Handbuch der Orientalistik, pt. 1: Nahe und Mittlere Osten, 73, 9–24. Leiden: Brill, 2003.
——. "A Unique Lamentation on Jerusalem by the Qaraite Author Yeshuaʿ b. Yehuda." Hebrew. In *Masʾat Moshe: Studies in Jewish and Islamic Culture Presented to Moshe Gil*, edited by Ezra Fleischer, Mordechai A. Friedman, and Joel L. Kraemer, 93–102. Jerusalem: Bialik Institute and Tel Aviv University, 1998.
Ben-Zvi, I. "The Codex of Ben-Asher." *Textus* 1, no. 7–9 (1960): 1–16.
Berkey, Jonathan P. *The Transmission of Knowledge in Medieval Cairo: A Social History of Islamic Education*. Princeton Studies on the Near East. Princeton: Princeton University Press, 1992.
Bernheimer, Teresa. "A Social History of the ʿAlid Family from the Eighth to the Eleventh Century." Ph.D. diss., Oxford University, 2006.
Bialik, H. N. and Y. H. Ravnitsky, eds. *Shirey Shelomo b. Yehuda ibn Gavirol*. 5 volumes. Tel Aviv, 1927.
Bianquis, Thierry. *Damas et la Syrie sous la domination fatimide 359–468/969–1076: Essai d'interprétation de chroniques arabes médiévales*. 2 vols. Damascus: Institut français de Damas, 1986.
Bickerman, Elias J. "Notes on Seleucid and Parthian Chronology." *Berytus* 8 (1943): 73–84.
Blau, Joseph L., ed. *Essays on Jewish Life and Thought Presented in Honor of Salo Wittmayer Baron*. New York: Columbia University Press, 1959.
Blau, Joshua. *A Dictionary of Mediaeval Judaeo-Arabic Texts*. Arabic, Hebrew, and English. Jerusalem: The Academy of the Hebrew Language and the Israel Academy of Sciences and Humanities, 2007.
Bloom, J. M. "The Mosque of the Qarafa in Cairo." *Muqarnas* 4 (1987): 7–20.
Bornstein, Ḥayim Yeḥiel. *Maḥloqet Rav Seʿadya Gaʾon u-Ven Meʾir*. Warsaw, 1904.
Bosworth, C. E. "Christian and Jewish Religious Dignitaries in Mamluk Egypt and Syria: Qalqashandi's Information on Their Hierarchy, Titulature, and Appointment." *International Journal of Middle East Studies* 3 (1972): 59–74 and 199–216.
——. *The New Islamic Dynasties: A Chronological and Genealogical Manual*. Rev. ed. New York: Columbia University Press, 1996.
——. "The Titulature of the Early Ghaznavids." *Oriens* 15 (1962): 210–33.
Brener, Anne. *Isaac ibn Khalfun: A Wandering Hebrew Poet of the Eleventh Century*. Hebrew Language and Literature Series 4. Leiden: Brill, 2003.
Brett, Michael, ed. *Northern Africa: Islam and Modernization*. London: Frank Cass, 1973.
Brinner, William M. "A Fifteenth-Century Karaite-Rabbanite Dispute in Cairo." In *The Majlis: Interreligious Encounters in Medieval Islam*, edited by Mark R. Cohen, Hava Lazarus-Yafeh, Sasson Somekh, and Sidney H. Griffith, 184–96. Wiesbaden: Harrassowitz, 1999.
Brody, Robert. *The Geonim of Babylonia and the Shaping of Medieval Jewish Culture*. New Haven: Yale University Press, 1998.
——. *The Textual History of the Sheʾiltot*. Hebrew. New York: American Academy for Jewish Research, 1991.
——. "Rav ʿAmram bar Sheshna—Gaʾon of Sura?" Hebrew *Tarbiẓ* 56 (1987): 327–45.
Bulliet, Richard W. *Conversion to Islam in the Medieval Period: An Essay in Quantitative History*. Cambridge: Harvard University Press, 1979.
——. *The Patricians of Nishapur: A Study in Medieval Islamic Social History*. Harvard Middle Eastern Studies 16. Cambridge: Harvard University Press, 1972.

Caetani, Leone, and Giuseppe Gabrieli. *Onomasticon Arabicum, ossia repertorio alfabetico dei nomi di persona e di luogo contenuti nelle principali opere storiche, biografiche e geografiche, stampate e manoscritte, relative all'Islām: Fonti–introduzione*. 2 vols. Vol. 1. Rome: Casa Editrice Italiana, 1915.
Cahen, Claude. *Mouvements populaires et autonomisme urbain dans l'Asie musulmane du moyen âge*. Leiden: Brill, 1959.
Catalogue de la collection Jack Mosseri, edité par l'Institut de Manuscrits Microfilmés Hébraïques avec le concours de nombreux spécialistes. Hebrew. Jerusalem: Jewish National and University Library, 1990.
Chamberlain, Michael. *Knowledge and Social Practice in Medieval Damascus, 1190–1350*. Cambridge: Cambridge University Press, 2002.
Chapira, E. D. "Mikhtav me-ha-ga'on R. Ṣemaḥ Ṣedeq bar Yiṣḥaq le-R. Elḥanan b. Shemarya mi-Miṣrayim." *Ginzei Qedem*, o.s. 3 (1925): 3–13.
——. "Lettre du Gaon Hai." *Revue des études juives* 82 (1926): 317–31.
Chesterton, G. K. *Orthodoxy*. Garden City: Image Books, 1959.
Chiesa, Bruno. *L'Antico Testamento ebraico secondo la tradizione palestinese*. Turin: Bottega di Erasmo, 1978.
——. *The Emergence of Hebrew Biblical Pointing*. Judentum und Umwelt. Frankfurt: Peter Lang, 1979.
——. "La tradizione babilonese dell'Antico Testamento ebraico." *Henoch* 6 (1984): 181–204.
Chiesa, Bruno, and Wilfrid Lockwood. *Yaqub al-Qirqisani on Jewish Sects and Christianity: A Translation of "Kitab al-anwar," Book 1, with Two Introductory Essays*. Judentum und Umwelt 10. Frankfurt: Peter Lang, 1984.
Cohen, Gerson D. *A Critical Edition with a Translation and Notes of the Book of Tradition (Sefer ha-qabbalah)*. Philadelphia: Jewish Publication Society, 1967.
——. "The Reconstruction of Gaonic History." In *Studies in the Variety of Rabbinic Cultures*, 99–155. Philadelphia: Jewish Publication Society, 1991.
——. "The Story of the Four Captives." *Proceedings of the American Academy of Jewish Research* 29 (1960): 55–123.
——. *Studies in the Variety of Rabbinic Cultures*. Philadelphia: Jewish Publication Society, 1991.
Cohen, Mark R. "Administrative Relations between Palestinian and Egyptian Jewry during the Fatimid Period." In *Egypt and Palestine: A Millennium of Association (868–1948)*, edited by Amnon Cohen and Gabriel Baer, 113–35. Jerusalem and New York: Ben-Zvi Institute for the Study of Jewish Communities in the East and St. Martin's Press, 1984.
——. "Jewish Communal Organization in Medieval Egypt: Research, Results and Prospects." *Judaeo-Arabic Studies* (1997): 73–86.
——. *Jewish Self-Government in Medieval Egypt: The Origins of the Office of Head of the Jews, ca. 1065–1126*. Princeton Studies on the Near East. Princeton: Princeton University Press, 1980.
——. "Jews in the Mamluk Environment: The Crisis of 1442 (a Geniza Study)." *Bulletin of the School of Oriental and African Studies* 47 (1984): 425–48.
——. "New Light on the Conflict over the Palestinian Gaonate, 1038–1042, and on Daniel b. ʿAzarya: A Pair of Letters to the Nagid of Qayrawan." *Association for Jewish Studies Review* 1 (1976): 1–37.
——. *Poverty and Charity in the Jewish Community of Medieval Egypt*. Jews, Christians, and Muslims from the Ancient to the Modern World. Princeton: Princeton University Press, 2005.
——. *Under Crescent and Cross: The Jews in the Middle Ages*. Princeton: Princeton University Press, 1994.
——. *The Voice of the Poor in the Middle Ages: An Anthology of Documents from the Cairo Geniza*. Princeton: Princeton University Press, 2005.
——. "What Was the Pact of ʿUmar? A Literary-Historical Study." *Jerusalem Studies in Arabic and Islam* 23 (1999): 100–156.
Cohen, Mark, and Sasson Somekh. "In the Court of Yaʿqūb ibn Killis: A Fragment from the Cairo Genizah." *Jewish Quarterly Review* 80 (1990): 283–315.
——. "Interreligious Majālis in Early Fatimid Egypt." In *The Majlis: Interreligious Encounters in Medieval Islam*, edited by Hava Lazarus-Yafeh, Mark Cohen, and Sasson Somekh, Studies in Arabic Language and Literature, 4. 128–36. Wiesbaden: Harrassowitz, 1999.
Conrad, Lawrence I. "A Nestorian Diploma of Investiture from the Tadhkira of Ibn Ḥamdūn: The Text and Its Significance." In *Studia Arabica et Islamica: Festschrift for Iḥsān ʿAbbās on His*

Sixtieth Birthday, edited by Wadād al-Qāḍī, 83–104. Beirut: American University of Beirut, 1981.
Cook, Michael. "Magian Cheese: An Archaic Problem in Islamic Law." *Bulletin of the School of Oriental and African Studies* 47 (1984): 449–67
Cortese, Delia, and Simonetta Calderini. *Women and the Fatimids in the World of Islam*. Edinburgh: Edinburgh University Press, 2006.
Coulson, Noel. *Succession in the Muslim Family*. Cambridge: Cambridge University Press, 1971.
Cowley, A. "Bodleian Geniza Fragments." *Jewish Quarterly Review*, o.s. 19 (1906–7): 250–56.
Crone, Patricia, and Martin Hinds. *God's Caliph: Religious Authority in the First Centuries of Islam*. Cambridge: Cambridge University Press, 1986.
Danzig, Neil. *Introduction to Halakhot Pesuqot with a Supplement to Halakhot Pesuqot*. Hebrew. 2d ed. New York: Jewish Theological Seminary of America, 1993.
Davidson, Israel. *The Book of the Wars of the Lord: Containing the Polemics of the Karaite Salmon ben Yeruhim against Saadia Gaon*. New York: Jewish Theological Seminary of America, 1934.
Davies, Rees. "The Medieval State: The Tyranny of a Concept?" *Journal of Historical Sociology* 16 (2003): 280–300.
De Goeje, M. J., ed. *Bibliotheca Geographorum Arabicorum*. 8 vols. Leiden: Brill, 1997 [1870–94].
Drory, Rina. *The Emergence of Jewish-Arabic Literary Contacts at the Beginning of the Tenth Century*. Sifrut, mashmaʿut, tarbut 17. Tel Aviv: Ha-Kibbutz ha-Meʾuḥad, 1988.
——. *Models and Contacts: Arabic Literature and Its Impact on Medieval Jewish Culture*. Brill's Series in Jewish Studies 25. Leiden: Brill, 2000.
——. "Le rôle de la littérature karaïte dans l'histoire de la littérature juive au xe siècle." *Revue des études juives* 159 (2000): 99–111.
Duby, Georges. *Love and Marriage in the Middle Ages*. Translated by Jane Dunnett. Chicago: University of Chicago Press, 1994.
Eldar, Ilan. *The Art of Correct Reading of the Bible*. Hebrew. Jerusalem: Academy of the Hebrew Language, 1994.
Eliash, J. "New Information on 11th Century Palestine." Hebrew. *Sefunot* 2 (1957–58): 7–25.
Elkin, Zeev, and Menaḥem Ben-Sasson. "Abraham Firkovich and the Cairo Genizas in the Light of His Personal Archive." Hebrew. *Peʿamim* 90 (2002): 51–95.
El-Leithy, Tamer. "Coptic Culture and Conversion in Medieval Cairo, 1293–1524 A.D." Ph.D. diss., Princeton University, 2005.
Elon, Menachem. *Jewish Law: History, Sources, Principles=Ha-mishpat ha-Ivri*. Edited by A. Philip and Muriel Berman. 4 vols. Philadelphia: Jewish Publication Society, 1994.
Ephrat, Daphna. *A Learned Society in a Period of Transition: The Sunnī ʿUlamāʾ of Eleventh Century Baghdad*. SUNY Series in Medieval Middle East History. Albany: SUNY Press, 2000.
Erder, Yoram. "The Mourners of Zion: The Karaites in Jerusalem of the Tenth and Eleventh Centuries." In *Karaite Judaism: A Guide to Its History and Literary Sources*, edited by Meira Polliack, Handbuch der Orientalistik, pt. 1: Nahe und Mittlere Osten, 73, 213–35. Leiden and Boston: Brill, 2003.
Fenton, Paul. "A Mystical Treatise on Perfection, Providence and Prophecy from the Jewish Sufi Circle." In The *Jews of Medieval Islam: Community, Society, and Identity*, edited by Daniel Frank, 301–34. Leiden: Brill, 1995.
Fischel, Walter J. *Jews in the Economic and Political Life of Medieval Islam*. New York: Ktav, 1969 [1937].
Fleischer, Ezra. "Pilgrims' Prayer at the Gates of Jerusalem." Hebrew. In *Masʾat Moshe: Studies in Jewish and Islamic Culture Presented to Moshe Gil*, edited by Ezra Fleischer, Mordechai A. Friedman, and Joel L. Kraemer, 298–327. Jerusalem: Bialik Institute and Tel Aviv University, 1998.
——. *The Proverbs of Saʿīd ben Bābshād*. Hebrew. Jerusalem: Ben-Zvi Institute, 1990.
——. "Qavim ḥadashim li-dmuto shel rav Daniʾel ben ʿAzarya, nasiʾ ve-gaʾon." *Shalem* 1 (1974): 53–74.
——. "Rabbi Sakan—payyeṭan ereṣ-yisraʾeli ba-meʾa ha-ʿasirit." In *Studies in Geniza and Sepharadi Heritage Presented to Shelomo Dov Goitein on the Occasion of his Eightieth Birthday*, edited by Shelomo Morag and Issachar Ben-Ami, with the assistance of Norman A. Stillman. Hebrew. 1–37. Jerusalem: Magnes Press, 1981.

——. "Saadya Gaon's Place in the History of Hebrew Poetry." Hebrew. *Pe'amim* 54 (1993): 4–17.
Fleischer, Ezra, Mordechai A. Friedman, and Joel L. Kraemer, eds. *Mas'at Moshe: Studies in Jewish and Arab Culture Dedicated to Moshe Gil.* Hebrew. Jerusalem: Bialik Institute and Tel Aviv University, 1998.
Flusser, David. *Judaism and the Origins of Christianity.* Jerusalem: Magnes Press, 1988.
Frank, Daniel. "Karaite Commentaries on the Song of Songs from Tenth-Century Jerusalem." In *With Reverence for the Word: Medieval Scriptural Exegesis in Judaism, Chrstianity, and Islam,* edited by Jane Dammen McAuliffe, Barry Walfish, and Joseph Ward Goering, 51–69. Oxford: Oxford University Press, 2003.
——. "Karaite Exegesis." In *Hebrew Bible, Old Testament: The History of Its Interpretation, vol. I: From the Beginnings to the Middle Ages (Until 1300). Part 2: The Middle Ages,* edited by Magne Sæbø, 110–28. Göttingen: Vandenhoeck & Ruprecht, 2000.
——. "Karaite Ritual." In *Judaism in Practice from the Middle Ages through the Early Modern Period,* edited by Lawrence Fine, 248–64. Princeton: Princeton University Press, 2001.
——. *Search Scripture Well: Karaite Exegetes and the Origins of the Jewish Bible Commentary in the Islamic East.* Leiden: Brill, 2004.
——. "The *Shoshanim* of Tenth-century Jerusalem: Karaite Exegesis, Prayer, and Communal Identity." In *The Jews of Medieval Islam: Community, Society, and Identity,* edited by Daniel Frank, 199–245. Leiden: Brill, 1995.
——. "The Study of Medieval Karaism, 1959–1989: A Bibliographical Essay." *Bulletin of Judaeo-Greek Studies* 6 (1990): 15–23.
——. "The Study of Medieval Karaism, 1989–1999." In *Hebrew Scholarship and the Medieval World,* edited by Nicholas De Lange, 3–22. Cambridge: Cambridge University Press, 2001.
——, ed. *The Jews of Medieval Islam: Community, Society, and Identity.* Etudes sur le judaïsme médiéval 16. Leiden: Brill, 1995.
Franklin, Arnold. "Cultivating Roots: The Promotion of Exilarchal Ties to David in the Middle Ages." *Association for Jewish Studies Review* 29 (2005): 91–110.
——. "Shoots of David: Members of the Exilarchal Dynasty in the Middle Ages." Ph.D. diss., Princeton University, 2001.
Frenkel, Miriam. *"The Compassionate and Benevolent": The Leading Elite in the Jewish Community of Alexandria in the Middle Ages.* Hebrew. Jerusalem: Ben-Zvi Institute for the Study of Jewish Communities in the East, Yad Izhak Ben-Zvi, and the Hebrew University of Jerusalem, 2006.
Frenkel, Miriam, and Nadia Zeldes. "The Sicilian Trade—Jewish Merchants in the Mediterranean in the Twelfth and Thirteenth Centuries." Hebrew. *Michael* 14 (1997): 99–137.
Freud, Sigmund. *Civilization and Its Discontents.* In *The Standard Edition of the Complete Psychological Works of Sigmund Freud,* translated and edited by James Strachey, vol. 21. London: Hogarth Press and the Institute for Psycho-Analysis, 1957.
Friedlander, Israel. "The Arabic Original of the Report of R. Nathan Hababli." *Jewish Quarterly Review,* o.s. 17 (1905): 747–61.
Friedman, M. A. *Jewish Marriage in Palestine: A Cairo Genizah Study.* 2 vols. Tel-Aviv: Tel-Aviv University, 1980.
——. *Jewish Polygyny: New Sources from the Cairo Geniza.* Hebrew. Jerusalem: Bialik Institute, 1986.
——. "Menstrual Impurity and Sectarianism in the Writings of the Geonim and of Moses and Abraham Maimonides." Hebrew. *Maimonidean Studies* 1 (1990): 1–21.
——. "On Marital Age, Violence and Mutuality in the Genizah Documents." In *The Cambridge Genizah Collections: Their Contents and Significance,* edited by Stefan C. Reif, 160–77. Cambridge: Cambridge University Press, 2002.
——. "On the Relationship of the Karaite and the Palestinian Rabbanite Marriage Contracts from the Geniza." Hebrew. *Te'uda* 15 (1999): 145–57.
——. "Qara'(im)=ben(ey) miqra'; ba'al(ey) miqra'." *Lĕšonénu* 39 (1976–77): 296–97.
Garcin, Jean-Claude. *Un centre musulman de la Haute-Egypte médiévale, Qus.* Textes arabes et études islamiques 6. Cairo: Institut français d'archéologie orientale du Caire, 1976.
Ghosh, Amitav. *In an Antique Land: History in the Guise of a Traveler's Tale.* New York: Knopf, 1993.
Gil, Moshe. *Documents of the Jewish Pious Foundations from the Cairo Geniza.* Leiden: Brill, 1976.

——. *A History of Palestine, 634–1099*. Translated by Ethel Broido. Cambridge: Cambridge University Press, 1992.
——. "Immigration and Pilgrimage in the Early Arab Period (634–1099)." Hebrew. *Cathedra* 8 (1978): 124–33.
——. *In the Kingdom of Ishmael*. Hebrew. 4 vols. Tel-Aviv and Jerusalem: Tel-Aviv University, the Ministry of Defense, and the Bialik Institute, 1997.
——. "The Jewish Community." In *The History of Jerusalem: The Early Muslim period, 638–1099*, ed. Joshua Prawer and Haggai Ben-Shammai, 163–200. Jerusalem: Yad Izhak Ben-Zvi and New York University Press, 1996.
——. *Jews in Islamic Countries in the Middle Ages*. Translated by David Strassler, Etudes sur le judaïsme médiéval 28. Leiden: Brill, 2004.
——. "The Jews in Sicily under Muslim Rule in the Light of the Geniza Documents." In *Italia Judaica: Atti del Convegno internazionale, Bari 18–22 maggio 1981*, 87–134. Rome: Ministero per i Beni Culturali e Ambientali, 1983.
——. "Maʿase be-ḥalom nifla' u-ve-misrat ṣibbur ba' ba-yamim." In *Studies in Geniza and Sepharadi Heritage Presented to Shelomo Dov Goitein on the Occasion of his Eightieth Birthday*, edited by Shelomo Morag and Issachar Ben-Ami, with the assistance of Norman A. Stillman, 67–75. Jerusalem: Magnes Press, 1981.
——. *Palestine during the First Muslim Period (634–1099)*. Hebrew. 3 vols. Tel Aviv: Tel Aviv University and the Ministry of Defense, 1983.
——. "Palestine during the First Muslim Period (634–1099): Additions, Notes, Corrections." Hebrew. *Te'uda* 7 (1991): 281–345.
——. "The Scroll of Evyatar as a Source for the History of the Struggles of the Yeshiva of Jerusalem during the Second Half of the Eleventh Century—A New Reading of the Scroll." Hebrew. In *Jerusalem in the Middle Ages: Selected Papers*, edited by Benjamin Z. Kedar, 39–106. Jerusalem: Yad Izhak Ben-Zvi, 1979.
——. *The Tustaris, Family and Sect*. Hebrew. Tel Aviv: Institute for Diaspora Research, 1981.
Gil, Moshe, and Ezra Fleischer. *Judah Halevi and His Circle: Fifty-Five Geniza Documents*. Hebrew. Jerusalem: World Union of Jewish Studies, 2001.
Ginzberg, Louis. *Geonica*. 2 vols. New York: Jewish Theological Seminary of America, 1909.
Ginzberg, Louis, Alexander Marx, and Israel Davidson. *Ginzey Schechter: Genizah Studies in Memory of Dr. Solomon Schechter*. 3 vols. New York: Jewish Theological Seminary of America, 1928.
Gladwell, Malcolm. *The Tipping Point: How Little Things Can Make a Big Difference*. New York: Little, Brown, 2000.
Glatzer, Mordechai. "The Aleppo Codex: Codicological and Paleographical Aspects." Hebrew. *Sefunot* 19 (1989): 167–276.
Goitein, S. D. "Additional Material from the Ibn ʿAwkal Archives on the Mediterranean Trade around 1000." Hebrew. *Tarbiẓ* 38 (1969): 18–42.
——. "Arbaʿ ketubbot ʿatiqot mi-Genizat Qahir" (Four ancient marriage contracts from the Cairo Geniza). *Lĕšonénu* 30 (1965–66): 197–215.
——. "Autographs of Yehuda Halevi." Hebrew. *Tarbiẓ* 25 (1956): 393–412.
——. "Bankers' Accounts from the Eleventh Century A.D." *Journal of the Economic and Social History of the Orient* 9 (1966): 28–68.
——. "A Caliph's Decree in Favour of the Rabbinite [*sic*] Jews of Palestine." *Journal of Jewish Studies* 5 (1954): 118–25.
——. "Commercial Mail Service in Medieval Islam." *Journal of the American Oriental Society* 84 (1964): 118–23.
——. "The Communal Activities of Elhanan b. Shemarya." Hebrew. In *Joshua Finkel Festschrift: In Honor of Joshua Finkel*, ed. S. B. Hoenig and L. D. Stitskin, 117–37. New York: Yeshiva University Press, 1974.
——. "Congregation versus Community: An Unknown Chapter in the Communal History of Jewish Palestine." *Jewish Quarterly Review* 44 (1954): 291–304.
——. "Contemporary Letters on the Capture of Jerusalem by the Crusaders." *Journal of Jewish Studies* 3 (1952): 162–77.

——. "Dani'el ben 'Azarya, nasi' ve-ga'on: berurim u-mismakhim ḥadashim." *Shalem* 2 (1975–76): 41–102.
——. "Early Letters and Documents from the Collection of the Late David Kaufmann." Hebrew. *Tarbiẓ* 20 (1950): 191–204.
——. "Geniza Sources for the Crusader Period: A Survey." In *Outremer: Studies in the History of the Crusading Kingdom of Jerusalem Presented to Joshua Prawer*, edited by B. Z. Kedar, H. E. Mayer, and R. C. Smail, 306–22. Jerusalem: Yad Izhak Ben-Zvi, 1982.
——. "Ibn Khalfun's Collection of Poems in 11th Century Egypt and Yemen." Hebrew. *Tarbiẓ* 29 (1959–60): 357–58.
——. *Jewish Education in Muslim Countries, Based on Records from the Cairo Geniza*. Hebrew. Jerusalem: Ben Zvi Institute and Hebrew University, 1962.
——. "Jewish Trade in the Mediterranean at the Beginning of the Eleventh Century (from the Archives of the Ibn 'Awkal Family)." Hebrew. *Tarbiẓ* 36 (1967): 366–95, 37 (1968): 48–77, 158–90.
——. "A Letter of the Gaon Samuel b. Ḥofni, Dated 998, and Its Implications for the Biography of the Spanish Poet Isaac b. Khalfon." Hebrew. *Tarbiẓ* 49 (1979–80): 199–201.
——. *Letters of Medieval Jewish Traders*. Princeton: Princeton University Press, 1973.
——. "Le-toldot ha-ge'onut be-ereṣ yisra'el" (On the history of the gaonate in Palestine). *Shalem* 1 (1974): 15–51.
——. "The Local Jewish Community in the Light of the Cairo Geniza Records." *Journal of Jewish Studies* 12 (1961): 133–58.
——. "A Maghrebi Living in Cairo Implores His Karaite Wife to Return to Him." *Jewish Quarterly Review* 73 (1982): 138–45.
——. "The Medieval Glass Industry as Reflected in the Cairo Geniza." *Readings in Glass History* 2 (1973): 18–26.
——. *A Mediterranean Society: The Jewish Communities of the Arab World as Portrayed in the Documents of the Cairo Geniza*. 6 vols. Berkeley: University of California Press, 1967–93.
——. "Mikhtavim me-Ereṣ Yisra'el mi-tequfat ha-ṣalbanim." *Yerushalayim: Meḥqerey Ereṣ Yisra'el* 2–5 (1955): 54–70.
——. "Minority Selfrule and Government Control in Islam." *Studia Islamica* 31 (1970): 101–16.
——. "New Documents from the Cairo Geniza." In *Homenaje a Millás-Vallicrosa*, 707–20. Barcelona: Consejo Superior de Investigaciones Científicas, 1954.
——. "New Sources on the Fate of the Jews during the Crusaders' Conquest of Jerusalem." Hebrew. *Zion* 17 (1952): 129–44.
——. "New Sources on the Palestinian Gaonate." In *Salo Wittmayer Baron Jubilee Volume on the Occasion of His Eightieth Birthday*, edited by Saul Lieberman and Arthur Hyman, 503–37. Jerusalem: American Academy for Jewish Research, 1974.
——. *Palestinian Jewry in Early Islamic and Crusader Times in Light of Geniza Documents*. Hebrew. Edited by Joseph Hacker. Jerusalem: Ben-Zvi Institute, 1980.
——. "Parents and Children: A Geniza Study on the Medieval Jewish Family." *Gratz College Annual of Jewish Studies* 4 (1975): 47–68.
——. "Petitions to the Fatimid Caliphs from the Cairo Geniza." *Jewish Quarterly Review* 45 (1954): 30–38.
——. "The President of the Palestinian Yeshiva (High Council) as Head of the Jews in the Fatimid Empire." Hebrew. In *Palestinian Jewry in Early Islamic and Crusader Times in Light of the Geniza Documents*, edited by Joseph Hacker, 52–69. Jerusalem: Ben-Zvi Institute, 1980.
——. "Rosh yeshivat ereṣ yisrae'el ke-rosh ha-yehudim ba-medina ha-faṭimit: mismakhim 'araviyim 'al ha-ge'onut ha-yisra'elit" (The head of the Palestinian yeshiva as the yead of the Jews in the Fatimid empire: Arabic documents on the Palestinian gaonate). *Eretz-Israel* 10 (1971): 100–113.
——. "Shemarya b. Elḥanan; With Two New Autographs." Hebrew. *Tarbiẓ* 32 (1962–63): 266–72.
——. "The Synagogue Building and Its Furnishings According to the Records of the Cairo Geniza." Hebrew. *Eretz-Israel* 7 (1964): 81–97.
——. "Three Letters from Qayrawan Addressed to Joseph ben Jacob ibn 'Awkal." Hebrew. *Tarbiẓ* 34 (1965): 162–82.
——. "Three Trousseaux of Jewish Brides from the Fatimid Period." *Association for Jewish Studies Review* 2 (1977): 77–110.

——. "The Title and Office of the Nagid: A Re-Examination." *Jewish Quarterly Review* 53 (1962): 93–119.
——. *The Yemenites: History, Communal Organization, Spiritual Life (Selected Studies).* Hebrew. Edited by Menahem Ben-Sasson. Jerusalem: Ben-Zvi Institute, 1983.
Golb, Norman. "Legal Documents from the Cairo Genizah." *Jewish Social Studies* 20 (1958): 17–46.
——. "The Topography of the Jews of Medieval Egypt, VI: Places of Settlement of the Jews of Medieval Egypt." *Journal of Near Eastern Studies* 33 (1974): 116–49.
Goldberg, Jessica L. "The Geographies of Trade and Traders in the Eastern Mediterranean 1000–1150: A Geniza Study." Ph.D. diss., Columbia University, 2005.
Goldziher, Ignaz. "Renseignements de source musulmane sur la dignité de resch-galuta." *Revue des études juives* 8 (1884): 121–25.
Goodblatt, David M. *Rabbinic Instruction in Sasanian Babylonia.* Studies in Judaism in Late Antiquity 9. Leiden: Brill, 1975.
Goodman, Martin. *The Oxford Handbook of Jewish Studies.* Oxford: Oxford University Press, 2002.
Goshen-Gottstein, M. H. "The Aleppo Codex and the Rise of the Massoretic Bible Text." *Biblical Archeologist* 42, no. 3 (1979): 145–63.
——. "The Authenticity of the Aleppo Codex." *Textus* 1 (1960): 17–19, 24.
——. "A Recovered Part of the Aleppo Codex." *Textus* 5 (1966): 53–59.
Gottheil, Richard J. H. "A Decree in Favour of the Karaites of Cairo Dated 1024." In *Festschrift zu Ehren des Dr. A Harkavy*, edited by Baron D. von Günzburg and Israel Markon, 115–25. St. Petersburg, 1908.
——. "An Eleventh-century Document Concerning a Cairo Synagogue," *Jewish Quarterly Review*, o.s. 19 (1907): 467–539.
——. "Tit Bits from the Geniza." In *Jewish Studies in Memory of Israel Abrahams*, edited by George Alexander Kohut, 149–69. New York: Press of the Jewish Institute for Religion, 1927.
Gottheil, Richard J. H., and William Hoyt Worrell. *Fragments from the Cairo Genizah in the Freer Collection.* New York: Macmillan, 1927.
Graetz, Heinrich. *Geschichte der Juden von den ältesten Zeiten bis auf die Gegenwart.* 4th ed. 11 vols. Leipzig, 1906–9.
Greenberg, Moshe. "The Stabilization of the Text of the Hebrew Bible, Reviewed in the Light of the Biblical Materials from the Judean Desert." *Journal of the American Oriental Society* 76 (1956): 157–67.
Greenstone, Julius H. "The Turkoman Defeat at Cairo." *American Journal of Semitic Languages and Literatures* 22 (1905–6): 144–75.
Greif, Avner. "Reputation and Coalitions in Medieval Trade: Evidence on the Maghribi Traders." *Journal of Economic History* 49 (1989): 857–82.
Grossman, Avraham. "The *Yeshiva* of Eretz Israel, Its Literary Output and Relationship with the Diaspora." In *The History of Jerusalem: The Early Muslim period*, 638–1099, edited by Joshua Prawer and Haggai Ben-Shammai, 225–69. Jerusalem: Yad Izhak Ben-Zvi and New York University Press, 1996.
Guillaume, A. "Further Documents on the Ben Meir Controversy." *Jewish Quarterly Review* 5 (1915): 543–57.
Gulak, Asher. *Oṣar ha-sheṭarot ha-nehugim be-Yisra'el* (Manual of Jewish legal documents). Jerusalem: Defus Poalim, 1926.
Guttman, Alexander. "Tractate Abot: Its Place in Rabbinic Literature." *Jewish Quarterly Review* 41 (1950): 181–93.
Hacker, Joseph. "Jewish Autonomy in the Ottoman Empire: Its Scope and Limits: Jewish Courts from the Sixteenth to the Eighteenth Centuries." In *The Jews of the Ottoman Empire*, edited by Avigdor Levy, 153–202. Princeton: Darwin Press, 1994.
Halevi, Judah. *Kitāb al-radd wa-l-dalīl fi l-dīn al-dhalīl (al-kitāb al-khazarī)* (The Book of Refutation and Proof on the Despised Faith [The Book of the Khazars], Known as the Kuzari). Edited by D. Z. Baneth and Haggai Ben-Shammai. Jerusalem: Magnes Press, 1977.
——. *The Kuzari=Kitab al Khazari: An Argument for the Faith of Israel.* Translated by Hartwig Hirschfeld. New York: Schocken Books, 1964.

Halivni, David. *Midrash, Mishnah, and Gemara: The Jewish Predilection for Justified Law*. Cambridge: Harvard University Press, 1986.

——. *Sources and Traditions: A Source Critical Commentary on the Talmud Tractate Bava Metzia*. Hebrew. Jerusalem: Magnes Press, 2003.

Halkin, Abraham S., ed. *Divulgatio mysteriorum luminumque apparentia, commentarius in Canticum Canticorum (Hitgallut ha-sodot ve-hofaʿat ha-meʾorot: perush Shir ha-shirim)*. Jerusalem: Meḳiẓe Nirdamim, 1964.

——. *Liber discussionis et commemorationis: poetica Hebraica*. Jerusalem: Meḳiẓe Nirdamim, 1975.

Hallaq, Wael B. *Authority, Continuity, and Change in Islamic Law*. Cambridge: Cambridge University Press, 2001.

——. "On the Origins of the Controversy about the Existence of Mujtahids and the Gate of Ijtihad." *Studia Islamica* 63 (1986): 129–41.

——. "Was the Gate of Ijtihād Closed?" *International Journal of Middle East Studies* 16 (1984): 3–41.

Halm, Heinz. "Der Treuhänder Gottes: Die Edikte des Kalifen al-Hakim." *Der Islam* 63 (1986): 11–72.

Halper, Ben-Zion. *Descriptive Catalogue of Genizah Fragments in Philadelphia*. Philadelphia: Dropsie College for Hebrew and Cognate Learning, 1924.

al-Ḥamawī, Yāqūt. *Muʿjam al-udabāʾ* (Compendium of literary authors). Beirut: Dār Iḥyāʾ al-Turāth al-ʿArabī, 1988.

Harkavy, Albert (Avraham Eliyyahu). *Meʾassef niddaḥim: meqorot be-toldot Yisraʾel u-ve-sifruto*. Jerusalem: Hoṣaʾat Qedem, 1970 [1879].

——. "Mikhtav mi-Yerushalayim mi-ketav yad asher be-Petersburg." *Oṣar ṭov* (1878): 77–81.

——. *Studien und Mittheilungen aus der Kaiserlichen Öffentlichen Bibliothek zu St. Petersburg vol. 8*. St. Petersburg, 1903.

Harris, Jay. *How Do We Know This? Midrash and the Fragmentation of Modern Judaism*. Albany: SUNY Press, 1995.

Harviainen, Tapani. "Abraham Firkovich." In *Karaite Judaism: A Guide to its History and Literary Sources*, edited by Meira Polliack, Handbuch der Orientalistik, pt. 1: Nahe und Mittlere Osten, 73, 875–93. Leiden: Brill, 2003.

——. "Abraham Firkovich, the Aleppo Codex, and Its Dedication." In *Jewish Studies at the Turn of the Twentieth Century: Proceedings of the 6th EAJS Congress, Toledo, July* 1998, edited by Judit Targarona Borrás and Angel Sáenz-Badillos, 131–36. Leiden: Brill, 1999.

——. "The Cairo Genizot and Other Sources of the Second Firkovich Collection in St. Petersburg." In *Proceedings of the Twelfth International Congress of the International Organization for Masoretic Studies* 1995, edited by E. J. Revell, 25–36. Atlanta: Society for Biblical Literature, 1996.

——. "The Karaites in Eastern Europe and the Crimea: An Overview." In *Karaite Judaism: A Guide to Its History and Literary Sources*, edited by Meira Polliack, Handbuch der Orientalistik, pt. 1: Nahe und Mittlere Osten, 73, 633–55. Leiden: Brill, 2003.

Hary, Benjamin. *Multiglossia in Judeo-Arabic, with an Edition, Translation, and Grammatical Study of the Cairene Purim Scroll*. Leiden: Brill, 1992.

Hary, Benjamin, and Marina Rustow. "Karaites at the Rabbinical Court: A Legal Deed from Mahdiyya Dated 1073." *Ginzei Qedem*, n.s. 2 (2006): 9–36.

Hezser, Catherine. *The Social Structure of the Rabbinic Movement in Roman Palestine*. Texte und Studien zum antiken Judentum 66. Tübingen: Mohr Siebeck, 1997.

Hildesheimer, Ezriel, ed. *Sefer Halakhot Gedolot*. 3 vols. Jerusalem: Meḳiẓe Nirdamim, 1971–87.

Hirschberg, H. Z. (J. W.). *A History of the Jews in North Africa*. 2 vols. Vol. 1: *From Antiquity to the Sixteenth Century*. Leiden: Brill, 1974.

——. "Links between the Jews of the Maghreb and Palestine in the Period of the Geonim." Hebrew. *Eretz-Israel* 5 (1958): 213–19.

——. "The Salars and Negidim of Qayrawan." Hebrew. *Ẓion* 23–24 (1958–59): 166–73.

——. "Concerning the Mount of Olives in the Gaonic Period." Hebrew. *Bulletin of the Jewish Palestine Exploration Society* 13 (1947): 156–64.

Hirschfeld, Hartwig. "A Karaite Conversion Story." In *Jews' College Jubilee Volume*, 81–100. London, 1906.

——. "An Unknown Grammatical Work by Abul-Faraj Harun." *Jewish Quarterly Review*, n.s. 13 (1922–23): 1–7.

Hirshman, Mark. "The Priest's Gate and Elijah b. Menaḥem's Pilgrimage." Hebrew. *Tarbiẓ* 55 (1986): 217–27.
——. "'R. Elijah Interpreted the Verse Concerning Pilgrims' (Shir Rabba 2, 14, 7): Another Medieval Interpolation and Again R. Elijah." Hebrew. *Tarbiẓ* 60 (1991): 275–76.
Hodgson, Marshall. "How Did the Early Shiʿa Become Sectarian?" *Journal of the American Oriental Society* 75 (1955): 1–13.
Horowitz, Elliott. *Reckless Rites: Purim and the Legacy of Jewish Violence*. Jews, Christians and Muslims from the Ancient to the Modern World. Princeton: Princeton University Press, 2006.
Humphreys, R. Stephen. *Islamic History: A Framework for Inquiry*. Rev. ed. Princeton: Princeton University Press, 1991.
Hurvitz, Nimrod. "From Scholarly Circles to Mass Movements: The Formation of Legal Communities in Islamic Societies." *American Historical Review* 108, no. 4 (2003): 985–1008.
——. "Schools of Law and Historical Context: Re-examining the Formation of the Ḥanbalī *madhhab*." *Islamic Law and Society* 7 (2000): 37–64.
Huygens, R. B. C., ed. *Guibert de Nogent: Dei gesta per Francos et cinq autres textes*, Corpus Christianorum, Continuatio Mediaevalis 127a. Turnhout: Brepols, 1996.
Hyatte, Reginald. *The Prophet of Islam in Old French: The Romance of Muhammad (1258) and The Book of Muhammad's Ladder (1264)*. Leiden: Brill, 1997.
Ibn al- Athīr, ʿIzz al-Dīn Abu l-Ḥasan ʿAlī. *al-Kāmil fi l-tārīkh* (Compendium of history). Edited by Carl Johan Tornberg. 14 volumes. Uppsala, 1851–76.
Ibn al-Fuwaṭī, Kamāl al-Dīn ʿAbd al-Razzāq b. Aḥmad (attributed to). *al-Ḥawādith al-jāmiʿa wa-l-tajārib al-nāfiʿa fi l-miʾa al-sābiʿa* (The comprehensive events and useful experiences of the seventh century). Edited by Muṣṭafā Jawād. Baghdad, 1932.
Ibn Khalaf, Abu l-Ḥasan ʿAlī al-Kātib. *Mawādd al-bayān* (The substances of eloquence). Edited by Fuat Sezgin, Manshūrāt Maʿhad Tārīkh al-ʿUlūm al-ʿArabiyya wa-l-Islāmiyya Series C, ʿUyūn al-turāth, vol. 39. Frankfurt: Institut für Geschichte der Arabisch-Islamischen Wissenschaften, 1986.
Ibn Khallikān, Aḥmad b. Muḥammad. *Wafayāt al-aʿyān wa-anbāʾ abnāʾ al-zamān* (Death-notices of notables and reports on people of the age). Edited by Iḥsān ʿAbbās. 8 volumes. Beirut, 1969–72.
Ibn Munqidh, Usāmah. *An Arab-Syrian Gentleman and Warrior in the Period of the Crusades: Memoirs of Usāmah ibn-Munqidh (Kitāb al-Iʿtibār)*. Translated by Philip Khuri Hitti. Records of Western Civilization. New York: Columbia University Press, 2000.
Ibn Muyassar, Tāj al-Dīn Muḥammad b. Yūsuf. *Akhbār Miṣr*. Edited by Henri Massé, Annales d'Égypte (les khalifes Fāṭimides). Cairo, 1919.
Ibn al-Qalānisī, Abū Yaʿlā Ḥamza b. Asad al-Tamīmī. *Dhayl tārīkh Dimashq* (Continuation of the history of Damascus). Edited by H. F. Amedroz. Beirut, 1908.
Ibn al-Sāʿī, Abū Ṭālib Tāj al-dīn ʿAlī b. Anjab. *al-Jāmiʿ al-mukhtaṣar* (The comprehensive abridgement). Edited by Muṣṭafā Jawād. Baghdad, 1934.
Ibn al-Ṣayrafī, Tāj al-Riʾāsa Amīn al-Dīn Abu l-Qāsim ʿAlī b. Munjib b. Sulaymān. *Qānūn dīwān al-rasāʾil*. Edited by ʿAli Bahjat. Cairo, 1905.
——. *al-Qānūn fī dīwān al-rasāʾil wa-l-ishāra ilā man nāla al-wizāra*. Edited by Ayman Fuʾād Sayyid. Cairo: al-Miṣrīyya al-Lubnānīyya, 1990.
al-Imad, Leila S. *The Fatimid Vizierate*, 969–1172. Islamkundliche Untersuchungen 133. Berlin: K. Schwarz, 1990.
Jaffee, Martin S. "The Oral-Cultural Context of the Talmud Yerushalmi: Greco-Roman Rhetorical Paideia, Discipleship, and the Concept of Oral Torah." In *Transmitting Jewish Traditions: Orality, Textuality, and Cultural Diffusion*, edited by Yaakov Elman and Israel Gershoni, 27–73. New Haven: Yale University Press, 2000.
——. *Torah in the Mouth: Writing and Oral Tradition in Palestinian Judaism, 200 BCE–400 CE*. New York: Oxford University Press, 2001.
al-Jāḥiẓ, ʿUthmān. *Kitāb al-ḥayawān* (The animals). Edited by A. M. Hārūn. Cairo: M. B. al-Ḥalabi, 1966.
Kahle, Paul. *The Cairo Geniza*. 2d ed. Oxford: Basil Blackwell, 1959 [1947].
——. "The Hebrew ben Asher Bible Manuscripts." *Vetus Testamentum* 1 (1951): 161–67.
——. *Masoreten des Westens*. 2 vols. Hildesheim: George Olms, 1967 [1927].

Kaplan, Yosef. "The Social Functions of the Ḥerem in the Portuguese Jewish Community of Amsterdam in the Seventeenth Century." In *Dutch Jewish History: Proceedings of the Symposium on the History of the Jews in the Netherlands*, edited by Jozeph Michman and Tirisah Levie, 111–55. Jerusalem: Tel Aviv University, 1984.

Katz, Jacob. "Rabbinic Authority and Authorization in the Middle Ages." In *Studies in Medieval Jewish History and Literature*, edited by I. Twersky, 128–45. Cambridge: Harvard University Press, 1979.

Kedar, Benjamin Z., ed. *Jerusalem in the Middle Ages: Selected Papers*. Jerusalem: Yad Izhak Ben-Zvi, 1979.

Kedar, B. Z., H. E. Mayer, and R. C. Smail, eds. *Outremer: Studies in the History of the Crusading Kingdom of Jerusalem Presented to Joshua Prawer*. Jerusalem: Yad Izhak Ben-Zvi, 1982.

Kellner, Menachem Marc. *Dogma in Medieval Jewish Thought: From Maimonides to Abravanel*. The Littman Library of Jewish Civilization. Oxford: Oxford University Press, 1986.

Khan, Geoffrey. "ʾAbūal-Faraj Hārūn and the Early Karaite Grammatical Tradition." *Journal of Jewish Studies* 48 (1997): 314–44.

——. *Arabic Legal and Administrative Documents in the Cambridge Genizah Collections*. Cambridge University Library Genizah Series 10. Cambridge: Cambridge University Press, 1993.

——. "The Early Karaite Grammatical Tradition." In *Jewish Studies at the Turn of the Twentieth Century: Proceedings of the 6th EAJS Congress, Toledo, July 1998*, edited by Judit Targarona Borrás and Angel Sáenz-Badillos, 1:72–80. Leiden: Brill, 1999.

——. *The Early Karaite Tradition of Hebrew Grammatical Thought: Including a Critical Edition, Translation and Analysis of the* Diqduq *of Abū Yaʿqūb Yūsuf ibn Nūḥ on the Hagiographa*. Leiden: Brill, 2000.

——, ed. *Exegesis and Grammar in Medieval Karaite Texts*. Journal of Semitic Studies Supplement 13. Oxford: Oxford University Press on behalf of the University of Manchester, 2001.

——. "The Historical Development of the Structure of Medieval Arabic Petitions." *Bulletin of the School of Oriental and African Studies* 53 (1990): 8–30.

——. *Karaite Bible Manuscripts from the Cairo Genizah*. Cambridge University Library Genizah Series 9. Cambridge: Cambridge University Press, 1990.

——. "The Medieval Karaite Transcriptions of Hebrew into Arabic Script." *Israel Oriental Studies* 12 (1992).

Khan, Geoffrey, María Ángeles Gallego, and Judith Olszowy-Schlanger. *The Karaite Tradition of Hebrew Grammatical Thought in Its Classical Form: A Critical Edition and English Translation of* al-Kitāb al-Kāfī fī al-Luġa al-ʿIbrāniyya *by ʾAbū al-Faraj Hārūn ibn al-Faraj*. Studies in Semitic Languages and Linguistics 37. Leiden: Brill, 2003.

al-Khaṭīb al-Baghdādī, Abū Bakr Aḥmad b. ʿAlī b. Thābit b. Aḥmad b. Mahdī al-Shāfiʿī. *Tārīkh Baghdād* (History of Baghdad). Cairo, 1931.

Kittel, Rudolf, Karl Elliger, Wilhelm Rudolph, Hans Peter Ruger, and G. E. Weil. *[Torah, Neviim u-Khetuvim]=Biblia Hebraica Stuttgartensia*. Edited by A. Schenker. 5th ed. Stuttgart: Deutsche Bibelgesellschaft, 1997.

Klar, Benjamin. *Megillat Aḥimaʿaṣ, be-ṣeruf kama hosafot, menuqqedet u-mevoʾeret bi-dey Binyamin Klar* (The Chronicle of Aḥimaʿaṣ, with notes, annotated and explained by Binyamin Klar). 2d rev. ed. Jerusalem: Sifre Tarshish, 1974 [1944].

——. *Meḥqarim ve-ʿiyyunim: ba-lashon, ba-shira u-va-sifrut*. Edited by A. M. Habermann. Tel-Aviv: Maḥbarot le-sifrut, 1954.

Klein, Elka. *Jews, Christian Society, and Royal Power in Medieval Barcelona*. Ann Arbor: University of Michigan Press, 2006.

Krämer, Gudrun. *The Jews in Modern Egypt*, 1914–1952. Seattle: University of Washington Press, 1989.

Lambert, Phyllis, ed. *Fortifications and the Synagogue: The Fortress of Babylon and the Ben Ezra Synagogue, Cairo*. Chicago: University of Chicago Press, 1994.

Lapidus, I. M. "The Conversion of Egypt to Islam." *Israel Oriental Studies* 2 (1972): 248–62.

Lasker, Arnold A., and Daniel J. Lasker. "642 Parts—More Concerning the Saadya–Ben Meir Controversy." Hebrew. *Tarbiz* 61 (1991): 119–28.

Lasker, Daniel J. "Judah Halevi and Karaism." In *From Ancient Israel to Modern Judaism; Intellect in Quest of Understanding. Essays in Honor of Marvin Fox*, edited by Jacob Neusner, Ernest S. Frerichs, and Nahum M. Sarna, 4 vols., 3:111–25. Atlanta: Scholars' Press, 1989.

——. "Karaism in Twelfth-Century Spain." *Journal of Jewish Thought and Philosophy* 1–2 (1992): 179–95.

Laskier, Michael M. *The Jews of Egypt, 1920–1970: In the Midst of Zionism, Anti-Semitism, and the Middle East Conflict.* New York: New York University Press, 1992.

Lazarus-Yafeh, Hava, Mark Cohen, and Sasson Somekh, eds. *The Majlis: Interreligious Encounters in Medieval Islam*, Studies in Arabic Language and Literature 4. Wiesbaden: Harrassowitz, 1999.

Le Goff, Jacques, ed. *Hérésies et sociétés dans l'Europe préindustrielle: 11e–18e siècles: Communications et débats du colloque de Royaumont: 27–30 mai 1962.* Paris: Mouton, 1968.

Le Strange, Guy. *The Lands of the Eastern Caliphate.* Cambridge: Cambridge University Press, 1905.

Lev, Yaacov. "The Fāṭimid Imposition of Ismāʿīlism on Egypt (358–386/969–996)." *Zeitschrift der Deutschen Morgenländischen Gesellschaft* 138 (1988): 313–25.

——. "The Fatimid Princess Sitt al-Mulk." *Journal of Semitic Studies* 32 (1987): 319–28.

——. "The Fatimid Vizier Yaʿqūb ibn Killis and the Beginning of the Fatimid Administration in Egypt." *Der Islam* 58 (1981): 237–49.

——. "The Fatimids and the Aḥdāth of Damascus, 386/996–411/1021." *Welt des Orients* 13 (1982): 98–106.

——. "Persecutions and Conversion to Islam in Eleventh-Century Egypt." *Asian and African Studies* 22 (1988): 73–91.

——. *State and Society in Fatimid Egypt.* Leiden: Brill, 1991.

Lewin, B. M. *The Epistle of Rav Sherira Ga'on.* Jerusalem: Maqor, 1971 [1921].

——. "Essa meshali le-RaSaG" (Seʿadya's 'I shall take up my parable'). In *Rav Seʿadya Ga'on: qoveṣ torani-maddaʿi*, edited by J. L. Fishman, 481–532. Jerusalem: Rav Kook Institute, 1943.

——. *Oṣar ha-ge'onim: The Responsa of the Babylonian Geonim and Their Commentaries According to the Order of the Talmud.* Jerusalem: Rav Kook Institute, 1928.

Lewis, Bernard. *Islam: From the Prophet Muhammad to the Capture of Constantinople.* 2 vols. Oxford: Oxford University Press, 1987 [1974].

——. "Palṭiel: A Note." *Bulletin of the School of Oriental and African Studies* 30 (1967): 177–81.

——. "The Qasida of Abu Ishaq against Joseph ibn Naghrella." In *Salo Wittmayer Baron Jubilee Volume on the Occasion of his Eightieth Birthday*, edited by Saul Lieberman and Arthur Hyman, 657–68. Jerusalem: American Academy for Jewish Research, 1974.

Libson, Gideon. "Gezerta and Ḥerem Setam in the Gaonic and Early Medieval Periods." Hebrew. Ph.D. diss., Hebrew University of Jerusalem, 1979.

——. "Halakha and Reality in the Gaonic Period: *Taqqanah*, *Minhag*, Tradition and Consensus: Some Observations." In *The Jews of Medieval Islam: Community, Society, and Identity*, edited by Daniel Frank, 67–99. Leiden: Brill, 1995.

——. *Jewish and Islamic Law: A Comparative Study of Custom during the Geonic Period.* Harvard Series in Islamic Law. Cambridge: Harvard University Press, 2003.

Little, Lester K. *Benedictine Maledictions: Liturgical Cursing in Romanesque France.* Ithaca: Cornell University Press, 1993.

Lobel, Diana. *Between Mysticism and Philosophy: Sufi Language of Religious Experience in Judah Ha-Levi's Kuzari.* SUNY Series in Jewish Philosophy. Albany: SUNY Press, 2000.

Madelung, Wilferd, and Sabine Schmidtke. *Rational Theology in Interfaith Communication: Abu l-Ḥusayn al-Baṣrī's Muʿtazilī Theology among the Karaites in the Fāṭimid Age.* Jerusalem Studies in Religion and Culture. Leiden: Brill, 2006.

Maimonides, Moses. *Responsa quae exstant ab ipso Arabice scripta ex schedis Cairensibus et libris tam manu scriptis quam.* Edited by Jehoshua Blau. 2d rev. ed. 4 vols. Jerusalem: Meḳiẓe Nirdamim, 1986.

Makdisi, Ussama. *The Culture of Sectarianism: Community, History and Violence in Nineteenth-Century Ottoman Lebanon.* Berkeley: University of California Press, 2000.

Malter, Henry. *Saadia Gaon, His Life and Works.* Philadelphia: Jewish Publication Society of America, 1921.

Mann, Jacob. "Early Ḳaraite Bible Commentaries." *Jewish Quarterly Review* 12 (1922): 435–526.

——. *The Jews in Egypt and in Palestine under the Fāṭimid Caliphs: A Contribution to Their Political and Communal History, Based Chiefly on Genizah Material Hitherto Unpublished.* 2 vols. London: Oxford University Press, 1920–22.

——. "A Note on 'Solomon b. Judah and Some of His Contemporaries'." *Jewish Quarterly Review* 9 (1918–19): 409–21.
——. "The Responsa of the Babylonian Geonim As a Source of Jewish History." *Jewish Quarterly Review* 7 (1917): 457–90, 8 (1918): 339–66, 9 (1919): 139–79, 10 (1919): 121–51, 309–65, 11 (1921): 433–71.
——. *The Responsa of the Babylonian Geonim As a Source of Jewish History.* New York: Arno Press, 1973.
——. "A Second Supplement to 'The Jews in Egypt and in Palestine under the Fāṭimid Caliphs'." *Hebrew Union College Annual* 3 (1926): 223–62.
——. *Texts and Studies in Jewish History and Literature.* New York: Ktav, 1972 [1931–35].
——. "A Tract by an Early Ḳaraite Settler in Jerusalem." *Jewish Quarterly Review* 12 (1921–22): 257–98.
al-Maqrīzī, Aḥmad b. ʿAlī. *Ittiʿaẓ al-ḥunafāʾ bi-akhbār al-aʾimma al-Fāṭimiyyīn al-khulafāʾ* (The Exhortation of Believers: On the History of the Fatimid Caliph-Imāms). Edited by Jamāl al-dīn al-Shayyāl. 3 volumes. Cairo: al-Majlis al-Aʿlā li-l-Shuʾūn al-Islāmiyya, 1967–73.
Marcus, Ivan. "History, Story, and Collective Memory: Narrativity in Early Ashkenazic Culture." In *The Midrashic Imagination: Jewish Exegesis, Thought, and History*, edited by Michael Fishbane, 255–79. Albany: SUNY Press, 1993.
Margariti, Roxani. *Aden and the Indian Ocean Trade: 150 Years in the Life of a Medieval Arabian Port.* Chapel Hill: University of North Carolina Press, 2007.
Margoliouth, G. "Ibn al-Hiti's Chronicle of the Karaite Doctors." *Jewish Quarterly Review* 9 (1897): 429–44.
Marmorstein, A. "Solomon Ben Judah and Some of His Contemporaries." *Jewish Quarterly Review* 8 (1917): 1–29.
Marx, Alexander. "The Importance of the Geniza for Jewish History." *Proceedings of the American Academy for Jewish Research* 16 (1946–47): 183–204.
Massé, Henri. "Ibn el-Çaïrafi: Code de la Chancellerie d'État (période fâtimide)," *Bulletin de l'Institut français d'archéologie orientale* 11 (1914): 65–120.
McSheffrey, Shannon. "Heresy, Orthodoxy and English Vernacular Religion." *Past & Present* 186 (2005): 47–80.
Mez, Adam. *The Renaissance of Islam.* Translated by Salahuddin Khuda Bukhsh and D. S. Margoliouth. New York: AMS Press, 1975 [1937].
Michaeli, Murad. "The Archive of Nahray b. Nissim: Merchant and Communal Leader in Egypt in the Eleventh Century." Hebrew. Ph.D. diss., Hebrew University, 1967.
Miller, Philip E. *Karaite Separatism in Nineteenth-Century Russia: Joseph Solomon Lutski's Epistle of Israel's Deliverance.* Monographs of the Hebrew Union College 16. Cincinnati: Hebrew Union College Press, 1993.
Mirsky, Aaron, ed. *Itzhak ibn Khalfun: Poems.* Hebrew. Jerusalem: Bialik Institute, 1961.
Modarressi, Hossein. *Crisis and Consolidation in the Formative Period of Shiʿite Islam: Abu Jaʿfar ibn Qiba al-Razi and His Contribution to Imamite Shiʿite Thought.* Princeton: Darwin Press, 1993.
Momigliano, Arnaldo. "The Origins of Universal History." *Annali della Scuola Normale Superiore di Pisa*, 3rd ser., 12 (1982): 533–60.
Morag, Shemuʾel. "On the Form and Etymology of Hai Gaʾon's Name." Hebrew. *Tarbiẓ* 31 (1961): 188–90.
Mottahedeh, Roy P. "Admistration in Buyid Qazwin." In *Islamic Civilisation* 950–1150, edited by D. S. Richards. Oxford: Bruno Cassirer, 1973.
——. "Bureaucracy and the Patrimonial State in Early Islamic Iran and Iraq." *al-Abhath* 29 (1981): 25–36.
——. *Loyalty and Leadership in an Early Islamic Society.* Princeton: Princeton University Press, 1980.
Müller, D. H., and D. Kaufmann. "Der Brief eines aegyptischen Rabbi an den Gaon [Salomo] Ben Jehuda." *Mittheilungen aus der Sammlung der Papyrus Erzherzog Rainer* 5 (1892): 127.
al-Muqaddasī (al-Maqdisī), Muḥammad b. Aḥmad. *Aḥsan al-taqāsīm fī maʿrifat al-aqālīm* (The best divisions for knowledge of the regions). Edited by M. J. de Goeje, Bibliotheca geographorum Arabicorum 3, 2d ed. Leiden, 1906.
——. *The Best Divisions for Knowledge of the Regions: Aḥsan al-taqāsīm fī maʿrifat al-aqālīm.* Translated by Basil Collins. Great Books of Islamic Civilization. London: Garnet Publishing, 2001.

al-Musabbiḥī, al-Amīr al-Mukhtār ʿIzz al-Mulk Muḥammad b. ʿUbaydallāh b. Aḥmad. *al-Juzʾ al-arbaʿūn min Akhbār Miṣr* (The fortieth chapter of the history of Egypt). Edited by Ayman Fuʾād Sayyid and Thierry Bianquis. Cairo: Institut français d'archéologie orientale, 1978.

Nemoy, Leon. "Anan ben David: A Reappraisal of the Historical Data." In *Semitic Studies in Memory of Immanuel Löw*, edited by Alexander Scheiber, 239–48. Budapest, 1947. Reprinted in *Karaite Studies*, edited by Philip Birnbaum, 309–18. New York: Hermon Press, 1971.

——. "The Epistle of Sahl ben Maṣlīaḥ." *Proceedings of the American Academy for Jewish Research* 38–39 (1970–71): 145–77.

——. *Karaite Anthology: Excerpts from the Early Literature*. Yale Judaica Series 7. New Haven: Yale University Press, 1952.

——. "Nissi ben Noah's Quasi-Commentary on the Decalogue." *Jewish Quarterly Review* 73 (1983).

——. "The Pseudo-Qumisian Sermon to the Karaites." *Proceedings of the American Academy of Jewish Research* 43 (1976): 49–105.

——. "al-Qirqisani's Account of the Jewish Sects and Christianity." *Hebrew Union College Annual* 7 (1930): 317–97.

——. "Two Controversial Points in the Karaite Law of Incest." *Hebrew Union College Annual* 49 (1978): 247–65.

Neubauer, A. "Egyptian Fragments II." *Jewish Quarterly Review*, o.s. 9 (1896): 24–38.

Neubauer, A., ed. *Mediaeval Jewish Chronicles and Chronological Notes, Edited from Printed Books and Manuscripts*. 2 vols. Oxford, 1887–95.

Neustadt (Ayalon), David. "Problems Concerning the 'Negidut' in Egypt during the Middle Ages." Hebrew. *Zion* 4 (1938–39): 126–49.

Nicholson, R. A. *Studies in Islamic Poetry*. Cambridge, 1921.

Obermeyer, Jacob. *Die Landschaft Babylonien im Zeitalter des Talmud und des Gaonats*. Frankfurt am Main, 1929.

Olszowy-Schlanger, Judith. "Karaite *Ketubbot* from the Cairo Geniza and the Origins of the Karaite Legal Formulae Tradition." Hebrew. *Teʿuda* 15 (1999): 127–44.

——. "Karaite Legal Documents." In *Karaite Judaism: A Guide to its History and Literary Sources*, edited by Meira Polliack, 255–74. Leiden: Brill, 2003.

——. *Karaite Marriage Documents from the Cairo Geniza: Legal Tradition and Community Life in Mediaeval Egypt and Palestine*. Etudes sur le judaïsme médiéval 20. Leiden: Brill, 1998.

——. "La lettre du divorce caraïte et sa place dans les relations entre caraïtes et rabbanites au moyen age: Une étude de manuscrits de la Geniza du Caire." *Revue des études juives* 155 (1996): 337–62.

Oppenheimer, Aharon, in collaboration with Benjamin Isaac and Michael Lecker. *Babylonia Judaica in the Talmudic Period*. Beihefte zum Tübinger Atlas des Vorderen Orients, ser. B (Geisteswissenschaften) No. 47. Wiesbaden: Dr. Ludwig Reichert, 1983.

Outhwaite, Benjamin. "Karaite Epistolary Hebrew: The Letters of Ṭoviyyah ben Moshe." In *Exegesis and Grammer in Medieval Karaite Texts*, edited by Geoffrey Khan, Journal of Semitic Studies Supplement 13, 195–234. Oxford: Oxford University Press on behalf of the University of Manchester, 2001.

Paul, André. *Ecrits de Qumran et sectes juives aux premiers siècles de l'Islam: Recherches sur l'origine du Qaraïsme*. Paris: Letouzey et Ané, 1969.

Pegg, Mark Gregory. *The Corruption of Angels: The Great Inquisition of* 1245–46. Princeton: Princeton University Press, 2001.

Penkower, Jordan S. "Maimonides and the Aleppo Codex." *Textus* 9 (1981): 40–43.

Petry, Carl F. "Educational Institutions as Depicted in the Biographical Literature of Mamluk Cairo: The Debate over Prestige and Venue." *Medieval Prosopography* 23 (2002): 101–23.

Pinsker, Simḥa. *Lickute Kadmoniot. Zur Geschichte des Karaismus und der karäischen Literatur*. Vienna, 1860.

Polliack, Meira. *The Karaite Tradition of Arabic Bible Translation: A Linguistic and Exegetical Study of Karaite Translations of the Pentateuch from the Tenth and Eleventh Centuries C.E.*, Etudes sur le judaïsme médiéval 17. Leiden: Brill, 1997.

——. ed. *Karaite Judaism: A Guide to its History and Literary Sources*, Handbuch der Orientalistik, Erste Abteilung: Nahe und der Mittlere Osten, 73. Leiden and Boston: Brill, 2003.

——. "Medieval Karaism." In *The Oxford Handbook of Jewish Studies*, edited by Martin Goodman, 295–326. Oxford: Oxford University Press, 2002.
Poznanski, Samuel. "Anan et ses écrits." *Revue des études juives* 44 (1902): 161–87.
——. "The Beginning of the Karaite Settlement in Jerusalem." Hebrew. *Jerusalem (edited by A. M. Luncz)* 10 (1913): 83–116, 321–23.
——. "Ephraim ben Schemaria de Fostat et l'académie palestinienne." *Revue des études juives* 48 (1904): 145–75.
——. *The Karaite Literary Opponents of Saadiah Gaon*. London: Luzac, 1908.
Prawer, Joshua. *The History of the Jews in the Latin Kingdom of Jerusalem*. Oxford: Clarendon Press, 1988.
Prawer, Joshua, and Haggai Ben-Shammai, eds. *The History of Jerusalem: The Early Muslim Period, 638–1099*. Jerusalem: Yad Izhak Ben-Zvi and New York University Press, 1996.
al-Qalqashandī, Abu l-ʿAbbās Aḥmad b. ʿAlī. *Ṣubḥ al-aʿshā fī ṣināʿat al-inshā* (Daybreak for the dim-sighted in the art of diplomatic). 14 vols. Cairo: al-Muʾassasa al-Miṣriyya al-ʿĀmma li-l-Taʾlīf wa-l-Tarjama wa-l-Ṭibāʿa wa-l-Nashr, 1964.
al-Qattan, Najwa. "Dhimmis in the Muslim Court: Legal Autonomy and Religious Discrimination." *International Journal of Middle East Studies* 31 (1999): 429–44.
al-Qirqisānī, Abū Yūsuf Yaʿqūb. *Kitāb al-anwār wa-l-marāqib: Code of Karaite Law*. Edited by Leon Nemoy. 5 vols. New York: Alexander Kohut Memorial Foundation, 1939–43.
al-Qūmisī, Daniʾel b. Moshe. *Pitron sheneym-ʿasar* (Commentary on the Twelve Minor Prophets). Edited by Israel Markon. Jerusalem: Meḳiẓe Nirdamim, 1948.
Rabin, Chaim, and Yigael Yadin, eds. *Aspects of the Dead Sea Scrolls*, Scripta Hierosolymitana 4. Jerusalem: Magnes Press, 1958.
Ray, Jonathan. *The Sephardic Frontier: The Reconquista and the Jewish Community in Medieval Iberia*. Conjunctions of Religion and Power in the Medieval Past. Ithaca: Cornell University Press, 2006.
Reif, Stefan C. *A Jewish Archive from Old Cairo: The History of Cambridge University's Genizah Collection*. Richmond, Surrey: Curzon Press 2000.
——. *Published Material from the Cambridge Genizah Collections: A Bibliography*, 1896–1980. Cambridge University Library Genizah Series 6. Cambridge: Cambridge University Press, 1988.
——. *Why Medieval Hebrew Studies? An Inaugural Lecture Given in the University of Cambridge, 11 November 1999*. Cambridge: Cambridge University Press, 2001.
——, ed. *The Cambridge Genizah Collections: Their Contents and Significance*. Cambridge University Library Genizah Series, vol. 1. Cambridge: Cambridge University Press, 2002.
Reiner, Elchanan. "Pilgrims and Pilgrimage to Ereṣ Yisraʾel, 1099–1517." Hebrew. Ph.D. diss., Hebrew University, 1988.
Richards, D. S. "Arabic Documents from the Karaite Community in Cairo," *Journal of the Economic and Social History of the Orient* 15 (1972): 105–62.
——. "A Fāṭimid Petition and 'Small Decree' from Sinai." *Israel Oriental Studies* 3 (1973): 140–58.
Rivkin, Ellis. "The Saadia–David Ben Zakkai Conflict: A Structural Analysis." In *Studies and Essays in Honor of Abraham A. Neuman, President, Dropsie College for Hebrew and Cognate Learning, Philadelphia*, edited by Bernard D. Weinryb, Meir Ben-Horin, and Solomon Zeitlin, 388–423. Philadelphia and Leiden: Brill for the Dropsie College, 1962.
Rivlin, Joseph. *Inheritance and Wills in Jewish Law*. Hebrew. Ramat Gan: Universitat Bar Ilan, 1999.
Rozenson, Yisraʾel. "'Be-ʿalot ʿam la-ḥog be-shalosh peʿamim': ʿal ʿaliyya le-regel le-har ha-zeytim ba-piyyuṭ ha-ereṣ-yisraʾeli ha-qadum." *Sinai* 117 (1997): 176–85.
Rubenstein, Jeffrey L. *The Culture of the Babylonian Talmud*. Baltimore: Johns Hopkins University Press, 2003.
al-Rūdhrāwarī, Abū Shujāʿ Muḥammad b. al-Ḥusayn. *Dhayl tajārib al-umam*. Edited by H. F. Amedroz and D. S. Margoliouth, *The Eclipse of the ʿAbbasid Caliphate*. 2 vols. Oxford, 1920–21.
Rustow, Marina. "Karaites Real and Imagined: Three Cases of Jewish Heresy." *Past & Present* 197 (2007): 35–74.
——. "Literacy, Orality, and Book Culture among Medieval Jews." *Jewish Quarterly Review*, forthcoming.

———. "Rabbanite-Karaite Relations in Fatimid Egypt and Syria: A Study Based on Documents from the Cairo Geniza." Ph.D. diss., Columbia University, 2004.
Rustow, Marina, Sharon Lieberman Mintz, and Elka Deitsch. *Scripture and Schism: Samaritan and Karaite Treasures from the Library of the Jewish Theological Seminary.* New York: The Jewish Theological Seminary of America, 2000.
Sachau, C. Edward. *Chronologie orientalischer Völker von alBīrūnī.* Leipzig: Deutsche Morgenländische Gesellschaft, F. A. Brockhaus, and Otto Harrassowitz, 1923.
———. *The Chronology of Ancient Nations: An English Version of the Arabic Text of the Ā thārul-bākiya of alBīrūnī.* Frankfurt: Minerva Verlag, 1984 [1879].
Sáenz-Badillos, Angel. *A History of the Hebrew Language.* Translated by John Elwolde. Cambridge: Cambridge University Press, 1993 [1988].
Safrai, Shmuel, ed. *The Literature of the Sages*, Compendia rerum Iudaicarum ad Novum Testamentum 2:3:1. Assen, Netherlands, and Philadelphia: Van Gorcum and Fortress Press, 1987.
Saleh, Abdel Hamid. "Une source de Qalqašandī, Mawādd al-Bayān, et son auteur, ʿAlī b. ʿḪalaf." *Arabica* 20 (1973): 192–200.
Salzman, Marcus. *The Chronicle of Ahimaaz.* Columbia University Oriental Studies 18. New York: Columbia University Press, 1924.
Schechter, Solomon. "Genizah Specimens: A Marriage Settlement." *Jewish Quarterly Review*, o.s. 13 (1901): 218–21.
———. *Saadyana: Geniza Fragments of Writings of R. Saadya Gaon and Others.* Cambridge, 1903.
Scheiber, Sandor. *Geniza Studies.* Hildesheim: Georg Olms, 1981.
Schirmann, Hayyim. *New Poems from the Geniza.* Hebrew. Jerusalem: Israel Academy of Science and Humanities, 1965.
Schlüter, Margarethe. *Auf welche Weise wurde die Mishna geschrieben? Das Antwortschreiben des Rav Sherira Gaon, mit einem Faksimile der Handschrift Berlin Qu. 685 (Or. 160) und des Erstdrucks Konstantinopel 1566.* Texts and Studies in Medieval and Early Modern Judaism 9. Tübingen: J. C. B. Mohr (Paul Siebeck), 1993.
Schmidtke, Sabine. "The Karaites' Encounter with the Thought of Abū l-Ḥusayn al-Baṣrī (d. 436/1044): A Survey of the Relevant Materials in the Firkovitch-Collection, St. Petersburg." *Arabica* 53 (2006): 108–42.
Scholem, Gershom. "Revelation and Tradition as Religious Categories in Judaism." In *The Messianic Idea in Judaism and Other Essays on Jewish Spirituality*, 282–303. New York: Schocken Books, 1971.
Schwarb, Gregor. "Sahl b. al-Faḍl al-Tustarī's *Kitāb al-īmā'*." *Ginzei Qedem* 2 (2006): 61–105.
———. "Capturing the Meanings of God's Speech: The Relevance of Uṣūl al-fiqh to an Understanding of Uṣūl al-tafsīr in Jewish and Muslim Kalām." In *A Word Fitly Spoken: Studies in Mediaeval Exegesis of the Hebrew Bible and the Qur'ān Presented to Haggai Ben-Shammai*, edited by Meir M. Bar-Asher, Simon Hopkins, Sarah Stroumsa, and Bruno Chiesa, 111–56. Jerusalem: Yad Izhak Ben-Zvi and the Hebrew University of Jerusalem, 2007.
Schwartz, Seth. "Big Men or Chiefs: Against an Institutional History of the Palestinian Patriarchate." In *Jewish Religious Leadership: Image and Reality*, edited by Jack Wertheimer, 155–73. New York: The Jewish Theological Seminary of America, 2004.
———. "Historiography on the Jews in the 'Talmudic Period' (70–630 CE)." In *The Oxford Handbook of Jewish Studies*, edited by Martin Goodman, 79–114. Oxford: Oxford University Press, 2003.
———. *Imperialism and Jewish Society, 200 BCE to 640 CE.* Jews, Christians, and Muslims from the Ancient to the Modern World. Princeton: Princeton University Press, 2001.
———. "Rabbinization in the Sixth Century." In *The Talmud Yerushalmi and Graeco-Roman Culture*, edited by Peter Schäfer, 55–69. Tübingen: Mohr Siebeck, 2002.
Scott, J. C. *Domination and the Arts of Resistance: Hidden Transcripts.* New Haven: Yale University Press, 1990.
Sela, Shulamit. "The Head of the Rabbanite, Karaite and Samaritan Jews: On the History of a Title." *Bulletin of the School of Oriental and African Studies* 57 (1994): 255–67.
———. "The Headship of the Jews in the Fāṭimid Empire in Karaite Hands." Hebrew. In *Mas'at Moshe: Studies in Jewish and Islamic Culture Presented to Moshe Gil*, edited by Ezra Fleischer,

Mordechai A. Friedman, and Joel L. Kraemer, 256–81. Jerusalem: Bialik Institute and Tel Aviv University, 1998.
Shaked, Shaul. *A Tentative Bibliography of Geniza Documents, Prepared under the Direction of D. H. Baneth and S. D. Goitein*. Ecole Pratique des Hautes Etudes, Sixième Section: Sciences Economiques et Sociales. Paris: Mouton, 1964.
Shtober, Shimon. "The Establishment of the Riʾāsat al-Yahūd in Medieval Egypt as Portrayed in the Chronicle Divrey Yosef: Myth or History?" *Revue des études juives* 164 (2005): 33–54.
——. "Questions Posed to R. Abraham b. Maimonides." Hebrew. *Shenaton ha-mishpat ha-ivri* 14–15 (1988–89): 245–81.
——, ed. *Sefer divrey Yosef by Yosef ben Yitzhak Sambari: Eleven Hundred Years of Jewish History under Muslim Rule*. Jerusalem: Ben-Zvi Institute, 1994.
Silverstein, Adam. *Postal Systems in the Pre-Modern Islamic World*. Cambridge Studies in Islamic Civilization. Cambridge: Cambridge University Press, 2007.
Simon, Uriel. *Four Approaches to the Book of Psalms: From Saadiah Gaon to Abraham Ibn Ezra*. Translated by Lenn J. Schramm. SUNY Series in Judaica: Hermeneutics, Mysticism, and Religion. Albany: SUNY Press, 1992 [1982].
Simonsohn, Shlomo. *The Jews in Sicily*, vol. 1: 383–1300. Leiden: Brill, 1997.
Simonsohn, Uriel. "Communal Boundaries Reconsidered: Jews and Christians Appealing to Muslim Authorities in the Medieval Near East." *Jewish Studies Quarterly* 14 (2007): 328–63.
Sklare, David. "A Guide to Collections of Karaite Manuscripts." In *Karaite Judaism: A Guide to its History and Literary Sources*, edited by Meira Polliack, 893–924. Leiden: Brill, 2003.
——. *Samuel ben Ḥofni Gaon and His Cultural World: Texts and Studies*. Etudes sur le judaïsme médiéval 18. Leiden: Brill, 1996.
——. "Yūsuf al-Baṣīr: Theological Aspects of his Halakhic Works." In *The Jews of Medieval Islam: Community, Society, and Identity*, edited by Daniel Frank, 249–70. Leiden: Brill, 1995.
Sklare, David, and Haggai Ben-Shammai, eds. *Judaeo-Arabic Manuscripts in the Firkovitch Collections: The Works of Yūsuf al-Basīr*. Jerusalem: Ben-Zvi Institute, 1997.
Skoss, S. L. *The Arabic Commentary of Ali ben Suleiman the Karaite on the Book of Genesis*. Philadelphia: Dropsie College, 1928.
Soloveitchik, Haim. "Rupture and Reconstruction: The Transformation of Contemporary Orthodoxy." *Tradition* 28 (1994): 64–130.
Sommerville, John C. "Interpreting Seventeenth-Century English Religion as Movements." *Church History* 69 (2000): 749–69.
Starr, Joshua. *The Jews in the Byzantine Empire*, 641–1204. Judaica Series 8. New York: B. Franklin, 1970.
Stemberger, Günter. *Il Giudaismo classico: Cultura e storia del tempo rabbinico (dal 70 al 1040)*. Translated by Daniela Leoni and Luigi Cattani. Rome: Città Nuova, 1991 [1979].
——. *Jews and Christians in the Holy Land: Palestine in the Fourth Century*. Translated by Ruth Tuschling. Edinbugh: T & T Clark, 2000 [1987].
Stern, S. M. *Fāṭimid Decrees: Original Documents from the Fatimid Chancery*. All Souls Studies 3. London: Faber and Faber, 1964.
——. "A Petition to the Fāṭimid Caliph al-Mustanṣir Concerning a Conflict within the Jewish Community." *Revue des études juives* 128 (1969): 203–22.
——. "Three Petitions of the Fāṭimid Period." *Oriens* 15 (1962): 172–209.
Stern, Sacha. *Calendar and Community: A History of the Jewish Calendar, Second Century BCE–Tenth Century CE*. Oxford: Oxford University Press, 2001.
Stewart, Devin J. *Islamic Legal Orthodoxy: Twelver Shiite Responses to the Sunni Legal System*. Salt Lake City: University of Utah Press, 1998.
——. "Popular Shiism in Medieval Egypt: Vestiges of Islamic Sectarian Polemics in Egyptian Arabic." *Studia Islamica* 84 (1996): 35–66.
Stillman, Norman A. "East-West Relations in the Islamic Mediterranean in the Early Eleventh Century: A Study of the Geniza Correspondence of the House of Ibn ʿAwkal." Ph.D. diss., University of Pennsylvania, 1970.
——. "The Eleventh Century Merchant House of Ibn ʿAwkal (A Geniza Study)." *Journal of the Economic and Social History of the Orient* 16 (1973): 15–88.

——. *The Jews of Arab Lands: A History and Source Book*. Philadelphia: Jewish Publication Society of America, 1979.

Sublet, Jacqueline. *Le voile du nom: Essai sur le nom propre arabe*. Paris: Presses Universitaires de France, 1991.

al-Suyūṭī, Abu l-Faḍl ʿAbd al-Raḥmān b. Abī Bakr. *Ḥusn al-muḥāḍara fī akhbār Miṣr wa-l-Qāhira* (The finest discourse on the history of Egypt and Cairo). Edited by Muḥammad Abu l-Faḍl Ibrāhīm. 2 vols. Cairo: ʿIsā al-Bābī al-Ḥalabī, 1968.

Swain, Joseph Ward. "The Theory of the Four Monarchies: Opposition History under the Roman Empire." *Classical Philology* 35 (1940): 1–21.

Talmon, Shemaryahu. "The Calendar Reckoning of the Sect from the Judaean Desert." In *Aspects of the Dead Sea Scrolls*, edited by Chaim Rabin and Yigael Yadin, 108–17. Scripta Hierosolymitana 4. Jerusalem: Magnes Press, 1958.

——. "Yom Hakkippurim in the Habakkuk scroll." *Biblica* 32 (1951): 563.

Tamani, Giuliano. *La letteratura ebraica medievale (secoli X–XVIII)*. Brescia: Morcelliana, 2004.

Tambiah, S. J. "The Magical Power of Words." *Man* 3 (1968): 175–208.

al-Thaʿālibī, Abū Manṣūr ʿAbd al-Malik b. Muḥammad b. Ismāʿīl. *Yatīmat al-dahr fī maḥāsin ahl al-ʿaṣr* (The incomparable of the age in the merits of its people). Edited by Muḥammad Muḥyi l-Dīn ʿAbd al- Ḥamīd. 4 vols. in 2. Cairo, al-Maktaba al-Tijāriyya al-Kubrā, 1956–58.

——. *Yatīmat al-dahr fī maḥāsin ahl al-ʿaṣr*. Edited by Ibrāhīm Shams al-Dīn. 6 vols. Beirut: Dār al-Kutub al-ʿIlmiyya, 2000.

Thackston, W. M. *Naser-e Khosraw's Book of Travels=(Safarnama)*. Persian Heritage Series 36. Albany: Bibliotheca Persica, 1986.

Tirosh-Becker, Ofra. "The Use of Rabbinic Sources in Karaite Writings." In *Karaite Judaism: A Guide to Its History and Literary Sources*, edited by Meira Polliack, Handbuch der Orientalistik, pt. 1: Nahe und Mittlere Osten, 73, 319–38. Leiden: Brill, 2003.

Toorawa, Shawkat. *Ibn Abī Ṭāhir Ṭayfūr and Arabic Writerly Culture: A Ninth-Century Bookman in Baghdad*. Richmond, Surrey: RoutledgeCurzon, 2005.

Udovitch, Abraham L. "Formalism and Informalism in the Social and Economic Institutions of the Medieval Islamic World." In *Individualism and Conformity in Classical Islam*, edited by Amin Banani and Spiros Vryonis, 61–81. Wiesbaden: Harrassowitz, 1977.

——. *Further Letters from the Eleventh-Century Correspondence of Nahray ben Nissim: Merchant, Banker and Scholar*. Judaeo-Arabic Studies at Princeton University 5. Princeton: Princeton University Press, 1992.

——. "Merchants and *Amirs*: Government and Trade in Eleventh-Century Egypt." *Asian and African Studies* 22 (1988): 53–72.

——. "Scenes from Eleventh-Century Family Life: Cousins and Partners—Nahray ben Nissim and Israel ben Natan." In *The Islamic World: From Classical to Modern Times*, edited by Charles Issawi, C. E. Bosworth, Roger Savory, and A. L. Udovitch. Princeton: Darwin Press, 1989.

——. "Time, the Sea, and Society: Duration of Commercial Voyages on the Southern Shores of the Mediterranean during the High Middle Ages." *Settimane di studio del Centro Italiano di Studi sull'Alto Medioevo* 25 (1978): 503–46.

Van Ess, Josef. *Chiliastische Erwartungen und die Versuchung der Göttlichkeit: Der Kalif al-Hakim (386–411 H.)*. Abhandlungen der Heidelberger Akademie der Wissenschaften, Philosophisch-Historische Klasse. Heidelberg: Winter, 1977.

Walker, Paul E. *Exploring an Islamic Empire: Fatimid History and Its Sources*. Ismaili Heritage Series 7. London: I.B. Tauris, 2002.

——. "The Ismaili Daʿwa in the Reign of the Fatimid Caliph al-Ḥākim." *Journal of the American Research Center in Egypt* 30 (1993): 160–82.

Wansbrough, J. E. *Lingua Franca in the Mediterranean*. Richmond, Surrey: Curzon Press, 1996.

Weber, Max. "Politik als Beruf." In *Gesammelte Politische Schriften*, 396–450. Munich, 1921.

Weiss, Gershon. "Legal Documents Written by the Court Clerk Halfon ben Manasse (dated 1100–1138): A Study in the Diplomatics of the Cairo Geniza." PhD diss., University of Pennsylvania, 1970.

Weitzman, Steven. "From Feasts into Mourning: The Violence of Early Jewish Festivals." *Journal of Religion* 79 (1999): 545–65.

Wertheimer, Jack, ed. *Jewish Religious Leadership: Image and Reality*. 2 vols. New York: Jewish Theological Seminary, 2004.
Wieder, Naphtali. *The Judean Scrolls and Karaism*. London: East and West Library, 1962.
Würthwein, Ernst. *The Text of the Old Testament: An Introduction to the Biblia Hebraica*. Translated by Erroll F. Rhodes. 4th ed. London: SCM Press, 1979 [1973].
Yahalom, Yosef. "The Transition of Kingdoms in Eretz Israel (Palestine) as Conceived by Poets and Homilists." Hebrew. *Shalem* 6 (1992): 1–22.
Yerushalmi, Yosef Hayim. *"Diener von Königen und nicht Diener von Dienern": Einige Aspekte der politischen Geschichte der Juden; Vortrag gehalten in der Carl Friedrich von Siemens Stiftung am* 19. *Oktober 1993*. Munich: Carl-Friedrich-von-Siemens-Stiftung, 1995.
——. *The Lisbon Massacre of* 1506 *and the Royal Image in the Shebet Yehuda*. Hebrew Union College Annual Supplements 1. Cincinnati: Hebrew Union College-Jewish Institute of Religion, 1976.
——. *"Servants of Kings and not Servants of Servants": Some Aspects of the Political History of the Jews*. Tenenbaum Family Lecture Series in Judaic Studies at Emory University. Atlanta: Emory University, 2007.
——. *Zakhor: Jewish History and Jewish Memory*. 2d ed. Seattle: University of Washington Press, 1996 [1982].
Young, M. J. L., J. D. Latham, and R. B. Serjeant, eds. *Religion, Learning, and Science in the 'Abbasid period*. Cambridge History of Arabic Literature. Cambridge and New York: Cambridge University Press, 1990.
Zeldes, Nadia, and Miriam Frenkel. "The Sicilian Trade: Jewish Merchants in the Mediterranean in the Twelfth and Thirteenth Centuries." In *Gli ebrei in Sicilia dal tardoantico al medioevo: Studi in onore di Monsignor Benedetto Rocco*, edited by Nicolò Bucaria, 243–56. Palermo: Flaccovio Editore, 1998.
Zer, Rafael. "Was the Masorete of the Aleppo Codex of Rabbanite or Karaite Origin?" Hebrew. *Sefunot* 23 (2003): 573–87.

INDEX

Pages in italics indicate illustrative material. Ha-kohen, ha-Levi, the definite articles *ha-* and *al-*, and *kunā* (in parentheses) do not affect alphabetization.

al-ʿArīsh, 24, 177
Ascalon, 177, 330, 331
Jews in, 186–87, 341–44
asceticism, Qaraite, 27–28
Asher the elder (father of Ben Asher dynasty), 46
Atsīz (Turcoman chief), 328–29
Augustine of Hippo, 233
Austin, J. L., 207–8
Avraham b. ʿAṭā (*nagid* of Qayrawān), 86, 151, 231
Avraham b. David. *See* Ibn Sughmār
Avraham b. Ḥiyya of Barcelona, 63
Avraham b. Sahlān (leader of Iraqis in Fustat), 150, 172n36, 172n38, 173–74, 186, 197n45
Avraham b. Shelomo (b. Yehuda Gaʾon), 174, 192–95, 213–14, 306–7
Avraham ha-Kohen b. Shelomo (b. Yehosef Gaʾon), 194
Avraham b. Sherira, 314
Avraham b. Yijū, 240
ʿayyārūn (gangs or militias), 310–11
ʿAzarya ha-Kohen b. Yisraʾel (b. Shemuʾel b. Ḥofni Gaʾon), 323
al-ʿAzīz (Fatimid caliph), 93, 123–27, 166

baʿaley miqraʾ
as designation for Masoretes, 45–46
as designation for Qaraites, 58
Babylonian gaonate and *geʾonim*
antiquity, claims of continuity with, 4–6
calendar controversy and, 15–20, 338
caliphal recognition of, 68–69
decline of in eleventh century, 5–6, 19–20, 313–14, 323–24
financial support from western Jews, seeking, 113, 136, 156, 157, 173
historiography on, 3–6, 22–23
independence of Fustat *midrash* from, 157–60, 171–72, 173–75
Palestinian submission to, evidence for and doubts regarding, 20–23
pilgrimage festival in Jerusalem as response to, 203
power of, 6–10
Qaraites, alliances with, 145–50, 297–302
trade network of. *See* trade connections
of twelfth and thirteenth centuries, 67n2, 12, 324
yeshivot, 3, 5–6, 19–21, 134–36, 145–50, 157–58, 313–14, 323–24. *See also* Pumbedita; Sura
see also names of individual geʾonim
Babylonian Rabbanites, 3–12
court clerks in Tyre, influences on, 281
earthquake in Palestine (1033), political use of, 292–93
excommunication in Egypt by Palestinian *gaʾon*, 174, 204–5, 208
Palestinian *gaʾon*'s jurisdiction over in Fatimid Egypt, 94–98, *95*
westward migration of, 5, 10–12, 48, 136, 324
Babylonian Talmud, 4–6, 22, 38–39
Bādīs (Zīrid *amīr*), 353
Badr al-Jamālī, 106, 328, 339
Baghdad
as Abbasid capital and seat of court, 7, 18, 68, 76, 149, 159, 160, 299n16, 361
Binyamin of Tudela's visit to, 69
Buwayhid takeover of, xxx, 10–11, 87
distance of Sura and Pumbedita from, 7–8n6
exilarch of. *See* exilarch
migration, travel, and pilgrimage from, 126, 135–36, 137, 269, 323–25
relocation of Babylonian *yeshivot* to, 5
trade networks with Mediterranean, 137–38, 281
yeshivot of. *See* Babylonian gaonate and *geʾonim*; Pumbedita; Sura
Baghdad, *geʾonim* of. *See* Babylonian gaonate and *geʾonim*
bans of excommunication. *See* excommunication
Bareket, Elinoar, 100, 101, 102, 198
al-Bargeloni, Yehuda b. Barzillay, 351
Baron, Salo Wittmayer, 46n20, 349, 350n6
al-Baṣīr, (Abū Yaʿqūb) Yūsuf b. Ibrāhīm, 32, 147, 259n49, 277
bayt al-māl (the fisc), 277
Bedouin, 51, 128, 177, 182, 195, 214n39
Beirut, 330
belief vs. praxis, misleading comparison of Judaism, Christianity, and Islam regarding, xviii*n3*
Ben Asher, Aharon, 44–47
Ben Asher, Moshe, 45, 48
Ben Asher family (Masoretes), 44–48
Ben Ezra synagogue, Fustat, xxvi–xxvii, 156, 318, 321. *See also* Cairo Geniza
Ben-Sasson, Menaḥem, 73–74, 203, 313
Ben-Shammai, Haggai, 54
Ben Shaʿyā, (Abū Saʿīd) Dāwūd b. Abū Naṣr, 252–53
Ben Shaʿyā, (Abu l-Faḍl) Sahl b. Yushaʿ, 85, 342, 344
Ben Shaʿyā family, 252, 287, 341–42
Berekhya, mercantile house of, 139, 145–47, 320
betrothal. *See* marriage
Bible
canonical books of, establishment of, 41
codices of, 44–47
text of, establishment of, 41–43. *See also* masoretic text
Binyamin of Tudela, 69, 232
birr (dutifulness, loyalty), 148–49

al-Bīrūnī, (Abū Rayḥān) Muḥammad b. Aḥ mad, 17n23, 47n23, 61, 78, 85, 87
Bomberg, Daniel, 22–23, 42
Book of the Wars of the Lord (Salmon b. Yeroḥam), 112, 220
Brener, Ann, 151
Brody, Robert, 41
brothers, division of business and community responsibilities between, 191
bureau. See *dīwān*
butchers and slaughterhouses, control of, 164, 283–84
Buxtorf, Johannes, 43
Byzantine Empire
  border skirmishes with Fatimids, 126–27, 135, 187
  captives from, 188–89
  Jews of, 49
  in late antiquity, 8n7, 14n16, 33, 71n7, 118, 159, 362
  Qaraites of, xxv, 24, 56, 61, 234, 262, 277

Caesarea, 331, 340
Cairo
  as Fatimid capital and seat of court, xxx, 10, 12, 106–7, 126–27, 339, 362
  Jewish courtiers and other notables of, *90*, 91, 102, 132, *165*, 168, 186, 282, 293–96, *295*, 316,
  Jews in and from, xx, 24, 138, 140, 143, 205, 244n11, 286, 287, 346
  Palestinian *ge'onim* in, 251n28
  Seljuk occupation of, 328
Cairo Codex of the Prophets, 45
Cairo Geniza, xix–xxii
  Firkovich's visit to, xxiii
  marriages between Qaraites and Rabbanites, representativeness of evidence regarding, 243–48
calendar(s)
  clauses regarding in marriage contracts between Qaraites and Rabbanites, 249, 250, 251, 337
  controversies between Babylonian and Palestinian Rabbanites, 15–20, 338
  controversies between Qaraites and Rabbanites, 57–65, 338
  dating and chronology, in contracts from Tyre, 281–82
  determining months, 16–17, 59–61
  Evyatar Ga'on's polemics on, 337–39
  history and historiography of differences between Qaraite and Rabbanite, 61–63
  intercalating the year, 16–17, 58–59
  months, determining, 59–61
  Palestinian monopoly on intercalation, claim of, 337–38
  pilgrimage festival in Palestine, proclamation of calendar at, 202–3
  of Qaraites from Tustar, 142
  Qaraites observing calculated, 19, 58,
  Rabbanites observing empirical, 17–19, 59–60
  second festival day, diaspora observance of, 63–65
caliphal rescripts. *See* rescripts
caliphs. *See* Abbasid caliphate; Fatimid caliphate; names of individual caliphs
cantors, 180
captives, ransoming, 269
  Ibn Dāwūd's myth of rabbinic transmission involving, 134–36, 157
  joint Rabbanite-Qaraite collections for, 188, 341–45
  petitions to Qaraite courtiers from Alexandrian Jews regarding, 187–91
charity, 190–91
  conversion and scholastic transfer as means of receiving, 254–57
  Qaraite recipients of from Palestinian Rabbanite system, 256
  for Rabbanites and Qaraites equally, penalties stipulating in marriage documents, 249–50, 253
Charlemagne, 104
checks. See *suftaja*
cheese, 283–86
Chesterton, G. K., 208n22
Chiesa, Bruno, 42n13, 43, 48, 50
Christianity and Christians
  belief vs. praxis, misleading comparison of Judaism, Christianity, and Islam regarding, xviii*n*3
  biblical transmission, shared Jewish-Christian interest in, 43
  children of Jewish-Christian marriages, 261–64
  codex used by, 38
  Copts, 106, 122
  courtiers, 120–25
  Jerusalem, pilgrimage to, 27–28
  Nestorian *katholikos*, 68, 69n4, 114, 115n8, 206
  persecution under al-Ḥākim, 176–77, 200
  pigs, as insult reserved for, 131, 132n50
  see also conversion; Crusades; Iberian peninsula
clerks or scribes. *See* legal reciprocity between Qaraites and Rabbanites
clothing requirements for Jews under Islamic rule, 119–20, 176
codex vs. scroll, 38, 42
Cohen, Mark, 86, 101, 105–6, 139, 160–62, 303n18, 311, 331, 339

Palestinian *yeshiva*'s move to, 340
Yūsuf ibn ʿAwkal's lack of position in, 139–40

gaonic period, 3–4
Gaza, 17n22, 21, 24, 182
genizot
of Ben Ezra synagogue, Fustat. *See* Cairo Geniza
of Dār Simḥa synagogue, Cairo, xx*n*4, 29n54, 365–66
defined, xix
ge'onim
Babylonian. *See* Babylonian gaonate
communal authority of. *See* communal autonomy under Muslim rule
on customary law, 267
Palestinian. *See* Palestinian gaonate
Qaraite *nesi'im* compared with, 29, 33–34
ra'īs al-yahūd and gaonate combined, 340
schism of. *See* schism of 1038–42
sons, role of, 18n28, 214
as title, 84, 87–88
Ghālib ha-Kohen b. Moshe, 218n49
al-Ghazzī b. Hārūn, Ibrāhīm, 256
ghiyār, 119–20
Ghosh, Amitav, 239
Gil, Moshe
on David b. Dani'el's marriage, 336
in historiography of Jewish community in Fatimid Egypt and Syria, xxv
on Jewish communal structure, 71–72, 74, 100
on petitions to Qaraite courtiers, 178, 180, 197, 198
on Qaraites of Tustar, 141–42
on schism of 1038–42, 305, 313
Ginzberg, Louis, 70–71, 105
giṭṭin, Qaraite vs. Rabbanite formulae for, 243
Goitein, S. D.
on communal autonomy, 71, 86, 89, 91, 92, 94, 99–100, 105–6
on excommunication of 1029, 208, 225, 235
in historiography of Qaraite and Rabbanite communities, xxv
on legal documents, 266
on marriages between Qaraites and Rabbanites, 240, 244
on observance of *dhimmī* clothing requirements, 120
on petition seeking confirmation of investiture of Shelomo b. Yehuda, 294
on petitions to Qaraite courtiers, 192
on treatment of female captives, 343
Goldberg, Harvey, 209n23
Goldberg, Jessica, 140
Graetz, Heinrich, 7, 70
Granada, 86, 151, 350, 353

Ḥabbūs (Zīrid *amīr*), 353
Hadassi, Yehuda, 234
Hadrian, 13
al-Ḥākim (Fatimid caliph)
communal autonomy under, 93
dhimmīs persecuted under, 120, 156, 160, 161, 176–77, 187
dhimmī public festivals forbidden by, 200
relationship between Qaraites and Jerusalem gaonate during reign of, 156, 160, 161, 164, 167–68
synagogues and churches destroyed or taken over by, 176–77, 184
Ḥalfon (Khalaf) b. Thaʿlab, 197, 203, 271–72
Ḥanan'el ben Ḥushi'el, 135
Ḥananya b. David, 55
(Abu l-Faraj) Hārūn b. al-Faraj. *See* Aharon b. Faraj
al-Ḥasan b. al-Mufarrij b. Daghfal b. Jarraḥ (Bedouin chief), 177, 191
Ḥasūn b. Yaʿqūb b. Yūsuf b. Kushnām, 31
Hayya b. Sherira
communal autonomy and, 86
death of, 313, 324
Fustat *midrash*'s relationship to, 158–59, 173
intellectual sensibilities of, 297–98
on oral and written literary transmission, 39, 63, 64
Qaraite mercantile houses, connection to, 145–47, 151, 297–302, 312
on Seʿadya's defense of second festival day, 64, 212
son of Shelomo b. Yehuda sent to study with, 20–21, 303
yeshiva as outward-looking under, 5
Hebrew
Tiberian Hebrew, belief in superiority of, 50–52
Tyrean preference for, 172n37
see also Aramaic vs. Hebrew
ḥemdat ha-yeshiva (title), 308
heresy
accusations of
as function of context, 201, 236, 261, 288, *317*, 318–19, 347–48
vs. indifference, 261, 347
power as shield against, 201, 236, 318–19
in Judaism, xviii–xix, xxxiii, 347–55
history of Qaraism, 55–57
on Iberian peninsula, treatment of, xxxiii, 345, 349–55
rabbinic terms for, xviii
Hilālī invasions of Ifrīqiya, 258, 324
Hillel b. Yehuda, 62–63
historical claims of Rabbanites and Qaraites, 37, 52–65
in calendar controversy, 57–65
retrojection in, 53–57

nishtevan (decree), 93n54, 185n19. *See also* petitions to caliph; *sijill*; *tawqīʿ*
Nizār (heir apparent to al-Mustanṣir), 339
Norman conquest of Sicily, 324

Olszowy-Schlanger, Judith, 242n6, 243n8, 247n22, 274n27
oral vs. written literary transmission, 36–52, 65–66
ʿOvadya ha-Kohen, 279n39
ʿOvadya ha-Kohen b. Yiṣḥaq, 279n39

Pact of ʿUmar, 120, 122–23, 184
Palestine, as geographical term, 361–62
Palestinian gaonate and *ge'onim*, 12–15
  Ananite *nesi'im* serving as, 33–34, 55, 60
  calendrical authority of, 337–38
  excommunication of Babylonian-rite followers in Egypt for slaughtering methods, 174
  Fustat *midrash*, relationship with, 157–63
  jurisdiction, administrative
    over Babylonian Rabbanites in Egypt, 94–98, *95*
    over Qaraites, 94, 99–107
  late antiquity, question of continuity with, 13–14
  list of, 363
  petitions of investiture for. *See* petitions to caliph
  petitions to Qaraite courtiers from. *See* petitions to Qaraite courtiers
  Qaraites, alliances with, xxx–xxxi, 156–75, 169–71
    documentary evidence suggesting, 156–57, 163–64
    Iraqi efforts to assert control over Fustat, as response to, 171–75
    Qaraite ascent at court as leading to, 164–69, *165*
    See also under petitions to caliph
  Rabbanite *nesi'im* as
    Dani'el b. ʿAzarya, 206, 301, 314, 323–28, 330–31, 334, 348
    David b. Dani'el, 324, 326, 327, 330–39
  ra'īs al-yahūd combined with, 340
  schism. *See* schism of 1038–42
  sources, limitations regarding, 13
  trade connections of, 136, 137, 139, 140
  western migration of Babylonian Rabbanites challenging, 11
  see also names of individual ge'onim
Palestinian Rabbanites, 12–23
  Babylonian triumph over, evidence for and doubts regarding, 20–23
  calendar controversy and, 15–20, 338
  court clerks in Tyre, influences on, 281–82
  ge'onim. *See* Palestinian *ge'onim*
  yeshiva, 3, 6, 12–15, 107, 197–99, 202, 322, 329–30, 332, 340
  see also excommunication controversy
Palestinian Talmud, 13, 14, 22, 41
papermaking, advances in, 37
patronage, xxvi, 75–76, 79–80, 81, 83, 108, 154
performative utterance, excommunications as, 207–8
Persia. *See* Iraq, Iran, and Persia
Petaḥya of Regensburg, 232
petitions to caliph
  by doll in Ibn al-Athīr, 124–25
  as Fatimid method of rule, 79–80
  use of honorifics and formulae in, 80–81
  for recognition of Iraqi exilarch, 68–69
  for recognition of Iraqi *ge'onim*, 67–68
  for recognition of Palestinian *ga'on*, 11, 69, 88–99
    intercessors, use of, 91–92, 93–94, 171–72, 183, 296
    petitions against threats by rivals, 91, 94–98, *95*, 173, 229, 293, 311–13
    petitions on becoming *ga'on*, 89, *90*, 91–93, 171–72, 183
    petitions to new caliphs, 89–91
  in schism of 1038–42, 293, 296, 311–13, 316–20, *317*, 347
  *sijill*s in response to, 166–67
  see also *tawqīʿ*
petitions to Qaraite courtiers, xxxi, 176–99
  from Alexandrian Jews seeking to ransom captives, 187–91
  from Ascalon Jews, 186–87
  Efrayim b. Shemarya, liberation of, 181–83
  events triggering, 176–77
  excommunication of 1029 and, 215
  from Palestinian gaonate
    for assistance in paying Jarrāḥid war tax, 183–84
    for caliphal recognition, 91–92, 93–94, 171–72, 183, 296
    for debtor relief during Jarrāḥid wars, 191–96, *193*
    for general relief of Jerusalem Jews, 196–97
    for *yeshiva* contributions, 197–99
  Qaraites petitioned, 176, 177–80
  for tax relief and assistance, 183–84, 190–91
  from Tripoli Jews seeking to reestablish synagogue, 184–86
philosophy and theology, Qaraite contributions to, xxvii, 23–24
pigs, as insult reserved for Christians, 131, 132n50
pilgrimage festival in Jerusalem
  excommunication of 1029 at, 200, 202–4

rennet, 284
rescript. See *tawqīʿ*
reshut, *reshuyot* (gaonic jurisdiction), 84n36, 173, 251n28
responsa from Baghdad, dissemination of, 8–9, 11
riʾāsa (leadership, authority), 49n29, 115, 162. See also *serara*
riʿāya (patronage), 315
rikkuv laws, 259–61
Rivqa (object of forged marriage contract), 287
rosh ha-gola, David b. Daniʾel as, 331–32, 334–35
ruqʿa. *See* petitions to caliph
Russia, and Qaraites in nineteenth century, xxii–xxiii

Sabbath observance, Qaraite vs. Rabbanite, 26, 249, 250, 251, 337
Ṣadoq ha-Levi b. Levi, 269
safeq mamzerim, Qaraites as, 345
Sahl b. Maṣliaḥ, 19, 30, 31, 119, 133
Sahlān b. Avraham (Iraqi Rabbanite leader of Fustat), 215, 217, 298–301, 311n42, 312, 314
Sahlawayh b. ḥayyim, 180, 197, 254, 269
Ṣahrajt, 24, 188
sajʿ (rhymed prose), 92, 102n74
Saladin (Ayyubid sultan), 124, 344
Ṣāliḥ b. Mirdās (Bedouin chief), 177, 191
Salmon b. Yeroḥam, 112, 115, 118–19, 216, 220, 222, 354
Samaritans, 94, 101n73, 103n77, 286n60
al-Sambarī, Yosef, 104
Sanhedrin, 14
sanī al-dawla (title), 85, 335
Sar Shalom ha-Levi, 344–45
Sara b. Ḥalfon (Khalaf) b. Thaʿlab, 271–72
Schechter, Solomon, xxiv, xxxi, 239, 247n22, 335
schism of 1038–42, xxxi–xxxii, 291–322
  consequences of, 321–22
  deposition of Natan and reinstatement of Shelomo, 321–22
  events leading up to
    confirmation of investiture from al-Mustanṣir sought by Shelomo b. Yehuda (1036), 293–96, *295*
    earthquake (1033), political manipulation of, 292–93
    excommunication of 1029, fallout from, 291, 293
    kingmaker positioning of Qaraites, 291, 296–302, 304–5
  historiography on, 302, 303n18
  nativist claims in, 302–4
  petitions to caliph in, 293, 296, 311–13, 316–20, *317*, 347
  pilgrimage festival of 1038, excommunication at, 18n28, 201, 231, 235, 305–7
  Qaraites and
    excommunication of 1038, 305–7
    heresy, accusations of, 347
    as kingmakers, 291, 296–302, 304–5, 321–22
    Natan b. Avraham's alliances with, 304–5, 307–10, 314–16, 320
    petitions to caliph and, 316–20
    Shelomo b. Yehuda's response to Natan's alliances with, 310–13
  Qayrawān plan of Shelomo b. Yehuda, 303, 310–14, 316, 320
  return of Natan b. Avraham to Palestine, 304–5
  typological argument against Natan b. Avraham's gaonate, 313–14
  Zirid governors of Ifrīqiya, appeal to caliphate via, 231, 302, 311
  see also Natan b. Avraham
Schwartz, Seth, 23n41, 62n62
scribes or clerks. *See* legal reciprocity between Qaraites and Rabbanites
scroll vs. codex, 38, 42
Seʿadya b. Yūsuf al-Fayyūmī
  anti-Qaraite polemics of, xv–xvii, 20, 24, 351
  calendar controversy, 15, 18, 19, 20, 34, 60, 61, 63, 308, 338
  claims of divinely revealed Oral Law, 26n48
  claims regarding rabbinic transmission, 53, 212
  David b. Zakkay and, 323
  as *gaʾon* of Sura, 5
  Hayya b. Sherira and, 64, 212, 297
  literary innovations adopted by, 41
  outsider status of, 302
  on second festival day, 64
  and self-conscious rabbinic tradition, 46–47
second festival day, diaspora observance of, 63–65
Second Purim, 331
"sect," Qaraites viewed as, xv–xvii, xxvi–xxix
Ṣedaqa b. ʿEzra, 271
Sefer ha-qabbala (Ibn Dāwūd), 113, 134–36, 157, 201, 232
Sela, Shulamit, 100–103, 199
Seleucus I, 281
Seljuks
  Damascus taken by, 328
  in Jerusalem, xxxii, 107, 329, 337
Ṣemaḥ b. Yiṣḥaq (*gaʾon* of Sura), 101, 157, 159
Ṣemaḥ b. Yoshiyyahu (Ananite *gaʾon* of Tiberias), 33–34, 55, 60, 326
serara (leadership, authority), 69, 162, 312
sexual practices, Qaraite vs. Rabbanite, 26, 249, 250, 251

CPSIA information can be obtained at www.ICGtesting.com
Printed in the USA
BVOW01s1924091014

369942BV00002B/6/P

9 780801 456503